EUROPEAN UNION LAW

EUROPEAN UNION LAW

Christian Dadomo and Noëlle Quénivet

Hall and Stott Publishing Ltd
27 Witney Close
Saltford
BS31 3DX

British Library Cataloguing in Publication Data
Data available

ISBN 978 0 993336 50 8

Typeset by Style Photosetting Ltd, Mayfield, East Sussex
Printed by Ashford Colour Press Ltd, Gosport, Hampshire

PREFACE

The years to come will be crucial years for the UK and the EU. The European Union Referendum Bill introduced into the House of Commons on 28 May 2015 provides in clause 1 that '[a] referendum is to be held on whether the United Kingdom should remain a member of the European Union' no later than 31 December 2017. This referendum could potentially lead to the withdrawal of the UK from the EU.

Would a Brexit make the teaching of EU law in UK universities redundant? Many students might be tempted to think so but nothing could be further from reality.

Since the European Communities Act 1972 introduced EU law into the UK legal system, giving the original Treaty of Rome and any of its subsequent amendments full legal effect in the UK, there is now virtually no part of its law that is not significantly affected or influenced by EU law.

Whatever the outcome of the planned referendum and whatever change in the nature of the relationships between the UK and the EU, the teaching of EU law will remain significant to any student who wishes to practise law. Access to the European internal market means compliance with EU regulations, rules and principles relating to the four freedoms of movement, competition, environmental and other significant policies. Suffice it to look at the situation of non-EU member States such as Norway, Iceland and Switzerland. Further, the intricate and complex intertwined relationship between EU and UK laws, the result of more than 40 years of mutual development, cannot be unravelled as easily as pulling the wool string of a knitted piece of clothing. It is no surprise that EU law is a taught element of law degrees in Swiss, Norwegian and Icelandic universities. There is no reason to believe it will be otherwise in UK universities in the years to come.

This book is the result of a teaching collaboration between Christian Dadomo, Senior Lecturer, and Noëlle Quénivet, Associate Professor in International Law, at the University of the West England (UWE). It started as a series of handouts we gave to students on the Graduate Diploma in Law at UWE in 2011–2012 to accompany our lectures, workshops and seminars.

As part-time and full-time GDL students have to study EU law over a short period of time, alongside other modules and often work commitments, the students appreciated the handouts all the more as they seemed to struggle to find a textbook that was covering the relevant legal area in a concise, yet not oversimplifying, manner. Attempting to bridge the gap between revision guides and classic textbooks in EU law, we decided to include a growing amount of information, such as cases and practical examples, in the handouts. Moreover, discussions with students brought to our attention the need to present the law in a more visual manner. In particular, diagrams and flowcharts were introduced to clarify or dissect certain points of the law or to explain a procedure in a chronological manner. Later, such handouts were also distributed to LLB students studying EU Law in their second year.

In 2013 we were contacted by Sue Hall and David Stott, the publishers of this book, who were looking to produce a textbook for GDL and LLB students. It was an excellent opportunity for us to offer students a more comprehensive support towards their learning and understanding of EU law. We hope that this textbook fills a gap in the market and that students will enjoy reading it.

Christian Dadomo
Noëlle Quénivet
University of the West England at Bristol

CONTENTS

PART V COMPETITION LAW

16 Core Concepts of Competition Law

17 Substantive Competition Rules Applicable to Undertakings

TABLE OF CASES

B

C

D

G

H

I

J

K

L

Q

R

T

TABLE OF LEGISLATION

TABLES OF EQUIVALENCES

Note. The Tables contain only the Treaty provisions referred to in the text.

Treaty on European Union

TEU Maastricht *Introduced by ToA	TEU (Amsterdam)	TEC (Amsterdam)	TEU (Lisbon)
A	1		1
			2
B	2		3
			4
		10	4(3)
		5 (3b TEC post Maastricht)	5
F	6		6
F.1*	7		7
G	8 (repealed)		9
			10
		191, first para	10(4)
			11
			12
H	9 (repealed)		13
			14
		189	14(1-2)
		190	14(1-3)
	4		15
			16
		202, first and second indents	16 (1)
		203	16(2) and (9)
		205(2) and (4)	16(4) and (5)
			17
		211	17(1)
		214	17(3) and (7)
		217(1), (3) and (4)	17(6)
		220	19
	10	11 and 11a	20
			22
J.1	11		24
J.5	15		29
	23		31
J.6	16		32

TEU Maastricht *Introduced by ToA	TEU (Amsterdam)	TEC (Amsterdam)	TEU (Lisbon)
			47
N	48		48
O	49		49
			50
			51

Treaty on the Functioning of the European Union

TEEC *Added or replaced by SEA	TEC Post Maastricht **Introduced by MT *** Introduced by ToA	TEC Post Amsterdam	TEU Post Amsterdam (TEU Maastricht)	TFEU
				2
				3
				4
				5
				6
				14
	191(a)***	255		15
	231(b)***	286		16
6	6	12		18
	6a***	13		19
				20
	8a**	18		21
	8b**	19		22
	8c**	20		23
	8d**	21		24
	8e**	22		25
8a*	7a	14		26
8c*	7c	15		27
9	9	23		28
10	10	24		29
12	12	25		30
28	28	26		31
29	29	27		32
30	30	28		34
34	34	29		35
36	36	30		36
37	37	31		37
38	38	32		38
48	48	39		45
49	49	40		46
50	50	41		47
51	51	42		48
52	52	43		49
55	55	45		51
56	56	46		52
57	57	47		53

TEEC *Added or replaced by SEA	TEC Post Maastricht **Introduced by MT *** Introduced by ToA	TEC Post Amsterdam	TEU Post Amsterdam (TEU Maastricht)	TFEU
58	58	48		54
59	59	49		56
60	60	50		57
66	66	55		62
	73i***	61	29 (K.1)	67
	73j***	62		77
	73m***	65		81
			31 (K.3)	82
			31 (K.3)	83
				86
			30 (K.2)	87
			32 (K.4)	89
75	75	71		91
85	85	81		101
86	86	82		102
87	87	83		103
89	89	85		105
90	90	86		106
95	95	90		110
99*	99	93		113
100a*	100a	95		114
100	100	94		115
102a*	102a**	98		120
103	103	99		121
	104c**	104		126
	105**	105		127
				139
	109j(1)**	121(1)		140(1)
119	119	141		157
	130**	157		173
130r*	130r	174		191
110	110	131		206
113	113	133		207
				216
228	228	300		218
229 to 231	229 to 231	302 to 304		220
138(3)	138(3)	190(4) and (5)		223
	138a**	191, second para		224
	138b, second para**	192, second para		225
	138c**	193		226
	138d**	194		227
	138e	195		228
139	139	196		229
140, second, third and fourth para	140, second, third and fourth para	197, second, third and fourth para		230
141	141	198		231

TEEC *Added or replaced by SEA	TEC Post Maastricht **Introduced by MT *** Introduced by ToA	TEC Post Amsterdam	TEU Post Amsterdam (TEU Maastricht)	TFEU
142	142	199		232
143	143	200		233
144	144	201		234
				236
147	147	204		237
148	148	205(1) and (2)		238
150	150	206		239
151	151	207		240
152	152	208		241
153	153	209		242
154	154	210		243
				244
157(2)	157(2)	213(2)		245
159	159	215		246
160	160	216		247
161	161	217(2)		248
162 and 156	162(2) and 156	218(2) and 212		249
163	163	219		250
165, second para	165, second para	221, second and third para		251
166, first and second para	166, first and second para	222		252
167	167	223		253
168a*	168a	225		256
		225a (inserted by Nice Treaty)		257
169	169	226		258
170	170	227		259
171	171	228		260
172	172	229		261
		229a (inserted by Nice Treaty)		262
173	173	230		263
174	174	231		264
175	175	232		265
176	176	233		266
177	177	234		267
178	178	235		268
				269
179	179	236		270
180	180	237		271
181	181	238		272
182	182	239		273
183	183	240		274
				275
				276

TEEC *Added or replaced by SEA	TEC Post Maastricht **Introduced by MT *** Introduced by ToA	TEC Post Amsterdam	TEU Post Amsterdam (TEU Maastricht)	TFEU
184	184	241		277
185	185	242		278
186	186	243		279
				282
	109a**	112		283
	109b**	113		284
206	188b	247		286
206b	188c	248		287
189	189	249		288
				289
145, third indent	145, third indent	202, third indent		290
145, third indent	145, third indent	202, third indent		291
149*	189b**	251		294
				295
190	190	253		296
191	191	254		297
				300
195	195	259		302
196	196	260		303
198	198	262		304
	198a**	263, second, third and fourth para		305
	198b**	264		306
	198c**	265		307
129	198d	266		308
130	198e	267		309
203(2) to (10)	203(2) to (10)	272(2) to (10)		314
206c	206	276		319
		11 and 11a (inserted by Nice Treaty)	27a to 27e, 40 to 40b and 43 to 45	326
		11 and 11a (inserted by Nice Treaty)	27a to 27e, 40 to 40b and 43 to 45	327
		11 and 11a (inserted by Nice Treaty)	27a to 27e, 40 to 40b and 43 to 45	328
		11 and 11a (inserted by Nice Treaty)	27a to 27e, 40 to 40b and 43 to 45	329
215	215	288		340
222	222	295		345
235	235	308		352
	236***	309		354

ToA = Treaty of Amsterdam; SEA = Single European Act; MT = Maastricht Treaty

ABBREVIATIONS

AG	Advocate General
AFSJ	area of freedom, security and justice
CCT	Common Customs Tariff
CDR	consensual dispute resolution
CFI	Court of First Instance
CJEU	Court of Justice of the European Union
CHEE	charge having equivalent effect
COREPER	*Comité des représentants permanents*
EC	European Community
ECB	European Central Bank
ECFR	Charter of Fundamental Rights of the European Union
ECHR	European Convention on Human Rights
ECSC	European Coal and Steel Community
ECJ	European Court of Justice
EEA	European Economic Area
EEC	European Economic Community
EESC	European Economic and Social Committee
EFTA	European Free Trade Area
EIB	European Investment Bank
EMU	European Monetary Union
ERASMUS	European Community Action Scheme for the Mobility of University Students
EU	European Union
EURATOM	European Atomic Energy Community
GATT	General Agreement on Tariffs and Trade
MEP	Member of the European Parliament
MHEE	measure having equivalent effect
NATO	North Atlantic Treaty Organization
NCA	national competition authority
OECD	Organisation for Economic Cooperation and Development
OJ	*Official Journal of the European Union*
QMV	qualified majority voting
R&D	research and development
SEA	Single European Act
SGP	Stability and Growth Pact
SIEC	significant impediment to effective competition
SMEs	small and medium-sized enterprises
SSNIP	small but significant and non-transitory increase in prices
TEC	Treaty Establishing the European Community
TEEC	Treaty Establishing the European Economic Community

TEU	Treaty on European Union
TFEU	Treaty on the Functioning of the European Union
TTA	technology transfer agreement
UK	United Kingdom
US	United States [of America]
WEU	Western European Union
WTO	World Trade Organization

THE FOUNDATIONS OF THE EUROPEAN UNION

chapter
1

Creation of the European Community and European Union

study points

After reading this chapter, you will be able to understand:
- the original aims and objectives behind the creation of the European Community and European Union
- the twin-track approach of widening and deepening the European Union project
- the relationship between the United Kingdom and the European Union.

1.1 Introduction

The idea of the creation of a united Europe is not a new one. Yet until the end of the Second World War, all plans to establish such a union failed. The War served as a catalyst, States realising the full impact of two global wars on the European continent. In 1946, Sir Winston Churchill famously made a speech calling for the creation of a United States of Europe, to be based on reconciliation between France and Germany. Various motives linked to the aftermath of the Second World War (see 1.2 below) led to the creation of a number of international organisations, among them the European Economic Community (EEC, 1957), which, through a series of treaties expanding its membership and competences, transformed into the contemporary European Union (EU) based on the 2007 Treaty of Lisbon. More recently, the United Kingdom's (UK's) attitude towards the EU, as well as its membership of the EU, has once again been questioned (see further 1.6 below).

1.2 Motives for European integration

In the years following the end of the Second World War, responding to the interests and needs of European States but also to the threats and challenges they faced, an array of international organisations was created on the European continent. There were three main reasons for this:

(a) The States were eager to build a peaceful and more stable future for Europe and themselves. The result of this wish to prevent further conflicts and to provide human rights to those living in European States, was the creation in 1949 of the Council of Europe, a forum within which the States of Europe could cooperate, especially on social, cultural and legal matters. Its greatest success was the adoption in 1950 of the Convention for the Protection of Human Rights and Fundamental Freedoms (commonly referred to as the European Convention on Human Rights (ECHR)) and its enforcement machinery.

(b) The economies of the European States had been devastated by two wars and needed to be rebuilt. It was acknowledged that cooperation, rather than coexistence, was essential for economic growth. The United States (US) provided financial assistance under the Marshall Plan, a European recovery programme that was administered by the Organisation for European Economic Cooperation (1948), which later became the Organisation for Economic Cooperation and Development (OECD). Undoubtedly this encouraged States to cooperate in the economic field.

(c) Security issues were also high on the agenda. The Western European Union (WEU) was established in 1948 by Belgium, France, Luxembourg, The Netherlands and the United Kingdom as a security alliance to prevent another war. However, the Berlin blockade in 1948–49 (during which the Soviet Union denied the Western Allies access to the sectors of Berlin under allied control) and the strain on the relationship between the US and the Soviet Union triggered the creation of the North Atlantic Treaty Organisation (NATO) in 1949, the primary objective of which was to defend European States against the rising Soviet threat.

In 1950 Pleven, then French Prime Minister, suggested the creation of a European Defence Community. Whilst the treaty was signed by France, Germany, Italy, Belgium, The Netherlands and Luxembourg, it failed owing to the lack of ratification by the French Parliament. This put an end to a European defence organisation. In 2011 the WEU ceased to exist.

Yet none of these organisations led to the creation of the EU.

1.3 The creation of international (European) organisations

The four organisations mentioned in 1.2 above are international organisations, ie structures established by States in order to fulfil a certain role:

- Council of Europe – peace, cultural/social/legal cooperation, protection of human rights
- OECD – economic cooperation
- NATO and WEU – military defence.

Likewise, the EU was set up to provide peace, security, a harmonious development of economic activities, economic stability, a raising of the standard of living and a guarantee of well-being for those living on the European continent.

International organisations are usually based on a treaty, an agreement between States that binds them on the international level once they have ratified it. Such organisations are endowed by States with powers (through a mechanism of transfer of sovereign powers) in order to achieve the aims and objectives set out in the specific treaty. This formal transfer of sovereign powers from the States to the international organisation was on several occasions recognised by the European Court of the Justice (ECJ), now the superior court of the Court of Justice of the European Union (CJEU), the judicial body of the European Union, in relation to the European Union (Case 26/62 *NV Algemene Transport- en Expeditie Onderneming van Gend & Loos v Netherlands Inland Revenue Administration* [1963] ECR 1; Case 6/64 *Costa v ENEL* [1964] ECR 585). An international organisation can act only if it has received such (delegated) powers. The treaty acts as the constitution of the international organisation, specifying its composition, its membership, its institutions and their working relations, its areas of competences, etc. Therefore it is important to read with care any treaty that establishes an international organisation.

Many organisations go through a dynamic process, in the sense that their powers and competences change over time as treaties are amended to fit the interests of the members. For example the Organisation for European Economic Cooperation mutated into the OECD. Likewise, the European Coal and Steel Community (ECSC, created in 1951 for a period of 50 years only) became part of the EC when the Treaty establishing it expired on 23 July 2002. The EU has transformed mainly through two mechanisms:

- *Functional integration*: the European organisation has been given more and more sectors/areas of competences.
- *Spill-over effect*: the European organisation was allowed to act in a certain field that nevertheless had effects on another one. States then endowed the European organisation with the powers to act in the latter field.

That being said, it must be borne in mind that this process was developed by States, and especially by statespersons, without the involvement of their citizens. Consequently, a pending and recurrent issue is the involvement of European citizens in the European integration project, and the challenge of making the EU a more democratic international organisation.

In Case 26/62 *NV Algemene Transport- en Expeditie Onderneming van Gend & Loos v Netherlands Inland Revenue Administration* [1963] ECR 1 and in Case 6/64 *Costa v ENEL* [1964] ECR 585, the ECJ explained that the States had voluntarily limited their sovereignty in favour of a *sui generis* legal order:

The objective of the [EU] Treaty, which is to establish [an internal] Market, the functioning of which is of direct concern to interested parties in the [EU], implies that this Treaty is more than an agreement which merely creates mutual obligations between the contracting states ...

The [EU] constitutes a new legal order of international law for the benefit of which the states have limited their sovereign rights, albeit within limited fields, and the subjects of which comprise not only Member States but also their nationals. (Case 26/62 *Van Gend en Loos*, 12)

Consequently,

[b]y contrast with ordinary international treaties, the [EU] Treaty has created its own legal system which ... became an integral part of the legal systems of the Member States and which their courts are bound to apply. By creating a [Union] of unlimited duration, having its own institutions, its own personality, its own legal capacity and capacity of representation on the international plane and, more particularly, real powers stemming from a limitation of sovereignty or a transfer of powers from the States to the [Union], the Member States have limited their sovereign rights ... and have thus created a body of law which binds both their nationals and themselves.

... [T]he law stemming from the treaty, an independent source of law, could not, because of its special and original nature, be overridden by domestic legal provisions, however framed, without being deprived of its character as [EU] law and without the legal basis of the [Union] itself being called into question.

The transfer by the states from their domestic legal system to the [Union] legal system of rights and obligations arising under the Treaty carries with it a permanent limitation of their sovereign rights against which a subsequent unilateral act incompatible with the concept of the [Union] cannot prevail. (Case 6/64 *Costa v ENEL*, 593–94)

1.4 Widening participation

The European project started with six Member States (France, Germany, Italy, The Netherlands, Belgium and Luxembourg). There are now 28 Member States in the EU (see **Figure 1.1**).

The UK, Ireland and Denmark joined in 1973. Norway had also agreed upon its terms for entry, but the Norwegian people rejected European Community membership in a referendum, mainly because of concerns about their principal industries, oil and fishing. Greece started accession negotiations in 1976 after the fall of the military junta and the restoration of democracy. She became a Member State in 1981. Two former dictatorships, Spain and Portugal, joined in 1986 after eight years of negotiations, complicated by the fact that Portugal was very poor, Spain had a huge fishing fleet, and both countries, as large-scale producers of fruits and vegetables, would compete with France and Italy. The next round of enlargement was straightforward, with the accession of Austria, Sweden and Finland in 1995. Norway also participated in the negotiations, but yet again its population rejected the proposal for membership. The Czech Republic, Slovakia, Latvia, Lithuania, Estonia, Hungary, Poland and Slovenia, all former Communist States, and Malta completed the process of preparing for EU membership, and were admitted as Member States in 2004. Cyprus was also admitted in 2004. That being said, the island is still divided between the Greek Cypriot south, whose government is legally recognised internationally as the only legitimate government of the whole island, and the Turkish Cypriot north, whose government is not legally recognised by any State except Turkey. It was hoped that enough pressure could be exerted by the EU to achieve a political settlement before Cyprus's entry, but this did not happen. In theory, the whole of Cyprus is part of the EU, but in practice only the Greek part is subject to EU law. Romania and Bulgaria were allowed to join in 2007 and Croatia in 2013.

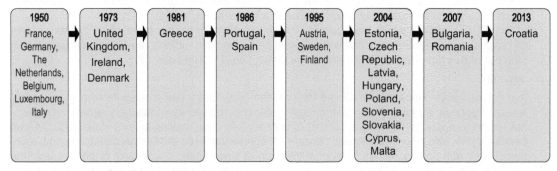

Figure 1.1   Membership of the EU (1950–2013)

In order to become a Member State of the EU, a State must fulfil a number of requirements that were set at the Copenhagen Summit in June 1993. The criteria are, first, that the State must have a stable government and institutions that are democratic and based on the rule of law and human rights (including the protection of minorities). It must also have a functioning market economy that is able to cope with the single market, which is the free trade and movement of labour, goods, services and capital. Moreover, the State must be able to accept the *acquis communautaire*, a French term that denotes all the rights and obligations that current members of the EU have (see 4.1). At the Madrid Summit in December 1995 it was explained that the candidate State must have created the conditions for its integration through adjustment of its administrative structures. A number of these requirements are now enshrined in Articles 2 and 3 TEU. A further criterion was set at the Helsinki Summit in 1999: good neighbourhood (no threat or action directed against a Member State and its sovereign rights). Candidate States then sign and ratify an accession treaty.

The prospect of EU membership has been offered to nine States: the Former Yugoslav Republic of Macedonia, Montenegro, Iceland, Albania, Bosnia-Herzegovina, Kosovo, Turkey and Serbia. Five of them have been granted official candidate status: Turkey, Former Yugoslav Republic of Macedonia, Serbia, Iceland and Montenegro. Turkey made repeated applications to join the EC, but until 2005 these were always rejected for three main reasons:

(a)   Turkey's economy is underdeveloped;
(b)   Turkey's human rights record is poor; and, most importantly,
(c)   Greece would not contemplate Turkey's admission until there was settlement of the Cyprus problem (see above).

Turkey has now been allowed to begin negotiations, and the prospect of its being admitted one day is being used as a bargaining counter in the tortuous process aimed at the settlement of the Cyprus problem. As Cyprus is now a Member State, it has the power to veto Turkish membership. Ukraine also expressed an interest in joining the EU, but owing to the ongoing armed conflict there, it is unlikely to become a Member State in the near future.

The only European States that seem happy to stay outside the EU are Norway and Switzerland. Norway is, however, a member of the European Economic Area (EEA), and Switzerland has signed an agreement with the EU; both are also part of the Schengen Area (see 1.5 below) and cooperation mechanism.

1.5   Deepening cooperation

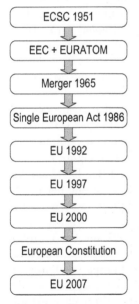

Figure 1.2   Deepening cooperation

The story of the European integration project started with the creation of the ECSC in 1951. A year earlier, Robert Schuman, the then French Foreign Minister, suggested a scheme (known to history as the Schuman Plan, although it was drafted by Jean Monnet) with the following aims:

(a)   to help the economic recovery and boost economic growth in Europe;
(b)   to remove competition between France and Germany that had led to two world wars;
(c)   to put the coal and steel industries of both Germany and France under the control of a supra-national body, ie a body that would be able to tell States what they could and could not do. This would ensure that Germany could not produce armaments.

Germany was happy to accept the scheme, and other States were invited to join. Belgium, The Netherlands, Luxembourg (which had already formed the Benelux economic union) and Italy all agreed, but the UK refused to join, partly out of insularity and partly because the then Labour Government had just nationalised both the coal and the steel industries.

In 1950, six States signed the Treaty of Paris, bringing into being the ECSC, the first genuinely supra-national body with a High Authority, an Assembly, a Council and a Court, organs that would later become the Commission, the European Parliament, the Council and the Court of Justice of the European Union. The aim of the ECSC was to remove barriers to trade in coal and steel, and to set up and manage common policies.

As the ECSC had proved very successful in revitalising the economies of the Member States, an intergovernmental committee, headed by Paul-Henri Spaak, presented a report in 1956 suggesting the establishment of an economic community and an atomic energy community. The result was the creation of the EEC and the European Atomic Energy Community (EURATOM) in Rome in 1957 (the Treaties of Rome). The aim of the EEC was to establish a common market, based on a customs union, the free movement of goods, persons and capital and common policies. It was decided that the three international organisations, the ECSC, the EEC and EURATOM, would have their own institutions but would share the Court of Justice and the Parliamentary Assembly. Later, in 1965, the Merger Treaty saw the creation of a single Council (of Ministers) and a Commission. Slowly, but assuredly, the three organisations were becoming one (see **Figure 1.3**).

The Single European Act 1986 was the first substantial revision of the original EEC Treaty. Its amendments attempted to ensure increased efficiency (use of qualified majority voting) and democracy (increased powers given to the European Parliament) in the (now) European Community (EC), and introduced an internal market, also referred to as a 'single market', to be attained by 1 January 1993 (see **Chapter 11**).

At this juncture it was obvious that States' cooperation went beyond mere economic collaboration. In 1985 five Member States (Belgium, France, Germany, Luxembourg and The Netherlands) adopted the Schengen Agreement, which gradually abolished border checks. In 1990 these States went further by adopting the Schengen Convention, which provided for, inter alia, the abolition of internal border controls and a common visa policy, thereby creating the Schengen Area. These treaties were independent of those operating the EC (see **20.2.1**).

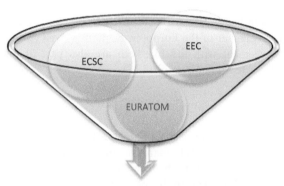

European Communities

Figure 1.3   The European Communities

The next major step was the Maastricht Treaty in 1992 (formally, the Treaty on European Union or TEU) that created the EU with increased powers and expanded areas of competences. In fact, the TEU worked as a framework treaty, setting up a three-pillar or temple structure to delineate these powers and competences (see **Figure 1.4**). The first pillar included the ECSC, EURATOM and the EC (the latter based on the European Community Treaty), ie the European Communities. The second pillar dealt with the Common Foreign Policy and Security, whilst the third pillar addressed issues relating to Justice and Home Affairs.

After two further amendments, the Treaty of Amsterdam 1997 and the Treaty of Nice 2000, the States agreed, in the Laeken Declaration in 2001, to set up a committee called 'European Convention' to draft a constitution for Europe. A European Constitution would have simplified matters since it aimed to incorporate all the aforementioned European Treaties into a single legal document. Although a text was agreed in 2004, it could not enter into force as it failed to be ratified by all the Member States. In 2007 the proposed treaty was formally abandoned and efforts were directed towards amending the Treaty of Nice.

A reform treaty was adopted in Lisbon in 2007 and took effect in December 2009. The Lisbon Treaty amended the founding Treaties by renaming the European Community Treaty as the Treaty on the Functioning of the European Union (TFEU) and renumbering the articles of the TEU and TFEU. Among the main changes introduced were:

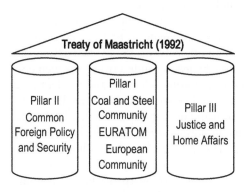

Figure 1.4   The three pillars of the EU under the Maastricht Treaty

- the creation of the High Representative of the Union for Foreign Affairs and Security Policy
- the recognition of the vital role played by the European Council
- a new definition of secondary EU law
- the insertion of the Charter of Fundamental Rights of the European Union into the TEU, giving it the same legal value as the Treaties
- the increased involvement of national parliaments in the law-making process, and
- the termination of the three-pillar structure described above.

The Lisbon Treaty is certainly not the last chapter in this chain of constitutional agreements. In the light of the recent financial and economic crisis, changes have already been suggested by several Member States.

in practice

The Lisbon Treaty renumbered the articles of the European Community Treaty and renamed it the Treaty on the Functioning of the European Union.

In parallel to the political and economic development in Europe, States attempted to create an economic and monetary union. In 1979 the European Exchange Rate Mechanism was established and the European Currency Unit (ECU) introduced with the aim to create monetary stability. The system operated outside of the then EEC. Economic and Monetary Union (EMU) became a reality under the Maastricht Treaty. While its economic aspects were defined in rather general terms, its monetary part was expressed in more coercive and specific ones. Indeed, the economic policy remains decentralised, with emphasis on coordination (Articles 120 and 121(1) TFEU), whilst the monetary and exchange-rate policies were centralised leading to the creation of a single currency in 1999, the euro, and the transfer of monetary powers to the European System of Central Banks headed by the European Central Bank (ECB) (see **2.5**), the primary objective of which is to 'maintain price stability' (Article 127(1) TFEU). This eurozone or euro area now consists of 19 Member States (Lithuania being the latest State to adopt the euro on 1 January 2015). While the UK and Denmark are still using their opt-outs obtained under the Maastricht Treaty, 'Member States with a derogation' (Article 139(1) TFEU) – Bulgaria, Croatia, the Czech Republic, Hungary, Poland, Romania and Sweden – are required, under the terms of their Accession Treaties, to adopt the Euro and join the eurozone as soon as they satisfy the euro convergence (or Maastricht) criteria under Article 140(1) TFEU, including successful participation in the European Exchange Rate Mechanism (ERM II) for at least two years.

The world financial crisis of 2008 emphasised the weaknesses and the incompleteness of the institutional design of the EMU, notably in respect of the economic policies where there was no EU institutional equivalent to the ECB. The blatant disregard by Member States of Treaty requirements relating to budget deficits and government debt led to sovereign debt crisis in four southern European countries (Portugal, Italy, Greece and Spain) and Ireland (PIIGS), threatening to undermine the economies of the rest of the Union and the very existence of the euro. While interest rates and monetary easing fell within the exclusive domain of the ECB, taxation and government expenditures remained national. In other words, the EU had a monetary union but no fiscal union. Following a proposal by Jean-Claude Trichet, the then head of the ECB, to adopt a form of fiscal union to guarantee adequate and prudent fiscal policies across the EU, in March 2011 the Member States first reformed the 1997 Stability and Growth Pact (SGP), designed to maintain stability within the EMU, with a view to strengthening its procedure and imposing automatic penalties for non-compliance with its deficit or debt rules. This reform was then followed by the adoption outside the framework of the EU Treaties, on 2 March 2012, of a new intergovernmental Treaty on Stability, Coordination and Governance in the Economic and Monetary Union (also referred to as TSCG or the Fiscal Stability Treaty). This Treaty, now known as the Fiscal Compact, signed by all Member States except the Czech Republic and the UK, entered into force on 1 January 2013 for the 16 Member States that ratified it before this date (a minimum of 12 ratifications were required). As from January 2015, the Treaty has been ratified by 25 EU States, of which 19 are eurozone States. The Fiscal Compact requires the ratifying States to keep their national budgets in balance or in surplus within a year of its entry into force for them, and to introduce a self-correcting mechanism to prevent future breaches. The Treaty also replicates the debt-brake rules contained in the SGP and requires States gradually to reduce their government debt to GDP ratio if it exceeds the 60% reference level.

1.6 The UK's attitude towards the European Union

The UK made its first application to join the then EEC in 1961, but this was rejected, mainly because of the opposition of De Gaulle, then President of France. A second application was made in 1967, but failed again due to France's hostility towards British membership. In January 1973, following the resignation of De Gaulle, the UK acceded to the EEC, and the European Communities Act 1972 took effect on 1 January 1973.

As the structure of the (now) EU underwent a number of changes in the course of its development, each treaty had to be ratified by every Member State. In 1988, UK Prime Minister Margaret Thatcher delivered a speech in Bruges setting out her view of Europe, which focused on opening the EU to Eastern European States and on criticising the intrusive nature of the European Commission. Whilst the pound joined the exchange rate mechanism of the European Monetary System in 1990, the UK made it clear that it would not join a single currency.

In 1992 the UK ratified the Maastricht Treaty that established the EU, but not without turmoil, as the vote in Parliament almost brought down the UK Government. Since then the UK has been able to negotiate agreement that certain issues be appended in a protocol to be separately agreed upon (Social Chapter in the Maastricht Treaty) or that opt outs be specifically granted (see now Protocol No 20 on the Application of Certain Aspects of Article 26 of the Treaty on the Functioning of the European Union to the United Kingdom and to Ireland; Protocol No 21 on the Position of the United Kingdom and Ireland in Respect of the Area of Freedom, Security and Justice; and Protocol No 30 on the Application of the Charter of

Fundamental Rights of the European Union to Poland and to the United Kingdom). This method allows EU States to enhance their cooperation (such as the incorporation of the Schengen Agreements into the Treaty of Amsterdam 1997) whilst giving the UK the right to opt out of participation in some policies. In 2000, as the EU institutions adopted the Charter of Fundamental Rights, the UK expressed its reservations about endowing it with legal status (though this was later given under the Lisbon Treaty) (see 4.6).

Throughout this period of time the UK has supported the Eastern enlargement of the EU, probably in the hope that a physical expansion of the Union would stymie further deepening of the European project. In 2008 the UK Parliament ratified the Treaty of Lisbon after a failed legal challenge to demand a referendum. In 2011 it passed the European Union Act, which not only requires any further transfer of powers to the EU to be accepted by way of referendum but also restates UK parliamentary sovereignty.

In 2012 the Government announced a review of the balance of competences in order to assess the impact of EU powers and competences on the UK. The review was completed in December 2014. Moreover, in light of growing discontent with EU migration and what is viewed as a lack of (parliamentary) sovereignty over domestic issues, the UK has planned to hold a referendum on UK membership before the end of 2017.

1.7 Further reading

Bulmer S and Lequesne C, *The Member States of the European Union* (Oxford University Press, 2013).

Craig P, 'The United Kingdom, the European Union and Sovereignty' in Rawlings R, Young A and Leyland P (eds), *Sovereignty and the Law, Domestic, European and International Perspectives* (Oxford University Press, 2013) 165.

Craig P, 'Britain in the European Union' in Jowell J and Oliver D (eds), *The Changing Constitution*, 7th edn (Oxford University Press, 2011) 92.

Craig P, 'The Treaty of Lisbon: Process, Architecture and Substance' (2008) 33 *EL Rev* 137.

Dinan D, *Ever Closer Union: An Introduction to European Integration*, 4th edn (Lynne Rienner, 2010)

Pinder J, *The Building of the European Union* (Oxford University Press, 1998).

Piris J-C, *The Lisbon Treaty: A Legal and Political Analysis* (Cambridge University Press, 2010).

Tatham AF, *Enlargement of the European Union* (Kluwer, 2009).

Wallace H, 'The UK: 40 Years of EU Membership' (2012) 8 *Journal of Contemporary European Research* 531.

summary

The EU is an international organisation created by States. It has evolved through a dynamic process involving further integration and expansion. Undoubtedly, the EU is a unique entity and has a complex structure. Often based on similarities rather than differences, the Member States have managed to create an integrated Europe. However, they do not always agree on the extent of such integration or 'deepening' of the Union. Furthermore, the European integration process seems to continue to be led by States rather than by the people it is supposed to bring together.

test your knowledge

1   Have the initial aims of the EEC been achieved?
2   Has the Lisbon Treaty brought the EU closer to its citizens?
3   What are the reasons for amending the Treaties, and do these amendments contribute to the process of the European integration?

The Institutional Framework of the European Union

After reading this chapter, you will be able to understand:

- the composition and functions of the seven EU institutions
- the sharing and division of powers and functions between such EU institutions
- the role played by other EU agencies and bodies
- how the principle of the separation of powers works in the EU.

2.1 Introduction

Article 13 of the Treaty on European Union (TEU) stipulates that the powers endowed by the Member States to the EU shall be exercised by seven institutions. Due to the composition and structure of these institutions, they represent different views, the idea being that as a result, a wide range of opinions can be expressed. Further, as the EU has developed, over time its institutions have changed, some growing in importance, others relinquishing their powers.

The EU has been criticised mainly on two issues:

(a) lack of democracy; and
(b) lack of the traditional separation of powers.

The institutions of the EU are complex, and thus warrant a thorough examination of their composition and powers.

2.2 Democracy and separation of powers within the European Union

2.2.1 Democracy in the EU

As mentioned in **2.1** above, the EU has often been criticised for its democratic deficit, notably because its institutions do not reflect the views of the EU citizens and were designed by States in view of the creation of an international organisation. This is certainly true of the institutions established by the predecessors of the EU.

Democracy is now one of the values upon which the Union is founded (Article 2 TFEU). The basic premise is that all public authority emanates from the people: people should take part in, or supervise, law making. The TEU envisages two forms of democracy in the Union:

(a) representative democracy (Article 10 TEU), whereby citizens as well as Member States are directly represented in the EU institutions. For example, the citizens directly elect their representatives in the European Parliament. Member States, on the other hand, nominate their government representatives (who are accountable to the national parliaments) in the Council. The part played by the European Parliament in law making reflects at Union level the 'fundamental democratic principle that the peoples should take part in the exercise of power through the intermediary of a representative assembly' (Case 138/79 *SA Roquette Frères v Council* [1980] ECR 3333, para 33);

(b) participatory democracy (Article 11 TEU), which enables citizens, Member States and other interested parties to air their views and make them known to the EU institutions through a range of formal and informal mechanisms. This form of democracy has the aim of leading to an open, transparent and regular dialogue among the stakeholders. This appeal to dialogue is specifically reflected in the obligation imposed on the Commission to consult widely and take note of any initiative put forward by a significant number of citizens (Articles 11(3) and 11(4) TEU). The European Citizens' Initiative allows groups of individuals to request the Commission to propose legislation in fields where the EU is competent to act. For example, the European Citizens' Initiative on water and sanitation as human rights was the first one to be examined by the European Commission (see **19.3.2.2**).

Moreover, the Lisbon Treaty has given national parliaments a formal role to play in the management and running of the EU (Article 12 TEU). This is examined in further detail in **5.3.1**.

2.2.2 The separation of powers in the EU

The separation of powers and the rule of law are two principles relating to democracy. A first approach towards the doctrine of separation of powers provides that the three types of government – executive, legislative and judicial – are allocated to three separate entities. A second approach is that the distribution of powers leads to a combination of powers that enables a system of checks and balances. It is the second conception that seems to have been espoused by the drafters of the EU, as the European Treaties have

> set up a system for distributing powers among different [Union] institutions, assigning to each institution its own role in the institutional structure of the [Union] and the accomplishment of the tasks entrusted to the [Union]. (Case C-70/88 *European Parliament v Council (Re Chernobyl)* [1990] ECR I-2041, para 21)

That being said, the powers are often shared in the EU: the legislative power (ie making laws) is shared between the Commission, the European Parliament and the Council; the executive power (ie proposing and implementing laws) is shared between the Commission and the Council; the judicial power (arbitrating laws in court) is in the hands of the Court of Justice of the European Union (though the European Commission also plays an important role with regard to the application and enforcement of the law (see **7.2**)). This is why the concept of **institutional balance** is to be preferred to that of separation of powers.

Two further powers can be now added to the three mentioned above:

- external competences and
- governmental control of financial markets.

See **Figure 2.1**.

2.3 The political institutions of the European Union

Article 13 TEU lists seven institutions, namely:

- the European Commission ('the Commission')

- the Council
- the European Parliament
- the Court of Justice of the European Union
- the European Council
- the European Central Bank, and
- the Court of Auditors.

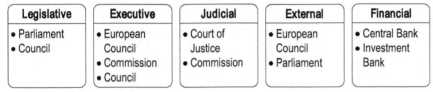

Legislative	Executive	Judicial	External	Financial
• Parliament • Council	• European Council • Commission • Council	• Court of Justice • Commission	• European Council • Parliament	• Central Bank • Investment Bank

Figure 2.1   Powers of the EU institutions

The political institutions – the Commission, the Council, the European Parliament and the European Council – are discussed in further detail in 2.3.1–2.3.4 below; the Court of Auditors is examined in 2.4; the Monetary Union institutions – the European Central Bank and the European System of Central Banks – are discussed in 2.5. The CJEU is discussed in detail in **Chapter 8** of this book.

2.3.1 The Commission

The Commission is the best place to start an examination of the institutions of the EU, not because it is the most important – it certainly is not – but because it is the starting-point for the making of EU law: it is the institution that springs to mind when the EU is mentioned, and it is entrusted with the promotion of the interests of the Union. It is based in Brussels, which is itself used as a shorthand term for the EU centre of power generally.

2.3.1.1 Constitution and appointment of the Commission

The Commission finds its legal bases in Article 17 TEU and Articles 244–250 TFEU. Since 1 November 2004 it consists of 28 Commissioners, one from each Member State (Article 17 TEU). However, with the future enlargement of the EU in mind, and in the interest of improving efficiency, the Lisbon Treaty introduced a new scheme of composition for the Commission that should have started on 1 November 2014. According to Article 17(4) TEU there should be a system of rotation based on the principle of equality to allocate places on the Commission corresponding to two-thirds of the number of Member States and 'reflecting the demographic and geographical range of all the Member States'. The implementing arrangements were to be adopted by the European Council (see **2.3.4**) acting unanimously. However, in 2009 the European Council decided that the Commission would continue to exist in its current form.

Commissioners are *not* representatives of their Member States. Legally, Commissioners are independent of the Member State that nominated them (Article 17(3) TEU; Article 245 TFEU). That being said, whilst Commissioners are not taking orders from their Member States, they keep a careful eye on matters affecting their home States. This is in fact useful to the Commission as a whole, as it enables it to get early warning of what will or will not be acceptable when drafting an act. From the perspective of Member States, there is often dissatisfaction that 'their' Commissioner is not protecting their interests.

The Commission is a collegiate body. Its workings are explained in the 2007 Governance Statement (30 May 2007) and the procedure is regulated by its 2011 Rules of Procedure ([2000] OJ L308/26 as amended by [2010] OJ L55/60 and [2011] OJ L296/58). All decisions are issued in the name of the whole Commission, not individual Commissioners. Yet each Commissioner has a particular area of responsibility: finance, transport, environment, etc. In practice, straightforward matters will be dealt with by individual Commissioners, their decisions being rubber-stamped by the others. However, all controversial matters will be discussed by the whole Commission at its Wednesday meetings, and decisions will, if necessary, be taken by simple majority vote. These meetings are not public and discussions are confidential.

Each Commissioner is assisted by a *cabinet*. Under the Commission there are 23 Directorates-General, each responsible for a particular policy area, headed by a Director-General and staffed by civil servants. There is a general public belief that the Commission is a huge bureaucracy, but this is not true. In fact, there are about 33,000 established posts, though there are also temporary, seconded and casual workers. This compares with the number of employees in an average-size County or City Council in the UK – and the Commission has the whole of Europe to look after.

- European Council nominates Commission President-elect (QMV)

- European Parliament approves Commission President-elect

- European Council by common accord with the Commission President adopts a list of candidate Commissioners

- European Parliament approves proposed Commission

- European Council appoints Commission

Figure 2.2   Procedure for appointment of the Commission

The President of the Commission is nominated by qualified majority voting by the European Council, taking account of the elections of the European Parliament (Article 17(7) TEU) and is then subject to approval by the European Parliament. The current President is Jean-Claude Juncker from Luxembourg. The other Commissioners are nominated by the President-elect and the European Council, after being put forward by the Member States. Thereafter the whole Commission is subject to the approval of the European Parliament, which usually questions the Commissioners individually before voting. However, the European Parliament cannot object to a specific Commissioner candidate, as it votes for or against the whole suggested Commission. However, it can exert enough political pressure to force a Member State to withdraw an unpopular nominee. Each Commissioner, including the President of the Commission, serves for a five-year term (renewable), which coincides with the term of the European Parliament. The kind of person chosen varies, but generally candidates have had a political career in their own Member State. The requirements for designation as member of the Commission are very broadly defined: nationality, competence and independence (Article 245 TFEU).

The Commission as a whole can be removed by a vote of censure by the European Parliament (Article 17(8) TEU; Article 234 TFEU). This possibility was used, though unsuccessfully, in 1999, as a result of which the Commission, headed by Jacques Santer, resigned. However, as mentioned above, it is not within the European

Parliament's powers to remove a specific Commissioner. That being said, under Article 247 TFEU the Commission or Council can seize the Court of Justice to 'retire' a Commissioner, and under Article 17(6) TEU the President of the Commission can ask a member to resign if he has the approval of the rest of the Commission.

2.3.1.2 Role of the Commission

The role of the Commission is set out in Article 17(1) TEU:

> 1. The Commission shall promote the general interest of the Union and take appropriate initiatives to that end. It shall ensure the application of the Treaties, and of measures adopted by the institutions pursuant to them. It shall oversee the application of Union law under the control of the Court of Justice of the European Union. It shall execute the budget and manage programmes. It shall exercise coordinating, executive and management functions, as laid down in the Treaties. With the exception of the common foreign and security policy, and other cases provided for in the Treaties, it shall ensure the Union's external representation. It shall initiate the Union's annual and multiannual programming with a view to achieving interinstitutional agreements.

The Commission formulates and suggests policy initiatives and legislative proposals (see **5.3.1**). Although it has the right of initiative, most proposals are on matters for which it has received instructions from the Council (**2.3.2**) or the European Council (**2.3.4**). Yet it remains the Commission's task to put the proposals into legislative form, and it is under no obligation to obey the Council's wishes. The Commission can also put forward its own ideas, but with no guarantee of acceptance.

The Commission acts as an executive of the Union. In fact, the Commission is in many ways the civil service of the EU, as it runs its everyday work and tends to act on the basis of simple majority votes (eg, competition policy and mergers control, the European Community Action Scheme for the Mobility of University Students (ERASMUS programme)).

The Commission has extensive rule-making powers, especially in relation to agriculture and trade, eg anti-dumping measures. Law-making powers may be categorised as those delegated by way of a legislative act (Article 290 TFEU) or implementing powers (Article 291(2) TFEU). With regard to such delegated acts, Article 290(1) TFEU explains that

> A legislative act may delegate to the Commission the power to adopt non-legislative acts of general application to supplement or amend certain non-essential elements of the legislative act.
>
> The objectives, content, scope and duration of the delegation of power shall be explicitly defined in the legislative acts. The essential elements of an area shall be reserved for the legislative act and accordingly shall not be the subject of a delegation of power.

Under Article 290(2)(a) TFEU, the European Parliament or the Council may revoke any such delegation. As for the implementing powers of the Commission, under Article 291(3) TFEU, their exercise can be controlled by rules and principles laid down in Regulation 182/2011 ([2011] OJ L55/13) (see further **5.4**).

The Commission drafts, manages and implements the EU budget. It drafts the budget within the overall guidelines agreed by the Council. It ensures that Member States pay their contributions, and is supposed to check that the money is spent properly. The Commission performs this duty under the supervision of the Council, the Parliament and the Court of Auditors (see **2.4**). The Commission also administers four European funds:

- the Social Fund
- the Development Fund
- the Agricultural Guidance and Guarantee Fund, and
- the Regional Development Fund.

As the guardian of the Treaties, the Commission ensures the proper application of the Treaties and other Union acts. When the time limit for implementing an EU act has been reached, the Commission will verify that Member States have implemented the act and, if they have not, has the power to initiate a procedure that might lead to a Member State being brought before the Court of Justice (see further **7.2**). The Commission perceives its role in the enforcement of laws as being as much political as legal. It will not take legal action against a Member State until it has tried negotiation, persuasion and compromise. However, the Commission is not the only body responsible for the correct application of EU law; this task belongs even more so to the national authorities, and especially to the national courts (see **9.1**).

The Commission also represents the EU at the international level. Where the EU is engaged in international negotiations as an entity separate from the Member States, it is the Commission that conducts the negotiations, under the guidance of the Council (eg negotiations at the World Trade Organization (WTO)). This role is specifically recognised in the field of the common commercial policy by Article 207(3) TFEU, and the procedures for the exercise of this role are set out within Article 218 TFEU. The EU can become a party to treaties in its own right, and besides negotiating international agreements, the Commission is also entrusted with maintaining all appropriate relations with international organisations (Article 220 TFEU) (eg the United Nations and its agencies, the Council of Europe). The Commission fulfils this role through the High Representative of the Union for Foreign Affairs and Security Policy (currently Federica Mogherini).

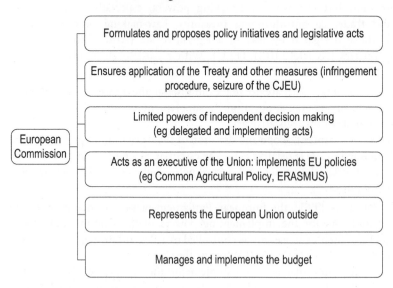

Figure 2.3   Role of the Commission

2.3.2 The Council

2.3.2.1 Configuration of the Council

The Council is the most powerful institution in the EU and is composed of representatives of the Member States (Ministers). The Council finds its legal bases in Article 16 TEU and Articles 237–243 TFEU. In particular, Article 16 TEU specifies:

1. The Council shall, jointly with the European Parliament, exercise legislative and budgetary functions. It shall carry out policy-making and coordinating functions as laid down in the Treaties.

2. The Council shall consist of a representative of each Member State at ministerial level, who may commit the government of the Member State in question and cast its vote.

3. The Council shall act by a qualified majority except where the Treaties provide otherwise.

The Council comprises one representative from each Member State, authorised to commit and act on behalf of that State (Article 16(2) TEU). This also means that Ministers are accountable to their national parliaments. Thus, the Council can claim democratic legitimacy, as Ministers are accountable, through national parliaments, to their own electorates. The exact configuration of the Council depends on the subject matter to be discussed (Article 16(6) TEU). There are currently 10 configurations. For example, the term 'Foreign Affairs Council' is used when it is the Foreign Ministers of the Member States who attend, whilst ECOFIN ('Economic and Financial Affairs') refers to the meeting of the Finance Ministers. All other meetings are called Technical Councils, and consist of the Ministers for the particular subject under discussion (eg agriculture, transport, environment, etc). However, there remains a single Council in that, regardless of the configuration of the Council that adopts a decision, that decision is always a Council decision, no mention being made of the configuration adopted in any particular case. The Council has the support of a secretariat, based in Brussels, which consists of international civil servants recruited from Member States.

Since the Treaty of Lisbon came into force, there is an overarching presidency for particular configurations within the Council, apart from the Foreign Affairs Council. Based on a system of equal rotation (Article 16(9) TEU), each presidency is determined by qualified majority voting (Article 236 TFEU). Acting as President is a tremendous opportunity for the politicians of a Member State, especially those of a small State. It is very hard work, but it gives the office-holder the chance to make a mark on the world stage. Most Member States like to set objectives to be attained during their candidate's term of office, and may lose face if they fail to achieve these.

2.3.2.2 Function of the Council

According to Article 16(1) TEU, the main function of the Council is passing legislation, and it is this that makes it the most important institution. It also has an important voice as regards policy development, coordination and harmonisation. Indeed, under Article 241 TFEU, the Council can ask the Commission to prepare proposals; in practice, the Council usually decides exactly what it wants and then asks the Commission to produce the formal legislative proposal. Articles 121 and 126 TFEU provide the Council with specific powers to coordinate the Member States' economic policies, and it may impose sanctions in this connection. The Council also concludes international agreements between the EU and other States or international organisations, develops the Common Foreign and Security Policy and coordinates cooperation in the field of justice and criminal matters. All of the Council's legislative deliberations are public, and most of its official documents are accessible to the public.

in practice

The Council is assisted by a body called by its French acronym, COREPER (*Comité des représentants permanents*), which was set up in 1958 but only formally recognised in the Merger Treaty of 1965. It comprises representatives of the Member States (Articles 16(7) TEU and 240 TFEU). In fact, each Member State keeps the equivalent of an embassy in Brussels, headed by the permanent representative and staffed by national civil servants.

The role of the COREPER consists in carrying out preliminary scrutiny of all the dossiers on the Council agenda, apart from agricultural issues that are left to be dealt with by the Special Committee on Agriculture. With this view, the COREPER works in two configurations:

A items: COREPER I: sectoral and technical policy areas (staffed by deputy permanent representatives); and

B items: COREPER II: issues that cover a range of policy areas and politically sensitive policy areas (staffed by permanent representatives from the EU Member States).

The items on the agenda for the meetings of the Council reflect this division: 'A items' are approved without discussion following agreement within the COREPER, whilst 'B items' are open for discussion. This system enables the Council to focus its attention on the more politically sensitive issues.

2.3.2.3 Council voting procedures

Under Article 238 TFEU, the Council can use three different voting procedures:

(a) *Unanimity* – each Member State is given the power to veto a measure. It is used for the most sensitive issues, such as the admission of new Member States, harmonising taxes and deciding whether a State can join the euro. In cases where unanimity is required and one State votes against a proposal, the whole proposal fails. Abstention cannot be used by Member State to stop the adoption of an EU measure requiring unanimity (Article 238(4) TFEU).

(b) *Simple majority voting* – this is used only for procedural matters, as it could lead to the large Member States being outvoted by the small Member States.

(c) *Qualified majority voting (QMV)* – the QMV system is meant to introduce the concepts of democracy and efficiency in law-making. According to Article 16(3) TEU, QMV is the rule. Each State has a number of votes, according to its size and importance, and a substantial majority is needed to make a decision. But that decision is then binding on all the Member States, even if they voted against it. With the current configuration of 28 Member States, there are 352 votes. Since 1 November 2014 a qualified majority is defined as

at least 55% of the members of the Council, comprising at least fifteen of them and representing Member States comprising at least 65% of the population of the Union. (Article 16(4) TEU)

In cases where one or more members of the Council do not take part in the vote as a result of an opt-out clause on the issue being voted upon, figures are adjusted accordingly.

That being said, under the TFEU and Article 3(2) of Protocol (No 36) on Transitional Provisions ([2012] OJ C115/322), a Member State may request that a different definition of qualified majority be used. First, under paragraph 3 of the Protocol, the weighting of Member States' votes is different. Secondly, paragraph 3 of the Protocol provides that when the proposal stems from the Commission, a majority is reached when at least 255 votes are cast in favour of the act, but that in other cases the majority is reached when these 255 votes represent at least two-thirds of the Member States. Thirdly, paragraph 4 of the Protocol introduces a safeguard, allowing Member States to ask if the qualified majority represents at least 62% of the total population of the EU. This system will end on 31 March 2017.

2.3.3 The European Parliament

2.3.3.1 Composition of the European Parliament

The European Parliament started life as a rather ineffectual body called the European Assembly, consisting of nominated individuals from the Member States. The most significant developments for this body were its change of name to 'Parliament' in 1962 (a change later formalised in the 1986 Single European Act) and the introduction of direct elections in 1979. However, the use of the term 'Parliament' is misleading. Usually a parliament is a jurisdiction's main law-making body, a legislature, but the European Parliament is not such a body as it shares its legislative functions with other institutions (see **2.2.2** above).

As the European Parliament is the only EU institution directly elected by the people of Europe it is endowed with democratic legitimacy. The main relevant legal provisions in relation to the European Parliament are Article 14 TEU and Articles 223–234 TFEU.

Members of the European Parliament (MEPs) are directly elected by EU citizens. Elections take place every five years (Article 14(3) TEU). There are currently 766 MEPs. The main criterion for allocation of seats is, broadly speaking, the population of the Member States concerned, but it should be borne in mind that representation is degressively proportional (Article 14(2) TEU), that is, more populous Member States will have more seats in the European Parliament, but there should be at least six and no more than 96 members for every Member State. The way MEPs are elected in their own States varies greatly, despite the fact that Article 223(1) TFEU provides for a uniform electoral procedure. Once elected, MEPs sit not by State, but by party group. In plenary sessions they sit in a hemicycle with parties of all types, from far left to far right, as MEPs are organised in cross-border political groupings (Article 10(4) TEU).

2.3.3.2 Functions of the European Parliament

The European Parliament has four main functions:

- legislative powers
- budgetary powers
- control of the Executive
- the right to litigate.

Legislative powers

Through the ordinary and special legislative procedures (see 5.3), the European Parliament is involved in the adoption of legislative acts of the EU (Article 14 TFEU). It can also ask the Commission to submit a proposal (Article 225(2) TFEU). This does not mean that the Commission has to do so, nor that the Council will agree to the Parliament's request, but it does give the European Parliament a formal input into the policy process.

Budgetary powers

The European Parliament has one of the main powers that a national parliament usually has, that of approving or disapproving the EU budget. The budget is drafted by the Commission, within overall financial guidelines agreed by the Member States, and adopted following a complex procedure set out in Article 314 TFEU. Prior to the Lisbon Treaty, the budget was divided into compulsory expenditures (eg Common Agricultural Policy and Common Foreign Policy) and non-compulsory expenditures (eg, research, aid, regional policy, social policy), and the European Parliament had the last word only with respect to the latter. Since the coming into force of the Lisbon Treaty, the European Parliament enjoys the same rights as the Council as regards the adoption of the annual budget in its entirety.

Control of the 'Executive'

Controlling the Executive is central to any democratic political system. As explained in 2.3.1.1 above, the Commission is approved and can be removed by the European Parliament. Furthermore, the European Parliament receives a variety of reports from both the Commission and the Council. According to Article 233 TFEU, the European Parliament is allowed to discuss the Commission's annual general reports, and according to Article 230 TFEU it has the power to question the Commission and the Council through a system of oral and written questions. It may also set up a Committee of Inquiry (Articles 226–227 TFEU) to look into violations or wrongful applications of Union law by Member States. One such committee was established, for example, at the time of the 'mad cow disease' outbreak in the mid-1990s, leading to the establishment of a European veterinary agency.

Right to litigate

Originally, the European Parliament did not have the right to litigate. Nonetheless, such a right was given to it by way of case law. The European Parliament is allowed to challenge another institution's failure to act before the CJEU (Case 13/83 *European Parliament v Council (Re Transport Policy)* [1985] ECR 1513; Article 265 TFEU; Case C-70/88 *European Parliament v Council (Re Chernobyl)* [1990] ECR I-2041), in order either to protect its own prerogatives (Case 302/87 *European Parliament v Council (Re Comitology)* [1988] ECR 5615) or if it so wishes to challenge, pursuant to Article 263 TFEU (see 10.2), the legality of the acts adopted by institutions.

Redress of individual grievances

In addition to the four main powers discussed above, the European Parliament provides a mechanism to redress individual grievances. First, MEPs may be used by individuals as a point of contact for dealing with problems. How willing MEPs are to do this will be determined by the practice of the individual Member State and the electoral system in use. Secondly, according to Article 227 TFEU, EU citizens have the right to petition the European Parliament. A committee of 34 members will examine the petition, which may present an individual request, a complaint or an observation concerning the application of EU law, or an appeal to the European Parliament to adopt a position on a specific matter. Thirdly, the Ombudsman (Article 228 TFEU) who is appointed by the European Parliament examines complaints about maladministration committed by the EU institutions, with a view to reaching an amicable solution in the instant case. More generally, the Ombudsman reports to the European Parliament. The petitioner receives a report on the issue raised but cannot enforce the conclusions of the Ombudsman. That being said, European institutions largely comply with the conclusions of the Ombudsman, and those that do not are required to explain what actions they have taken six months after the report is issued.

2.3.4 The European Council

From 1974 onwards, Heads of State or Governments of the Member States decided to meet up regularly, despite the lack of a legal basis for such meetings in the Treaties. In the Single European Act 1986, these meetings were formally recognised under the title of the European Council and the membership was laid down: the Heads of State or Government, the Foreign Ministers, the President of the Commission and one other Commissioner, to discuss matters outside the formal scope of the Treaties (eg international crises).

According to Article 15(2) TEU, the European Council now comprises:

* Heads of State or Government of the Member States
* the President of the European Council
* the President of the Commission, and
* the High Representative of the Union for Foreign Affairs and Security Policy.

The European Council is headed by a President for a term of two and a half years, who has been elected by qualified majority (Article 15(5) TEU). The current President is Donald Tusk, who took over from Herman van Rompuy on 1 December 2014.

The Lisbon Treaty recognised that the European Council was an institution on its own that should provide the Union with the impetus for reform and closer cooperation (Article 15(1) TEU). All really important decisions are taken at its meetings (eg admission of new States, new treaties and major policy decisions like the introduction of the euro). The agenda can easily get cluttered with whatever politically sensitive issues are hot news at the time. The meetings take place four times a year (or more, should the situation so require), and there is a combination of formal sessions, informal meetings and bilateral discussions. Decisions are taken by consensus under Article 15(4) TEU. The President also reports to the European Parliament (Article 15(6)(d) TEU).

2.4 The European Court of Auditors

The relevant legal provisions for the European Court of Auditors are Articles 285–287 TFEU. The Court of Auditors is an independent supervisory body whose task it is to examine the accounts of all revenue and expenditure of the Union. Despite its name, it is not a court, as it has no judicial functions. It comprises one national from each Member State. Both the Council and the European Parliament are involved in the appointment procedure. Under Article 286(1) TFEU, auditors must be chosen from among persons who belong or have belonged in their respective States to external audit bodies or who are especially qualified for this office. Their independence must be beyond doubt.

Under Article 319 TFEU, the European Court of Auditors is responsible for auditing the EU's accounts, making sure that all the money has been spent properly and can be accounted for. It then reports to the European Parliament, which has the power to vote formally to discharge the budget, ie declare itself satisfied with the records of how the money has been spent. On occasion, including 1984 and 1996, the European Parliament has refused to grant a discharge, because the auditors' report revealed that money had gone astray and could not be traced. This virtually amounts to censuring the Commission.

2.5   The Monetary Union institutions: the European Central Bank and the European System of Central Banks

The European Central Bank (ECB) is governed by Articles 282–284 TFEU and Protocol (No 4) on the Statute of the European System of Central Banks and of the European Central Bank. Based in Frankfurt (Germany), it is part of the European System of Central Banks, which comprises the ECB and the national central banks of all Member States irrespective of whether or not they have adopted the euro. Its key task is to conduct the Union's monetary policy and maintain the euro's purchasing power, and thus price stability in the euro area (also known as the 'eurozone'). The euro area comprises the 19 EU Member States that have introduced the euro since 1999: Austria, Belgium, Cyprus, Estonia, Finland, France, Germany, Greece, Ireland, Italy, Latvia, Lithuania, Luxembourg, Malta, Netherlands, Portugal, Slovakia, Slovenia and Spain.

The ECB's Governing Council is made up of the governors of the central banks of Member States whose currency is the euro, and the members of the ECB's Executive Board. The Board consists of the President, Vice-President and four members (Article 283 TFEU), who are appointed by the European Council for a non-renewable eight-year term.

The Governing Council formulates the Union's monetary policy, whilst the Executive Board implements that policy and gives the necessary directions to the national central banks. The ECB's activities are not funded from the EU budget but rather from the national central banks.

2.6   The Union's advisory bodies

In addition to the seven institutions listed in Article 13 TEU, the EU has created a range of entities (eg the Committee of Transport, the Economic and Finance Committee, the Committee on the European Social Fund, the Office for Veterinary and Plant Health Inspection, the European Environmental Agency, Europol and the European Union Agency for Fundamental Rights) to play an executive or advisory role. Owing to their diversity, it is not possible to categorise them, although there is a distinction between those based on the Treaties and those set up by Union legislation.

Three noteworthy advisory bodies are:

*   the **European Economic and Social Committee** (EESC; Articles 300–304 TFEU). This is a long-standing body of the EU as it was included in the original Treaty of Rome. It comprises no more than 350 representatives of various groups of

economic and social activity, appointed for a five-year renewable term by the Council after consultation with the European Parliament. Its opinions are non-binding, though compulsory in some areas such as the Common Agricultural Policy, mobility of labour or transport, etc.

- the **Committee of the Regions** (Articles 300 and 305–307 TFEU). The Committee consists of no more than 350 representatives appointed by the Council acting unanimously on a proposal from the Commission. As the Committee of the Regions is meant to represent regional and local bodies of the Member States, its members must either be elected members of regional or local authorities, or be politically answerable to an elected assembly. Its opinions are non-binding, but the Committee of Regions must be consulted in a number of areas such as vocational training, cross-border cooperation and transport, protection of the environment, etc. The Treaty of Lisbon has granted the Committee of the Regions additional rights, such as the right to start proceedings under Article 263 TFEU to defend its prerogatives (see **10.2.4.2**), and under Protocol (No 2) on the Application of the Principles of Subsidiarity and Proportionality to ensure the correct application of the principle of subsidiarity (see **3.4**).
- the **European Investment Bank** (EIB; Articles 308–309 TFEU). This bank, owned by and representing the interests of the EU Member States, provides financial expertise for investment projects contributing to developing EU policy objectives. It further offers loans and financial support for such projects.

2.7 Further reading

Chiti E, 'An Important Part of the EU's Institutional Machinery: Features, Problems and Perspectives of European Agencies' (2009) 46 *CML Rev* 1395.

Conway G, 'Recovering a Separation of Powers in the European Union' (2011) 17 *European Law Journal* 304.

Curtin D, *Executive Power of the European Union* (Oxford University Press, 2009).

Lang JT, 'Checks and Balances in the European Union: The Institutional Structure and the "Community Method"' (2006) 12 *European Public Law* 127.

Moravcsik A, 'In Defence of the "Democratic Deficit": Reassessing Legitimacy in the European Union' (2002) 40 *Journal of Common Market Studies* 603.

Nugent N, *The Government and Politics of the European Union*, 7th edn (Palgrave, 2010).

Schmidt VA, 'Re-envisioning the European Union: Identity, Democracy, Economy' (2009) 47 *Journal of Common Market Studies* 17.

Sieberson SC, 'The Treaty of Lisbon and its Impact on the European Union's Democratic Deficit' (2007-2008) 14 *Columbia Journal of European Law* 445.

Tsadiras A, 'The Position of the European Ombudsman in the Community System of Judicial Remedies' (2007) 32(5) *EL Rev* 607.

Wallace H, Pollack M and Young A, *Policy-Making in the EU*, 6th edn (Oxford University Press, 2010).

There are seven main institutions in the EU:

- the Commission
- the Council
- the European Parliament
- the European Council,
- the Court of Justice of the European Union
- the European Court of Auditors, and
- the European Central Bank.

There is no separation of powers in the EU in the way this concept is understood at national level. One rather refers to the concept of 'institutional balance'.

Democracy in the EU is ensured through representative and participative democracy.

1 It has been argued that the division of competences between (i) the European Parliament and the European Commission, (ii) the Council and (iii) the CJEU reflects broadly the classical division between the legislative, executive, and judicial powers. To what extent does this statement reflect the reality of the EU?

2 By using the example of at least one of the EU institutions, critically analyse whether the EU lacks democratic legitimacy.

3 By what means can the European Parliament control the activities of the other EU institutions?

3 Division of Competences between the Union and the Member States

After reading this chapter, you will be able to understand:

- the distinction between powers and competences
- the principle of conferral
- the delineation of competences between the European Union and the Member States
- the limits to the competences of the European Union.

3.1 Introduction

International organisations such as the EU, which has been granted legal personality under Article 47 TEU, are endowed with powers and competences. Powers allow the EU to act in a certain way, eg legislative power. In contrast, a 'competence' refers to the ability and responsibility to act in a given field, and this usually relates to a particular area or policy specified in the Treaties. For example, the EU has the competence to legislate in the field of the customs union. Undoubtedly the two concepts are intertwined, and it is common to see them used interchangeably.

After explaining the powers of the EU, and notably the principle of conferral, this chapter investigates the delineation of competences between the EU and the Member States. Lastly, it examines the limits to the competences of the EU.

3.2 Powers

3.2.1 Principle of conferral

Member States confer upon the Union some of their sovereign powers, if and when they consider that their interests are better served by common action. As a result, in order for the EU to act, it must ensure that the Member States have conferred upon it the power to do so. Under the **principle of conferral** stipulated in Article 5(2) TEU, 'the Union shall act only within the limits of the competences conferred upon it by the Member States in the Treaties to attain the objectives set out therein'. Competences not conferred upon the Union in the Treaties remain with the Member States. Consequently, for the EU to act, its actions must be founded upon a legal basis laid down in the Treaties.

There are two consequences:

- The EU does not have the power to confer powers on itself (this is known as *Kompetenz-Kompetenz*). In other words, its powers are delegated by the Member States (and can be reclaimed by Member States by, say, amending the Treaties) and it cannot expand its powers.

- If the EU acts beyond its powers (an *ultra vires* act) then the action is invalid since the Union did not have the power to take it. It is therefore possible to bring an action for annulment before the CJEU under Article 263 TFEU (see **10.2**).

Thus powers are *expressly* delegated in the Treaties.

3.2.2 Implied powers

Although powers are expressly delegated to the EU by the Member States, the ECJ has through its case law extended the existing powers of the EU, notably by using the theory of implied powers (Case 8/55 *Fédération Charbonnière de Belgique v High Authority* [1954-1956] ECR 292). Implied powers are defined as powers that do not result directly and expressly from treaty provisions but which are derived from general objectives set out in the particular treaty. For example, the ECJ expanded the powers of the Union in the internal (eg Joined Cases 281, 283–285 and 287/85 *Germany and Others v Commission* [1987] ECR 3203) and the external (Case 22/70 *Commission v Council (Re ERTA)* [1971] ECR 263) spheres of action of the EU.

case example

In Case 22/70 *Commission of the European Communities v Council of the European Communities (ERTA)* [1971] ECR 263, five of the six original Member States had signed a treaty on the working practices of international road transport crews (ERTA), which, however, did not enter into force owing to an insufficient number of ratifications. Renegotiations started at a later stage, but by this time the (then) European Community had adopted measures falling within that field. The Commission challenged the Council that had passed a resolution setting out the Member States' position vis-à-vis the negotiations, on the basis that the European Community, rather than the individual Member States, should negotiate the treaty.

In *ERTA* the ECJ explained that the internal powers of the EU should be mirrored externally. As a result, whenever the EU adopts common rules, Member States no longer have the right to undertake agreements with third States that would affect these rules. The *ERTA* jurisprudence allowed the ECJ to develop the **doctrine of parallelism**, whereby the internal powers of the EU are matched externally (*Opinion 2/91 (Re ILO Convention 170)* [1993] ECR I-1061 and *Opinion 1/76 (Re Rhine Navigation Case)* [1977] ECR 741).

3.2.3 Residual powers

Besides the **doctrine of implied powers** discussed in **3.2.2** above, Article 352(1) TFEU stipulates:

> If action by the Union should prove necessary, within the framework of the policies defined in the Treaties, to attain one of the objectives set out in the Treaties, and the Treaties have not provided the necessary powers, the Council, acting unanimously on a proposal from the Commission and after obtaining the consent of the European Parliament, shall adopt the appropriate measures ...

This means that in the case where the Treaties have not provided the EU with the necessary powers to take appropriate measures to reach the aims specified in the Treaties, the Council can 'authorise' such powers, provided it follows a set procedure. This provision is referred to as the **residual powers clause** since it can be used for two purposes:

- to endow the EU with further powers in a policy area in which it is already competent under the Treaties but which does not provide the EU with sufficient powers to achieve the objectives set in the Treaties; or
- to develop a policy area that is not mentioned in the Treaties. For example, the environmental policy of the EU was developed under the former EEC version of this provision in the early 1970s, long before the formal inclusion of this policy in the Single European Act 1986.

The use of Article 352 TFEU, which could lead to a considerable expansion of the powers of the EU, is limited both by the Treaty itself (Article 352(3) and (4) TFEU) and by case law (see eg *Opinion 2/94 [Accession by the Community to the European Convention for the Protection of Human Rights and Fundamental Freedoms]* [1996] ECR I-1759). Moreover, the new procedure in place to adopt measures under Article 352 TFEU has been tightened with the view to limiting the use of the procedure.

3.3 Union competences

Once powers have been granted to the EU, it is imperative to consider exactly how they are divided between the EU institutions and the Member States. The TFEU refers to this as the **allocation of competence**. Until the Treaty of Lisbon there was no clear delineation of competences between the EU and the Member States. To enshrine such a division of competences in the Treaty became necessary as Member States complained about the 'creeping competences drift' in favour of the EU, and EU citizens feared that the Union would acquire more competences without democratic oversight. The Treaty of Lisbon takes a different approach to the allocation of competences depending on policy areas. Thus specific provisions in the Treaty form the basis for conferring competences upon the EU.

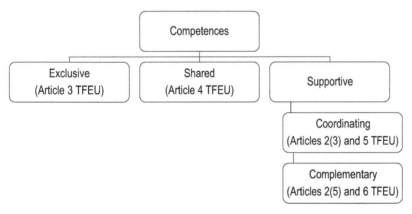

Figure 3.1 Competences of the EU and Member States

3.3.1 Exclusive competences

Article 2 TFEU distinguishes between exclusive and shared competences. Exclusive competences relate to specific areas where only the Union institutions can act. Member States are thus prevented from acting unilaterally or collectively in those areas. This provision endorses the doctrine of implied powers used in the *ERTA* case (see 3.2.2 above), as it enshrines the Commission's external competence in the fields listed in Article 3 TFEU. The areas listed in that article include customs union, competition rules, monetary policy for those Member States whose currency is the euro, etc.

3.3.2 Shared competences

The concept of shared competences relates to specific areas in which both the Union institutions and the Member States can act. Article 4 TFEU provides a non-exhaustive list of areas of competences, eg economic and social cohesion, consumer protection, transport, energy, etc. Areas not mentioned in Article 3 and Article 6 TFEU also fall within the remit of shared competences. Member States can act only if the Union has not yet exercised its right to act, or has decided to cease exercising its right to act (Article 2(2) TFEU). This means that a Member State cannot adopt measures contrary to the EU's principles and values, or in breach of the **principle of sincere cooperation** (Article 4(3) TEU).

This **idea of pre-emption**, which could have led to the EU exercising its rights and thereby grabbing all the competences for itself, is nonetheless tempered by:

(a) exceptions to the rule (eg Articles 4(3) (research, technological development and space) and 4(4) TFEU (development, cooperation and humanitarian aid)). States cannot be prevented from exercising their competences in these areas.

(b) Protocol No 25 on the Exercise of Shared Competence ([2012] OJ C326/307), the Sole Article of which stipulates that 'the scope of this exercise of competence only covers those elements governed by the Union act in question and therefore does not cover the whole area'.

(c) the principles of subsidiarity and proportionality (see 3.4 below).

3.3.3 Supportive competences

There are two further categories of competences:

(a) *Coordinating competences.* According to Articles 2(3) and 5 TFEU, the EU is allowed to issue guidelines and suggest initiatives to foster further coordination among the Member States in relation to economic policy, employment policy and social policy.

(b) *Complementary competences.* In pursuance of Articles 6 and 2(5) TFEU, the EU is allowed to take action to support, coordinate or supplement the action of the Member States in fields such as health, industry, culture, tourism and education. In these fields Union action does not supersede the Member States' competences and binding acts of the Union must not entail harmonisation.

3.3.4 The enhanced cooperation procedure

The Treaties allow for differential integration, a multi-speed Europe in areas that do not fall within the exclusive competence of the EU. In such areas, where a limited number of Member States have decided to cooperate further, a specific and complex procedure under Article 329(1) TFEU has been set up.

To avoid potential conflicts between EU law and the enhanced procedure, Article 20 TEU specifies that '[e]nhanced cooperation shall aim to further the objectives of the Union, protect its interests and reinforce its integration process'. Moreover, Articles 326 and 327 TFEU explain that the procedure should not undermine the internal market and must respect the competences, rights and obligations of the non-participating Member States. The enhanced cooperation framework must remain open to non-participating Member States should they wish to join later (Article 328 TFEU).

Although enhanced cooperation was originally introduced by the Amsterdam Treaty in 1997, it has been used for the first time only recently with the adoption of Council Regulation (EU) No 1259/2010 of 20 December 2010 implementing enhanced cooperation in the area of the law applicable to divorce and separation ([2010] OJ L343/10). This enhanced cooperation was established by 14 Member States: Belgium, Bulgaria, Germany, Spain, France, Italy, Latvia, Luxembourg, Hungary, Malta, Austria, Portugal, Romania and Slovenia. A second recent example of enhanced cooperation is that of Regulation (EU) No 1257/2012 of the European Parliament and of the Council of 17 December 2012 implementing enhanced cooperation in the area of the creation of unitary patent protection ([2012] OJ L361/1).

3.4 Limits to competences

Article 5(1) TEU unambiguously spells out that the competences of the EU are limited by two principles: the **principle of subsidiarity** and the **principle of proportionality**. This is reiterated in Article 1 of Protocol No 2 on the Application of the Principles of Subsidiarity and Proportionality ([2012] OJ C326/206).

3.4.1 Principle of subsidiarity

Subsidiarity is a concept that relates to the level of governance – EU, national, regional or local – at which action should be taken, the aim being that decisions are taken as closely as possible to the citizens of the EU. This principle is not new; it was initially articulated by the ECJ as a general principle of EU law (see **4.5**) and is now enshrined in the Treaty and in Protocol No 2. The principle applies to all kinds of EU acts, except those that fall within the exclusive competence of the EU.

Under the principle of subsidiarity, in areas that do not fall within its exclusive competence, the Union shall act only if and in so far as the objectives of the proposed action cannot be sufficiently achieved by the Member States, either at central level or at regional and local level, but rather, by reason of the scale or effects of the proposed action, can be better achieved at Union level (Article 5(3) TEU).

Compliance with the principle of subsidiarity may be achieved by fulfilling two requirements:

(a) *Necessity test*. For the EU to act, it must demonstrate that it is not possible for Member States individually or collectively to sufficiently achieve the objectives set out in the Treaty.

(b) *Greater benefits test*. Further, the EU must show that the circumstances are such that the objectives can be better achieved at Union level. Action by the EU institutions must bring added value over and above that which can be achieved by Member States (see Case C-84/94 *United Kingdom v Council (Re Working Time Directive)* [1996] ECR I-5755).

In other words, there is a built-in bias in favour of action at the lowest possible level.

The principle of subsidiarity is guaranteed by a number of procedural safeguards enshrined in the Protocol on the Application of the Principles of Subsidiarity and Proportionality and the Protocol on the Role of National Parliaments in the European Union ([2012] OJ C326/203):

(a) The Commission must consult widely (at national, regional and local level) before proposing legislative acts.

(b) All draft legislative acts must include a statement (usually featuring in the preamble) whereby the institution proposing the act demonstrates that the proposal complies with the principle of subsidiarity. The reasons given must be substantiated by qualitative and, wherever possible, quantitative indicators.

(c) National parliaments have been granted extensive powers to monitor the application of the principle of subsidiarity. Indeed, draft legislative acts, regardless of the originator, must be notified to national parliaments, which have eight weeks to send a response on why a particular act does not comply with the principle of subsidiarity. Each Member State has two votes (usually one for the upper and one for the lower chamber). Further:

   (i) the initiator of the draft legislative act must take into account the opinions of the national parliaments;

   (ii) if a third of all votes cast indicate that there is a violation of the principle of subsidiarity then the act must be reviewed by the Commission ('yellow card'). This procedure was used for the first time in September 2012, when parliaments in 12 Member States declared a Commission's proposal to re-examine the Posted Workers Directive (96/71/EC) to be in breach of the principle of subsidiarity. Instead of redrafting the proposal, the Commission chose to withdraw it;

   (iii) if a majority believes there is a violation then the Commission must provide a reasoned opinion as to why it still believes the act to be in conformity with the principle ('orange card'). The reasoned opinion and those of all the national parliaments must be appended to the act and given to the European Parliament and the Council, which must first vote on whether the principle of subsidiarity has been complied with. If either the European Parliament or the Council believes it does not comply with the principle then the act is dismissed. The use of the orange card is available only when acts are passed under the ordinary legislative procedure (see 5.3).

(d) The CJEU is competent to deal with actions on grounds of infringement of the principle of subsidiarity. Such actions might be brought by an EU institution (Article 263 TFEU; see 10.2), a Member State (Article 263 TFEU and Protocol on the Application of the Principles of Subsidiarity and Proportionality), a Member State on behalf of its national parliament (Protocol on the Application of the Principles of Subsidiarity and Proportionality) or the Committee of Regions to protect its prerogatives (Article 263 TFEU and Protocol on the Application of the Principles of Subsidiarity and Proportionality). Additionally, it might be possible for national courts and tribunals to refer a question of interpretation of the principle of subsidiarity through the preliminary ruling procedure under Article 267 TFEU (see **Chapter 9**). Unfortunately, the Court has shown great reluctance to grapple with the concept and has, so far, not struck down any legislation on the ground of subsidiarity (see eg Case C-84/94 *Re Working Time Directive*, above; Case C-377/98 *Netherlands v European Parliament and Council* [2001] ECR I-7149; Case C-58/08 *R (Vodafone Ltd, Telefónica O2 Europe plc, T-Mobile International AG, Orange Personal Communications Services Ltd) v Secretary of State for Business, Enterprise and Regulatory Reform* [2010] ECR I-4999).

(e) According to Article 9 of the Protocol on the Application of the Principles of Subsidiarity and Proportionality the Commission must submit an annual report to the European Council, the European Parliament, the Council and national parliaments on the application of Article 5 TEU.

(f) When amending draft legislative acts, both the Council and the European Parliament must take into account the principle of subsidiarity.

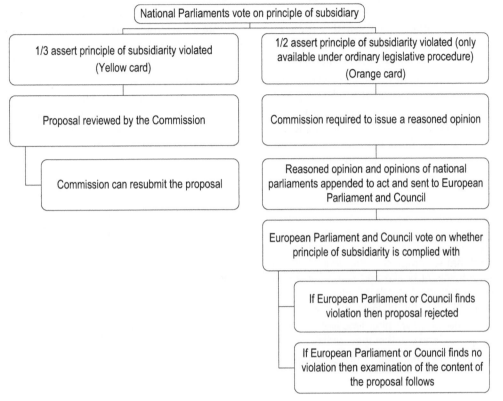

Figure 3.2   Procedural safeguards for the principle of subsidiarity

This undoubtedly demonstrates that the principle of subsidiarity is secured by mechanisms that can be used before, during and after the passing of a legislative act.

3.4.2   Principle of proportionality

The principle of proportionality, which applies in relation to the form and content of the measure suggested by the European institutions, is a further limit on the competences of the EU.

Under the principle of proportionality, the content and form of Union action shall not exceed what is necessary to achieve the objectives of the Treaties (Article 5(4) TEU).

Each draft legislative act must contain an explanation as to how the principle of proportionality is complied with. The concept stems from the German legal system (*Verhältnismässigkeit*) and was initially adopted into EU law (eg Case 8/55 *Fédération Charbonnière de Belgique v High Authority* [1954-1956] ECR 292) as a general principle of law (see **4.5**). The principle requires the action to be both appropriate to attain its objectives and not go beyond what is necessary to achieve them (Case C-491/01 *R v Secretary of State for Health, ex parte British American Tobacco (Investments) Ltd and*

Imperial Tobacco Ltd [2002] ECR I-11453). In practical terms this means that there is a need to show a link between the nature and scope of the measures taken and the object in view:

> In the present case the general principle of proportionality must be the only test in determining whether the infringement of this fundamental right serves a purpose which is in itself acceptable, whether it is such as to enable this objective to be attained and whether it does not constitute an arbitrary and intolerable burden. (Case 114/76 *Bela-Mühle Josef Bergman KG v Grows-Farm GmbH & Co KG (Re Skimmed-Milk Powder)* [1977] ECR 1211, 1217)

Consequently when an EU institution has a choice between various types of measures, it should opt for the one that is the least restrictive and the least burdensome, and the disadvantages of which must not be disproportionate to the aims pursued (Case C-331/88 *Fedesa et al* [1990] ECR I-4023). Unlike the principle of subsidiarity (see **3.4.1** above), the CJEU has found a number of measures to be in contravention of the principle of proportionality.

case example

In Case C-84/94 *United Kingdom v Council (Re Working Time Directive)* [1996] ECR I-5755, the UK Government argued that the Working Time Directive (2003/88/EC) had been adopted in breach of the principles of subsidiarity and proportionality.

The ECJ held that with regard to the principle of subsidiarity the Directive was necessary, as the aim was to raise the levels of health and safety across the EU, and this could be achieved only by the EU rather than by the individual Member States.

As for the principle of proportionality, the ECJ examined

> whether the means which [the directive] employ[ed] [were] suitable for the purpose of achieving the desired objective and whether they [did] not go beyond what [was] necessary to achieve it ...

and concluded that the measures in the Directive did not exceed what was necessary to achieve such objective.

3.5 Further reading

Conway G, 'Conflicts of Competence Norms in EU Law and the Legal Reasoning of the ECJ' (2010) 11 *German Law Journal* 966.

Craig P, 'Subsidiarity: A Political and Legal Analysis' (2012) 50(S1) *Journal of Common Market Studies* 72.

Craig P, *The Lisbon Treaty: Law, Politics and Treaty Reform* (OUP, 2010).

Davies G, 'Subsidiarity: The Wrong Idea, in the Wrong Place, at the Wrong Time', (2006) 43 *CMLR* 63.

Fabbrini F and Granat K, '"Yellow Card, but not Foul": The Role of the National Parliaments under the Subsidiarity Protocol and the Commission Proposal for an EU Regulation on the Right to Strike' (2013) 50 *CMLR* 115.

Harbo T-I, 'The Function of the Proportionality Principle in EU Law' (2010) 16(2) *European Law Journal* 158.

Horsley T, 'Subsidiarity and the European Court of Justice: Missing Pieces in the Subsidiarity Puzzle' (2012) 50 *Journal of Common Market Studies* 267.

Kiiver P, 'The Conduct of Subsidiarity Checks of EU Legislative Proposals by National Parliaments: Analysis, Observations and Practical Recommendations' (2012) 12(4) *ERA Forum* 535.

Weber A, 'The Distribution of Competences between the Union and the Member States' in Blank H-J and Mangiameli S (eds), *The European Union after Lisbon* (Springer, 2012) 311.

Wohlfahrt C, 'The Lisbon Case: A Critical Summary' (2009) 10 *German Law Journal* 1277.

summary

The EU is based on the principle of conferral of powers, but the implied powers theory and the residual powers clause have been used to expand such powers.

The Treaty of Lisbon distinguishes between three main types of competences: exclusive competences, shared competences and supportive competences.

Any measure adopted by the EU institutions must be founded on a legal basis in the Treaty, as this is where the delineation of competences is stipulated and where the various policy areas for which the EU is competent are spelled out.

The main limitations to the competences of the EU are the principle of subsidiarity (only with regard to shared competences) and the principle of proportionality. Whilst the latter principle has been used on numerous occasions by the ECJ to strike down legislation, the former remains a concept of political, rather than legal, application.

test your knowledge

(This is a fictional situation.) A heatwave in Europe in 2013 led to the death of about one-sixth of the cattle transported in road vehicles. In November 2014 the Commission issued a report suggesting ways to improve the transport of cattle across Europe. At about the same time, 1 million EU citizens, representing a significant number of Member States, have invited the Commission to propose a regulation to improve the treatment of farm animals in transit. A lobby group has submitted a proposal to the Commission, which is willing to initiate the process of adoption of such a piece of legislation.

1 Has the EU the competence to issue such a piece of legislation?
2 Should the EU legislate on the issue?
3 Can the EU negotiate and sign a treaty with Ukraine on the issue?

The Sources of European Law

After reading this chapter, you will be able to understand:
- the primary sources that are the Treaties
- the secondary sources adopted under the Treaties
- the case law of the Court of Justice of the European Union
- other sources of European Union law.

4.1 Introduction

As noted by the European Court of Justice (ECJ), 'the member States have limited their sovereign rights ... and have thus created a body of law which binds both their nationals and themselves' (Case 6/64 *Costa v ENEL* [1964] ECR 585, 593). This body of law comprises the sources of EU law that are collectively referred to as the *acquis communautaire*, as shown in **Table 4.1**. *Acquis communautaire* is a French term referring to the cumulative body of EU laws. It includes all the Treaties, acts passed by the European institutions and judgments laid down by the CJEU. The *acquis* is undoubtedly dynamic, constantly developing as the EU evolves, and fundamental. All Member States are bound to comply with the *acquis communautaire*. Moreover, acceptance of the *acquis* is one of the key criteria as regards the admission of new Member States.

Regulations	Charter of Fundamental Rights	CJEU case law
Directives	The Treaties (TEU and TFEU)	Recommendations and Opinions
Decisions	General principles of EU law	International agreements

Table 4.1   Sources of EU law – the acquis communautaire

The sources of EU law form a comprehensive hierarchy of norms. Some, the primary sources (eg the Treaty on the European Union (TEU) and the Treaty on the Functioning of the European Union (TFEU)), are more important than others, such as the secondary sources of law (eg regulations, directives). Moreover, sources may be categorised into legislative/enacted and judicial/non-enacted sources of law (see **Table 4.2**).

Legislative/Enacted	Judicial/Non-enacted	
Primary Sources	Secondary Sources	Secondary Sources
TEU	Listed in Art 288 TFEU (acts of the Institutions)	CJEU case law
TFEU	International agreements	General principles
Charter of Fundamental Rights		

Table 4.2 *Enacted and non-enacted sources of law*

in practice

Following the Continental model, all legislation, information and notices are published in the *Official Journal of the European Union* (OJ), which consists of two series and a supplement:

- the L Series (Legislation) – legislative acts, publication of which is required under the Treaties and other acts
- the C Series (Communication) – any information that is not of a legislative character
- the S Series (Supplement) – invitations to tender for public works and supply contracts.

Since 1 January 2015, the numbering of EU legal acts in the L Series has changed. Documents are now presented in the following manner: (domain) YYYY/N where the domain may be EU, Euratom, CFSP, etc, followed by the year of the publication and the sequential number of the document for a given year.

4.2 Primary sources

The EU is founded on treaties of equal value, the TEU and TFEU; these establish the framework and authority of the EU. A treaty is defined as an international agreement between States, usually in written form, that is binding upon States. It is the fundamental rule of international law that States obey the treaties they have ratified (*pacta sunt servanda*). Member States of the EU are thus bound by the terms of the TEU and the TFEU.

Initially, there were three founding treaties, as there were three distinct communities:

- the European Coal and Steel Community (ECSC) (expired on 23 July 2002; not published)
- the European Atomic Energy Community (EURATOM) (Consolidated Version [2012] OJ C327/01), and
- the European Economic Community (EEC) (Consolidated Version [2002] OJ C325/33) (see 1.4).

Over time, the three communities became one, and in 1993, with the entry into force of the Maastricht Treaty, the EEC was renamed the 'European Community' (EC). As the EC branched out into new policy areas, as its institutions became more coordinated and as more Member States joined, the original Treaties were gradually amended. In 2004 a draft Treaty Establishing a Constitution for Europe proposed the codification of the Treaties into a single text, but this failed to be ratified and thus the paper trail of numerous treaties remained. The current Treaties – the TEU and TFEU, referred to as 'The Treaties' – were amended by the Treaty of Lisbon 2007 (which entered into force on 1 December 2009). These latest changes revised both the content and the organisation of the Treaties.

in practice

The Treaty of Lisbon enumerates the changes made to the previous treaties and is not used as such. As it would be too difficult to find the current version of a specific provision, bearing in mind the number of times it has been amended since the original Treaties, the European Union creates consolidated versions of the TEU and TFEU (as published in the *Official Journal of the European Union* ([2012] OJ C326/01 and [2012] OJ C326/47), which incorporate the modifications made by the Treaty of Lisbon. The most up-to-date versions of the consolidated Treaties are available on the website of the EU at <http://eur-lex.europa.eu/collection/eu-law/treaties.html>.

The Treaties are self-executing (ie they do not need to be transposed into national law and are directly applicable). However, some Member States, such as the UK, Germany and Belgium, have historically followed a dualist system, which means that the Treaties must be formally implemented into domestic law by national legislation. In the UK, the European Communities Act 1972 (as amended) provides for the implementation of the Treaties. In monist States such as France and The Netherlands, once duly ratified the Treaties automatically become law without the need for further legislation.

The Treaties contain the founding principles that govern and drive the EU, forming its constitution. In *Opinion 1/91 on the Draft Agreement between the EEC and the EFTA* [1991] ECR 6079, the ECJ stated:

> The [TFEU], albeit concluded in the form of an international agreement, nonetheless constitutes the constitutional charter of a [Union] based on the rule of law. As the Court of Justice has consistently held, the [Union] Treaties established a new legal order for the benefit of which the States had limited their sovereign rights, in ever wider fields, and the subjects of which comprised not only the Member States but also their nationals. (para 21)

The Treaties resemble a constitution inasmuch as they set out the objectives of the EU, its competences and the institutional framework of the EU, as well as spelling out some of the rights of EU citizens. Article 3 TEU lists the broad objectives of the EU, which mainly relate to the internal market (Article 3(3)), the area of freedom, security and justice (Article 3(2)), economic and monetary union (Article 3(4)), and relations with the wider world (Article 3(5)).

Article 13(1) TEU establishes seven EU institutions:

- the European Parliament
- the European Council
- the Council
- the European Commission
- the Court of Justice of the European Union
- the European Central Bank, and
- the Court of Auditors.

See further **Chapter 2**.

Although the Treaties do not contain an exhaustive list of the rights of EU citizens, they do confer a number of rights (eg the right not to be discriminated against on the basis of nationality under Article 18 TFEU, the right to seek work under Article 45 TFEU) that can be enforced directly in the national courts in accordance with the **principle of direct effect** (see **6.3**).

According to the **principle of conferral** enshrined in Article 5(1) TEU (see **3.2.1**), the EU can act only in those areas in which it has competence (Articles 2–6 TFEU), which means that all the work carried out by the EU institutions must be done under the authority of the Treaties, the Protocol on the Application of the Principles of Subsidiarity and Proportionality, and the Protocol on the Role of National Parliaments in the European Union (see **3.3**). As a result, if an EU institution acts *ultra vires* (ie beyond its conferred powers), its action may be challenged and struck down under the judicial review procedure laid out in Article 263 TFEU (see **10.2**).

New policy areas cannot be developed and legislated for without prior agreement of the Member States by way of treaty amendment. Amending the Treaties is a difficult and lengthy process because it is essentially a political process requiring the unanimous agreement of all 28 Member States, which will have variable sensitivity, contention and, sometimes, opposition towards certain policy areas.

According to the ordinary revision procedures stipulated by Article 48(2)–(5) TEU, any Member State, the European Parliament or the Commission may submit to the Council proposals for amendment, which are forwarded to the European Council whilst national parliaments are notified of their submission. If the European Council accepts to examine the amendments, a Convention (comprising representatives of the national parliaments, the Heads of State or Government of the Member States, the European Parliament and the Commission) will be convened. The European Council may also, however, subject to the consent of the European Parliament, decide by a simple majority not to convene such a Convention but to set up an Intergovernmental Conference directly. Otherwise, it is the Convention that recommends the setting up of such a Conference. All Member States are invited to participate in the Intergovernmental Conference, and any amendment to the Treaties must be ratified by all the Member States in pursuance of their own domestic requirements.

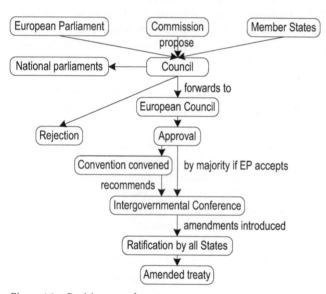

Figure 4.1   Revision procedure

Amendments enter into force once all Member States have ratified them according to their constitutional arrangements. Article 48(6) and (7) TEU also provide for a simplified revision procedure. See further **Figure 4.1**.

A number of protocols, annexes and declarations are attached to the Treaties. Whilst the protocols and annexes are an integral part of the Treaties (Article 51 TEU), declarations are legally effective only if they are adopted by the Council. There are three types of declarations:

- declarations concerning provisions of the Treaties
- declarations concerning protocols annexed to the Treaties, and
- declarations by Member States explaining their position in relation to a specific provision or issue.

in practice

For the purpose of the study of EU law, the most notable protocols are Protocol No 1 on the Role of National Parliaments in the European Union, Protocol No 2 on the Application of the Principles of Subsidiarity and Proportionality, and Protocol No 30 on the Application of the Charter of Fundamental Rights of the European Union to Poland and to the United Kingdom.

The most relevant declarations are Declaration No 1 concerning the Charter of Fundamental Rights of the European Union, Declaration No 17 concerning Primacy, and Declaration No 18 in Relation to the Delimitation of Competences.

4.3 Secondary sources

Secondary sources are by far the most substantial part of EU law. Indeed, the Treaties provide for the creation of five types of secondary sources of EU law under Article 288 TFEU, known as the legal acts of the Union (EU acts):

> To exercise the Union's competences, the institutions shall adopt regulations, directives, decisions, recommendations and opinions.

It must be noted that the sequence in which these acts are listed in Article 288 TFEU does not provide a hierarchy. That being said, the Treaty of Lisbon introduced a hierarchy among secondary sources, reflected in Articles 289, 290 and 291, creating three types of norms:

- Legislative acts as stipulated in Article 289 TFEU. These acts must be adopted in accordance with (ordinary or special) legislative procedure.
- Non-legislative or delegated acts of general application. According to Article 290 TFEU, these acts are enacted by the Commission to supplement or amend non-essential elements of the legislative act. However, the Commission can act only if the original legislative act allows it to do so. The legislative act also sets out the objectives, content, scope and duration of the delegation of power, as well as the conditions to which the delegation is subject.
- Implementing acts as provided under Article 291 TFEU, whereby the Commission – and sometimes the Council – has implementing powers. In this case the Commission uses the comitology system under Regulation 182/2011 ([2011] OJ L55/13). Under this procedure the Commission must seek the opinion of a committee comprising State representatives on proposed measures. Article 2 of the Comitology Regulation lays down two procedures:
  (a) the examination procedure used for acts of general scope and for acts potentially having an important impact relating to, eg, the environment, security and safety, or protection of the health or safety, of humans, animals or plants; and
  (b) the advisory procedure used for all other implementing acts.

It must be borne in mind that under all three types of norms, it is possible to find regulations, directives and decisions.

Figure 4.2   Legal acts of the EU

The legal effect of an EU act depends upon its specific nature. It is thus essential to be aware of the legal characterisation of the act in order to assess, for example, whether it is binding and whether it can be challenged under Article 263 TFEU (see 10.2).

A number of acts not mentioned under Article 288 TFEU also play an important role in the legal order of the EU. These are declarations and interinstitutional agreements, as well as acts relating to the Common Foreign and Security Policy.

4.3.1   Validity of EU acts

In order for an EU act to be valid, certain requirements need to be fulfilled. The act must:

- address an issue that is within the competences of the EU
- contain a reference to a legal basis (Article 296 TFEU)
- contain a reference to a preliminary act (Article 296, second paragraph TFEU)
- include a statement of the reasons why this act is necessary (Article 296, second paragraph TFEU; Case 24/62 *Germany v Commission (Re Brennwein)* [1963] ECR 63)
- be signed by the appropriate person/institution, and
- be published in the *Official Journal of the European Union* or notified to the relevant addressee.

Failure to fulfil all these requirements means that the act can be challenged before the CJEU, which can declare it void (see **10.2**).

In many areas of EU competence, the Treaties stipulate the type of legal act to be adopted. When no type is specified, Article 296, first paragraph TFEU explains that

the institutions shall select it on a case-by-case basis, in compliance with the applicable procedures and with the principle of proportionality.

The choice of the legal basis is particularly important since it determines which law-making procedure is used (ordinary or special legislative

```
Legal Basis
├── Specific
│   ├── Field in which action by EU is possible
│   ├── Type of act made possible
│   ├── Procedure to follow
│   └── Sometimes degree of harmonisation
└── General
    ├── Article 114 TFEU
    ├── Article 115 TFEU
    └── Article 352 TFEU
```

Figure 4.3   Legal basis of an EU act

procedure), which institutions will be involved in the law-making procedure (Council, European Parliament, national parliaments, etc), how the Council votes (unanimity, single majority, qualified majority voting), the extent of the European Parliament's participation (see **5.3**) and the content of the act itself, as the EU is not allowed to legislate in fields in which it is not competent (see **3.3** above). Moreover, failure to use the correct legal basis means that the act can be challenged and declared void (Case C-376/98 *Germany v European Parliament and Council (Re Tobacco Advertising)* [2000] ECR I-8419). In other words, the CJEU has the last word as to whether a particular EU act was passed using the appropriate legal basis. In the case where the act covers two areas then the procedural requirements of both must be satisfied (Case 165/87 *Commission v Council (Re Commodity Coding)* [1988] ECR 5545, para 11). Exceptions to the rule are when it is impossible to fulfil all requirements or when it would be against the rationale of the procedural requirements, eg the law-making procedures are different (Case C-300/89 *Commission v Council (Re Titanium Dioxide)* [1991] ECR I-2867, paras 18–21), to do so.

4.3.2 Article 288 TFEU

Among the five legal acts stipulated in Article 288 TFEU, three of them, regulations, directives and decisions, are legally binding (see **4.3.2.1** below). Non-legally binding EU acts are discussed in further detail in **4.3.2.2** below.

4.3.2.1 Binding EU acts: regulations, directives and decisions

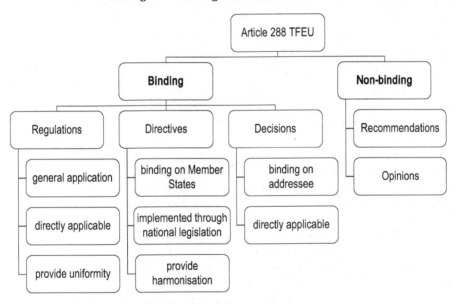

Figure 4.4   Binding and non-binding EU acts

Regulations

Article 288 TFEU explains that

> [a] regulation shall have general application. It shall be binding in its entirety and directly applicable in all Member States.

Regulations are perhaps the most powerful type of EU act because they can be used to achieve uniformity in law across the Union. Member States usually do not like regulations because they are outside their control.

Regulations have three key characteristics:

- they are of general application as they are 'applicable not to a limited number of persons, defined or identifiable' (Joined Cases 789–790/79 *Calpak SpA v Commission* [1980] ECR 1949, 1961) 'but to categories of persons viewed abstractly and in their entirety' (Joined Cases 16–17/62 *Confédérations de producteurs de fruits et légumes and others v Council* [1962] ECR 471, 479);
- they are binding in their entirety; and
- they are directly applicable, which means that they do not need to be transposed into national law and that national implementation measures are invalid (Case 34/73 *Fratelli Variola SpA v Amministrazione italiana delle Finanze* [1973] ECR 981). As a consequence, regulations can be applied by the domestic courts as soon as they become operative.

Directives

In contrast to a regulation:

> A directive shall be binding as to the result to be achieved upon each state to which it is addressed, but shall leave to the national authorities the choice of form and methods. (Article 288 TFEU)

Directives are used to encourage harmonisation in law across the EU, but they leave the method of achieving this to the Member States, thereby providing them with some flexibility. This explains why directives are binding as to the result. Member States are left to decide the form and method of achieving the end result, though in some instances directives can contain specific provisions that leave little discretion to the Member States. In other words, directives are not directly applicable as they must first be transposed into national law to be given legal effect.

Member States will be given a certain time within which to implement a directive into their own law, depending on how difficult that will be – anything from months to years. A directive will enter into force on the date specified in the directive or, if no date is stipulated, 20 days after its publication in the *Official Journal*. If a Member State fails to enforce the directive by the implementation deadline, it can be subject to enforcement proceedings by the Commission under the provisions in Articles 258–260 TFEU (see 7.2).

Decisions

According to Article 288 TFEU,

> [a] decision is binding in its entirety upon those to whom it is addressed.

A decision is not really a general law, but is used to give legal effect to a ruling affecting one Member State or even an individual company. Decisions are usually addressed to a Member State, as in the case of *Plaumann* (Case 25/62 *Plaumann and Co v Commission* [1963] ECR 95, in which Plaumann challenged a decision addressed by the Commission to Germany – see 10.2.4.3), or to a natural or legal person (eg, in competition law cases such as Case T-201/04 *Microsoft Corp v Commission* [2007] ECR II-3601), and they will be binding upon the addressee upon notification. However, a decision that does not specify those to whom it is addressed must be published in the *Official Journal* and will enter into force on the date stipulated by the decision, or, if there is no such date, on the 20th day following publication in the *Official Journal* (Article 297(2) TFEU).

4.3.2.2 Non-binding EU acts: recommendations and opinions

Article 288 TFEU also provides for two types of acts that are not legally binding, recommendations and opinions:

> Recommendations and opinions shall have no binding force.

According to case law, an act is binding when it 'brings about a distinct change in the legal position of a party' (Case 60/81 *IBM v Commission* [1981] ECR 2639, para 9).

In line with Article 17(1) TEU, the Commission can, in the general interest of the Union, formulate recommendations or deliver opinions. Although these are forms of soft law, ie non-legally binding, they can be used to clarify the meaning of legal provisions and often indicate how the law may develop in the future. They can be endowed with persuasive authority if they are referred to by the CJEU. In contrast, they must be taken into account by national courts when interpreting EU measures (Case C-322/88 *Grimaldi v Fonds des Maladies Professionnelles* [1989] ECR 4407).

4.3.3 Other acts

Besides the acts mentioned under Article 288 TFEU, there are various forms of acts in EU law such as:

- recommendations, communications (eg Commission Communication (2011/C 12/01) on fines for non-compliance with a CJEU judgment) (see **7.2.1.2**), and acts on the organisation and running of the institutions, such as inter-institutional agreements (eg the Framework Agreement on Relations between the European Parliament and the European Commission ([2010] OJ L304/47) (see **5.2.1**);
- green papers (aimed at stimulating discussion amongst stakeholders at European level) – green papers may lead to legislative developments outlined in white papers (which contain proposals for EU action in a specific area); staff working documents (SWD), which give a description, though non-exhaustive, of EU existing or proposed legislation and serve as guidance; and action programmes used by the Commission to agree on long-term objectives of the EU (eg, the 7th General Union Environment Action Programme to 2020, 'Living well, within the limits of our planet' (Decision 1386/2013/EU, [2013] OJ L354/171));
- acts relating to the external policies and actions of the EU, such as decisions under Articles 22, 29 and 31 TEU;
- acts adopted in the framework of enhanced cooperation under Article 20 TEU.

4.4 Case law of the Court of Justice of the European Union

Some of the most significant developments in EU law have come from the decisions of the CJEU (see **Chapter 8**), which have established fundamental doctrines (eg **principle of direct effect** (see **6.3**), **principle of supremacy** (see **6.2**)) securing the authority of EU law (eg **principle of Member State liability** (see **7.3**)). This derives partly from the Court's power to ensure observance of Treaty objectives through Article 267 TFEU on preliminary references (see **Chapter 9**), partly from its creativity in comparison to the relative inertia of the legislative bodies, and partly from its role of filling the gaps left by the Treaties and EU acts.

There is a fierce debate among academics as to whether the activities of the CJEU are legitimate, or whether the judges have trespassed on the sovereignty of Member States (idea of judicial activism) (see 8.6).

4.5 General principles of EU law

Article 19(1) TEU provides:

> [The CJEU] shall ensure that in the interpretation and application of the Treaties the law is observed.

The phrase 'law is observed' is interpreted so as to take into account not only EU law, but also any rule of law relating to the application and interpretation of treaties more generally. This means that other sources of (international) law, such as general principles of law, may assist in understanding the meaning of the provisions enshrined in the Treaties.

There are two types of general principles of EU law:

(a) principles that have been derived from the legal traditions of the Member States; and

(b) principles that have been established by the CJEU.

General principles can be used in order to clarify the intention behind legislation, as well as to test the validity of acts of the institutions.

On occasion a general principle is formally incorporated into the Treaties (eg the **principle of equality** in Article 2 TEU, the **principle of proportionality** in Article 5(1) TEU (see **3.4.2**), the **principle of subsidiarity** in Article 5(1) TEU (see **3.4.1**)). Other examples of general principles of EU law are the concept of **legal certainty** (see **5.2.2**) (Case 70/83 *Kloppenburg v Finanzamt Leer* [1984] ECR 1075).

It must be noted that prior to the Charter of Fundamental Rights of the European Union (see further **4.6** below), human rights were secured in the EU under the general principles of EU law (Case 29/69 *Stauder v City of Ulm, Sozialamt* [1969] ECR 419, 425). Whilst this illustrates the potential of general principles to be formally adopted into codified law, it should be noted that Article 6(3) TEU still recognises that fundamental rights that result from the constitutional traditions common to the Member States shall constitute general principles of the Union's law.

4.6 Fundamental rights: the Charter of Fundamental Rights of the European Union and the European Convention on Human Rights

The original treaties of the European Communities made no reference to respect for human rights. However, as explained in **4.5**, the CJEU recognised the need to respect fundamental rights as an integral part of the general principles of EU law. The Treaties now acknowledge the importance of the protection and promotion of human rights. In its current version, Article 2 TEU states:

> The Union is founded on the values of respect for human dignity, freedom, democracy, equality, the rule of law and respect for human rights, including the rights of persons belonging to minorities. These values are common to the Member States in a society in which pluralism, non-discrimination, tolerance, justice, solidarity and equality between women and men prevail.

4.6.1 Charter of Fundamental Rights of the European Union

In reflection of the development of jurisprudence in the field of human rights, the Charter of Fundamental Rights of the European Union was signed on 7 December 2000, but it was not legally binding at the time. The Charter includes civil, political, economic, social and societal rights that stem from a variety of European and national sources. The Charter was amended on 12 December 2007 and formally adopted by the Member States under the Treaty of Lisbon 2007; it is now, in pursuance of Article 6(1) TEU (and Declaration No 1 concerning the Charter of Fundamental Rights of the European Union [2012] OJ C326/339), considered to be a primary source of EU law in the same way as the Treaties:

> The Union recognises the rights, freedoms and principles set out in the Charter of Fundamental Rights of the European Union of 7 December 2000, as adapted at Strasbourg, on 12 December 2007, which shall have the same legal value as the Treaties. (Article 6(1) TEU)

The Charter binds EU institutions, as well as Member States, when the latter implement EU law (Article 51 of the Charter and Joined Cases C-411/10 and C-493/10 *NS v Secretary of State for the Home Department* and *ME and Others v Refugee Applications Commissioner and Minister for Justice, Equality and Law Reform* [2011] ECR I-13905, para 119). The Court has specified a number of requirements that should be examined to establish whether national legislation 'involves the implementation of EU law for the purposes of Article 51 of the Charter' (Case C-206/13 *Cruciano Siragusa v Regione Sicilia,* 6 March 2014, ECLI:EU:C:2014:126, para 25). The Charter does not create rights that are of general application in domestic law and applies only within the remit of EU law as specified by Declaration No 1:

> The Charter does not extend the field of application of Union law beyond the powers of the Union or establish any new power or task for the Union, or modify powers and tasks as defined by the Treaties.

Further, under Protocol No 30, the UK and Poland sought reassurance that the Charter does not create additional rights for individuals in their States. Whilst Protocol No 30 is sometimes viewed as an 'opt out', the CJEU has in Joined Cases C-411/10 and C-493/10 (above) explained in clear terms that

> Article 1(1) of Protocol (No 30) explains Article 51 of the Charter with regard to the scope thereof and does not intend to exempt the Republic of Poland or the United Kingdom from the obligation to comply with the provisions of the Charter or to prevent a court of one of those Member States from ensuring compliance with those provisions. (para 120)

Yet the CJEU has also stressed that

> [i]n addition, according to the sixth recital in the preamble to that protocol, the Charter reaffirms the rights, freedoms and principles recognised in the Union and makes those rights more visible, but does not create new rights or principles. (para 119)

4.6.2 European Convention on Human Rights

Article 6(3) TEU provides:

> Fundamental rights, as guaranteed by the European Convention for the Protection of Human Rights and Fundamental Freedoms and as they result from

the constitutional traditions common to the Member States, shall constitute general principles of the Union's law.

This repeats similar wording used by the ECJ in Case C-260/89 *ERT* [1991] ECR 2925, para 41. The TEU thus formally acknowledges that the ECHR forms part of the EU's fundamental principles when EU law is being interpreted and applied. However, the Luxembourg Court has 'no power to examine the compatibility with the European Convention on Human Rights of national legislation lying outside the scope of [Union] law' (Case 12/86 *Demirel v Stadt Schwäbisch Gmünd* [1987] ECR 3719, para 28).

Article 6(2) TEU provides that the EU shall accede to the ECHR, which means that the ECHR will be directly applicable to the EU and that the EU will be required by virtue of international law to abide by its provisions. In other words, judgments of the CJEU could be challenged before the European Court of Human Rights. The accession negotiations started in May 2010 and a Draft Accession Agreement of the European Union to the European Convention on Human Rights (<http://www.coe.int/t/dghl/standardsetting/hrpolicy/accession/Meeting_reports/47_1(2013)008rev2_EN.pdf>) was finalised on 5 April 2013. Yet on 18 December 2014 the CJEU in *Opinion 2/13*, 18 December 2014, ECLI:EU:C:2014:2454 declared this agreement to be incompatible with EU law, mainly on the basis that it would disregard the intrinsic nature of the European Union and affect the division of powers between the EU and its Member States.

4.7 International agreements

Lastly, we should consider international law as part of the corpus of the *acquis*. The EU has legal personality under Article 47 TEU, and Article 216 TFEU provides that agreements entered into with third countries are to be binding on both the EU and the Member States. This includes multilateral and bilateral treaties to which the EU is a party. For example, the EU is a party to the World Trade Organization (WTO) Agreement and the United Nations Convention on the International Sale of Goods. The ECJ held, in Joined Cases 21–24/72 *International Fruit Company NV and others v Produktschap voor Groenten en Fruit* [1972] ECR 1219 that the General Agreement on Tariffs and Trade (GATT) 1947 was binding on the EU; and in Case 70/87 *Fédération de l'industrie de l'huilerie de la CEE (Fediol) v Commission* [1989] ECR 1781 and Case C-69/89 *Nakajima v Council* [1991] ECR I-2069 the Court held that companies could, in specific circumstances, challenge the legality of an EU measure in light of GATT 1947, and now in respect of the WTO Agreement.

4.8 Further reading

Cartabia M, 'Fundamental Rights and the Relationship among the Court of Justice, the National Supreme Courts and the Strasbourg Court' in Court of Justice of the European Union, *50th Anniversary of the Judgment in Van Gend en Loos 1963–2013*, Conference Proceedings, 13 May 2013 (OPUE, Luxembourg, 2013) 155.

Driessen B, 'Delegated Legislation after the Treaty of Lisbon: An Analysis of Article 290 TFEU' (2010) 35 *EL Rev* 837.

Gragl P, 'A Giant Leap for European Human Rights? The Final Agreement on the European Union's Accession to the European Convention on Human Rights' (2014) *CML Rev* 13.

Gragl P, *The Accession of the European Union to the European Convention on Human Rights* (OUP, 2013).

Harpaz G, 'The European Court of Justice and its Relations with the European Court of Human Rights: The Quest for Enhanced Reliance, Coherence and Legitimacy' (2009) 46 *CML Rev* 105.

Hoffman H, 'Legislation, Delegation and Implementation under the Treaty of Lisbon: Typology Meets Reality' (2009) 15(4) *European Law Journal* 482.

Lenaerts K and Gutiérrez-Fons JA, 'The Role of General Principles of EU Law' in A Arnull et al (eds), *A Constitutional Order of States? Essays in EU Law in Honour of Alan Dashwood* (Hart Publishing, 2011) 179.

Weiss W, 'Human Rights in the EU: Rethinking the Role of the European Convention on Human Rights after Lisbon' (2011) 7 *European Constitutional Law Review* 64.

summary

European Union law comprises a variety of sources that may be classified as (i) primary sources (TEU and TFEU) and (ii) secondary sources (Article 288 TFEU) which include legally binding EU acts, such as regulations, directives and decisions, and soft law, such as recommendations and opinions. The CJEU also plays an important role in the creation and development of EU law through its case law and use of general principles of (EU) law.

test your knowledge

1   What is the role of general principles of law in the creation of EU law?
2   What is meant by the legal basis of an EU act, and why is it important?
3   What are the key differences between regulations and directives?

chapter

5

The Law-making Process in the European Union

After reading this chapter, you will be able to understand:
- the principles of law-making
- the difference between the various legislative procedures
- the difference between the legislative and non-legislative procedures.

5.1 Introduction

The **principle of representative democracy** (see 2.2) has been reinforced by extending the application of the ordinary legislative procedure, whereby the Council and the European Parliament legislate together in a range of areas of EU policies. Moreover, this procedure involves national parliaments, thereby proving that the EU is based on the concept of representative democracy.

There are two approaches towards defining what legislation is. First, the focus is on the procedural aspect (formal approach): the procedure used for passing legislation determines the quality of the law. Secondly, according to a functional or material approach, it is important to examine the content of the law, ie whether it is an abstract rule of general application. The drafters of the Lisbon Treaty have adopted the first approach, inasmuch as Article 289(3) TFEU states that '[l]egal acts adopted by legislative procedure shall constitute legislative acts'.

The case law of the CJEU further supports this approach, as the General Court explained in *Inuit* (Case T-18/10 *Inuit Tapiriit Kanatami v European Parliament and Council* [2011] ECR II-5599, para 65, as upheld by the Court of Justice in Case C-583/11P *Inuit Tapiriit Kanatami v European Parliament and Council*, 3 October 2013, ECLI:EU:C:2013:625, para 61) that the distinction between legislative and regulatory acts was based solely on the procedure used to pass the particular act (see further 10.2).

In the law-making process the EU institutions are guided by a number of key principles, discussed at 5.2 below. There are two legislative procedures: the ordinary legislative procedure (5.3.1), and the special legislative procedure (5.3.2). Further the Commission can enact other EU acts using its delegated and implementing powers, examined at 5.4.

5.2 The principles of law-making

In the law-making procedure, a number of principles must be complied with. Whilst some relate to the institutions, others concern the content and the procedure itself.

5.2.1 Principles relating to the institutions

One of the key principles of law-making is the **principle of cooperation** between all institutions involved in the law-making process. As this process involves three main institutions – the Commission, the Council and the European Parliament – it is known as a 'trilogue'.

In order to organise and facilitate cooperation between these institutions, as well as to improve the efficiency of the procedure and ensure that there is a constant discussion between the institutions, they have integrated the informal 'trilogue' into their rules of procedure. For example, in 2012 the European Parliament reviewed Rule 70 (interinstitutional negotiations in legislative procedures) of its Rules of Procedure. Further, the institutions have adopted a number of agreements. In particular, Article 295 TFEU recognises their capacity to conclude legally binding interinstitutional agreements:

> The European Parliament, the Council and the Commission shall consult each other and by common agreement make arrangements for their cooperation. To that end, they may, in compliance with the Treaties, conclude interinstitutional agreements which may be of a binding nature.

The key agreements with regard to the law-making process are the Interinstitutional Agreement on Better Law-Making ([2003] OJ C321/1), the Joint Declaration on Practical Arrangements for the Co-Decision Procedure ([2007] OJ C145/5), the Framework Agreement on Relations between the European Parliament and the European Commission ([2010] OJ L304/47) and the Interinstitutional Agreement on Budgetary Discipline, on Cooperation in Budgetary Matters and on Sound Financial Management ([2013] OJ C373/1). The thrust of these instruments is that these institutions will consult each other before a legislative act is drafted and throughout the law-making process.

A second significant principle is the **principle of institutional balance**. This may be defined in the following terms (see Article 13(2) TEU):

- each institution must act within its powers defined by the Treaties (ie no extension or transfer of powers)
- each institution must exercise its powers with due regard for the powers of the other institutions (**principle of mutual and sincere cooperation**)
- each institution plays a role in the law-making procedures of the EU.

That being said, it must be borne in mind that interinstitutional rivalry also exists, as each institution wishes to guard its areas of competence. The **principle of institutional balance** (see 2.2.2) is safeguarded by the Court of Justice (see Case 138/79 *SA Roquette Frères v Council* [1980] ECR 3333) in the sense that the Court will declare invalid an act that has been adopted in breach of this principle.

5.2.2 Principles relating to content and procedure

In relation to content and procedure, the main principles are:

(a) the principles of subsidiarity and proportionality (see 3.4);
(b) the principle of legal certainty:

> [Union] legislation must be certain and its application foreseeable by individuals. The principle of legal certainty requires that every measure of the institutions having legal effects must be clear and precise and must be brought to the notice of the person concerned in such a way that he can ascertain exactly the time at which the measure comes into being and starts to have legal effects. (Case T-115/94 *Opel Austria GmbH v Council* [1997] ECR II-39, para 124)

(c) the **principle of transparency** (Articles 1 and 15 TEU). This is achieved by ensuring the broadest possible access to documents of all EU institutions, and by requiring the European Parliament to meet in public and the Council to open its deliberations and votes on draft legislative acts to the public. As the Court of Justice explained:

> [This openness] enables citizens to participate more closely in the decision-making process and guarantees that the administration enjoys greater legitimacy and is more effective and more accountable to the citizen in a democratic system.
>
> …
>
> Openness … contributes to strengthening democracy by allowing citizens to scrutinize all the information which has formed the basis of a legislative act. The possibility for citizens to find out the considerations underpinning legislative action is a precondition for the effective exercise of their democratic rights. (Joined Cases C-39/05 P and C-52/05 P *Sweden and Turco v Council* [2008] ECR I-4723, paras 45–46)

As a result of increased transparency, the **principle of democratic legitimacy** and the **principle of accountability** are more likely to be fulfilled.

(d) The **principles of simplicity, clarity and consistency** in the drafting of the acts (Interinstitutional Agreement on Better Law-making ([2003] OJ C321/1) also enable the principle of transparency to be complied with.

5.3 The legislative procedures

The Lisbon Treaty provides for two law-making procedures:

(a) the ordinary legislative procedure; and
(b) the special legislative procedure (see **Figure 5.1**).

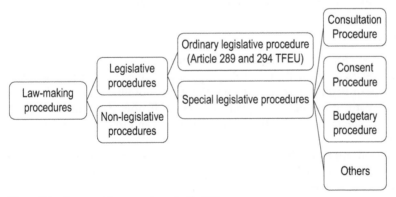

Figure 5.1   Law-making procedures in the EU

By stipulating that the ordinary legislative procedure, which involves the European Parliament, is the standard procedure, the aim of the Treaty of Lisbon was to strengthen the democratic legitimacy of the EU by extending the European Parliament's powers.

It must be noted that a range of actors is involved in the law-making process, on both the national and the European levels.

5.3.1 The ordinary legislative procedure

The ordinary legislative procedure is explained in Article 289(1) TFEU and defined in Article 294 TFEU (see below):

> *Article 289*
>
> 1. The ordinary legislative procedure shall consist in the joint adoption by the European Parliament and the Council of a regulation, directive or decision on a proposal from the Commission. This procedure is defined in Article 294.

The ordinary legislative procedure applies in 83 areas of law and policy, which means that most of the legislation in the Union is passed under this procedure. The noteworthy elements of the procedure are:

- Two readings by the European Parliament, which gives that body a real opportunity to take part in the legislative process.
- A positive action being required for amendments and rejection of a proposal.
- A constant trilogue between the Council, the European Parliament and the Commission at all stages of the procedure.

Whilst these practices have increased the efficiency of the procedure, they have also been criticised for lacking transparency and accountability.

The procedure is as follows (Article 294 TFEU):

Submission of proposal

- The Commission submits a proposal to the Parliament and the Council.
- The national parliaments are informed of the draft legislative act and can comment on whether they deem the act to comply with the principle of subsidiarity.

First reading

- The European Parliament adopts a position and communicates it to the Council.
- If the Council approves the position it will adopt the act concerned. If it does not, it will submit its own proposal to the European Parliament. The Commission will also inform the European Parliament of its position.

Second reading

- If within three months the European Parliament approves the Council's position or does not take a decision, the Council's proposal is deemed to have been adopted. If the European Parliament rejects the position by an absolute majority, the act is deemed not to have been adopted. However, if the Parliament suggests amendments, the text will be returned to the Council and to the Commission for an opinion.
- If the Council approves the amendments within three months by a qualified majority, the act is deemed to have been adopted. If the Council cannot agree upon the amendments, a Conciliation Committee will be formed.

Conciliation procedure

- The Committee, comprising an equal number of members of the Council and the European Parliament, is convened within six weeks. The Commission also takes part in the discussions. If no joint text can be agreed, or that is not possible within the six-week window, the text shall be deemed not to have been adopted.
- If a joint text is approved within six weeks, both the Council and the European Parliament are given six weeks to approve the text. If they do not approve the joint text, the act is not adopted.

5.3.2 The special legislative procedure

A special legislative procedure is provided for by the Treaties in the following cases:

- An act is adopted by the European Parliament with the participation of the Council (Article 289(2) TFEU).
- An act is adopted by the Council with the participation of the European Parliament (Article 289(2) TFEU).
- An act is adopted on the initiative of a group of Members States or of the European Parliament, on a recommendation from the European Central Bank, or at the request of the Court of Justice or the European Investment Bank (Article 289(4) TFEU).

Under the Treaty of Lisbon, the special legislative procedure has replaced the consultation, budgetary and consent procedures. However, these procedures still apply in respect of specified areas in the Lisbon Treaty. In this regard, the TFEU refers to the following procedures:

- **Consultation.** Under Article 289 TFEU, consultation is a special legislative procedure whereby the European Parliament (as well as the European Economic and Social Committee and the Committee of the Regions – see **2.6**) is asked for its opinion on proposed legislation before the Council adopts it. However, there is no legal obligation upon the Council to amend the proposal in the light of the comments of the European Parliament. Nevertheless, failure to consult the European Parliament means that the act can be declared void by the Court of Justice (Case 138/79 *Roquette Frères*, **5.2.1** above), as consultation with the European Parliament is understood to be an 'essential procedural requirement' (see **10.2.2**). Also, if the Council intends to amend the proposal substantially, it is required to consult the European Parliament again (Case C-65/90 *European Parliament v Council* [1992] ECR I-4593, para 16). On the other hand, the European Parliament should not unnecessarily delay giving its opinion (Case C-65/93 *European Parliament v Council* [1995] ECR I-643). This procedure is applicable in a limited number of legislative areas, such as internal market exemptions and competition law. Consultation of the European Parliament is also required, as a non-legislative procedure, where international agreements are being adopted under the Common Foreign and Security Policy.
- **Consent.** The European Parliament is requested to give its consent, thereby endowing it with a right of veto. This usually applies to the ratification of certain agreements negotiated by the EU, or is applicable most notably in the cases of serious breach by a Member State of Article 2 TEU values on which the EU is founded (Article 7(1) and (2) TEU), or for the accession of new EU Member States (Article 49, first paragraph TEU) or as regards arrangements for withdrawal from the EU (Article 50(2) TEU). Furthermore, it is used when new legislation on combating discrimination is being adopted and when the subsidiary general legal basis is applied in line with Article 352 TFEU (see **3.2.3**).
- **Budgetary procedure.** This complex procedure, under which the European Parliament and the Council establish the Union's annual budget, is described in Article 314 TFEU. It is not proposed to examine this in further detail in this book.
- **Other procedures** under, for example, Article 7(4) and (5) TEU and Article 354 TFEU (suspension of certain rights resulting from Union membership), Article 49, second paragraph TEU (ratification of accession agreement by Member States) and Article 218 TFEU (international agreements).

5.4 The adoption of regulatory acts

The Treaty, as well as case law, distinguishes between legislative and other, ie regulatory, acts (see **4.3**). Prior to the Lisbon Treaty, non-legislative acts were adopted according to what used to be called the 'comitology' procedure. Under this procedure, the Commission would consult a supervisory committee, comprising national civil servants presided over by a non-voting Commission member, before adopting implementing measures. Such a mechanism was legitimised by the ECJ in *Köster* (Case 25/70 *Einfuhr- und Vorratsstelle für Getreide und Futtermittel v Köster and Berodt & Co* [1970] ECR 1161) and then subject to a number of Council decisions.

As the mechanism lacked transparency, appeared complex and did not allow the European Parliament to exercise supervisory powers, a number of Council decisions attempted to remedy these problems, but only partially. As the Treaty of Lisbon introduced two types of non-legislative acts – delegated acts (Article 290 TFEU) and implementing acts (Article 291(2) TFEU) – it also spelled out specific procedures for their adoption. In the process it (partially) did away with the comitology procedure.

Council Note 8753/11 (2011), entitled 'Common Understanding – Delegated Acts', explains the procedure to be followed for the adoption of delegated acts referred to in Article 290 TFEU. The Commission prepares a draft act and consults with experts from the relevant national authorities (which will later have to implement the act). It also transmits the delegated act to the European Parliament and the Council. The legislator (ie the institution(s) that has/have passed the act delegating powers to the Commission) has two months from the submission of the draft act either to revoke the delegation, or to express its objections to the act. If objections are expressed then the Commission cannot adopt the act. In that case it is free either to adopt a new draft act, or to amend the rejected draft act or to do nothing.

Article 291(2) TFEU provides that the Commission (or the Council in special circumstances) may exercise implementing powers when the legislative act so provides and '[w]here uniform conditions for implementing legally binding Union acts are needed'. In 2011, the European Parliament and the Council adopted Regulation 182/2011 ([2011] OJ L55/13) to set out the way implementing acts are agreed upon. In fact, the mechanisms are reminiscent of the comitology procedures. According to the Regulation there are two procedures, the examination procedure and the consultative/advisory procedure, both using committees comprising representatives of Member States, scientific experts and representatives from business and industry, and presided over by a non-voting representative of the Commission. The committees act as a forum for discussion between the Commission and the national authorities. Under the examination procedure, the Commission can adopt an implementing act only if the relevant committee positively agrees to it. Under the consultative procedure, the Commission may adopt an implementing act despite a negative opinion expressed by the relevant committee. That being said, an appeal committee set up after the adoption of the act may, by delivering a negative opinion, repeal the act.

5.5 Further reading

Blom-Hansen K and Brandsma GJ, 'The EU Comitology System: Intergovernmental Bargaining *and* Deliberative Supranationalism?' (2009) 47 *Journal of Common Market Studies* 719.

Christiansen T, 'The European Union after the Lisbon Treaty: An Elusive "Institutional Balance"?' in Biondi A et al (eds), *EU Law after Lisbon* (OUP, 2012).

Corbett R, 'The Evolving Roles of the European Parliament and of National Parliaments' in Biondi A et al (eds), *EU Law after Lisbon* (OUP, 2012).

Craig P, 'The Treaty of Lisbon, Process, Architecture and Substance' (2008) 33 *EL Rev* 137.

Devuyst Y, 'The European Union's Institutional Balance after the Treaty of Lisbon: "Community Method" and "Democratic Deficit" Reassessed' (2008) 39 *Georgetown Journal of International Law* 247.

Driessen B, 'Interinstitutional Conventions and Institutional Balance' (2008) 33 *EL Rev* 550.

Kardasheva R, 'The Power to Delay: The European Parliament's Influence in the Consultation Procedure' (2009) 47 *Journal of Common Market Studies* 385.

Kliver P, 'Reflections on the Lisbon Judgment – How the Judges at Karlsruhe Trust neither the European Parliament nor their National Parliament' (2009) 16 *Maastricht Journal of European and Comparative Law* 263.

Pechtold A and Sneller J, 'Democratic Control of the European Union' (2007-2008) 24 *Merkourios-Utrecht Journal of International and European Law* 48.

Reh C, 'The Informal Politics of Co-Decision: Towards a Normative Assessment', Paper prepared for the UACES Conference on *Exchanging Ideas on Europe*, University of Edinburgh, 1–3 September 2008.

Sieberson SC, 'The Treaty of Lisbon and its Impact on the European Union's Democratic Deficit' (2007-2008) 14 *Columbia Journal of European Law* 445.

Special Issue of *Journal of European Public Policy* (2003) 20(7) on Twenty Years of Legislative Codecision in the European Union.

Stie, A E, *Democratic Decision-making in the EU: Technocracy in Disguise?* (Routledge, 2013)

Türk A, 'Lawmaking after Lisbon' in A Biondi et al (eds), *EU Law after Lisbon* (OUP, 2012).

summary

- The law-making procedure is based on principles that relate to the institutions (cooperation between institutions and institutional balance), and to content and procedure.
- The ordinary legislative procedure is the usual law-making procedure by default. According to this procedure, the Council and the European Parliament are on an equal footing, with the result that no act can be adopted without both bodies' agreement.

test your knowledge

1   Do you agree that in the EU, the concept of 'institutional balance' is more appropriate than the notion of 'separation of powers' to explain the sharing and division of functions between the institutions?

2   It is argued that Member States have little influence on the EU law-making process and are being subjected to rules to which they have not consented. To which extent does this statement reflect the reality?

3   Your Spanish friend Miguel has been working for the Spanish armed forces for the past two years. Miguel has passed all the required fitness tests set by the Spanish armed forces, and there are no other requirements to work in the Spanish armed forces. However, he has recently heard that the European Commission is drafting an EU act (to be adopted under the ordinary legislative procedure) that would oblige all Member States to recruit members of the armed forces who are at least 1.70m tall, and that this would apply three years retroactively. If the EU act is passed, Miguel, who is 1.68m tall, would automatically be made redundant.

Advise Miguel whether and at which stages of the ordinary legislative procedure he could influence the EU and national institutions.

part

II

THE RELATIONSHIP BETWEEN EU LAW AND NATIONAL LAWS

chapter 6

The Constitutional Pillars of European Union Law

study points

After reading this chapter, you will be able to understand:

- the rationale of the principles of supremacy and direct effect of EU law
- the relationship between EU law and domestic law
- the difference between vertical and horizontal direct effect
- the application of the principle of direct effect to treaty provisions, EU acts and international agreements
- the Court of Justice's answer to limits on the principle of direct effect: indirect effect, incidental effect and application of the general principles of EU law.

6.1 Introduction

The CJEU explains in *Opinion 2/13*, 18 December 2014, ECLI:EU:C:2014:2454 that the

> founding treaties of the EU … have established a new legal order, possessing its own institutions, for the benefit of which the Member States thereof have limited their sovereign rights, in ever wider fields, and the subjects of which comprise not only those States but also their nationals … (para 157)

As a result the EU has its own constitutional framework and founding principles, and

> EU law is characterised by the fact that it stems from an independent source of law, the Treaties, by its primacy over the laws of the Member States … and by the direct effect of a whole series of provisions which are applicable to their nationals and to the Member States themselves … (para 166).

This means that the relationship between EU law and national law is governed by two principles:

- the **principle of supremacy**, and
- the **principle of direct effect**.

The principle of supremacy (also called 'principle of primacy') denotes the superior hierarchical status of the Union legal order over the domestic legal orders. As a result, EU law has the capacity to override and pre-empt domestic law. Direct effect simply means that an EU norm can be invoked by an individual in, and applied by, a national court.

6.2 Supremacy of EU law

The original Treaty of Rome did not expressly state the supremacy of European Community (EC) law. As a result, it was envisaged that there would be occasions when national courts would have to apply EC laws. But this could cause difficulties if there was also a national law dealing with the same issue. Which law should the courts apply? When there are two conflicting laws, the normal rule is that under the *lex posterior* doctrine, the most recent law is applied. But that would not work in this context, as it would allow Member States to breach EC laws by subsequently passing conflicting legislation. The Treaty did not actually specify the answer to this problem. Did this consequently mean that supremacy was a matter to be determined by national law? Furthermore, both the dualist and monist systems (see 4.2) pose a threat to the unity of the Union legal order. For dualist Member States, the status of EU law depends on the national act incorporating the European Treaties into their domestic legal order. Where this is done by a parliamentary act, any subsequent parliamentary acts could in fact repeal the incorporating law. Within the British tradition, this follows from the classic doctrine of parliamentary sovereignty. Even for monist Member States, in which duly ratified international laws are automatically incorporated into national law and are given precedence over subsequent national laws, the supremacy of EU law finds a limit in the individual State's constitutional structures.

It was left to the Court of Justice to find a solution and establish the **principle or doctrine of supremacy**. In Case 6/64 *Costa v ENEL* [1964] ECR 585, Costa was trying to get out of paying his electricity bill by claiming that an Italian statute nationalising the electricity industry was contrary to EC law. The statute had been passed after Italy joined the EC, so on the normal time rule, it would prevail over EC law. But the Court of Justice ruled that EC law always prevails over national law, whichever law was passed first. The Court explained (at 593–94):

> By contrast with ordinary international treaties, the [EU] Treaty has created its own legal system which, on the entry into force of the Treaty, became an integral part of the legal systems of the Member States and which their courts are bound to apply. ... The executive force of [EU] law cannot vary from one State to another in deference to subsequent domestic laws, without jeopardising the attainment of the objectives of the Treaty. ... It follows from all these observations that the law stemming from the Treaty, an independent source of law, could not, because of its special and original nature, be overridden by domestic legal provisions, however framed, without being deprived of its character as [EU] law and without the legal basis of the [Union] itself being called into question.

The Court went even further in *Internationale Handellgesellschaft* (Case 11/70 *Internationale Handelsgesellschaft mbH v Einfuhr- und Vorratstelle für Getreide und Futtermittel* [1970] ECR 1125), where it held that EC law would prevail not only over national laws but also over the constitutions of Member States, though in the given case it managed to interpret the EC law in question so that it did not conflict with the German Constitution.

These cases placed national courts in an awkward position, especially where national law restricted their power to rule a national law invalid. In *Simmenthal II* (Case 106/77 *Amministrazione delle Finanze v Simmenthal* [1978] ECR 629), an Italian judge was faced with a conflict between EC and Italian law. Under Italian law, only the Constitutional Court or the Parliament can declare a national law invalid. What should the court do – refer the case to the Constitutional Court, or declare the law invalid itself? The ECJ held that every national court must apply EC law in its entirety and set aside any provision of national law that conflicts with it. In other words disapplication, rather than invalidation, of the domestic law is required of national courts.

In the UK, a key development in relation to supremacy was Case C-213/89 *R v Secretary of State for Transport, ex parte Factortame Ltd* (*Factortame (No 1)*) [1990] ECR I-2433, which concerned the compatibility of the Merchant Shipping Act 1988 with the

EC Treaty. Following a preliminary ruling (see **Chapter 9**), the national court found that

> [s]upremacy ... was certainly well established in the jurisprudence of the ECJ long before the UK joined the Community. Thus, whatever limitation of its sovereignty Parliament accepted when it enacted the ECA 1972 it was entirely voluntary ... [I]t has always been clear that it was the duty of a United Kingdom court ... to override any rule of national law found to be in conflict with any directly enforceable rule of Community law. ([1991] 1 AC 603, per Lord Bridge at 658)

As a result, the English courts were given the power to issue injunctions against the Crown and disapply an Act of Parliament that conflicted with EC law.

This absolute vision of the supremacy of EU law is not shared by the Member States. The supremacy of EU law is seen as relative once it is granted, and limited by national constitutional law. The history of the relationship between the German Constitutional Court and the Court of Justice is particularly revealing in this regard. The national limits to supremacy have been expressed in three contexts:

(a) Some Members States have fought a battle over human rights within the Union legal order. At the inception of the application of the doctrine of supremacy, it was claimed that EC law could not violate national fundamental rights. In the famous '*Solange I*' judgment (*Solange I*, decision of 29 May 1974, BVerfGE 37, 271, [1974] CMLR 540), the German Constitutional Court initially rejected this absolute vision of supremacy of EC law, explaining that *so long as* (hence '*Solange*') the then EC lacked a codified catalogue of fundamental rights, the German Constitutional Court would disapply EC law that conflicted with the fundamental rights guaranteed in the German Constitution. Thus national limits were put on the supremacy of EC law, though such limits were relative, as they depended on the evolution and nature of EC law. Indeed, in a second famous '*Solange II*' ruling (*Solange II*, decision of 22 October 1986, BVerfGE 73, 339, [1987] 3 CMLR 225) the German Constitutional Court inverted the 'so long as' condition: it promised not to question the supremacy of EC law so long as the latter guaranteed fundamental rights substantially similar to those recognised by the German Constitution.

(b) The second constitutional battle is that over the expansive exercise of legislative and judicial competences of the Union. Whilst the Member States accept the supremacy of EU law within limited fields, they contest that the EU can exclusively delimit these fields. The *ultra vires* question was at the heart of the famous *Maastricht* ruling of the German Constitutional Court:

> Thus, if European institutions and agencies were to treat or develop the Union Treaty in a way that was no longer covered by the Treaty in the form that is the basis for the Act of Accession, the resultant legislative instruments would not be legally binding within the sphere of German sovereignty. (*Maastricht*, decision of 12 October 1993, BVerfGE 89, 155, [1994] 1 CMLR 57, para 99)

This national review power was subsequently confirmed in the *Lisbon* decision (*Lisbon*, decision of 30 June 2009, BVerfGE 123, 267, [2010] 3 CMLR 276) and then limited and refined in the *Honeywell* case (*Honeywell*, decision of 6 July 2010, 2 BvR 2661/06, [2011] 1 CMLR 1067) that was the result of the *Mangold* case

(Case C-144/04 *Mangold v Helm* [2005] ECR I-9981) (see below **6.3.5.4**). In the latter case, the German Constitutional Court accepted a presumption that the Union would generally act within the scope of its competences, and that only for clear and exceptional violations would the German Constitutional Court challenge the supremacy of EU law.

(c) The 'State identity limit' was added by the German Constitutional Court as a further constitutional limit on European integration. In the *Lisbon* judgment (see (b) above), the German Constitutional Court identified a number of essential areas of democratic formative action, such as:

decisions on substantive and formal criminal law; on the disposition of the monopoly on the use of force by the police within the state and by the military towards the exterior; fundamental fiscal decisions on public revenue and public expenditure, the latter being particularly motivated, inter alia, by social policy considerations; decisions on the shaping of living conditions in a social state; and decisions of particular cultural importance, for example on family law, the school and education system and on dealing with religious communities. ([2010] 3 CMLR 276, 341)

That being said, the principle of supremacy is now firmly enshrined in EU law. Declaration No 17 Concerning Primacy ([2012] OJ C326/346) affirms that

in accordance with well settled case law of the Court of Justice of the European Union, the Treaties and the law adopted by the Union on the basis of the Treaties have primacy over the law of Member States, under the conditions laid down by the said case law.

The Declaration cites the Opinion of the Council Legal Service of 22 June 2007 (11197/ 07 (JUR 260)):

It results from the case-law of the Court of Justice that primacy of [EU] law is a cornerstone principle of [EU] law ... According to the Court, this principle is inherent to the specific nature of the European [Union]. At the time of the first judgment of this established case law (*Costa/ENEL* 6/64) there was no mention of primacy in the treaty. It is still the case today. The fact that the principle of primacy will not be included in the future treaty shall not in any way change the existence of the principle and the existing case-law of the Court of Justice.

6.3 Direct effect

6.3.1 The principle of direct effect

Under international law, a State is obliged to abide by treaty provisions. If it does not, usually only the injured State can lodge a complaint against the State that has failed to comply with the treaty (see eg proceedings before the International Court of Justice). Some treaties, however (eg European Convention on Human Rights), provide for individuals to access an international court. The Treaty of Rome did not provide for any such mechanism. It nevertheless allowed the Commission to investigate allegations of non-compliance with the Treaty or other legislative acts enacted by the EU institutions. Having said that, the Commission might not take up the case, or might not pursue it through the courts, accepting the Member State's excuses and promises of future obedience (see further 7.2). Even if it did, it might take two to three years before the Member State was held to be in breach and thus obliged to put its law right. In other words, the mechanism of remedies afforded in the original Treaty was not favourable to individuals.

The ECJ, in the seminal *Van Gend en Loos* ruling (Case 26/62 *NV Algemene Transport- en Expeditie Onderneming van Gend & Loos v Netherlands Inland Revenue Administration* [1963] ECR 1, 12), confirmed the independence of the European legal order from classical international law:

> The objective of the [EU] Treaty, which is to establish a common market, the functioning of which is of direct concern to interested parties in the [Union], implies that this Treaty is more than an agreement which merely creates mutual obligations between the contracting States.

According to the Court, (now) EU law is directly applicable in the national legal orders, and it is to be enforced by national courts.

In Case 26/62 *NV Algemene Transport- en Expeditie Onderneming van Gend & Loos v Netherlands Inland Revenue Administration* [1963] ECR 1, the company imported a chemical from Germany to The Netherlands; it was then told that the chemical had been reclassified so the customs duty payable had increased. This was clearly a breach of former Article 12 TEEC (now Article 30 TFEU), which forbade the imposition of new customs duties between Member States. Van Gend sued the Dutch authorities to get its money back. The case was referred to the ECJ for a preliminary ruling under former Article 177 TEEC (now Article 267 TFEU). The Advocate General (see **8.2**) argued that the Treaty imposed obligations on Member States that were enforceable only through former Article 169 TEEC (now Article 258 TFEU) (see **7.2**). But the Court went much further. It said that the then EEC constituted a 'new legal order' and that EEC law conferred rights on individuals that become part of their legal heritage. They could therefore enforce these rights directly before the national court; the rights had direct effect. The Court admitted that the reason it made this decision was to provide an additional way to force Member States to obey EEC law. Any individual could then claim rights under EEC law and the national court would enforce them, with a preliminary ruling if required (see **Chapter 9**). It was no longer necessary to wait for the Commission to take action. The Court held (at 152):

> [T]he [EU] constitutes a new legal order of international law for the benefit of which the States have limited their sovereign rights, albeit within limited fields, and the subjects of which comprise not only Member States but also their nationals. Independently of the legislation of the Member States, [EU] law therefore not only imposes obligations on individuals but is also intended to confer on them rights which become part of their legal heritage. These rights arise not only where they are expressly granted by the Treaty, but also by reason of obligations which the Treaty imposes in a clearly defined way upon individuals as well as upon Member States.

The *Van Gend en Loos* case set a two-pronged test for individuals claiming direct effect:

(a) the specific EU provision must provide Member States and individuals with rights and obligations; and

(b) such rights and obligations can be enforced in national courts.

Indeed, the ECJ explained in the *Francovich* case (Joined Cases C-6 and 9/90 *Francovich and Others v Italy* [1991] ECR I-5357, para 12) that in order to determine whether a provision has direct effect, a court must be able to:

- identify persons who are entitled to the right
- ascertain the content of that right, and
- identify the person or body that is liable to provide that right.

Having established the **principle of direct effect**, the ECJ had to elaborate exactly when a Treaty provision would be regarded as conferring directly effective rights on an individual. To be enforceable, a norm must be 'justiciable' or 'executable', that is, it must be capable of being applied by a public authority in a specific case. The qualities required by a provision, spelled out in para 152 of the *Van Gend en Loos* decision, are as follows:

(a)   the provision must be clear and precise;

(b)   the provision must be unconditional, ie no conditions are attached to it; and

(c)   the provision is not subject, 'in its implementation or effects, to the taking of any measure either by the institutions of the [EU] or by the Member States'.

Moreover, if a specific provision is found to have direct effect, it binds all the authorities of the Member States, which include not only governments, parliaments and national courts but also decentralised authorities such as *Länder*, regions, towns, cities and municipalities (Case C-429/09 *Fuß v Stadt Halle* [2010] ECR I-12167, para 85).

6.3.2   Direct effect of Treaty provisions

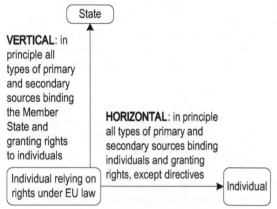

Figure 6.1   Vertical and horizontal effects of EU law

In *Van Gend en Loos* (**6.3.1** above), the ECJ explained that individuals could derive rights directly from the Treaty. In that case the Court held only that an individual could assert his rights as spelled out in the Treaties against the State; but in Case 43/75 *Defrenne v Sabena* [1976] ECR 455, it went further. The applicant here complained that her employer, an airline company, was paying female air stewardesses less than male ones, contrary to former Article 119 TEEC (now Article 157 TFEU, which requires equal pay for equal work). The Court held that Treaty provisions, such as that article, have direct effect against everyone: **vertical effect**, obliging the State to act in conformity with the Treaty provisions; and **horizontal effect**, compelling individuals and companies to abide by the Treaty provisions (see **Figure 6.1**). Yet it cannot be assumed that all TEU or TFEU provisions have direct effect, for they still have to fulfil the direct effect test (**6.3.1** above).

6.3.3   Direct effect of EU acts

The Court of Justice has expanded the doctrine of direct effect to EU acts, namely, to regulations, directives and decisions, as well as to international agreements. Non-binding measures, such as recommendations and opinions, do not have direct effect. Given that it is not possible to give horizontal direct effect to directives (ie effect as between individuals) (see **6.3.3.2** below), the Court has applied a variety of techniques to ensure that individuals are still able to enforce the rights they have been guaranteed by EU law.

6.3.3.1   Direct effect of regulations

After establishing the direct effect of Treaty provisions, the Court pushed the concept further by looking at regulations. According to Article 288(2) TFEU, regulations are directly applicable, that is, they do not need any implementation measure to be considered valid law at national level (see **4.3.2.1**). The Court therefore had no problem extending direct effect to regulations, because the Treaty already made them directly applicable, in other words they are directly incorporated into the law of Member States. If they are unconditional, clear and precise, there is no problem giving regulations vertical (Case 9/70 *Grad v Finanzamt Traunstein* [1970] ECR 825) and horizontal (Case 34/73 *Fratelli Variola v Amministrazione delle Finanze* [1973] ECR 981) direct effect, so they can be enforced against both the Member State and private individuals.

That being said, it must be noted that it is not the entire regulation that has direct effect but the specific provision that fulfils the test (Case C-403/98 *Azienda Monte Arcosu Srl v Regione Autonoma della Sardegna, Organismo Comprensoriale no 24 della Sardegna and Ente Regionale per l'Assistenza Tecnica in Agricoltura (ERSAT)* [2001] ECR I-103):

> [A]lthough, by virtue of the very nature of regulations and of their function in the system of sources of [EU] law, the provisions of those regulations generally have immediate effect in the national legal systems without its being necessary for the national authorities to adopt measures of application, some of their provisions may none the less necessitate, for their implementation, the adoption of measures of application by the Member States.
>
> ...
>
> In the light of the discretion enjoyed by the Member States in respect of the implementation of those provisions, it cannot be held that individuals may derive rights from those provisions in the absence of measures of application adopted by the Member States. (paras 26 and 28)

At this juncture, it must be highlighted that whereas *direct applicability* refers to the incorporation and the internal effect of an EU act within national legal orders, *direct effect* refers to the individual effect of a binding act in specific cases. Direct effect requires direct applicability, but not the other way around. The direct applicability of an act simply makes its direct effect possible.

6.3.3.2 Direct effect of directives

The situation in relation to directives is more complicated. It would seem clear that directives could not possibly have direct effect, as they are only instructions to the Member State to create or amend a national law so as to comply with the substance laid down in the directive. How could anyone claim any rights until the directive has been implemented into national law? Nevertheless, the Court was worried by the fact that not all Member States implemented all directives, not only on time but also correctly. Should individuals be deprived of their rights by the failure of a Member State to meet its obligations? The Court answered this question in the negative by extending direct effect to directives in the landmark *Van Duyn* case (Case 41/74 *Van Duyn v Home Office* [1974] ECR 1337). This decision was and is controversial, because it could be argued that it is plainly contrary to what the drafters of the Treaty might have originally intended when they invented directives.

In Case 41/74 *Van Duyn v Home Office* [1974] ECR 1337, Miss Van Duyn, a Dutch woman, wished to take up a job as a secretary with the Church of Scientology, but was refused admission to the UK on the ground of public policy because the activities of the Church of Scientology were then being thought to be socially harmful (see further **20.5.2.1**). She challenged this refusal on the basis of her right of freedom of movement for workers under Article 48 EEC (now Article 45 TFEU), Regulation 1612/68 (now Regulation 492/2011) (see further **15.4.2**) and, notably, Article 3(1) of former Directive 64/221/EEC on the co-ordination of special measures concerning the movement and residence of foreign nationals which are justified on grounds of public policy, public security or public health. However, the UK had not adopted the wording of Article 3(1) of the directive and so argued that Miss Van Duyn could have no rights. The Court held that even a directive could have direct effect, provided it was unconditional, clear and precise.

As a result of this decision, the difference between directives and regulations is rather limited. Perhaps as a consequence of this concern, the Court attached two restrictions to the direct effect of directives. First, *no directive can have direct effect until after the date for implementation has passed* (Case 148/78 *Criminal proceedings against Ratti* [1979] ECR 1629). Until that date, there is no obligation to implement a directive, and therefore no right can be derived from it. But if a Member State passes legislation in advance of the deadline, it is obliged to refrain from adopting measures that might compromise the result prescribed in the directive (Case C-129/96 *Inter-Environnement Wallonie SBL v Région Wallone* [1997] ECR I-7411). In *Ratti*, the Court held that the justification for applying direct effect to directives was to stop a Member State from relying on its own failure to implement, a form of estoppel. However, this could apply only where the defendant was a Member State body.

The second restriction is that *directives can only have vertical direct effect*. In Case 152/84 *Marshall v Southampton and South-West Hampshire Area Health Authority* [1986] ECR 723, Ms Marshall complained that under the Social Security Act 1975, she was forced to retire at the age of 62 whereas men could work until they reached the age of 65. This was regarded as discrimination on the ground of age contrary to the 1976 EC Directive on Equal Treatment, which required equal retirement ages. However, the UK had not implemented the Directive. If the defendant was a private body, it would be unfair to blame it for the non-implementation of the Directive. This locates the rationale for the direct effect of directives not in the nature of the instrument itself, but in the behaviour of the Member State. As the Court observed,

> according to Article [288 TFEU] the binding nature of a directive, which constitutes the basis for the possibility of relying on the directive before a national court, exists only in relation to 'each member state to which it is addressed'. It follows that a directive may not of itself impose obligations on an individual and that a provision of a directive may not be relied upon as such against such a person ... (para 48)

As Ms Marshall worked in the public sector (an emanation of the State – see below), she could rely on the 1976 Directive.

This ruling of course produces all kind of anomalies. If Ms Marshall had worked in the private sector, she could not have relied on the directive. Some therefore argue that the Court should push the law on and give horizontal direct effect to directives. Yet in *Faccini Dori* (Case C-91/92 *Faccini Dori v Recreb Srl* [1994] ECR I-3325), the ECJ reiterated its position. This ruling is based on the idea that to grant horizontal direct effect to directives would override the distinction between directives and regulations as set out originally in the EC Treaty and now in the TFEU.

As a consequence, it becomes extremely important to define what counts as a public body. There are some obvious ones: government, central and local, health authorities and the police. Yet the Court adopted a broad definition of the State in order to mitigate the effect of the lack of horizontal direct effect of directives. In Case C-188/89 *Foster and others v British Gas plc*[1990] ECR I-3133, the ECJ spelled out three criteria to determine whether a particular body is an 'emanation of the State'. The body must:

(a)   be made responsible by the Member State for providing a public service;

(b)   provide the service under the control of the State;

(c)   have special powers to provide that service.

This wide definition consequently covers private bodies endowed with public functions, such as:

(a)   regional and local government (Case 103/88 *Fratelli Costanzo v Milano* [1989] ECR 1839);

(b)   a Chief Constable (Case 222/84 *Johnston v Chief Constable of the Royal Ulster Constabulary* [1986] ECR 1651);

(c)   a corporation under State control (although some conditions have been attached) (*Doughty v Rolls Royce Plc* [1992] 1 CMLR 1045);

(d)   a school receiving State funding (*NUT v St Mary's School* [1997] 3 CMLR 630).

6.3.3.3   Direct effect of decisions

Decisions are directly applicable (see **4.3.2.1**) and thus, as with regulations, it was relatively easy for the ECJ to state that decisions or provisions thereof had direct effect. In Case 9/70 *Grad v Finanzamt Traunstein* [1970] ECR 825, the Court explained that the direct effect of a provision depended on the 'nature, background and wording of the provision', and that the provision in question had to be 'unconditional and sufficiently clear and precise to be capable of producing direct effects in the legal relationship between the Member States and those subject to their jurisdiction' (para 9). That being said, only the decision's specific addressees may rely on it.

6.3.4   Direct effect of international agreements

Article 216(2) TFEU stipulates that:

> [a]greements concluded by the Union are binding upon the institutions of the Union and on its Member States.

The ECJ has expressly stated that such agreements are part of the European legal system from the moment they enter into force, and this without the need for an act of incorporation (Case 181/73 *R & V Haegeman v Belgium* [1974] ECR 449, para 5).

The rulings of the Court have ensured some consistency in the application and interpretation of such agreements. In particular, the Court has spelled out a two-stage test to determine the direct effect of international agreements:

(a)   The Court examines whether the agreement as a whole is capable of containing effective provisions (Case 104/81 *Hauptzollamt Mainz v CA Kupferberg & Cie KG aA* [1982] ECR 3641, para 17). If it is not, then the Court looks at the agreement's purpose and nature (Case 12/86 *Demirel v Stadt Schwäbisch Gmünd* [1987] ECR 3719, para 14), as well as at its spirit and general scheme, to determine whether it has direct effect (Joined Cases 21–24/72 *International Fruit Company NV and others v Produktschap voor Groenten en Fruit* [1972] ECR 1219, para 20).

(b) Then the Court investigates whether the specific provision at stake has direct effect, in other words whether it is clear, precise and unconditional (*Demirel*, para 14).

That being said, the Court has exercised great judicial restraint, and few agreements and provisions thereof have been deemed to have direct effect. The Court has explained that agreements that are the subject of international negotiations are better left to the legislative and executive bodies of the EU:

> To accept that the role of ensuring that [EU] law complies with those rules devolves directly on the [Union] judicature would deprive the legislative or executive organs of the [Union] of the scope for manoeuvre enjoyed by their counterparts in the [Union's] trading partners. (Case C-149/96 *Portugal v Council* [1999] ECR I-8395, para 46)

When provisions of international agreements do have direct effect, such direct effect is both vertical and horizontal (Case C-138/00 *Deutscher Handballbund eV v Kolpak* [2003] ECR I-4135). When they do not have direct effect, it might be possible to use the principle of indirect effect (see **6.3.5.1** below). One approach, based on the principle of consistent interpretation, is to ensure that EU acts are interpreted in the light of the agreements (Case C-61/94 *Commission v Germany (Re IDA)* [1996] ECR I-3989, para 52). Another approach, based on the principle of implementation, has two strands:

(a) either the EU act is adopted with a view to implementing an obligation specified in an agreement (Case C-69/89 *Nakajima All Precision Co Ltd v Council* [1991] ECR I-2069); or

(b) the EU act expressly refers to the provision in the agreement (Case 70/87 *Fédération de l'industrie de l'huilerie de la CEE (Fediol) v Commission* [1989] ECR 1781) and then the concept of indirect effect can be used (see eg Case T-19/01 *Chiquita Brands International, Inc and Others v Commission* [2005] ECR II-315).

6.3.5 Circumventing the lack of horizontal direct effect of directives: indirect effect, triangular situations, incidental effect and the fundamental rights approach

6.3.5.1 Indirect effect

Owing to the limitations of direct effect, the Court has developed another means to protect the rights of EU citizens where the Member States have not done so: the **indirect effect** of directives (for an overview of the CJEU's methods in developing the doctrine of indirect effect, see **8.6**). The Court created in the *Von Colson* case (Case 14/83 *Von Colson and Kamann v Land Nordrhein-Westfalen* [1984] ECR 1891) the concept of indirect effect, which provides that domestic law has to be interpreted in the light of the directive. To some extent this is similar to the principle of consistent interpretation with regard to international agreements (see **6.3.4.** above). In the *Von Colson* case, the domestic law was an attempt at transposing the directive.

In Case 14/83 *Von Colson and Kamann v Land Nordrhein-Westfalen* [1984] ECR 1891, two women were discriminated against in seeking work, one in the public sector and one in the private sector. The 1976 EC Directive on Equal Treatment required Member States to set up a system for giving redress to victims of sex discrimination. Germany had given them a right to sue, but only for wasted travelling expenses. With regard to this specific requirement, the Directive did not have direct effect, and would in any case have helped only one of the women. The ECJ held that the national courts were obliged to try to interpret their own domestic law in such a way as to give effect to EC laws, including unimplemented directives and directives that did not have direct effect. In this case it was relatively easy to find an interpretation of the German law that would give effect to the directive. Indeed, the German law had been intended all along to comply with EC law, and it would be normal for a national court to try hard to find a way of interpreting a law that would give the effect intended. As a result, the duty of consistent interpretation may lead to the indirect implementation of a directive.

The rationale for this concept derives from the **principle of sincere cooperation** under now Article 4(3) TEU (former Article 5 TEEC), whereby Member States are required to

> take any appropriate measure, general or particular, to ensure fulfilment of the obligations arising out of the Treaties or resulting from the acts of the institutions of the Union.

The principle is binding on all national authorities, including the courts. As a result,

> in applying the national law and in particular the provisions of a national law specifically introduced in order to implement [a] Directive …, national courts are required to interpret their national law in the light of the wording and the purpose of the directive in order to achieve the result referred to in the third paragraph of Article [288]. (*Von Colson*, para 26)

However, this could prove more difficult where the national law pre-dates the directive and cannot therefore have been intended to give effect to it. Nonetheless, in Case C-106/89 *Marleasing SA v La Comercial Internacional de Alimentaciòn SA* [1990] ECR I-4135, the Court held that the Spanish courts had the duty to interpret national law as far as possible in the light of EU law, and this duty would extend to all national law, including national law that pre-exists EU law (here, the interpretation of a provision of the Spanish Civil Code in light of Company Directive 68/151 which had not been yet implemented by Spain). However, where domestic law had been specifically enacted to implement a directive, the national courts must operate under the presumption 'that the Member State, following its exercise of the discretion afforded to it under that provision, had the intention of fulfilling entirely the obligations arising from the directive concerned' (Joined Cases C-397/01 to C-403/01 *Pfeiffer et al v Deutsches Rotes Kreuz, Kreisverband Waldshut eV* [2004] ECR I-8835, para 112).

The tricky element is the expression 'as far as possible' in the Court's decision in *Marleasing* (above). How far is the national court supposed to go? Clearly, if the national law is ambiguous, it will be easy for the court to give preference to the interpretation that would give effect to the directive. In contrast, the Court of Justice has recognised that the clear and unambiguous wording of a national provision constitutes an absolute limit to its interpretation. As a result, if it is impossible to interpret domestic law in conformity with a directive then national law should be disapplied (Case C-555/07 *Kücükdeveci v Swedex GmbH & Co KG* [2010] ECR I-365, para 49). Thus, a national court is not obliged to invent or import novel interpretative methods but is required 'to do whatever lies within its jurisdiction, having regard to the whole body of rules of national law' (*Pfeiffer*, para 118).

Under EU law there are a number of limitations on the principle of indirect effect:

(a) Indirect effect can be used only after the deadline for transposition has expired (Case C-212/04 *Adeneler and Others v Ellinikos Organismos Galaktos (ELOG)* [2006] ECR I-6057).

(b) There is no obligation on the national court to interpret domestic law in light of an EU directive if it leads to the imposition on an individual of an obligation under an unimplemented directive (Case C-456/98 *Centrosteel Srl v Adipol GmbH* [2000] ECR I-6007), especially if criminal liability is involved (Case C-168/95 *Criminal Proceedings against Arcaro* [1996] ECR I-4705).

(c) The interpretation that results from the application of the principle of indirect effect cannot go against the general principles of EU law, and more particularly the principles of legal certainty (see **10.2.2.3**) and non-retroactivity (see **10.2.2.3**). For example, this type of interpretation cannot be used to increase penalties, as criminal law is subject to particularly strict rules of interpretation. In Case 80/86 *Criminal proceedings against Kolpinghuis Nijmegen BV* [1987] ECR 3969, the accused was prosecuted for filling bottles with tap water and selling it as mineral water. This was an offence only if Dutch law was interpreted in the light of the 1980 EC Directive on the exploitation and marketing of natural mineral waters, not yet implemented in the Netherlands. The Court held that it would be unfair to take an unimplemented directive into account, with the effect of determining or aggravating the criminal liability of an individual acting in contravention of the directive.

See **Figure 6.2**.

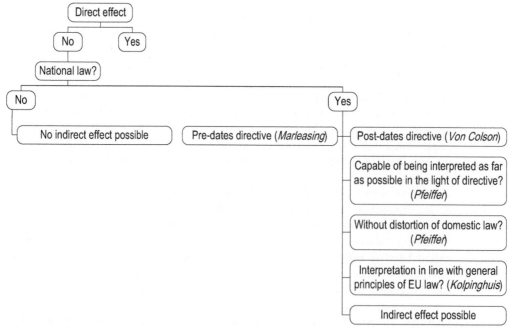

Figure 6.2   Direct and indirect effect in EU law

6.3.5.2   Triangular situations

One way of obtaining some form of horizontal direct effect is by claiming that a directive has negative consequences for another individual who is not a party to the domestic court proceedings. In this case, the individual brings a case against the Member State when in fact the true target of the legal action is another individual. Typical cases involve a permit holder and someone who objects to the permit, usually on the basis of EU environmental law, or a public contract being awarded to a third party although it appears to be in violation of a directive. In this context, the failure of the competent authorities delivering the permit triggers a duty of sincere cooperation for the national court to revoke or suspend the consent decision or, alternatively, award compensation for the harm suffered.

case example

In Case C-201/02 *R (Wells) v Secretary of State for Transport, Local Government and the Regions* [2004] ECR I-748, the applicant, Ms Delena Wells, owned a house next to a disused quarry. The quarry was granted a permit to start its mining operations. Ms Wells claimed that such a permit had been delivered without an environmental impact assessment having been carried out, which, she argued, did not comply with Directive 85/337/EEC. The Court held that

the principle of legal certainty prevents directives from creating obligations for individuals. For them, the provisions of a directive can only create rights ... Consequently, an individual may not rely on a directive against a Member State where it is a matter of a State obligation directly linked to the performance of other obligation falling, pursuant to that directive, on a third party ...

On the other hand, mere adverse repercussions on the rights of third parties, even if the repercussions are certain, do not justify preventing an individual from invoking the provisions of a directive against the Member State concerned. ... (paras 56 and 57)

The Court agreed that the directive had been violated, and as a consequence the consent had to be withdrawn from the quarry or suspended in order that an environmental impact assessment might be carried out.

6.3.5.3   Incidental effect

Incidental effect, whereby an individual uses a directive to require the Member State to give another individual a right or deprive him of one, is another way of claiming some form of horizontal direct effect. Incidental effect is defined as the application of a directive that incidentally affects the legal position of a private party but does not impose any obligations on the individual (Case C-194/94 *CIA Security International SA v Signalson SA and Securitel SPRL* [1996] ECR I-2201 and Case C-443/98 *Unilever Italia SpA v Central Foods SpA* [2000] ECR I-7535).

In Case C-443/98 *Unilever Italia SpA v Central Foods SpA* [2000] ECR I-7535, Directive 83/ 189 prescribed certain procedures to be followed when a Member State intended to adopt technical regulations. The purpose of those procedures was to facilitate the proper functioning of the internal market by obviating the restrictions on the free movement of goods that might arise from Member States' technical requirements for goods marketed or used within their territories. A Member State that intended to adopt such provisions was required to notify those provisions in advance and then refrain from enacting them for a specified standstill period, in order to allow the Commission and the other Member States to submit observations concerning possible obstacles to trade at a stage at which they could be taken into account, and to allow the legislature, if it thought fit, to adopt an act regulating the field in question. The question referred to the Court by an Italian court concerned civil proceedings between individuals arising from a contract, and whether a national court should disapply a national technical regulation that, although notified to the Commission in accordance with Council Directive 83/189, was adopted before the expiry of the 'standstill' period applicable under that Directive. In its ruling, the Court responded:

> … a national court is required, in civil proceedings between individuals concerning contractual rights and obligations, to refuse to apply a national technical regulation which was adopted during a period of postponement of adoption prescribed in Article 9 of Directive 83/189. (para 52)

6.3.5.4 The general principles approach

Another tool used by the Court of Justice is to refer to the **general principles of EU law**. In *Mangold* (Case C-144/04 *Mangold v Helm* [2005] ECR I-9981), the *Arbeitsgericht* (Labour Court) of Munich referred to the ECJ three questions on the interpretation of Council Directive 1999/70/EC of 28 June 1999 concerning the framework agreement on fixed-term work (concluded by the European Trade Union Confederation, the Union of Industrial and Employers' Confederations of Europe (renamed 'BusinessEurope' in 2007) and the European Centre of Enterprises with Public Participation and of Enterprises of General Economic Interest) and Council Directive 2000/78/EC of 27 November 2000 establishing a general framework for equal treatment in employment and occupation. The national court wished to know whether, in the context of a dispute between private parties, those directives precluded a national rule allowing older people to be employed on fixed-term contracts with no restrictions. In essence, without giving horizontal direct effect to the directives concerned, the Court concluded that:

> The principle of non-discrimination on grounds of age must thus be regarded as a general principle of [EU] law. …
>
> Consequently, observance of the general principle of equal treatment, in particular in respect of age, cannot as such be conditional upon the expiry of the period allowed the Member States for the transposition of a directive intended to lay down a general framework for combating discrimination on the grounds of age, in particular so far as the organisation of appropriate legal remedies, the burden of proof, protection against victimisation, social dialogue, affirmative action and other specific measures to implement such a directive are concerned.
>
> … It is the responsibility of the national court to guarantee the full effectiveness of the general principle of non-discrimination in respect of age, setting aside any provision of national law which may conflict with [EU] law, even where the period prescribed for transposition of that directive has not yet expired. (paras 75, 76 and 78)

A similar position was adopted in Case C-555/07 *Kücükdeveci v Swedex GmbH & Co KG* [2010] ECR I-365. Again on a reference from a German court, this case was an opportunity for the Court of Justice to clarify the legal rules governing the general principle of non-discrimination on grounds of age, and the function which that principle fulfils in a situation in which the time-limit for the transposition of the abovementioned Council Directive 2000/78/EC had expired and the proceedings involved two private parties. According to Advocate General Bot, directives should have horizontal direct effect in certain circumstances, notably when they apply fundamental principles, such as non-discrimination.

> Most of all, it cannot be accepted that the protection of individuals against discrimination which is contrary to [EU] law is reduced after the expiry of that period even though the purpose of the rule in question is to increase their protection. To my mind, therefore, it should be possible to rely on Directive 2000/78 in proceedings between private parties in order to exclude a national provision which is contrary to [EU] law …
>
> … To adopt such an approach in the present case would not force the Court to reverse its earlier case-law concerning the absence of horizontal direct effect of directives. All that is at stake in the present case is the exclusion of a national provision contrary to Directive 2000/78 … to allow the national court to apply the remaining provisions of that paragraph, namely the periods of notice calculated on the basis of the length of the employment relationship. Directive 2000/78 is not therefore to be applied to independent private conduct not subject to any particular State rule, such as the decision of an employer to take on workers over the age of 45 or under the age of 35. Only that situation would call into question the appropriateness of recognising that the directive has genuine horizontal direct effect. (paras 87 and 88)

Again, without resorting to horizontal direct effect, the Court of Justice confirmed the *Mangold* ruling:

> It is for the national court, hearing proceedings between individuals, to ensure that the principle of non-discrimination on grounds of age, as given expression in Directive 2000/78, is complied with, disapplying if need be any contrary provision of national legislation, independently of whether it makes use of its entitlement, in the cases referred to in the second paragraph of Article 267 TFEU, to ask the Court of Justice of the European Union for a preliminary ruling on the interpretation of that principle. (*Kücükdeveci*, para 56)

The Court of Justice has thus found a number of ways to mitigate the lack of horizontal direct effect of directives.

6.4 Further reading

Avbelj M, 'Supremacy or Primacy of EU Law – (Why) Does it Matter?' (2011) 17 *European Law Journal* 744.

Craig P, 'The Legal Effect of Directives: Policy, Rules and Exception' (2009) 34 *EL Rev* 349.

Cremona M, 'The Judgment – Framing the Argument' in Court of Justice of the European Union, *50th Anniversary of the Judgment in Van Gend en Loos 1963–2013*, Conference Proceedings, 13 May 2013 (OPUE, Luxembourg, 2013) 23.

Dougan M, 'In Defence of Mangold?' in Arnull A et al (eds), *A Constitutional Order of States? Essays in EU Law in Honour of Alan Dashwood* (Hart Publishing, 2011) 219.

Dougan M, 'When Worlds Collide! Competing Visions of the Relationship between Direct Effect and Supremacy' (2007) 44 *CML Rev* 931.

Doukas D, 'The Verdict of the German Federal Constitutional Court on the Lisbon Treaty: Not Guilty, but Don't Do it Again!' (2009) 34 *EL Rev* 866.

Drake S, 'Twenty Years after *Von Colson*: The Impact of "Indirect Effect" on the Protection of the Individual's Community Rights' (2005) 30 *EL Rev* 329.

Grosser A, 'The Federal Constitution Court's *Lisbon* Case: Germany's "Sonderweg": An Outsider's Perspective' (2009) 10 *German Law Journal* 1263.

Lackoff K and Nyssens H, 'Direct Effect of Directives in Triangular Situations' (1998) 23 *EL Rev* 397.

Lenaerts K and Corthaut T, 'Of Birds and Hedges: The Role of Primacy in Invoking Norms of EU Law' (2006) 31 *EL Rev* 287.

Martines F, 'Direct Effect of International Agreements of the European Union' (2014) 25(1) *European Journal of International Law* 149.

Moens G and Trone J, 'The Effect of EU Law upon National Law' in Moens G and Trone J (eds), *Commercial Law of the European Union* (Springer Verlag, 2010) 367.

Niedobitek M, 'The *Lisbon* Case of 30 June 2009: A Comment from the European Law Perspective' (2009) 10 *German Law Journal* 1267.

Payandeh M, 'Constitutional Review of EU Law after *Honeywell*: Contextualising the Relationship between the German Constitutional Court and the EU Court of Justice' (2011) 48 *CML Rev* 9.

Pernice I, 'The Autonomy of the EU Legal Order – Fifty Years After Van Gend' in Court of Justice of the European Union, *50th Anniversary of the Judgment in Van Gend en Loos 1963–2013*, Conference Proceedings, 13 May 2013 (OPUE, Luxembourg, 2013) 55.

Roes T, 'Case Law: Case C-555/07, *Seda Kucukdeveci v. Swedex Gmbh & Co KG*' (2010) 16 *Columbia Journal of European Law* 497.

Schiek D, 'The ECJ Decision in *Mangold*: A Further Twist on Effects of Directives and Constitutional Relevance of Community Equality Legislation' (2006) 35 *Industrial Law Journal* 329.

Thüsing G and Horler S, 'Case Note: *Seda Kucukdeveci v Swedex*' (2010) 47 *CML Rev* 1161.

Weiler JHH, 'Revisiting *Van Gend en Loos*: Subjectifying and Objectifying the Individual' in Court of Justice of the European Union, *50th Anniversary of the Judgment in Van Gend en Loos 1963–2013*, Conference Proceedings, 13 May 2013 (OPUE, Luxembourg, 2013) 11.

The principles of supremacy and direct effect ensure that individuals who have been endowed with rights by EU law can benefit from these rights. In particular, the Court of Justice has ensured that these rights are effective, for they can be raised in national courts, which are then obliged to use a range of techniques, such as disapplying domestic law or interpreting domestic law in the light of EU law.

The principle of supremacy has been challenged, especially by national higher and constitutional courts, but is generally accepted. The principle of direct effect applies to Treaty provisions, EU acts and international agreements, but to varying degrees. For example, directives have only vertical direct effect in contrast to Treaty provisions, international agreements and other EU acts, which also have horizontal effect. However, to minimise the legal effect of the lack of horizontal direct effect of directives, the Court of Justice has established the principle of indirect effect and the principle of incidental effect, as well as used the general principles of EU law.

1   Critically evaluate the doctrines of direct effect and supremacy as the twin constitutional pillars of EU law.

2   Trace the development of the doctrine of direct effect from its inception in the case law of the Court of Justice, with reference to primary and secondary EU legislation, and explain the extent of its contributions to EU law and the development of the rights of the individual.

3   The doctrine of indirect effect addresses appropriately the shortcomings of the rules relating to direct effect. Discuss.

4   Jacek, a Polish national, works in the UK as a fruit and vegetable picker. He is paid the minimum wage, irrespective of how many kilos of fruit and vegetables he picks. In contrast, British nationals are paid the minimum wage plus a productivity bonus, which can be up to 20% of their harvest. Moreover, although he has been working for Fruit & Veg Ltd for the last two years, Jacek is hired on a temporary basis (two-month contracts). (Fictitious) Directive 888/2013 stipulates that if an individual has been continuously employed for two years with the same company, the employer is obliged to offer a contract of employment of at least one year's duration. Although the deadline for the application of this directive has passed, the UK has still not implemented it. In contrast, the (fictitious) Employment Act 2009 stipulates that such employers are required to incrementally lengthen the contract periods provided to temporary workers. Jacek tells his employer that he has rights under the European Treaties and Directive 888/2013, but the employer replies that EU law is irrelevant in the UK, and even if it was relevant, national law would prevail. Jacek contacts you as his lawyer and asks you:
    (a)   Whether EU law is irrelevant, and whether national law does indeed prevail as the employer claims?
    (b)   If he goes to court:
          (i)   Can he rely on EU law to ensure that he is not discriminated against with regard to the entitlement to a productivity bonus?
          (ii)   Can he rely on the directive against his employer with regard to the entitlement to a one-year contract?

chapter 7

The Effectiveness of European Union law

study points

After reading this chapter, you will be able to understand:
* the enforcement procedure under Article 258 TFEU
* the role played by the Commission as the guardian of the Treaties and by the CJEU as the judicial body enforcing EU law
* the principle of Member State liability as established and developed by the CJEU.

7.1 Introduction

Under traditional international law, disputes concerning infringements of a treaty are settled among the States that are parties to it. Article 259 TFEU accordingly enables a Member State to bring proceedings before the CJEU against another Member State that it considers to be in breach of its Treaty obligations. However, that procedure has hardly ever been used (eg Case 141/78 *France v United Kingdom* [1979] ECR 2923, Case C-388/95 *Belgium v Spain* [2000] ECR 3123). Rather, EU law is enforced via Article 258 TFEU, which endows the Commission and the CJEU with the power to enforce EU law, and via the case law-based concept of State liability, to ensure that EU law is effective in the legal order of each Member State.

7.2 Enforcement actions against Member States under Articles 258 to 260 TFEU

Article 258 TFEU gives the Commission the power to bring before the CJEU any Member State that is believed to have failed to fulfil the obligations imposed upon it by the Treaties. Article 258 TFEU provides:

> If the Commission considers that a Member State has failed to fulfil an obligation under the Treaties, it shall deliver a reasoned opinion on the matter after giving the State concerned the opportunity to submit its observations.
>
> If the State concerned does not comply with the opinion within the period laid down by the Commission, the latter may bring the matter before the Court of Justice of the European Union.

Indeed, in pursuance of Article 17(1) TEU, the Commission is the guardian of the Treaties:

> The Commission shall promote the general interest of the Union and take appropriate initiatives to that end. It shall ensure the application of the Treaties, and of measures adopted by the institutions pursuant to them. It shall oversee the application of Union law under the control of the Court of Justice of the European Union. …

The aims and purposes of Article 258 TFEU are:

(a) to ensure compliance with and full application of EU law, as well as to deter Member States from potential violations;

(b) to provide a procedure for dispute settlement;

(c) to clarify the law for Member States so that they apply it in a correct manner.

Article 258 TFEU clearly sets up two separate phases in the enforcement procedure: an administrative or pre-judicial phase, and a judicial phase. In cases where the Member State does not comply with the ruling of the CJEU finding it to be in breach of EU law, the Commission can then take the State to Court again and request financial penalties to be imposed upon the Member State.

7.2.1 The procedure

The Commission may become aware of a possible infringement of the Treaties by a Member State through its own monitoring of the application of EU law, a complaint by a private party, petitions submitted to and questions asked by the European Parliament, information in the media, etc. The White Paper on European Governance issued by the European Commission on 25 July 2001 (COM (2001) 428) explains how the Commission decides whether or not to act upon possible breaches of EU law.

> The Commission will focus on:
> – The effectiveness and quality of transposition of directives as the most effective way of avoiding individual problems arising at a later stage.
> – Situations involving the compatibility of national law with fundamental [Union] principles.
> – Cases that seriously affect the [Union] interest (eg cases with cross-border implications) or the interests that the legislation intended to protect.
> – Cases where a particular piece of European legislation creates repeated implementation problems in a Member State.
> – Cases that involve Union financing.
> Such cases should be handled as a priority in the framework of formal infringement procedures. In other cases, other forms of intervention could be explored before launching formal infringement proceedings. (at 25)

In most instances, the Commission deals with cases relating to violations of the Treaties, EU acts and international agreements. In practice there are three types of infringements:

(a) non-communication of measures transposing directives (eg the State has failed to notify the Commission of the implementation measures);

(b) non-conformity of national measures (eg the State has failed to remove existing law that conflicts with EU law or to implement a directive (correctly));

(c) poor application of EU law (eg to put EU law into practice).

Cases can be brought against the legislature, the government, the judiciary, federal entities as well as against the population (Case C-265/95 *Commission v France (Re Spanish Strawberries)* [1997] ECR I-6959) as they are all deemed to be components of the Member State. Right from the beginning, the Court explained that

> … the liability of a Member State under Article [258 TFEU] arises whatever the agency of the State whose action or inaction is the cause of the failure to fulfil its obligations, even in the case of a constitutionally independent institution. (Case 77/69 *Commission v Belgium* [1970] ECR 237, para 15)

Although the Commission relies heavily on individual complaints, it is not bound to pursue them. For example, in Case T-47/96 *SDDDA v Commission* [1996] ECR II-1559, the then Court of First Instance (now the General Court, see **8.3**) explained:

> The Commission is not bound to initiate an infringement procedure against a Member State; on the contrary, it has a discretionary power of assessment, which rules out any right for individuals to require it to adopt a particular position. (para 42)

In many cases, the Commission will decide not to act, especially when politically sensitive issues are present, and will try to find a settlement with the Member State concerned instead. If it declines to initiate proceedings, its decision cannot be challenged in the CJEU.

If the Commission decides to pursue a possible infringement, the Treaty requires it to follow a lengthy procedure, involving not just a judicial phase but also a pre-judicial or administrative phase that involves an informal and formal stage.

7.2.1.1 The pre-judical (administrative) phase

Informal phase

The formal pre-judicial phase is always preceded by an informal stage, in which the Commission will investigate the complaint, making discreet inquiries with the Permanent Representative of the Member State concerned. It must be noted that this phase is not expressly mentioned in Article 258 TFEU. This phase will give the Member State the opportunity to explain its position:

> It is settled case-law that the purpose of the pre-litigation procedure is to give the Member State concerned an opportunity, on the one hand, to comply with its obligations under [EU] law and, on the other, to avail itself of its right to defend itself against the charges formulated by the Commission. (Case C-147/03 *Commission v Austria* [2005] ECR I-5969, para 22)

The majority of cases are cleared up at this point, particularly since Member States have, under Article 4(3) TEU, a legal duty to cooperate with the Commission's investigations:

> Moreover, it should be noted that the failure to reply to the Commission's requests has made the achievement of its task under the Treaty more difficult, and that it therefore breaches the obligation of cooperation laid down by [Article 4(3) TEU]. (Case 375/92 *Commission v Spain* [1994] ECR I-1985, para 25)

If a State refuses to cooperate, then the Commission can use Article 258 TFEU for breach of the **principle of sincere cooperation** to obtain the required information (Case 240/86 *Commission v Greece* [1988] ECR 1835). States are usually given a period of two months to answer. Then, depending on the nature and substance of the information received, the Commission will or not start fresh proceedings under Article 258 TFEU.

Formal phase

If the Commission is not satisfied with the answer it receives, it will move on to the formal stage, in which the Member State concerned is informed by the Commission of the essence of the case against it in a formal letter. The Commission should spell out in clear terms what the allegations are (Case 211/81 *Commission v Denmark* [1982] ECR 4547, paras 7–9), bearing in mind that the Commission must refer to an existing rather than a hypothetical or potential violation of EU law (Case C-341/97 *Commission v Netherlands* [2000] ECR I-6611):

> Also, in order for a letter of formal notice to be issued, a prior failure by the Member State concerned to fulfil an obligation owed by it must be alleged.
>
> However, it is clear that, at the time when a detailed opinion under Directive 83/189 is delivered, the Member State to which it is addressed cannot have infringed Community law, since the measure exists only in draft form.
>
> The contrary view would result in the detailed opinion constituting a conditional formal notice whose existence would be dependent on the action taken by the Member State concerned in relation to the opinion. The requirements of legal certainty, which are inherent in any procedure capable of becoming contentious, preclude such incertitude. (paras 18–20)

The Member State is then given an opportunity to submit observations within a certain period of time (generally two months, less in case of urgency, or more taking into account the complexity of the matter). This was affirmed in the Case 293/85 *Commission v Belgium (Re University Fees)* [1988] ECR 305:

> [T]he *Commission must allow Member States a reasonable period to reply to the letter of formal notice and to comply with a reasoned opinion, or, where appropriate, to prepare their defence.* In order to determine whether the period allowed is reasonable, account must be taken of all the circumstances of the case. Thus, very short periods may be justified in particular circumstances, especially where there is an urgent need to remedy a breach of where the Member State concerned is fully aware of the Commission's views long before the procedure starts. (para 14, emphasis added)

The Commission usually decides within a year either to close the case, or to proceed on to the next step, ie the issuance of a reasoned opinion.

Reasoned opinion

If the Commission is not satisfied with the Member State's response, it issues a reasoned opinion laying down a deadline for compliance. The reasoned opinion is a detailed explanation of the reasons that led the Commission to the conclusion that a Member State has failed to fulfil its obligation under EU law:

> Consequently, the reasoned opinion and the proceedings brought by the Commission must be based on the same complaints as those set out in the letter of formal notice initiating the pre-litigation procedure. ... [T]he reasoned opinion ... must contain a cogent and detailed exposition of the reasons which led the Commission to the conclusion that the Member State concerned had failed to fulfil one of its obligations under the Treaty. (Case C-441/02 *Commission v Germany* [2006] ECR I-3449, para 60)

Whilst there are no set deadlines imposed on this stage (to allow sufficient time for negotiations), the Commission may set a time limit for compliance. If that deadline expires without the requisite steps having been taken, the Commission may then, and only then, initiate proceedings before the Court (Case 7/61 *Commission v Italy* [1961] ECR 317, 326). That being said, as the Court established in Case 247/87 *Star Fruit Company SA v Commission* [1989] ECR 291, the Commission is not obliged to bring the case before the Court:

[I]t is clear from the scheme of Article [258] of the Treaty that the Commission is not bound to commence the proceedings provided for in that provision but in this regard has a discretion which excludes the right for individuals to require that institution to adopt a specific position.

It is only if it considers that the Member State in question has failed to fulfil one of its obligations that the Commission delivers a reasoned opinion. Furthermore, in the event that the State does not comply with the opinion within the period allowed, the institution has in any event the right, but not the duty, to apply to the Court of Justice for a declaration that the alleged breach of obligations has occurred. (paras 11 and 12)

Generally, proceedings cannot be brought by the Commission if the breach is terminated before the deadline set in the reasoned opinion (Case C-439/99 *Commission v Italy* [2002] ECR I-351, para 17) but, exceptionally, the Commission may still bring proceedings if it is able to prove that the Member State is guilty of a general and persistent failure to abide by EU law (Case C- 494/01 *Commission v Ireland* [2005] ECR I-3331, para 32).

The scope of the proceedings is limited to the infringements specified in the reasoned opinion. This means that no charges other than those in the reasoned opinion or in the original formal letter can be added to the court action:

[T]he letter of formal notice from the Commission to the Member State concerned and then the reasoned opinion issued by it delimit the subject-matter of the dispute, so that it cannot thereafter be extended. Consequently, the reasoned opinion and the application must be based on the same complaints. (Case C-147/03 *Commission v Austria* [2005] ECR I-5969, para 23)

If any new charges materialise then the Commission must start a new Article 258 procedure.

7.2.1.2 The judicial phase

Where an application is made to the Court, the Commission is required to prove that the obligation in question has not been fulfilled. The burden on the Commission is not easy to discharge (Case 96/81 *Commission v The Netherlands* [1982] ECR 1791, para 6).

The procedure(s)

There are two procedures. The first one, enshrined in Articles 258 and 260(1) TFEU, pre-dates the Lisbon Treaty and is the most common one. This is the procedure discussed in detail below.

One of the novelties in the Lisbon Treaty is the addition of Article 260(3) TFEU according to which, if the action concerns a breach of the obligation to notify measures transposing a directive adopted under the legislative procedure, the Commission may bring the matter before the Court under Article 258 TFEU and combine it with a request to impose a lump sum or penalty payment for a specific amount. The reason for the existence of this new procedure is to give Member States stronger incentive to implement directives within deadlines and to ensure that EU legislation is genuinely effective. It must be stressed that often these directives confer rights to EU citizens. The Commission can request a lump sum or a penalty payment for both a complete and a partial failure to notify measures adopted to transpose the directive (2011 Commission Communication (2011/C 12/01), para 19). As under the procedure under Article 258 TFEU, the Commission is not obliged to use Article 260(3); it is within its discretion to use its powers. It has mainly issued actions for a declaration that a Member State has failed to fulfil its obligations in cases where the period for transposition of the directive was exceeded by two years. However, unlike the situation under Article 260(2) TFEU (see 7.2.2 below), the Court may not in such cases impose amounts higher than those specified by the Commission (2011 Commission Communication, para 9).

in practice

According to the Commission 31st Annual Report on the Monitoring of the Application of EU law (2013) (COM(2014) 612 final):

> In 2013, the Commission continued to refer a number of late transposition infringements to the Court of Justice with a request for daily penalties under Article 260(3) TFEU. Nine Member States were involved in 14 such decisions in 2013: Belgium, Bulgaria, Estonia, Romania, the United Kingdom (two cases each) and Austria, Cyprus, Poland and Portugal (one each). The proposed daily penalty range from EUR 4 224 to EUR 148 177,92. Most of the penalty proposals for late transposition of directives have been made in the policy area of energy. The Commission has not yet proposed the Court to apply lump sum payments.
>
> Member States increased their efforts to achieve complete transposition before the judgment of the Court of Justice during 2013. However, taken together with the other cases based on Article 258 and 260(3) TFEU that were launched in the previous years, there remained a total of twelve open late transposition infringement cases with a referral decision proposing daily penalties: two cases each against Estonia, Romania and Slovenia and one case each against Austria, Belgium, Cyprus, Germany, Poland and Portugal. (at 6)

Defences

Most cases brought by the Commission before the Court under Article 258 TFEU are won by the Commission. This is because, whilst there is a range of defences available to Member States, the Court will only accept a few of them. The Court will examine the defences presented before ruling on whether there has been a breach of EU law or not. In Case C-215/98 *Commission v Greece* [1999] ECR I-4913, the Court held that:

> an action based on Article [258 TFEU] requires only an objective finding of a failure by a Member State to fulfil its obligations and not proof of any inertia or opposition on the part of the Member State concerned. (para 15)

Defences that are accepted fall within two categories: procedural errors and substantive errors made by the Commission. First, the defendant Member State may argue that the Commission has failed to comply with the procedural requirements imposed on it by the Treaties, notably whether time limits in the formal letter and the reasoned opinion are reasonable (see 7.2.1.1; Case 42/87 *Commission v Belgium* [1988] ECR 5445), that the scope of the case in the formal letter and the reasoned opinion is identical (Case 7/69 *Commission v Italy* [1970] ECR 111), and whether the Commission has indicated which measures the Member State is required to take to comply with its obligations. Secondly, the Member State may seek to establish that the Commission's view of what EU law requires, or its understanding of national law or of what the Member State concerned has actually done, is incorrect (Case C-418/04 *Commission v Ireland* [2007] ECR I-10947).

In cases where a Member State claims that the initial EU action was erroneous, the Court tends to remind the Member State that it could have challenged the legality of the

EU measure under Article 263 TFEU. As a result, such a defence is limited to cases of 'serious and manifest defects' of an EU decision (Case C-226/87 *Commission v Greece* [1988] ECR 3611), the illegality of a regulation (Case 116/82 *Commission v Germany* [1986] ECR 2519) and where the Member State had exclusive competence (Case 6/69 *Commission v France* [1969] ECR 523).

The Court also accepts the possibility of *force majeure* but is not usually sympathetic to such claims:

> [A]lthough it is true that the bomb attack, which took place before 18 January 1979, may have constituted a case of *force majeure* and created insurmountable difficulties, its effect could only have lasted a certain time, namely the time which would in fact be necessary for an administration showing a normal degree of diligence to replace the equipment destroyed and to collect and prepare the data. The Italian government cannot therefore rely on that event to justify its continuing failure to comply with its obligations years later. (Case 101/84 *Commission v Italy* [1985] ECR 2629, para 16)

Member States cannot use the principle of reciprocity either, claiming that other Member States have similarly not implemented the EU legislation (Joined Cases 52 and 55/95 *Commission v France* [1995] ECR I-4443; Case 232/78 *Commission v France (Re Restrictions on Imports of Lamb)* [1979] ECR 2729).

It is no defence to argue that a provision of national law that is incompatible with the Treaties is not in practice applied (Case 167/73 *Commission v France (Re French Merchant Seamen)* [1974] ECR 359). The Court rejects this defence on the basis that the very existence of such a national law breaches EU obligations (Case C-381/92 *Commission v Ireland* [1994] ECR 215). Furthermore, administrative measures are not accepted as proper implementation:

> As the Court has consistently held in judgments concerning the implementation of directives, mere administrative practices, which by their nature are alterable at will by the authorities and are not given the appropriate publicity, cannot be regarded as constituting the proper fulfilment of a Member State's obligations under the Treaty. (Case C-236/91 *Commission v Ireland* [1992] ECR I-5933, para 6)

Likewise, the Court will not accept the defence that the necessary amending legislation has been held up in parliament. Internal circumstances are not accepted as justification either. In Case C-39/88 *Commission v Ireland* [1990] ECR I-4271, the Court held that

> ... [it] is well established in the case law of the Court ... that a Member State may not plead internal circumstances in order to justify a failure to comply with obligations and time-limits resulting from [EU] law. Moreover, it has been held on several occasions ... that practical difficulties which appear at the stage when an [EU] measure is put into effect cannot permit a Member State unilaterally to opt out of fulfilling its obligations. (para 11)

In particular, the Member State cannot claim that the lack of implementation or the incorrect implementation is due to the division of powers between central and regional authorities. In Case C-87/02 *Commission v Italy* [2004] ECR I-5975, the Court clearly spelled this out:

> First of all, it should be recalled that the fact that a Member State has conferred on its regions the responsibility for giving effect to directives cannot have any bearing on the application of Article [258 TFEU]. The Court has consistently held

that a Member State cannot plead conditions existing within its own legal system in order to justify its failure to comply with obligations and time-limits resulting from [EU] directives. While each Member State may freely allocate internal legislative powers as it sees fit, the fact remains that it alone is responsible towards the [EU] under Article [258 TFEU] for compliance with obligations arising under [EU] law ... (para 38)

A Member State may even incur liability as a result of the actions of private individuals, if the Court decides that it has not done enough to protect the proper functioning of the internal market. This was established in the *Spanish Strawberries* case decided in 1997 (Case C-265/95 *Commission v France* [1997] ECR I-6959), involving acts of violence committed by French farmers:

[I]n the present case the French Government has manifestly and persistently abstained from adopting appropriate and adequate measures to put an end to the acts of vandalism which jeopardize the free movement on its territory of certain agricultural products originating in other Member States and to prevent the recurrence of such acts. (para 65)

Neither is it a good defence to argue that the aim of the infringement was to correct the effects of a breach by someone else, such as another Member State or an EU institution. In relation to an alleged violation by the EU institutions, the Court explained in Joined Cases 90 and 91/63 *Commission v Luxembourg and Belgium* [1964] ECR 625:

[T]he Treaty is not limited to creating reciprocal obligations between the different natural and legal persons to whom it is applicable ... [E]xcept where otherwise expressly provided, the basic concept of the Treaty requires that the Member States shall not take the law into their own hands. Therefore the fact that the Council failed to carry out its obligations cannot relieve the defendants from carrying out theirs. (para 631)

After all,

[a] Member State cannot under any circumstances unilaterally adopt, on its own authority, corrective measures or measures to protect trade designed to [obviate] any failure on the part of another Member State to comply with the rules laid down by the Treaty. (Case 232/78 *Commission v France (Re Restrictions on Imports of Lamb)* [1979] ECR 2729, para 9)

See **Figure 7.1**.

Interim measures

It must be borne in mind that interim measures can be granted by the Court under Article 279 TFEU:

The Court of Justice of the European Union may in any cases before it prescribe any necessary interim measures.

Figure 7.1   Defences to enforcement actions against Member States

Indeed, as the time between the case being lodged with the Court and the Court's judgment is often over two years, some activities can cause irreversible damage. The Court explained in Case C-246/89 R *Commission v UK* [1989] ECR 3125:

Under Article 83(2) of the Rules of Procedure, interim measures such as those requested may not be ordered unless there are circumstances giving rise to urgency and factual and legal grounds establishing a prima facie case for the measures applied for. (para 21)

As a result, the Court has been rather reluctant to impose interim measures.

For an example of interim measures, see Cases C-503/06 R *Commission v Italy* [2006] ECR I-141 and C-76/08 R *Commission v Malta* [2008] ECR I-64, where Member States were ordered by the Court to stop hunting activities.

Effect of the Court's ruling

If the Commission's application to the Court is successful, the Court will declare that the Member State concerned has failed to fulfil its obligations under the Treaties. As Article 260(1) TFEU provides:

> If the Court of Justice of the European Union finds that a Member State has failed to fulfil an obligation under the Treaties, the State shall be required to take the necessary measures to comply with the judgment of the Court.

The Court will specify the act or omission giving rise to the failure. The Member State will have to infer which measures are necessary to comply with the judgment:

> [W]hile, in proceedings for failure to fulfil obligations under Article [258 TFEU], the Court is only required to find that a provision of [Union] law has been infringed, it is clear from Article [260(1) TFEU] that the Member State concerned is required to take the measures necessary to comply with the judgment of the Court. (Case C-126/03 *Commission v Germany* [2004] ECR I-11197, para 26)

The Court will not itself quash any national measure that it finds unlawful, but the Treaties require the Member State in question to do what is necessary to comply with the judgment. In Joined Cases 314–316/81 and 83/82 *Procureur de la République v Waterkeyn* [1982] ECR 4337, the Court stipulated:

> [I]f the Court finds in proceedings under Articles [158–159 TFEU] that a Member State's legislation is incompatible with the obligations which it has under the Treaty the courts of that State are bound by virtue of Article [260(1)] to draw the necessary inferences from the judgment of the Court. However, it should be understood that the rights accruing to individuals derive, not from that judgment, but from the actual provisions of [EU] law having direct effect in the internal legal order. (para 16)

The defaulting Member State can only be required to comply with an Article 258 judgment; the Court cannot compel the Member State to comply by means of injunction, nor can it annul a national measure declared incompatible with EU law. Thus, it is not surprising that Member States have a tendency to ignore such rulings (Case C-494/01 *Commission v Ireland* [2005] ECR I-3331, paras 127 and 139).

7.2.2 Financial penalties

The vast majority of the cases in which infringement proceedings are brought are settled before they are referred to the Court of Justice, which suggests that the threat of court proceedings is usually enough to secure compliance. However, the 1980s saw a marked increase in the number of cases brought against Member States for failing to comply with previous rulings against them, a development that may have been attributable to the increased enthusiasm shown by the Commission between the late

1970s and the early 1990s for pursuing delinquent Member States. Furthermore, non-compliance became such a serious problem in the 1980s that the Maastricht Treaty empowered the Court to impose pecuniary sanctions against a defaulting Member State. However, the power is triggered only if the Commission brings the matter back to the Court: no sanctions may be imposed in the initial proceedings under Article 258 TFEU except under Article 260(3) (see **7.2.1**).

Article 260(2) TFEU provides:

> If the Commission considers that the Member State concerned has not taken the necessary measures to comply with the judgment of the Court, it may bring the case before the Court after giving that State the opportunity to submit its observations. It shall specify the amount of the lump sum or penalty payment to be paid by the Member State concerned which it considers appropriate in the circumstances.
>
> If the Court finds that the Member State concerned has not complied with its judgment it may impose a lump sum or penalty payment on it.
>
> This procedure shall be without prejudice to Article 259.

According to the Commission in its Working Document on the Impact of the Lisbon Treaty on infringement proceedings (COCOM 10-08):

> [T]he second modification introduced by the Lisbon Treaty speeds up the system of pecuniary sanctions (lump sum and/or penalty payment) in the event a Member State fails to comply with a judgment of the Court of Justice establishing an infringement …
>
> It follows from the above that, in contrast with the previous infringement rules, the Commission has no longer the obligation to issue a reasoned opinion before the second referral to the Court of Justice. If the Commission considers that a Member State does not comply with an earlier judgment it will issue a letter of formal notice. If, after the letter of formal notice, the Commission is not yet satisfied with the measures taken it will refer the matter directly to the Court of Justice. The referral will be accompanied by a proposal for a penalty payment and/or a lump sum.
>
> This modification applies immediately, ie from 1 December 2009, including infringement proceedings pending at that time, which were opened under the old regime of Article 228 EC.
>
> Member States should also be aware of the fact that once the Commission decision on the second referral of the case to the Court of Justice is adopted the Commission will no longer withdraw the case and the Member State concerned will have to pay at least the lump sum penalising the continuation of the infringement between the judgment on noncompliance and the judgment delivered under Article 260 TFEU.

Article 260(2) TFEU offers a choice between two types of pecuniary sanctions: a lump sum or a penalty payment. The basic objective of the whole infringement procedure is to secure compliance as rapidly as possible. The sanctions are not meant to compensate for the damage caused by the Member State, but to place it under pressure so as to put an end to the breach. Often the Commission considers that a penalty payment is the most appropriate instrument for achieving this (see former Memorandum on applying Article 228 of the EC Treaty, [1996] OJ C242/6, para 4). Usually the Commission will ask for a lump sum if it wishes to punish past behaviour (dissuasive function as it is based on the assessment of the detrimental effects caused by the failure to comply with the initial judgment), or for a periodic penalty payment to ensure future compliance (persuasive function as it serves to induce the Member State to put an end as soon as possible to a breach that would tend to persist). It is nonetheless possible that the Commission will request both a lump sum and a period penalty payment:

> That being so, recourse to both types of penalty provided for in Article [260(2) TFEU] is not precluded, in particular where the breach of obligations both has continued for a long period and is inclined to persist. (Case C-304/02, *Commission v France* [2005] ECR I-6263, para 82)

The Court's ruling allowing for the imposition of both types of sanctions is now anchored in the 2011 Commission Communication – Implementation of Article 260(3) of the Treaty (2011/C 12/01), Section IV.

However, as the Treaty does not cover the method of calculation of those sanctions, the Commission established clear criteria in successive Communications, the first one being the 2005 Commission Communication (SEC(2005) 1658) that took notice of the guidance provided by the Court in Case C-387/97 *Commission v Greece* [2000] ECR I-5047:

> The basic criteria which must be taken into account in order to ensure that penalty payments have coercive force and [EU] law is applied uniformly and effectively are, in principle, the duration of the infringement, its degree of seriousness and the ability of the Member State to pay. In applying those criteria, regard should be had in particular to the effects of failure to comply on private and public interests and to the urgency of getting the Member State concerned to fulfil its obligations. (para 92)

The current methods of calculation of the penalties and lump sum payments are set out in the 2011 Communication, which must be read in conjunction with the 2005 Communication. Moreover, as stipulated in para 23 of the 2011 Communication, these methods of calculation also apply in cases relating to Article 260(3) (see **7.2.1**). In setting the penalty, three fundamental criteria are taken into account (para 13):

(a) the seriousness of the infringement. This is measured in reference to the provision breached, the effects of infringements on general or particular interests, the actions taken by the States to comply at least partially with the judgment, etc (2005 Communication, para 16);

(b) its duration;

(c) the need to ensure that the sanction itself is a deterrent to further infringements.

That being said, the calculations take into account the capacity of the Member State to pay and the number of votes it has in the Council (2005 Communication, paras 14 and 18). Further, the sanctions proposed by the Commission must be foreseeable and respect the **principles of proportionality**, **equal treatment** and **transparency** (2011 Communication, para 14). Last but not least, the amount must be appropriate, 'in order to ensure the deterrent effect of the sanction'. After all a purely symbolic payment would render the exercise useless (2011 Communication, para 15).

The lump sum, on the other hand, is calculated by using the method set out in paras 19–24 of the 2005 Communication. It must be noted that the day from which the period to be taken into account when calculating the lump starts running is, under Article 258, the day after the first judgment (2005 Communication, para 22) and, under Article 260(3), the day after the time limit for the transposition of the directive (2011 Communication, para 28).

The macro-economic data used to calculate lump sum and penalty payments are constantly being revised. The latest update is dated 6 August 2015 ([2015] OJ C257/1). It must be stressed, however, that the guidelines contained in these Communications are not binding on the Court, though they contribute to ensuring that the Commission's actions are 'transparent, foreseeable and consistent with legal certainty' (Case C-304/02 *Commission v France*, para 85).

Article 260(3) TFEU further explains that

> [i]f the Court finds that there is an infringement it may impose a lump sum or penalty payment on the Member State concerned not exceeding the amount specified by the Commission. The payment obligation shall take effect on the date set by the Court in its judgment.

In other words, the Commission may calculate the penalty but the suggestions do not bind the Court, they merely constitute a useful point of reference. Ultimately the decision belongs with the Court, as it stated in Case C-278/01 *Commission v Spain* [2003] ECR I-14141:

> In that connection it must be pointed out that the Commission's suggestions cannot bind the Court and merely constitute a useful point of reference. In exercising its discretion, it is for the Court to fix the lump sum or penalty payment that is appropriate to the circumstances and proportionate both to the breach that has been found and to the ability to pay of the Member State concerned. (para 41)

It is in fact the combination of the powers of the Commission and the Court that makes this procedure an effective tool to ensure that EU law is enforced in all Member States. See **Figure 7.2**.

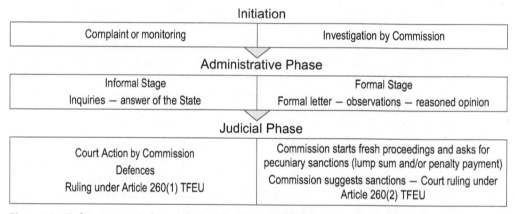

Figure 7.2   Enforcement procedure under Articles 258 to 260 TFEU

case example

The Commission claimed that the Portuguese transposition of Directive 89/665/EEC on the coordination of the laws, regulations and administrative provisions relating to the application of review procedures to the award of public supply and public works contracts, was incorrect and incomplete. Following an exchange of information, the Commission, dissatisfied with Portugal's reply on 26 July 1995, sent a *formal letter of notice* on 8 September 1995, asking Portugal to transpose the directive correctly and fully. On 7 July 1997 the Commission then issued a *reasoned opinion*, and on 9 February 2001 it sent a complementary reasoned opinion in the light of discussions with Portugal. The Commission referred to two specific breaches: (a) the domestic act did not cover all relevant activities mentioned in the Directive, and (b) Decree-Law No 48 051 that limited compensation possibilities had not yet been repealed. As Portugal did not abide by the deadline set in the reasoned opinion, the Commission seized the Court, which issued a *judgment* on 14 October 2004 (Case C-275/03 *Commission v Portugal* ECLI:EU:C:2004:632) demanding that Portugal repeal Decree-Law No 48 051. The *defences* that the law was not applied by the judges, that Portugal was facing some internal challenges and that some legislative changes had been made after the expiry of the deadline were dismissed by the Court.

By letter of 4 November 2004, the Commission requested Portugal to inform it of the measures adopted to comply with the judgment. Replying on 19 November 2004, Portugal explained that a change of government had delayed the bill repealing Decree-Law No 48 051, a defence the Commission did not accept in its *formal letter of notice* on 21 March 2005. The Commission further explained that the draft law did not comply with Directive 89/665. A *reasoned opinion* (NB: since the Lisbon Treaty a reasoned opinion is no longer required) was issued on 13 July 2005 following an unsatisfactory reply by Portugal, reminding Portugal to fulfil its obligations under Article [260(1) TFEU]. Portugal informed the Commission on 12 December 2005 that it was in the process of repealing Decree-Law No 48 051. On 7 February 2006, as Portugal had not complied with the ruling, the Commission started fresh proceedings seeking the imposition of a penalty payment. The Court, satisfied that Decree-Law No 48 051 had not been repealed and that there were no acceptable defences, ruled that Portugal had failed to fulfil its obligations (Case C-70/06 *Commission v Portugal* [2008] ECR I-1). The Commission proposed a penalty payment of €21,450 per day of delay. Whilst the Court agreed that a penalty was a means to be adopted to induce Portugal to repeal Decree-Law No 48 051, its application of the criteria of seriousness of the breach, duration of the infringement and Member State's ability to pay differed, to the effect that Portugal was asked to pay a penalty payment of €19,392 per day from the date of delivery of the judgment, ie 10 January 2008.

In the meantime Portugal adopted a law that repealed Decree-Law No 48 051 and established a new system of compensation. The Commission, however, felt the new system to be lacking in the light of the Directive, and thus as not compliant with the 2004 judgment. A second Portuguese law was passed. Consequently the Commission sought payment by Portugal for the period from 10 January to 17 July 2008 (date when the second law was adopted). Portugal challenged the decision of the Commission determining the amount to be paid, on the basis that the Court ruling had only asked that Decree-Law No 48 051 be repealed, and that had been done as of 30 January 2008 when the first law entered into force. The Court reminded the Commission that it was not entitled to decide whether the law complied with the Directive, only whether Decree-Law No 48 051 had been repealed in accordance with the Court judgment (Case T-33/09 *Portugal v Commission* [2011] ECR II-1429). If the Commission was of the opinion that the system in place was not in conformity with the Directive, the Commission should have initiated fresh infringement proceedings.

7.3 Member State liability for breaches of EU law

Most EU rules are enforced through national legal systems. Thus it appears normal that individuals who are granted rights by virtue of EU law also use the national court system to obtain compensation for violation of such rights. Whilst the **principle of supremacy** (see **6.2**) and the **principle of direct effect** (see **6.3**) ensure that individuals can assert their rights in domestic courts, there was initially no right to seek and receive compensation.

7.3.1 Background to and rationale of the principle

The principle of Member State liability was established in the *Francovich* case (Joined Cases C-6 and 9/90 *Francovich and Others v Italy* [1991] ECR I-5357). The principle holds that Members States can be found liable for damages suffered by individuals as a result of the Member States' failure to comply with EU law. The objective of the Court was to try to make EU law more effective.

In Joined Cases C-6 and 9/90 *Francovich and Others v Italy* [1991] ECR I-5357, Italy had failed to implement a directive designed to protect employees in the event of their employer's insolvency. Francovich had been employed by an Italian company but had received hardly any wages. Having brought proceedings against his employer, the latter had gone insolvent. For that reason Francovich brought a separate action against the Italian State to cover his losses. In the course of these second proceedings, the national court asked the ECJ whether the State itself would be obliged to cover the losses of the employees.

Based on the principles of supremacy and direct effect, the Court explained:

It should be borne in mind at the outset that the Treaty of Rome as amended had created its own legal system, which is integrated into the legal systems of the Member States and which their courts are bound to apply. The subjects of that legal system are not only the Member States but also their nationals.

Just as it imposes burdens on individuals, [EU] law is also intended to give rise to rights, which become part of their legal patrimony. Those rights arise not only where they are expressly granted by the Treaty but also by virtue of obligations which the Treaty imposes in a clearly defined manner both on individuals and on the Member States and the [EU] institutions (see the judgments in Case 26/62 *NV Algemene Transport- en Expeditie Onderneming van Gend & Loos v Netherlands Inland Revenue Administration* [1963] ECR 1 and Case 6/64 *Costa v ENEL* [1964] ECR 585). (paras 31 and 32)

Thus, the Court wished to give individuals a means to seek redress:

The full effectiveness of [EU] rules would be impaired and the protection of the rights, which they grant, would be weakened if individuals were unable to obtain redress when their rights are infringed by a breach of [EU] law for which a Member State can be held responsible.

The possibility of obtaining redress from the Member State is particularly indispensable where, as in this case, the full effectiveness of [EU] rules is subject to prior action on the part of the State and where, consequently, in the absence of such action, individuals cannot enforce before the national courts the rights conferred upon them by [EU] law.

It follows that the principle whereby a State must be liable for loss and damage caused to individuals as a result of breaches of [EU] law for which the State can be held responsible is inherent in the system of the Treaty. (paras 33–35)

The Court set out the three criteria for Member State liability in *Francovich*:

The first of those conditions is that the result prescribed by the [EU provision] should entail the *grant of rights to individuals.*

The second condition is that it should be possible *to identify the content of those rights* on the basis of the provisions of the directive.

Finally, the third condition is the existence of a *causal link between the breach of the State's obligation and the loss and damage suffered by the injured parties.* (para 40, emphasis added)

7.3.2 Author of the violation: definition of a State

The author of the violation of an EU obligation must be the Member State. Yet the definition of a State encompasses 'whatever be the organ of the State whose act or omission was responsible for the breach' (Joined Cases C-46 and 48/93 *Brasserie du Pêcheur SA v Germany* and *R v Secretary of State for Transport, ex parte Factortame Ltd and Others* [1996] ECR I-1029, para 32). This means that the following organs of the State can be held to be in breach of EU law and, if the criteria set out in the *Factortame* case (see below 7.3.3) are fulfilled, individuals can seek damages against the State:

(a) national legislatures (*Factortame*);

(b) national executives (Case C-5/94 *R v Ministry of Agriculture, Fisheries & Food, ex parte Hedley Lomas (Ireland) Ltd* [1996] ECR I-2553);

(c) national Supreme Courts (Case C-224/01 *Köbler v Austria* [2003] ECR I-10239 confirmed in Case C-173/03 *Traghetti del Mediterraneo SpA v Italy* [2006] ECR I-5177). The ECJ, however, added that in this instance State liability would only arise 'in the exceptional case where the court has manifestly infringed the applicable law' (para 53);

(d) regional authorities (Case C-302/97 *Konle v Austria* [1999] ECR I-3099);

(e) autonomous public law bodies (Case C-424/97 *Haim v Kassenzahnärztliche Vereinigung Nordrhein* [2000] ECR I-5123);

(f) State officials (Case C-470/03 *AGM-COS MET Srl v Suomen valtio and Lehtinen* [2007] ECR I-2749).

7.3.3 Development of the principle

The original criteria set out in the *Francovich* case were later refined in the *Factortame* case:

> In such circumstances, [EU] law confers a right to reparation where three conditions are met: the rule of law infringed must be intended to confer rights on individuals; the breach must be sufficiently serious; and there must be a direct causal link between the breach of the obligation resting on the State and the damage sustained by the injured parties. (para 51)

The criterion of the *intention to confer rights on individuals* is usually fulfilled when the provision is directly effective (*Factortame*). Yet non-directly effective provisions can also confer rights on individuals (*Francovich* and Case C-91/92, *Faccini Dori v Recreb Srl* [1994] ECR I-3325). However, not every provision of EU law will be covered (Case C-72/95 *Aannemersbedrijf PK Kraaijeveld BV v eav Gedeputeerde Staten van Zuid-Holland* [1996] ECR I-5403 and Case C-443/98 *Unilever Italia SpA v Central Foods SpA* [2000] ECR I-7535).

The second criterion requires the *breach of EU law to be sufficiently serious*. The test is 'whether the Member State or the [EU] institution concerned *manifestly and gravely disregarded the limits on its discretion*' (*Factortame*, para 55, emphasis added). In order to determine whether a Member State has indeed manifestly and gravely disregarded the limits on its discretion, the following factors are taken into account:

• the clarity and precision of the EU rule breached (Case C-392/93 *R v HM Treasury, ex parte British Telecommunications plc* [1996] ECR I-1631 and Joined Cases C-283, 291 and 292/94 *Denkavit International BV, VITIC Amsterdam BV and Voormeer BV v Bundesamt für Finanzen* [1996] ECR I-5063)

- the measure of discretion left by that rule to the national or EU authorities (*Hedley Lomas* and Joined Cases C-178–179 and 188–190/94 *Dillenkofer, Erdmann, Schulte, Heuer, Werner and Knor v Germany* [1996] ECR I-4845)
- whether the infringement and the damage caused were intentional or involuntary (*Dillenkofer*, para 28)
- whether any error of law was excusable or inexcusable (*Factortame*, para 56)
- the fact that the position taken by an EU institution might have contributed towards the omission (*Factortame*, para 56), and
- the adoption or retention of national measures or practices contrary to EU law (*Factortame*, para 56).

In other words, the less discretion the Member State has, the greater its liability (*Haim*, para 38).

The last criterion is the proof of a *causal link* between the alleged breach and the damage incurred by the individual. In this regard it must be noted that this determination is left in the hands of the national courts:

> As for the third condition, it is for the national courts to determine whether there is a direct causal link between the breach of the obligation borne by the State and the damage sustained by the injured parties. (*Factortame*, para 65)

7.3.4 Procedural autonomy and domestic responsibilities

In principle, national courts apply the above-mentioned criteria for Member State liability (Case C-446/04 *Test Claimants in the FII Group Litigation v Commissioners of Inland Revenue* [2006] ECR I-11753, para 210), as this ensures some autonomy of the national courts whilst asserting their role as enforcers of EU law (see further **9.1**). However, in some instances, when the Court of Justice believes it has sufficient information, it may proceed to determine whether the conditions for Member State liability are satisfied (see eg Case C-392/93 *Ex parte British Telecommunications* (see **7.3.3** above) and Case C-429/09 *Fuß v Stadt Halle* [2010] ECR I-12167). It can be particularly difficult for a national court to determine whether there is a sufficiently serious breach based on a variety of factors to be applied to a specific set of circumstances.

It must be borne in mind, though, that the Court has always stressed, as in Case 33/76 *Rewe-Zentralfinanz eG et Rewe-Zentral AG v Landwirtschaftskammer für das Saarland* [1976] ECR 1989, that

> [i]t is for the domestic legal system of each member state to designate the courts having jurisdiction and to determine the procedural conditions governing actions at law intended to ensure the protection of the rights which citizens have from the direct effects of [Union] law … (para 5)

Despite being given clear autonomy, the domestic courts must abide by the **principles of equivalence** and **effectiveness**, ie the conditions for reparation 'must not be less favourable than those relating to similar domestic claims and must not be so framed as to make it virtually impossible or excessively difficult to obtain reparation' (*Francovich*, para 43). The equivalence principle requests national courts to extend existing national remedies to similar actions based on EU law. For example, in *Transportes Urbanos* (Case C-118/08 *Transportes Urbanos y Servicios Generales SAL v Administración del Estado* [2010] ECR I-635), the ECJ found that the requirement of exhaustion of domestic remedies before bringing a State liability claim for breach of EU law violated the principle of equivalence. In contrast the effectiveness principle demands that these national remedies must not make the enforcement of EU law excessively difficult. The Court has held that whilst EU law does not rule out Member State liability in conditions that are less restrictive than those provided for in EU law, it precludes the imposition of any additional conditions (*Fuß*, para 66).

When determining the type and amount of reparation to be granted to the individual who suffered from the failure of the Member State to apply EU law, the national court uses the relevant domestic law (*Francovich*). However, the Court has indicated that the reparation 'must be commensurate with the loss or damage sustained' (*Factortame*, para 82). Further, the Court has specified that the amount claimed must be actual, certain and concrete (Case 138/79 *SA Roquette Frères v Council* [1980] ECR 3333), and there is no compensation for anticipated profits. Moreover, injured parties are expected to show reasonable diligence in limiting the extent of the loss or damage (mitigation) or risk having to bear the loss or damage themselves (Joined Cases C-104/89 and C-37/90 *Mulder and others and Heinemann v Council and Commission* [1992] ECR I-3061, para 33). Nonetheless, this does not go so far as to oblige an individual to request compliance with a directly effective provision of EU law as a precondition for obtaining compensation as this would breach the principle of effectiveness (*Fuß*, para 78).

Whilst the principle of State liability makes EU law more effective, its application in EU Member States varies considerably. After all it is a remedy offered under national law. Moreover, given the choice between asking for the application of the principles of supremacy and direct effect of EU law and compensation for violation of EU law, individuals tend to favour the former.

7.4 Further reading

Albors-Llorens A, 'Remedies against the EU Institutions after Lisbon: An Era of Opportunity?' (2012) 71 *Cambridge Law Journal* 507.

Beutler B, 'State Liability for Breaches of Community Law by National Courts: Is the Requirement of a Manifest Infringement of the Applicable Law an Insurmountable Obstacle?' (2009) 46 *CML Rev* 773.

Breuer M, 'State Liability for Judicial Wrongs and Community Law: The Case of *Gerhard Köbler v Austria*' (2004) 29 *EL Rev* 243.

Lock T, 'Is Private Enforcement of EU Law through State Liability a Myth? An Assessment 20 Years after *Francovich*' (2012) 49 *CML Rev* 1675.

Pavlovic V, 'Some Observations on the European Court of Justice's Post-*Francovich* Jurisprudence' (2009) 4 *Croatian Yearbook of European Law and Policy* 179.

Peers S, 'Sanctions for Infringement of EU Law after the Treaty of Lisbon' (2012) 18 *European Public Law* 33.

Prete L and Smulders B, 'The Coming of Age of Infringement Proceedings' (2010) 47 *CML Rev* 9.

Smith M, 'Inter-institutional Dialogue and the Establishment of Enforcement Norms: A Decade of Financial Penalties under Article 228 EC (now Article 260 TFEU)' (2010) 16 *European Public Law* 547.

Steunenberg B, 'Is Big Brother Watching? Commission Oversight of the National Implementation of EU Directives' (2010) 11 *European Union Politics* 359.

Zingales N, 'Member State Liability vs. National Procedural Autonomy: What Rules for Judicial Breach of EU Law?' (2010) 11 *German Law Journal* 419.

The EU has no harmonised remedies or procedural rules to ensure the enforcement of its norms. The two main remedies are the Article 258 TFEU enforcement procedure, which can only be initiated by the Commission, and the application of the concept of Member State liability that has been created and developed by the Court of Justice. This clearly shows that the main guardians of EU law are the Commission and the CJEU, assisted by the national courts.

test your knowledge

1   In 2013 the Council of Ministers issued a Directive laying down minimum standards for the manufacture of door locks, to try to reduce the amount of burglary in the EU. The Directive was due to be implemented by April 2014. However, in response to lobbying from UK-based lock manufacturers, the UK Government failed to implement it. Instead, it issued informal guidance to lock manufacturers, recommending them to take the EU Directive into account when designing locks.

Lock Your Door, a German company manufacturing door locks, argues that it has been adversely affected by the lack of implementation of the Directive. Indeed, manufacturing locks according to the Directive (which has been correctly implemented in Germany) is more costly, and thus the sale price of locks is higher than that of locks produced in the UK.

Lock Your Door has alerted the European Commission that the UK Government has failed to implement the Directive. After informal discussion with the UK, the Commission has now issued a reasoned opinion, warning the UK that it will face legal proceedings if it does not implement the Directive. The UK has made the following points in response:

(a)   The informal guidance it has issued is sufficient to comply with its obligation to implement the Directive.

(b)   The Directive is invalid because it had been adopted using the wrong voting procedure.

(c)   Spain has also failed to implement the Directive, but no proceedings have been taken against Spain.

(d)   As soon as most UK-based lock manufacturers have changed their designs, a UK law complying with the Directive will be introduced.

After briefly explaining at which stage of the procedure we are, advise the Commission as to the validity of the British arguments and how it may proceed against the UK. What will happen if the UK refuses to implement the Directive?

2   Cryptonia (a fictional Member State) has failed to implement a Directive that has now passed the date for transposition. As a result, Carbon-Co, a leading consultancy firm on environmental matters in Cryptonia, has suffered major losses and expects to be forced into liquidation within six months. Cryptonia, a federal State, has relied on its regional assemblies to implement the Directive but, whilst some have done so, others have not. Meanwhile, it has come to Carbon-Co's attention that the Council, when adopting the Directive, not only failed to follow the correct voting procedure but also ignored advice that the measure breached the right to property, a fundamental right protected by the general principles of EU law.

Advise Carbon-Co.

THE EUROPEAN JUDICIARY

The Court of Justice of the European Union

After reading this chapter, you will be able to understand:

- the structure of the Court of Justice of the European Union (CJEU)
- the workings and role of the CJEU
- the methods of interpretation used by the CJEU to develop and clarify EU law
- the so-called judicial activism of the CJEU.

8.1 Introduction

In the first decades of the European Communities (EC), only one court, the European Court of Justice (ECJ), handled cases relating to EC law. Gradually the ECJ became clogged up with cases. This was not so much the result of the expansion of the Court, the number of judges increasing at every stage of the enlargement of the then EC alongside deepening European integration. Rather, this evolution quite naturally led to more litigation. It was therefore agreed in 1986, under the Single European Act, to set up a Court of First Instance (CFI) to deal with the bulk of the cases, such as complaints by EU staff, with a right of appeal on points of law to the ECJ. Gradually the jurisdiction of the CFI was extended in an effort to keep pace with the growing number of cases. But there remained a problem of overload, and thus a further layer of courts, called judicial panels, was set up to deal with minor cases. The first of these, the Civil Service Tribunal, was established to deal with staff cases. The CFI heard more and more matters that used to fall within the jurisdiction of the ECJ, leaving the latter to concentrate on the really important cases. In effect there is now a whole hierarchy of courts, just as there is in Member States.

in practice

The CJEU should never be confused with the European Court of Human Rights, which sits in Strasbourg and deals with States both within and outside the EU. The European Court of Human Rights is completely separate and does not have jurisdiction to adjudicate EU law. It is the judicial body of the European Convention on Human Rights, and examines cases relating to the protection of human rights and fundamental freedoms in the Member States of the Council of Europe, an international organisation separate from the EU (see **1.2** above).

The Lisbon Treaty reorganised the court system. The CJEU now consists of the Court of Justice (former ECJ – **8.2** below), the General Court (former CFI – **8.3** below) and specialised courts (Article 19(1) TEU – **8.4** below), and has the duty to 'ensure that in the interpretation and application of the Treaties the law is observed' (Article 19(1) TEU). The CJEU certainly is one of the strongest indicators of the supranational nature of the EU (see eg *Opinion C-2/13* of 18 December 2014, ECLI:EU:C:2014:2454), and has been described as one of the most Union-minded and most independent from national interests of all the EU's institutions. Furthermore, it has driven the Union towards further integration through its interpretation of the Treaties and secondary legislation (often referred to as judicial activism). The legal provisions relating to the CJEU are Articles 19 TEU and Articles 251–281 TFEU, Protocol No 3 on the Statute of the Court of Justice of the European Union (the Statute of the Court) and the Rules of Procedure (of the Court of Justice ([2012] OJ L265) and of the General Court ([2015] OJ L105/1) respectively).

8.2 The Court of Justice

The Court of Justice consists of 28 judges, one for each Member State, appointed by common accord of the Member States (though in practice each State appoints its own judge and the other States accept them) after consultation of a panel responsible for giving an opinion on prospective candidates' suitability to perform the duties concerned. The judges serve for a renewable six-year term, with half retiring every three years to preserve continuity (Article 253 TFEU). They, in turn, elect their President from among themselves. Judges are individuals whose independence is beyond doubt, and are either qualified for the highest judicial office in their own State or are jurisconsults (academic lawyers) of recognised competence (Article 253 TFEU).

The Court is entitled to set up chambers, which means that it can multiply itself into a variety of 'miniature courts' that enjoy the powers of the full Court. Article 251 TFEU indeed specifies that '[t]he Court of Justice shall sit in chambers or in a Grand Chamber', but exceptionally it 'may also sit as a full Court'. The Court may sit either as a full court in a Grand Chamber of 15 judges or in Chambers of three or five judges.

The Court of Justice is currently assisted by nine Advocates General (AGs), who must have the same qualifications as the judges (a former judge at the General Court (see **8.3** below) might be appointed as an Advocate General – see, eg, AG Nils Wahl who was a judge at the General Court from 7 October 2006 to 28 November 2012 before being appointed Advocate General at the Court of Justice). They are appointed by common accord (Article 252 TFEU), which means that in practice the larger Member States expect to have one Advocate General and the smaller Member States take turns. By virtue of Article 253 TFEU, their job is to act with complete impartiality and independence to make in open court reasoned submissions in order to assist the Court. This idea derives from French administrative courts, where a person called the *Commissaire du Gouvernement* addresses the court on behalf of the public interest. In contrast to most domestic legal systems where the highest court has before it the judgments of one or two lower courts and can ask itself whether they were right or wrong, the Court of Justice rarely has this privilege. Moreover, the Court has several roles (see **8.2.1** below). To facilitate the task of the judges, Advocates General present their views after the judges have heard the arguments of the parties. In other words, Advocates General are independent advisers to the Court, who produce an 'opinion' or a 'view' (in the case of an opinion of the Court pursuant to Article 228(11) TFEU (eg, *Opinion C-1/13* of 14 October 2014, ECLI:EU:C:2014:2303) or an urgent preliminary ruling (eg, Case C-129/14 PPU *Criminal proceedings against Spasic* of 2 May 2014, ECLI:EU:C:2014:586)) that is not legally binding on the Court.

The Court, which sits in Luxembourg, is administered by a registrar and staff. Each judge and Advocate General is free to appoint and employ up to four legal secretaries, also known as *référendaires*. These are legally trained persons who assist the judge or the Advocate General with research and drafting.

8.2.1 The aims and roles of the Court of Justice

There are three central objectives that the Court of Justice strives to achieve:

(a) to ensure that in application and interpretation the law is observed;
(b) to provide a forum for resolving disputes between institutions, Member States and individuals;
(c) to protect individual rights.

The Court has several roles and acts as:

(a) a constitutional court, considering the powers of the institutions, bodies, agencies and offices, and of the Member States and/or the relations between them (see further **Chapter 2**);
(b) an administrative court, providing judicial review of acts of the EU institutions (see further **10.2**);
(c) an appeal court, dealing with points of law in appeals against judgments or orders of the General Court under Article 256(1)(sub 2) TFEU;
(d) an advisory court, providing preliminary rulings on an interpretation of EU law upon request by a national court (Article 267 TFEU) (see further **Chapter 9**) and, when requested by a Member State, the Council, the Commission or the European Parliament, also providing an Opinion as to whether an agreement envisaged by the EU is compatible with the Treaties (Article 218(11) TFEU – see **8.2.2.2** below);
(e) a fining body, that is, in certain circumstances, the Court can impose fines (see further **7.2.2**) or review fines imposed by the General Court in competition law cases; and
(f) a reviewer of decisions of the General Court against decisions of the Civil Service Tribunal.

The Court of Justice may take action against Member States of the EU or the institutions of the EU in six circumstances:

(a) Article 267 references from national courts for a preliminary ruling on an interpretation of European Union law (see further **Chapter 9**);
(b) Articles 258 and 259 actions against Member States for failing to implement Treaty obligations (see further **7.2**);
(c) Article 263 actions against an institution for abuse of power brought by privileged applicants. The Court of Justice has sole jurisdiction over proceedings brought by Member States against the Council (with the exception of measures on State aid, dumping and implementing powers) and/or the European Parliament, and over actions brought by one EU institution against another (see further **10.2**);
(d) Article 265 proceedings instituted by privileged applicants against an institution for failing to act (see further **10.3**);
(e) appeals on points of law from the General Court (Article 256(1)(sub 2) TFEU);
(f) review of decisions of the General Court against decisions of the Civil Service Tribunal.

See further **Figure 8.1**.

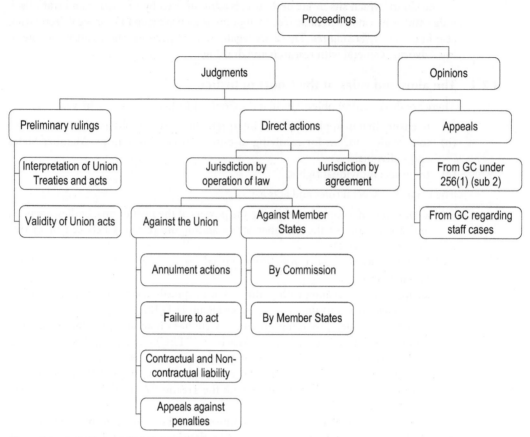

Figure 8.1   Jurisdiction of the Court of Justice

8.2.2   The procedure

8.2.2.1   Judicial proceedings

The procedure in the Court of Justice is very much based on the Continental model, with the bulk of the proceedings being written, not oral. The procedure is governed by Protocol No 3 on the Statute of the Court of Justice of the European Union.

As the Court is multilingual, there have to be rules to govern which language is used in any particular case. If a natural or legal person sues an EU institution, the applicant can choose which of the official languages is used. If the action is against a Member State, it is that State's language that will be used. If the case is on reference from the court of a Member State, again it will be that court's language that is used. All official proceedings will take place in that language, all documents will be translated into that language and the version of the judgment in that language will be the authoritative one. That being said, lawyers addressing the Court will use their own language and all judgments are translated into and reported in all the official languages of the EU. However, the Court's working language has always been and remains French. This means that judges and Advocates General need to speak and read French to a high standard. The judgment is usually drafted in French before being translated into the official language of the case and then in all other languages.

Cases may begin either with a request from a national court for a preliminary ruling or as a direct action. The applicant submits an application to the Court, stating in detail the whole case. Since September 2011, documents may be filed online via e-Curia at <http://curia.europa.eu/jcms/jcms/P_78957/> (see Decision of the Court of Justice on the Lodging and Service of Procedural Documents by Means of e-Curia (2011/C 289/06). No fee is payable though it is obligatory to employ a lawyer, presumably to save everyone's time.

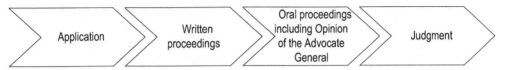

Figure 8.2   Procedure in the Court of Justice

Upon registration of the case, the application is served on the defendant who may lodge a defence. Each party has the right to reply to the other. Thereafter the Court takes over the initiative by assigning a Judge-Rapporteur to the case and allocating it to an Advocate General. Also the Court will assign the case to a chamber or the full Court, depending on the importance of the case. The Judge-Rapporteur's first job is to decide whether a preliminary inquiry, an inquisitorial process in which the Court itself hears witnesses of fact and expert witnesses and demands documents, is necessary. The Judge-Rapporteur then investigates the legal issues and prepares a summary of the case. At this stage, emphasis is put on written proceedings.

EU institutions and Member States have a right of third party intervention. It is quite common and very useful for the Commission, for example, to intervene to clarify the meaning of a directive's provisions. Also, Member States may be keen to have their say about a law that might affect them. For example, in Case C-304/02 *Commission v France* [2005] ECR I-6263 (regarding non-compliance with an enforcement judgment under former Article 228 TEC (now Article 258 TFEU) (see further 7.2)), the Commission as well as 17 Member States presented their views at the oral hearing.

After reading the report of the Judge-Rapporteur and hearing the views of the Advocate General, the Court decides whether any further preparatory inquiries are needed, the type of formation to which the case should be assigned and whether a hearing should be held for oral argument. The Judge-Rapporteur's report summarising the facts, the procedure and the arguments of the parties is then made public. The case is finally argued at a public hearing at which the parties' lawyers address the court for no more than 30 minutes. Weeks later, the Advocate General delivers an impartial, independent Opinion before the Court of Justice, again in open court. The recommendation in the Opinion of the Advocate General is not binding on the Court or on the parties but it may be used and cited (if the Court chooses to do so), as Opinions of Advocates General often contain very detailed and high standards of legal analysis. This marks the end of the oral stage of the proceedings.

The judges of the Court of Justice then deliberate on the basis of the draft judgment drawn up by the Judge-Rapporteur and are expected to agree on a final and single judgment. The reasoning of the Court in its judgment may not be as comprehensive and fully argued as the Opinion of the Advocate General given that the Court must reach a single judgment. The deliberations of the judges are strictly secret. No one else is allowed in, not even interpreters, hence the need for the judges to have a common language, French. They will try to reach consensus but if need be they will take a vote. Yet, following the Continental method, no one ever knows how the result is reached, the idea being that judgments are collegial. No dissenting opinions are recorded either. All judicial differences must be settled in the decision of the Court, which sometimes leads to judgments that read like an 'edited collection'. However, the collective and secret nature of the judgment is like a shield designed to protect the independence of the European judiciary.

Judgments are signed by all the judges who took part in the deliberation and their operative part is pronounced in open court. Judgments are also published: the operative part in the *Official Journal of the European Union* and the whole judgment, together with the Advocate General's Opinion, in the official law reports (European Court Reports or ECR). Preliminary rulings brought under Article 267 TFEU go back to the referring national court to be dealt with (see 9.7). For all other cases, judgments are declaratory. Pursuant to Article 260(1) TFEU (enforcement action) (see 7.2.1.2) and Article 266, first paragraph TFEU (judicial review actions) (see 10.2.5), the Court's judgments are binding and it is assumed that they will be obeyed. Whilst EU institutions abide by the rulings of the Court, some Member States fail to comply with its judgments. As a result, the 1992 Maastricht Treaty introduced a procedure whereby a Member State may in certain circumstances be taken back to the Court and fined an unlimited amount (see 7.2.2).

8.2.2.2 Orders and Opinions

In addition to judgments, the Court of Justice also has the power to give 'Orders' and 'Opinions'. Orders may result from an application for interim measures (see 7.2.1.2). An Order will thus typically precede a judgment. Opinions, on the other hand, may be requested with regard to the compatibility of international agreements with the EU Treaties. The Court's Opinion in this regard is more than just advisory; should it give a negative Opinion, the EU institutions cannot enter into the particular agreement unless either the agreement or the EU Treaties are revised (Article 218(11) TFEU). As a result, the Court's opinions have been instrumental in shaping the law of the external relations of the EU. For example, the Court issued *Opinion 2/94 (Accession to ECHR)* [1996] ECR I-1759, in which it declared that the EU could not at the time accede to the ECHR as it would be beyond the scope of what is now Article 352 TFEU. The Court was of the view that only a subsequent treaty amendment could provide a legal basis for the EU to become a party to the ECHR. This power has now been granted to the EU by virtue of Article 6(2) TEU. Yet, in spite of the amendment, in its *Opinion 2/13* ECLI:EU:C:2014:2454, the Court declared that the 2013 draft Agreement on the Accession of the EU to the ECHR was incompatible with Article 6(2) TEU or with Protocol (No 8) relating to Article 6(2).

in practice

Since 1989 case numbers include a letter to indicate the court that made the ruling. Citations of cases decided by the General Court start with 'T-', as the General Court used to be called the '*tribunal de première instance*' in French ('Court of First Instance' in English). For example, Case T-201/04 *Microsoft Corp v Commission* [2007] ECR II-3601.

Citations of cases decided by the Court of Justice start with 'C-'. For example, Case C-376/98 *Germany v European Parliament and Council (Re Tobacco Advertising)* [2000] ECR I-8419.

In 2014 the European Union introduced the European Case Law Identifier (ECLI) that is composed of a number for each judgment, which identifies the originating jurisdiction, the code of the court that rendered the judgment, the year of the judgment and its number. Each element is separate by a colon. For example, ECLI:EU:T:2014:1095 for Case T-400/10 *Hamas v Council* of 17 December 2014 (nyr).

8.3 The General Court

The General Court was originally established under the name 'Court of First Instance' on 1 January 1989 by Council Decision 88/591 ([1988] OJ L319/1) in accordance with the provisions of the Single European Act 1986. The General Court, governed by Article 256 TFEU and its own Rules of Procedure, also has 28 judges of the same calibre as the judges of the Court of Justice (see **8.2** above). Judges can act as Advocates General, if necessary.

The General Court hears cases involving:

(a)   annulment actions under Article 263, fourth paragraph TFEU brought by natural or legal persons against acts of EU institutions, bodies, offices or agencies which are addressed to them (eg, a case brought by a company against a Commission decision imposing a fine on that company, as in competition law) or which are of direct and individual concern to them; or against regulatory acts which are of direct concern to them and do not entail implementing measures (see **10.2.4.3**);

(b)   actions under Article 265 TFEU brought by natural or legal persons against a failure to act on the part of EU institutions, bodies, offices or agencies (see **10.3**);

(c)   actions under Article 263 TFEU brought by the Member States against the Commission (see **10.2**);

(d)   actions under Article 263 TFEU brought by Member States against the Council's acts in the field of State aid, 'anti-dumping' measures and acts by which the Council exercises implementing powers;

(e)   actions under Articles 268 and 340 TFEU seeking compensation for damage caused by EU institutions, bodies, offices or agencies or their staff (see further **10.5**);

(f)   actions based on agreements made by EU institutions (eg, a grant agreement between the Commission and a university) and which expressly give jurisdiction to the General Court (see **10.5**);

(g)   actions relating to EU trade marks and designs against decisions of the Office for Harmonisation in the Internal Market;

(h)   actions brought against decisions of the Community Plant Variety Office or of the European Chemicals Agency;

(i) appeals on points of law against the decisions of the EU Civil Service Tribunal (see **8.4** below).

The General Court also sits in Luxembourg and is administered by a registrar and staff. Each judge is free to appoint and employ up to three *référendaires* (see **8.2**).

8.4 Specialised courts

Article 257 TFEU provides for the creation of Specialised Courts by the European Parliament and the Council, acting in accordance with the ordinary legislative procedure. At the moment there is only one such court, the EU Civil Service Tribunal, which was established by Decision 2004/752 ([2004] OJ L333/7). Made up of seven judges appointed for a renewable six year term of office, this tribunal deals at first instance with disputes between the EU institutions, bodies, offices and agencies and their respective servants on matters ranging from working relations to social security (Article 270 TFEU). It also hears and determines disputes involving certain specific employees such as, notably, those of the European Central Bank, the European External Action Service, Eurojust, Europol and the Office for Harmonisation in the Internal Market. The Civil Service Tribunal decisions may, within two months, be appealed against on points of law to the General Court (see **8.3**) and, in turn, the General Court decisions on appeal may in exceptional circumstances be re-examined before the Court of Justice (see **8.2.1**).

8.5 Methods of interpretation

Interpretation is a process of expressing implicit meanings, and it is thus often considered as lying between art and science. It is creative in its construction of meaning. Yet, by insisting on judicial rules of construction, it has a scientific soul. The methods which the Court employs when interpreting EU law are, in some respects, very different from those used by the judiciary in the UK. In *Bulmer v Bollinger SA* [1974] 4 Ch 401, at 411 (CA), Lord Denning stated:

> The [EU] Treaty is quite unlike any of the enactments to which we have become accustomed … It lays down general principles. It expresses its aims and purposes. All in sentences of moderate length and commendable style. But it lacks precision. It uses words and phrases without defining what they mean. An English lawyer would look for an interpretation clause, but he would look in vain. There is none. All the way through the Treaty there are gaps and lacunae. These have to be filled by the judges, or by regulations or directives.
>
> It is the European way … Seeing these differences, what are the English courts to do when they are faced with a problem of interpretation? They must follow the European pattern. No longer must they argue about the precise grammatical sense. They must look to the purpose and intent … They must divine the spirit of the Treaty and gain inspiration from it. If they find a gap, they must fill it as best as they can … These are the principles, as I understand it, on which the European Court acts.

The methods of interpretation used by the Court of Justice are derived from international law and more specifically from Articles 31 to 33 of the Vienna Convention on the Law of Treaties. Yet the Court has altered these methods of interpretation to suit its needs. All in all, there are three main methods the Court employs when interpreting EU law:

(a) **Literal.** The ordinary dictionary meaning of the words is used to interpret the law. The grammatical or literal interpretation of EU texts causes a significant problem, mainly because these documents are authentic in all the languages that are recognised by the EU. As a result, this approach to interpreting the law is limited.

(b) **Contextual or systematic.** This method involves looking at EU law as a whole. It entails examining not only the provision as such but also the provision in its context, that is the entire act (especially the preamble, the section or chapter in which the provision is included, etc). Further, the Court may interpret the provision by reference to other related acts, such as a Protocol to the Treaty of the EU. The meaning of the norm is constructed by reference to its place within the general scheme of the legislative, treaty or constitutional system.

(c) **Purposive.** The law is interpreted in a way that furthers the purposes of the EU. This method is frequently used by the Court. Any EU act lends itself to this method owing to the usually lengthy preamble setting out the aims and objectives of the act in question. In other words, a functional perspective is adopted, for the Court tries to achieve the broad goals set in primary law. In *Opinion 2/13* the Court explained that 'the implementation of the process of integration ... is the *raison d'être* of the EU itself' (para 172).

A fourth method, the historical interpretation, which searches for the original meaning of a rule, is not used much by the Court of Justice. The reasons for this are that the legislative history of EU law is often complex and not published in its entirety, and that EU law is the result of compromises. Whilst the Court could refer to the recitals in the preamble of EU acts to understand the history of a particular EU act, it prefers to use them for a purpose-orientated interpretation of the act. It also refuses to consider minutes of meetings of the Commission, the Council and the European Parliament as reflections of the history of the act, unless specifically referred to in the wording of a provision of secondary legislation (Case C-404/06 *Quelle AG v Bundesverband der Verbraucherzentralen und Verbraucherverbände* [2008] ECR I-2685, para 32).

The Court makes little recourse to comparative law, although many EU acts are inspired by legislation in Member States. It may also seem surprising that judges from such a variety of legal systems do not use their knowledge of their own legal systems. It is argued that the reason for avoiding references to national legal systems, and thus not adopting a comparative approach to interpreting EU law, is that the Court endeavours to prevent the autonomy of the EU legal system being undermined by references to particular State legal systems. For EU norms and principles to be implemented in an autonomous and consistent manner, their interpretation must be independent of national preconceptions. After all, the Treaties have created a 'new legal order'.

In practice, the Court often uses a combination of the second and third methods set out above. For example, based on the **practical effectiveness** (*effet utile*) **doctrine**, the Court accepted that if individuals were entitled to invoke a specific measure before the national courts, the measure would have greater relevance and impact. Therefore, the Court thought it would be suitable for certain provisions to be directly effective. For example, the Court stated in Case C-223/98 *Adidas AG* [1999] ECR I-7081 that:

> In interpreting a provision of [EU] law it is necessary to consider not only its *wording* but also the *context* in which it occurs and the *objects* of the rules of which it is part ... [W]here a provision of [EU] law is open to several interpretations,

only one of which can ensure that the provision retains its *effectiveness*, preference must be given to that interpretation. (paras 23–24, emphasis added)

In essence, the interpretation of EU law rests on three principles: uniformity, effectiveness and the protection of individual rights. This approach is illustrated by the extension of the concept of a 'worker' under EU law to part-time employees (Case 53/81 *Levin v Staatssecretaris van Justitie* [1982] ECR 1035), individuals undertaking training (Case C-3/90 *Bernini v Minister van Onderwijs en Wetenschappen* [1992] ECR I-1071), job-seekers (Case C-292/89 *R v Immigration Appeal Tribunal, ex parte Gustaff Desiderius Antonissen* [1991] ECR I-745), doctoral candidates (Case C-94/07 *Raccanelli v Max-Planck-Gesellschaft zur Förderung der Wissenschaften eV* [2008] ECR I-5939) and individuals earning so little that their wages had to be supplemented by public assistance (Case 139/85 *Kempf v Staatssecretaris van Justitie* [1986] ECR 1741) (see further 15.2.1).

In Case T-18/10 *Inuit Tapiriit Kanatami v European Parliament and Council* [2011] ECR II-5599, the General Court had to interpret the new Article 263, fourth paragraph TFEU that introduced the concept of 'regulatory act' (see **10.2.4.3**). To do so, the Court used the literal, contextual, historical and teleological methods of interpretation. After using a *literal* approach and comparing the old and the new modified article, the Court concluded that the word 'regulatory' covers a limited number of acts of general application (paras 41–43). A *contextual* approach revealed that in light of Article 263, first paragraph TFEU, two categories of acts are subject to review – (i) legislative acts, and (ii) 'other binding acts intended to produce legal effects vis-à-vis third parties' (para 44) – which, read in conjunction with Article 263, fourth paragraph TFEU, means that judicial review proceedings may be instituted by individuals '(i) against a legislative or regulatory act of general application which is of direct and individual concern to them and (ii) against certain acts of general application, namely regulatory acts which are of direct concern to them and do not entail implementing measures' (para 45). An examination of the *history* of the process that led to the adoption of Article 263, fourth paragraph TFEU shows that the drafters wanted to distinguish between legislative and regulatory acts, and limit the ability of individuals to challenge legislative acts (para 49). Last but not least, the Court investigated the purpose of the provision, which is to enable judicial review of acts of general application (though not legislative acts) so as to avoid the situation whereby a natural or a legal person would have to infringe the law to have access to the court (para 50). As a conclusion, the Court stated:

In view of the foregoing, it must be held that the meaning of 'regulatory act' for the purposes of the fourth paragraph of Article 263 TFEU must be understood as covering all acts of general application apart from legislative acts. Consequently, a legislative act may form the subject-matter of an action for annulment brought by a natural or legal person only if it is of direct and individual concern to them. (para 56)

8.6 The CJEU as a constitutional court and judicial activism

The jurisdiction of the CJEU is set out by Articles 256 to 279 TFEU. The CJEU does not have 'residual' or 'inherent' powers and can exercise its powers only within the jurisdiction conferred upon it (Article 13(2) TEU). For example, in any non-Union policy area, the CJEU's jurisdiction is either excluded or limited by various articles in the Treaty: Article 24(1) TEU and Article 275 TFEU rule out judicial review of provisions pertaining to the Common Foreign and Security Policy.

Using the methods of interpretation discussed in **8.5** above, the Court has undeniably become a motor for integration, ensuring and extending the primacy of EU law. In particular it has fashioned the constitutional framework of the EU by its interpretation of the primary sources (see **4.2**). For example, the CJEU has:

(a) created new concepts – the **principle of direct effect** (Case 26/62 *NV Algemene Transport- en Expeditie Onderneming van Gend & Loos v Netherlands Inland Revenue Administration* [1963] ECR 1) (see further **7.3**) and the **principle of supremacy** (Case 6/64 *Costa v ENEL* [1964] ECR 585) (see further **7.2**);

(b) created new liability regimes – **Member State liability** (Joined Cases C-6 and 9/90 *Francovich and Bonifaci and others v Italy* [1991] ECR I-5357) (see further **7.3**);

(c) declared that fundamental rights are to be protected under EU law (Case 29/69 *Stauder v City of Ulm* [1969] ECR 419) and specified and extended EU fundamental freedoms (see further **4.6**);

(d) broadened certain definitions (eg definition of 'measures having an equivalent effect' to quantitative restrictions (Case 8/74 *Procureur du Roi v Dassonville and Dassonville* [1974] ECR 837; Case 120/78 *Rewe-Zentral AG v Bundesmonopolverwaltung für Branntwein* [1979] ECR 649) (see further **13.2.3**); given new powers to the EU, eg the power to negotiate, sign and ratify international treaties in fields in which it has competence internally (Case 22/70 *Commission v Council (Re ERTA)* [1971] ECR 263) (see further **3.2.2**).

Thus, the Court has established a fully-fledged legal system. Yet its interpretation of EU law has raised concerns. Some Member States and scholars accuse the CJEU of going beyond the letter of the Treaties in its development of EU law. By its so-called judicial activism the Court, it is argued, has acted as a law-maker, reshaping the architecture of the EU without the consent of the Member States. In defence of the Court, it should be noted that the original treaty was a framework treaty that needed to be fleshed out, as it regulated only a few topics in exhaustive detail. Moreover, treaties are the result of compromises made during negotiations, are often formulated in vague terms and present a patchwork of legal provisions. The multilingual character of EU law also offers numerous opportunities for the Court to choose a suitable interpretation of the law. A new doctrine or principle is usually introduced in a ground-breaking judgment. Then, in subsequent cases, the Court gradually clarifies the scope of application of the doctrine or principle by specifying conditions, expanding the initial scope of application or assisting authorities in the application of the law.

in practice

The way the Court proceeds in introducing and developing a doctrine as well as specifying its limits can be seen in the example of the **doctrine of indirect effect** (see further **6.3.5.1**).

Introducing the doctrine

Case 14/83 *Von Colson and Kamann v Land Nordrhein-Westfalen* [1984] ECR 1891.

Limitations

- A directive may have indirect effect only after the deadline for its implementation has expired (Case C-212/04 *Adeneler and Others v Ellinikos Organismos Galaktos (ELOG)* [2006] ECR I-6057).
- Interpretation of a provision cannot result in a conflict with a general principle of EU law (Case 80/86 *Criminal proceedings against Kolpinghuis Nijmegen BV* [1987] ECR 3969).
- There are no obligations on individuals if there was no proper implementation of a directive (Case C-456/98 *Centrosteel Srl v Adipol GmbH* [2000] ECR I-6007 (especially if criminal liability involved (Case C-168/95 *Criminal proceedings against Arcaro* [1996] ECR I-4705)).

Assistance in the application

- Interpretation can go only 'so far as possible' (Case C-91/92 *Faccini Dori v Recreb Srl* [1994] ECR I-3325)
- National courts must consider the whole body of national rules and interpret them, so far as possible, in the light of the wording and purpose of the directive in order to achieve an outcome consistent with the objectives of the directive (Joined Cases C-397/01 to C-403/01 *Pfeiffer et al v Deutsches Rotes Kreuz, Kreisverband Waldshut eV* [2004] ECR I-8835).
- National law may be disapplied if it is impossible to interpret it in conformity with the directive (Case C-555/07 *Kücükdeveci v Swedex GmbH & Co KG* [2010] ECR I-365).

At the same time, the Court has also been criticised for not being activist enough and for trying to limit the ability of natural and legal persons to question the work of the EU and its institutions. For example, for a long time, the requirements for EU liability (see **10.5**) were more difficult to fulfil than the requirements for Member State liability (see **7.3**). Also, the Court has been reluctant to offer a broad interpretation of the requirements for action for annulment initiated by a legal or natural person, even pointing out that such an interpretation would go against the Treaty and was best left to be amended by the Member States (see **10.2.4.3**), or to accept the principle of damages liability where it concerns EU acts (see **10.5**). However, others have argued that the Court is merely doing what it was set up to do: helping to create the 'ever closer union' mentioned in the original Treaty and reaffirmed in later Treaties.

8.7 Further reading

Arnull A, *The European Union and its Court of Justice*, 2nd edn (OUP, 2006).
Barents R, 'The Court of Justice after the Treaty of Lisbon' (2010) 47 *CML Rev* 709.
Burrows N and Greaves R, *The Advocate General and EC Law* (OUP, 2007).

Dawson M, De Witte B and Muir E (eds), *Judicial Activism at the European Court of Justice* (Edward Elgar Publishing, 2013).

De Waele H, 'The Role of the European Court of Justice in the Integration Process: A Contemporary and Normative Assessment' (2010) 6 *Hanse Law Review* 3.

Itzcovich G, 'The Interpretation of Community Law by the European Court of Justice' (2009) 10 *German Law Journal* 537.

Jacobs F, 'The Lisbon Treaty and the Court of Justice' in Biondi A *et al* (eds), *EU Law after Lisbon* (OUP, 2012) 197.

Poiares Maduro M, 'Interpreting European Law: Judicial Adjudication in a Context of Constitutional Pluralism' (2007) 1 *European Journal of Legal Studies* 1.

Solanke I, '"Stop the ECJ"?: An Empirical Analysis of Activism at the Court' (2011) 17(6) *EL Rev* 764.

Tamm D, 'The History of the Court of Justice of the European Union since its Origin' in Court of Justice of the European Union, *Justice and the Construction of Europe: Analyses and Perspectives on Sixty Years of Case-Law* (Asser Press, 2013) 9.

summary

The CJEU is not a single judicial body; rather, it is composed of the Court of Justice, the General Court and specialised courts. The procedure before the Court is mainly written and its judgments are collegiate.

As the Court has adopted specific methods of interpretation that allow it to provide a broad interpretation of EU law and its principles, it has often been accused both by Member States and by academics of judicial activism.

test your knowledge

1 Critically discuss, by using relevant examples, whether you believe that the CJEU has gone beyond its powers.

2 The CJEU has been the motor for integration since its inception. Now that the Member States (via the Treaties) and the European institutions (via secondary legislation) have created a comprehensive set of EU norms, there is no longer a need for judicial activism. Discuss.

Preliminary Ruling Procedure on Interpretation and Validity

After reading this chapter, you will be able to understand:

- the aim of the Article 267 TFEU preliminary ruling procedure and the division of tasks between the 'national court or tribunal' and the CJEU
- the type of questions that can be referred to the CJEU
- which national courts and tribunals can refer questions to the CJEU
- when a national court or tribunal is obliged to refer questions to the CJEU
- when the CJEU might refuse to hear a preliminary ruling
- the special preliminary ruling procedures
- the effects of the preliminary ruling.

9.1 Introduction

Much of the responsibility for applying the rules laid down in the EU treaties and acts belongs to the national courts of the Member States. Indeed, Article 19(1) TFEU stipulates:

> Member States shall provide remedies sufficient to ensure effective legal protection in the fields covered by Union law.

In *Opinion 1/09* of 8 March 2011 [2011] ECR I-1137, this provision has been held by the Court of Justice, to turn national courts into 'the guardians of [the European] legal order' and to make it clear that 'the judicial system of the European Union [comprises] the Court of Justice and the courts and tribunals of the Member States' (para 66). After all, the Court continues, '[t]he national court, in collaboration with the Court of Justice fulfils a duty entrusted to them both of ensuring that in the interpretation and application of the Treaties the law is observed' (para 69). In *Opinion 2/13* of 18 December 2014, ECLI:EU:C:2014:2454, the Court of Justice reiterated that 'it is for the national courts and tribunals and for the Court of Justice to ensure the full application of EU law in all Member States and to ensure judicial protection of an individual's rights under that law' (para 175).

From a functional perspective, national courts are effectively decentralised courts of EU law. However, from an institutional perspective, they are distinct, and the CJEU is not a European court of appeal (**principle of judicial autonomy**).

Yet this state of affairs gives rise to a potential problem. If the internal market is to work properly, the relevant rules must have the same effect in all the EU Member States. The nature of the judicial process and varying legal traditions mean that, left to their own devices, it would be highly unlikely that courts in, say, London would always apply EU law in the same way as courts in, say, Paris. However, it is of the utmost importance for the CJEU to secure uniformity in the EU legal order (Case 166/73 *Rheinmühlen-Düsseldorf v Einfuhr- und Vorratsstelle für Getreide und Futtermittel (No 1)* [1974] ECR 33; *Opinion 1/09*, para 83 and *Opinion 2/13*, para 176). To help safeguard the uniform application of EU law, Article 267 TFEU lays down a procedure that enables national courts to ask the CJEU for guidance on the interpretation or validity of provisions of EU law they must apply before giving judgment in cases brought before them (*Opinion 1/09*, para 83).

The **preliminary ruling procedure** is primarily an instrument of cooperation between the CJEU and the national courts, and thus the relationship between the courts is not hierarchical (*Opinion 1/09*, para 84) but one of dialogue (*Opinion 2/13*, para 176). Generally, the principle of cooperation between national courts and the CJEU must be understood as part of the broader **principle of cooperation** between the Member States and the EU enshrined in Article 4(3) TEU:

> Pursuant to the principle of sincere cooperation, the Union and the Member States shall, in full mutual respect, assist each other in carrying out tasks which flow from the Treaties.
>
> The Member States shall take any appropriate measure, general or particular, to ensure fulfilment of the obligations arising out of the Treaties or resulting from the acts of the institutions of the Union.
>
> The Member States shall facilitate the achievement of the Union's tasks and refrain from any measure which could jeopardise the attainment of the Union's objectives.

Both sets of courts have distinct, albeit complementary, roles to play in finding a solution to a case, which is consistent with EU law.

In a report prepared for the 1996 Inter-Governmental Conference, the preliminary reference procedure was described as 'the veritable cornerstone of the operation of the internal market' (*Report of the Court of Justice on Certain Aspects of the Application of the Treaty on European Union*, May 1995). It is under this procedure that the CJEU has created or further developed major principles that have shaped the EU legal order and law, such as supremacy (see **6.2**), direct effect (see **6.3**), Member State liability (see **7.3**), free movement of goods (see **Chapters 12–14**), European citizenship (see **Chapter 19**), etc. Undoubtedly, references from national courts now often represent the largest category of cases brought before the Court in a single year. For example, in 2014, out of 719 cases dealt with by the Court of Justice (701 cases completed in 2013), 428 (59%) were preliminary references. The average duration of cases brought for preliminary rulings amounted to 15 months in 2014 (16.3 months in 2013) (see CJEU Press Release 27/15). These figures clearly demonstrate the importance of this procedure in the EU judicial system.

9.2 Jurisdiction of the Court of Justice of the European Union and division of tasks

The CJEU has interpreted its jurisdiction under Article 267, first paragraph in a strict manner, entrusting national courts with the application of EU law and thus ensuring a clear division of tasks between the CJEU and the national courts.

9.2.1 Jurisdiction of the Court of Justice of the European Union

The jurisdiction of the CJEU as regards the preliminary reference procedure is spelled out in Article 267, first paragraph TFEU, which provides:

The Court of Justice of the European Union shall have jurisdiction to give preliminary rulings concerning:

(a) the interpretation of the Treaties;

(b) the validity and interpretation of acts of the institutions, bodies, offices or agencies of the Union.

...

Moreover, the General Court has competence to hear Article 267 applications in certain areas laid down by the Statute of the Court of Justice (Article 256(3) TFEU). In other words, preliminary references may be made in relation to two judicial functions:

(a) the interpretation of EU law (regarding the meaning of EU law); and

(b) the validity of EU law (regarding the validity of binding secondary EU measures (eg directives) in the light of EU law and international law that binds the EU).

These two functions are, however, limited:

(a) the CJEU does not concern itself with the facts of the case pending before the national court, and does not rule on the validity of national law (Case 26/62 *NV Algemene Transport- en Expeditie Onderneming van Gend & Loos v Netherlands Inland Revenue Administration* [1963] ECR 1) (see **9.2.1** below); and

(b) it will not examine the validity of EU law if this could have been done under Article 263 TFEU (see further **10.2**).

See **Figure 9.1**.

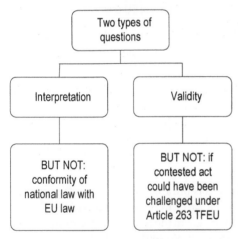

Figure 9.1 contents:

Two types of questions → Interpretation; Validity

Interpretation → BUT NOT: conformity of national law with EU law

Validity → BUT NOT: if contested act could have been challenged under Article 263 TFEU

Figure 9.1   Jurisdiction of the CJEU in the preliminary reference procedure

The jurisdiction of the CJEU is not limited to the treaties and the acts of the institutions. In practice, the CJEU will agree to examine any form of law, whether binding or not. For example, in Case C-322/88 *Grimaldi v Fonds des Maladies Professionnelles* [1989] ECR 4407, the Court looked at a recommendation. Moreover, the Court also examines international agreements between the EU and other States (Case 181/73 *R & V Haegeman v Belgium* [1974] ECR 449).

Various types of questions may be the subject of a reference to the Court of Justice for a preliminary ruling. The Court may be asked what the Treaty or an act of one of the institutions means. It may also be asked whether such an act is valid or not. References may in addition be made on whether a provision of EU law produces direct effect, that is whether it confers rights on private parties (such as individuals and companies) which national courts must protect (see **6.3** on direct effect).

9.2.2   Division of tasks

The role of the Court of Justice in the preliminary reference procedure is limited to answering questions of EU law raised in the case pending before the national court. It is for this reason that the Court's ruling is described as 'preliminary'. The answers given by the Court are couched in abstract terms. Indeed the application of EU law is not within the power of the Court, as the Court noted in Case 6/64 *Costa v ENEL* [1964] ECR 585, 592 that Article 267 TFEU 'gives the Court no jurisdiction to apply the Treat[ies] to a specific case'.

Yet the distinction between interpretation and application is hard to make. The Court has tried to explain it as follows:

> When it gives an interpretation of the Treat[ies] in a specific action pending before a national court, the Court limits itself to deducing the meaning of the [European] rules from the wording and spirit of the Treat[ies], it being left to the national court to apply in the particular case the rules which are thus interpreted. (Joined Cases 28–30/62 *Da Costa en Schaake NV and Others v Netherlands Inland Revenue Administration* [1963] ECR 31, at 38)

It is for the national court to decide questions of national law and questions of fact, and to apply the ruling of the Court of Justice to the dispute between the parties. This means that it is the national court, not the Court of Justice, which in the last resort decides whether national law satisfies the requirements of EU law. This is important, because democratic States, which respect the rule of law, do not disregard judgments of their own courts. This also means that the relationship between national courts and the CJEU is based on their voluntary cooperation. See **Figure 9.2**.

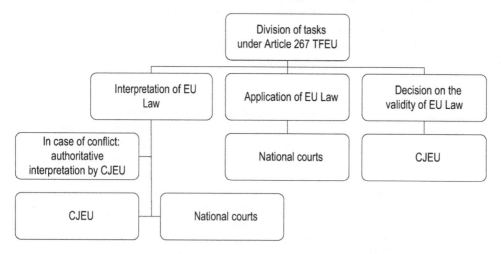

Figure 9.2   Division of tasks under Article 267 TFEU

Yet sometimes, owing to the way the question is phrased, the CJEU finds it difficult to interpret the law without applying it to the case. In some instances, the CJEU's rulings leave the national court with little room for manoeuvre (see, for example, the 'Arsenal cases': *Arsenal Football Club plc v Matthew Reed* [2001] 2 CMLR 23 (ChD); Case C-206/01 *Arsenal Football Club plc v Matthew Reed (No 2)* [2003] 1 CMLR 13 (ChD); *Arsenal Football Club plc v Matthew Reed* [2003] 2 CMLR 25 (CA)). In other instances, the Court has crossed the line between interpretation and application by stating that some national rules were incompatible with the EU law (see, for example, the 'Sunday trading cases': Case C-145/88 *Torfaen Borough Council v B & Q plc* [1989] ECR 3851 and Case C-169/91 *Council of the City of Stoke-on-Trent v B & Q plc* [1992] ECR I-6635). The CJEU might also refer to EU law provisions that were not mentioned by the national court in its questions (Case C-92/02 *Kristiansen v Rijksdienst voor Arbeidsvoorziening* [2003] ECR I-14597). Although this might be viewed as an extension of the Court's power, it is for the benefit of the national court to understand the broader EU context within which the question is asked. That being said, the CJEU cannot answer questions that are not asked (Case C-236/02 *Slob v Productschap Zuivel* [2004] ECR I-1861).

The success of the procedure depends on the willingness of the national courts to apply the rulings of the Court of Justice faithfully. The **principle of precedence or primacy** and the notion that directives might have direct effect encountered resistance in some national courts, particularly those of Germany and France. However, by and large, the national courts have played their part in the procedure remarkably conscientiously.

9.3 Which 'national court or tribunal' can make a reference?

This is not an appeal procedure. It is not up to the parties to the dispute to request a preliminary reference but to 'any court or tribunal of a Member State' to do so. This means that any court or tribunal within the legal system of a Member State of the EU is entitled to request a preliminary ruling. Naturally, for the purpose of an effective application of Article 267 TFEU, the CJEU had to interpret the concepts of 'court or tribunal' and of a court or tribunal 'of a Member State', rather than leaving them to the laws of the Member States.

At first sight, a direct reference to judicial authorities appears to exclude indirectly administrative authorities (eg the licensing and control authority of a broadcasting authority). Nonetheless, the Court has traditionally taken a relatively broad view on the matter and has not regarded the body's status under national law as decisive. Whether a national body satisfies that description is a question of EU law for the Court of Justice to determine. In fact, the Court of Justice considers the function of the body making the reference rather than its name. The Court has explained, in Case C-54/96 *Dorsch Consult Ingenieurgesellschaft mbH v Bundesbaugesellschaft Berlin* [1997] ECR I-4961, that

> [i]n order to determine whether a body making a reference is a court or tribunal for the purposes of Article [267] of the Treaty, which is a question governed by [Union] law alone, the Court takes account of a number of factors, such as whether the body is established by law, whether it is permanent, whether its jurisdiction is compulsory, whether its procedure is *inter partes*, whether it applies rules of law and whether it is independent ... (para 23)

The relevant criteria to be applied in determining whether a body is a court or tribunal may be remembered using the mnemonic **EPICAR**, that is the body:

- must be   Established by law
- must be   Permanent
- must be   Independent
- must have   Compulsory jurisdiction
- must have an   Adversarial procedure (*inter pares* procedure), and
- must apply the   Rule of law.

As a result, administrative tribunals (*Van Gend en Loos*), an Appeals Committee for General Medicine (Case 246/80 *Broekmeulen v Huisarts Registratie Commissie* [1981] ECR 2311) and a University Appeals Board (Case C-407/98 *Abrahamsson and Anderson v Fogelqvist* [2000] ECR I-5539) have been allowed to request a preliminary ruling, while tribunals established in pursuance of a private contract have not (Case 102/81 *Nordsee v Reederei Mond* [1982] ECR 1095). As for administrative and financial authorities, it appears that the criterion of independence is the most important one (Case C-210/06

Cartesio Oktató és Szolgáltató bt [2008] ECR I-9641, para 57; Case C-53/03 *Syfait et al v GlaxoSmithKline* [2005] ECR I-4609; and Case C-516/99 *Schmid* [2002] ECR I-4593, para 37).

The Court has also applied the expression 'court or tribunal of a Member State' to courts in special territories, such as the courts of the Isle of Man (Case C-355/89 *DHSS (Isle of Man) v Barr and Montrose Holdings Ltd* [1991] ECR-I 3479) or the administrative court of Papeete (Case C-100/89 *Kaefer and Procacci v France* [1990] ECR I-4647), as well as to courts that are common to more than one Member State, such as the Benelux Court of Justice (Case C-337/95 *Parfums Christian Dior v Evora BV* [1997] ECR I-6013). These courts may thus also make preliminary references.

9.4 Obligation and discretion to refer

Article 267, third paragraph TFEU draws a distinction between courts whose decisions are subject to appeal in the national system and courts whose decisions are final (either generally or in the specific case):

> Where any [preliminary] question is raised in a case pending before a court or tribunal of a Member State against whose decisions there is no judicial remedy under national law, that court or tribunal shall bring the matter before the Court.

Generally, lower courts have the discretion whether or not refer a question when there is a point of EU law that needs to be decided. They can either ask for a preliminary ruling, or decide the point for themselves. In principle, a lower national court is the sole judge of whether a reference is necessary and the relevance of the questions put to the Court of Justice. As the Court explained in Case C-2/06 *Willy Kempter v Hauptzollamt Hamburg-Jonas* [2008] ECR I-411:

> [T]he system of references for a preliminary ruling is based on a dialogue between one court and another, the initiation of which depends entirely on the national court's assessment as to whether a reference is appropriate and necessary. (para 42)

In particular, in Case C-138/09 *Todaro Nunziatina & C Snc v Assessorato del Lavoro, della Previdenza Sociale, della Formazione Professionale e dell'Emigrazione della regione Sicilia* [2010] ECR I-4561, the Court stated that

> [i]t must be borne in mind that it is solely for the national court before which the dispute has been brought, and which must assume responsibility for the subsequent judicial decision, to determine, in the light of the particular circumstances of the case, both the need for a preliminary ruling in order to enable it to deliver judgment and the relevance of the questions which it submits to the Court. (para 25)

Initially, the ECJ adopted a flexible approach (Joined Cases 36 and 71/80 *Irish Creamery Milk Suppliers Association v Government of Ireland* [1981] ECR 735), though it warned of the perils of non-referral in Case 283/81*Srl CILFIT and Lanificio di Gavardo SpA v Ministry of Health* [1982] ECR 3415).

The only instance in which lower courts are obliged to refer the case is when they investigate the validity of an EU law provision. In this case they are under the duty to refer the case to the CJEU.

In Case 314/85 *Foto-Frost v Hauptzollamt Lübeck Ost* [1987] ECR 4199, the Court held that national courts had no power to declare EU acts invalid because of the danger that measures intended to apply throughout the Member States would be declared invalid in some but not in others. This means that where the validity of an EU measure is seriously questioned in national court proceedings and the issue needs to be resolved in order for the national judgment to be given, then a reference to the Court of Justice *must* be made. This is so regardless of whether or not the national court is one whose decisions are subject to appeal. Clearly, this approach has the merit of avoiding contradictory decisions between the CJEU and national courts and also between national courts. Moreover this approach contains a strong integrating element as it ensures the uniform and effective application of EU law, which is the aim of Article 267 TFEU.

The only exception, where the Court of Justice has been prepared to recognise the power of national courts to suspend provisionally the validity of EU acts, is where the national court has been asked to grant provisional relief pending final judgment in the case. The urgency of such cases might make it impractical to wait for a preliminary ruling, so the Court of Justice has accepted that national courts may declare EU acts invalid in such circumstances, provided a number of strict conditions are met. In Joined Cases C-143/88 and 92/89 *Zuckerfabrik Süderdithmarschen AG v Hauptzollamt Itzehoe* [1991] ECR I-415, the Court explained:

> Suspension of enforcement of a national measure adopted in implementation of a [Union] regulation may be granted by a national court only:
> (i) if that court entertains serious doubts as to the validity of the [Union] measure and, should the question of the validity of the contested measure not already have been brought before the Court, itself refers that question to the Court;
> (ii) if there is urgency and a threat of serious and irreparable damage to the applicant; and
> (iii) if the national court takes due account of the [Union's] interests. (para 33)

In contrast, courts whose judgments are final have no discretion: they must refer such points to the Court of Justice. Indeed, if the case is pending before a court or tribunal of a Member State against whose decisions there is no judicial remedy under national law – for example the Supreme Court (UK), the *Cour de Cassation* (France), the *Bundesgerichtshof* (Germany) – that court or tribunal shall bring the matter before the Court of Justice. The purpose of this rule is to prevent the emergence of a body of national case law that is not in accordance with EU law (Case 107/76 *Hoffmann La Roche v Centrafarm* [1977] ECR 957).

Two theories have been advanced to explain when there is an obligation upon tribunals to refer the matter to the CJEU. The abstract or institutional theory stipulates that it is the highest court in the Member State that is obliged to ask for a preliminary ruling. The concrete or procedural theory, on the other hand, examines whether there is in reality a possibility of appeal to the highest judicial authority in the Member State. If there is, that is if the case is able to reach the highest court, then the court is not obliged to ask for a preliminary reference. The CJEU has declared that as long as there is a possibility of an appeal (even if leave to appeal might be refused), there is no obligation upon the court to ask for a preliminary ruling. In Case C-99/00 *Criminal proceedings against Lyckeskog* [2002] ECR I-4839, the ECJ explained:

Decisions of a national appellate court which can be challenged by the parties before a supreme court are not decisions of a 'court or tribunal of a Member State against whose decisions there is no judicial remedy under national law' within the meaning of Article [267 TFEU]. The fact that examination of the merits of such appeals is subject to a prior declaration of admissibility by the supreme court does not have the effect of depriving the parties of a judicial remedy.

That is so under the Swedish system. The parties always have the right to appeal to the *Högsta domstol* [Supreme Court] against the judgment of a *hovrätt* [Court of Appeal], which cannot therefore be classified as a court delivering a decision against which there is no judicial remedy. Under Paragraph 10 of Chapter 54 of the *Rättegångsbalk* [Code of Procedure], the *Högsta domstol* may issue a declaration of admissibility if it is important for guidance as to the application of the law that the appeal be examined by that court. Thus, uncertainty as to the interpretation of the law applicable, including [Union] law, may give rise to review, at last instance, by the supreme court.

If a question arises as to the interpretation or validity of a rule of [Union] law, the supreme court will be under an obligation, pursuant to the third paragraph of Article [267 TFEU], to refer a question to the Court of Justice for a preliminary ruling either at the stage of the examination of admissibility or at a later stage. (paras 16–18)

There are two instances when a court's Treaty obligation to refer a case to the CJEU is waived:

(a) when, under the *acte clair* doctrine, the answer to the question raised is clear (see 9.6 below); and

(b) when the question is 'materially identical' to a question that has already been addressed in a previous preliminary ruling (eg in *Da Costa* a question identical to one raised in *Van Gend en Loos* was asked), or when the CJEU has already dealt with the point of law in question (*CILFIT*). The Court will deal with this type of request only if there are new facts or new arguments presented by the national court (*Da Costa*). As a result, a system of precedent is emerging by default.

For a summary of when a question must be referred, see **Figure 9.3**.

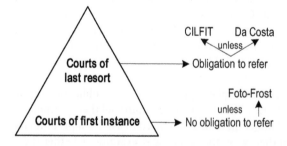

Figure 9.3   Courts having an obligation to refer under Article 267 TFEU

9.5   Can the Court of Justice of the European Union refuse to hear a preliminary reference?

Article 267, second paragraph TFEU stipulates:

Where such a question [preliminary reference] is raised before any court or tribunal of a Member State, that court or tribunal may, if it considers that a decision on the question is necessary to enable it to give judgment, request the Court to give a ruling thereon.

The Court explained in Case C-379/98 *PreussenElektra AG v Schhleswag AG* [2001] ECR I-2099:

It should remembered that it is settled law that in the context of the cooperation between the Court of Justice and the national courts provided for by Article [267] of the Treaty it is solely for the national court before which the dispute has been brought, and which must assume responsibility for the subsequent judicial decision, to determine in the light of the particular circumstances of the case both the need for a preliminary ruling in order to enable it to deliver judgment and the relevance of the questions which it submits to the Court. Consequently, where the questions submitted by the national court concern the interpretation of [Union] law, the Court of Justice is, in principle, bound to give a ruling. (para 38)

The Court originally took a very liberal attitude to questions referred to it, reformulating them if they were badly drafted or missed the point, and doing its best to establish the background from the material submitted to it where this had not been explained adequately by the national court. This helped to establish a good working relationship with national judges and encouraged them to make use of the procedure.

More recently, the growing volume of cases has led the Court to take a stricter approach. First, it has issued recommendations to the national courts and tribunals in relation to the initiation of preliminary rulings proceedings (2012/C 338/01) (replacing the former 2011 information note on references from national courts for a preliminary ruling), which contain a wealth of information concerning, notably, the stage at which to submit a reference for a preliminary ruling (paras 18–19) and the form and content of the request for a preliminary ruling (paras 20–28). (See also Article 94 of the 2012 Rules of Procedure of the Court of Justice, [2013] OJ L265/1.)

Secondly, the CJEU has stated that it will not look into certain cases, such as those where:

(a) the dispute is not connected with any of the situations contemplated by the Treaty provisions or EU acts. As the CJEU has no jurisdiction with regard to national legislation lying outside the scope of EU law, it cannot answer the request of the national court (Case C-299/95 *Kremzow v Austria* [1997] ECR I-2629);

(b) there is no real dispute between the parties (Case 104/79 *Foglia v Novello (No 1)* [1980] ECR 745 and Case 244/80 *Foglia v Novello (No 2)* [1981] ECR 3045);

(c) the case is hypothetical (Case 138/80 *Borker* [1980] ECR 1975; Case C-83/91 *Meilicke v ADV/ORGA FA Meyer AG* [1992] ECR I-4871) or the application of EU law to the case is hypothetical (Case C-16/12 *Hermes Hitel és Faktor Zrt v Nemzeti Földalapkezelö Szervezet*, 6 July 2012, ECLI:EU:C:2012:426);

(d) the question is irrelevant to the actual case (Case C-318/00 *Bacardi-Martini SAS, Cellier des Dauphins v Newcastle United FC* [2003] ECR I-905; *CILFIT*, **9.4** above; Case C-147/02 *Alabaster v Woolwich plc and Secretary of State for Social Security* [2004] ECR I-3101);

(e) the court cannot understand the question (Joined Cases C-320–322/90 *Telemarsicabruzzo SpA and Others v Circostel and Others* [1993] ECR I-393);

(f) the court deems that there is not enough information (Case C-176/96 *Lehtonen, Castors Canada Dry Namur-Braine ASBL v Fédération Royale Belge des Sociétés de*

Basket-ball ASBL (FRBSB) [2000] ECR I-2681). As the Article 267 TFEU procedure is one based on cooperation between national courts and the CJEU, the latter expects to be provided by the former with the factual and legal framework in which the question is asked (Case C-75/12 *Criminal proceedings against Abdel* [2012] OJ C303/15). However, in Case C-316/93 *Vaneetveld v Le Foyer SA and Le Foyer SA v Fédération des Mutualités Socialistes et Syndicales de la Province de Liège* [1994] ECR I-763, the Court admitted:

> It is true that the Court has held that the need to arrive at an interpretation of [Union] law which is useful for the national court requires that court to define the factual and legislative context of the questions, or at least to explain the factual hypotheses on which they are based ... None the less, that requirement is less pressing where the questions relate to specific technical points and enable the Court to give a useful reply even where the national court has not given an exhaustive description of the legal and factual situation. (para 13)

(g) the validity of judgments of the CJEU is questioned (Case C-69/85 *Wünsche Handelsgesellschaft GmbH & Co v Germany* [1986] ECR 947);

(h) the CJEU has already dealt with the question on a previous occasion (*CILFIT*, **9.4** above; Case C-466/93 *Atlanta Fruchthandelsgesellschaft mbH and others v Bundesamt für Ernährung und Forstwirtschaft* [1995] ECR I-3799 and *Da Costa*; and Article 99 of the 2012 Rules of Procedure of the Court of Justice);

(i) subject to the linguistic proviso (*CILFIT*, **9.4** above, paras 16–19), the correct interpretation is so obvious as to leave no scope for reasonable doubt (known as *acte clair* in French administrative law) (*CILFIT*, **9.4** above; Article 99 of the 2012 Rules of Procedure of the Court of Justice). Before reaching that conclusion, the national court has to be convinced that the matter would be equally obvious to the courts of other Member States and to the Court of Justice. This means taking account of the characteristic features of EU law and the special difficulties to which its interpretation gave rise;

(j) proceedings in the national court are already terminated (Case 338/85 *Fratelli Pardini SpA v Ministero del Commercio con l'Estero* [1988] ECR 2041); or

(k) one of the parties has withdrawn from the proceedings and it is therefore no longer necessary to give a ruling (Joined Cases C-422–424/93 *Zabala Erasun and others v Instituto Nacional de Empleo* [1995] ECR I-1567).

See Figure 9.4.

9.6 The special preliminary ruling procedures

In pursuance of Article 23a of Protocol No 3 on the Statute of the Court of Justice of the European Union, there are two special preliminary ruling procedures:

(a) the expedited procedure; and

(b) the urgent procedure.

Both are dealt with in chapters 2 and 3 of Title III of the 2012 Rules of Procedure of the Court of Justice. Under these procedures the case may be decided, within a short time, without a written submission from the Advocate General, that is the submission may be made orally.

The use of the *expedited preliminary ruling procedure*, described in Articles 105 to 106 of the Rules of Procedure of the Court of Justice, may be requested by the referring court or tribunal (very few such requests are made and only about one-third are granted) or, on his own motion, by the President of the Court after hearing the Judge-Rapporteur and the Advocate General. A strict time limit for the submissions is then set, and the President may request submissions to focus on the essential points of law raised in the reference.

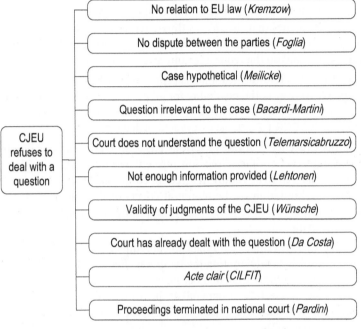

Figure 9.4   *Grounds on which the CJEU may refuse a referral*

The *urgent preliminary ruling procedure*, which was introduced in 2008, may be used only for issues covered by Title V of Part III of the TFEU, that is, the area of freedom, security and justice. It can be triggered either by the referring court or tribunal submitting a request for the urgent procedure to be applied, or, failing that, by the President of the Court of Justice, if 'the application of that procedure appears, prima facie, to be required', in which case a Court Chamber will consider whether or not it is necessary to deal with the reference under that procedure (Article 107(3) of the Rules of Procedure). When submitting such a request, the referring court or tribunal will have to explain why this procedure is required and, ideally, propose its own answer to the questions referred (Article 107(2) of the Rules of Procedure). A decision as to the urgency of the procedure will then have to be made by the designated chamber (Article 108 of the Rules of Procedure) before ruling on the substance after hearing the Advocate General (Article 112 of the Rules of Procedure). Should the application of the urgent procedure be deemed unnecessary, the normal reference procedure will continue to apply (Article 109(6) of the Rules of Procedure). In 2014, the urgent preliminary ruling procedure was used in four cases and was completed within two months on average (CJEU Press Release 27/15).

9.7   The effects of the ruling of the Court of Justice of the European Union

Preliminary rulings cannot bind the parties in the national dispute, since the CJEU will not decide their case. However, the ruling of the CJEU 'is binding on the national court as to the interpretation of the [Union] provisions and acts in question' (Case 52/76 *Benedetti v Munari Fratelli SAS* [1977] ECR 163, para 26).

It must be remembered that, as the Court explained in Case C-2/06 *Willy Kempter v Hauptzollamt Hamburg-Jonas* [2008] ECR I-411, para 35, 'a preliminary ruling does not create or alter the law but is purely declaratory, with the consequence that in principle it takes effect from the date on which the rule interpreted entered into force'. Furthermore, the ruling affects all legal relationships, whether established before or after the ruling. The Court clearly explained in Case 61/79 *Amministrazione delle Finanze dello Stato v Denkavit Italiana* [1980] ECR 1205 that a preliminary ruling on the interpretation of a rule of Union law

> … clarifies and defines where necessary the meaning and scope of that rule as it must be or ought to have been understood and applied from the time of its coming into force. It follows that the rule as thus interpreted may, and must, be applied by the [national] courts even to legal relationships arising and established before the judgment ruling on the request for interpretation … (para 16)

The CJEU has nevertheless acknowledged that exceptionally, where legal certainty requires it, it is acceptable to restrict the possibility for all persons concerned of relying on the Court's interpretation of an EU provision. In Case C-577/08 *Rijksdienst voor Pensioenen v Brouwer* [2010] ECR I-7489, the Court acknowledged that

> [i]n addition to the existence of a risk of serious economic repercussions due in particular to the large number of legal relationships entered into in good faith on the basis of rules considered to be validly in force, an additional factor to take into account to justify the limitation of the temporal effects of the judgment is the existence of significant objective uncertainty regarding the implications of [Union] provisions. (para 36)

That being said, the Court has specified that financial consequences resulting from the preliminary ruling do not solely justify limiting the temporal effects of the ruling (Case C-209/03 *R, on the application of Bidar v London Borough of Ealing and Secretary of State for Education and Skills* [2005] ECR I-2119, para 68) as this would diminish the judicial protection of the rights individuals have under EU law (Case C-35/97 *Commission v France* [1998] ECR I-5325, para 52).

Further references regarding the same case are allowed by the national court, as the Court explained in Case 14/86 *Pretore di Salò v Persons unknown* [1987] ECR 2545:

> … the fact that judgments delivered on the basis of references for a preliminary ruling are binding on the national courts does not preclude the national court to which such a judgment is addressed from making a further reference to the Court of Justice if it considers it necessary in order to give judgment in the main proceedings. Such a reference may be justified when the national court encounters difficulties in understanding or applying the judgment, when it refers a fresh question of law to the Court, or again when it submits new considerations which might lead the Court to give a different answer to a question submitted earlier. (para 12)

The preliminary ruling must also be taken into consideration by all courts in all Member States of the EU (Case 66/80 *International Chemical Corporation v Amministrazione delle Finanze* [1981] ECR 1191) and may be treated as authoritative. This is explained by the fact that the ruling is meant to declare and interpret pre-existing law. The Court has nonetheless never meant to attribute general binding force to interpretative preliminary rulings.

In the case of an EU act being declared invalid, the CFI explained in Case T-220/97 *H & R Ecroyd Holdings Ltd v Commission* [1999] ECR II-1677 that

> … [the Court's] decision has the legal effect of requiring the competent [Union] institutions to adopt the measures necessary to remedy that illegality … In those

circumstances, they are to take the measures that are required in order to comply with the judgment containing the ruling in the same way as they are, under Article [266 TFEU], in the case of a judgment annulling a measure or declaring that the failure of a [Union] institution to act is unlawful … [W]hen a [Union] measure is held to be invalid by a preliminary ruling, the obligation laid down by Article [266 TFEU] applies by analogy. (para 49)

9.8 Further reading

Anagnostaras AG, 'Preliminary Problems and Jurisdiction Uncertainties: The Admissibility of Questions Referred by Bodies Performing Quasi-Judicial Functions' (2005) 30 *EL Rev* 878.

Bermann GA, 'New Frontiers in the Relationship between National and European Courts' (2008-2009) 32 *Fordham International Law Journal* 525.

Bobek M, 'Learning to Talk: Preliminary Rulings, the Courts of the Member States and the Court of Justice' (2008) 45 *CML Rev* 1611.

Broberg M, 'The Preliminary Reference Procedure and Questions of International and National Law' (2009) 28 *Yearbook of European Law* 362.

Broberg M and Fenger N, *Preliminary References to the European Court of Justice*, 2nd edn (OUP, 2014).

Komarek J, 'In the Court(s) we Trust? On the Need for Hierarchy and Differentiation in the Preliminary Ruling Procedure' (2007) 32 *EL Rev* 467.

Lenaerts K, 'The Rule of Law and the Coherence of the Judicial System of the European Union' (2007) 44 *CML Rev* 1625.

Lenz CO, 'The Role and Mechanism of the Preliminary Ruling Procedure' (1994) 18 *Fordham International Law Journal* 388.

Tridimas T, 'Knocking on Heaven's Door: Fragmentation, Efficiency and Defiance in the Preliminary Reference Procedure' (2003) 40 *CML Rev* 9.

Tridimas T, 'Constitutional Review of Member State Action: The Virtues and Vices of an Incomplete Jurisdiction' (2011) 9 *ICON* 737.

summary

Provided certain requirements are fulfilled, the preliminary ruling procedure enables national courts and tribunals to ask the CJEU to interpret EU Treaties and acts, as well as to determine the validity of EU acts. Unless their judgment is final, national courts have discretion to determine whether it is necessary or not to make a referral to the CJEU. This is not deemed necessary when the CJEU has already answered the question, or where the answer to the question is so obvious as to leave no room for doubt. Because the CJEU does not act as an appeal court and does not deal with the facts of the case pending before the referring court, its answer is formulated in abstract terms so as to leave the concrete application of the law to the national court.

You are the chair of a professional arbitration tribunal that deals with complaints stemming from members of the Association of Chiropractors. Decisions of this tribunal are legally binding. Next week you are to hear a case brought by a disabled employee involving an allegation of discrimination, contrary to a recently enacted domestic Utopian law that was passed to implement an (imaginary) EU Directive. The employee concerned is being supported by a pressure group, because it is hoped that the case will publicise the issue of disabled rights. The employer concerned is a medium size private company. The company's lawyer is apparently intending to raise questions about the validity of the EU Directive and the legal definition of 'disability' in the Directive. There is a right of appeal from decisions of the Tribunal to the Employment Appeal Tribunal, but only on a point of law.

1   Are you entitled to make a request for a preliminary reference? If so, are you obliged to make such a request?
2   Would your answer to the questions above differ if the CJEU had already given a judgment on the meaning of the term 'disability' in the Directive?
3   At which stage of the proceedings would it be best to make such a request?
4   If you were to use your powers, how would you formulate your request to ensure that you are provided with an adequate answer?
5   What kind of answer do you expect from the CJEU?

chapter 10

Judicial Supervision of European Union Institutions

After reading this chapter, you will be able to understand:
- the different judicial actions available to ensure that EU institutions act in compliance with the Treaties
- the judicial review process and the hurdles faced by individuals in seeking such review
- the possibility of invoking a plea of illegality while proceedings are engaged under another procedure
- the opportunity for institutions and individuals to spur the EU into action by alleging that it has failed to act despite its obligation to do so
- the conditions under which the EU's extra-contractual liability is engaged.

10.1 Introduction

The TFEU gives the EU institutions wide powers to adopt legislation. As a result, it would have been incompatible with the legal traditions of the Member States and with the rule of law for these powers to escape judicial control. Whilst it is hoped that they carry out their functions in the way specified in the Treaty and according to general principles of EU law (see Article 13(1) and (2) TEU), the possibility remains that they may act beyond their limited competences. To avoid this, Article 263 TFEU provides for a procedure for judicial review, and Article 277 TFEU allows a plea of illegality in proceedings engaged on a basis different from Article 263 TFEU. Furthermore, to oblige EU institutions to comply with their Treaty obligations, it is possible to lodge a complaint for failure to act under Article 265 TFEU. In cases where the EU institutions' actions and omissions have led to damage, individuals and institutions alike can have recourse to Article 340 TFEU and claim compensation.

10.2 Annulment of EU acts

Article 263 TFEU establishes a procedure known as the **action for annulment**, under which the CJEU may review the legality of any acts adopted by other institutions that are intended to have legal effects. Article 263 TFEU offers legal protection to those who are adversely affected by instruments that are or may be in fact illegal.

10.2.1 Reviewable acts

According to Article 263, first paragraph TFEU:

> The Court of Justice of the European Union shall review the legality of legislative acts, of acts of the Council, of the Commission and of the European Central Bank, other than recommendations and opinions, and of acts of the European Parliament and of the European Council intended to produce legal effects vis-à-

vis third parties. It shall also review the legality of acts of bodies, offices or agencies of the Union intended to produce legal effects vis-à-vis third parties.

In other words, the following acts may be challenged:

(a) legislative acts of the European Parliament and Council, acts of the Council, of the Commission and of the European Central Bank in the form of regulations, directives and decisions, but not recommendations or opinions since they are not intended to have legally binding force;

(b) acts of the European Parliament and the European Council that have legal effects on third parties;

(c) acts of bodies, offices and agencies that have legal effects on third parties.

All acts and measures that are intended to have legally binding force, ie have an effect on someone's legal rights, may be reviewed, eg acts of the Council (Case 22/70 *Commission of the European Communities v Council of the European Communities (ERTA)* [1971] ECR 263) or of the Commission (Case 8-11/66 *SA Cimenteries CBR Cementsbedrijven NV and others v Commission (Noordwijks Cement Accord)* [1967] ECR 75). Regulatory acts may also be challenged according to Article 263, fourth paragraph TFEU. Acts that cannot be reviewed are, for example, informal communications such as telex messages, unless they have legal effects, and internal instructions, unless they are in fact decisions, etc.

10.2.2 Grounds of review

Article 263, second paragraph TFEU provides that

> [the Court] shall for this purpose have jurisdiction in actions brought ... on grounds of lack of competence, infringement of an essential procedural requirement, infringement of this Treaty or of any rule of law relating to its application, or misuse of powers.

See **Figure 10.1**.

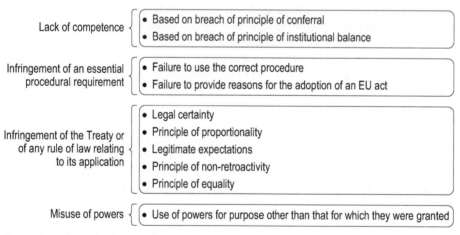

Figure 10.1   Grounds of review of EU acts

10.2.2.1 Lack of competence

Equivalent to the concept of substantive *ultra vires* in English law, the review of EU law for excess of power extends to primary and secondary law. The review of primary legislation originates in the **principle of conferral** (see 3.2.1). With regard to secondary legislation, the Court of Justice not only may review whether the institution has acted within the scope of the powers delegated, but must also ensure that the absolute limits to such a delegation have not been violated. This follows from the **principle of institutional balance** (see 2.2.1 and 5.2.1). This is well illustrated in Case C-327/91 *France v Commission* [1994] ECR I-3641, in which France successfully challenged, on the ground of lack of competence, an act of the Commission seeking to conclude an agreement with the USA on the application of EC and US competition laws. Under former Article 228(1) TEEC, the power to conclude the agreement belonged to the Council (the whole procedure of negotiation and conclusion of international agreements is now covered by Article 218 TFEU).

10.2.2.2 Infringement of an essential procedural requirement

This ground is equivalent to procedural impropriety in English law. The Court has specified that an essential procedural step is breached when the EU adopts an act under a procedure that leaves out an institution that was entitled to be involved (Case 17/74 *Transocean Marine Paint Association v Commission* [1974] ECR 1063; Case 138/79 *SA Roquette Frères v Council* [1980] ECR 3333).

Also, not providing reasons for the adoption of an EU measure is considered an infringement of an essential procedural requirement. In Case C-378/00 *Commission v European Parliament and Council* [2003] ECR I-937 the Court explained:

> First, the statement of reasons for [a Union] measure must appear in that measure (see, to that effect, Case C-291/98 P *Sarrió v Commission* [2000] ECR I-9991, paragraphs 73 and 75) and, second, it must be adopted by the author of the measure (see, to that effect, Case C-137/92 P *Commission v BASF* [1994] ECR I-2555, paragraph 67), so that, in the present case, a declaration adopted by the Council alone cannot in any event serve as a statement of reasons for a regulation adopted jointly by the Parliament and the Council ... (para 66)

What is more, the statement of reasons must fulfil some substantial requirements. In Joined Cases C-27/00 and 122/00 *R v Secretary of State for the Environment, Transport and the Regions, ex parte Omega Air* [2002] ECR I-2569, the Court spelled out that

> ... it should be borne in mind that it is settled case-law that the statement of reasons required by Article [263 TFEU] must be adapted to the nature of the act in question. It must disclose in a clear and unequivocal fashion the reasoning followed by the [Union] institution which adopted the measure in such a way as to make the persons concerned aware of the reasons for the measure and to enable the Court to exercise its power of review. It follows from the case-law that it is not necessary for details of all relevant factual and legal aspects to be given. The question whether the statement of the grounds for an act meets the requirements of Article [263 TFEU] must be assessed with regard not only to its wording but also to its context and to all the legal rules governing the matter in question. ...
>
> The Court has also held that if the contested measure clearly discloses the essential objective pursued by the institution, it would be excessive to require a specific statement of reasons for the various technical choices made ...

... [T]he statement of reasons in a regulation of general application cannot be required to specify the various facts, frequently very numerous and complex, on the basis of which the regulation was adopted, nor a fortiori to provide a more or less complete evaluation of those facts ... That is particularly the case where the relevant factual and technical elements are well known to the circles concerned. (paras 46–47 and 51)

10.2.2.3 Infringement of the Treaty or of any rule of law relating to its application

Under this heading the Court of Justice has examined cases whereby the general principles of EU law were breached. The introduction of these principles (see 4.5) has added a substantive dimension to the rule of law in the EU. It has been used to review the content of EU legislation against notably fundamental rights. Among the general principles of EU law are:

(a) *Legal certainty* (Case 169/80 *Gondrand Frères and Garancini* [1981] ECR 1931 and Case C-439/01 *Cipra and Kvasnicka v Bezirkshauptmannschaft Mistelbach* [2003] ECR I-745). The principle of legal certainty, which is a general principle of EU law (see 4.5), requires that the law be certain, clear and precise as well as predictable.

(b) *Legitimate expectations* (Case 120/86 *Mulder v Minister van Landbouw en Visserij* [1988] ECR 2321 and Joined Cases C-104/89 and 37/90 *Mulder and Others v Council and Commission* [1992] ECR I-3061). This principle has its roots in the principles of legal certainty and good faith. The idea is that if someone acts and follows in good faith the law, they should not be frustrated in their expectations. In other words, it is not possible for an EU institution to renege on its earlier position.

(c) *Non-retroactivity*. Whilst the Court protects the principle of non-retroactivity (Case 63/83 *R v Kirk* [1984] ECR 2689), it accepts that exceptionally some EU measures can take effect from a point in time before their publication (Case 98/78 *Racke v Hauptzollamt Mainz* [1979] ECR 69).

(d) *Proportionality* (Case C-491/01 *R v Secretary of State, ex parte British American Tobacco* [2002] ECR I-11453) (see 3.4.2).

(e) *Equality* (Case 61/77 *Commission v Ireland* [1978] ECR 417), which is now integrated in Articles 18 and 19(1) TFEU. The principle of equality means that different cases must not be treated in the same way, save where there is an adequate justification.

10.2.2.4 Misuse of powers

This ground is equivalent to that of improper purpose in English law. The rationale behind it is the prohibition on pursuing an objective that is different from the one underpinning the legal competence (Case 105/75 *Giuffrida v Council* [1976] ECR 1395). The Court has further clarified, in Case C-491/01 *R v Secretary of State, ex parte British American Tobacco* [2002] ECR I-11453, that

... a measure is vitiated by misuse of powers only if it appears on the basis of objective, relevant and consistent evidence to have been taken with the exclusive or main purpose of achieving an end other than that stated or evading a procedure specifically prescribed by the Treaty for dealing with the circumstances of the case (Case C-331/88 *Fedesa et al* [1990] ECR I-4023, para 24; Case C-156/93 *Parliament v Commission* [1995] ECR I-2019, para 31; and Case C-48/96 P

Windpark Groothusen v Commission [1998] ECR I-2873, para 52, and Case C-110/
97 *Netherlands v Council* [2001] ECR I-8763, para 137). (para 189)

10.2.3   Time limits

Article 263, sixth paragraph TFEU stipulates that

> The proceedings provided for in this Article shall be instituted *within two months*
> of the publication of the measure, or of its notification to the plaintiff, or, in the
> absence thereof, of the day on which it came to the knowledge of the latter, as the
> case may be. (emphasis added)

This is supplemented by Article 59 of the Rules of Procedure of the General Court (see
Chapter 8), which specifies:

> Where the time limit allowed for initiating proceedings against a measure
> adopted by an institution runs from the publication of that measure in the *Official
> Journal of the European Union*, that time limit shall be calculated, for the purposes
> of Article 58(1)(a), from the end of the fourteenth day after such publication.

As a result, the Court has clearly spelled out that the main criteria are the date of
publication in the *Official Journal* for regulations and directives, or the date of
notification if the measure is a decision addressed to the applicant. If, and only if,
neither of those applies will the Court look at the date when the measure came to the
applicant's attention:

> It is clear simply from the wording of that provision [Article 263] that the
> criterion of the day on which a measure came to the knowledge of an applicant, as
> the starting point of the period prescribed for instituting proceedings, is
> subsidiary to the criteria of publication or notification of the measure. (Case
> C-122/95 *Germany v Council* [1998] ECR I-973, para 35)

Based on the **principle of legal certainty**, the Court has refused to adopt a wide
interpretation of the Treaty with regard to the time limit, as can be seen in Joined Cases
T-121/96 and 151/96 *Mutual Aid Administration Services NV v Commission* [1997] ECR
II-1355:

> It is settled case-law that the time-limit prescribed for bringing actions under
> Article [263] of the Treaty is a matter of public policy and is not subject to the
> discretion of the parties or the Court, since it was established in order to ensure
> that legal positions are clear and certain and to avoid any discrimination or
> arbitrary treatment in the administration of justice ... (para 38)

That being said, the Court has granted some protection to individuals. For example, in
Case C-143/95 P *Commission v Sociedade de Curtumes a Sul do Tejo Lda (Socurte) and
Others* [1997] ECR I-1, it has declared that the notification must meet certain
requirements:

> ... notification of the [EU] acts referred to in [Article 263] and Article [297
> TFEU] necessarily involves the communication of a detailed account of the
> contents of the measure notified and of the reasons on which it is based. In the
> absence of such an account, the third party concerned would be denied precise
> knowledge of the contents of the act in question and of the reasons for which it
> was adopted, which would enable him to bring proceedings effectively against
> that decision. (para 31)

10.2.4 *Locus standi* – who may seek annulment of an EU act?

Annulment proceedings may be brought by three categories of applicants (see **Figure 10.2**). The distinction between the members of each category lies in the nature of the interest they must show in order to establish a right to bring an action.

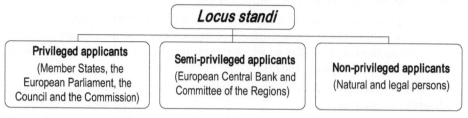

Figure 10.2   Locus standi in annulment proceedings

The purpose of *locus standi*, which is separate from the merits of the action, is to prevent the Court being swamped and the legislation process being disrupted by a large number of challenges to the legality of legislation. The balance between this consideration and the rule of law can be a hard one to strike and a strict approach to standing is likely to be controversial, as is the case in the context of EU law.

10.2.4.1   Privileged applicants

Article 263, second paragraph TFEU specifies that the Court

> shall for this purpose [of review of EU acts] have jurisdiction in actions brought by a Member State, the European Parliament, the Council or the Commission …

The first category of applicants is called 'privileged' because they are exempt from any rule on standing. Member States, the European Parliament, the Council and the Commission have an automatic right to challenge any binding EU act.

10.2.4.2   Semi-privileged applicants

Article 263, third paragraph TFEU provides:

> The Court shall have jurisdiction under the same conditions in actions brought by the Court of Auditors and by the European Central Bank and by the Committee of the Regions for the purpose of protecting their prerogatives.

This second category of applicants is referred to as 'semi-privileged' because they are allowed to bring an action for annulment only for the purpose of protecting their prerogatives, which include the right to participate in the decision-making process as and when provided by the TFEU.

10.2.4.3   Non-privileged applicants

Article 263, fourth paragraph TFEU gives individuals the right to request the judicial review of a European Union act:

> Any natural or legal person may, under the conditions laid down in the first and second paragraphs, institute proceedings against an act addressed to that person or which is of *direct and individual concern* to them, and against a *regulatory act which is of direct concern to them and does not entail implementing measures.* (emphasis added)

This third category of applicant is the most controversial, comprising 'natural persons' (individuals) and 'legal persons' (bodies with legal personality). Whilst the definition of a natural person is uncontested, the Court has set certain requirements for applicants to qualify as a legal person. In Case T-161/94 *Sinochem Heilongjiang v Council* [1996] ECR II-695 the Court explained:

> ... It is settled law that, under the [Union] judicial system, an applicant is a legal person if, at the latest by the expiry of the period prescribed for proceedings to be instituted, it has acquired legal personality in accordance with the law governing its constitution ... or if it has been treated as an independent legal entity by the [Union] institutions. ... (para 31)

These applicants are called 'non-privileged' because they have to satisfy strict standing requirements in order to establish their right to challenge an EU act. The Court's approach to the interpretation of those requirements has not been entirely consistent, but the general effect of the case law is to make it extremely difficult for non-privileged applicants to challenge acts other than decisions addressed to them. It should also be noted that most applications stem from this group.

There is a striking contrast between the importance attached by the Court of Justice to the individual in the context of the rights he or she enjoys against the Member States through **direct effect** (6.3) and **State liability** (7.3), and its approach to the right of individuals to bring annulment proceedings. It can be argued that the Court's case law has not kept pace with developments in many national systems where rules on standing have been progressively relaxed.

An interest in bringing proceedings must be clearly demonstrated by an individual applicant. In Joined Cases T-480/93 and T-483/93 *Antillean Rice Mills v Commission* [1995] ECR II-2305, the Court noted:

> It is settled law that a claim for annulment is not admissible unless the applicant has an interest in seeing the contested measure annulled ... Such an interest can be present only if the annulment of the measure is of itself capable of having legal consequences ...
>
> In that regard, it must be borne in mind that, under Article [266 TFEU], an institution whose act has been declared void is required to take the necessary measures to comply with the judgment. Those measures do not concern the elimination of the act as such from the [Union] legal order, since that is the very essence of its annulment by the Court. They involve, rather, the removal of the effects of the illegalities found in the judgment annulling the act. The annulment of an act which has already been implemented or which has in the meantime been repealed from a certain date is thus still capable of having legal consequences. Such annulment places a duty on the institution concerned to take the necessary measures to comply with the judgment. The institution may thus be required to take adequate steps to restore the applicant to its original situation or to avoid the adoption of an identical measure ... (paras 59 and 60)

Whilst, before the entry into force of the Treaty of Lisbon in 2009, natural or legal persons had to prove that the decision was addressed to them, or that the decision was in the form of a regulation or a decision addressed to another person, but was of direct and individual concern to them, Article 263 TFEU refers to an 'act', thereby dropping the distinction between regulations and decisions. Consequently, there are now three types of EU act that an applicant may challenge (see **Figure 10.3**):

(a) an act addressed to the individual;

(b) an act of direct and individual concern to the applicant; and

(c) a regulatory act of direct concern, with no implementing measures.

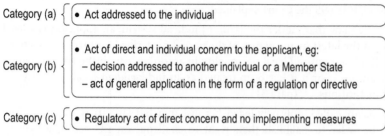

Figure 10.3 *Categories of acts that may be challenged by an applicant*

Category (a) remains unchanged and is fairly straightforward, in that a legal or natural person may challenge an act (an individual decision) addressed to that person.

As regards category (b), the expression 'direct and individual concern' remains unchanged in the Treaty. In Case 25/62 *Plaumann & Co v Commission* [1963] ECR 95, the Court explained that an act could be challenged by an individual if it could be proved that the act at issue was of *direct* and *individual* concern to the applicant. Recent case law shows that the *Plaumann* jurisprudence is still valid. In Case T-259/10 *Ax v Council* [2011] ECR II-176, the Court has reiterated and applied the 'direct and individual concern' test. That being said, the Court sometimes does not clearly separate the two elements (eg Case T-351/09 *Acetificio Marcello de Nigris Srl v Commission* [2011] ECR II-216).

In Case 25/62 *Plaumann v Commission* [1963] ECR 95, the German Government had asked the Commission for permission to suspend the collection of taxes on imports of clementines into Germany from non-Member States. The Commission refused. The applicant, Mr Plaumann, an importer of clementines, challenged the decision of the Commission, which had been addressed to the German Government. The Court explained that

[p]ersons other than those to whom a decision is addressed may only claim to be individually concerned if that decision affects them by reason of certain attributes which are peculiar to them or by reason of circumstances in which they are differentiated from all other persons and by virtue of these factors distinguishes them individually just as in the case of the person addressed. In the present case the applicant is affected by the disputed decision as an importer of clementines, that is to say, by reason of a commercial activity which may at any time be practised by any person and is not therefore such as to distinguish the applicant in relation to the contested decision as in the case of the addressee. (at 107)

The act must be of 'direct concern', which is defined as an act that:

(a) directly affects the legal position and rights of the individual; and

(b) does not endow the national authorities with any discretionary power (margin of appreciation) with regard to the implementation of the act.

In relation to the first requirement, the Court explained in Joined Cases 41–44/70 *NV International Fruit Company v Commission* [1971] ECR 411 that there is no need to show the existence of a direct causal link between the challenged EU act and the impact on the individual, but only that the act directly affects the complainant. In relation to the second requirement, the Court stated in Case 294/83 *Parti Ecologiste 'Les Verts' v European Parliament* [1986] ECR 1339 that

> [a] measure will be of direct concern to an applicant where it constitutes 'a complete set of rules which are sufficient in themselves and which require no implementing provisions', since in such circumstances the application of the measure 'is automatic and leaves no room for any discretion.' (para 31)

Indeed, if the national authorities had some discretionary power then the act could be challenged at the national level. To sum it up, in Case C-486/01 P *Front National v European Parliament* [2004] ECR I-6289 the Court clarified that

> ... it is appropriate to bear in mind that, by virtue of settled case-law, the condition that the decision forming the subject-matter of the proceedings must be of 'direct concern' to a natural or legal person, as it is stated in the fourth paragraph of Article [263 TFEU], requires the [Union] measure complained of *to affect directly the legal situation of the individual and leave no discretion to the addressees of that measure, who are entrusted with the task of implementing it, such implementation being purely automatic and resulting from [EU] rules without the application of other intermediate rules.* (para 34, emphasis added)

Further, the concern must be 'individual'. The Court will consider the concern to be 'individual'

> ... only if the act affects [the individual] by reason of certain attributes peculiar to them or by reason of a factual situation which differentiates them from all other persons and thereby distinguishes them individually in the same way as the addressee. (Case T-49/07 *Fahas v Council* [2010] ECR II-5559, para 33)

This means that the expression 'individual concern' is to be defined narrowly, in the sense that it covers a limited and identifiable group (Joined Cases 106 and 107/63 *Toepfer und Getreide-Import Gesellschaft v Commission* [1965] ECR 405). Clearly, individuals must prove that they are in a position that distinguishes them from other persons. This was again spelled out in Case 26/86 *Deutz und Geldermann, Sektkellerei Breisach (Baden) GmbH v Council* [1987] ECR 941:

> In order for a measure to be of individual concern to the persons to whom it applies, it must affect their legal position because of a factual situation which differentiates them from all other persons and distinguishes them individually in the same way as a person to whom it is addressed. (para 9)

And in Case C-309/89 *Codorníu SA v Council* [1994] ECR I-1853:

> Codorniu registered the graphic trade mark 'Gran Cremant de Codorniu' in Spain in 1924 and traditionally used that mark both before and after registration. By reserving the right to use the term 'crémant' to French and Luxembourg producers, the contested provision prevents Codorniu from using its graphic trade mark.
>
> It follows that Codorniu has established the existence of a situation which from the point of view of the contested provision differentiates it from all other traders. (paras 21 and 22)

However, if the measure affects all individuals in a similar manner, the measure cannot be said to be of individual concern. For example, in Case T-99/94 *Asociación Española de Empresas de la Carne v Council* [1994] ECR II-871, the Court stressed that

... [u]nlike the regulation in question in Case C-309/89 [*Codorniu*] ... the directive now under consideration has not affected specific rights of the applicant or its members.

On the contrary, the applicant and its members are – like all traders in the [Union] operating in the sector in question – subject to the national measures adopted for the purposes of transposing the directive. (paras 20–21)

The *Plaumann* test has on numerous occasions been considered unduly restrictive. Advocate General Jacobs, in Case C-50/00 P *Unión de Pequeños Agricultores v Council* [2002] ECR I-6677, suggested a new test:

The only satisfactory solution is ... to recognise that an applicant is individually concerned by [an EU] measure where the measure has, or is liable to have, a substantial adverse effect on his interests. (para 102)

This was accepted by the General Court in Case T-177/01 *Jégo-Quéré et Cie SA v Commission* [2002] ECR II-2365:

... [I]n order to ensure effective judicial protection for individuals, a natural or legal person is to be regarded as individually concerned by [an EU] measure of general application that concerns him directly if the measure in question affects his legal position, in a manner which is both definite and immediate, by restricting his rights or by imposing obligations on him. The number and position of other persons who are likewise affected by the measure, or who may be so, are of no relevance in that regard. (para 51)

The Court of Justice refused to follow the opinion of the Advocate General for two main reasons:

... [I]t is for the Member States to establish a system of legal remedies and procedures which ensure respect for the right to effective judicial protection.

... [I]n accordance with the principle of sincere cooperation laid down in Article [4] of the Treaty, national courts are required, so far as possible, to interpret and apply national procedural rules governing the exercise of rights of action in a way that enables natural and legal persons to challenge before the courts the legality of any decision or other national measure relative to the application to them of a [Union] act of general application, by pleading the invalidity of such an act. ...

While it is, admittedly, possible to envisage a system of judicial review of the legality of [Union] measures of general application different from that established by the founding Treaty and never amended as to its principles, it is for the Member States, if necessary, in accordance with Article 48 [TEU], to reform the system currently in force. (paras 41–42 and 45)

In paras 41 and 42 of the judgment, the Court confirms that individuals can still use national remedies, a position it reiterated in the *Acetificio* case (above). The Court also refers in para 45 to its inability to offer a different interpretation of the relevant provision. Although the Court acknowledges that there must be some form of effective judicial remedy, it does not believe that it can go beyond the wording of the Article (see, eg, *Acetificio*), and has explained in Case T-18/10 *Inuit Tapiriit Kanatami v European Parliament and Council* [2011] ECR II-5599 that

[a]ccording to settled case-law, the Courts of the European Union may not, without exceeding their jurisdiction, interpret the conditions under which an individual may institute proceedings against a regulation in a way which has the

effect of setting aside those conditions, expressly laid down in the Treaty, even in the light of the principle of effective judicial protection. (para 51)

That being said, as the Charter of Fundamental Rights of the European Union is now legally binding, it is possible that individuals might challenge the strict test imposed by the Court, pleading that it fails to provide them with an effective remedy, as required under Article 47, first paragraph, of the Charter.

As mentioned above, to some extent it is sometimes possible for non-privileged applicants to contest the validity of EU acts in the national courts instead of seeking their annulment in Luxembourg. Indeed, under the Article 267 TFEU procedure (see **Chapter 9**), national courts can question the validity of EU acts. This system has an array of advantages, in that, indirect challenges:

(a) can be brought against any Union act (even those of a non-binding nature), on any grounds (even those outside Article 263, second paragraph TFEU);

(b) can be launched by anyone (without regard to the 'direct and individual concern' test); and

(c) can be brought at any time.

Nonetheless, the Court held in Case C-188/92 *TWD Textilwerke Deggendorf v Germany* [1994] ECR I-833 that this option was not available when the applicant could clearly have challenged the act in annulment proceedings but failed to do so before the expiry of the two-month time limit laid down in Article 263 TFEU. Where the applicant's standing is uncertain, the Court is, however, more generous (Case C-408/95 *Eurotunnel SA and Others v SeaFrance* [1997] ECR I-6315).

The downsides of indirect review are numerous too. For example:

(a) the preliminary reference procedure under Article 267 TFEU can be used only if a national court has jurisdiction, and this may not be the case where there are no national implementing acts to challenge;

(b) the applicant may need to breach EU law before challenging the legality of the act on which the illegal behaviour rests;

(c) individual applicants have no right to demand indirect review of EU law, as it is left in the hands of the national courts to decide whether it is necessary to ask for a preliminary reference (see **Chapter 9**).

The dividing line between the second (b) and third (c) categories of EU acts that may be challenged has become the new legal battlefield post-Lisbon. The third category of acts, category (c), that may be challenged by non-privileged applicants is new, inasmuch as regulatory acts are a new type of measure introduced by the Treaty of Lisbon. There is no definition of a 'regulatory act' in the TFEU, and this has led a number of academics to suggest that it could be a regulation, a legislative act, an implementing act, etc. The General Court clarified the matter in the *Inuit* case (above) by stating that

> ... the meaning of 'regulatory act' for the purposes of the fourth paragraph of Article 263 TFEU must be understood as covering all acts of general application apart from legislative acts. (para 56)
>
> [The] categorisation [of an act] as a legislative act or a regulatory act according to the FEU Treaty is based on the criterion of the procedure, legislative or not, which led to its adoption. (para 65)

This definition has been criticised for taking a procedural, rather than substantive, approach. Provided that they are of general application, acts adopted under the comitology procedure (see **4.3**) can be classed as regulatory acts (eg Case T-262/10 *Microban International Ltd and Microban (Europe) Ltd v Commission* [2011] ECR II-7697). It is also likely that measures adopted pursuant to other forms of *ad hoc* procedures by the Commission qualify as regulatory acts. Likewise delegated acts adopted pursuant to Article 290 TFEU can be understood as regulatory acts, since the Treaty expressly specifies that these are 'non-legislative acts of general application' and clearly distinguishes them from legislative acts.

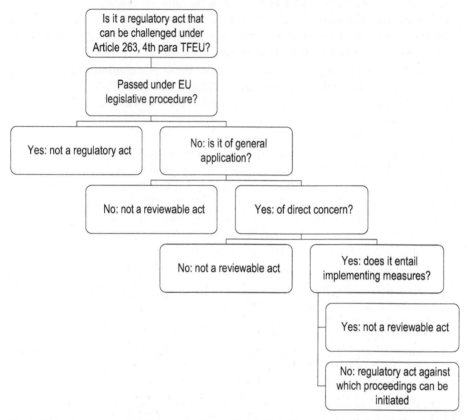

Figure 10.4   Summary of regulatory acts that may be challenged under Article 263, fourth paragraph TFEU

It must be noted that for this category, the act only needs to be of direct concern to the individual. The definition used of 'direct concern' is the same as the one for category (b). There is no requirement that the act be of individual concern. This may lead to some absurd results. Indeed, a prohibition included in a non-legislative act could be challenged on the basis that it is only of direct concern, whilst the same prohibition enshrined in a legislative act would need to be challenged on the basis that it is of direct *and* individual concern to the applicant.

In addition to being of 'direct concern', the regulatory act in question does not entail any implementing measures. In Case C-274/12 *Telefónica SA v Commission*, 19 December 2013, ECLI:EU:C:2013:852, the Court of Justice argued that the purpose of the introduction of this new wording to Article 263, fourth paragraph TFEU was to prevent an individual from being denied access to legal remedies. If the responsibility for the implementing measures lies with the Member State, the act may be challenged at the national level by claiming that it is invalid, thereby obliging the national court to request a preliminary ruling from the Court (see Chapter 9). Where the responsibility lies with EU institutions, the act may be challenged under Article 263 TFEU or by way of a plea of illegality under Article 277 TFEU (see below 10.4). If there are no such implementing measures then the act (provided it is a regulatory act) may be reviewed under Article 263, fourth paragraph TFEU.

When defining 'implementing measures', the Court explained that it needs to assess these measures by reference to the position of the applicant and the subject matter of the action (paras 30–31). For example, in *Microban* (above) the act did not entail any implementing measures as it prohibited with immediate effect the marketing of a substance without the need for Member States to take any action. See **Figure 10.4**.

10.2.5 Effect of annulment

By virtue of Article 264 TFEU:

> If the action is well founded, the Court of Justice of the European Union shall declare the act concerned to be void.
>
> However, the Court shall, if it considers this necessary, state which of the effects of the act which it has declared void shall be considered as definitive.

Furthermore, Article 266 TFEU specifies that

> The institution whose act has been declared void or whose failure to act has been declared contrary to the Treaties shall be required to take the necessary measures to comply with the judgment of the Court of Justice of the European Union.
>
> This obligation shall not affect any obligation which may result from the application of the second paragraph of Article 340.

An example of the application of Article 266 is Case C-13/83 *European Parliament v Council (Re Transport Policy)* [1985] ECR 1513. Moreover, in Case C-310/97 P *Commission v Assi Domän Kraft Products* [1999] ECR I-5363 the Court explained that:

> Where a number of similar individual decisions imposing fines have been adopted pursuant to a common procedure and only some addressees have taken legal action against the decisions concerning them and obtained their annulment, the principle of legal certainty … precludes any necessity for the institution which adopted the decisions to re-examine, at the request of other addressees, in the light of the grounds of the annulling judgment, the legality of the unchallenged decisions and to determine, on the basis of that examination, whether the fines paid must be refunded. (para 63)

If the EU institution fails to comply then the individual can start an action for damages on the basis of the EU non-contractual liability under Article 340 TFEU (see **10.5** below).

10.3 Failure to act

Failure to act is the counter-point to the annulment action examined in **10.2** above. Article 265 TFEU provides:

> Should the European Parliament, the European Council, the Council, the Commission or the European Central Bank, in infringement of the Treaties, fail to act, the Member States and the other institutions of the Union may bring an action before the Court of Justice to have the infringement established. This

Article shall apply, under the same conditions, to bodies, offices and agencies of the Union which fail to act.

The action shall be admissible only if the institution, body, office or agency concerned has first been called upon to act. If, within two months of being so called upon, the institution, body, office or agency concerned has not defined its position, the action may be brought within a further period of two months.

Any natural or legal person may, under the conditions laid down in the preceding paragraphs, complain to the Court that an institution, body, office or agency of the Union has failed to address to that person any act other than a recommendation or an opinion.

Institutions that are liable are the European Parliament, the European Council, the Council, the Commission and the European Central Bank, as well as the bodies, offices and agencies of the Union (see **Chapter 4**). Neither the Court of Auditors nor the CJEU can be liable for failure to act.

The acts that have failed to be adopted encompass acts similar to those covered under Article 263 TFEU, that is, legally binding acts as well as other acts such as preparatory acts (Case 377/87 *European Parliament v Council of the European Communities (Re Budgetary Procedure)* [1988] ECR 4045). In other words, the material scope of Article 265 TFEU is wider. Proceedings can be initiated in the CJEU where there is either a lack of action by, or a decision not to act taken by, one of the aforementioned institutions. However, the failure to adopt an act because it is rejected in the law-making procedure cannot be challenged before the Court (eg Case C-27/04 *Commission v Council (Re Deficit Procedure)* [2004] ECR I-6679, para 34).

The applicant must clearly pinpoint which specific act or action was expected to be taken, to the extent that the missing EU act can be 'identified individually'. For example:

> It follows that the Parliament's first claim, even if it is substantiated, can be upheld only in so far as the absence of a common transport policy with which the Council is charged is due to failure to take measures the scope of which can be sufficiently defined for them to be identified individually and adopted in compliance with the Court's judgment pursuant to Article [266]. (*Re Transport Policy,* para 37)

The aim of this procedure is to ensure the implementation of the Treaty. Indeed, the TFEU imposes positive legal duties upon EU institutions. Should they fail to carry out such duties it is possible to bring an action before the CJEU under Article 265 TFEU. It is thus imperative that the applicant shows that the Treaty obliges an institution to act. If the Treaty refers to an institution having only the right, rather than the duty, to take some action, the 'failure to act' procedure cannot be engaged. For example, in the enforcement proceedings under Article 258 TFEU (see **Chapter 7**) the Commission has a right but not a duty to commence judicial proceedings. Therefore, if the Commission does not start such proceedings, there is no possibility to commence an action under Article 265 TFEU (Case 247/87 *Start Fruit Company SA v Commission* [1989] ECR 291, paras 10–11). When there is institutional discretion the CJEU views it as excluding an obligation to act. In the light of the fact that the 'duties' specified in the Treaties are in reality 'powers', many applications are inadmissible.

Similar to, albeit different from, Article 263 TFEU, privileged and non-privileged applicants have *locus standi*. Privileged applicants – the EU Member States, the European Parliament, the Commission, the Council, the European Council and the European Central Bank – have an automatic and absolute right to bring an action. For example, the European Parliament brought an action for failure to act against the Council in 1985, for not having adopted a comprehensive Common Transport Policy (*Re Transport Policy*). This procedure allows EU institutions and Member States to become guardians of the Treaty, ensuing that what the Member States agreed by way of treaty is indeed implemented.

In contrast, natural and legal persons have limited standing, as they can lodge an application only if the institution has failed to address an act to them (other than an opinion or a recommendation). In other words, such applicants have to prove that they would have been the actual addressees (Case 246/81 *Bethell v Commission* [1982] ECR 2277). In fact the Court has made clear that the applicant must demonstrate direct and individual concern (Case C-107/91 *Empresa Nacional de Urânio SA v Commission* [1993] ECR I-599).

The procedure is divided into a pre-judicial or administrative phase, whereby the applicant must first call upon the institution to act within two months and indicate which measures the applicant would like the institution to take (Joined Cases 114–117/79 *Fournier and Others v Commission* [1980] ECR 1529, 1531). Only after giving the institution the opportunity to reply to this call can the applicant bring an action before the Court. Should the institution fail to define its position, the applicant has a further two months to bring an action. Given that the institution only needs to explain its position, very few actions under Article 265 TFEU have been successful.

In Case T-74/92 *Ladbroke Racing Deutschland GmbH v Commission* [1995] ECR II-115, Ladbroke asked the Commission to explain the denial of access for the televising of horse racing, which, it believed, breached competition rules under Articles 85 and 86 TEEC (now Articles 101 and 102 TFEU). As the Commission failed to clarify its position, Ladbroke brought an action under Article 175 TEEC (now Article 265 TFEU). The Court ruled that the Commission had

> failed to address to the applicant a measure other than a recommendation or an opinion, in so far as it failed either to initiate the procedure for establishing breach of Article [102] of the Treaty, so that a decision confirming such a breach could be adopted, or to dismiss the complaint after having sent the applicant a letter under Article 6 of Regulation No 99/63, or, finally, to make a duly reasoned decision not to pursue the complaint on the ground of lack of [EU] interest. (para 69)

This means that if an institution decides not to pursue an investigation or to act, this may in itself constitute a decision that can then be challenged as failure to act (Case C-39/93 *SFEI and others v Commission* [1994] ECR 2681, paras 27–28).

A ruling by the Court stating the failure to act obliges the institution to take the necessary measures under Article 266 TFEU (see **10.2.5** above):

> The effect of that declaration, under Article [266], is that the defendant institution is required to take the necessary measures to comply with the judgment of the Court, without prejudice to any actions to establish non-contractual liability to which the aforesaid declaration may give rise. (*Re Budgetary Procedure*, para 9)

That being said, the Court does not issue directions to the institutions or substitute itself for them (Case T-19/90 *Von Hoessle v Court of Auditors* [1991] ECR II-615, para 30). This means that the institutions are given discretion as to how best to implement the ruling. Further, a reasonable period of time is given to the particular institution to remedy the omission (*Re Transport Policy*, para 69).

10.4 Plea of illegality

Article 277 TFEU offers an additional, incidental form of action to Article 263 TFEU. It states:

> Notwithstanding the expiry of the period laid down in Article 263, sixth paragraph, any party may, in proceedings in which an act of general application adopted by an institution, body, office or agency of the Union is at issue, plead the grounds specified in Article 263, second paragraph, in order to invoke before the Court of Justice of the European Union the inapplicability of that act.

The provision may be used during proceedings (eg within the framework of enforcement proceedings under Article 258 TFEU (see **Chapter** 7)) before the CJEU only when the argument of illegality is brought forward in relation to the subject matter of the procedure. In practice, rather than being an action, it is an argument. As the Court has stressed in Joined Cases 87/77, 130/77, 22/83, 9/84 and 10/84 *Salerno and others v Commission and Council* [1985] ECR 2523:

> [T]he sole purpose of Article [277] is to protect parties against the application of an unlawful regulation where the regulation itself can no longer be challenged owing to the expiry of the period laid down in Article [263]. However, in allowing a party to plead the inapplicability of a regulation, Article [277] does not create an independent right of action; such a plea may only be raised indirectly in proceedings against an implementing measure, the validity of the regulation being challenged in so far as it constitutes the legal basis of that measure. (para 36)

Consequently, it is a collateral review of a parent act.

The plea of illegality is often used to challenge decisions based on EU regulations (parent act), the validity of which is questioned. Yet, to limit recourse to this type of plea, the Court has explained that whilst it allows for a party to raise this argument after the deadline set out in Article 263 TFEU has passed, it will not entertain such a plea if the party had the opportunity to challenge it earlier under Article 263 TFEU but failed to do so. For example, in Case 156/77 *Commission v Belgium* [1978] ECR 1881, the Court refused to consider the plea of illegality of a Member State addressee of a decision as this could have been done under Article 263 TFEU.

Generally, the Court has been reluctant to grant privileged applicants under Article 263 TFEU legal standing under Article 277 TFEU. Whereas the Court accepts that individuals faced with the hurdles of proving *locus standi* under Article 263 TFEU can use Article 277 TFEU on the basis that they were unable to challenge the act under Article 263 TFEU, it refuses to give standing to individuals under Article 277 TFEU if there is no doubt that they would have had *locus standi* under Article 263 TFEU (Case C-188/92 *TWD Textilwerke Deggendorf GmbH v Germany* [1994] ECR I-833). In other words, Article 277 TFEU compensates for the tight *locus standi* rules for non-privileged applicants under Article 263 TFEU (Case 92/78 *SpA Simmenthal v Commission* [1979] ECR 777, paras 39–41).

Furthermore, the Court will not examine such a plea if the matter is pending before a national court. Indeed, Article 277 TFEU should not be used as a means to make a direct request to the CJEU for a preliminary ruling (Joined Cases 31/62 and 33/62 *Milchwerke Heinz Wöhrmann & Sohn KG and Alfons Lütticke GmbH v Commission* [1962] ECR 155, at 507). This is to ensure a clear division of jurisdiction between the CJEU and the national courts.

Any act of general application capable of producing legally binding effects may be challenged. The grounds for review are identical to those under Article 263 TFEU (lack of competence, infringement of procedural requirement, infringement of the Treaty, misuse of power).

The effect of a successful plea of illegality is that the act is declared inapplicable to the applicant's case, though it is not annulled as it cannot be challenged under Article 263 TFEU any longer. However, to comply with a ruling under Article 266 TFEU, the institution that adopted the act often amends or repeals it.

10.5   Extra-contractual liability

The TFEU contains rules regarding the liability of the Union for damage caused by its institutions, which can mainly be divided into contractual liability (Article 340, first paragraph TFEU) and extra-contractual liability (Article 340, second paragraph TFEU).

Article 340, second paragraph TFEU provides that:

> In the case of non-contractual liability, the Union shall, in accordance with the general principles common to the laws of the Member States, make good any damage caused by its institutions or by its servants in the performance of their duties.

This is another mechanism to ensure that the European institutions act in accordance with EU law. As a result, Article 268 TFEU stipulates that:

> The Court of Justice of the European Union shall have jurisdiction in disputes relating to compensation for damage provided for in the second and third paragraphs of Article 340.

10.5.1   Admissibility of the action

Although EU liability is based on a Treaty provision, the Court has developed a regime of liability in accordance with the general principles common to the laws of the Member States (see **4.3**). In Joined Cases C-46 and 48/93 *Brasserie du Pêcheur SA v Germany and R v Secretary of State for Transport, ex parte Factortame Ltd and Others* [1996] ECR I-1029, the Court explained:

> The principle of the non-contractual liability of the [Union] expressly laid down in Article [340] of the Treaty is simply an expression of the general principle familiar to the legal systems of the Member States that an unlawful act or omission gives rise to an obligation to make good the damage caused. That provision also reflects the obligation on public authorities to make good damage caused in the performance of their duties. (para 29)

It is noteworthy that fault is not a prerequisite for liability. In fact, EU institutions may be held liable for any damage caused by a lawful act (however, this is not dealt with in this chapter). The aim of Article 340, second paragraph TFEU is to provide compensation for such damage, but not to obtain the abolition of the measure itself or oblige an institution to take action. Separate proceedings need to be lodged for these purposes.

Historically, what is now Article 340, second paragraph TFEU could be invoked only if it had been preceded by a successful annulment action under what is now Article 263 TFEU (*Plaumann* (see **10.2.4.3**), at 108). This link was removed in Case 5/71 *Aktien-Zuckerfabrik Schöppenstedt v Council* [1971] ECR 975, the Court describing what is now Article 340, second paragraph as an autonomous form of action against acts of the EU institutions:

> The action for damages provided for by Articles [268] and [340], paragraph 2, of the Treaty was introduced as an autonomous form of action, with a particular purpose to fulfil within the system of actions and subject to conditions on its use dictated by its specific nature. It differs from an application for annulment in that its end is not the abolition of a particular measure, but compensation for damage caused by an institution in the performance of its duties. (para 3)

Similarly, what is now Article 340, second paragraph TFEU could not be invoked if it had not been preceded by a successful ruling declaring that an EU institution had failed to act. This bond between Article 340, second paragraph TFEU and Article 265 TFEU was removed in Case 4/69 *Alfons Lütticke GmbH v Commission* [1971] ECR 325 (see para 6).

The parties involved are the party who suffered damage and the specific institution whose action or omission is at issue. In contrast to other forms of actions against EU institutions, there are no limitations as to who can bring such an action (Case 118/83 *CMC Cooperativa muratori e cementisti and others v Commission* [1985] ECR 2325, para 31):

> Any person who claims to have been injured by such acts or conduct must therefore have the possibility of bringing an action, if he is able to establish liability, that is, the existence of damage caused by an illegal act or by illegal conduct on the part of the [Union].

Action must, however, be brought against an official act of an institution of the Union or its civil servants. In Case C-370/89 *Société Générale d'Entreprises Electro-Mécaniques SA (SGEEM) and Etroy v European Investment Bank* [1992] ECR I-6211, the Court clarified that a broad definition must be given to the word 'institution'. As a result, proceedings may also be brought against the European Ombudsman (Case C-234/02 P *European Ombudsman v Lamberts* [2004] ECR I-2838). Furthermore, the act must be attributable to a specific institution or institutions (see eg Case T-383/00 *Beamglow Ltd v European Parliament and Others* [2005] ECR II-5465) and not to the EU as a whole (Joined Cases 63 to 69/72 *Werhahn Hansamühle and others v Council* [1973] ECR 1229) or to the Member States (Case 169/73 *Compagnie Continentale France v Council* [1975] ECR 117).

In accordance with Article 46 of the Statute of the Court of Justice, an applicant needs to start proceedings within five years from the time of the injury. Article 46 also stipulates:

> The period of limitation shall be interrupted if proceedings are instituted before the Court of Justice or if prior to such proceedings an application is made by the aggrieved party to the relevant institution of the Union. In the latter event the proceedings must be instituted within the period of two months provided for in Article 263 of the Treaty on the Functioning of the European Union; the provisions of the second paragraph of Article 265 of the Treaty on the Functioning of the European Union shall apply where appropriate.

However, the Court has interpreted that provision in Case 145/83 *Adams v Commission* [1985] ECR 3539

> as meaning that the expiry of the limitation period cannot constitute a valid defence to a claim by a person who has suffered damage where that person only

belatedly became aware of the event giving rise to it and thus could not have had a reasonable time in which to submit his application to the Court or to the relevant institution before the expiry of the limitation period. (para 50)

10.5.2 Requirements for a right to damages

The history of the criteria to be fulfilled for an action for damages for EU liability has been rather confusing. This is mainly due to the fact that, as with judicial review under Article 263 TFEU (**10.2** above), the Court of Justice was initially very wary of actions being brought against EU institutions. That being said, following its *Francovich* ruling on Member State liability (Joined Cases C-6 and 9/90 *Francovich v Italy* [1991] ECR I-5357; see **7.3**), the Court has attempted to simplify and to unify Member State and EU liability regimes.

The initial requirements for liability were specified in *Alfons Lütticke* (**10.5.1** above):

> By virtue of the second paragraph of Article [340] and the general principles to which this provision refers, the liability of the [Union] presupposes the existence of a set of circumstances comprising *actual damage, a causal link between the damage claimed and the conduct alleged against the institution, and the illegality of such conduct.* (para 10, emphasis added)

The Court has stated that the amount claimed must be actual, certain and concrete (Case 26/74 *Société Roquette Frères v Commission* [1976] ECR 677). If the actual damage cannot be established, it must be at least imminent (Joined Cases 56 to 60/74 *Kurt Kampffmeyer Mühlenvereinigung KG and others v Commission and Council* [1976] ECR 711) and foreseeable with sufficient certainty. Furthermore, the Court stipulated in *Mulder and others* (Joined Cases C-104/89 and 37/90 *Mulder and Others v Council and Commission* [1992] ECR I-3061) that the extent of 'the damage alleged must go beyond the bounds of the normal economic risks inherent in the activities in the sector concerned' (para 13). In addition, there can be no compensation for anticipated profits (Case 74/74 *Comptoir national technique agricole (CNTA) SA v Commission* [1975] ECR 533*)*.

This strict approach to the definition of 'damage' is explained by the fact that there must be a direct causal link between the breach and the damage suffered. The Court explained in Joined Cases 64 and 113/76, 167 and 239/78, 27, 28 and 45/79 *P Dumortier Frères SA and others v Council* [1979] ECR 3091 that there is no obligation for the Union 'to make good every harmful consequence, even a remote one, of unlawful legislation'; the damage alleged must 'be a sufficiently direct consequence of the unlawful conduct' of the institution concerned (para 21).

The burden of proving the causal link is on the applicant (Case 40/75 *Société des produits Bertrand SA v Commission* [1976] ECR 1). The causal link may be severed, however, by contributory negligence in the sense that contributory negligence will lessen the amount of damages awarded to the individual (*Adams* (**10.5.1** above) and Case T-351/03 *Schneider Electric SA v Commission* [2007] ECR II-2251).

The most difficult requirement to fulfil is to prove that the Union and its institutions are liable. Indeed, the Court has distinguished three situations under which the Union might be held liable (see **Figure 10.5**):

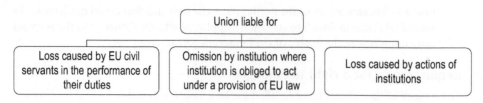

Figure 10.5   Circumstances in which the Union might be liable

(a)   The first situation involves loss caused by servants of the EU in the performance of their duties. The Court has interpreted this liability criterion in a very strict manner (see, eg, Case 9/69 *Sayag and SA Zurich v Leduc, Thonnon and SA La Concorde* [1969] ECR 329; Joined Cases 169/83 and 136/84 *Leussink and others v Commission* [1986] ECR 2801).

(b)   The second situation involves an omission by an institution where the institution concerned had a legal obligation to act under a provision of EU law. As the Court explained in Case C-146/91 *Koinopraxia Enóséon Georgikon Synetairismon Diacheiríséos Enchorion Proïonton Syn PE (KYDEP) v Council and Commission* [1994] ECR I-4199:

> As a preliminary point it should be remembered that omissions by the [Union] institutions give rise to liability on the part of the [Union] only when the institutions have infringed a legal obligation to act under a provision of [EU] law. (para 58)

(c)   The third and more usual type of action relates to the EU's liability for loss caused by the actions of its institutions.

For many years, the Court distinguished between claims involving administrative acts and those involving legislative acts. Administrative acts placed EU institutions under a duty of good administration (eg, adopting satisfactory procedures; obtaining the relevant facts before making decisions and not giving misleading information; adequately supervising bodies to whom power has been delegated). If illegal conduct, damage and a causal link could be established for administrative acts then liability could be proven.

As for legislative acts, they were categorised into those involving 'economic policy choices' and other acts. Establishing EU liability for the former faced a graver hurdle, involving the so-called *Schöppenstedt* formula:

> Where legislative action involving measures of economic policy is concerned, the [Union] does not incur non-contractual liability for damage suffered by individuals as a consequence of that action, by virtue of the provisions contained in Article [340], second paragraph, of the Treaty, unless *a sufficiently flagrant violation of a superior rule of law for the protection of the individual has occurred.* For that reason the Court, in the present case, must first consider whether such a violation has occurred. (Case 5/71 *Aktien-Zuckerfabrik Schöppenstedt v Council* [1971] ECR 975, para 11, emphasis added)

In other words, for such a legislative act to be considered as 'illegal conduct', three requirements had to be met:

(a)   There had to be a breach of a superior rule of law (eg, the principle of legitimate expectation in *Comptoir national technique agricole*, above).

(b)   The breach must have been sufficiently serious. This was understood to mean that the institution had 'manifestly and gravely disregarded the limits on the exercise of its power' (Joined Cases 83 and 94/76, 4, 15 and 40/77 *Bayerische HNL Vermehrungsbetriebe GmbH & Co KG and others v Council and Commission (Re Skimmed-Milk Powder)* [1978] ECR 1209) (see further discussion below).

(c)   The superior rule of law must have been one for the protection of the individual. For example, in *Kampffmeyer* (above) the Court explained that the support for agricultural markets was intended to benefit the interests of individuals such as importers.

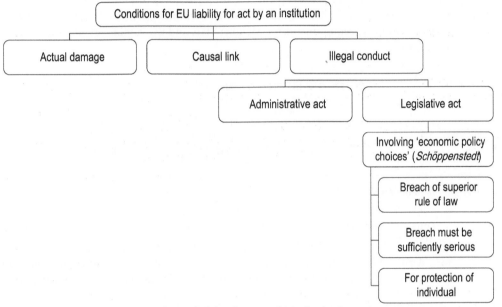

Figure 10.6   Historical conditions for EU liability for an act by an institution

The Court justified its strict interpretation of the EU liability regime in the following manner:

> The strict approach taken towards the liability of the [Union] in the exercise of its legislative activities is due to two considerations. First, even where the legality of measures is subject to judicial review, exercise of the legislative function must not be hindered by the prospect of actions for damages whenever the general interest of the [Union] requires legislative measures to be adopted which may adversely affect individual interests. Second, in a legislative context characterized by the exercise of a wide discretion, which is essential for implementing a [Union] policy, the [Union] cannot incur liability unless the institution concerned has *manifestly and gravely disregarded the limits on the exercise of its powers* (Joined Cases 83/76, 94/76, 4/77, 15/77 and 40/77 *Bayerische HNL and others v Council and Commission* [1978] ECR 1209, paragraphs 5 and 6). (*Brasserie du Pêcheur/ Factortame*, para 45, emphasis added)

The Court nevertheless recognised that the conditions under which the EU, on the one hand, and the Member States, on the other, incurred liability for breaching EU law were different, and this had to be remedied. It stressed in Case C-352/98P *Laboratoires Pharmaceutiques Bergaderm SA and Goupil v Commission* [2000] ECR I-5291, para 41:

> The Court has stated that the conditions under which the State may incur liability for damage caused to individuals by a breach of [Union] law cannot, in the absence of particular justification, differ from those governing the liability of the [Union] in like circumstances. The protection of the rights which individuals derive from [EU] law cannot vary depending on whether a national authority or a [EU] authority is responsible for the damage (*Brasserie du Pêcheur/Factortame*, para 42).

The *Bergaderm* ruling removed the requirement for a superior rule of law to be breached and the distinction between administrative and legislative acts. Consequently, the requirements for Member State and EU liability are now similar (see Figure 10.7).

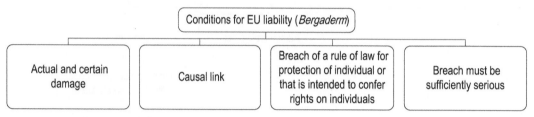

Figure 10.7   Current conditions for EU liability

Thus, besides proving the causal link between the actual damage and the illegal conduct, *Bergaderm* requires two elements to be met (para 42):

(a) A rule of law for the protection of the individual, or intended to confer rights on individuals must be infringed. For example, the principle of non-discrimination (Case T-166/98 *Cantina sociale di Dolianova Soc coop rl and Others v Commission* [2004] ECR II-3998), the duty of confidentiality of the EU institutions and general principles such as legitimate expectations fulfil this requirement. However, the fact that the Commission exceeds the powers it has been granted by the Council, thereby violating the division of powers, is not to be considered as a rule for the protection of the individual; rather, the **principle of institutional balance** (see 2.2.1 and 5.2.1) is a rule for the benefit of the EU (Joined Cases T-64/01 and T-65/01 *Afrikanische Frucht-Compagnie GmbH and Internationale Fruchtimport Gesellschaft Weichert and Co v Council and Commission* [2004] ECR II-527).

(b) The breach must be sufficiently serious. The Court stresses that 'the decisive test for finding that a breach of [Union] law is sufficiently serious is whether the Member State or the [EU] institution concerned manifestly and gravely disregarded the limits on its discretion' (*Bergaderm*, para 43).

In Case C-312/00 P *Commission v Camar Srl and Tico Srl* [2002] ECR I-11355, the Court also clearly abandoned the distinction between administrative and legislative acts, stating that 'the decisive test for determining whether there has been such an infringement is not the individual nature of the act in question, but the discretion available to the institution when it was adopted' (para 55). The Court thereby highlights that the nature of the act is important only inasmuch as it is a pointer to the degree of discretion enjoyed by the institution.

In cases where there is no or limited discretion, the mere infringement of EU law may be sufficient to determine the existence of a 'sufficiently serious breach' (*Bergaderm*, para 44). Similarly, a breach of a general obligation of diligence (Case C-308/87 *Grifoni v European Atomic Energy Community (No 1)* [1990] ECR I-1203), or a misapplication of the relevant substantive or procedural rules (*Kampffmeyer*), may lead to a finding of a 'sufficiently serious breach'.

In cases where the institution has been provided with some degree of discretion, the applicant must demonstrate some degree of blameworthiness:

> On the other hand, the right to compensation for damage resulting from the conduct of the institution becomes available where such conduct takes the form of action manifestly contrary to the rule of law and seriously detrimental to the interests of persons outside the institution and cannot be justified or accounted for by the particular constraints to which the staff of the institution, operating normally, is objectively subject. (*Schneider Electric SA v Commission*, para 124)

Following Case C-282/05 P *Holcim (Deutschland) AG v Commission* [2007] ECR I-2941 the Court, in addition to examining the margin of discretion available to the author of the act in question, examines the complexity of the situations that need to be regulated, the difficulty in the application or interpretation of the legislation and, more particularly, the margin of discretion available to the author of the act in question. An example of a serious breach is the infringement of the fundamental right to have a case dealt with within a reasonable time (Case C-385/07 P *Der Grüne Punkt – Duales System Deutschland GmbH v Commission* [2009] ECR I-6155, paras 167–96, esp 188: General Court's failure to complete within a reasonable time proceedings concerning the infringement of competition rules).

Lastly, in its judgment on liability, the Court will specify the obligation of the EU to pay compensation and fix the amount of damages awarded.

10.6 Further reading

Balthasar S, 'Locus Standi Rules for Challenges to Regulatory Acts by Private Applicants: The New Article 263(4) TFEU' (2010) 35 *EL Rev* 542.

Craig P, 'The ECJ and Ultra Vires Action: A Conceptual Analysis' (2011) 48 *CML Rev* 395.

Gutman K, 'The Evolution of the Action for Damages against the European Union and its Place in the System of Judicial Protection' (2011) 48 *CML Rev* 695.

Kornezov A, 'Locus Standi of Private Parties in Actions for Annulment: Has the Gap been Closed?' (2014) 73 *Cambridge Law Journal* 25.

Peers S and Costa N, 'Judicial Review of EU Acts after the Treaty of Lisbon; Order of 6 September 2011, Case T-18/10 *Inuit Tapiriit Kanatami and Others* v. *Commission* & Judgment of 25 October 2011, Case T-262/10 *Microban* v. *Commission*' (2012) 8 *EuConst* 82.

Turk A, *Judicial Review in EU Law* (Edward Elgar, 2009).

Wakefield J, 'The Changes in Liability of EU Institutions: Bergaderm, FIAMM and Schneider' (2012) 12 *ERA Forum* 625.

Werkmeister C, Pötters A and Traut J, 'Regulatory Acts within Article 263(4) TFEU – A Dissonant Extension of *Locus Standi* for Private Applicants' (2012) 13(1) *Cambridge Yearbook of European Legal Studies* 311.

In conformity with the principle of the rule of law, the drafters of the EU Treaties have set up a comprehensive system (judicial review, plea of illegality, failure to act, EU extra-contractual liability) to ensure that acts of the EU may be reviewed and challenged in a court of law. That being said, whilst the Court has consistently reiterated that individuals should be provided with effective remedies at the national level (through **the principles of supremacy, direct effect** and **State liability**), it has been more reluctant to grant individuals such remedies against EU acts.

test your knowledge

1   At a family occasion on 1 August 2015, your cousin, David, tells you that in June 2015 the Shale Gas Industries Association informed him that on 10 March 2015 the European Parliament and the Council passed an EU Regulation that will adversely affect his business. There are about 50 registered companies in the Association, many of which will, as a result of this Regulation, have to make extensive and expensive changes to their method of extracting gas. The smaller companies (including David's company) will not be able to afford such changes and will have to wind down. David is very upset because a previous Regulation had offered financial support for the creation of small companies in the oil industry. If such financial support had not been given, David would not have set up his company. During the conversation, David asks you whether it is possible to have this EU Regulation repealed.

(a)   What are the grounds on the basis of which this Regulation can be reviewed?
(b)   Would David be able to challenge it under Article 263, fourth paragraph TFEU?
(c)   Would David be able to obtain compensation under Article 340, second paragraph TFEU?

2   There was a surplus of Kabuli-chickpeas within the EU in 2014, and as a result (fictitious) Council Regulation 11/2015 was enacted on 25 January 2015. Exporters of Kabuli-chickpeas during 2015 were entitled under the Regulation to incentives of £100 per ton of Kabuli-chickpeas exported. On 26 January 2015, B-Eyed Peas Ltd applied for a licence to export 1,000 tons of Kabuli-chickpeas. The company was granted the licence on the payment of a deposit of £5,000, which would be forfeited if the company did not comply with the requirements of the licence.

In February 2015 there was serious disruption of the Kabuli-chickpea crop, which resulted in a shortage of Kabuli-chickpeas in the EU, and on 22 February 2015 the Commission enacted Regulation 13/2015, which eliminated the refund subsidies of Kabuli-chickpeas, making exporters liable instead for a levy of £5 per ton exported. Regulation 13/2015 specifically included those who had already exported Kabuli-chickpeas in the 2015 marketing year, but did not contain reasons for its issue.

B-Eyed Peas Ltd exported 400 tons of its quota before 22 February 2015 and is now presented with a levy of £2,000. It must export the remaining quantity of its quota (600 tons) or lose the deposit of £5,000. Exporting the 600 tons will, however, make it liable to a further levy of £3,000.

Advise B-Eyed Peas Ltd on whether, and on what grounds, if any, it may successfully challenge Regulation 13/2015.

3 Article 340, second paragraph TFEU is one of the essential safeguards in the EU legal order for ensuring that EU institutions act in compliance with the Treaties. Do you agree?

4 It is argued that despite the wide range of actions possible against acts of the EU institutions, there are situations where an aggrieved individual is left without any judicial remedy whatsoever. Is this true? Discuss.

part

IV

TRADE WITHIN THE
INTERNAL MARKET

11 The Internal Market and Harmonisation

study points

After reading this chapter, you will be able to understand:

- the concept of the internal market
- its development from the Single European Act
- the challenges faced by the internal market in the 21st century
- the Single Market Acts
- the estimated benefits of the internal market
- the internal market as the main object of the harmonisation process
- the methods of harmonisation.

11.1 Introduction

The idea of the internal market, which enshrined the objective of exponential economic prosperity through the abolition of all trade barriers and the liberalisation of exchanges of goods, services and capital, was conceived of by the drafters of the Treaty of Rome, but only became a reality in January 1993. Although a Customs Union had been achieved on 1 July 1968, progress in eliminating national technical rules governing products and the provision of services, anti-competitive practices and State aid was rather slow. The maintenance of internal frontiers meant that the European market was a common market in name only.

The objective of creating a genuine single market was reinvigorated under the Single European Act 1986 (SEA). This first amendment to the Treaty of Rome formalised the concept of the 'internal market' as an area without internal borders, within which the free movement of human and materials resources is ensured. It also set a clear timetable and deadline for the removal of all existing barriers. Although there is clear evidence that the impact of the launch of the internal market under the SEA has been positive, the internal market cannot be taken for granted, and is an ongoing process that now has to face, and adapt to, new challenges from globalisation, EU enlargement, innovation, and social and environmental developments.

The internal market covers not only the 28 EU Member States, but also three European Free Trade Area (EFTA) States – Iceland, Liechtenstein and Norway – as a result of their membership of the European Economic Area (EEA) Agreement, and Switzerland as a result of agreements with the EU.

Harmonisation of national legislation is one of the most effective instruments to ensure freedom of movement of goods, services, capital and persons in a single market. Yet, although provided for in the Treaty of Rome, harmonisation proved to be a long, cumbersome process, which hampered rather than supported the common market. Combined with a new requirement of qualified majority voting (see 2.3.2.3), introduced under the SEA and replacing the original requirement for unanimity, the new approach (see 11.3.3.2), developed by the European Commission in its 1985

White Paper, *Completing the Internal Market* (COM(85) 310 final, 14 June 1985), became instrumental in the creation and the completion of the 1993 internal market.

11.2 From the common market to the internal market

Original Article 8 of the European Economic Community (EEC) Treaty provided for the progressive establishment of the common market over a transitional period of 12 years, divided up into three stages of four years each and ending on 1 January 1970. Yet the Customs Union was achieved by a decision of the Council of Ministers of 1 July 1968, 18 months before the deadline.

However, if customs duties and quantitative restrictions were abolished by the end of the transitional period, the free movement of goods, persons, services and capital was far from being completed by then. The economic recession in the 1970s further hindered this process. As Member States were increasingly seeking to protect their markets and national industries, non-tariff barriers, far from being abolished, multiplied, and provisions on restrictions to the freedom to provide services failed to be implemented, not only during the transitional period but at all.

11.2.1 The road to the Single European Act

At the European summits of Copenhagen in 1982, Fontainebleau in June 1984 and Dublin in December 1984, the Heads of State and Governments pledged themselves to give the completion of the common market the highest priority. The Commission was finally called upon by the European Council, at the summit of March 1985, to draw up a detailed programme of measures and a timetable, with a view to abolishing the remaining obstacles to that goal. The Commission, under the chairmanship of Lord Cockfield, its Vice-President responsible for the internal market, drafted a White Paper within seven weeks, entitled *Completing the Internal Market*. This was presented to the European Council of Milan in June 1985. The Commission pointed out that, despite the long existence of the then European Community, the common market was still plagued with barriers to free movement. It notably identified three types of such remaining obstacles:

(a) physical barriers, ie customs formalities for goods and individuals;
(b) technical barriers, such as sets of national rules and measures intended to obstruct free trade directly or indirectly, thus making standardisation or mutual recognition of technical standards necessary; and
(c) fiscal barriers arising from various national rates of indirect taxes, such as value added tax or excise duties.

The Commission laid down a comprehensive programme and schedule for the abolition of these barriers, the approximation of legislation and taxes, and further monetary cooperation.

For the implementation of this programme to be possible, the Member States adopted the SEA (on 17 and 28 February 1986) in order to amend the EEC Treaty, as well as the European Coal and Steel Community (ECSC) and the European Atomic Energy Community (EAEC) or EURATOM Treaties. This was the first major revision of the Treaties of Rome and Paris (see **1.5**).

11.2.2 The Single European Act and the internal market

11.2.2.1 Common market and internal market

With the SEA, the new term 'internal market' was coined to replace 'common market'. Article 13 SEA added a new Article 8a to the EEC Treaty (now Article 26(2) TFEU), which reads:

> The internal market shall comprise an area without internal frontiers in which the free movement of goods, persons, services and capital is ensured in accordance with the provisions of this Treaty.

Although the expressions 'common market', on the one hand, and 'internal market' (or 'single market' as it is often referred to by the European Commission), on the other, had been treated as synonymous, it had been argued that the two concepts have different scopes.

A broad definition of the concept of 'common market' can be found in the ruling of the Court of Justice in Case 15/81 *Schul Douane Expediteur BV v Inspecteur der Invoerrechten en Accijnzen, Roosendaal* [1982] ECR 1409:

> The concept of common market as defined by the Court in a consistent line of decisions involves the elimination of all obstacles to intra-[Union] trade in order to merge the national markets into a single market bringing conditions as close as possible to those of a genuine internal market. It is important that not only commerce as such but also private persons who happen to be conducting an economic transaction across national frontiers should be able to enjoy the benefits of that market. (para 33)

From this extract it is clear that, from 1982, the Court used the three expressions 'common market', 'internal market' and 'single market' interchangeably. But were the concepts of 'internal market' or 'single market' similar to that of 'common market', or did their content and objectives have to be understood in a wider context?

Article 13 SEA defined the internal market as an 'area without internal frontiers in which the free movement of goods, persons, services and capital is ensured'. In a literal sense, the notion of 'internal market' or 'single market' would be confined to the achievement of the four fundamental freedoms. In this respect, those notions appeared to be more limited in scope than that of 'common market', which also encompassed the common commercial policy and the competition policy. However, this strict interpretation could not reflect the ambitious objectives of the drafters of the SEA. First, Article 13 did not alter the fundamental framework and principles laid down for the purpose of achieving the common market, nor did it replace them. Secondly, Article 13 SEA introduced an innovative element into the concept of 'common market', by defining it as an 'area without internal frontiers', making it a genuine unified area, with no internal customs and free of all technical, fiscal, physical and monetary barriers.

Having said that, former Articles 2 and 3(1)(h) TEC still referred to a 'common market', while former Article 3(1)(c) TEC described the internal market as being 'characterised by the abolition of obstacles to the free movement of goods, persons, services and capital', and former Article 3(1)(g) TEC provided that the activities of the European Community included a 'system ensuring that competition in the internal market is not distorted'.

The 2009 Lisbon Treaty put an end to the dual reference to the common market and internal market. Article 3(3) TEU now identifies the establishment of an internal market as one of the objectives of the Union, and the Treaty on the Functioning of the European Union contains a specific title in Part Three on the 'Internal Market'.

11.2.2.2 The internal market: a gradual process of creation

Former Article 8a TEEC (now repealed) provided:

> The Community shall adopt measures with the aim of progressively establishing the internal market over a period expiring on 31 December 1992 ...

In order to ensure that the internal market was established and completed in a balanced way throughout the then European Community, the SEA imposed a few essential conditions on the Community institutions and the Member States for the adoption of their legislative programme.

First, Article 14 provided that EC legislative measures had to take into account a 'balanced progress in all the sectors concerned', thus clearly emphasising their interdependence in a global economic environment.

Secondly, Article 15 SEA (now Article 27 TFEU) provided:

> When drawing up its proposals ... the Commission shall take into account the extent of the effort that certain economies showing differences in development will have to sustain during the period of establishment of the internal market and it may propose appropriate provisions.
>
> If these provisions take the form of derogations, they must be of a temporary nature and must cause the least possible disturbance to the functioning of the internal market.

This obliged the Commission to take account of the economic differences existing between the Member States, their regions, and between overseas territories and other European economies.

Thirdly, according to Article 18(3) SEA, adding new Article 100a EEC (now 114 TFEU):

> The Commission, in its proposals envisaged in paragraph 1 concerning health, safety, environmental protection and consumer protection, will take as a base *a high level of protection.* (emphasis added)

Furthermore, the achievement of an internal market would not be complete, were it not accompanied and supplemented by new common European policies. New policies were expressly inserted in the Treaty of Rome by the SEA, to give the internal market a new dimension. These were as follows:

- Cooperation in economic and monetary policy under former Article 102a TEEC (now economic and monetary policy under Articles 119–144 TFEU), designed to ensure the convergence of economic and monetary policies within the competence of the European Community at that time. This chapter on economic and monetary policy was later fully rewritten under the Maastricht Treaty.
- Social policy under former Articles 118a and 118b TEEC (now Articles 151–161 TFEU), regarded as a fundamental part of the 1993 objectives by the Commission in its communication of 14 September 1988 (COM(88) 1148 final). The achievement of the single market would have indeed been absurd if the standard of living and social welfare fought for and enjoyed by European citizens were to be put into question. For that purpose, the SEA supplemented the numerous

provisions of the EEC Treaty in the social area, either by adding new provisions or by extending the powers of the European Community. Furthermore, an EC Charter of Social Rights was adopted at Strasbourg on 9 December 1989 by 11 Member States (thus excluding the UK), which was later incorporated into the EEC Treaty by the Maastricht Treaty.

- Economic and social cohesion under former Articles 130a–130e TEEC (now the economic, social and territorial cohesion policy under Articles 174–178 TFEU), 'aiming at reducing disparities between various regions within the EC and the backwardness of the least-favoured regions'.

- Research and technological development under former Articles 130f–130q TEEC (now research and technological development and space under Articles 179–190 TFEU), aiming at strengthening the scientific and technological dimension of European industry by adopting multi-annual framework programmes (MFP) implemented through specific programmes, such as ESPRIT (information technologies), RACE (telecoms), BRITE (new technologies applied to traditional industries), EURAM (conception and production of new material), and JET (controlled thermonuclear fusion).

- Environmental protection, which was formally incorporated by the SEA into the Treaty of Rome under former Articles 130r–130t TEEC (now Articles 191–193 TFEU). Until then, and since 1972, European environmental policy had been based on former Articles 100 TEEC (approximation of national laws) and 235 TEEC (residual powers – see 3.2.3), as the European Community had no original competences in that domain. The SEA was thus instrumental in turning environmental protection into one of the fundamental objectives of the European Community, and in establishing core principles of European environmental law such as the **prevention principle** or the **integration principle**.

By the end of the eight-year internal programme, 264 of the 282 proposals had been adopted and 18 proposals remained, of which five were not given high priority. This certainly was an unprecedented legislative achievement, and the work on the single market was remarkably successful, in particular with respect to the movement of goods, services and capital.

11.2.2.3 The internal market after the first 10 years

The benefits of the internal market were first assessed by the Commission in its Staff Working Paper, 'The Internal Market – Ten Years without Frontiers' (Brussels, 7.1.2003 SEC (2002) 1417). Painting a broad-brush picture of the achievements of the SEA, the Commission asserted that

> [t]he benefits of the measures set out in the White Paper [were] clearly being felt, as more and more individual citizens and businesses [took] advantage of the opportunities on offer. The Internal Market has not of course been the only factor at work: other major forces [were] also transforming our economies – ie rapid and accelerating globalisation and the rise of new technologies, in particular the internet. The relationship between these forces and the Internal Market is complex and mutually reinforcing. Together, they have contributed to opening up the Member States' economies to more competition and brought immense benefits in terms of increased efficiency and competitiveness.
>
> Moreover, the Internal Market has been further developed and strengthened in the last ten years. It has been extended into new sectors, such as air transport,

telecommunications energy and financial services, which are crucial to the competitiveness of the economy as a whole. Consumer and environmental protections have been significantly enhanced. ... And now, with the arrival of the euro, the pace of economic integration has been stepped up and many of the benefits of the Internal Market have been reinforced. (at 4)

The following are some of the perceived and estimated economic benefits of the internal market:

- EU GDP in 2002 was 1.8% (or €164.5 billion) higher than in 1992
- about 2.5 million jobs were created in the EU after 1992
- there was more created wealth, to the value of €877 billion, between 1992 and 2002
- the ability of EU businesses to compete in global markets was enhanced
- there was an increase in EU exports to third countries, from 6.9% of EU GDP in 1992 to 11.2% in 2001
- there was a doubling of the percentage of EU GDP of foreign direct investment into the EU
- trade within the borders of the EU was made easier as a result of the elimination of border bureaucracy, shorter delivery times and reduced costs, and the harmonisation of different, complex national standards and requirements
- new export markets opened up to small and medium-sized enterprises (SMEs)
- cross-border sales of companies exporting to more than five EU countries received a boost
- public procurement opened up, enabling companies to bid for contracts to supply goods and services to public authorities in other Member States.

Citizens and consumers have also directly benefited from the opening up of national markets and the resulting increased in competition. For instance, they enjoyed:

- a wider choice of goods and services at cheaper prices;
- lower telecommunications tariffs and lower airfares as a result of technology combined with internal market liberalisation;
- work, retirement, or study in another country (it was estimated that more than 15 million EU citizens had moved across borders for one or more of those purposes);
- full consumer rights when shopping outside their own country.

11.2.3   The internal market of the 21st century

While many barriers have been removed, others have reappeared, and new challenges are arising. Despite many achievements, the internal market is far from being complete 22 years on, and much remains to be done to turn it into a genuinely integrated market. Far from being finite, it is an ongoing process.

In its Communication, 'A Single Market for Citizens – Interim report to the 2007 Spring European Council' (COM(2007) 60 final, 21 February 2007), the Commission pointed out that the internal market should now 'evolve to make markets work better and deliver even more tangible benefits for European citizens, entrepreneurs, workers and consumers alike in an enlarged EU' (at 3). To that effect, on 20 November 2007, the Commission presented an overall plan to realise the potential of the internal market and position it to adapt to new realities of globalisation, the fast pace of innovation, and social and environmental evolution. On 29 June 2009, it also made a Recommendation 'on measures to improve the functioning of the single market' (2009/527/EC, [2009] OJ L176/17).

In 2010, at the request of the Commission, former Commissioner Mario Monti submitted a report entitled *A New Strategy for the Single Market*, in which he proposed 'a new strategy to safeguard the single market from the risk of economic nationalism, to extend it into new areas key for Europe's growth and to build an adequate degree of consensus around it' (at 7). This strategy was articulated around three broad sets of initiatives aimed at:

(a) 'removing the remaining bottlenecks and plugging the gaps and missing links that hamper innovation and dampen growth potential in the single market' (at 8). This included ensuring the better functioning of the single market for citizens, consumers and SMEs; creating a digital single market; supporting green growth and Europe's transition to a low-carbon and resource-efficient economy; maximising the potential of the single market for services; encouraging labour mobility in the single market; and establishing the 'physical' infrastructure for the single market;

(b) addressing 'the concerns identified through the consultation and thus building consensus on a stronger single market' (at 8). These concerns were notably about reconciling economic freedoms and workers' rights; guaranteeing a place for social services within the single market; the integrating of the EU's policy goals in public procurement policy; using tax coordination to safeguard national tax sovereignty within further market integration; balancing competitiveness and cohesion within the single market through regional development policies; fostering an active industrial policy; and ensuring that the single market remains open without being powerless vis-à-vis competitors from outside;

(c) improving the tools needed to boost the single market, notably through ensuring light but effective regulation in the single market; and reinforcing enforcement of EU rules through a coherent system in which 'infringement actions, informal problem solving mechanisms and private enforcement form a seamless web of remedies against breaches of EU law' (at 9).

Finally, under the leadership of Michel Barnier, former Commissioner for the Internal Market, the Commission presented an action plan in the form of 50 proposals in a Communication entitled 'Towards a Single Market Act. For a highly competitive social market economy. 50 proposals for improving our work, business and exchanges with one another' (COM(2010) 608 final, 27 October 2010). This was supplemented by another Communication of 13 November 2011, entitled 'Single Market Act. Twelve levers to boost growth and strengthen confidence. "Working together to create new growth"' (COM(2011) 206 final), and another of 3 October 2012 on 'Single Market Act II. Together for new growth' (COM(2012) 573 final).

Because the 'single market integration is not an irreversible process, and the continued existence of the single market should not be taken for granted' (Report of the European Parliament, *On Delivering a Single Market to Consumers and Citizens* (A7-0132/2010) at 6), the Single Market Acts aim to achieve a highly competitive social market economy, and are designed to boost the single market through 12 key drivers for growth, competitiveness and social progress, including:

• greater workers' mobility (modernising the rules for mutual recognition of professional qualifications) (see **15.5**)
• better access to finance for SMEs (common rules for venture capital funds)
• improved consumer protection (non-judicial means of redress)
• strengthened standardisation for services

- new EU tax legislation to meet the challenge of sustainable development
- reinforced intellectual property (unitary patent protection for inventions)
- stronger European transport, energy and electronic communications networks
- the modernisation of the public procurement legislative framework
- the development of a Digital Single Market.

11.3   Harmonisation

Alongside instruments of negative harmonisation, whereby barriers to free movement of goods, persons, services and capital are removed, EU institutions can also resort to positive harmonisation to prevent those barriers from reappearing. Harmonisation of national legislation is in this respect a very efficient instrument to achieve the objectives of 'establishing or ensuring the functioning of the internal market', as set out in Article 26 TFEU (Article 114(1) TFEU).

Harmonisation aims to deal with disparities between the laws of the Member States in areas where they are liable to prevent free movement and subsequently distort competition. Such disparities need not be current. Indeed, in Case C-66/04 *United Kingdom v European Parliament and Council of the European Union* [2005] ECR I-10573, interpreting the concept of harmonisation broadly, the Court of Justice stated that former Article 95 TEC (now Article 114 TFEU) authorised the EU legislature to intervene by adopting appropriate measures

> [w]here there are obstacles to trade, or *it is likely that such obstacles will emerge in the future, because the Member States have taken, or are about to take, divergent measures* with respect to a product or a class of products which bring about different levels of protection and thereby prevent the product or products from moving freely within the [EU] ... (para 41, emphasis added)

Yet the 'mere finding of disparities between national rules is not sufficient to justify having recourse to Article [114 TFEU]' (see Case C-434/02 *Arnold André GmbH & Co KG v Landrat des Kreises Herford* [2004] ECR I-11825, para 30; and Joined Cases C-154/04 and C-155/04 *R, on the application of Alliance for Natural Health and Nutri-Link Ltd v Secretary of State for Health and R, on the application of National Association of Health Stores and Health Food Manufacturers Ltd v Secretary of State for Health and National Assembly for Wales* [2005] ECR I-6451, para 28). Furthermore, harmonisation under Article 114 TFEU must aim 'to improve the conditions of the establishment and functioning of the internal market' (*UK v EP and Council of the EU*, above, para 44).

11.3.1   The legal basis of harmonisation

With the exception of the provisions concerning the Area for Freedom, Security and Justice, notably Article 82 TFEU (Judicial cooperation on criminal matters through measures establishing minimum rules facilitating mutual recognition of judgments and judicial decisions) and Article 83 TFEU (Directives establishing minimum rules regarding the definition of criminal offences and sanctions, particularly for serious crime with a cross-border dimension), and common policies provisions (eg the transport policy under Article 91 TFEU, competition policy under Article 103 TFEU, or the environmental policy under Article 191 TFEU, etc), the main instruments and procedure of harmonisation are spelled out in Chapter 3 of the TFEU on

'Approximation of Laws', under Title VII on 'Common Rules on Competition, Taxation and Approximation of Laws'.

The main harmonisation provision is Article 114(1) TFEU, which provides:

> Save where otherwise provided in the Treaties, the following provisions shall apply for the achievement of the objectives set out in Article 26. The European Parliament and the Council shall, acting in accordance with the ordinary legislative procedure and after consulting the Economic and Social Committee, adopt the measures for the approximation of the provisions laid down by law, regulation or administrative action in Member States which have as their object the establishment and functioning of the internal market.

Formerly Article 95 TEC, this provision is a direct product of the SEA, and is aimed at the 'establishment and functioning of the internal market'. It was designed to remedy the shortcomings of its predecessor, Article 100 TEEC, especially as a result of the unanimity rule requirement (see **2.3.2.3**), which obstructed progress.

However, the drafters of the SEA originally regarded this provision as a derogation from the uninamity requirement laid down in former Article 94 TEC (now Article 115 TFEU) and as subordinate to the latter. Indeed former Article 95 TEC originally started with the words 'By way of derogation from Article 94'. Yet, because of its flexibility of use owing to the qualified majority rule (see **2.3.2.3**), former Article 95 TEC proved to be the main driver for the establishment of the internal market and the vast harmonisation programme, as set out in the 1985 Commission White Paper. Furthermore, the scope of application of former Article 95 was much clearer and more precise than that of former Article 94 TEC. Indeed, while the former covered harmonising measures that 'have as their object the establishment and functioning of the internal market', the latter referred to the approximation of such national laws 'as directly [affecting] the establishment or functioning of the common market'.

Article 115 TFEU now provides:

> Without prejudice to Article 114, the Council shall, acting unanimously in accordance with a special legislative procedure and after consulting the European Parliament and the Economic and Social Committee, issue directives for the approximation of such laws, regulations or administrative provisions of the Member States as directly affect the establishment or functioning of the internal market.

It is now more than clear that the process of harmonisation has as its main object and purpose the establishment and functioning internal market, within the framework of Articles 114 and 115 alike.

It is also to be noted, though, that, with the exceptions mentioned above, under Article 114(2) TFEU, the scope of application of Article 114 TFEU does not extend to fiscal harmonisation (covered by Article 113 TFEU), to the free movement of persons, or to provisions relating to the rights and interests of employed persons.

11.3.2 Harmonisation, approximation or coordination?

As in the original provisions of the Treaty of Rome, notably Articles 99 and 100 TEEC, different and inconsistent terminology is used in the TEU and the TFEU to describe harmonisation. For instance, while Article 113 TFEU refers to 'harmonisation of legislation' with regard to taxation, Article 114(1) and Article 115 use the expression 'approximation of the provisions laid down by law, regulation or administrative action in Member States'. Yet the words 'harmonisation measure' are used in Article 114(4), (5), (7) and (10).

Furthermore, the reference to coordination of the provisions laid down by law, regulation or administrative action in Member States is also made in other parts of the TFEU, such as in Article 53(1) (right of establishment), Article 145 ('coordinated strategy for employment'), Article 150, first paragraph ('coordination between Member States on employment and labour market policies'), Article 156, first paragraph ('coordination of [the Member States'] action in all social policy fields') and Article 173(2) (coordinated action in industry policy to the exclusion of 'any harmonisation of the laws and regulations of the Member States' under Article 173(3)). Even Article 32 TEU provides that 'Member States shall ensure, *through the convergence of their actions*, that the EU Union is able to assert its interests and values on the international scene' (emphasis added), for the purpose of determining a common action on any matter of Common Foreign and Security Policy.

It might be suggested that the difference in the terminology used reflects a difference in degree in the process of harmonisation, with 'coordination' being the lowest form of harmonisation, and 'approximation' and 'harmonisation' being the more elaborate forms. Coordination could even be presented as the opposite of, or as an alternative to, harmonisation, as seems to be the case under Article 173(2) and (3) TFEU. Yet there is nothing in the Treaties to suggest that this is the case or that each of the terms used has a fundamentally different meaning.

11.3.3 Methods of harmonisation

Former Article 100 TEEC was silent about the methods of harmonisation, and the whole process, notably because of the unanimity rule (see 2.3.2.3), originally seemed to have been cumbersome. It certainly proved to be a slow process, and was the main cause of the paralysis of the common market. In order to accelerate the harmonisation process, the Commission proposed a new approach in its 1985 White Paper, based on less and lighter regulation. As it put it then,

> [t]he general thrust of the Commission's approach in this area [goods and services] will be to move away from the concept of harmonisation towards that of mutual recognition and equivalence. But there is a continuing role for the approximation of Member States' law and regulations, as laid down in Article 100 of the Treaty. Clearly, action under this Article would be quicker and more effective if the Council were to agree not to allow the unanimity requirement to obstruct progress where it could otherwise be made. (at 6 and 7)

11.3.3.1 Original methods of harmonisation

Before the White Paper and the SEA, four main methods of harmonisation were primarily used at the full discretion (see Case C-66/04 *United Kingdom v European Parliament and Council*, paras 45–46) of the European legislative bodies:

(a) exhaustive harmonisation;
(b) partial harmonisation;
(c) optional harmonisation; and
(d) mutual recognition.

Harmonisation is said to be exhaustive or total when a European Directive imposes a single standard throughout the EU that replaces the national standards, even though it allows Member States to adopt stricter standards or provides for strictly controlled derogations (see Case C-374/05 *Gintec International Import- Export GmbH v Verband Sozialer Wettbewerb eV* [2007] ECR I-9517, regarding complete harmonisation under Directives 2001/83/EC on the Community code relating to medicinal products for human use ([2001] OJ L311/67) and 92/28/EEC on the advertising of medicinal products for human use ([1992] OJ L113/13)). Under such harmonisation measures, Member States may generally no longer justify their own standards under Article 36 TFEU or on the basis of mandatory requirements (see **Chapter 14**).

Harmonisation will be partial when a directive covers only some of the national standards, leaving others untouched. Directive 2000/13/EC on the approximation of the laws of the Member States relating to the labelling, presentation and advertising of foodstuffs ([2000] OJ L109/29) provides an example of full (labelling) and partial (advertising) harmonisation (as illustrated in Case C-239/02 *Douwe Egberts NV v Westrom Pharma NV and Souranis* [2004] ECR I-7007, para 34 and Case C-315/05 *Lidl Italia Srl v Comune di Arcole (VR)* [2006] ECR I-11181).

Under optional harmonisation, the application of common standards set under a directive is optional, and Member States remain free to set their own production and marketing rules for goods intended purely for their national markets. This means that manufacturers need comply with European standards only where they intend to trade across the EU, but can choose to follow or not the Directive in its entirety if they trade only at national level.

Mutual recognition is the lowest form of harmonisation and, with the exception of Article 53 TFEU on mutual recognition of professional qualifications, is not expressly mentioned in the Treaties. Indeed, mutual recognition is an implied form of harmonisation in trade between the Member States, as the marketing of imported products or services is allowed on the basis that they implicitly comply with the national standards of the importing country. It naturally facilitates market access. Originally taken into consideration by EEC institutions in the early 1970s, in an attempt to avoid dual imposition of technical and administrative controls on goods both in the country of origin and in the country of export, the **principle of mutual recognition** was formally elaborated and laid down in the *Cassis de Dijon* case (Case 120/78 *Rewe-Zentral AG v Bundesmonopolverwaltung für Branntwein* [1979] ECR 649) (see **13.2.3.2**). In relation to a German ban on the marketing of alcoholic beverages not meeting a minimum alcoholic content rule, the Court held that '[t]here is ... no reason why, provided that they have been lawfully produced and marketed in one of the Member States, alcoholic beverages should not be introduced into any other Member State' (para 14).

This basic principle was further codified by the Commission in its Communication concerning the consequences of the judgment given by the Court of Justice on 20 February 1979 in Case 120/78 ('*Cassis de Dijon*') ([1980] OJ C-256/2). In the absence of harmonisation, the principle of mutual recognition simply means that

> a Member State may not in principle prohibit the sale in its territory of a product lawfully produced and marketed in another Member State even if the product is produced according to technical or quality requirements which differ from those imposed on its domestic products. Where a product 'suitably and satisfactorily' fulfils the legitimate objective of a Member State's own rules (public safety, protection of the consumer or the environment, etc), the importing country cannot justify prohibiting its sale in its territory by claiming that the way it fulfils the objective is different from that imposed on domestic products.

Restrictions on marketing can only be justified on the grounds set out under Article 36 TFEU (see **14.2.1**), or on the basis of imperative requirements, provided they are proportionate to the objective pursued (see **14.3**).

Although this principle should be regarded as a fairly simple one to apply, the Commission observed in recitals 4 and 5 of the preamble to Regulation 764/2008/EC laying down procedures relating to the application of certain national technical rules to products lawfully marketed in another Member State and repealing Decision No 3052/95/EC ([2008] OJ L218/21) (the Mutual Recognition Regulation or 'MRR') that

> [m]any problems still exist as regards the correct application of the principle of mutual recognition by the Member States. It is therefore necessary to establish procedures to minimise the possibility of technical rules creating unlawful obstacles to the free movement of goods between Member States. The absence of such procedures in the Member States creates additional obstacles to the free movement of goods, since it discourages enterprises from selling their products, lawfully marketed in another Member State, on the territory of the Member State applying technical rules. Surveys have shown that many enterprises, in particular small and medium-sized enterprises (SMEs), either adapt their products in order to comply with the technical rules of Member States, or refrain from marketing them in those Member States ...

and that

> [c]ompetent authorities also lack appropriate procedures for the application of their technical rules to specific products lawfully marketed in another Member State. The lack of such procedures compromises their ability to assess the conformity of products in accordance with the Treaty.

Effective as from 13 May 2009, the Mutual Recognition Regulation was adopted on 9 July 2008, with the view to setting rules and procedures to be followed by national authorities when taking administrative measures based on technical rules that are likely to hinder the free movement of a product lawfully marketed in another Member State and not covered by harmonised standards at European level. The Regulation sets out a framework for the assessment of product conformity with national technical standards. National authorities must comply with the rules and procedures regarding:

(a) the collating of information on the product concerned;

(b) the recognition of certificates or test reports issued by recognised conformity assessment bodies in accordance with Regulation No 765/2008/EC setting out the requirements for accreditation and market surveillance relating to the marketing of products and repealing Regulation (EEC) No 339/93 ([2008] OJ L218/30);

(c) the assessment of the need to apply a technical rule, notably its proportionality based on its technical or scientific elements; and

(d) the temporary suspension of the marketing of a product, which is prohibited unless the product concerned poses a serious risk, or is prohibited in a Member State on grounds of public morality or public security.

Furthermore, the Regulation provides that a Product Contact Point is to be set up by each Member State in order to provide information on the technical rules applicable in the territory of the Member State, the contact details of the competent authorities and the remedies available.

The MRR applies in all EU Member States, and in those EFTA States that are parties to the Agreement on the EEA (Iceland, Lichtenstein and Norway). It does not, however, apply to EU–Turkey relations, even though the **mutual recognition principle** does (see Articles 5–7 of Decision 1/95 of the EC–Turkey Association Council of 22 December 1995 on implementing the final phase of the Customs Union ([1996] OJ L35), on the elimination of measures having an effect equivalent to quantitative restrictions between the EU and Turkey).

In its Working Document on 'The concept of "lawfully marketed" in the Mutual Recognition Regulation (EC) No 764/2008' (COM(2013) 592 final, 16 August 2013), noting that the concept 'lawfully marketed' is not defined in the MMR or in the case law of the Court of Justice, the Commission has offered the following definition of the concept 'lawful marketing' (at 5 and 6), as meaning the supply taking place in:

(a) another Member State, in accordance with the applicable national legislation; or

(b) an EFTA state that is a contracting party to the EEA Agreement in accordance with the applicable national legislation.

Additionally, with regard to products intended for (or which may be used by) consumers, products placed on the EU market are subject to the requirements and safety criteria laid down by the Directive on general product safety. As regards products imported from third countries, they must lawfully be marketed in a Member State or in an EFTA State that is a contracting party to the EEA Agreement in order to benefit from mutual recognition.

11.3.3.2 The new approach

The creation of a single market by 31 December 1992 could not have been achieved without a new regulatory technique and strategy laid down in the Council Resolution of 7 May 1985 on the new approach to technical harmonisation and standards ([1985] OJ C136/1).

This new approach is based on the following principles:

- Harmonisation is limited to essential requirements set out in annexes to directives, and to be satisfied by products before being placed on and put into service in the European market.
- The technical specifications of products meeting the essential requirements set out in the directives are laid down in harmonised standards.
- The application of harmonised or other standards remains voluntary, and manufacturers have the option to apply other technical specifications to meet the requirements.
- Products that comply with national standards transposing harmonised standards are presumed to conform with the corresponding essential requirements.

Essential requirements are mandatory and lay down the elements necessary to protect the public interest. They are designed to ensure a high level of protection in particular with regard to the protection of the health and safety of users, consumers and workers. They may relate to certain hazards associated with the product, such as physical and mechanical resistance, flammability, chemical, electrical or biological properties, hygiene, radioactivity, accuracy; or to the product's characteristics or its performance, such as materials, design, construction, manufacturing process, instructions drawn up by the manufacturer. It is for the manufacturer to carry out risk analysis in order to determine the essential requirement applicable to the particular product. The purpose of essential requirements is only to define the objectives to be achieved or the hazards to be dealt with, not to specify the technical solutions for doing so. This allows manufacturers to choose the way they wish to adopt to satisfy the requirements.

Harmonised standards are European standards, defined as technical specifications elaborated and adopted by European standards organisations (ESOs), namely the European Committee for Standardisation (CEN), the European Committee for Electrotechnical Standardisation (CENELEC) and the European Telecommunication Standards Institute (ETSI). These standards are adopted in accordance with the 2003 General Guidelines for the Cooperation between CEN, CENELEC and ETSI, the European Commission and EFTA ([2003] OJ C91/04). The internal rules of these organisations provide that European standards must be transposed at national level. Harmonised standards must match the essential requirements of the relevant directives.

New approach directives are total harmonisation directives (see 11.3.3.1). As a result, Member States are, in principle, not allowed to maintain or introduce more stringent rules than those provided for in the particular directive. Examples of such directives are:

- the Toy Safety Directives (Directives 88/378/EEC and 2009/48/EC ([2009] OJ L170))
- the Packaging and Packaging Waste Directive (Directive 2005/20/EC amending Directive 94/62/EC on packaging and packaging waste ([2005] OJ L70))
- the Low Voltage Directive (Directive 2006/95/EC ([2006] OJ L374))
- the Machinery Directive (2006/42/EC ([2006] OJ L157)).

in practice

Consumers are very familiar with the CE mark, which can be found on most common goods such as smart phones, laptops, tablets and toys, but very few know exactly what it means.

The CE mark is simply an indication that a product is compliant with EU legislative requirements (eg, a harmonised level of health or safety laid down in applicable directives), so as to enable its free movement within the European Economic Area (EEA). It is the sole responsibility of the manufacturers to declare that their products, whether manufactured within or outside the EEA, meet all the legal requirements for the CE mark. Affixing the mark to their products means that those products can be sold throughout the EEA.

The CE mark is therefore an indication not of origin but that the product has been assessed before being marketed within the EEA. It is the manufacturers' responsibility to:

- verify that their products comply with all relevant essential requirements laid down in the applicable directive;
- ensure that the products have been examined by an independent conformity assessment body, if so required by the applicable directive; and
- carry out all conformity assessment, create the technical file, issue the declaration of conformity and affix the CE mark to the product.

For their part, distributors must check that the CE mark has been appropriately affixed to the product and that the supporting documentation is correct.

Importers of products manufactured outside the EEA must check that all the necessary steps for declaration of conformity have been taken by the manufacturer and that the relevant documentation is readily available.

11.4 Further reading

Chalmers D, 'Repackaging the Internal Market' (1994) 19 *EL Rev* 385.

Curral J, 'Some Aspects of the Relation between Articles 30–36 & Article 100 of the EEC Treaty, with a Closer Look at Optional Harmonisation' (1984) 4 *Yearbook of European Law* 169.

Dougan M, 'Minimum Harmonization & the Internal Market' (2000) 37 *CML Rev* 853.

Ehlermann CD, 'The Internal Market Following the Single European Act' (1987) 24 *CML Rev* 361.

Gormley WL, 'Competition and Free Movement: Is the Internal Market the Same as a Common Market?' (2002) *European Business Law Review* 517.

Govaere I, 'The Future Direction of the EU Internal Market: On Vested Values and Fashionable Modernism' (2009) 16 *Columbia Journal of European Law* 67.

Hervey TK, 'Community & National Competence in Health after Tobacco Advertising' (2001) 38 *CML Rev* 1421.

Oliver P and Roth WR, 'The Internal Market and the Four Freedoms' (2004) 41 *CML Rev* 407.

Mortelmans K, 'The Common Market, the Internal Market, and the Single Market, What's in a Market?' (1998) 35 *CML Rev* 101.

Mostl M, 'Preconditions and Limits of Mutual Recognition' (2010) 47 *CML Rev* 405.

Pelkmans J, 'The New Approach to Technical Harmonisation and Standardisation' (1987) 25 *Journal of Common Market Studies* 249.

Rott P, 'Minimum Harmonization for the Completion of the Internal Market?' (2003) 40 *CML Rev* 1107.

Slot PJ, 'Harmonisation' (1996) 21 *EL Rev* 378.

Smith MP, 'Single Market, Global Competition' (2010) 17 *Journal of European Public Policy* 936.

summary

The internal market is the cornerstone of the whole EU law project. Defined as an 'area without frontiers within which the free movement of goods, persons, services and capital is ensured', the internal market was completed under the Single European Act on 1 January 1993 thanks to an ambitious programme of removal of remaining barriers to the free movement of persons and of material resources, and of harmonisation of national laws with a view to reducing disparities between national rules, a process improved and accelerated under a new approach introduced by the European Commission in 1985. Yet, despite the many achievements in 1993 and the clear benefits of the creation of the internal market in the 10 years that followed, much remains to be done to ensure that the internal market meets the challenges arising from globalisation, technological innovation, and social and environmental evolution. To that end, in 2011 and 2012 the European Commission put forward, in two Communications on the Single Market Act, a number of proposals to achieve a highly competitive social market economy and to boost the internal market through 12 key drivers for growth, competitiveness and social progress.

test your knowledge

1   To what extent can one say that the Single European Act achieved the Single European Market?

2   'Two decades after the adoption of the Single European Act, and 14 years after the launch of the Single Market, the majority of the evidence received by the Committee suggests that its impact, so far, has been positive. It has facilitated the creation of a home market of 500 million consumers, making the EU the world's largest trading bloc, and "a very attractive investment location" with a strong position in the global economy (Harbour, Purvis, Wilcox p 221)' (House of Lords EU Committee, 5th Report of Session 2007/08, *The Single Market: Wallflower or Dancing Partner? Inquiry into the European Commission's Review of the Single Market* (HL Paper 36-I, 2008) para 23)
    Discuss.

3   To what extent is it true to say that 'Mutual recognition is not always a miracle solution for ensuring free movement ... in the single market. Harmonisation or further harmonisation remains without doubt one of the most effective instruments, both for economic operators and for the national administration'? (Commission, *Second Biennial Report on the Application of the Principle of Mutual Recognition in the Single Market* (COM(2002) 419 final, 23 July 2002, para 3)

chapter 12

The Free Movement of Goods: The Customs Union and the Abolition of Tariff Barriers

After reading this chapter, you will be able to understand:

- the aim of the free movement of goods provisions
- the concept of the Customs Union, and its internal and external dimensions
- the definition of a charge having equivalent effect to customs duties
- the definition of discriminatory internal taxations

12.1 Introduction

The free movement of goods is one of the fundamental principles of the Treaty (Case C-265/95 *Commission v France* (*Re Spanish Strawberries*) [1997] ECR I-6959, para 24; Case C-320/03 *Commission v Austria* [2005] ECR I-9871, para 63) and one of the fundamental freedoms in EU law (Case C-108/09 *Ker-Optika bt v ÀNTSZ Dél-dunántúli Regionális Intézete* [2010] ECR I-12213, para 43). In fact, given the wording of Article 26(2) TFEU, which defines the internal market, the principle of free movement of goods holds first place amongst the four fundamental freedoms:

> 2. The internal market shall comprise an area without internal frontiers in which the free movement of goods, persons, services and capital is ensured in accordance with the provisions of the Treaties.

Indeed, with the exception of Article III-130(2) of the unratified Treaty Establishing a Constitution for Europe of 29 October 2004, which put individuals at the heart of European integration, the free movement of goods has always been listed as the first fundamental freedom, and the Treaty of Lisbon has preserved that order. This is in no way surprising, as Member States have always given priority to the free movement of goods and the liberalisation of markets, over the free movement of persons.

This principle ensures that national businesses have open and free access to the ability to export domestic products to all other Member States, without restrictions; indeed, this is one of the principal reasons for joining the EU. Free movement of goods across the EU is seen as increasing economic efficiency by increasing competitive pressure, driving up quality and driving down prices, widening consumer choice and developing the EU's competitiveness in world markets.

The free movement of goods can operate either within a free trade area, within which Member States retain a wide discretion, or within a Customs Union, which favours a high level of economic integration and limits Member States' discretion. In the aftermath of the Second World War, while the majority of European States, under the leadership of the UK, created the European Free Trade Area (EFTA), the six original EEC Member States opted for a Customs Union (see 1.5). The Customs Union is the foundation of the EU, and is the core element in the existence and functioning of the internal market (see 1.5).

12.2 The Customs Union

12.2.1 The creation of the Customs Union

The Customs Union was solidly established on three pillars:

- *A standstill clause.* Former Article 12 TEEC prevented Member States from introducing new customs duties on imports and exports, or any charges having equivalent effect, or increasing those already applied in their trade with each other (Case 26/62 *NV Algemene Transport- en Expeditie Onderneming van Gend & Loos v Netherlands Inland Revenue Administration* [1963] ECR 1).

- *A timetabled removal of all customs duties and quantitative restrictions over a transitional period of 12 years (Article 14 TEEC).* Under Article 14 TEEC, this transitional period was divided up into three stages of four years each. Customs duties were to be reduced by 30% in the first two stages and by 40% in the remaining period. Owing to a favourable economic climate, this process was accelerated, and Member States agreed on 12 May 1960 and 15 May 1962 to reduce those duties by 30% as of 1 July 1960 and by 50% as of 1 July 1962. By 1 January 1966, the basic duties were reduced by 80% (against 60% as scheduled), and duties on industrial products were abolished on 1 July 1968, 18 months before the end of the transitional period.

Industrial products			level	duties remaining
	EEC Treaty	Acceleration process	(as a percentage of the basic duties at 1 January 1957)	
first stage	1 Jan 1959 1 July 1960	1 Jan 1961	10% 10% 10%	90% 80% 70%
second stage	1 Jan 1959 1 July 1963 1 Jan 1965	1 July 1962	10% 10% 10% 10%	60% 50% 40% 40%
third stage	1 Jan 1966 1 July 1967 1 July 1968		10% 5% 15%	20% 15% 0%

Table 12.1   Timetable for the abolition of customs duties under former Article 14 TEEC

- *A Common Customs Tariff.* Regulation 950/68/EEC ([1968] OJ L172/1) gradually established a Common Customs Tariff (CCT), by approximating the then four customs tariffs of Benelux, France, Germany and Italy. Member States were to apply this CCT from 1 July 1968 to goods imported from third countries, and eliminate any customs duties chargeable between them on those goods. This CCT simply consists of a list of categories of goods, updated each year, setting out the duty payable on the products coming from a non-Member State into the EU; the duty is normally an *ad valorem* duty (based on the value of the products) and, although collected by Member States' authorities, is one of the EU's own resources.

12.2.2 The Union Customs Code

A Community Customs Code was established under Council Regulation 2913/92/EEC, which consolidated and codified all rules and procedures applicable to goods originating from third countries. This Customs Code was later modernised under Regulation 450/2008/EC of the European Parliament and of the Council of 23 April 2008 laying down the Community Customs Code (Modernised Customs Code) (in order to incorporate new, simplified customs procedures and methods, rationalise international trade and reduce costs for businesses). This was repealed by Regulation 952/2013/EU of the European Parliament and the Council of 9 October 2013, which establishes a Union Customs Code that will provide, as from 1 May 2016, the new EU legislative framework on customs rules and procedures. The purposes of the Code are to rationalise and simplify customs legislation, rules and procedures, provide legal certainty and uniformity to economic operators and greater clarity for EU customs officials, and to offer compliant economic operators a swifter customs procedure through a complete paperless electronic process. This Code may be regarded as the ultimate instrument of Customs integration.

12.2.3 The internal and external aspects of the Customs Union

Under Article 28(1) TFEU:

> The Union shall comprise a customs union which shall cover all trade in goods and which shall involve the prohibition between Member States of customs duties on imports and exports and of all charges having equivalent effect, and the adoption of a common customs tariff in their relations with third countries.

It is clear from this provision that the Customs Union has an internal and an external dimension. Internally, the Member States are required to abolish all tariff barriers (customs duties (see below **12.4.1**) and charges having equivalent effect (see below **12.4.2**)) with a view to establishing a single customs area. Externally, the Member States must apply the same duties on goods entering the EU, a common customs tariff, which in turn has become an important instrument of the European Common Commercial Policy. Conducted 'in the context of principles and objectives of the Union's external action' (Article 207(1) TFEU), this policy is a Union instrument to support 'the harmonious development of world trade, the progressive abolition of restrictions on international trade and on foreign direct investment, and the lowering of customs and other barriers' (Article 206 TFEU).

The Customs Union	
Internal Aspects	**External Aspects**
Abolition of tariff barriers (Art 30 TFEU)	Common Customs Tariff (CCT) (Arts 31 and 32 TFEU (ex Arts 26 and 27 TEC)) Applies to goods imported into the EU (Art 29 TFEU) European Common Commercial Policy (CCP) (Art 207(1) TFEU)

Figure 12.1 Aspects of the Customs Union

Article 29 TFEU further provides:

Products coming from a third country shall be considered to be in free circulation in a Member State if the import formalities have been complied with and any customs duties or charges having equivalent effect which are payable have been levied in that Member State, and if they have not benefited from a total or partial drawback of such duties or charges.

The Customs Union therefore has a wider dimension than a free trade area, which only involves the removal of customs duties and quotas on goods circulating within the area, and within which the participating States' powers to regulate their trading relations and policies with third countries remain untouched.

12.3 The definition of 'goods'

While the TFEU prohibits all barriers to the trade of goods, Article 28 TFEU offers no definition of the terms 'goods' or 'products'. In contrast, 'agricultural products' are clearly defined under Article 38(1) TFEU. The lacunae in the Treaty gave the ECJ the opportunity to define the term 'goods' in the widest sense. In Case 7/68 *Commission v Italy (Re Art Treasures)* [1968] ECR 423, the Court rejected the argument raised by the Italian Government, according to which the provisions on free movement of goods would not apply to a charge levied on the export of goods of historic or artistic interest. The Court ruled that such goods can be 'valued in money and ... are capable, as such, of forming the subject of commercial transactions' (at 428).

As a result, the nature of the good, its commercial value or its final use being irrelevant, the concept has been applied to goods as varied as collectable coins (Case 7/78 *R v Thompson, Johnson and Woodiwiss* [1978] ECR 2247), recyclable and non-recyclable waste (Case C-2/90 *Commission v Belgium (Re Walloon Waste)* [1992] ECR I-4431, para 28; Case C-221/06 *Stadtgemeinde Frohnleiten and Gemeindebetriebe Frohnleiten GmbH v Bundesminister für Land- und Forstwirtschaft, Umwelt und Wasserwirtschaft* [2007] ECR I-9643, para 37), wild and domesticated animals (Case 100/08 *Commission v Belgium (Re Birds Born and Bred in Captivity)* [2009] ECR I-140; Case C-219/07 *Nationale Raad van Dierenkwekers en Liefhebbers VZW and Andibel VZW v Belgium* [2008] ECR I-4475), human blood products (Case C-421/09 *Humanplasma GmbH v Austria* [2010] ECR I-12869), slot machines (Case C-124/97 *Läärä, Cotswold Microsystems Ltd and Oy Transatlantic Software Ltd v Kihlakunnansyyttäjä (Jyväskylä) and Suomen valtio (Finnish State)* [1999] ECR I-6067) and even electricity (Case 393/92 *Municipality of Almelo v Energibedriff Ijsselmij* [1994] ECR I-1477). In contrast, lottery advertisements and tickets (Case C-275/92, *Her Majesty's Customs and Excise v Schindler and Schindler* [1994] ECR I-1039) and fishing rights and angling permits (Case C-97/98 *Jägerskiöld v Gustafsson* [1999] ECR I-7319) do not constitute goods, and are covered by the provisions on freedom to provide services; while the cross-border movement of banknotes and coins that are still legal tender is covered by the provisions on free movement of capital (Joined Cases C-358/93 and C-416/93 *Criminal proceedings against Bordessa, Marí Mellado and Barbero Maestre* [1995] ECR I-361).

12.4 The elimination of tariff barriers

As Article 28 TFEU provides, the Customs Union '... shall involve the prohibition between Member States of customs duties on imports and exports and of all charges having equivalent effect ...'. The latter charges, in particular, constitute surreptitious but efficient national protectionist measures, which for decades slowed down the completion of a genuine European internal market. Equally, Member States used their fiscal policies, control of which they retain and fiercely protect, in a way that offered protection to their domestic products against imported goods similar to, or in competition with, those domestic products (discriminatory internal taxation). Both charges having equivalent effect and discriminatory internal taxation are protectionist pecuniary measures that hinder the free movement of goods and free and fair competition within the single market.

It is always tempting for governments and national authorities to try to protect their own domestic economies by making it more difficult for imported products to enter their national markets and compete against domestic products, or to make the imported goods more expensive so that domestic consumers are more likely to buy domestic goods. It is only necessary to read the 1985 Commission White Paper ('Completing the Internal Market' (COM(85) 310 final)), which made a negative assessment of the then common market, to understand how its completion as a true single market and the objective of the EC Treaties, to create a European economic system and level playing field across the Union, were frustrated by a number of persisting physical, technical and fiscal barriers.

But while the White Paper led to the adoption of the 1986 SEA, aimed at eliminating those remaining barriers, the ECJ actively participated in the process of the abolition of tariff barriers by interpreting the Treaty provisions relating to them in such a way as to give them the widest possible scope of application.

12.4.1 The abolition of customs duties

Under Article 30 TFEU:

> Customs duties on imports and exports and charges having equivalent effect shall be prohibited between Member States. This prohibition shall also apply to customs duties of a fiscal nature.

Article 30 applies to both imports and exports. The large majority of cases relate to imports, perhaps obviously, as Member States are more likely to try to hinder imports into their markets than to try to prevent domestically produced goods from being exported. However, there have been cases where Member States have tried to prevent goods leaving their territory, as in *Commission v Italy (Re Art Treasures)* (see **12.3** above) and Case C-173/05 *Commission v Italy (Re Environmental Tax)* [2007] ECR I-4917 (Italian environmental tax on methane imported from Algeria and subsequently exported to other Member States).

Customs duties can easily be identified as duties imposed on imported or exported goods on the basis of their value, and are usually designated as such. Such duties were dealt with by the ECJ in the early case of *Van Gend en Loos*, which ruled that the now repealed Article 12 TEEC had direct effect (see **Chapter 6**). Article 12 TEEC provided that

> Member States shall refrain from introducing between themselves any new customs duties on imports or exports or any charge having equivalent effect, and from increasing those which they already apply in their trade with each other.

However, as can be seen from the straightforward wording of this provision, a charge having equivalent effect (CHEE) is not defined. It was for the ECJ to formulate a precise definition of this concept.

12.4.2 Charges having equivalent effect to customs duties

Summarily mentioned in Article 30 TFEU, the concept of charges having equivalent effect to customs duties developed exponentially soon after the creation of the Customs Union.

In Case 2-3/62 *Commission v Belgium and Luxembourg (Re Gingerbread)* [1962] ECR 425, the ECJ ruled that the duty on imported gingerbread was a CHEE, as it made imports more expensive by equalising the price of gingerbread. The charge concerned was a national special duty on imported gingerbread that did not contain rye. It was designed to compensate the disadvantage suffered by gingerbread producers in Luxembourg and Belgium as a result of the high domestic tax on rye, one of the principal ingredients of the product in those countries.

It was not until Case 24/68 *Commission v Italy (Re Statistical Levy)* [1969] ECR 193 and Joined Cases 2 and 3/69 *Sociaal Fonds voor de Diamantarbeiders v SA Ch Brachfeld & Sons and Chougol Diamond Co (Diamantarbeiders)* [1969] ECR 211 that the Court defined a CHEE as follows:

> Any pecuniary charge, however small and whatever its designation and mode of application, which is imposed unilaterally on domestic or foreign goods by reason of the fact that they cross a frontier, and which is not a customs duty in the strict sense, constitutes a charge having equivalent effect ... even if it is not imposed for the benefit of the State, is not discriminatory or protective in effect and if the product on which the charge is imposed is not in competition with any domestic product. (*Diamantarbeiders*, para 15; *Statistical Levy*, para 9)

Commission v Italy was concerned with a charge of 10 lira on every 100 kg or every metric ton of goods imported or exported, to cover the cost of collecting trade statistics. In *Sociaal Fonds voor de Diamantarbeiders*, a Belgian law imposed a tax of 0.33% on unworked imported diamonds, which was collected to help fund the pensions of employees in the Belgian diamond industry.

There are formal and substantive elements in this complete and rich definition, in which every word counts.

12.4.2.1 The nature of the charge

The pecuniary nature of the charge is the first element of the Court's definition. This helps distinguish charges having equivalent effect from measures having equivalent effect, which are covered by Article 34 TFEU (see 13.2.3). The amount of the charge is irrelevant ('however small'). This clearly suggests that the Court is more concerned with the mechanical effect of the charge on the free movement of goods, as the tax will inevitably increase the costs of the good (see Case 46/76 *WJG Bauhuis v The Netherlands* [1977] ECR 5).

In the *Statistical Levy* case, the Court observed:

> The very low rate of the charge cannot change its character with regard to the principles of the Treaty which, for the purpose of determining the legality of those charges, do not admit of the substitution of quantitative criteria for those based on the nature of the charge. (para 14)

This suffices to render the charge unlawful. (See also Case 193/85 *Cooperativa Co-Frutta Srl v Amministrazione delle finanze dello Stato* [1987] ECR 2085, para 10.)

Furthermore, the Court will ignore the designation (tax, fiscal or parafiscal charge, due, fee, etc) (see Case 229/87 *Commission v Greece* [1988] ECR 6347) or mode of application of the charge (whether the charge is collected by customs, financial or fiscal authorities is irrelevant) (see Case 94/74 *Industria Gomma Articoli Vari IGAV v Ente nazionale per la cellulosa e per la carta ENCC* [1975] ECR 699, in which ENCC was an autonomous institution governed by public law and devoid of any commercial character).

12.4.2.2 The origin of the charge

As suggested in former Article 12 TEEC, and in its new wording under Article 30 TFEU, which refers to charges 'between Member States', a CHEE is 'unilaterally imposed' by a national authority. National authorities are to be understood in a wide sense so as to include local government authorities or private bodies vested with public powers, such as a professional body financing general interest activities, as in Case C-72/92 *Firma Herbert Scharbatke GmbH v Germany* [1993] ECR I-5509 (parafiscal charge credited to the German fund for the marketing of agricultural, forestry and food products).

12.4.2.3 The tax point of the charge

Whether imposed on imports or exports, a charge is a CHEE by reason of the fact that the good crosses a national border. As a result, a charge imposed solely on national agricultural products would not satisfy this criterion (see Case C-355/00 *Freskot AE v Elliniko Dimosio* [2003] ECR I-5263, para 40).

The concept of a national border extends to regional, internal State borders. In Case C-163/90 *Administration des Douanes et Droits Indirects v Léopold Legros and others* [1992] ECR I-4625, an *octroi de mer* (dock due) applicable on the entry of goods imported from another Member State into Réunion, a French overseas territory, was deemed to be a CHEE despite the fact that such charge was also imposed on goods entering that territory from another part of France (para 27) (see also Case C-363/93 *René Lancry SA v Direction Générale des Douanes and Société Dindar Confort* [1994] ECR I-3957). This ruling also applied to an *ad valorem* charge imposed on the import and export of goods in the Dodecanese region of Greece (Joined Cases C-485 and 486/93 *Simitzi v Dimos Kos* [1995] ECR I-2655). In Case C-72/03 *Carbonati Apuani Srl v Comune di Carrara* [2004] ECR I-8027, a charge levied by the town of Carrara on marble excavated within its territory that was being transported across the boundaries of a municipal territory, was regarded as a CHEE on exports, 'despite the fact that it is imposed also on goods the final destination of which is within the Member State concerned' (para 23). Soon after, the Court confirmed this ruling in a case concerning a charge imposed by the Jersey Potato Export Marketing Board on the export of Jersey potatoes to the United Kingdom (Case C-293/02 *Jersey Produce Marketing Organisation Ltd v States of Jersey and Jersey Potato Export Marketing Board* [2005] ECR I-9543).

12.4.3 Permissible charges

Although there is no express derogation from Article 30 TFEU, a charge imposed by a Member State that would otherwise be a breach of Article 30 will not be a CHEE if it relates to a general system of internal dues applied systematically and in accordance with the same criteria to domestic products and imported products alike ..., it constitutes payment for a service in fact rendered to the economic operator of a sum in proportion to the service ..., or again, subject to certain conditions, it attaches to inspections carried out to fulfil obligations imposed by [EU] law ... (Case 18/87 *Commission v Germany (Re Inspection Fees on Live Animals)* [1988] ECR 5427, para 6)

12.4.3.1 Charges as fees for services rendered by the Member State

A common defence used by the Member State suspected of levying unlawful charges is that the disputed charge 'constitutes consideration for a service rendered' and 'is in the nature of *quid pro quo*' (*Statistical Levy*, 12.4.2 above, para 15).

The ECJ has accepted the validity of such defence, provided the disputed charge satisfies three criteria. In Case 340/87 *Commission v Italy (Re Inspections and Formalities Outside Customs Office Hours)* [1989] ECR 1483 the Court observed that

[t]he Court has consistently held that a charge imposed on goods by reason of the fact that they cross a frontier is not a charge having equivalent effect prohibited by the Treaty if it constitutes consideration for a specific service actually and individually rendered to the trader, in an amount proportionate to that service (see the judgment of 26 February 1975 in Case 63/74 *W Cadsky v Istituto Nazionale per il Commercio Estero* [1975] ECR 281). For that to be so there must be a specific or individual benefit provided to the trader. (para 15)

The service must be effective and genuine

A service is a genuine one when a real benefit is provided to the trader, as opposed to general administrative formalities imposed on all traders in consideration of which a fee is levied.

In Case 266/81 *Società Italiana per l'Oleodotto Transalpino (SIOT) v Ministero delle finanze* [1983] ECR 731, the Court accepted that an Italian charge imposed on a company running a transalpine oil pipeline, for crude oil imported from countries that were not parties to the General Agreement on Tariffs and Trade (GATT) and transported to Germany and Austria, was a charge for a genuine service. Indeed, the company used 'harbour waters or installations for the navigability and maintenance of which the public authorities were responsible' (para 23). By contrast, the costs of inspections and administrative formalities carried out during the normal business hours of customs offices at frontier posts, in accordance with a European directive, could not be regarded as payments for genuine services (*Re Inspections and Formalities Outside Customs Office Hours*).

From this it follows that the service must be optional and cannot be mandatory (Case C-119/92 *Commission v Italy (Re Customs Forwarding Agents)* [1994] ECR I-393). As a result, the Court has always rebutted any attempts by Member States to justify veterinary, sanitary and technical inspections as genuine optional services on the ground that such inspections would encourage free movement of goods (Case 87/75 *Bresciani v Amministrazione Italiana delle Finanze* [1976] ECR 129), even in a case where the inspection is 'provided for by an international convention intended to encourage the free importation of plants into the countries of destination by establishing a system of inspections in the exporting State, recognised and organised on a reciprocal basis' (Case C-111/89 *Netherlands v P Bakker Hillegom BV* [1990] ECR I-1735).

The service is for the sole benefit of the trader

The service must be provided specifically to the trader. Any charge for a service rendered in the general interest of traders would be deemed a CHEE. This would be the case as regards fees for veterinary or sanitary inspections, or quality controls imposed on agricultural products. This is well illustrated by Case 63/74 *W Cadsky SpA v Istituto Nazionale per il Commercio Estero* [1975] ECR 281, in which the Court ruled that an Italian quality control on fruit and vegetables for export, coupled with a prohibition on exporting products that did not meet the quality standards, could not be regarded as a service provided for the benefit of an individual exporter, as its alleged benefit related to the general interest of all Italian exporters (paras 7 and 8).

Equally, in Case C-389/00 *Commission v Germany (Re Export of Waste)* [2003] ECR I-2001 a German mandatory contribution to a solidarity fund for the return of illegally exported waste, imposed on shipments of waste to other Member States, was not deemed to be related to a service provided specifically to the German exporters of waste, since this contribution was collected on all waste shipments and was determined according to the type and quantity of waste to be shipped. The Court then concluded that 'the disputed contribution [could] not be considered as payment for a service actually provided specifically to the economic operators in question' (para 37).

The charge must be proportionate to the actual cost of the service

The fee must only cover the actual cost of the genuine service. Any fee calculated according to the weight, or length or invoice value of a good would be regarded as a CHEE, even if the total amount charged did not exceed the total amount of the costs of the service (Case C-111/89 *Netherlands v Bakker Hillegom* [1990] ECR I-1735). The fee must therefore be calculated precisely, and could in no case be calculated on an *ad valorem* basis (Case 170/88 *Ford España SA v Spain* [1989] ECR 2305).

In Case 209/89 *Commission v Italy* [1991] ECR 1575, the Commission brought an enforcement action against the Italian Government for a declaration that the Italian system of charges payable by businesses where customs formalities were completed outside the customs area or outside normal office hours was contrary to former Articles 9, 12, 13 and 16 TEEC (now Article 30 TFEU), on the ground that where services were rendered simultaneously to several businesses in connection with customs formalities, each business was required to pay a single payment based on the nature and length of the most expensive service provided. According to the Commission, this single payment was disproportionate to the actual cost of the service rendered to each business, and therefore constituted a CHEE. Where the service required concerned a single consignment of goods belonging to several owners, the service was deemed to have been provided in respect of a single owner. Furthermore, in calculating the charges payable by the businesses, any fraction of an hour's work by the Italian customs officers was reckoned as a full hour. The Court ruled that while a fee could be calculated on the basis of a fixed-rate assessment of costs, such as a fixed hourly rate, 'the method of calculation applied in Italy [could] lead, for example, to five traders each being required to pay the charge per hour for a total of 30 minutes' work'. Such charge would therefore be deemed to be in excess of the actual cost of the customs inspection.

12.4.3.2 Charges attached to inspections required under EU law

It is also important to distinguish a CHEE from a charge attached to a service or an inspection required under EU law or an international agreement binding on the EU. Such charge is lawful (*Bauhuis*, see **12.2.4.1**), provided the charge satisfies four criteria set out by the ECJ in *Re Inspection Fees on Live Animals* (**12.4.3** above). The Court ruled that fees on the importation of live animals from other Member States to cover the costs of veterinary inspections carried out under Council Directive 81/389/EEC of 12 May 1981

> [m]ay not be classified as charges having an effect equivalent to a customs duty if the following conditions are satisfied:
> (a) they do not exceed the actual costs of the inspections in connection with which they are charged;
> (b) the inspections in question are obligatory and uniform for all the products concerned in the [EU];
> (c) they are prescribed by [EU] law in the general interest of the [EU];
> (d) they promote the free movement of goods, in particular by neutralizing obstacles which could arise from unilateral measures of inspection adopted in accordance with Article 36 of the Treaty. (para 8)

(See also Case 89/76 *Commission v Netherlands* [1977] ECR 1355 (phytosanitary inspections on exportation provided for by an International Convention) and Case 1/83 *IFG v Freistaat Bayern* [1984] ECR 349 (charge for health controls on fresh meat imported from non-Member countries under a 1972 EC Directive on health problems affecting intra-European trade in fresh meat).)

Charges imposed on domestic goods only

The Court of Justice accepts a degree of reverse discrimination against domestic goods when no goods are crossing a State border. It is then a purely internal matter with no EU element.

In Case 222/82 *Apple and Pear Development Council v KJ Lewis Ltd* [1983] ECR 4083 (see **13.2.1.1** and **13.2.3.3.1**), a number of UK growers challenged a compulsory levy imposed on apples and pears grown in the UK. The levy was imposed to fund the A&PDC (a semi-public body that conducted research, compiled statistics and provided information, publicity and promotion), but was not imposed on apples and pears imported into the UK. The Court ruled that since the levy did not apply to imports, there was no breach of former Articles 9 to 16 TEEC (now Article 30 TFEU) (para 30).

Charges imposed on domestic and imported goods

What happens if a charge is imposed on both imports and domestic products of the charging Member State? Whether a charge imposed on both imported and domestic goods breaches Article 30 TFEU will depend on:

(a) the nature of the charge;
(b) the method of calculation; and
(c) the use to which the charge is put (who benefits from the charge).

Charges that are identical and imposed as part of a general system of tax may or may not be prohibited under Article 110 TFEU as discriminatory internal taxes (see **12.4.4** below) but are not subject to Article 30 TFEU. However, if the same charges are imposed on all goods but are imposed in a different way on the imported goods, they will be in breach of Article 30. In Case 29/72 *SpA Marimex v Italian Finance Administration* [1972] ECR 1309, imported meat was subject to an inspection and to a veterinary inspection tax. Domestic meat was subject to the same rate of charge, but it was imposed on different criteria and by a different national body. The Court concluded that the charge on imported meat constituted a CHEE.

Equally, if the same charge is imposed on both imported and domestic goods but the benefits of the charge are enjoyed exclusively by the domestic goods, this will constitute a CHEE (Case 77/72 *Capolongo v Azienda Agricola Maya* [1973] ECR 611, regarding a charge on egg boxes, the benefit of which went to the Italian paper and cardboard industry; and Case 77/76 *Fratelli Cucchi v Avez SpA* [1977] ECR 987, regarding a charge on domestic and imported sugar intended to finance the Italian beet producers and sugar industry).

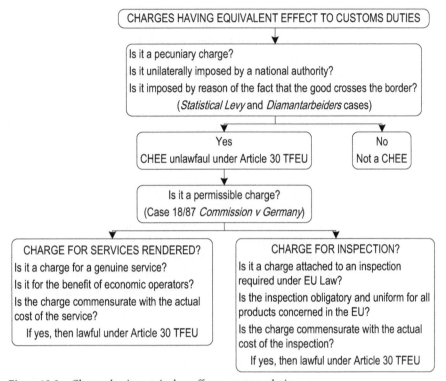

Figure 12.2   Charges having equivalent effect to customs duties

12.4.4 The prohibition of discriminatory internal taxation

It is for each Member State to determine its own systems of taxation and rates of internal tax. Politically, this is a very important issue, as the ability of a Member State to set its own taxes is seen as a question of sovereignty by individual Member States. All British governments, Conservative and Labour, have constantly said that they will not compromise on this.

The Court of Justice also recognises that Member States have wide discretion over taxation policy, as it observed in Case 243/84 *John Walker & Sons Ltd v Ministeriet for Skatter og Afgifter* [1986] ECR 875:

> [EU] law at its present stage of development does not restrict the freedom of the Member States to lay down arrangements which differentiate between certain products on the basis of objective criteria, such as the nature of the raw materials used or the production process employed.

Such differentiation is compatible with [EU] law if it pursues objectives of economic policy which are themselves compatible with the requirements of the [TFEU] and its secondary legislation, and if the detailed rules are such as to avoid any form of discrimination, direct or indirect, in regard to imports from other Member States or any form of protection of competing domestic products. (para 22)

Under Article 110 TFEU:

No Member State shall impose, directly or indirectly, on the products of other Member States any internal taxation of any kind in excess of that imposed directly or indirectly on similar domestic products.

Furthermore, no Member State shall impose on the products of other Member States any internal taxation of such a nature as to afford indirect protection to other products.

Article 110 TFEU does not prohibit Member States from setting their own taxation, but rather seeks to prevent discrimination in the rate and application of such taxation as between domestic and imported goods. As such, these provisions have to be seen as complementing those of Article 30 TFEU, as the Court observed in Case C-290/05 *Nádasdi v Vám- és Pénzügyörség Észak-Alföldi Regionális Parancsnoksága* and Case C-333/05 *Németh v Vám- és Pénzügyörség Dél-Alföldi Regionális Parancsnoksága* [2006] ECR I-10115:

[W]ithin the system of the [TFEU], Article [110 TFEU] supplements the provisions on the abolition of customs duties and charges having equivalent effect. Its aim is to ensure free movement of goods between the Member States in normal conditions of competition by the elimination of all forms of protection which may result from the application of internal taxation that discriminate against products from other Member States ... (para 45)

Naturally, and logically, if Articles 30 and 110 complement each other, they are mutually exclusive. In Case C-221/06 *Stadtgemeinde Frohnleiten* (12.3 above), the Court made it clear that

[TFEU] provisions relating to charges having equivalent effect and those relating to discriminatory internal taxation cannot be applied together, so that under the system of the Treaty the same measure cannot belong to both categories at the same time. (para 26)

12.4.4.1 'Genuine tax'

The distinction between a CHEE and an internal tax is a very important one to make, as the former is by definition presumed to be unlawful (save in exceptional circumstances) while the latter is always presumed lawful unless it is discriminating against imported goods (Case C-228/98 *Charalampos Dounias v Ypourgio Oikonomikon* [2000] ECR I-577, paras 39–41).

Furthermore, while a CHEE is levied when goods cross a national border, an internal tax is part of the national fiscal policy and is not concerned with the provenance of the goods. As the Court put it in Case 90/79 *Commission v France (Re Levy on Reprographic Machines)* [1981] ECR 283, an internal taxation measure is part of '[a] general system of internal dues applied systematically to categories of products in accordance with objective criteria irrespective of the origin of the product' (para 14). For instance, an Austrian standard fuel consumption tax (*Normverbrauchsabgabe*) imposed on motor vehicles belonging to individuals by reason of their registration in Austria upon the owners' transfer of their residence to Austria, was regarded as an internal tax whose compatibility with EU law could only be examined under Article 110 TFEU and not Article 30 TFEU (Case C-387/01 *Weigel and Weigel v Finanzlandesdirektion für Vorarlberg* [2004] ECR I-4981, para 81; see also Case C-290/05 *Nadasdi* and C-333/05 *Németh* [2006] ECR I-10115, paras 40–42; and Case C-313/05 *Brzezinski v Dyrektor Izby Celnej w Warszawie* [2007] ECR I-513, paras 22–24).

However, there is sometimes a very fine line between the two types of taxes, and the distinction between them is not always as clear-cut as the Court's definition of an internal tax might suggest. Indeed, while a tax may be part of a general system of dues, it might alternatively be a 'de facto' tax levied on imported products in the absence of similar domestic products. This was the situation, for instance, in *Cooperativa Co-Frutta Srl*, in which an Italian tax was levied on the consumption of fresh bananas originating from Colombia and imported from the Benelux, in circumstances in which there was only a very small domestic production of bananas in Sicily (120 tonnes as opposed to 357,500 tonnes of imported bananas). In this case the Court observed:

> The essential feature of a charge having an effect equivalent to a customs duty which distinguishes it from an internal tax therefore resides in the fact that the former is borne solely by an imported product as such whilst the latter is borne both by imported and domestic products.
>
> The Court has however recognized that even a charge which is borne by a product imported from another Member State, when there is no identical or similar domestic product, does not constitute a charge having equivalent effect but internal taxation within the meaning of Article [110] of the Treaty if it relates to a general system of internal dues applied systematically to categories of products in accordance with objective criteria irrespective of the origin of the products. (paras 9, 10)

As a result, even if in some circumstances low domestic production could be equated with non-existence of a product, a levy would not necessarily be regarded as a CHEE, especially if it is part of a general system of taxation, as was the case as regards the Italian tax concerned.

In *Stadtgemeinde Frohnleiten* (12.3 above), which involved the Austrian taxation of a deposit of waste coming from Italy at the Frohnleiten municipal waste disposal site, the Court decided that the measure was an internal tax, as it was levied irrespective of the origin of the waste and not because the waste crossed the Austrian border. However, it was considered as discriminatory under Article 110 TFEU on the ground that some of the exemptions from the levy benefited only domestic waste (para 73). By contrast, in Case C-109/98 *CRT France International SA v Directeur régional des impôts de Bourgogne* [1999] ECR I-2237 the Court found that a French flat-rate tax on transmitting-receiving sets operating on two-way channels ('CB sets') could not be regarded as an internal tax as it was undisputed that there was no domestic production of CB sets.

Therefore, in deciding whether a tax is a genuine internal tax, one needs to consider whether it fits into the overall system of internal taxation of the Member State, or whether it has been superimposed on the system for a particular purpose, in which case it is more likely to be subject to Article 30 TFEU.

12.4.4.2   Application of Article 110 TFEU

As the Court of Justice put it in Case C-167/05 *Commission v Sweden (Re Beer and Wine Taxes)* [2008] ECR I-2127:

> Article [110 TFEU], as a whole, has the aim of ensuring free movement of goods between the Member States in normal conditions of competition through the elimination of all forms of protection which may result from the application of internal taxation that discriminates against products from other Member States and the complete neutrality of internal taxation as regards competition between domestic products and imported products. (para 40)

As with Article 30 TFEU, the Court of Justice has held that Article 110 TFEU has direct effect (Case 57/65 *Alfons Lütticke GmbH v Hauptzollamt Sarrelouis* [1966] ECR 205, at 211).

'Similar products'

Under the first paragraph of Article 110 TFEU, Member States must not discriminate directly or indirectly against imported products by imposing on them any internal taxation in excess of that imposed on similar domestic products. In other words, the same tax rate must be applied to similar imported and domestic products.

In Case C-74/06 *Commission v Greece (Re Taxes on Second-Hand Cars)* [2007] ECR I-7585, the Court observed that

> [The first paragraph of] Article [110 TFEU] is infringed where the taxation on the imported product and that on the similar domestic product are calculated in a different manner on the basis of different criteria which lead, even if only in certain cases, to higher taxation being imposed on the imported product. (para 25)

Article 110 TFEU does not require the domestic and imported products to which the discriminatory tax applies to be identical; it only requires them to be 'similar'.

Consistent with its approach to the interpretation of other Treaty provisions, the Court of Justice has defined 'similar products' widely, so as to catch as many discriminatory internal taxes as possible. Two tests have been used over time by the Court of Justice:

(a) On the one hand, under the formal test, the Court examines whether the products in question come within some fiscal, customs or statistical classification. Case 27/67 *Firma Fink-Frucht GmbH v Hauptzollamt München-Landsbergerstrasse* [1968] ECR 223, in which the Court was dealing with a German equalization tax imposed on imported sweet peppers, is a good illustration of this test:

> Similarity between products within the meaning of the first paragraph of Article [110] exists when the products in question are normally to be considered as coming within the same fiscal, customs or statistical classification, as the case may be. (at 232)

(b) On the other hand, the broad test combines a factual comparison of the products with an economic analysis of their use. In Case 106/84 *Commission v Denmark (Re Taxes on Wine)* [1986] ECR 833, in which the Commission brought an action for annulment against Denmark for taxing wine made from grapes at a higher rate than wine made from other fruit, the Court considered the objective characteristics of the products and their capability of meeting the same need from the customer's point of view:

In order to determine whether products are similar within the terms of the prohibition laid down in the first paragraph of Article [110] it is necessary to consider ... whether they have similar characteristics and meet the same needs from the point of view of consumers. The Court endorsed a broad interpretation of the concept of similarity in its judgments of 27 February 1980 in Case 168/78 (*Commission v France* [1980] ECR 347) and 15 July 1982 in Case 216/81 (*Cogis v Amministrazione delle Finanze dello Stato* [1982] ECR 2701) and assessed the similarity of the products not according to whether they were strictly identical, but according to whether their use was similar and comparable. Consequently, in order to determine whether products are similar it is necessary first to consider certain objective characteristics of both categories of beverages, such as their origin, the method of manufacture and their organoleptic properties, in particular taste and alcohol content, and secondly to consider whether or not both categories of beverages are capable of meeting the same need from the point of view of consumers. (para 12)

Case C-302/00 *Commission v France (Re Tobacco)* [2002] ECR I-2055 can be regarded as an even better illustration of this test. The Commission brought an action for annulment against a French law imposing different tax rates on dark-tobacco and light-tobacco cigarettes, to the disadvantage of the latter. The Court observed:

According to the settled case-law of the Court, which has interpreted the concept of similarity widely, in order to determine whether products are similar it is necessary to consider whether they have similar characteristics and meet the same needs from the point of view of consumers, the test being not whether they are strictly identical but whether their use is similar and comparable ...

It is important to note as a preliminary point that dark- and light-tobacco cigarettes are manufactured from different types of the same base product, tobacco, using comparable processes. While the organoleptic characteristics of dark- and light-tobacco cigarettes, such as their taste and smell, are not identical they are nevertheless similar.

... [T]he difference between dark and light-tobacco cigarettes is one of degree. Under [the French] provision, cigarettes which contain a minimum of 60% of certain types of tobacco are considered to be dark-tobacco cigarettes while all the rest are considered to be light-tobacco cigarettes.

Further, the two types of products can satisfy the same needs of consumers, given their similar properties, since they are intended for tobacco consumption in the typical form of cigarettes, that is ready-made cylinders of tobacco rolled in sheets of paper. The fact that the average age of consumers of dark-tobacco is clearly higher than the average age of consumers of light-tobacco cannot cast doubt on that finding.

Moreover, the similarity of dark- and light-tobacco cigarettes is recognised by the [EU] legislature which, in Directives 95/59 and 92/79, provides for uniform tax treatment for all cigarettes. (paras 23–27)

'Products in competition'

Under the second paragraph of Article 110 TFEU, no Member State shall impose on products from other Member States any internal taxation of such a nature as to afford indirect protection to other products. The domestic and imported products do not need to be 'similar' for the second paragraph of Article 110 to apply. However, this provision will apply to any form of indirect tax protection of domestic products over imported products that, although not necessarily 'similar', are nevertheless in partial, indirect or potential competition. In effect, the second paragraph of Article 110 is wider in its application than the first paragraph.

The Commission has brought cases against Member States under the enforcement procedure concerning domestic taxes relating to alcohol that allegedly favoured domestic products over imported alcohol. One such case was *Commission v Sweden*, which was concerned with a Swedish law imposing internal taxes of such a nature as to afford indirect protection to beer, mainly produced in Sweden, as compared with wine, which was mainly imported from other Member States. The Court applied an economic test, using cross-elasticity of demand and past and future consumer preference:

> [I]t is appropriate to determine whether the higher taxation of wine as compared with strong beer is such as to have the effect, on the market in question, of reducing potential consumption of imported products to the advantage of competing domestic products ...
>
> In that respect, account must be taken of the difference between the selling prices of the products in question and the impact of that difference on the consumer's choice, as well as to changes in the consumption of those products ...
>
> To arrive at that assessment, a method of comparison finally accepted by both parties, based on a litre of beer and a litre of wine, must be used, since the Commission has failed to establish the relevance to the present case of any other method.
>
> ...
>
> The comparison of the relationship between the selling prices of a litre of strong beer and a litre of wine in competition with strong beer thus makes it clear that the difference in price between those two products is virtually the same before taxation as after taxation. In those circumstances, even though the difference between the respective selling prices of beer and competing wines is narrower than that found by the Court in *Commission v Belgium*, it must be pointed out that the difference in selling price found in the present case is nevertheless such that the difference in the tax treatment of those two products is not liable to influence consumer behaviour in the sector concerned. (paras 52–54 and 57)

In another landmark case, Case 170/78 *Commission v UK (Re Excise Duties on Wine)* [1980] ECR 417, in which the UK imposed a higher rate of tax on wine than on beer, the Commission accepted that beer and wine were not 'similar products' under the first paragraph of Article 110, but claimed a breach of the second paragraph of Article 110 as the different taxes indirectly protected UK alcohol (most beer consumed in the UK was domestically produced) over imported alcohol (most wine consumed in the UK was imported). The case involved a close economic analysis of the competitive relationship between beer and wine. The Court ruled that when considering whether different products are 'in competition' with each other, one must take into account whether:

(a) the products are capable of meeting the same needs of consumers (when consumers need a drink, do they need beer or wine, or just alcohol?); and

(b) there is a degree of substitution or interchangeability between the different products known as price elasticity or cross-elasticity of demand (how much does the price of beer have to go up before consumers transfer their preference to wine, and vice versa).

The Court stated:

> As regards the question of competition between wine and beer, the Court considered that, to a certain extent at least, the two beverages in question were capable of meeting identical needs, so that it had to be acknowledged that there was a degree of substitution, one for the other. It pointed out that, for the purpose of measuring the possible degree of substitution, attention should not be confined to consumer habits in a Member State or in a given region. Those habits, which were essentially variable in time and space, could not be considered to be immutable; the tax policy of a Member State must not therefore crystallize given consumer habits so as to consolidate an advantage acquired by national industries concerned to respond to them.
>
> …
>
> In view of the substantial differences in the quality and, therefore, in the price of wines, the decisive competitive relationship between beer, a popular and widely consumed beverage, and wine must be established by reference to those wines which are the most accessible to the public at large, that is to say, generally speaking, the lightest and cheapest varieties. Accordingly, that is the appropriate basis for making fiscal comparisons by reference to the alcoholic strength or to the price of the two beverages in question. (paras 8 and 12)

The Court of Justice will take into account different competitive criteria, such as respective prices, strengths of alcohol, consumer drinking habits, etc. Further, it considers not only the present situation, but also possible future developments (for example, consumer trends towards increasingly substituting wine for beer). The Court was somewhat visionary in this regard, for since the case was heard in 1980, the consumption of wine has become much more commonplace in the UK, and now accounts for a larger percentage of the overall alcohol market than it did 35 years ago.

Overall, the fiscal policy of a Member State should not be allowed to prevent future and potential competitiveness, by taxing more heavily the potentially competing imported goods.

12.4.4.3 Direct and indirect discrimination

In deciding whether there is any direct or indirect discrimination, the Court of Justice will insist on strict equality as regards the treatment of both domestic and imported goods. To that purpose, it will consider not only the rate of tax but also the basis of assessment and the rules for collection, including disproportionately high penalties for non-payment (or late payment) on imported goods.

Two types of discrimination are prohibited under the first paragraph of Article 110 TFEU:

(a) direct discrimination, where an internal tax is imposed on imports only; and
(b) indirect discrimination, where a national taxation measure applies to all relevant goods, imported and domestic, but falls more heavily on imported goods.

Direct discrimination

A national tax that is directly discriminatory cannot be justified by the Member State and will automatically be in breach of Article 110 TFEU since it is imposed on imports only. In Case 55/79 *Commission v Ireland (Re Taxation of Alcohol)* [1980] ECR 489, the discriminatory application of provisions relating to the deferment of payment of excise duty on spirits, beer and wine in Ireland, where importers had to pay the tax on imports immediately on importation while domestic producers were given a number of weeks to pay the tax, was ruled to be a breach of former Article 95 TEEC (now Article 110 TFEU), although the same tax was imposed on both domestic and imported goods (see also *Lütticke* (only imports were taxed) and Case C-90/94 *Haahr Petroleum Ltd v Åbenrå Havn and others* [1997] ECR I-4085 (imports were taxed at a higher rate than domestic products)).

Indirect discrimination

In Case 112/84 *Humblot v Directeur des services fiscaux* [1985] ECR 1367, France imposed a tax on cars that was calculated by reference to the power of their engines. As it happened, the most powerful vehicles (which were all imported, as there were no French cars as powerful) were subject to a disproportionately high tax. The cut-off point was 16 CV. Below this (covering all French cars), the tax was determined on a sliding scale up to a maximum of 1,100 FF; but for cars over 16 CV, there was a significant increase, with the tax rising to 5,000 FF. The Court found the French tax constituted indirect discrimination, as the same rules applied to both imports and domestically produced cars:

> [T]here are two distinct taxes: a differential tax which increases progressively and is charged on cars not exceeding a given power rating for tax purposes and a fixed tax on cars exceeding that rating which is almost five times as high as the highest rate of the differential tax. Although the system embodies no formal distinction based on the origin of products it manifestly exhibits discriminatory or protective features contrary to Article [110] since the power rating determining liability to the special tax has been fixed at a level such that only imported cars, in particular from other Member States, are subject to the special tax whereas all cars of domestic manufacture are liable to the distinctly more advantageous differential tax. (para 14)

Furthermore, there was no objective justification for the high tax to be charged on the (highly-powered) imported cars:

> Article [110 TFEU] prohibits the charging on cars exceeding a given power rating for tax purposes of a special fixed tax the amount of which is several times the highest amount of the progressive tax payable on cars of less than the said power rating for tax purposes, where the only cars subject to the special tax are imported, in particular from other Member States. (para 16)

There will not be a breach of Article 110 TFEU in respect of an indirectly discriminatory domestic tax if the Member State can show that the criteria for imposing the indirectly discriminatory tax are objectively justified, that is, for reasons not based on the nationality of the products. In Case 140/79 *Chemial Farmaceutici SpA v DAF SpA* [1981] ECR 1, Italy taxed synthetic ethyl alcohol (made from a petro-chemical derivative) more highly than natural (fermented) ethyl alcohol. Very small quantities of synthetic ethyl alcohol were produced in Italy, and most of the product sold in Italy was imported. Italy claimed that the relevant petro-chemical derivative should be saved for more important uses than producing synthetic ethyl alcohol. The Court ruled that the Italian tax was justified on objective criteria, as it was not based on the nationality of the goods. Therefore there was no breach of Article 110 TFEU:

As the Court has stated on many occasions …, in its present stage of development [EU] law does not restrict the freedom of each Member State to lay down tax arrangements which differentiate between certain products on the basis of objective criteria, such as the nature of the raw materials used or the production processes employed. Such differentiation is compatible with [EU] law if it pursues economic policy objectives which are themselves compatible with the requirements of the Treaty and its secondary law and if the detailed rules are such as to avoid any form of discrimination, direct or indirect, in regard to imports from other Member States or any form of protection of competing domestic products.

Differential taxation such as that which exists in Italy for denatured synthetic alcohol on the one hand and denatured alcohol obtained by fermentation on the other satisfies these requirements. It appears in fact that that system of taxation pursues an objective of legitimate industrial policy in that it is such as to promote the distillation of agricultural products as against the manufacture of alcohol from petroleum derivatives. That choice does not conflict with the rules of [EU] law or the requirements of a policy decided within the framework of the [EU]. (paras 14–15)

In Case 243/84 *John Walker & Sons Ltd v Ministeriet for Skatter og Afgifter* [1986] ECR 875, the Danish Østre Landsret referred to the Court of Justice for a preliminary ruling questions concerning the compatibility with former Article 95 TEEC (now Article 110 TFEU) of a system of differential taxation applied under Danish tax legislation to Scotch whisky and fruit wine of the liqueur type. Fruit wine of the liqueur type of an alcoholic strength not exceeding 20% by volume was subject to a specific duty, calculated per litre of the product. Scotch whisky, however, like other spirits, as well as fruit wine of the liqueur type of an alcoholic strength exceeding 20% by volume and grape wine of the liqueur type exceeding 23% by volume, was subject to a levy consisting of a specific duty imposed per litre of pure ethyl alcohol and a duty proportionate to the highest selling price charged by wholesalers. The Danish tax legislation did not define 'fruit wine'.

With regard to determining the similarity between Scotch whisky and fruit wine, the Court of Justice first considered certain objective characteristics of both alcohols, such as their origin, the method of manufacture and their organoleptic properties, in particular taste and alcohol content; and, secondly, considered whether or not both alcohols were capable of meeting the same needs from the point of view of consumers. The Court noted that they exhibited different characteristics. Fruit wine of the liqueur type was a fruit-based product obtained by natural fermentation, whereas Scotch whisky was a cereal-based product obtained by distillation. The organoleptic properties of the two products were also different. For the products to be regarded as similar, the raw material (here alcohol) also had to be present in more or less equal proportions in both products. In that regard, the alcoholic strength of Scotch whisky was 40% by volume, whereas the alcoholic strength of fruit wine of the liqueur type, to which the Danish tax legislation applied, did not exceed 20% by volume. The Court therefore concluded that Scotch whisky and fruit wine of the liqueur type could not be regarded as similar products. The Court then examined whether the two products could be regarded as being in competition. On the basis of the documents and observations presented to the Court, it concluded that

without there being any need to ascertain whether there exist[ed] a competitive relationship between Scotch whisky and fruit wine of the liqueur type, … at the present stage of its development, [EU] law … did not preclude the application of a system of taxation which differentiated between certain beverages on the basis of objective criteria. Such a system did not favour domestic producers if a significant proportion of domestic production of alcoholic beverages fell within each of the relevant tax categories. (para 23)

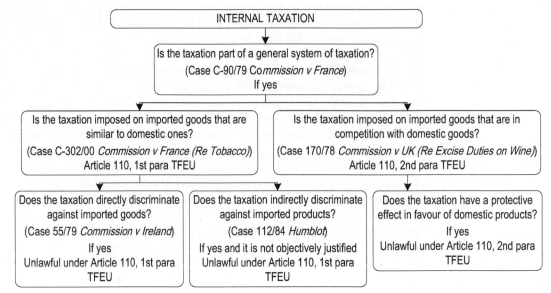

Figure 12.3 Discrimination in internal taxation

12.5 Further reading

Banks K, 'The Application of the Fundamental Freedoms to Member State Tax Measures: Guarding against Protectionism or Second-guessing National Policy Choices?' (2008) 33 *EL Rev* 482.

Barents C, 'Charges of Equivalent Effect to Customs Duties' (1978) 15 *CML Rev* 415.

Cordewener A, Kofler G and Van Thiel S, 'The Clash Between European Freedoms and National Direct Tax Law: Public Interest Defences Available to the Member States' (2009) 46 *CML Rev* 1951.

Easson A, 'The Spirits, Wine and Beer Judgments: A Legal Mickey Finn?' (1980) 5 *EL Rev* 318.

Oliver P and Enchelmaier S, 'Recent Developments in the Case-Law' (2007) 44 *CML Rev* 649.

Snell J, 'Non-Discriminatory Tax Obstacles in Community Law' (2007) 56 *ICLQ* 339.

At the heart of the European internal market, within which the free movement of goods is ensured, is the Customs Union. The European Customs Union represents a more advanced form of economic integration than a simple free trade area like the European Free Trade Area (EFTA), the North American Free Trade Area (NAFTA) or the ASEAN Free Trade Area (AFTA). It involves not only the abolition between Member States of all customs duties and charges having equivalent effect on imports and exports, but also the adoption of a common customs tariff applicable to all goods imported from third countries into the European single market. Furthermore, while Member States have wide discretion over taxation policy, they may not use internal taxes in such a way as to discriminate against products of other Member States that are either similar to or in competition with domestic products.

test your knowledge

1   The British Freight Transport Association (BFTA), which represents most UK lorry owners and drivers, seeks your advice on the compatibility of the following measures with Article 30 TFEU:

    (a)   Lorries waiting at Calais to embark on cross-Channel ferries are often targeted by asylum-seekers. Because of complaints from BFTA about poor security, the French authorities have just opened a new high-security lorry park, protected by barbed wire and patrolled by armed guards. However, the charge for using the lorry park is €50 an hour, and as lorries may have to wait up to 24 hours for a ferry, the cost can be very high.

    (b)   The UK Government believes that the recent outbreak of foot and mouth disease originated in the arrival in the UK of infected animals. It has therefore ordered extra inspections of imported animals, for which a charge of £50 per lorry will be made.

2   The BFTA considers it unfair that, while its members have to pay heavy taxes to use lorries on British roads, Irish lorries contribute nothing. The BFTA would like the British Government to impose a tax on all Irish lorries arriving at British ports that are going to drive across Britain to Continental Europe.

    Alternatively, the Association would like special tolls to be imposed, payable by all lorries, on roads connecting Irish sea ports to the British motorway network.

    Analyse whether those suggested taxes would come under Article 30 TFEU or Article 110 TFEU, and whether they would be lawful under one or the other Treaty provision.

The Free Movement of Goods: The Abolition of Non-tariff Barriers

chapter 13

study points

After reading this chapter, you will be able to understand:

- the definition of a quantitative restriction
- the definition of a measure having equivalent effect to quantitative restrictions under the *Dassonville* formula
- the *Cassis de Dijon* principle of mutual recognition
- the limits of the *Dassonville* formula
- the concept of measures governing 'certain selling arrangements'
- the market access approach
- measures having equivalent effect under Article 35 TFEU.

13.1 Introduction

The process of free movement of goods is articulated around the prohibitive and preventive approaches (negative and positive harmonisation). Both have gradually become more complementary since the early 1980s, even though the first approach still seems to prevail today. With the creation of the Customs Union, the prohibitive approach aimed to abolish or prohibit any measure from a Member State constituting a hindrance to trade within the European single market. It therefore specifically targets individual behaviour of Member States that is incompatible with their Treaty obligations. Used in Articles 25–28 and 110 TFEU for tariff barriers (see 12.4), this approach is also at the heart of Articles 34–37 TFEU on non-tariff barriers.

In contrast, the preventive approach is more holistic, being designed to anticipate and prevent the emergence of new obstacles to trade within the single market, and to reduce discrepancies between national laws by creating the conditions for their convergence. The Notification Directive (Directive 83/189/EEC codified by Directive 98/34/EC ([1998] OJ L204/37), as amended by Directive 98/48/EC ([1998] OJ L217/18)) was the first instrument to adopt this approach. It plays a fundamental role in the management of the internal market by preventing the adoption of national technical regulations and standards setting up new trade barriers. This is achieved through a mechanism of transparency and mutual exchange of information, whereby the Member States inform each other and the Commission of any proposed technical legislation, with the view to eliminating at source any new potential barriers to trade. According to the 2011 Commission Report, *The Operation of Directive 98/34/EC in 2009 and 2010* (COM(2011) 853 final),

> [t]he information procedure has brought transparency to standards at national and thus also European level and has encouraged National Standards Bodies (NSBs) to continue to take initiatives at European level, in turn promoting European harmonisation. ...

... [T]he notification to the Commission of national technical regulations prior to their adoption has proved to be an effective instrument of prevention of barriers to trade and of cooperation between the Commission and the Member States and among the Member States themselves as well as improving the regulatory framework. (at 3)

The second main instrument was the early warning and rapid intervention system created under Council Regulation (EC) No 2679/98 on the functioning of the internal market in relation to the free movement of goods among the Member States ([1998] OJ L337/8). Under this information and monitoring mechanism, the Member States must inform the European Commission of any major obstacles to trade that might seriously disrupt the free movement of goods and/or cause individuals serious loss, such as border blockades (Case C-265/95 *Commission v France (Re Spanish Strawberries)* [1997] ECR I-6959: blockades and destruction of lorry-loads by French farmers protesting against the import of fruit and vegetables from Spain), or demonstrations (Case C-112/00 *Eugen Schmidberger, Internationale Transporte und Planzüge v Austria* [2003] ECR I-5659: political demonstrations by environmentalists leading to the closure of major routes) or even road works concerning important routes.

Regulation 2679/98 was supplemented by the 'New Legislative Framework' for the marketing of products, the purpose of which is to improve and strengthen the working of the internal market for goods and the placing of industrial products in this market. This Framework, comprising two Regulations and one Decision, was adopted on 9 July 2008:

- Regulation (EC) No 764/2008 laying down procedures relating to the application of certain national technical rules to products lawfully marketed in another Member State ([2008] OJ L218/21). This Regulation aims to improve the application of the principle of mutual recognition by laying down, in non-harmonised sectors, rules and procedures that authorities of Member States must follow when they take or intend to take measures that could hinder the free movement of goods lawfully marketed in another Member State.
- Regulation (EC) No 765/2008 setting out the requirements for accreditation and market surveillance relating to the marketing of products ([2008] OJ L218/30). This Regulation organises market surveillance, which ensures that products placed on the market do not put at risk the health and safety of consumers and workers or any public interest, and that any measures are taken to stop the marketing of products that do not comply with EU harmonisation legislation requirements. In accordance with the principle of subsidiarity (see 2.4), while the requirements for market surveillance are set out in the Regulation, its organisation and practice are carried out at national level.
- Decision No 768/2008/EC on a common framework for the marketing of products ([2008] OJ L218/82). This Decision sets out common conformity assessment procedures, whereby products undergo testing, inspection and certification to ensure that they meet the requirements of applicable European technical harmonisation legislation. Combined with the Regulation on market surveillance, the Decision forms an overall and consistent framework for the marketing of products.

While the preventive approach has made undeniable progress, it is unlikely to replace or even marginalise the prohibitive approach, since Member States are always tempted to introduce new, disguised, indirect obstacles to trade. The prohibitive, repressive approach seems to remain the most efficient instrument against all attempts at protectionism.

13.2 The prohibition of physical and technical barriers

The previous chapter examined financial charges imposed by Member States. This section considers non-financial restrictions imposed by a Member State, ie national rules that impose administrative hurdles that may ultimately cost money to ensure compliance with such administrative practices, without involving any form of payment of dues.

Under Article 34 TFEU:

> Quantitative restrictions on imports and all measures having equivalent effect shall be prohibited between Member States.

And under Article 35 TFEU:

> Quantitative restrictions on exports, and all measures having equivalent effect, shall be prohibited between Member States.

Both provisions have been held to be directly applicable and to have vertical direct effect (Case 74/76 *Iannelli & Volpi SpA v Ditta Paolo Meroni* [1977] ECR 557, para 13; Case 83/78 *Pigs Marketing Board v Raymond Redmond* [1978] ECR 2347, para 66).

13.2.1 Measures caught under Articles 34 and 35 TFEU

By definition, Articles 34 and 35 TFEU are directed at Member States, and therefore cover primarily national measures that are taken by central or local authorities (see **13.2.1.1**). This means that measures taken by private individuals or purely internal ones are, in principle, not covered by those provisions (see **13.2.1.2**). Furthermore, although one would assume that Articles 34 and 35 would not apply to EU measures, the Court has ruled to the contrary (see **13.2.1.3**).

13.2.1.1 National measures

All measures of Member States are subject to Articles 34 and 35 TFEU. These include not only legally binding measures of central public authorities (Acts of Parliament and secondary legislation), but also measures by local authorities as well as administrative practices (see Case C-41/02 *Commission v The Netherlands* [2004] ECR I-11375: consistent policy of the Dutch Health Minister on granting derogations from the legal prohibition on the marketing of foodstuff fortified with micronutrients).

Articles 34 and 35 apply also to rules of State-sponsored bodies or of private bodies exercising public powers. In 1978 the Irish Goods Council, a private company, launched the 'Buy Irish Campaign' to promote goods made in Ireland. The Commission brought an enforcement action against Ireland (Case 249/81 *Commission v Ireland (Re Buy Irish Campaign)* [1982] ECR 4005) for breach of the former Article 30 TEEC (now Article 34 TFEU). The Irish Government raised three potential defences:

- The 'Buy Irish Campaign' was created by the Irish Goods Council as a private company, and as such was not subject to the free movement of goods provisions.
- The 'Buy Irish Campaign' was not legally binding on the Irish public as it was not law (the Irish Goods Council could not force the Irish public to buy Irish goods, nor deter them from buying imported goods).

- The 'Buy Irish Campaign' had clearly failed, as the evidence produced by the Irish Government showed that the Irish consumers had bought more imported goods following the campaign.

The Court of Justice rejected all arguments. The Irish Goods Council was to be treated as part of the Irish Government as a State-sponsored body:

> It is … apparent that the Irish Government appoints the members of the Management Committee of the Irish Goods Council, grants it public subsidies which cover the greater part of its expenses and, finally, defines the aims and the broad outline of the campaign conducted by that institution to promote the sale and purchase of Irish products. In the circumstances the Irish Government cannot rely on the fact that the campaign was conducted by a private company in order to escape any liability it may have under the provisions of the Treaty.
>
> …
>
> … [T]he campaign cannot be likened to advertising by private or public undertakings, or by a group of undertakings, to encourage people to buy goods produced by those undertakings. Regardless of the means used to implement it, the campaign is a reflection of the Irish Government's considered intention to substitute domestic products for imported products on the Irish market and thereby to check the flow of imports from other Member States. (paras 15 and 23)

The campaign was capable of hindering the pattern of trade between Member States, as it was capable of influencing trade and therefore of frustrating the aims of the free movement of goods:

> Such a practice cannot escape the prohibition laid down by Article [34] of the Treaty solely because it is not based on decisions which are binding upon undertakings. Even measures adopted by the government of a Member State which do not have binding effect may be capable of influencing the conduct of traders and consumers in that State and thus of frustrating the aims of the [EU] … (para 28)

In a later decision, Case 222/82 *Apple and Pear Development Council v KJ Lewis Ltd* [1983] ECR 4083, the Court had to examine whether the promotion of the consumption of apples and pears by a series of advertisements – featuring typically English varieties, such as Cox's Orange Pippin apples and Conference pears – by the Apple and Pear Development Council (APDC), a semi-public body, could be regarded as national measures subject to Article 34 TFEU. The Court observed that

> … a publicity campaign to promote the sale and purchase of domestic products may, in certain circumstances, fall within the prohibition contained in Article [34] of the Treaty, if the campaign is supported by the public authorities. In fact, a body such as the Development Council, which is set up by the government of a Member State and is financed by a charge imposed on growers, cannot under [EU] law enjoy the same freedom as regards the methods of advertising used as that enjoyed by producers themselves or producers' associations of a voluntary character. (para 17)

Rules adopted by a professional body within a Member State can also constitute a 'measure' subject to Article 34 if the rules are capable of affecting trade between the Member States. In Joined Cases 266 and 267/87 *The Queen v Royal Pharmaceutical Society of Great Britain* [1989] ECR 1295, the Court ruled that to decide if a particular professional body has sufficient authority to establish measures that could fall foul of Article 34, the Court will consider the:

(a) legal status of the professional body;
(b) requirements of mandatory membership by relevant professionals;
(c) power to enact rules of ethics;
(d) existence of disciplinary powers; and
(e) sanctions that the professional body can invoke if members break the rules (paras 14–16).

In Case C-171/11 *Fra.bo SpA v Deutsche Vereinigung des Gas- und Wasserfaches eV (DVGW) – Technisch-Wissenschaftlicher Verein* of 12 July 2012, ECLI:EU:C:2012:453, the question was raised as to whether a non-profit body governed by private law, which set technical standards for products used in the drinking water supply sector in order to certify products in compliance with those standards, had to comply with Article 34 TFEU 'where the national legislation considers the products certified by that body to be compliant with national law and that has the effect of restricting the marketing of products which are not certified by that body' (para 32). The Court ruled in the affirmative.

Even measures or actions taken by non-State bodies or individuals, which might hinder the free movement of goods, could fall foul of Article 34 TFEU, should the State fail to take steps to prevent them. In *Re Spanish Strawberries* (**13.1** above), in which French farmers prevented imports of Spanish strawberries into France by blockading roads and intercepting lorries and destroying their loads, the Commission brought an action against the French Government on the ground that it should have taken steps to prevent such acts by the French farmers. The Court of Justice agreed with the Commission, and notably ruled that,

> [a]s an indispensable instrument for the realization of a market without internal frontiers, Article [34] therefore does not prohibit solely measures emanating from the State which, in themselves, create restrictions on trade between Member States. It also applies where a Member State abstains from adopting the measures required in order to deal with obstacles to the free movement of goods which are not caused by the State. (para 30)

Given the fundamental nature of Article 34 TFEU, and in view of Article 4(3) TEU, which requires Member States to 'take all necessary and appropriate measures' to ensure that, notably, the EU's fundamental freedoms are respected (**principle of sincere cooperation**, see **2.3.2**), Member States are required to take positive action to prevent their own nationals from acting in a way that is incompatible with the EU Treaty (see *Re Spanish Strawberries*, para 32).

In contrast, Austria was not found guilty of a breach of Article 34 TFEU when it authorised a demonstration against pollution along the Brenner pass, which blocked traffic on that transit route (*Schmidberger*).

13.2.1.2 'Purely internal measures'

The Treaty provisions on free movement of goods naturally imply that the national measure affects cross-frontier movement between Member States. Consequently, a measure that affects trade within a single State only, with no cross-border element, will be deemed to be a purely internal measure and will not be subject to Articles 34 or 35 TFEU. In Case 286/81 *Criminal proceedings against Oosthoek's Uitgeversmaatschappij BV* [1982] ECR 4575, the Court observed, in the context of a Dutch law prohibiting the offering of free books to purchasers of an encyclopaedia for sales promotion purposes, that

> ... it must be stated that the application of the Netherlands legislation to the sale in the Netherlands of encyclopaedias produced in that country is in no way linked to the importation or exportation of goods and does not therefore fall within the scope of [Article 34 and Article 35 TFEU]. However, the sale in the Netherlands of encyclopaedias produced in Belgium and the sale in other Member States of encyclopaedias produced in the Netherlands are transactions forming part of intra-[EU] trade. ... [I]t is therefore necessary to determine whether provisions of the type contained in the Netherlands legislation are compatible with both [Article 34 and Article 35 TFEU]. (para 9)

It appears from the case law of the Court that the scope of purely internal measures is increasingly shrinking. Joined Cases C-321/94 *Criminal proceedings against Pistre Michèle*, C-322/94 *Barthes*, C-323/94 *Milhau* and C-324/94 *Oberti* [1997] ECR I-2343 provide a good illustration of this tendency. Here, the Court held that a French law preventing the use of indications of 'mountain' provenance for agricultural products and foodstuffs without prior administrative authorisation was to be regarded as a measure having equivalent effect (MHEE) to a quantitative restriction (see **13.2.3** below), on the ground that

> ... whilst the application of a national measure having no actual link to the importation of goods does not fall within the ambit of Article [34] of the Treaty ... Article [34] cannot be considered inapplicable simply because all the facts of the specific case before the national court are confined to a single Member State. (para 44)

Similarly, in Case C-448/98 *Criminal proceedings against Guimont* [2000] ECR I-1663, the Court rejected the argument of the French Government that former Article 30 TEC (now Article 34 TFEU) did not apply to the French Decree reserving the designation 'Emmenthal' for cheeses with 'a hard, dry rind, of a colour between golden yellow and light brown', which Mr Guimont was accused of infringing, since the Decree did not, in practice, apply to imported products and it 'was designed to create obligations solely for national producers and [did] not therefore concern intra-[EU] trade in any way' (para 14). First, the Court observed that former Article 30 TEC was not

> designed to ensure that goods of national origin enjoy the same treatment as imported goods in every case, and a difference in treatment as between goods which is not capable of restricting imports or of prejudicing the marketing of imported goods does not fall within the prohibition contained in that article. (para 15)

Then, it held that the mere fact that the French law, which was applicable without distinction to both French and imported products, did not apply to imported products in practice, did 'not exclude the possibility of it having effects which indirectly or potentially hinder intra-[EU] trade' (paras 16 and 17).

13.2.1.3 EU measures

The Court was also asked to analyse whether EU measures could potentially be MHEEs (see further 13.2.3 below). Generally, especially in relation to EU rules relating to the common organisation of markets or limiting the production or marketing of certain agricultural products, the Court would answer in the negative, as in Case 15/83 *Denkavit Nederland BV* [1984] ECR 2171, paras 16–17. Yet, the principle that '[t]he prohibition of quantitative restrictions and of all measures having equivalent effect applies not only to national measures but also to measures adopted by the [EU] institutions' was reiterated by the Court (see *Denkavit*, para 15, as confirmed in Case C-51/93 *Meyhui NV v Schott Zwiesel Glaswerke AG* [1994] ECR I-3879, para 11, and Case C-114/96 *Kieffer and Thill* [1997] ECR I-3629, para 27). Along those lines, in Case C-47/90 *Établissements Delhaize frères and Compagnie Le Lion SA* [1992] ECR I-3669, para 26 and Case C-315/92 *Verband Sozialer Wettbewerb eV v Clinique Laboratoires SNC and Estée Lauder Cosmetics GmbH* [1994] ECR I-317, para 12, the Court confirmed that 'all [EU] secondary legislation, [must] be interpreted in the light of the Treaty rules on the free movement of goods'. As a result, provided they satisfy the proportionality test, EU measures may equally be justified under Article 36 TFEU (see **14.2.1**), as in Case C-210/03 *R (Swedish Match AB and Swedish Match UK Ltd) v Secretary of State for Health* [2004] ECR I-11893 in which the Court ruled that

> [w]hile the prohibition of marketing tobacco products for oral use under Article 8 of Directive 2001/37 constitutes one of the restrictions referred to in Articles [34 and 35 TFEU], it is nevertheless justified … on grounds of the protection of human health. It cannot therefore, in any event, be regarded as having been adopted in breach of the provisions of Articles [34 and 35 TFEU]. (para 61)

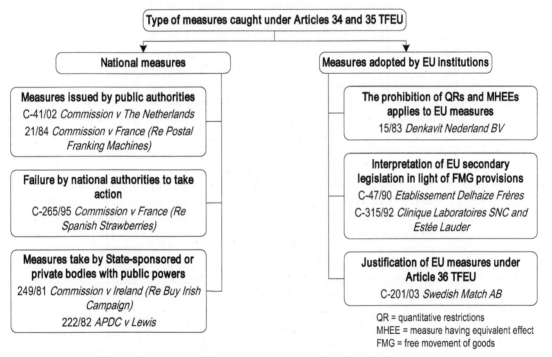

Figure 13.1   Type of measures caught under Articles 34 and 35 TFEU

13.2.2   Quantitative restrictions

Quantitative restrictions were classically defined by the Court in Case 2/73 *Geddo v Ente Nazionale Risi* [1973] ECR 865, as 'measures which amount to a total or partial restraint of, according to the circumstances, imports, exports or goods in transit' (at 879). These are quotas artificially imposed by a Member State to restrict by value or quantity the import of certain products into that Member State. As such, a total ban on imports is regarded as a quantitative restriction, as in Case 34/79 *R v Henn and Darby* [1979] ECR 3795. In this case, Henn and Darby were prosecuted in the UK for importing certain pornographic material, contrary to a UK law imposing a complete ban on the importation of such items. The defendants claimed that the UK law was unlawful as it hindered trade between Member States and constituted a MHEE under former Article 30 TEEC (now Article 34 TFEU). Contrary to the interpretation of the Court of Appeal, which did not hold a ban to be the same as a quantitative restriction, the Court of Justice ruled that

> [i]t is clear that [Article 34] includes a prohibition on imports inasmuch as this is the most extreme form of restriction. The expression used in Article [34] must therefore be understood as being the equivalent of the expression 'prohibitions or restrictions on imports' occurring in Article 36.
>
> … [T]herefore … a law such as that referred to in this case constitutes a quantitative restriction on imports within the meaning of Article [34] of the Treaty. (paras 12 and 13)

13.2.3 Measures having equivalent effect to quantitative restrictions on imports

Like the notion of charges having equivalent effect (see **12.4.2**), the notion of measures having equivalent effect (MHEE) is not defined in the Treaty. Therefore the Commission and the Court of Justice were able to shape this concept into an efficient means of limiting the impact of new national protectionist measures that arose at the end of the transitional period in 1970, when all customs duties and quantitative restrictions had been abolished.

The Commission was first to attempt to define a 'measure having equivalent effect' in Directive 70/50 of 22 December 1969 ([1971] OJ L013/29). This Directive was designed to act as guidance at the end of the transitional period. While it no longer has legal effect, it still offers good examples of such measures, and notably distinguishes between two categories:

(a) Article 2 provides a non-exhaustive list of measures that apply exclusively to, and have adverse effects on, imports or favour domestic products. These are therefore directly discriminatory (distinctly applicable measures). These include measures which, for example, impose maximum or minimum prices on imports, or subject imported products only to conditions relating to shape, size, weight, composition, presentation, or identification, or 'subject imported products to conditions which are different from those for domestic products and more difficult to satisfy', etc.

(b) Article 3 refers to

> … measures governing marketing of products which deal, in particular, with shape, size, weight, composition, presentation, identification or putting up and which are equally applicable to domestic and imported products, where the restrictive effect of such measures on the free movement of goods exceeds the effects intrinsic to trade rules.

These are indistinctly or equally applicable measures.

13.2.3.1 The *Dassonville* formula

The Court of Justice went one step further by offering a wide and holistic definition of 'measures having equivalent effect'. In Case 8/74 *Procureur du Roi v Dassonville and Dassonville* [1974] ECR 837, the Court was asked to examine the compatibility with former Article 30 TEEC of a Belgian law that required importers of Scotch whisky to produce certificates of origin demonstrating that the whisky was effectively produced in Scotland. Dassonville purchased Scotch whisky in France, but was unable to produce a certificate of origin from the seller. Consequently, he was prosecuted in Belgium for not having a certificate. His defence was that the Belgian measure was a MHEE contrary to Article 30 TEEC (now Article 34 TFEU). The Court ruled that

> the requirement by a Member State of a certificate of authenticity which is less easily obtainable by importers of an authentic product which has been put into free circulation in a regular manner in another Member State than by importers of the same product coming directly from the country of origin constitutes a measure having an effect equivalent to a quantitative restriction as prohibited by the Treaty. (para 9)

But, more importantly, it produced the following definition, known as the '*Dassonville* formula':

> All trading rules enacted by Member States which are capable of hindering, directly or indirectly, actually or potentially, intra-[EU] trade are to be considered as measures having an effect equivalent to quantitative restrictions. (para 5)

The crucial element of this definition is the possible effect of a national measure on trade between the Member States. There is no need to show an intent to discriminate on the part of the Member State, or, indeed, actual hindrance of trade. Consequently, the *de minimis* rule used in competition law (see **17.2.2.2**), that is the degree to which trade is affected, is not used by the Court to assess the effect on trade of national measures (Joined Cases 177 and 178/82 *Criminal proceedings against van de Haar and Kaveka de Meern BV* [1984] ECR 1797, para 13).

Unlike the Commission, the Court of Justice does not make express the distinction between distinctly and indistinctly applicable measures: both are caught by the *Dassonville* formula. However, the Court has been more strict in its application of Article 34 TFEU, catching a wider range of national measures than the Commission had suggested in Directive 70/50, particularly in respect of indistinctly applicable measures as defined in Article 3 of the Directive (see **13.2.3** above).

13.2.3.2 The *Cassis de Dijon* approach

Following Member States' complaints about its approach, the Court retreated slightly from the broad definition of a MHEE in the *Dassonville* formula by developing a new approach in the *Cassis de Dijon* case (Case 120/78 *Rewe-Zentral AG v Bundesmonopolverwaltung für Branntwein* [1979] ECR 649). There, the Court applied the *Dassonville* formula but laid down two principles to help regulate its application:

(a) the rule of reason (first principle) (see **14.3.1**); and
(b) the principle of mutual recognition or equivalence (second principle) (see below).

The ruling

In *Cassis de Dijon*, a German law, the *Branntweinmonopolgesetz*, set a minimum alcohol level of 32% for certain spirits, whether domestic or imported – therefore an indistinctly applicable measure – including for Cassis de Dijon, a French blackcurrant liqueur the alcohol content of which was only 15–20%. Consequently, Cassis de Dijon was prevented from being imported into Germany, since it did not satisfy the German rules. On a preliminary reference from the Hesse Finance Court, the Court ruled:

> It is clear from the foregoing that the requirements relating to the minimum alcohol content of alcoholic beverages do not serve a purpose which is in the general interest and such as to take precedence over the requirements of the free movement of goods, which constitutes one of the fundamental rules of the [Union].
>
> In practice, the principle [*sic*] effect of requirements of this nature is to promote alcoholic beverages having a high alcohol content by excluding from the national market products of other Member States which do not answer that description.
>
> It therefore appears that the unilateral requirement imposed by the rules of a Member State of a minimum alcohol content for the purposes of the sale of alcoholic beverages constitutes an obstacle to trade which is incompatible with the provisions of Article [34] of the Treaty.
>
> There is therefore no reason why, provided that they have been lawfully produced and marketed in one of the Member States, alcoholic beverages should not be introduced into any other Member State ... (para 14)

Consequently, the Court ruled that

> the concept of 'measures having an effect equivalent to quantitative restrictions on imports' contained in Article [34] of the Treaty is to be understood to mean that the fixing of a minimum alcohol content for alcoholic beverages intended for human consumption by the legislation of a Member State also falls within the prohibition laid down in that provision where the importation of alcoholic beverages lawfully produced and marketed in another Member State is concerned. (para 15)

The principle of mutual recognition or equivalence

In this landmark case of *Cassis de Dijon*, the Court rejected the German Government's argument that obstacles to trade had been reduced by recourse to the procedure for the harmonisation of national standards on the manufacture and marketing of goods as they directly affected the establishment and functioning of the then common market. Until such standards had been harmonised, former Article 30 TEEC (now Article 34 TFEU) was to be applied only in so far as those provisions led to discrimination against imported goods in relation to domestic goods. The German Government further argued that

> [m]easures which are applicable without distinction to domestic products and imported products [did] not, according to Directive No 70/50, have effects equivalent to those of quantitative restrictions and [did] not therefore, in principle, fall within the scope of Article [34]. (at 655)

Laying down the principle of equivalence or mutual recognition, the Court explained that such a national rule cannot be relied upon in order to prohibit in a general manner the import and marketing of products that have been 'lawfully produced and marketed' in other Member States. Far from being an issue of intrinsic validity of the national rule, it is rather one of reliance on the rule to prevent the marketing of imported goods.

As a result, as the Commission explained in its Communication concerning the consequences of the judgment given by the Court of Justice on 20 February 1979 in Case 120/78 ('*Cassis de Dijon*') ([1980] OJ C256/2):

> Any product imported from another Member State must in principle be admitted to the territory of the importing Member State if it has been lawfully produced, that is, conforms to rules and processes of manufacture that are customarily and traditionally accepted in the exporting country, and is marketed in the territory of the latter.
>
> This principle implies that Member States, when drawing up commercial or technical rules liable to affect the free movement of goods, may not take an exclusively national viewpoint and take account only of requirements confined to domestic products. The proper functioning of the [single] market demands that each Member State also give consideration to the legitimate requirements of the other Member States. (at 2)

The principle of mutual recognition is still applicable in the absence of common rules relating to the production and marketing of goods (see 11.3).

That being said, the national rule might be justified under Article 36 TFEU (see 14.2.1), or on the ground of any of the 'imperative requirements' mentioned in para 8 of this judgment, namely effectiveness of fiscal supervision, the protection of public health, the fairness of commercial transactions and the defence of the consumer (see 14.3.1).

The economic significance of *Cassis de Dijon*

If the overall aim of economic integration is to be achieved, it is the consumers and not the national laws that will decide which goods will sell and which will not. It is possible that consumers in a Member State will stick with their domestic products, but if national producers are to maintain their market share, it must be because of the quality of the goods and their ability to persuade consumers that their products are best, not through taking advantage of the protectionist national laws of their Member State.

From *Cassis de Dijon*, the Court of Justice clearly has tried to empower consumers. This is particularly well illustrated in the German *Re Law of Purity of Beer* case (see 13.2.3.3 and 14.3.1.2), in which the 1516 *Reinheitsgebot* (the regulation concerning the production of beer in Germany) could not be relied upon to prohibit the marketing of imported beer in Germany. Yet this ruling did not have the effect of preventing German breweries from producing and marketing their beers according to the *Reinheitsgebot*. As a result, German consumers have now a wider choice, and can still enjoy a German lager as well as Scottish or Belgian ale, or English bitter or stout.

13.2.3.3 Examples of measures having equivalent effect

Distinctly applicable measures

Measures imposing conditions on imported goods only

The issue of new or old car registrations provides an abundance of cases concerning the question of national supplementary and excessive requirements being imposed on cars imported from other Member States. For instance, in Case C-524/07 *Commission v Austria* [2008] ECR I-187, the Court found that an Austrian law requiring used motor vehicles previously registered in and imported from other Member States to comply with stricter technical requirements, with regard to exhaust emissions and noise pollution in compliance with Directive 93/59/EEC ([1993] OJ L186/21), at the time of registration in Austria, was a MHEE, because vehicles having the same characteristics and which were already authorised for use on the roads in Austria were not subject to the same requirements in the case of their re-registration.

Import licences

In Joined Cases 51–54/71 *International Fruit Company NV v Produktschap voor groenten en fruit* [1971] ECR 1107, national provisions requiring import or export licences, even if granted automatically or as a formality, or any other similar procedure, were deemed to be MHEEs by their very nature.

Similarly, in Case C-170/04 *Rosengren and others v Riksåklagaren* [2007] ECR I-4071, a Swedish law on alcohol provided that the wholesale import of alcohol could be undertaken only by persons who were approved warehouse keepers or registered recipients of alcoholic goods, and that such goods could be imported into Sweden only by authorised persons. Rosengren and others ordered cases of bottles of wine from Spain, directly by correspondence and without declaring them to the Swedish customs authorities. The bottles were confiscated on the ground that they had been unlawfully imported in breach of the law on alcohol. The Court found that the provisions of the *Alkohollagen*, under which private individuals were prohibited from importing alcoholic beverages, amounted to a quantitative restriction on imports under former Article 28 TEC (now Article 34 TFEU) and could not be justified under former Article 30 TEC (now Article 36 TFEU).

Inspections

A large number of MHEEs can be found in the numerous cases dealing with unjustified, unilaterally imposed veterinary, sanitary and technical inspections. Where there is no, or incomplete, European harmonising legislation, Member States have some discretion to require that imported products be inspected, provided that such additional inspections or controls do not impose any additional burden on imported goods (see Case C-14/02 *ATRAL SA v Belgium* [2003] ECR I-4431).

For instance, in Case 251/78 *Firma Denkavit Futtermittel GmbH v Minister für Ernährung, Landwirtschaft und Forsten des Landes Nordrhein-Westfalen* [1979] ECR 3369, a trader, who imported feeding-stuffs containing products of animal origin into Germany from the Netherlands, questioned the compatibility with former Article 30 TEEC (now Article 34 TFEU) of a 1957 regional regulation from the Land of North Rhine-Westphalia on animal health measures applicable on the importation and transit of feeding-stuffs containing products of animal origin from abroad. Under the regulation concerned, the feeding-stuffs could only be imported if two conditions were fulfilled:

(a) that a certificate from the competent authorities in the exporting country was produced, confirming that the goods had undergone a heating process during or after dehydration in order to destroy *Salmonellae* which might have been present and;

(b) that the feeding-stuffs had to be subject upon importation to a preliminary inspection, in the form of samples taken for inspection purposes by veterinary experts and examined in an official veterinary inspection institute in Germany, after which their importation would only be possible once it had been established by bacteriological analysis that the goods were free from *Salmonellae*.

The Court of Justice ruled that the German regional regulation fell within the prohibition of former Article 30 TEEC (now Article 34 TFEU) unless justified under former Article 36 TEEC (now Article 36 TFEU).

More recently, in Case C-170/07 *Commission of the European Communities v Republic of Poland* [2008] ECR I-87, Polish legislation requiring imported second-hand vehicles to undergo a roadworthiness test prior to their registration, whereas domestic vehicles with the same characteristics were not subject to such a requirement, was deemed to be in breach of former Article 28 TEC (now Article 34 TFEU).

Measures favouring or promoting domestic products

Campaigns promoting domestic goods over imports Any advantage given exclusively to domestic products will fall foul of Article 34 TFEU. The Court will regard as unlawful any form of indirect State aid, such as advertising campaigns promoting or favouring domestic products.

For instance, in the *Buy Irish Campaign* case (above **13.2.1.1**), the campaign had the potential to give Irish goods a preference over imported goods. Through this campaign, the Irish Government sought to promote Irish goods and to achieve a 3% switch in customer spending from imports to Irish products. A number of means were adopted for that purpose:

(a) an information service, indicating to consumers which products were made in Ireland and where they could be obtained;

(b) exhibition facilities for Irish goods;

(c) encouragement of the use of a 'Buy Irish' symbol for goods made in Ireland; and

(d) the organisation of a publicity campaign by the Irish Goods Council.

Following intervention by the Commission, only the first two measures were dropped. In an enforcement ruling, the Court observed that the Irish Government, which appointed the members of the Irish Goods Council and were its main founders, was thus responsible for the Council's activities, even though they were run by a private body, and that '[t]he advertising campaign to encourage the sale and purchase of Irish products cannot be divorced from its origin as part of the government programme' (para 26). Consequently, the third and fourth activities listed above

> amount[ed] to the establishment of a national practice, introduced by the Irish Government and prosecuted with its assistance, the potential effect of which on imports from other Member States is comparable to that resulting from government measures of a binding nature. (para 28)

And

> [s]uch a practice cannot escape the prohibition laid down by Article [34] of the Treaty solely because it is not based on decisions which are binding upon undertakings. Even measures adopted by the government of a Member State which do not have binding effect may be capable of influencing the conduct of traders and consumers in that State and thus of frustrating the aims of the [EU]. (para 29)

A similar situation occurred in the UK in the *Apple and Pear Development Council* case (see **13.2.1.1**), in which the Council, a professional body vested with statutory powers, engaged in an advertising campaign, including the slogan 'Polish up your English', intended to encourage consumers to purchase domestically grown apples and pears. Following the *Buy Irish Campaign* case, the Court confirmed that 'a publicity campaign to promote the sale and purchase of domestic products may, in certain circumstances, fall within the prohibition contained in Article [34] of the Treaty, if the campaign is supported by the public authorities' (para 17). As the Council was a semi-public body set up by the British Government, and was financed by a charge imposed on growers, it could not 'under [EU] law enjoy the same freedom as regards the methods of advertising used as that enjoyed by producers themselves or producers' associations of a voluntary character' (para 17). As a result, such a body

> is under a duty not to engage in any advertising intended to discourage the purchase of products of other Member States or to disparage those products in the eyes of consumers. Nor must it advise consumers to purchase domestic products solely by reason of their national origin. (para 18)

However, the Council could draw attention, in its publicity, to specific qualities of domestic fruit, or organise campaigns to promote the sale of certain varieties, mentioning their particular properties (eg apples being 'crisp' or 'crunchy'), even if these varieties were typically national products.

Therefore, by contrast with the *Buy Irish Campaign* case, a Member State is not prohibited from running a campaign based on the quality of the goods concerned, even though the qualities promoted by the campaign are those that are primarily found in domestic (rather than imported) goods, provided that predominance is given to quality and not origin. To prefer domestic goods over imported goods solely on the grounds of origin would be a breach of Article 34 TFEU.

Measures making imports more costly or more difficult Any national measure imposing on imported products conditions that are not imposed on domestic ones would have the effect of increasing the cost of the former or hindering their market access, thus putting them at a commercial disadvantage.

In Case 113/80 *Commission v Ireland (Re Irish Souvenirs)* [1981] ECR 1625, 'Irish' souvenirs produced outside of Ireland had to be marked 'foreign', or with the country of their origin, whereas souvenirs produced in Ireland did not have to be marked in this way. The Commission brought an enforcement action claiming breach of former Article 30 TEEC (now Article 34 TFEU). The Irish Government did not dispute that the measure was in breach of the free movement of goods provision, but it argued that it was justified, notably, to protect consumers under the first *Cassis de Dijon* principle (see **14.3.1**). The Court disagreed, and concluded that it was a MHEE.

Public procurement measures or contracts designed to favour domestic firms In Case 72/83 *Campus Oil Limited and others v Minister for Industry and Energy and others* [1984] ECR 2727, Irish rules imposing an obligation on importers of petroleum products to purchase a certain proportion of their supply at prices fixed by the competent minister from a State-owned company that operated a refinery in Ireland, were regarded as incompatible with former Article 30 TEEC (now Article 34 TFEU).

Similarly, in Case C-398/98 *Commission v Greece* [2001] ECR I-7915, a Greek system for stocks of petroleum products was found to be a MHEE. Under this system, companies marketing those products could only free themselves from the obligation to store them at their installations if they obtained supplies from refineries established in Greece, but could not do so if they bought their products from refineries situated in other Member States. The Court found that, by making their marketing more difficult, this system clearly discriminated against petroleum products from refineries established in other Member States.

Administrative practices favouring domestic goods　As pointed out in 13.2.1.1 above, the free movement provisions may be infringed by national administrative practices under the cloak of general legally binding rules.

In Case 21/84 *Commission v France (Re Postal Franking Machines)* [1985] ECR 1356, a leading UK manufacturer claimed that the French postal administration repeatedly refused to approve its postal franking machines, even though they had been approved in a considerable number of other countries. On an action for enforcement, the Court of Justice ruled that the consistent and general administrative discrimination, consisting in delays in replying to applications for approval or refusing approval because of inaccurate alleged technical faults and without proper justification, was a breach of former Article 30 TEEC (now Article 34 TFEU).

Failure to take adequate steps to prevent obstacles to the free movement of goods also constitutes a 'manifest and persistent failure by the State', as in *Re Spanish Strawberries* (see **13.1**), in which acts of obstruction, vandalism and violence, such as the interception of lorries transporting fruit and vegetables originating in Spain, the destruction of their loads, violence towards the lorry drivers, threats to wholesalers and retailers, and the damaging of those goods on display, were perpetrated by French farmers. The Court ruled that such acts 'unquestionably created obstacles to intra-[EU] trade in those products' (para 38) and that the French authorities had

> … manifestly and persistently abstained from adopting appropriate and adequate measures to put an end to the acts of vandalism which jeopardise the free movement on its territory of certain agricultural products originating in other Member States and to prevent the recurrence of such acts. (para 65)

Indistinctly applicable measures

Price restrictions

In the 1970s and 1980s, it was quite common for Member States to try to regulate the sale price of goods. This was always viewed with suspicion by the European Commission, the theory being that the price of products should be determined by the economic operation of the market, rather than by Member State governments.

Maximum selling price　In Case 65/75 *Tasca* [1976] ECR 29, the Italian authorities prescribed a maximum selling price for refined sugar. While the Court of Justice did not view a maximum selling price applicable to domestic and imported products as constituting a MHEE in itself, it ruled that

> … it may have such an effect, however, when it is fixed at a level such that the sale of imported products becomes, if not impossible, more difficult than that of domestic products. A maximum price, in any event in so far as it applies to imported products, constitutes therefore a measure having an effect equivalent to a quantitative restriction, especially when it is fixed at such a low level that, having regard to the general situation of imported products compared to that of domestic products, dealers wishing to import the product in question into the Member State concerned can do so only at a loss. (para 13)

Since imported sugar was more expensive than Italian processed sugar, and importers had to reduce their profit margin or even sell at a loss in order to meet the Member State maximum price, the Italian rule had the potential to make imports more costly and therefore more difficult.

Minimum selling price   Artificially keeping prices high is inherently bad, as it hinders the free movement of goods and prevents effective competition, which should drive down prices.

In Case 82/77 *Openbaar Ministerie of the Netherlands v van Tiggele* [1978] ECR 25, in which the Dutch authorities prescribed, under a 1975 regulation concerning the price of spirits, a minimum selling price for gin, the ECJ observed that '[w]hilst national price-control rules applicable without distinction to domestic products and imported products cannot in general produce such an effect they may do so in certain specific cases' (para 13). This could be the case when

> ... a national authority fixes prices or profit margins at such a level that imported products are placed at a disadvantage in relation to identical domestic products either because they cannot profitably be marketed in the conditions laid down or because the competitive advantage conferred by lower cost prices is cancelled out. (para 14)

Maximum profit margin on retail sales   A profit margin is the difference between the retailer's sale price and the expense of buying the products for re-sale. In Case 78/82 *Commission v Italy* [1983] ECR 1955, the Court of Justice did not view an Italian measure prescribing a maximum profit margin of 8% on the retail sale of cigarettes as a MHEE per se, since maximum profit margins did not hinder trade between the Member States. The Italian rule did not affect

> ... the freedom of producers to fix the retail prices of their products. Competition [could] be freely pursued in the essential field of retail prices. Foreign producers of tobacco products [were] free either to take advantage of more competitive production costs or to pass on higher production costs in their entirety. It [was] not contested that the uniform margin represent[ed] an adequate remuneration to tobacconists for the retailing of tobacco products, whether they [were] imported or domestic products. (para 17)

Production and marketing restrictions

National requirements affecting the characteristics of goods provide a wealth of examples of MHEEs.

Indications of origin   Case 207/83 *Commission v United Kingdom* [1985] ECR 1201 concerned a UK measure, requiring all clothing, whether imported or domestic, to be sold retail in the UK, to have a label indicating the country of origin. The UK Government claimed that the measure was necessary to protect consumers. Rejecting this defence, the Court of Justice ruled that the measure was designed to persuade British consumers to buy British clothing, and that it 'enabled consumers to assert their nationalistic prejudices which they may have against foreign products'. Thus,

> ... the origin-marking requirement not only makes the marketing in a Member State of goods produced in other Member States ... more difficult; it also has the effect of slowing down economic interpenetration in the [EU] by handicapping the sale of goods produced as the result of a division of labour between Member States. (para 17)

Production or manufacturing requirements   The majority of cases involving indistinctly applicable measures concern the regulation of the specific characteristics of a product. A few examples of such cases will illustrate how Member States tend to use national standards in order to limit or prohibit the marketing of foreign products. Such standards might comprise a requirement that the product be manufactured and marketed in a particular form or shape.

A typical example is Case 261/81 *Walter Rau v de Smedt* [1982] ECR 3961, which concerned a Belgian measure requiring that all margarine sold in Belgium – whether imported or domestic – be contained in cube boxes, allegedly to help prevent confusion with butter amongst consumers. The Court of Justice rejected the Belgian Government's reliance on mandatory requirements (first *Cassis de Dijon* principle – see **14.3.1**). Indeed, although the measure applied to both imported and domestic products, its effect on imported margarine was clearly disproportionate, as the objective of preventing confusion with butter (protection of consumers) could have been achieved in a less restrictive manner, eg by the use of adequate labelling. While domestic producers all produced and packaged their margarine in cube boxes, importers had to re-package their margarine, which imposed on importers a requirement to have a separate production line for cubed containers, thus making production more expensive and hindering imports and competition.

Other requirements involve the content of a product. In Case 788/79 *Gilli and Andres* [1980] ECR 2071, importers of apple vinegar from Germany to Italy were prosecuted for fraud, because they had sold vinegar in Italy that was not made from the fermentation of wine as prescribed by Italian law. Such a requirement was deemed to be a MHEE. This was also the case as regards French legislation that restricted the use of the name 'Edam' to cheese with a fat content of 40%. In Case 286/86 *Ministère public v Deserbais* [1988] ECR 4907, Mr Deserbais, the director of a dairy product company, was prosecuted for importing from Germany and marketing in France Edam cheese with a fat content of 34.3%, in contravention of the French law.

More interesting is Case 178/84 *Commission v Germany (Re Law of Purity of Beer)* [1987] ECR 1227. Under German rules (the *Biersteuergesetz*, the law on beer duty, which provides that bottom-fermented beers may be manufactured only from malted barley, hops, yeast and water), the marketing of imported beers that used different ingredients and manufacturing processes, under the designation 'beer', was prohibited. The same requirements also applied to the manufacture of top-fermented beer, but here the rules authorised the use of other malts, technically pure cane sugar, beet sugar or invert sugar, and glucose and colourants obtained from those sugars. Furthermore, imports into Germany of beers containing additives were absolutely prohibited under the 1974 Law on foodstuffs, tobacco products, cosmetics and other consumer goods. The Court ruled that

> … by prohibiting the marketing of beers lawfully manufactured and marketed in another Member State if they do not comply with Articles 9 and 10 of the *Biersteuergesetz*, the Federal Republic of Germany has failed to fulfil its obligations under Article [34 TFEU]. (para 54)

13.2.3.4 Marketing restrictions: chronicle of a jurisprudence foretold

The *Dassonville* formula (see **13.2.3.1**) was set out in the context of a national measure that imposed marketing restrictions. Such measures gave rise to many challenges in national courts, whether they concerned a ban on canvassing and selling at private places (Case 382/87 *R Buet and Educational Business Services (EBS) v Ministère public* [1989] ECR 1235), a German rule prohibiting the transport and delivery of bread to consumers and retailers at night (Case 155/80 *Oebel* [1981] ECR 1993), a Belgian ban on storing and selling spirits in premises open to the public (Case 75/81 *Blesgen v Belgium* [1982] ECR 1211), a Dutch law that allowed tax collectors to seize goods if

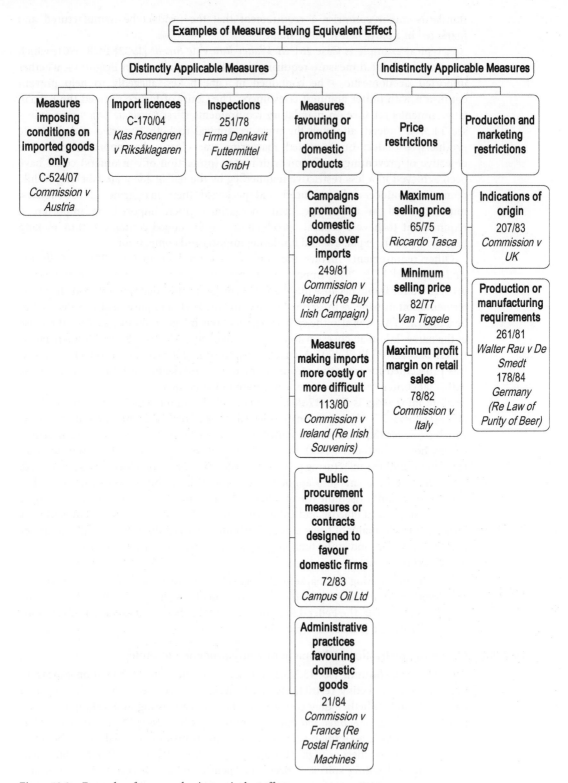

Figure 13.2   Examples of measures having equivalent effect

purchasers failed to discharge their tax debts, even if those goods belonged to a supplier in another Member State (Case C-69/88 *H Krantz GmbH & Co v Ontvanger der Directe Belastingen and Netherlands State* [1990] ECR I-583), or, as in Case C-23/89 *Quietlynn Limited and Richards v Southend Borough Council* [1990] ECR I-3059, the prohibition of sale of lawful sex goods from unlicensed sex establishments. All these national measures fell outside the scope of application of former Article 30 TEEC (now Article 34 TFEU) as they did not seek to control or affect trade between Member States.

In a further series of cases, the Court of Justice was asked to rule on the compatibility of national laws prohibiting or restricting the employment of staff on Sundays and Sunday trading. In Case C-312/89 *Union départementale des syndicats CGT de l'Aisne v SIDEF-Conforama* [1991] ECR I-997 and Case C-332/89 *Criminal proceedings against Marchandise* [1991] ECR I-6457, the Court held that French and Belgian rules, respectively, prohibiting workers from working on Sundays, were not excessive and thus were compatible with former Article 28 TEC (now Article 34 TFEU). In Case C-145/88 *Torfaen Borough Council v B & Q plc* [1989] ECR 3851 and Cases C-169/91 *Council of the City of Stoke-on-Trent and Norwich City Council v B & Q plc* [1992] ECR I-6635, the Court ruled that former Article 28 TEC did not apply to legislation such as the Shops Act 1950, prohibiting retailers from opening shops on Sunday, because it 'reflected certain choices relating to particular national or regional socio-cultural characteristics' (para 11), and its restrictive effects on trade were not excessive to the social aim pursued by such legislation (para 12).

From these cases, the development of a new line of jurisprudence was perceptible. It was based on a distinction between national measures governing product characteristics, such as composition, characteristics and presentation of products, and national measures regulating market circumstances, such as place, time, manner, or authorised persons, etc. Only the former would be caught under the free movement of goods provisions. However, this distinction also led to a lot of confusion. In this context, the *Keck and Mithouard* ruling marked a greater evolution of this jurisprudence, by introducing a new important distinction between national measures governing product requirements and those concerning methods of sale.

13.2.3.5 Review of the scope of application of Article 34 TFEU: *Keck and Mithouard*

Owing to the wide application of the *Dassonville* formula and the increasing number of cases involving the first *Cassis de Dijon* principle, the Court of Justice felt it necessary and appropriate to reassess its case law on the application of former Article 30 TEEC (now Article 34 TFEU) and the concept of MHEE. In Joined Cases C-267 and C-268/91 *Criminal proceedings against Keck and Mithouard* [1993] ECR I-6097, the Court indeed observed that

[i]n view of the increasing tendency of traders to invoke Article [34] of the Treaty as a means of challenging any rules whose effect is to limit their commercial freedom even where such rules are not aimed at products from other Member States, the Court considers it necessary to re-examine and clarify its case law on this matter. (para 14)

In this case, a French competition rule prohibited the sale or resale in France of imported or domestic products in an unaltered state at less than their purchase price, ie at a loss. Keck and Mithouard separately imported products and sold them at a loss, with a view to making inroads into the French market. They were prosecuted for breach of the French measure in the Strasbourg Court, but claimed that the French law prohibiting resale at a loss was a MHEE. In contrast, the French authorities argued that the measure was justified, as it was aimed at preventing predatory pricing, whereby a supplier sells at a loss in order to drive competitors out of the market, only then to take advantage of being the only supplier, enabling it to put up the price again and recover its loss. In the long term, such a strategy is not regarded as being in the best interests of consumers.

After reiterating the *Dassonville* formula (para 11), the Court of Justice confirmed that a national law 'imposing a general prohibition on resale at a loss is not designed to regulate trade in goods between Member States' (para 12). Indeed, even if it may restrict the volume of sales, and 'therefore the volume of sales of products from other Member States, in so far as it deprives traders of a method of sales promotion', this is not sufficient to regard such law as a 'measure having equivalent effect to a quantitative restriction' on imports (para 13). Then, after recalling the principles laid down in the *Cassis de Dijon* case (para 15), the Court stated:

> By contrast, contrary to what has previously been decided, the application to products from other Member States of national provisions restricting or prohibiting certain selling arrangements is not such as to hinder directly or indirectly, actually or potentially, trade between Member States within the meaning of the *Dassonville* judgment, so long as those provisions apply to all relevant traders operating within the national territory and so long as they affect in the same manner, in law and in fact, the marketing of domestic products and of those from other Member States. (para 16)

In other words, the Court stated that national measures that restrict or prohibit certain selling arrangements, automatically fall outside the scope of application of Article 34 TFEU and therefore are not MHEEs within the *Dassonville* formula, provided that they:

(a) apply to all traders within the Member State (principle of universality); and

(b) affect in the same manner, in law and in fact, the marketing of domestic and imported goods (principle of neutrality).

In such circumstances, imported goods are not impeded in the Member State by the national measure any more than domestic goods are, in which case the measure does not fall foul of Article 34 TFEU in the first place.

Thus, the Court drew a sharp distinction between:

(a) obstacles to the free movement of goods arising from rules laying down requirements to be met by the goods, ie their physical characteristics (size, weight, composition, presentation, labelling and packaging), such rules falling within the scope of the *Dassonville* formula; and

(b) national rules relating to the prohibition or restriction of methods of sale ('selling arrangements'), such national rules being deemed not to hinder intra-EU trade, provided they satisfy the principles of universality and neutrality.

Examples of national measures governing 'certain selling arrangements'

The principle in *Keck* was applied in numerous subsequent cases, such as Case C-292/92 *Hünermund and others v Landesapothekerkammer Baden-Württemberg* [1993] ECR I-6787, which concerned a rule of professional conduct laid down by a German regional pharmacists' association, prohibiting pharmacists from advertising outside the pharmacy quasi-pharmaceutical products that they were allowed to sell. The Court ruled that such rule was not caught by former Article 30 TEEC (now Article 34 TFEU) as it was not directed towards intra-EU trade and applied equally to all domestic and imported goods. As such, advertising falls within *Keck*'s concept of 'selling arrangements', and escaped the scope of application of former Article 30 TEEC.

This was confirmed in the subsequent Case C-412/93 *Société d'Importation Edouard Leclerc-Siplec v TF1 Publicité SA and M6 Publicité SA* [1995] ECR I-179. In this case, French rules prohibited the fuel distribution sector from advertising on national television. Other forms of advertising were available however. The Court ruled that, provided that the principles of universality and neutrality were satisfied,

> the application of such rules to the sale of products from another Member State meeting the requirements laid down by that State is not by nature such as to prevent their access to the market or to impede access any more than it impedes the access of domestic products ... (para 21)

The French rules concerned selling arrangements, since they prohibited 'a particular form of promotion (televised advertising) of a particular method of marketing products (distribution)' (para 22), and therefore they fell outside the scope of former Article 30 TEEC.

A restriction on the opening hours of outlets was also deemed to concern selling arrangements in Joined Cases C-401 and 402/92 *Criminal proceedings against Tankstation 't Heukske vof and JBE Boermans* [1994] ECR I-2199 (petrol station opening hours); Case C-391/92 *Commission v Greece (Re Infant Formula)* [1995] ECR I-1621 (Greek law requiring processed milk for infants to be sold only by pharmacies) and Joined Cases C-69 and 258/93 *Punto Casa SpA v Sindaco del Comune di Capena and Comune di Capena and Promozioni Polivalenti Venete Soc coop arl (PPV) v Sindaco del Comune di Torri di Quartesolo and Comune di Torri di Quartesolo* [1994] ECR I-2363 (prohibition of certain kinds of Sunday trading).

National measures not regarded as governing 'certain selling arrangements' As the Court has deliberately avoided defining clearly the notion of 'selling arrangements', preferring to deal with national provisions on a case-by-case basis, this concept remains unclear. Depending on the angle from which a national measure is analysed, it may be deemed to deal with selling arrangements or not. Consequently, certain rules that seem to fall into the category of selling arrangements are in fact treated as rules relating to products.

This was indeed the case as regards a German rule prohibiting the sale of Mars ice-cream bars with a '+10%' marking on the packaging (Case C-470/93 *Verein gegen Unwesen in Handel und Gewerbe Köln eV v Mars GmbH* [1995] ECR I-1923, para 13) and Austrian legislation prohibiting publishers from including prize competitions, such as crossword puzzles, in newspapers or magazines (Case C-368/95 *Vereinigte Familiapress Zeitungsverlags- und vertriebs GmbH v Heinrich Bauer Verlag* [1997] ECR I-3689, para 11). Equally, a Danish prohibition on the keeping on Læso Island of bees other than the Læso brown bees, was not deemed to govern a selling arrangement as it concerned the intrinsic characteristics of bees (Case C-67/97 *Criminal proceedings against Bluhme* [1998] ECR I-8033, para 21).

In Joined Cases C-158/04 *Alfa Vita Vassilopoulos AE* and C-159/04 *Carrefour Marinopoulos AE v Elliniko Dimosio and Nomarchiaki Aftodioikisi Ioanninon* [2006] ECR I-8135, the Court held that a Greek measure classifying frozen 'bake-off' products as bread, and thus requiring licences to operate ovens and the fulfilment of certain building requirements, was aimed to specify production conditions for baked products, and therefore constituted 'a barrier to imports which [could not] be regarded as establishing a selling arrangement as contemplated in *Keck and Mithouard*' (para 19).

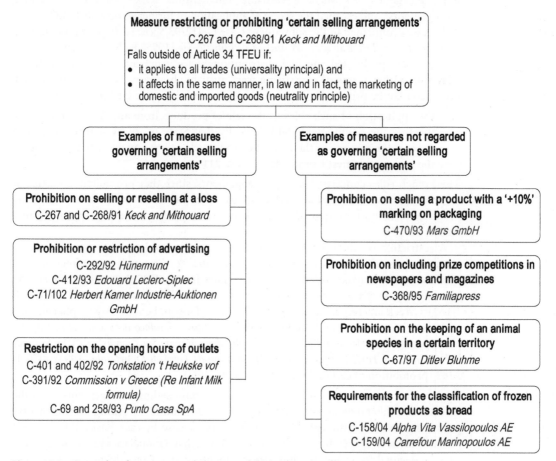

Figure 13.3   Examples of measures restricting or prohibiting 'certain selling arrangements'

The limits of the *Keck and Mithouard* approach

The distinction operated by the Court in *Keck and Mithouard* was criticised from its outset in the Court itself, by Advocates General and academics, for being too rigid. In his Opinion in Case C-412/93 *Leclerc-Siplec* [1995] ECR I-179, Advocate General Jacobs criticised the *Keck and Mithouard* approach and offered an alternative analysis. In his view,

> the Court's reasoning – although not the result – in *Keck* is unsatisfactory for two reasons. First, it is inappropriate to make rigid distinctions between different categories of rules, and to apply different tests depending on the category to which particular rules belong. The severity of the restriction imposed by different rules is merely one of degree. Measures affecting selling arrangements may create extremely serious obstacles to imports. For example, a rule permitting certain products to be sold only in a handful of small shops in a Member State would be almost as restrictive as an outright ban on importation and marketing. (para 38)

And

> [s]econdly, the exclusion from the scope of Article [34 TFEU] of measures which 'affect in the same manner, in law and in fact, the marketing of domestic products and those from other Member States' amounts to introducing, in relation to restrictions on selling arrangements, a test of discrimination. That test, however, seems inappropriate. ... If an obstacle to inter-State trade exists, it cannot cease to exist simply because an identical obstacle affects domestic trade ... (para 39)

On the assumption that the 'principle should be that all undertakings should have unfettered access to the whole of the [single] market', he then proposed the *de minimis* test as an alternative, which assesses whether there is a substantial restriction on access to this market (para 42).

According to Advocate General Poaires Maduro, in his Opinion in Joined Cases C-158 and 159/04 *Alfa Vita Vassilopoulos* [2006] ECR I-8135, *Keck* has 'proved to be a source of uncertainty for economic operators', as

> ... [i]n some cases, it is difficult to distinguish selling arrangements from national rules relating to the characteristics of products, for the very reason that the existence of a restriction on trade is dependent on the method of application of a rule and its concrete effects. In other cases, it is impossible to include a measure within one or other of these categories because the variety of rules which may be called into question does not fit easily into such a restricted framework. (para 31)

He identified three criteria, applied by the Court, amounting to identifying discrimination against the exercise of freedom of movement, namely:

(a) the Court maintains that any discriminatory provisions, direct or indirect, are prohibited (para 43);
(b) imposing supplementary costs on goods in circulation in the EU or on traders' cross-border activities has to be duly justified. Selling arrangements (such as resale at a loss, or the prohibition of Sunday trading) do not normally impose such costs, but if they did they should be regarded as MHEEs (para 44);
(c) any national measure impeding access to the market and the putting into circulation of products from other Member States is to be considered to be a MHEE (para 45).

The Court of Justice has never contemplated adopting the *de minimis* test, and is unlikely to do so. However, the test whereby a national measure must affect both domestic and imported products, in the same manner, in law and in fact (principle of neutrality) has proved difficult to apply at times, thus forcing the Court to apply a market access test, as the cases below illustrate.

National measures that limit market access

In paragraph 17 of the *Keck and Mithouard* ruling, the Court made a reference to 'market access'. Indeed, it observed that, provided the conditions set out in *Keck* were fulfilled by national rules relating to selling arrangements, their application to the sale of products from another Member State meeting the requirements laid down by the importing State 'is not by nature such as to prevent their access to the market or to impede access any more than it impedes the access of domestic products'.

case example

The issue of access to the national market would arise, should one of the *Keck* criteria not be fulfilled by a national rule. In Joined Cases C-34-36/95 *Konsumentombudsmannen (KO) v De Agostini (Svenska) Förlag AB and TV-Shop i Sverige AB* [1997] ECR I-3843, the Court was requested to examine the compatibility with (then) EC law of, first, a Swedish partial ban on television advertising of a magazine called *Everything About Dinosaurs*, directed at children under the age of 12 (Case C-34/95); and, secondly, a ban on the broadcast of infomercials for 'Body De Lite' skin-care products (Case C-35/95) and detergents (Case C-36/95). The Court held that the Swedish law related to a selling arrangement, but it could not 'be excluded that an outright ban, applying in one Member State, of a type of promotion for a product which is lawfully sold there might have a greater impact on products from other Member States' (para 42). It particularly noted that 'television advertising was the only effective form of promotion enabling De Agostini to penetrate the Swedish market, since it had no other advertising methods for reaching children and their parents' (para 43). Consequently,

> an outright ban on advertising aimed at children less than 12 years of age and of misleading advertising, ... is not covered by Article [34] of the Treaty, unless it is shown that the ban does not affect in the same way, in fact and in law, the marketing of national products and of products from other Member States. (para 44)

In the latter case, in particular where the national measure imposes the same burden in law but a different one in fact (as seemed to be the case as regards the Swedish ban, as strongly suggested by the Court in para 43), the measure would have to be necessary to satisfy a mandatory requirement (see **14.3.1**), or be justified under Article 36 TFEU, and be proportionate for that purpose (para 47).

A similar situation occurred in Case C-405/98 *Konsumentombudsmannen (KO) v Gourmet International Products AB (GIP)* [2001] ECR I-1795, which concerned a Swedish ban on advertising alcohol on radio, television and in magazines. Although the Swedish law could be viewed as relating to a selling arrangement, in the case of products like alcohol,

> the consumption of which is linked to traditional social practices and to local habits and customs, a prohibition of all advertising directed at consumers in the form of advertisements in the press, on the radio and on television, the direct mailing of unsolicited material or the placing of posters on the public highway is liable to impede access to the market by products from other Member States more than it impedes access by domestic products, with which consumers are instantly more familiar. (para 21)

In such a case, a breach of Article 34 TFEU would have to be justified, under Article 36 or the first *Cassis de Dijon* principle (see **Chapter 14**), on the ground of protection of public health against the harmful effects of alcohol, provided that could be ensured by measures having less effect on intra-EU trade (para 34).

More significantly, it is very clear from the wording of paragraph 18 of this ruling that the Court based its reasoning on the concept of market access. Indeed, it stated that if

> ... national provisions restricting or prohibiting certain selling arrangements are to avoid being caught by Article [34] of the Treaty, they must not be of such a kind as to *prevent access to the market* by products from another Member State or to impede access any more than they impede the access of domestic products. (emphasis added)

This approach was further confirmed in Case C-239/02 *Douwe Egberts NV v Westrom Pharma NV and Souranis* [2004] ECR I-7007, which dealt with a Belgian law prohibiting references in the advertising of coffee products imported from other Member States to 'slimming' and to 'medical recommendations, attestations, declarations or statements of approval'. Referring to its ruling in *Gourmet*, the Court confirmed that 'an absolute prohibition of advertising the characteristics of a product is liable to impede access to the market by products from other Member States more than it impedes access by domestic products, with which consumers are more familiar' (para 53).

The sale of products over the Internet has also been an issue analysed by the Court under the market access lens. An interesting decision is Case C-322/01 *Deutscher Apothekerverband eV v 0800 DocMorris NV and Waterval* [2003] ECR I-14887. DocMorris, a Dutch company, ran a 'standard' pharmaceutical business in a pharmacy in the Netherlands, and was selling medicinal products by mail order over the Internet. Both activities were covered by a licence issued by the Dutch authorities. In 2000, DocMorris started to offer prescription and non-prescription medicines for human use for sale online, for end consumers in Germany. The sale of medicines by DocMorris over the Internet to German consumers was challenged in a Frankfurt court by the German pharmacists' association, on the ground that a German 1998 law on medicinal products did not permit the sale by mail order of medicinal products that could only be sold in pharmacies. The Court held that the prohibition of sales of medicines over the Internet was

> more of an obstacle to pharmacies outside Germany than to those within it. Although there is little doubt that as a result of the prohibition, pharmacies in Germany cannot use the extra or alternative method of gaining access to the German market consisting of end consumers of medicinal products, they are still able to sell the products in their dispensaries. However, for pharmacies not established in Germany, the Internet provides a more significant way to gain direct access to the German market. A prohibition which has a greater impact on pharmacies established outside German territory could impede access to the market for products from other Member States more than it impedes access for domestic products. (para 74)

National measures that impose a ban on, or restriction on, use of products legally produced and marketed

In more recent cases, the Court has had to analyse the effect on the free movement of goods of national measures banning or restricting the use of products lawfully produced and marketed in other Member States.

In Case C-265/06 *Commission v Portugal* [2008] ECR I-2245, Advocate General Trstenjak approached the Portuguese measure, a ban on the fixing of tinted film onto vehicle windows, through the *Dassonville* formula (see 13.2.3.1). However, although indistinctly applicable and non-discriminatory, she viewed the prohibition as being capable of limiting opportunities for intra-EU trade in the products in question, and as hampering imports and the marketing of such products. Following its Advocate General, the Court applied the *Dassonville* formula to find the restriction on the use of tinted film to be a MHEE, as potential purchasers would in practice have no interest in buying the product, knowing that fixing it to vehicle windows was prohibited (para 33).

In Case C-110/05 *Commission v Italy (Re Trailer)* [2009] ECR I-519, Advocate General Léger also followed *Dassonville* with regard to the Italian measure, which prohibited the towing of trailers by motorcycles. Although indistinctly applicable and non-discriminatory, like Advocate General Trstenjak in the case above, Advocate General Léger regarded the prohibition as likely to limit opportunities for intra-EU trade in the products in question, and as hampering imports and the marketing of such products. In a second opinion, Advocate General Bot advised the Court not to apply *Keck* to the restriction/prohibition of use of a product, but rather to apply a straightforward market access test/approach. He argued that a measure that hinders, prevents or make more difficult market access is in breach of former Article 28 TEC (now Article 34 TFEU), and found the Italian measure to be a MHEE.

The Grand Chamber of the Court analysed the problem from the viewpoint of market access. It distinguished between trailers specifically designed for motorcycles and those capable of being towed by other vehicles. As regards the former, the Court accepted the Commission's argument that the Italian prohibition was a MHEE. Indeed, it argued, the prohibition on use of a product exercises a considerable effect on the behaviour of consumers, which in turn affects the access of that product to the market of the Member State.

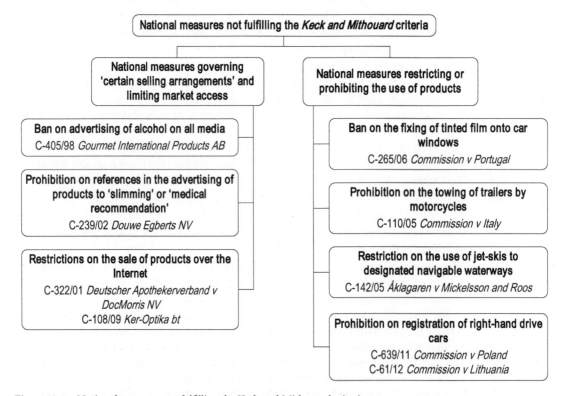

Figure 13.4   National measures not fulfilling the Keck and Mithouard criteria

In Case C-142/05 *Åklagaren v Mickelsson and Roos* [2009] ECR I-4273, Advocate General Kokott preferred to rationalise the Swedish restriction on the use of jet-skis under the *Keck* formula, and considered the measure to be excluded from the scope of former Article 28 TEC (now Article 34 TFEU) unless it prevented access to the market for imports. A marginal possibility of using the product was equated with absolute prevention of market access. However, the Court confirmed that former Article 28 TEC captured measures that not only prohibited but also restricted the use of products, here the use of jet-skis being restricted to designated navigable waterways.

13.2.4 Quantitative restrictions and measures having equivalent effect on exports

Although Article 35 TFEU is worded in terms similar to those of Article 34, the Court of Justice seems to have been more tolerant of national measures that have the potential to hinder only exports. A national measure will be in breach of Article 35 TFEU only if it is overtly or covertly protectionist, that is it has

> as [its] specific object or effect the restriction of patterns of exports and thereby the establishment of a difference in treatment between the domestic trade of a Member State and its export trade in such a way as to provide a particular advantage for national production or for the domestic market of the State in question at the expense of the production or of the trade of other Member States. (Case 15/79 *PB Groenveld BV v Produktschap voor Vee en Vlees* [1979] ECR 3409 para 7)

Three criteria must therefore be satisfied:

(a) a restriction of patterns of exports;
(b) a difference in treatment between a Member State's domestic trade and its export trade; and
(c) an unfair advantage for domestic trade.

These conditions were confirmed in Case 172/82 *Inter-Huiles and Others* [1983] ECR 555, para 12, and in Case C-209/98 *Entreprenørforeningens Affalds/Miljøsektion (FFAD) v Københavns Kommune* [2000] ECR I-3743, para 34. In the latter case, the Court held that a system for the collection and receipt of non-hazardous building waste destined for recovery, set up by the Municipality of Copenhagen, under which a limited number of undertakings were authorised to process waste produced in the municipality, was in breach of former Article 34 TEC (now Article 35 TFEU) and could not be justified under Article 36 TEC (now Article 36 TFEU) or in the interest of environmental protection.

On the basis of the criteria listed above, the Court found that a Dutch law prohibiting certain ingredients from being used in Gouda and Edam cheese made in Holland and for consumption in Holland, but leaving imported cheese unaffected, was not in breach of former Article 34 TEEC (now Article 35 TFEU) (Case 237/82 *Jongeneel Kaas BV and others v State of the Netherlands and Stichting Centraal Orgaan Zuivelcontrole* [1984] ECR 483). The *Groenveld* criteria above did not apply to provisions that 'lay down minimum standards of quality for cheese production, without making any distinction as to whether the cheese is intended for the domestic market or for export' (para 22).

In contrast, a measure such as a French law requiring that watches intended for export had to submit to inspection before getting an export licence, whereas there was no such requirement of inspection for watches intended for the domestic market, was deemed to be in breach of former Article 34 TEEC. It was a distinctly applicable measure as it applied only to exports, and it discriminated against exports as it made it more difficult for consumers in other Member States to purchase the French watches

(Case 53/76 *Procureur de la République de Besançon v Les Sieurs Bouhelier and others* [1977] ECR 197, paras 15 and 16).

Equally, a measure such as a Spanish law limiting the quantity of Rioja wine available for export in bulk to other Member States was deemed to fall foul of former Article 34 TEEC, as it had the 'specific effect of restricting exports of wine in bulk and in particular, of procuring a special advantage for bottling undertakings situated in the region of production' (Case C-47/90 *Établissements Delhaize frères and Compagnie Le Lion SA v Promalvin SA and AGE Bodegas Unidas SA* [1992] ECR I-3669). However, on a re-examination of the same rules in Case C-388/95 *Belgium v Spain* [2000] ECR I-3123, the Court decided that instead of considering whether or not bottling in the region of production of Rioja should be regarded as a stage in the process of production of that wine, it should rather focus on the reasons for which bottling should be carried out in the region of production, and on whether those reasons were capable of justifying the Spanish measure, intended to ensure that the '*denominación de origen calificada*' fulfilled its function of guaranteeing the origin of the wine. In light of European legislation aimed at enhancing the quality of agricultural products, especially in the wine sector, in order to promote their reputation through, notably, the use of designations of origin, and in light of Council Regulation (EEC) No 2081/92 of 14 July 1992 on the protection of geographical indications and designations of origin for agricultural products and foodstuffs, the Court accepted that '[d]esignations of origin fall within the scope of industrial and commercial property rights … They are intended to guarantee that the product bearing them comes from a specified geographical area and displays certain particular characteristics' (para 54). And that

> [t]he rules governing the Rioja '*denominación de origen calificada*' are designed to uphold those qualities and characteristics. By ensuring that operators in the wine growing sector of the Rioja region, at whose request the designation of origin was granted, control bottling as well, they pursue the aim of better safeguarding the quality of the product and, consequently, the reputation of the designation, for which they now assume full and collective responsibility. (para 58)

Generally, such national rules are not very common, as it is not usual for a Member State to want to pass rules that effectively make export of the goods more difficult. This could explain why the Court treated MHEEs on imports and on exports differently. However, following a number of criticisms, the Court reviewed its position in Case C-205/07 *Lodewijk Gysbrechts and Santurel Inter BVBA* [2008] ECR I-9947.

Gysbrechts was the founder and manager of Santurel, a business specialising in the wholesale and retail sale of food supplements, with a big part of its sales being made online by means of the company's Internet site. Once ordered, the goods were sent to the purchasers by post. Both Gysbrecht and Santurel were prosecuted in Belgium for breaching the provisions on distance selling in the 1991 Belgian Law on Consumer Protection, and notably for disregarding its prohibition, under Article 80(3), on requiring consumers to provide a deposit or any form of payment before the expiry of the period of seven working days, within which withdrawal from the contract was permitted. Santurel and Gysbrechts argued that the prohibition concerned was an unjustified obstacle to the free movement of goods, notably to the export of national goods.

The Court noted that the prohibition laid down in Article 80(3) of the Belgian Law was within the scope of Directive 97/7/EC ([1997] OJ L144/19). However, harmonisation under this Directive was not exhaustive, thus allowing Member States to introduce more stringent consumer protection rules, provided they were Treaty compliant. The Court therefore held that Article 80(3) of the Belgian Law could be examined in light of former Article 28 TEC (now Article 34 TFEU), and more specifically of Article 29 TEC (now Article 35 TFEU), as the Belgian provision had been applied in a case relating to the exports of goods from Belgium to other Member States (paras 32–36).

The Court observed, first, that traders were deprived of an efficient tool to guard themselves against the risk of non-payment by the prohibition against requiring an advance payment; secondly, that such a prohibition had more significant consequences in cross-border sales made directly to consumers by means of the Internet, notably because of the difficulties in suing any defaulting consumers in another Member State; thirdly, that the effect of such prohibition was greater on goods leaving the market of the exporting Member State than on the marketing of goods in its domestic market, even if the prohibition applied to all traders operating in that Member State (paras 41–43). The Court then concluded that

> a national measure … prohibiting a supplier in a distance sale from requiring an advance or any payment before expiry of the period for withdrawal constitutes a measure having equivalent effect to a quantitative restriction on exports. The same is true of a measure prohibiting a supplier from requiring that consumers provide their payment card number, even if the supplier undertakes not to use it to collect payment before expiry of the period for withdrawal. (para 44)

Although the Court referred in this ruling to the *Groenveld* criteria (para 40; see above), it is clear that the Court interpreted a MHEE under former Article 29 TEC (now Article 35 TFEU) in a manner consistent with its interpretation of former Article 28 TEC (now Article 34 TFEU). By emphasising the fact that the Belgian prohibition had a greater effect on exports than on the marketing of the goods in the domestic market, the Court focused on its hindering effect on trade. This realignment of the interpretation of Article 34 is further confirmed by the fact that the Court accepted for the first time that a restriction on exports could also be justified 'by overriding requirements of public interest, provided that the measure is proportionate to the legitimate objective pursued' (para 45) (see **14.3.1**).

13.3 Further reading

Derlin M and Lindholm J, 'Article 28 EC and Rules on Use: A Step Towards a Workable Doctrine on Measures Having Equivalent Effect to Quantitative Restrictions' (2010) 16 *Columbia Journal of European Law* 191.

Gormley L, 'Free Movement of Goods and their Use – What is the Use of it? (2010) 33 *Fordham International Law Journal* 1589.

Gorywoda L, 'The New European Legislative Framework for the Marketing of Goods' (2009) 16 *Columbia Journal of European Law* 161.

Hojnik J, 'Free Movement of Goods in a Labyrinth. Can *Buy Irish* Survive the Crises? (2012) 49 *CML Rev* 291.

Jansson M and Kalimo H, 'De Minimis Meets "Market Access": Transformations in the Substance – and the Syntax – of EU Free Movement Law? (2014) 51 *CML Rev* 523.

Möstl M, 'Preconditions and Limits of Mutual Recognition' (2010) 47 *CML Rev* 405.

Oliver P, 'Of Trailers and Jet Skis: Is the Case Law on Article 34 TFEU Hurtling in a New Direction?' (2010) 33 *Fordham International Law Journal* 1423.

Prete L, 'Of Motorcycle Trailers and Personal Watercrafts: the Battle over *Keck*' (2008) 35(2) *Legal Issues of Economic Integration* 133.

Shuibhne N, 'The Treaty is Coming to Get You' (2012) 37(4) *EL Rev* 367.

Snell J, 'The Notion of Market Access: A Concept or a Slogan?' (2010) 47 *CML Rev* 437.

Szydlo M, 'Export Restrictions within the Structure of the Free Movement of Goods. Reconsiderations of an Old Paradigm' (2010) 47 *CML Rev* 753.

Tryfonidou A, 'Further Steps on the Road to Convergence among the Market Freedoms' (2010) 35(1) *EL Rev* 36.

Wenneras P and Moen K, 'Selling Arrangements, Keeping Keck' (2010) 35(3) *EL Rev* 387.

Wilsher D, 'Does Keck Discrimination Make Any Sense? An Assessment of the Non-discrimination Principle within the European Single Market' (2008) 33(1) *EL Rev* 3.

Non-tariff barriers are prohibited under Articles 34 and 35 TFEU. These include quantitative restrictions on imports and exports, as well as measures having equivalent effect (MHEEs). Owing to the deliberate general wording of those Treaty provisions, it was left to the ECJ to define and refine those two concepts. While the former was easily defined by the Court in the *Geddo* case, the latter proved more problematic. At first the Court offered a broad definition of a 'measure having an equivalent effect' in the *Dassonville* judgment, with a view to covering all existing and future national trade restrictions. This approach was further supported by the elaboration of the principle of mutual recognition in the second key case of *Cassis de Dijon*. However, recognising that this approach showed its practical limitations, in the third key ruling of *Keck and Mithouard*, the Court drew a distinction between national measures affecting product characteristics and national measures restricting or prohibiting 'certain selling arrangements', the latter falling outside the scope of Articles 34 and 35 TFEU, provided they are universal and neutral in law and in fact.

Notwithstanding the lack of definition of 'selling arrangements', this new approach also showed its own limitation, especially in the case of national measures that are neutral in law but not in fact. This situation led the Court to refine its definition of MHEEs further, by gradually referring to the concept of market access, whereby any national measure prohibiting or restricting access to a national market is to be regarded as prohibited under the Treaty. However, it is to be noted that the Court has not opted for a full application of the market access test as the sole criterion for the application of Article 34 TFEU at the expense of the *Dassonville*, *Cassis de Dijon* and *Keck* approaches, as had been suggested by Advocate General Bot in his Opinion in Case C-110/05 *Commission v Italy (Re Trailer)* [2009] ECR I-519.

1 Brocks Organic, one of the biggest manufacturers of cordials in the UK, has concerns over various issues of EU law. Advise Brocks Organic, in the following scenarios, as to whether there is a breach of Article 34 TFEU:

   (a) The Estonian authorities require cordials to be packaged in glass bottles, so that Estonian citizens can distinguish them from fruit-flavoured bottled water that is packaged in plastic bottles. Brocks Organic packages its drinks in plastic bottles only.

   (b) The Danish state television companies ban the advertising of cordials before the watershed of 21:00, as there are concerns that the high sugar content of these drinks could have a detrimental effect on children's teeth.

2 'La Selle' is a new brand of horse saddles manufactured by the French company, Equus SA. It has become very popular with horse riders throughout Europe for its particular ergonomic features. However, British manufacturers of riding equipment are not too happy about the detrimental effect this has had on their industry, and have exerted pressure on the British Government to take action to limit imports of this new product. The managing director of Equus SA, Pauline Chevalier, has recently learnt that the British authorities are:

   (a) imposing inspections, on the ground that, according to the latest research conducted in the UK, some of the French saddles may cause irreversible back injuries to horses;

   (b) prohibiting the advertising of Equus saddles in UK horse-riding magazines; and

   (c) prohibiting the use of Equus saddles in horse trials in the UK, such as at Badminton and Gatcombe Park.

   Advise Pauline Chevalier on the lawfulness of the British measures under Article 34 TFEU.

14 The Free Movement of Goods: Derogations and Justifications

study points

After reading this chapter, you will be able to understand:

- the derogations from the free movement of goods provided for under Articles 36 and 114 TFEU
- the justifications for the free movement of goods under the first *Cassis de Dijon* principle, and under general principles of law as developed by the CJEU
- the conditions for the application of those derogations and justifications.

14.1 Introduction

At the time of the drafting of the Treaty of Rome, it was not conceivable that a general and rigid principle prohibiting non-fiscal trade barriers could be laid down, without allowing Member States the ability to justify some barriers on the ground of protection of legitimate national interests. This flexibility was allowed within the strict framework of the provisions of Article 30 of the Treaty of Rome (now Article 36 TFEU), which set out a limited list of grounds for derogations from the principle of prohibition of trade barriers, and laid down the strict conditions under which these might be relied upon by the Member States (see **14.2**). Later on, the 1986 Single European Act introduced new derogations under former Article 95 TEEC (now Article 114 TFEU), on the approximation of national laws (see **14.2.2**). Furthermore, as the original Treaty derogations proved to be insufficient to embrace new forms of justification for the protection of general public interests, in the *Cassis de Dijon* case the Court created new derogations, known as mandatory requirements (see **14.3.1.3**).

14.2 Treaty derogations

Originally provided for in a limited way in Article 30 of the Treaty of Rome (now Article 36 TFEU), justifications for trade barriers were further expanded under former Article 95 TEEC (now Article 114 TFEU).

14.2.1 Derogations under Article 36 TFEU

Under Article 36 TFEU:

> The provisions of Articles 34 and 35 shall not preclude prohibitions or restrictions on imports, exports or goods in transit justified on grounds of public morality, public policy or public security; the protection of health and life of humans, animals or plants; the protection of national treasures possessing artistic, historic or archaeological value; or the protection of industrial and commercial property. Such prohibitions or restrictions shall not, however, constitute a means of arbitrary discrimination or a disguised restriction on trade between Member States.

14.2.1.1 General considerations

Scope of application of Article 36 TFEU

It is first important to note that Article 36 refers to the provisions of Articles 34 and 35 TFEU and, as such, cannot be relied upon to justify tariff barriers prohibited under Article 30 TFEU (Case 7/68 *Commission v Italy (Art Treasures)* [1968] ECR 423, 430). Secondly, the Court repeatedly held, as in Case 153/78 *Commission v Germany (Re Restrictions on Imports of Meat Products)* [1979] ECR 2555, that

> ... the purpose of Article 36 of the Treaty is not to reserve certain matters to the exclusive jurisdiction of the Member States; it merely allows national legislation to derogate from the principle of the free movement of goods to the extent to which this is and remains justified in order to achieve the objectives set out in the article. (para 5)

Thirdly, the list of derogations in Article 36 is exhaustive, but it reflects what were seen as priorities in 1957. In particular, it does not include the protection of the environment, of consumers or culture, etc. (See Case 229/83 *Association des Centres distributeurs Édouard Leclerc and others v SARL 'Au blé vert' and others* [1985] ECR 17, para 30.) Article 36 has never been amended. The Court has always interpreted those derogations restrictively (Case 46/76 *W J G Bauhuis v The Netherlands* [1977] ECR 5, para 12; Case 113/80 *Commission v Ireland (Re Irish Souvenirs)* [1981] ECR 1625, para 7).

Article 36 TFEU cannot be relied upon by Member States to protect economic interests (Case 95/81 *Commission v Italy* [1982] ECR 2187, para 27; Case 72/83 *Campus Oil Limited and others v Minister for Industry and Energy and others* [1984] ECR 2727, para 35; Case C-120/95 *Decker v Caisse de maladie des employés privés* [1998] ECR I-1831, para 39). Nor can it be relied upon once EU measures of harmonisation have been adopted (Case 5/77 *Tedeschi v Denkavit Commerciale srl* [1977] ECR 1555, para 35; Case 197/08 *Commission v France* [2010] ECR I-1599, paras 49–50). In such a context, Member States cannot impose stricter requirements under Article 36 TFEU than those laid down by a directive, unless expressly provided for in the directive or where harmonisation is only partial (*Carlo Tedeschi v Denkavit*, above, para 49).

Conditions of application of Article 36 TFEU

If a national measure appears to be justifiable on one of the grounds set out in Article 36 TFEU, it must not be:

(a) an 'arbitrary discrimination', that is a measure which is not justified on objective grounds. For example, in Case 152/78 *Commission v France* [1980] ECR 2299, para 18, a French measure restricting the advertising of grain spirits but not that of wine spirits could not be justified on objective grounds and was found to amount to arbitrary discrimination; and/or

(b) a 'disguised restriction' on trade between the Member States, or a measure presented as protecting one of the national interests under Article 36 while in fact being adopted for some other, illegitimate reason. In Case 40/72 *Commission of the European Communities v United Kingdom (Re Newcastle Disease – Import of Poultry Meat)* [1982] ECR 2793, para 40, the reintroduction of a slaughter policy by the UK Government had no valid justification, as it was not necessary to deal with the risk of infection of national flocks by imported poultry products; in fact, under pressure from British poultry producers to block these imports, the Government had hurriedly introduced its new policy, without informing the Commission and the Member States concerned in good time, thus resulting in French Christmas turkeys being excluded from the British market for the 1981 season.

The Court further requires that the national measure:

(a) is necessary to protect the identified permitted ground (Case 274/87 *Commission v Germany (Re Ban on the Importation of Meat Products)* [1989] ECR 229, para 6; Case C-170/07 *Commission v Poland (Re Technical Controls on Cars)* [2008] ECR I-87, para 46; Case C-443/10 *Bonnarde v Agence de Services et de Paiement* [2011] ECR I-9327, para 32); and

(b) does not go beyond what is necessary to achieve the permitted ground, that is, it must be proportionate. A measure is regarded as proportionate if it is not possible to protect the identified permitted ground in any less restrictive way (*Re Technical Controls on Cars*, above, para 46; *Bonnarde*, above, para 32; Case C-421/09 *Humanplasma GmbH v Austria* [2010] ECR I-12869, para 34).

Another condition of substitutability, also known as minimal hindrance, adds further to the two requirements, of necessity and proportionality, listed above. It ensures that the hindrance to trade is the least restrictive possible, even if it is proportionate. In this respect, the Court will offer alternative measures that are less restrictive of trade (Case 298/87 *Smanor SA* [1988] ECR 4489, para 19; Case 261/81 *Walter Rau Lebensmittelwerke v De Smedt PVBA* [1982] ECR 3961, para 19; Case C-161/09 *Kakavetsos-Fragkopoulos AE Epexergasias kai Emporias Stafidas v Nomarchiaki Aftodioikisi Korinthias* [2011] ECR I-915, para 60). Normally, an outright ban will be found to be disproportionate, yet in Case C-473/98 *Kemikalieinspektionen v Toolex Alpha AB* [2000] ECR I-5681, a Swedish ban on trichloroethylene, a proven carcinogen, was found to be proportionate (para 49).

According to the settled case law of the Court, the burden of proof is always on the Member States. It is for the national authorities to show that they could not take any less restrictive measure (Case 251/78 *Firma Denkavit Futtermittel GmbH v Minister für Ernährung, Landwirtschaft und Forsten des Landes Nordrhein-Westfalen* [1979] ECR 3369, para 24; Case 227/82 *Criminal proceedings against Leendert van Bennekom* [1983] ECR 3883, para 40; Case C-265/06 *Commission v Portugal* [2008] ECR I-2245, para 39).

14.2.1.2 Grounds for justification

With the exception of the protection of national treasures possessing artistic, historic or archaeological value, which has given rise to very few cases, the grounds for derogations provided for under Article 36 TFEU can be grouped into three main categories, as discussed below.

Public morality, public policy and public security

All three concepts are at the core of national sovereignty, and the Court of Justice has recognised, in Case 34/79 *R v Henn and Darby* [1979] ECR 3795, that '[i]n principle, it is for each Member State to determine in accordance with its own scale of values and in the form selected by it the requirements of public morality in its territory' (para 15).

Under this principle, Member States have a wide discretion to protect within their territories public morality, policy and security, and may justify restrictions on imports on those grounds. Because of the contingent character of those concepts, as they vary from State to State and over time, the Court has always avoided defining them strictly. However, the Court will always examine whether the national measure is truly justified on one of those grounds, and, notably, whether it is an arbitrary measure or a disguised restriction. In other words, if

> ... [m]ember States are free to establish their own standards concerning public morality, that freedom is subject to the principle that Member States may not apply conditions to imports which are stricter than those applicable to the manufacture and marketing of the same products within their territory. (Case 121/85 *Conegate Limited v HM Customs & Excise* [1986] ECR 1007, para 12)

Public morality

In *R v Henn & Darby*, a consignment of obscene films and magazines imported from Rotterdam into the UK was seized by British customs authorities under the Customs and Excise Act 1952, and the importers were prosecuted. The Court held that the UK law prohibiting the import of pornographic materials was a measure having equivalent effect (MHEE) to a quantitative restriction (para 13). However, this prohibition was genuinely applied to protect public morality, as there was no domestically produced material permitted by the UK legislation on sale of pornographic material. Therefore no domestically produced material would have benefited from the import ban (paras 21–22).

By contrast, in *Conegate v HM Customs & Excise*, the Court held that the seizure by HM Customs of inflatable dolls, on the ground that they were contrary to the UK prohibition on importing 'indecent and obscene' products, was an unjustifiable breach of former Article 30 TEEC. Indeed, there was no ban on the production and sale of such products in the UK – a ban applied only on the sale of products 'likely to deprave or corrupt', yet inflatable dolls could be sold in the UK if the premises from which they were sold were licensed. Since it was not illegal to produce and sell such products in the UK, the Court held that to ban the importation of such products could hinder trade between Member States (para 16).

It might be difficult to see the obvious distinction between the two cases (the UK law concerned is the same in both cases), but it turns on the fact that in *Henn & Darby*, the Court accepted that there were no UK products on the market in the UK that were of a type that could be sold but which could not have been imported.

Public policy

The Court has construed 'public policy' narrowly, and Member States will rarely succeed in trying to rely on this ground to justify measures that have purely economic ends (Case 95/81 *Commission v Italy* [1982] ECR 2187, para 27). In this case, Italian rules required that all importers of goods coming from other Member States had to provide a security or a bank guarantee of up to 5% of the value of the goods when payment was made in advance. The Court rejected the Italian Government's argument that the rules were justified on the ground of public policy, in that its objective was the safeguarding of the defence of its currency, a fundamental interest of the State.

This narrow approach was confirmed in later cases, such as Case 231/83 *Cullet v Centre Leclerc* [1983] ECR 305, in which the Court held that the French requirement to sell petrol at a minimum price because of a threat to public order and security through violence, as an anticipated reaction of retailers affected by unrestricted competition, was unjustified (para 33). In Case C-265/95 *Commission v France (Re Spanish*

Strawberries) [1997] ECR I-6959, the Court ruled that the failure by the French authorities to adopt necessary and proportionate measures, to prevent the free movement of fruit and vegetables from being obstructed by actions of private individuals, could not be justified on the ground that 'determined action by the competent authorities might provoke violent reactions by those concerned, which would lead to still more serious breaches of public order or even to social conflict' (para 54). Equally, in Case C-239/90 *SCP Boscher, Studer et Fromentin v SA British Motors Wright and others* [1991] ECR I-2023, the Court held that a French law, which imposed on a seller the requirement of prior entry in the trade register at the place where the auction sale took place, was liable to impede the free movement of goods and could not be justified on grounds of public policy.

By contrast, the public policy justification was successful in Case 7/78 *R v Thompson, Johnson and Woodiwiss* [1978] ECR 2247, which concerned a UK ban on exporting silver coins in order to prevent their being melted down or destroyed in another Member State – a criminal offence in UK – even though they were no longer legal tender. The Court held that this ban was justified on grounds of public policy, because 'it stems from the need to protect the right to mint coinage which is traditionally regarded as involving the fundamental interests of the State' (para 34).

Public security

The Court accepted that an Irish measure, requiring that importers of crude oil bought a minimum of 35% of their requirements from the Irish national oil company at prices fixed by the Irish Government, was justified on grounds of public security, though discriminatory and protectionist, since the measure helped to preserve the Irish national oil industry, which was vital in times of national crisis (Case 72/83 *Campus Oil Limited and others v Minister for Industry and Energy and others* [1984] ECR 2727).

It appears that this case was decided on its own particular facts, and that a similar defence now would be unlikely to succeed, as shown in Case C-398/98 *Commission v Greece* [2001] ECR I-7915. There, Greece required petrol companies to hold minimum stocks of petrol at their own installations. The companies were entitled to transfer their storage obligations to Greek government-owned refineries, provided the companies had bought large amounts of petrol from these refineries in the previous year. The Greek system on the compulsory maintenance of emergency stocks of petroleum products was deemed to be in breach of Article 30 TEC (now Article 36 TFEU), which could not be justified on grounds of public security. The Court notably pointed out that, although 'the maintenance on national territory of a stock of petroleum products allowing continuity of supplies to be guaranteed constitutes a public security objective' (para 29), in this case the arguments of the Greek Government were purely economic ones.

However, in Case C-367/89 *Criminal proceedings against Richardt and Les Accessoires Scientifiques SNC* [1991] ECR I-4621, the Court held that 'the concept of public security within the meaning of Article 36 of the Treaty covers both a Member State's internal security and its external security', and that 'the importation, exportation and transit of goods capable of being used for strategic purposes may affect the public security of a Member State, which it is therefore entitled to protect pursuant to Article 36 of the Treaty' (para 22). Consequently, in this case, Luxembourg legislation requiring a special transit licence for the export and import of goods of a strategic nature, under which the customs authorities seized bubble memory circuits imported from the USA for export to the USSR via Luxembourg, was regarded as justifiable.

Protection of health and life of humans, animals and plants

The protection of health and life of humans, animals and plants is the ground of justification most relied on by Member States, and the Court itself has acknowledged, in Case C-170/04 *Rosengren and others v Riksåklagaren* [2007] ECR I-4071, that

> ... the health and life of humans rank foremost among the assets or interests protected by Article [36 TFEU] and it is for the Member States, within the limits imposed by the Treaty, to decide what degree of protection they wish to assure ... (para 39)

The Court accepts that, in the absence of European harmonisation, Member States enjoy a certain degree of discretion with regard to the protection of public health. However, to be successfully justified under this heading, the national measure taken to control the movement of goods must be part of a seriously considered and coherent health policy.

When exercising its supervision the Court will proceed in two stages. First, the Court will determine whether the protection of public health is the real purpose behind the Member State's action, or whether it is designed to protect domestic products (*Re Newcastle Disease – Import of Poultry Meat*, **14.2.1.1** above). In Case 124/81 *Commission v UK (Re UHT Milk)* [1983] ECR 203, a UK measure, requiring that all domestic and imported milk be packaged and sold through approved dairies or distributors, was deemed to be a MHEE. Its effect was that imported milk had to be repackaged, thus increasing its costs. The Court rejected the claim by the UK Government that the measure was designed to ensure the milk was free from infection. The Court held that the evidence was that milk in all Member States was subject to similar controls and was of similar quality. Therefore the measure could not be justified on grounds of public health.

By contrast, in Case C-67/97 *Criminal Proceedings against Bluhme* [1998] ECR I-8033, the Court accepted that a Danish law forbidding the importation into and the keeping of any species of bees on the island of Læso, in order to protect a very special type of indigenous brown bee (*Apis mellifera mellifera*) and ensure it would not be endangered by crossbreeding, was a measure that contributed to the maintenance of biodiversity by preserving a rare and threatened species and, as such, fell within the protection of the health and life of animals under Article 36 (para 33).

Secondly, the Court will consider whether a claim is justified in the absence of a consensus on the scientific or medical impact of certain substances. In Case 53/80 *Officier van justitie v Koninklijke Kaasfabriek Eyssen BV* [1981] ECR 409, which concerned the compatibility with the Treaty of a Dutch law prohibiting the use of the preservative nisin in processed cheese, the ECJ held that the Dutch authorities did not have to prove conclusively that there was a risk to public health, and that the Dutch prohibition was justified by the fact that the risk was known and an established possibility. Indeed the Court recognised that it was not disputed that 'the addition of preservatives to foodstuffs ... call[ed] for the adoption of national measures designed to regulate the use of such additives in the interest of the protection of human health', and that the use of nisin in milk and other processed food products

> ... has revealed the need, both at national level in certain countries and at international level, to study the problem of the risk which the consumption of

products containing the substance presents, or may present, to human health and has led certain international organisations ... to undertake research into the critical threshold for the intake of that additive. (para 13)

However, the Court observed that 'those studies [had] not as yet enabled absolutely certain conclusions to be drawn regarding the maximum quantity of nisin which a person may consume daily without serious risk to his health' (para 13), and concluded that

> [t]he difficulties and uncertainties inherent in such an assessment may explain the lack of uniformity in the national laws of the Member States regarding the use of this preservative and at the same time justify the limited scope which the prohibition of the use of the additive in a given product, such as processed cheese, has in certain Member States, including the Netherlands, which prohibit its use in products intended for sale on the domestic market while permitting it in products intended for export to other Member States where the requirements for the protection of human health are assessed differently according to dietary habits of their own population. (para 14)

This approach was confirmed in the Case 174/82 *Criminal proceedings against Sandoz* [1983] ECR 2445, where the Dutch authorities refused to grant authorisation for the importation of muesli bars with added vitamins from Germany where they were lawfully marketed. While vitamins are not harmful substances per se, and are rather recognised as necessary for the human body, the Court observed that 'excessive consumption of them over a prolonged period may have harmful effects, the extent of which varies according to the type of vitamin: there is generally a greater risk with vitamins soluble in fat than with those soluble in water' (para 11). However, as 'scientific research does not appear to be sufficiently advanced to be able to determine with certainty the critical quantities and the precise effects' (para 11), the Court concluded that

> ... in so far as there are uncertainties at the present state of scientific research it is for the Member States, in the absence of harmonisation, to decide what degree of protection of the health and life of humans they intend to assure, having regard however for the requirements of the free movement of goods within the [Union]. (para 16)

In another vitamins case (Case C-192/01 *Commission v Denmark* [2003] ECR I-9693), the Danish Government tried to justify, on the basis of the *Sandoz* ruling, an administrative practice prohibiting the marketing of foodstuffs with added vitamins lawfully produced or marketed in other Member States, unless it was demonstrated that such vitamin enrichment met a nutritional need in Danish consumers. In line with *Sandoz*, the Court observed that as long as 'scientific uncertainty persists as regards the existence or extent of real risks to human health', and provided the risk assessment is not based on purely hypothetical considerations, 'it must be accepted that a Member State may, in accordance with the precautionary principle, take protective measures without having to wait until the reality and seriousness of those risks are fully demonstrated' (para 49). The Court further asserted that

> [w]here it proves to be impossible to determine with certainty the existence or extent of the alleged risk because of the insufficiency, inconclusiveness or imprecision of the results of studies conducted, but the likelihood of real harm to

public health persists should the risk materialise, the precautionary principle justifies the adoption of restrictive measures … (para 52)

However, the Court disagreed with the Danish Government's interpretation of the *Sandoz* judgment, and ruled that while 'the criterion of the nutritional need of the population of a Member State can play a role in its detailed assessment of the risk which the addition of nutrients to foodstuffs may pose for public health' (para 54), a total prohibition cannot be justified under Article 36 TFEU on the sole basis of the absence of such a need. For that reason, the Court regarded the Danish administrative practice as disproportionate (see para 55).

Provided they satisfy the proportionality test (see 14.2.1.1 above), national laws on the production and marketing of medicinal products are generally considered favourably in the case law of the Court. For instance, in Joined Cases 266 and 267/87 *R v Royal Pharmaceutical Society of Great Britain* [1989] ECR 1295, the rules in the Code of Ethics and Guidance Notes of the Pharmaceutical Society of Great Britain, prohibiting a pharmacist from substituting, except in an emergency, any other medicinal product for a product specifically named in the prescription, even if he believed that the former product had identical therapeutic effect and quality, were regarded as justified under Article 36 of the Treaty. By contrast, a French Decree that imposed an obligation to state the registration number of medical reagents on their external packaging, and to mention that registration on the notice accompanying the reagents, ie chemical or biological substances specially prepared for use in vitro for medical biological analyses, was not regarded as satisfying the proportionality test, as

> [m]entioning the registration, in particular by stating the registration number, merely guarantees the user that the reagent has been registered with the competent authorities, and does not provide any additional information which might effectively protect public health … (Case C-55/99 *Commission v France* [2000] ECR I-11499, para 43)

The advertising of imported medicinal products has also been the object of national regulation. A national prohibition on the sale by mail order of medicinal products that may be sold only in pharmacies in the Member State of import is a MHEE, but may be justified if the prohibition covers medicinal products subject to prescription. However, an absolute prohibition on the sale by mail order of medicinal products that are not subject to prescription in the Member State of import cannot be justified (Case C-322/01 *Deutscher Apothekerverband eV v 0800 DocMorris NV and Waterval* [2003] ECR I-14887). By contrast, in Case C-143/06 *Ludwigs-Apotheke München Internationale Apotheke v Juers Pharma Import-Export GmbH* [2007] ECR I-9623, the Court ruled that a German law prohibiting all advertising of medicinal products not approved in Germany but lawfully put into circulation in another State, products which are acquired in that State by pharmacists in small quantities in response to individual orders, was deemed to be in breach of former Articles 28 and 30 TEC (now Articles 34 and 36 TFEU) on the ground that the importation of those products was 'authorised only on an exceptional basis, which contain[ed] no information other than that concerning the trade name, packaging size, dose and price' (para 44), and could not be justified on grounds of the protection of the health and life of humans (para 42).

The distinction between medicinal and food products has become a key issue in this context. It is particularly well illustrated in Case C-319/05 *Commission v Germany* [2007] ECR I-9811, regarding the regulation of the marketing of a garlic preparation in capsule form, legally marketed as a food supplement in a number of Member States but classified as a medicinal product in Germany under Directive 2001/83/EC ([2001] OJ L311/67) and, as such, as subject to a marketing authorisation. The Court noted, first, that the main purpose of this Directive was to remove obstacles to trade in medicinal products within the single market, but it did not constitute complete harmonisation of national legislation on the production and marketing of those products. As a result, 'the fact that a product is classified as a foodstuff in another Member State cannot prevent it from being classified as a medicinal product in the Member State of importation, if it displays the characteristics of such a product' (para 37). Following an examination of the garlic preparation under Directive 2001/83/EC, the Court then concluded that it did not satisfy the definition of 'medicinal product by presentation', as it was 'not indicated or recommended as a product for treating or preventing disease, whether on the label, the information printed on the external packaging, or in any other way' (para 45). Nor did it satisfy the definition of 'medicinal product by function', which covers products the pharmacological properties of which have been scientifically observed and which are genuinely designed to make a medical diagnosis or to restore, correct or modify physiological functions. Indeed, the garlic preparation did not have a significant effect on the metabolism, and was not capable of restoring, correcting or modifying physiological functions (see para 68). Carrying on with further scrutiny of the German practice under former Articles 28 and 30 TEC (now Articles 34 and 36 TFEU), the Court ruled that the German reclassification of the garlic preparation as a medicinal product was not based on a 'detailed assessment of the risks to health', and making this product subject to a strict marketing authorisation procedure could not be justified. Instead, as the Court suggested, Germany could have 'prescribed suitable labelling warning consumers of the potential risks related to taking this product' (para 95). In doing so, it would have complied with the principle of proportionality, and 'the protection of public health would thus have been ensured without such serious restrictions on the free movement of goods' (para 95).

In Case C-108/09 *Ker-Optika bt v ÀNTSZ Dél-dunántúli Regionális Intézete* [2010] ECR I-12213, in the context of sales over the Internet, the Court ruled that Hungarian legislation authorising the sale of contact lenses solely in medical supply shops, and therefore prohibiting the sale of contact lenses via the Internet, was a MHEE that could not be objectively justified, as

> the objective of ensuring protection of the health of users of contact lenses can be achieved by measures which are less restrictive than those provided for under the legislation at issue in the main proceedings, namely measures which subject to certain restrictions only the first supply of lenses and which require the economic operators concerned to make available a qualified optician to the customer. (para 74)

Where a Member State adopts legislation such as the Hungarian law, 'it exceeds the limits of [its] discretion ... and that legislation must therefore go beyond what is necessary to attain the objective the Member State claims to pursue' (para 75).

Protection of industrial and commercial property

Article 36 TFEU also provides for a derogation permitting a national law to protect industrial and commercial property rights (IPRs). It must be noted that under Article 345 TFEU, '[t]he Treaties shall in no way prejudice the rules in Member States governing the system of property ownership'. Read jointly, Articles 36 and 345 TFEU appear to ensure that national rules regarding industrial and commercial property rights are not affected by Articles 34 and 35 of the Treaty.

The notion of 'industrial and commercial property' in Article 36 TFEU is a very broad one and covers rights over an invention (patents), a design and a brand (trade marks). It also covers literary or artistic work (copyrights) (Joined Cases 55 and 57/80 *Musik-Vertrieb membran GmbH and K-tel International v GEMA* [1981] ECR 147), a breeder's right over a new plant variety (Case 258/78 *LC Nungesser KG and Eisele v Commission* [1982] ECR 2015), and product names (Case C-220/98 *Estée Lauder Cosmetics GmbH & Co OHG v Lancaster Group GmbH* [2000] ECR I-117) as well as protected designations of origins (Case C-388/95 *Belgium v Spain* [2000] ECR I-3123, on the prohibition on selling and exporting Rioja '*denominación de origen calificada*' wine in bulk (see **13.2.4**); Case C-108/01 *Consorzio del Prosciutto di Parma and Salumificio S Rita SpA v Asda Stores Ltd and Hygrade Foods Ltd* [2003] ECR I-512, regarding the slicing and packaging of Parma ham in the region of production; Case C-478/07 *Budějovický Budvar, národní podnik v Rudolf Ammersin GmbH* [2009] ECR I-7721, concerning the designation 'Bud' and the use of the mark 'American Bud').

All in all, Article 36 TFEU covers all intellectual property rights. However, the issue is that IPRs can be in direct conflict with the free movement of goods and free competition, in that:

(a) such rights are territorial in nature and application (normally within a Member State). National systems of IPRs in a Member State can therefore result in the EU single market's being divided into 28 separate markets for IPR purposes. Furthermore, IPRs sometimes last for long periods, giving the IPR owner monopoly rights to exploit it, thus potentially perpetuating the separation of markets within the EU. This can clearly conflict with the idea of a single market throughout the EU (see **Chapter 11**);

(b) this exclusive, monopoly right to exploit an IPR can undermine the objectives of free competition (see **Chapter 16**) within the single market.

As the TFEU does not deal with or attempt to resolve this conflict, the ECJ has tried to achieve a balance between the following two conflicting objectives:

(a) allowing IPRs to act as an incentive for individuals and enterprises to invest in research and development to develop new products, by giving them certain exclusive rights; and, on the other hand,

(b) preventing the use of IPRs with the effect of undermining the economic objectives of free movement of goods and free competition within the EU.

Most problems have resulted from 'parallel imports'. Such situation occurs when:

- X owns the IPR to certain goods in Member State 1 and Member State 2
- X sells goods in Member State 1 for less than he sells the goods in Member State 2, because consumers in Member State 2 are prepared to pay more than consumers in Member State 1
- X sells goods in Member State 1 to Y, who wants to export them to (import them into) Member State 2 and resell them for less than X sells the goods in Member State 2, but at a profit compared to what Y paid for them in Member State 1
- X attempts to enforce its IPR in Member State 2, to try to prevent Y from selling in Member State 2.

The question is whether X should be allowed to enforce his IPR in Member State 2 where the effect is to prevent the free movement of goods between Member State 1 and Member State 2 by Y, and free competition in the goods between X and Y within Member State 2.

The exploitation of (or reliance on) IPRs has been controlled and restricted by the ECJ in two broad ways:

(a) first, by applying Article 101 TFEU (see 17.2) to prevent the enforcement of an IPR within a potentially anti-competitive agreement. For example, the owner of an IPR purports to enter into an agreement (eg, a licence) with a licensee, giving the licensee absolute territorial protection in the distribution of the goods in a particular Member State (see Joined Cases 56 and 58/64 *Établissements Consten SàRL and Grundig-Verkaufs-GmbH v Commission* [1966] ECR 299, in which the Court ruled that the use of an IPR in this way was capable of being (and, on facts, was) a breach of competition rules (at 345)); and

(b) secondly, by applying Article 34 TFEU to prevent the enforcement of an IPR where there is no agreement caught under Article 101 TFEU.

In order to tackle the issue of parallel imports, the ECJ resorted to the principle of 'exhaustion of rights', as in Case 78/70 *Deutsche Grammophon Gesellschaft mbH v Metro-SB-Großmärkte GmbH & Co KG* [1971] ECR 487. The 'exhaustion of rights' principle permits the existence of a national IPR, but only its limited exercise, at which point the right is said to be exhausted and no further exercise of it will be permitted.

The analysis of the ECJ is as follows:

(a) The protection given by a national IPR is compatible with Article 34 TFEU only to the extent that it is permitted by Article 36 TFEU. A national IPR rule is a distinctly applicable MHEE within the *Dassonville* formula (see 13.2.3.1) in so far as it prevents imports (or certainly makes imports more difficult), unless the exercise of the IPR is justified under the Article 36 TFEU derogation for the protection of industrial and commercial property.

(b) Article 36 TFEU permits restrictions on the free movement of goods caused by the enforcement of an IPR only to the extent that they are justified for enforcing rights that are the specific subject matter of such an IPR. The national IPR rule will be permitted if proportionate and necessary to achieve the objective of protection of industrial property (see *Deutsche Grammophon Gesellschaft*, para 11).

(c) The ECJ shall decide what rights are the 'specific subject matter' of each type of IPR, that is, which IPR is capable of being protected under Article 36 TFEU, and the extent of their protection. For instance, in Case 15/74 *Centrafarm BV and de Peijper v Sterling Drug Inc* [1974] ECR 1147, the subject matter of a patent was

> ... the guarantee that the patentee, to reward the creative effort of the inventor, has the exclusive right to use an invention with a view to manufacturing industrial products and putting them into circulation for the first time, either directly or by the grant of licences to third parties, as well as the right to oppose infringements. (para 9)

(d) The right being the 'specific subject matter' of the IPR exists, but can be exercised only until such right has been exhausted. Therefore, there is a distinction between the existence of a national IPR (permitted by Article 36 TFEU) and the exercise of such IPR (the exercise of the right being prohibited once the right has been exhausted).

(e) As such, an IPR is protected within the territorial monopoly granted under a national law, but only to the extent that the relevant good, to which the IPR applies, has been lawfully put onto the market in one Member State in accordance with the national IPR by the IPR owner, or by anyone else with the owner's consent. Once the goods have been put on the market of one Member State by, or with the consent of, the owner, it would no longer be justified for the owner of the IPR to try to enforce the national IPR further in another Member State to protect the 'specific subject matter' of that IPR (see, in the context of patents, *Centrafarm*, above, para 11). Therefore, any further exercise of an IPR in the Member State of sale or any other Member State, will be prohibited under Article 34 TFEU and unjustifiable under Article 36 TFEU (see Case 187/80 *Merck & Co Inc v Stephar BV and Exler* [1980] ECR 2063, para 14).

(f) The principle of exhaustion of rights can be mitigated, however. For instance, in the case of trade marks, an IPR owner can object to its use by a third person in order to prevent counterfeiting or confusion amongst consumers. In the context of a coffee trade mark, the ECJ ruled that a company that was the owner of a trade mark protected in a Member State, could oppose the importation from another Member State of similar goods lawfully bearing in the latter State an identical trade mark, or one which would be liable to be confused with the protected mark, even if the mark under which the goods were imported originally belonged to a subsidiary of the company that opposed the importation and was acquired by a third company after the expropriation of that subsidiary (Case 192/73 *Van Zuylen frères v Hag AG (Hag I)* [1974] ECR 731 and Case C-10/89 *SA CNL-SUCAL NV v HAG GF AG (Hag II)* [1990] ECR I-3711). Similarly, a subsidiary trading in Member State A of a car manufacturer established in a Member State B, could be prevented from using the mark 'Quadra' for a four-wheel-drive car in its own State and elsewhere, on the ground that another car manufacturer has a trade mark right to use 'Quattro' in Member State A, even if this word has a numerical connotation, the meaning of which is discernible in other Member States (Case C-317/91 *Deutsche Renault AG v AUDI AG* [1993] ECR I-6227).

14.2.2 Derogations under Article 114 TFEU

Article 114(1) TFEU provides:

> Save where otherwise provided in the Treaties, the following provisions shall apply for the achievement of the objectives set out in Article 26. The European Parliament and the Council shall, acting in accordance with the ordinary legislative procedure and after consulting the Economic and Social Committee, adopt the measures for the approximation of the provisions laid down by law, regulation or administrative action in Member States which have as their object the establishment and functioning of the internal market.

Harmonisation directives (see 11.3) are adopted in Council by qualified majority voting under Article 114(1) TFEU, except for fiscal provisions and those relating to the free movement of persons, and to the rights and interests of employed persons (Article 114(2) TFEU). In the fields of health, safety, environmental protection and consumer protection, harmonisation directives must take 'as a base a high level of protection, taking account in particular of any new development based on scientific facts' (Article

114(3) TFEU). A directive may include a safeguard clause, which authorises a Member State to take provisional measures for non-economic reasons under Article 36 TFEU and subject to a Union control procedure (Article 114(10) TFEU).

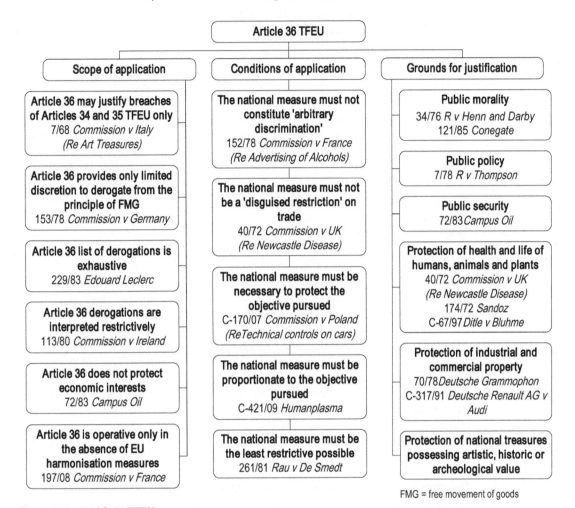

Article 36 TFEU

Scope of application

Article 36 may justify breaches of Articles 34 and 35 TFEU only
7/68 *Commission v Italy (Re Art Treasures)*

Article 36 provides only limited discretion to derogate from the principle of FMG
153/78 *Commission v Germany*

Article 36 list of derogations is exhaustive
229/83 *Edouard Leclerc*

Article 36 derogations are interpreted restrictively
113/80 *Commission v Ireland*

Article 36 does not protect economic interests
72/83 *Campus Oil*

Article 36 is operative only in the absence of EU harmonisation measures
197/08 *Commission v France*

Conditions of application

The national measure must not constitute 'arbitrary discrimination'
152/78 *Commission v France (Re Advertising of Alcohols)*

The national measure must not be a 'disguised restriction' on trade
40/72 *Commission v UK (Re Newcastle Disease)*

The national measure must be necessary to protect the objective pursued
C-170/07 *Commission v Poland (Re Technical controls on cars)*

The national measure must be proportionate to the objective pursued
C-421/09 *Humanplasma*

The national measure must be the least restrictive possible
261/81 *Rau v De Smedt*

Grounds for justification

Public morality
34/76 *R v Henn and Darby*
121/85 *Conegate*

Public policy
7/78 *R v Thompson*

Public security
72/83 *Campus Oil*

Protection of health and life of humans, animals and plants
40/72 *Commission v UK (Re Newcastle Disease)*
174/72 *Sandoz*
C-67/97 *Ditle v Bluhme*

Protection of industrial and commercial property
70/78 *Deutsche Grammophon*
C-317/91 *Deutsche Renault AG v Audi*

Protection of national treasures possessing artistic, historic or archeological value

FMG = free movement of goods

Figure 14.1   Article 36 TFEU

After the adoption of a directive, a Member State may maintain national provisions for non-economic reasons under Article 36 TFEU, or for the protection of the environment or the working environment, in which case the Member State must notify the Commission of these provisions (Article 114(4) TFEU).

14.3   Justifications in the case law of the Court of Justice

14.3.1   The first *Cassis de Dijon* principle

The concept of 'mandatory requirements' (also referred to as 'imperative requirements' or 'overriding requirements in the public interest') was first mentioned in the *Cassis de Dijon* case (Case 120/78 *Rewe-Zentral AG v Bundesmonopolverwaltung für Branntwein* [1979] ECR 649 (see **13.2.3.2**). After establishing the principle of mutual recognition, and after pointing out that

> [i]n the absence of common rules relating to the production and marketing of alcohol ... it is for the Member States to regulate all matters relating to the production and marketing of alcohol and alcoholic beverages on their own territory ... (para 8)

the Court confirmed for the first time that, outside the scope of application of Article 36 TFEU,

> [o]bstacles to movement within the Community resulting from disparities between the national laws relating to the marketing of the products in question must be accepted in so far as those provisions may be recognised as being necessary in order to satisfy mandatory requirements relating in particular to the effectiveness of fiscal supervision, the protection of public health, the fairness of commercial transactions and the defence of the consumer. (para 8)

This is known as the first *Cassis de Dijon* principle.

14.3.1.1 Legal basis of 'mandatory requirements'

This category of justifications cannot be legally based on Article 36 TFEU, by reason of the very wording of that provision and its restrictive interpretation by the Court. Indeed, the Court had consistently held that the list of derogations contained in Article 36 is exhaustive (see **14.2.1.1** and *Re Irish Souvenirs*, paras 7–8). As a result, mandatory requirements can only be raised under Article 34 TFEU, in spite of the fact that Article 34 merely lays down a general principle prohibiting quantitative restrictions and MHEEs, without explicitly providing for exceptions to this principle. Consequently, if justified by a mandatory requirement, a trade barrier will not be regarded as a MHEE in the first place since it will then fall outside the scope of Article 34 TFEU. By contrast, a national measure that is justified under Article 36 will first be regarded as a MHEE since it falls within the scope of Article 34. The first *Cassis de Dijon* principle acts therefore as a 'rule of reason', in the sense that it softens the harshness of the prohibitive principle laid down in Article 34 TFEU. It is to be noted, however, that the Court of Justice has never referred to this rule as such in its case law.

14.3.1.2 Relationship between the first *Cassis de Dijon* principle and Article 36 TFEU

While distinctly applicable measures (applying to imported goods only, or applying differently to imports) (see **13.2.3.3**) can only be justified under Article 36 TFEU, as they are discriminatory by nature, indistinctly applicable measures (applying equally to both domestic and imported goods without prima facie discrimination) (see **13.2.3.3**) can be justified either under Article 36, or under the first *Cassis de Dijon* principle. This is well illustrated by *Re Irish Souvenirs* (see **14.2.1.1**), which concerned an Irish requirement that only 'Irish' souvenirs produced outside of Ireland had to be marked 'foreign' or with the country of their origin. The Irish Government did not dispute that the measure was in breach of the free movement of goods provision, but it argued that it was necessary to protect consumers and the fairness of commercial transactions (two mandatory requirements) by distinguishing 'genuine' Irish souvenirs from those made abroad. Observing that the Irish measure was only applied to imported goods, the Court ruled that it could not be justified under the first *Cassis de Dijon* principle. The measure could not be justified under Article 36 TEEC (now Article 36 TFEU) either, as the two grounds for justification relied upon by the Irish Government were not included in that provision. The Court concluded that the requirement was a MHEE.

However, as with Article 36 derogations, Member States can rely upon mandatory requirements only in the absence of EU measures of harmonisation (see **14.2.1.1**) (Case C-470/93 *Verein gegen Unwesen in Handel und Gewerbe Köln eV v Mars GmbH* [1995] ECR I-1923, para 12), and provided that their measures satisfy the proportionality test. In the *Cassis de Dijon* case, the German Government had argued that the minimum alcohol content of 32% for certain spirits, whether domestic or imported, imposed under the *Branntweinmonopolgesetz*, was a necessary measure for the protection of consumers – since low-alcohol drinks might easily induce alcohol tolerance – and for guaranteeing fairness of commercial transactions – since cheaper, lower-strength alcohol might force manufacturers to reduce the alcohol content in their own beverages owing to competitive pressures from imported lower-alcohol drinks (para 12). The ECJ rejected Germany's arguments. The German measure was deemed disproportionate, since the protection of the consumer could have been achieved by national measures much less restrictive on imports, such as an effective labelling.

In order for a national measure to be justified, the Member State must therefore show that its measure:

(a) has as its sole purpose to satisfy a mandatory requirement;

(b) is part of a serious and coherent policy to meet that identified mandatory requirement; and

(c) is 'reasonably necessary' (proportionate) to the purpose of the measure (the identified mandatory requirement).

In Case 178/84 *Commission v Germany (Re Law of Purity of Beer)* [1987] ECR 1227, the Commission brought an enforcement action against Germany for prohibiting the marketing of beers, lawfully manufactured and marketed in other Member States, if they did not comply with Articles 9 and 10 of the *Biersteuergesetz* (Law on beer duty). This law covered manufacturing rules (Article 9), which applied only to breweries in Germany, and rules on the use of the designation '*Bier*' (beer) (Article 10), which applied both to beer brewed in Germany and to imported beer. The manufacturing rules notably provided that bottom-fermented beers could be manufactured only from malted barley, hops, yeast and water, according to the old German tradition of the *Reinheitsgebot* (purity of beer). And, under Article 10, only fermented beverages satisfying the requirements set out in Article 9 of the *Biersteuergesetz* could be marketed under the designation '*Bier*'. Furthermore, imported beers containing additives would face an absolute prohibition on marketing under the Law on foodstuffs, tobacco products, cosmetics and other consumer goods. The German Government tried to justify those rules on the ground of the protection of consumers (mandatory requirement) and the protection of human health (under the then Article 36 TEEC (now Article 36 TFEU)). The Court rejected the first argument on the ground that

… consumers' conceptions which vary from one Member State to the other are also likely to evolve in the course of time within a Member State. The establishment of the [internal] market is, it should be added, one of the factors that may play a major contributory role in that development. Whereas rules protecting consumers against misleading practices enable such a development to be taken into account, legislation of the kind contained in Article 10 of the Biersteuergesetz prevents it from taking place. As the Court has already held in another context …, *the legislation of a Member State must not 'crystallize given consumer habits so as to consolidate an advantage acquired by national industries concerned to comply with them'*. (para 32, emphasis added)

Furthermore with regard to the designation '*Bier*', the Court pointed out:

> It is admittedly legitimate to seek to enable consumers who attribute specific qualities to beers manufactured from particular raw materials to make their choice in the light of that consideration. However ..., *that possibility may be ensured by means which do not prevent the importation of products which have been lawfully manufactured and marketed in other Member States* and, in particular, 'by the compulsory affixing of suitable labels giving the nature of the product sold'. By indicating the raw materials utilised in the manufacture of beer '*such a course would enable the consumer to make his choice in full knowledge of the facts and would guarantee transparency in trading and in offers to the public*'. It must be added that such a system of mandatory consumer information must not entail negative assessments for beers not complying with the requirements of Article 9 of the Biersteuergesetz. (para 35, emphasis added).

Following the Commission, the Court also rejected the second argument, and ruled that an absolute ban on the marketing of beers containing additives could not be justified on protection of human health grounds under Article 36 TEEC (now Article 36 TFEU). The Court observed that

> ... it appears from the tables of additives authorised for use in the various foodstuffs submitted by the German Government itself that some of the additives authorised in other Member States for use in the manufacture of beer are also authorised under the German rules, in particular the Regulation on Additives, for use in the manufacture of all, or virtually all, beverages. *Mere reference to the potential risks of the ingestion of additives in general and to the fact that beer is a foodstuff consumed in large quantities does not suffice to justify the imposition of stricter rules in the case of beer.* (para 49, emphasis added)

Dismissing as a 'disguised means of restricting trade between Member States' (para 51) a further argument by Germany relating to the lack of technological need for additives in beer, the Court concluded that

> ... in so far as the German rules on additives in beer entail a general ban on additives, their application to beers imported from other Member States is contrary to the requirements of [EU] law as laid down in the case law of the Court, since that prohibition is contrary to the principle of proportionality and is therefore not covered by the exception provided for in Article [36 TFEU]. (para 53)

14.3.1.3   'Mandatory requirements'

If the list of derogations under Article 36 TFEU is exhaustive, that of mandatory requirements is not, as suggested by the words 'in particular' in paragraph 8 of the *Cassis de Dijon* case (see **14.3.1**). The original paragraph 8 list of mandatory requirements has subsequently been expanded by the Court of Justice so as to include:

- the improvement of working conditions (Case 155/80 *Summary Proceedings against Oebel* [1981] ECR 1993, a German rule prohibiting delivery of bakery products to consumers and retailers during the night and before 4 am)
- protection of the environment (Case 302/86 *Commission v Denmark* [1988] ECR 649, a Danish law requiring all containers for beer and soft drinks to be returnable, and Case C-320/03 R *Commission v Austria* [2005] ECR I-7929, an Austrian law prohibiting lorries weighing more than 7.5 tonnes from being driven on a section of the A12 motorway in the Inn Valley, to improve air quality so as to ensure lasting protection of human, animal and plant health)
- the maintenance of press diversity (Case C-368/95 *Vereinigte Familiapress Zeitungsverlags- und vertriebs GmbH v Heinrich Bauer Verlag* [1997] ECR I-3689, a German newspaper publisher selling newspapers in Germany and Austria, in

which readers were offered the opportunity to take part in games with prizes, was accused of acting in breach of the Austrian Unfair Competition Act 1992)

- protection of the cinema industry as a form of cultural expression (Joined Cases 60 and 61/84 *Cinéthèque SA and others v Fédération nationale des cinémas français* [1985] ECR 2605, a French law prohibiting the sale or hire of films within a year of their first showing in cinema theatres, thus restricting the import of videos from other Member States)

- protection of a national social security system (Case C-120/95 *Decker v Caisse de maladie des employés privés* [1998] ECR I-1831, prior authorisation requirement from a Luxembourg competent social security institution before reimbursement of costs for glasses purchased in another Member State)

- protection of national or regional socio-cultural characteristics (Case C-145/88 *Torfaen Borough Council v B & Q plc* [1989] ECR 3851, concerning the compatibility with Article 30 TEEC of the Shops Act 1951 prohibiting Sunday trading – note that such a rule would now be caught under the *Keck* ruling, see **13.2.3.4**).

See Case C-639/11 *Commission v Poland* of 20 March 2014, ECLI:EU:C:2014:173 and Case C-61/12 *Commission v Lithuania (Re Obligation, for the purpose of registration, to reposition to the left-hand side the steering equipment of passenger vehicles positioned on the right-hand side)* of 20 March 2014, ECLI:EU:C:2014:172. Over recent years, the Commission had received a series of complaints from Polish and Lithuanian citizens, who exercised a professional activity in the United Kingdom and Ireland and who had bought a passenger vehicle there. On their return to Poland and to Lithuania they wanted to register their vehicles, but were obliged, under Polish and Lithuanian legislation, to reposition the steering-wheel of their vehicle on the left-hand side. Such modification can be very complicated.

The Commission considered that such a requirement amounted to a prohibition on registration in Poland and Lithuania of vehicles with the steering-wheel positioned on the right, and that the refusal to register those vehicle constituted, with regard to new vehicles, an infringement of Article 4(3) of Directive 2007/46/EC ([2007] OJ L263/1) and of Article 2a of Directive 70/311/EEC ([1970] OJ L133/10), which require national authorities to register new vehicles irrespective of the position of the steering-wheel. The refusal also constituted an infringement of Article 34 TFEU with regard to vehicles that had been registered in another Member State. The Commission invited those two States to terminate those infringements and, following the pre-litigation procedure under Article 258 TFEU, it decided to bring an action against them in the Court of Justice.

With regard to Article 34 TFEU, relying on the *Dassonville* and *Cassis de Dijon* rulings, and on the ruling in Case C-110/05 *Commission v Italy (Re Trailer)* [2009] ECR I-519, the Court found that the Polish and Lithuanian laws constituted

> ... measure[s] having equivalent effect to quantitative restrictions on imports ..., in so far as [their] effect [was] to hinder access to the [Polish and Lithuanian] market[s] for vehicles with steering equipment on the right, which are lawfully constructed and registered in Member States other than [Poland and Lithuania] ... (para 52 and para 57 respectively)

However, these laws could be justified in order to satisfy imperative requirements, 'on condition that [they were] appropriate for securing the attainment of the objective pursued and that [they did] not go beyond what is necessary in order to attain that objective' (para 53 and para 58 respectively). Following an examination of the justification put forward by Poland and Lithuania, namely the need to ensure road safety, which constitutes an imperative requirement relating to the public interest, the Court held that it did not appear that the national measures concerned could be considered to be necessary to attain the objective pursued, and that they were not compatible with the principle of proportionality. (para 64 and para 69 respectively)

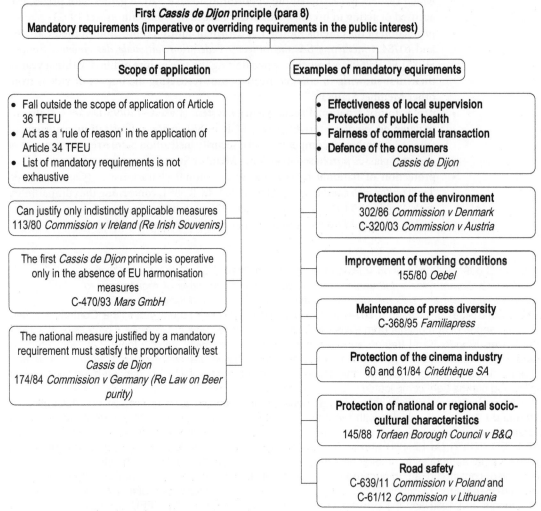

Figure 14.2   Mandatory requirements

14.3.2   Principles of law

Enshrined in primary legislation, the precautionary principle (Article 191(2) TFEU) and the protection of fundamental rights (Article 6(3) TEU) have also been incorporated and interpreted by the Court of Justice to justify certain restrictions on the free movement of goods.

14.3.2.1   The precautionary principle

Originating in environmental law and first introduced by the Maastricht Treaty, the precautionary principle was rapidly extended to the free movement of goods through the concept of protection of public health. Unlike the preventive principle, the precautionary principle presupposes only some uncertainty as to the existence or extent of risks to human health.

It was in the late 1990s, following the BSE or 'mad cow disease' crisis, that the precautionary principle first appeared in order to justify limits to the free movement of goods. Yet it was not in the first BSE case (Case C-180/96 *United Kingdom v Commission* [1998] ECR I-2265, where the UK sought the annulment of Commission Decision 96/239/EC of 27 March 1996 on emergency measures to protect against bovine spongiform encephalopathy, effectively banning all exports from the UK of all bovine animals and derived products to the EU and third countries) but in the second one that the principle was raised. While in the former case the Court simply justified the ban imposed by the Commission on the export of British beef on the 'risks regarded as a serious hazard to public health' posed by BSE-infected products, without the need to refer explicitly to the precautionary principle, in Case C-1/00 *Commission v France* [2001] ECR I-9989, the Court rejected the argument of the French Government, based on the precautionary principle, to justify the Government's refusal to comply with the Commission's decisions lifting the ban on British beef.

The precautionary principle was also raised with regard to genetically modified organisms (GMOs) and their presence in certain foodstuffs. In Case C-132/03 *Ministero della Salute v Codacons and Federconsumatori* [2005] ECR I-4167, an Italian decree provided that the presence of GMOs in a proportion not exceeding 1% of the ingredients making up baby foods, caused by adventitious contamination, needed not be indicated on the labelling of such food and formulae. The issue was whether the decree was covered by the exemption from the obligation to state on the labelling of foodstuffs that material derived from certain GMOs was present, under Articles 2(1) and 3 of Council Regulation (EC) No 1139/98 ([1998] OJ L159/4) concerning the compulsory indication on the labelling of certain foodstuffs produced from genetically modified organisms. The Court not only answered in the affirmative, but also stressed that this 'interpretation [could] not be called into question on the basis of the precautionary principle' (para 56), as

> [t]he GMOs to which Regulation No 1139/98 refers can be placed on the market only if they have first been authorised following a risk assessment intended to ensure that, in the light of the conclusions of the assessment, they are safe for the consumer. The precautionary principle, where relevant, is part of such a decision-making process ... (para 63)

The clash between the precautionary principle and the principle of free movement of goods is, however, better and more clearly illustrated in Case C-41/02 *Commission v The Netherlands* [2004] ECR I-11375, which concerned a Dutch legal prohibition on the marketing of foodstuffs fortified with micronutrients and vitamins. Derogations could be granted by the Health Minister only in the event that the addition did not pose a risk to public health and met an actual nutritional need. After recalling that

> [EU] law does not ... preclude legislation of a Member State prohibiting in accordance with the precautionary principle, save for prior authorisation, the marketing of foodstuffs when nutrients other than those whose addition is lawful under that legislation have been added thereto ... (para 44)

and that, 'it follows from the case-law of the Court that the precautionary principle may also apply in policy on the protection of human health which, ... aims at a high level of protection' (para 45), the Court ruled that

> [a] proper application of the precautionary principle requires, in the first place, the identification of the potentially negative consequences for health of the proposed addition of nutrients, and, secondly, a comprehensive assessment of the

risk for health based on the most reliable scientific data available and the most recent results of international research …

Where it proves to be impossible to determine with certainty the existence or extent of the alleged risk because of the insufficiency, inconclusiveness or imprecision of the results of studies conducted, but the likelihood of real harm to public health persists should the risk materialise, the precautionary principle justifies the adoption of restrictive measures … (paras 53–54)

As the Dutch Government failed to produce scientific studies showing that any intake over the recommended daily allowance of any of the nutrients concerned entailed a real risk to public health, the systematic prohibition of the marketing of fortified foodstuffs was regarded as contrary to EU law.

14.3.2.2 Protection of fundamental rights

The protection of fundamental rights as a means to justify a limitation on the free movement of goods is best demonstrated in Case C-112/00 *Eugen Schmidberger, Internationale Transporte und Planzüge v Austria* [2003] ECR I-5659. The Court ruled that the fact that the Austrian authorities did not ban a demonstration on the Brenner motorway, resulting in traffic by road being obstructed 'on a single route, on a single occasion and during a period of almost 30 hours', was not to be regarded as a breach of former Article 30 TEC (now Article 36 TFEU). Contrasting this situation with that which arose in the *Spanish Strawberries* case (see **14.2.1.2**), the Court held that the impact on the free movement of goods was limited, and that the inaction of the national authorities was justified on the ground that the demonstrators exercised their legitimate fundamental rights of expression and protest, and that the 'purpose of that public demonstration was not to restrict trade in goods of a particular type or from a particular source' (para 86).

However, the Court set limits to the challenge of national measures on the ground of fundamental freedoms. In Case C-71/02 *Herbert Karner Industrie-Auktionen GmbH v Troostwijk GmbH* [2004] ECR I-3025, the UWG, an Austrian law on unfair competition, prohibited retailers from indicating to consumers that goods came from an insolvent estate where they no longer constituted part of that estate. Karner and Troostwijk were two companies that engaged in the sale by auction of industrial goods and the purchase of the stock of insolvent companies. In 2001, Troostwijk acquired the stock of an insolvent construction company in which Karner also showed interest. With a view to selling the goods from the insolvent company in an auction sale to take place a few months later, Troostwijk advertised the auction in a sales catalogue and on the Internet, stating that it was an insolvency auction and that the goods were from the insolvent estate of the company. Karner challenged Troostwijk's advertising in the Vienna Commercial Court, on the ground that it was contrary to the UWG. On appeal to the Vienna Higher Regional Court, Troostwijk questioned the compatibility of the UWG with former Article 28 TEC and Article 10 ECHR concerning freedom of expression. With regard to the freedom of expression argument, the Court observed:

It is common ground that the discretion enjoyed by the national authorities in determining the balance to be struck between freedom of expression and the abovementioned objectives varies for each of the goals justifying restrictions on that freedom and depends on the nature of the activities in question. When the exercise of the freedom does not contribute to a discussion of public interest and, in addition, arises in a context in which the Member States have a certain amount of discretion, review is limited to an examination of the reasonableness and proportionality of the interference. This holds true for the commercial use of freedom of expression, particularly in a field as complex and fluctuating as advertising ...

In this case it appears, having regard to the circumstances of fact and of law characterising the situation which gave rise to the case in the main proceedings and the discretion enjoyed by the Member States, that a restriction on advertising as provided for in Article 30 of the UWG is reasonable and proportionate in the light of the legitimate goals pursued by that provision, namely consumer protection and fair trading. (paras 51–52)

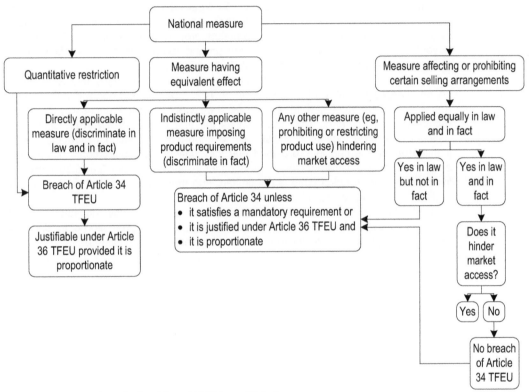

Figure 14.3   How a breach of Article 34 TFEU is established

14.4 Further reading

Caro De Sousa P, 'Through Contact Lenses, Darkly: Is Identifying Restrictions to Free Movement Harder than Meets the Eye? Comment on Ker-Optika' (2012) 37(1) *EL Rev* 79.

Harbo TI, 'The Function of the Proportionality Principle in EU Law' (2010) 16(2) *European Law Journal* 158.

Maduro PM, 'Harmony and Dissonance in Free Movement' (2001) 4 *Cambridge Yearbook of European Legal Studies* 315.

Oliver P and Enchelmaier S, 'Free Movement of Goods: Recent Developments in the Case Law' (2007) 44 *CML Rev* 649.

Schrauwen A, 'Case C-320/03, *Commission v Republic of Austria*, Judgment of the Court (Grand Chamber) of 15 November 2005, nyr' (2006) 43 *CML Rev* 1447.

Weatherill S, 'Free Movement of Goods' (2012) 61 *ICLQ* 541.

Unlike custom duties and charges having equivalent effect under Article 30 TFEU, quantitative restrictions and measures having equivalent effect (MHEEs) under Article 34 and 35 TFEU can be expressly justified under Article 36 TFEU. Article 36 provides for an exhaustive list of six non-economic grounds for justification, which can be relied upon by Member States to justify MHEEs, provided the national measures are not discriminatory or disguised restrictions on trade and provided there are no EU harmonisation measures. The Court further requires that the national measure is necessary to protect the identified permitted ground (necessity) and does not go beyond what is necessary to achieve the ground (proportionate). In addition, those derogations are always interpreted strictly by the Court.

Later on, in the *Cassis de Dijon* case, the Court acknowledged that, outside the scope of application of what is now Article 36 TFEU, barriers to trade within the internal market could be accepted in so far as they were deemed necessary to satisfy mandatory requirements. This is known as the first *Cassis de Dijon* principle. Only national measures that apply indistinctly to imported and national products can be justified under this principle, provided that they satisfy the requirements of necessity and proportionality. Unlike the list of grounds for justification under Article 36 TFEU, the list of mandatory requirements is not limited, and many were created by the Court in addition to the original four *Cassis* requirements.

Finally, the Court has also gradually, albeit in a limited way, accepted that EU principles of law such as the precautionary principle and the protection of fundamental rights can justify national restrictions on trade between Member States.

1   Spirituality, an (imaginary) EU Member State, seeks to fight alcoholism, binge-drinking and alcohol-related health problems, and envisages taking a number of measures to achieve those objectives. Advise its government on whether the following proposed measures could be justified under either Article 36 TFEU or the first *Cassis de Dijon* principle:

(a)   to set a minimum price per unit of alcohol;

(b)   to prohibit all advertising of alcohol on television or on the radio, and in magazines;

(c)   to prohibit the use of screw tops on all bottles of alcohol.

2   AutoPlus is a French company that makes components for the European car industry. Should these following national measures be in breach of Article 34 TFEU, AutoPlus seeks your advice as to whether they could be justified under either Article 36 TFEU or the first *Cassis de Dijon* principle:

(a)   The customs authorities in Spain insist on unpacking and inspecting all consignments of halogen bulbs for headlights. Because the bulbs are very fragile, many of them get broken during this process, and the importers then refuse to pay AutoPlus for them.

(b)   The German Government has recently enacted a law requiring all cars sold in Germany to be labelled according to the percentage of German-made components they contain. This was in response to complaints from German trade unions that too many components are being imported.

(c)   Sweden has enacted a law stating that windscreen wipers on all cars sold in Sweden must be able to operate effectively at a temperature as low as –20°c. AutoPlus's windscreen wipers are only guaranteed to work at a temperature as low as –10°c.

15 Freedom to Exercise an Economic Activity

After reading this chapter, you will be able to understand:

- the free of movement of workers and the concept of worker
- the free movement of the self-employed and the right of establishment
- the freedom to provide and receive services
- the principle of equal treatment of workers and the self-employed
- the principle of mutual recognition of professional qualifications
- the public service and official authority exceptions to the right of free movement of workers and the self-employed.

15.1 Introduction

The right of workers, self-employed persons and legal persons to move and reside freely anywhere within the internal market, with the view to taking up and exercising an economic activity, was recognised in the original Treaty establishing the European Communities. Its objective was indeed to provide economically active persons free access to Member States' markets.

The freedom to exercise an economic activity firmly rests on Treaty provisions relating to the freedom of movement of workers, the right of establishment and the freedom to provide services. Further, the Treaties provide that EU legislation on the mutual recognition of professional qualifications shall be adopted, in order to make it easier to take up and exercise an economic activity.

This freedom is also reinforced by the principle of non-discrimination on the ground of nationality, a core principle of EU law, which guarantees that EU migrants are accorded equal treatment with the nationals of the host Member State. However, equal treatment does not extend to activities that involve the exercise of powers conferred by public law or of official authority.

15.2 Free movement of workers

The right of free movement for workers is guaranteed under Articles 45 to 48 TFEU, and in secondary legislation adopted under Article 46 TFEU with a view to 'setting out the measures required to bring about the freedom of movement for workers, as defined in Article 45'.

Article 45(1) TFEU lays down the basic principle by stating that '[f]reedom of movement for workers shall be secured within the Union'. This provision enables any EU national who wishes to take up employment as an employed worker – rather than setting up a business or otherwise providing services as a self-employed person – to do so in any other Member State.

15.2.1 The concept of worker

In the absence of an express definition of the term 'worker' in the Treaty or secondary legislation, the European Court of Justice (ECJ) gave a very wide, common European meaning to the concept of worker in order to prevent different and restrictive national interpretations of the term and, hence, give full effect to a fundamental freedom of the EU (Case 53/81 *Levin v Staatssecretaris van Justitie* [1982] ECR 1035).

15.2.1.1 A European law concept

Very early on, in Case 75/63 *Hoekstra (née Unger) v Bestuur der Bedrijfsvereniging voor Detailhandel en Ambachten* [1964] ECR 178, the Court made it clear that

> [i]f the definition of [the term worker] were a matter within the competence of national law, it would therefore be possible for each Member State to modify the meaning of the concept of 'migrant worker' and to eliminate at will the protection afforded by the Treaty to certain categories of person. (at 184)

To allow national law to define and modify this concept unilaterally would deprive the Treaty provisions on the free movement of workers of all effect, and frustrate the objectives of the Treaty in this respect.

Noting that the wording of former Articles 48 to 51 of the EEC Treaty (now Articles 45 to 48 TFEU) did not leave the definition of the term 'worker' to national legislation, and that former Article 48(2) referred to 'certain elements of the concept of "workers" such as employment and remuneration', the Court concluded that those provisions attributed a European meaning to the concept of 'workers'.

In Case 66/85 *Lawrie-Blum v Land Baden-Württemberg* [1986] ECR 2121, Deborah Lawrie-Blum, a British national, passed, at the University of Freiburg, the examination for the profession of teacher at a German secondary school. She was refused admission by the Stuttgart Secondary Education Office, however, to the period of preparatory service leading to the Second State Examination, which qualifies successful candidates for appointment as teachers in secondary schools, on the ground of her nationality. During that period of preparatory service, a trainee was regarded as a civil servant and received payment.

The issue was whether trainee teachers could be regarded as 'workers', even if they give lessons for only a few hours a week and were paid remuneration below the starting salary of a qualified teacher.

In this case, the Court defined a worker as

> a person who is obliged to provide services to another in return for monetary reward and who is subject to the direction or control of the other person as regards the way in which the work is done (para 14).

On that basis,

> a trainee teacher who, under the direction and supervision of the school authorities, is undergoing a period of service in preparation for the teaching profession during which he provides services by giving lessons and receives remuneration must be regarded as a worker. (para 22)

A worker must therefore be engaged in a relationship based on subordination, where the individual is under the control of an employer. The nature of the employment is therefore a determining factor. Furthermore, to be a worker, an individual must be 'engaged in an economic activity' (Case 36/74 *Walrave and Koch v Association Union Cycliste Internationale and others* [1974] ECR 1405: the practice of sport is an economic activity when it has the character of gainful employment or remunerated service) that is 'effective and genuine', be it on a full- or part-time basis (*Levin*, 15.2.1 above, para 17), and irrespective of the fact that the level of remuneration is below the minimum level of subsistence and is supplemented by other lawful, privately- or publicly-funded means (Case 139/85 *Kempf v Staatssecretaris van Justitie* [1986] ECR 1741, para 14). A 'genuine and effective activity' could comprise an activity performed by members of a religious community as part of the commercial activities of that community, provided the services offered by the community to its members can be regarded as the 'indirect quid pro quo for [their] genuine and effective work' (Case 196/87 *Steymann v Staatssecretaris van Justitie* [1988] ECR 6159, para 14).

A genuine activity excludes one that is 'on such a small scale as to be regarded as purely marginal and ancillary', as in Case 344/87 *Bettray v Staatssecretaris van Justitie* [1989] ECR 1621 (paid activity provided under a Dutch social employment law as a means of rehabilitation or reintegration). The duration of the activities is also a factor that may be taken into account to assess whether those activities are effective and genuine, or rather purely marginal and ancillary. Therefore, 'a very limited number of hours in a labour relationship may be an indication that the activities exercised are purely marginal and ancillary' (see Case C-357/89 *Raulin v Minister van Onderwijs en Wetenschappen* [1992] ECR I-1027, para 14: waitress who worked 60 hours over a period of 16 days under an on-call contract, and Case C-413/01 *Ninni-Orasche v Bundesminister für Wissenschaft, Verkehr und Kunst* [2003] ECR I-13187).

15.2.1.2 Work seekers

Article 45(3)(a) and (b) TFEU give an EU national the right to enter another Member State to 'accept offers of employment actually made' and 'to move freely within [its] territory ... for this purpose', and Article 45(3)(c) gives the right to 'stay in the Member State for the purpose of employment'. Do these provisions cover an individual who enters another Member State to look for work? According to a strict wording of Article 45(3)(a) and (b), EU nationals would be given the right to move freely to and within another Member State for the purpose only of accepting offers of employment actually made, and, interpreted restrictively, the right to stay in that Member State, under Article 45(3)(c), would be for the purpose of employment only.

In Case C-292/89 *R v Immigration Appeal Tribunal, ex parte Antonissen* [1991] ECR I-745, the ECJ observed that '[s]uch an interpretation would exclude the right of a national of a Member State to move freely and to stay in the territory of the other Member States in order to seek employment there, and cannot be upheld' (para 10). Indeed, a narrow interpretation would render Article 45(3) ineffective, as it 'would jeopardise the actual chances that a national of a Member State who is seeking employment will find it in another Member State' (para 12) and, as a result, fewer workers would move between Member States.

Therefore, Article 45(3) TFEU must be interpreted as covering work seekers. This interpretation is further corroborated by the wording of Articles 1 and 5 of former Regulation 1612/68 (now Regulation (EU) 492/2011 on the Freedom of Movement for Workers within the Union ([2011] OJ L141/1)). The former Regulation refers to the 'right to take up an activity as an employed person', and the latter covers more specifically the right of a national of a Member State who seeks employment in the territory of another Member State to 'receive the same assistance there as that afforded by the employment offices in that State to their own nationals seeking employment'.

That being said, the status of a work seeker does not equate fully to that of a worker, as the right of those seeking employment to stay in a Member State may be subject to a reasonable time limit, unless they '[provide] evidence that [they are] continuing to seek employment and that [they have] genuine chances of being engaged' (*ex parte Antonissen*, para 22). This difference in status was later on enshrined in Article 14(4)(b) of Directive 2004/38/EC ([2004] OJ L158/77), which provides that Union citizens entering another Member State in order to seek employment 'may not be expelled for as long as the Union citizens can provide evidence that they are continuing to seek employment and that they have a genuine chance of being engaged'.

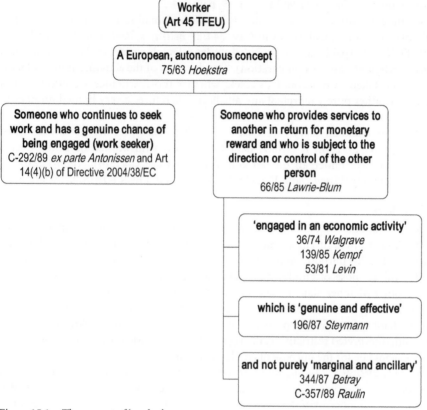

Figure 15.1   The concept of 'worker'

15.2.2 The worker's rights

Under Article 45 TFEU, and subject to the restrictions on grounds of public policy, public security or public health under Article 45(3) (see **20.5**), EU nationals have the rights to enter another Member State, and to move and reside freely within it for the purpose of seeking employment or taking up an activity as a worker. Article 45(3)(d) also gives them the right to stay in a Member State after having been employed in that State.

Article 7(1)(a) of Directive 2004/38/EC further provides that EU migrant workers have a right of residence for more than three months. Should they cease to be workers, their worker status and their right of residence are protected under Article 7(3)(a)–(d) of the Directive. This is the case where:

(a)   they are unable to work following an illness or accident;

(b) they are involuntarily unemployed after more than one year of employment, and have registered as job seekers;

(c) they are in involuntary unemployment on completion of a fixed-term employment contract of less than a year's duration, or during the first 12 months of employment, and have registered as job seekers. The status of worker can then be retained for no less than six months; or

(d) they take up vocational training, which, except in the case of involuntary unemployment, must be related to the previous employment for worker status to be retained.

---

case example

In Case C-507/12 *Jessy Saint Prix v Secretary of State for Work and Pensions* of 19 June 2014, ECLI:EU:C:2014:2007, Ms Saint Prix, a French national, entered the United Kingdom on 10 July 2006, where she worked as a teaching assistant for a year before enrolling on a Post-Graduate Certificate in Education course at the University of London, running from September 2007 until the end of June 2008. During that period she became pregnant and withdrew from the course, registering with an employment agency in the hope of finding work in secondary school. As no work was available, she took agency positions working in nursery schools instead. When she was nearly six months pregnant, she stopped that work because the demands of caring for nursery school children had become too strenuous for her.

Three months before her expected date of confinement, Ms Saint Prix claimed income support. Her claim was refused by the Secretary of State by a decision in May 2008, as she did not meet one of the requirements to receive income support, namely, that she had lost her right of residence in the UK. She appealed against that decision before the First Tier Tribunal.

In August 2008, three months after the premature birth of her child, Ms Saint Prix resumed work. The case was eventually brought before the Supreme Court.

By way of preliminary reference, the Supreme Court asked whether a pregnant woman who had temporarily given up work because of her pregnancy could still be considered a 'worker' under Article 45 TFEU and Article 7 of Directive 2004/38/EC.

Rejecting the British Government's argument that Article 7(3) of Directive 2004/38/EC lists exhaustively the circumstances in which a migrant worker who is no longer in employment may retain that status, the Court held that

Article 45 TFEU must be interpreted as meaning that a woman who gives up work, or seeking work, because of the physical constraints of the late stages of pregnancy and the aftermath of childbirth retains the status of 'worker', within the meaning of that article, provided she returns to work or finds another job within a reasonable period after the birth of her child. (para 47)

Furthermore, Article 45(2) TFEU and Regulation 492/2011/EU protect workers against any discrimination on the ground of nationality with regard to employment, remuneration and other working conditions. These equal treatment rights are discussed below (15.4).

15.3 Freedom of establishment and freedom to provide services

The freedom of establishment and the freedom to provide services are the other two freedoms of movement available to economically active EU migrants.

15.3.1 The concept of establishment

According to Article 49, second paragraph TFEU,

> Freedom of establishment shall include the right to take up and pursue activities as self-employed persons and to set up and manage undertakings, in particular companies or firms ...

Like the freedom of movement of workers, the freedom of establishment has two components: the right to take up an activity, and the right to pursue it.

The concept of establishment implies the permanent or semi-permanent settlement of a natural or legal person for the purpose of pursuing an economic activity, 'through a fixed establishment in another Member State for an indefinite period' (Case C-221/89 *R v The Secretary of State for Transport, ex parte Factortame Ltd and others* [1991] ECR I-3905, para 20). The Court described this concept as

> a very broad one, allowing a [EU] national to participate, on a stable and continuous basis, in the economic life of a Member State other than his State of origin and to profit therefrom, so contributing to economic and social interpenetration within the [EU] in the sphere of activities as self-employed persons. (Case C-55/94 *Gebhard v Consiglio dell'Ordine degli Avvocati e Procuratori di Milano* [1995] ECR I-4165, para 25)

In order to determine whether an activity in a Member State can be regarded as permanent, stable and continuous, the Court has offered in Case C-202/97 *Fitzwilliam Executive Search Ltd v Bestuur van het Landelijk instituut sociale verzekeringen* [2000] ECR I-883 (para 43) a non-exhaustive list of criteria to be considered in each specific case, such as:

- the place where the undertaking has its seat and administration;
- the number of administrative staff working in the Member State in which the undertaking is established and in the other Member State;
- the place where posted workers are recruited, and the place where the majority of contracts with clients are concluded;
- the law applicable to the employment contracts concluded by the undertaking with its workers, on the one hand, and with its clients, on the other hand; and
- the turnover during an appropriately typical period in each Member State concerned.

15.3.2 The concept of services

Related to the right of establishment is the right of an individual, partnership or company based in one Member State to provide services temporarily in another Member State, rather than establishing a permanent business in the latter State. Under Article 56, first paragraph TFEU:

> Restrictions on freedom to provide services within the Union shall be prohibited in respect of nationals of Member States who are established in a Member State other than that of the person for whom the services are intended.

This provision applies to services 'in so far as they are not governed by the provisions relating to freedom of movement for goods, capital and persons' (Article 57, first paragraph).

Drawing a distinction between freedom of establishment and the freedom to provide services, Article 57, third paragraph TFEU also provides:

> Without prejudice to the provisions of the Chapter relating to the right of establishment, the person providing a service may, in order to do so, temporarily

pursue his activity in the Member State where the service is provided, under the same conditions as are imposed by that State on its own nationals.

In *Gebhard*, a German lawyer residing in Italy initially practised as an associate in Italian chambers of lawyers in Milan before opening his own chambers, in which he worked in collaboration with Italian lawyers. Following complaints lodged with the Milan Italian Bar, the latter initiated disciplinary proceedings against Gebhard on the ground that he had contravened Italian law by pursuing a professional activity in Italy on a permanent basis in chambers set up by himself whilst using the title of '*avvocato*'. He was suspended from pursuing his professional activity for six months. Gebhard challenged that decision on the ground that Directive 77/249/EEC (to facilitate the effective exercise by lawyers of freedom to provide services, [1977] OJ L78/17) gave him the right to pursue his professional activities from his own chambers in Milan.

As the Court explained, whether Article 52 TEC (now Article 49 TFEU) or Article 59 TEC (now Article 56 TFEU) is to apply to any particular situation is to be determined by the temporary nature of the provision of the services. Referring to its Advocate General's opinion, the Court confirmed that 'the temporary nature of the activities in question has to be determined in the light, not only of the duration of the provision of the service, but also of its regularity, periodicity or continuity' (para 27). That being said, as the Court further stated in the same paragraph,

[t]he fact that the provision of services is temporary does not mean that the provider of services ... may not equip himself with some form of infrastructure in the host Member State (including an office, chambers or consulting rooms) in so far as such infrastructure is necessary for the purposes of performing the services in question.

This was indeed the case, for instance, as regards a leasing company that supplied cars to customers established in another Member State, and which was contacted through self-employed intermediaries also established in that State (see Case C-190/95 *ARO Lease BV v Inspecteur van de Belastingdienst Grote Ondernemingen te Amsterdam* [1997] ECR I-4383).

Furthermore, only services 'normally provided for remuneration' are to be considered to be 'services' within the meaning of the Treaty. Not expressly defined, the term 'remuneration' has been interpreted broadly by the Court. It does not necessarily mean that the service must be paid for by those for whom it is performed, as in Joined Cases C-51/96 and C-191/97 *Deliège v Ligue Francophone de Judo* [2000] ECR I-2549, para 56 (high-ranking athlete's participation in an international competition involving the provision of a number of separate, related services, such as the organisation of sports events which are attended by the public, are broadcast on television, and attract advertisers and sponsors), or in Case 352/85 *Bond van Adverteerders and others v The Netherlands* [1988] ECR 2085, para 16 (distribution by operators of cable networks established in a Member State of television programmes supplied by broadcasters established in other Member States, a service for which the cable network operators were paid in the form of fees, which they charged their subscribers rather than the broadcasters).

The 'essential characteristic' of remuneration 'lies ... in the fact that it constitutes consideration for the service in question, and is normally agreed upon between the provider and the recipient of the service' (Case 263/86 *Belgium v Humbel and Edel* [1988] ECR 5365, para 17). Such a characteristic is, for instance, missing in courses that form part of a secondary education provided under a national education system funded from the public purse (*Humbel*, para 18). In contrast, if the distribution by Irish student associations of information about the identity and location of abortion clinics involved in the lawful termination of pregnancies in another Member State cannot be regarded as a service, since the clinics had no involvement in the distribution of the information (Case C-159/90 *Society for the Protection of Unborn Children Ireland Ltd v Grogan and others* [1991] ECR I-4685, paras 24–27), the lawful termination of pregnancy is 'a medical activity which is normally provided for remuneration and may be carried out as part of a professional activity', and as such, is a service within the meaning of Article 57 TFEU (paras 18–21). Equally, medical treatment provided in one Member State and paid for by the patient is a service, even if the patient can apply for reimbursement of the costs of that treatment under another Member State's sickness insurance legislation (Case C-157/99 *BSM Geraets-Smits v Stichting Ziekenfonds VGZ* [2001] ECR I-5473, para 55).

Under Article 57, second paragraph, a service notably includes activities of an industrial or commercial character, and activities of craftsmen or of the professions, but also, more generally, any genuine and effective economic activities. These include sporting activities, such as in international competitions (*Deliège v Ligue Francophone de Judo*), the transmission of television signals (Case 155/73 *Sacchi* [1974] ECR 409), the broadcasting of advertisements (Case 352/85 *Bond van Adverteerders and Others v Netherlands State* [1988] ECR 2085), the grant of credit on a commercial basis (Case C-452/04 *Fidium Finanz AG v Bundesanstalt für Finanzdienstleistungsaufsicht* [2006] ECR I-9521), lottery activities (Case C-275/92 *Schindler* [1994] ECR I-1039), betting on sporting events (Case C-67/98 *Questore di Verona v Zenatti* [1999] ECR I-7289; Case C-409/06 *Winner Wetten GmbH v Bürgermeisterin der Stadt Bergheim* [2010] ECR I-8015), online gambling (Joined Cases C-447/08 and C-448/08 *Criminal proceedings against Sjöberg and Gerdin* [2010] ECR I-6921), etc.

Moreover, the freedom to provide services covers both the providers and the recipients of services (Joined Cases 286/82 and 26/83 *Luisi and Carbone v Ministero del Tesoro* [1984] ECR 377, para 16; and Case C-42/07 *Liga Portuguesa de Futebol Profissional and Bwin International Ltd v Departamento de Jogos da Santa Casa da Misericórdia de Lisboa* [2009] ECR I-7633, para 51).

The service concerned will not be covered by Articles 56 and 57 TFEU unless it has a cross-border element. This can occur in four different situations:

(a) the service provider travels to another Member State;
(b) the service recipient travels to another Member State;
(c) both service provider and recipient, based in the same State, travel to the host State where the service is provided; or
(d) the service itself is provided across the border by post, telecommunication or electronic communication (television broadcast, phone communication, fax transmission, online service).

15.3.3 The beneficiaries of the freedom of establishment and the freedom to provide services

Both physical and legal persons are granted the rights of establishment and to provide services.

15.3.3.1 Natural persons

Nationals of the EU are the primary beneficiaries of Articles 49 and 56 TFEU, which give them the right to take up and exercise an activity as self-employed persons or set up and manage a company in another Member State, and the right to provide services in another Member State. They must, however, reside in an EU Member State in order either to set up agencies, branches or subsidiaries (secondary establishment), or to provide services in another Member State.

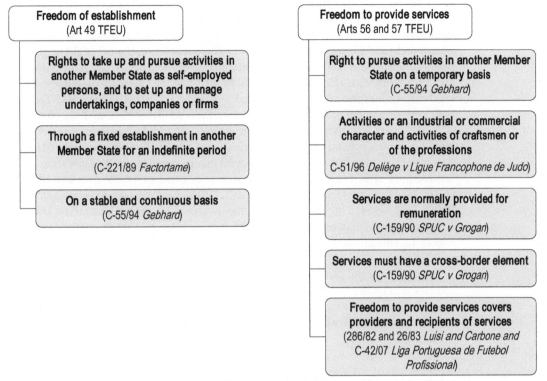

Figure 15.2 Freedom of establishment and freedom to provide services

Those rights extend to the family members of EU nationals, whether they are EU nationals or not (Article 23 of Directive 2004/38/EC; see Case 131/85 *Gül v Regierungspräsident Düsseldorf* [1986] ECR 1573).

Third-country nationals who are not family members of an EU national can rely on those provisions on the basis of:

(a) the Agreement on the European Economic Area (EEA) ([1994] OJ L1/3) or the EU–Swiss Agreement on the free movement of persons ([2002] OJ L114/6), which give EEA and Swiss citizens rights of establishment and to supply services; or

(b) association or cooperation agreements between the EU and third countries (eg, Turkey, Morocco, Algeria); or

(c) Council Directive 2003/109/EC concerning the status of third-country nationals who are long-term residents ([2004] OJ L16/44).

Although Article 56, second paragraph TFEU provides that the freedom to provide services may be extended to third-country nationals who are established within the EU and provide services, no EU secondary legislation has been adopted yet.

15.3.3.2 Legal persons

Articles 54 and 62 TFEU also extend the right of establishment and the right to provide services to companies or firms that have their registered office, central administration or principal place of business within the EU. 'Companies or firms' means companies or firms 'constituted under civil or commercial law' of a Member State, and include 'cooperative societies, and other legal persons governed by public or private law, save for those which are non-profit-making' (Article 54, second paragraph TFEU).

In order to benefit from those freedoms, companies must be incorporated under the legislation of a Member State and have their registered office, real head office, central management and control or principal place of business within the EU (right to primary establishment). However, since companies are, in the absence of EU harmonisation, 'creatures of national law', and 'exist only by virtue of the varying national legislation which determines their incorporation and functioning' (Case 81/87 *R v HM Treasury and Commissioners of Inland Revenue, ex parte Daily Mail and General Trust plc* [1988] ECR 5483, para 19), they cannot rely on Articles 49 and 54 TFEU to 'transfer their central management and control and their central administration to another Member State while retaining their status as companies incorporated under the legislation of the first Member State' (para 24) if the company law of that first State does not allow it. This ruling was later confirmed in Case C-210/06 *Cartesio Oktató és Szolgáltató bt* [2008] ECR I-9641, in which a company incorporated under Hungarian law was prohibited under that law from transferring its seat to Italy while continuing to be subject to Hungarian law. Hungarian law did not breach the company's right of establishment.

Having a principal place of business in a Member State, companies can then set up agencies, branches and subsidiaries in another Member State (secondary establishment). Such a right cannot be restricted by a Member State on the ground that the branch or subsidiary carries out its entire business where it has been created.

In Case C-212/97 *Centros Ltd v Erhvervs- og Selskabsstyrelsen* [1999] ECR I-1459, Mrs Bryde, a Danish national, set up Centros Ltd in the UK, and then sought to set up its subsidiary in Denmark. The Danish authorities refused to register the branch on the ground that Centros did not trade in the UK and Mrs Bryde was in fact seeking to establish in Denmark a principal establishment by circumventing the Danish rules, notably those regarding the paying up of a higher minimum capital share. Rejecting the argument of the Danish Government, which was that this situation was purely internal to Denmark, the Court ruled not only that it fell within the scope of former Article 52 TEC (now Article 49 TFEU), but also that 'it is immaterial that the company was formed in the first Member State only for the purpose of establishing itself in the second, where its main, or indeed entire, business is to be conducted' (para 17).

While a Member State is entitled to prevent some of its nationals from taking advantage of EU law provisions in an attempt to circumvent improperly their national legislation, it cannot prevent them from forming a company under the rules of company law of a Member State which seem the least restrictive, and then setting up branches in other Member States. Such behaviour 'cannot, in itself, constitute an abuse of the right of establishment', since '[t]he right to form a company in accordance with the law of a Member State and to set up branches in other Member States is inherent in the exercise, in a single market, of the freedom of establishment guaranteed by the Treaty' (para 27).

Company transformation operations, such as cross-border mergers (Case C-411/03 *SEVIC Systems AG* [2005] ECR I-10805: refusal of registration in the national commercial register of the merger of a company by dissolution without liquidation and transfer of its assets to another company) and cross-border conversions (Case C-378/10 *VALE Építési kft*, 12 July 2012, ECLI:EU:C:2012:440: cross-border transfer of a company by removal from the commercial register under the law of one Member State and its reincorporation as a company under the law of another Member State), also

> constitute particular methods of exercise of the freedom of establishment, important for the proper functioning of the internal market, and are therefore amongst those economic activities in respect of which Member States are required to comply with the freedom of establishment laid down by Article [49 TFEU]. (*SEVIC*, para 19)

15.3.4 The Services Directive

In its Report on *The State of the Internal Market for Services* (COM(2002) 441 final), the Commission concluded that 10 years after the completion of the internal market, 'there [was still] a huge gap between the vision of an integrated EU economy and the reality as experienced by European citizens and European service providers'. On 13 January 2004, the Commission published its proposal on services in the internal market (COM(2004) 2 final), later called the Bolkenstein Directive after the Commissioner who initiated it. Its objective was

> to provide a legal framework that will eliminate the obstacles to the freedom of establishment for service providers and the free movement of services between the Member States, giving both the providers and recipients of services the legal certainty they need in order to exercise these two fundamental freedoms enshrined in the Treaty. (at 3)

It was intended to cover a wide range of economic service activities and to apply only to service providers established in a Member State. The proposed Directive was based on the quintessential principle of the 'country of origin', whereby 'a service provider is subject only to the law of the country in which he is established and Member States may not restrict services from a provider established in another Member State' (at 3).

Although this principle was simply another form of the principle of mutual recognition (eg, as applied to the free movement of goods – see 13.2.3.2), allowing service providers to export their business and commercial models, it was rapidly perceived as carrying the risk of social dumping and lowering standards of services. Owing to a lack of consensus about it and the controversy and hostility that it generated, the 'country of origin' rule was simply abandoned in the text adopted by the European Parliament in the first reading. The scope of application of the proposed Directive was also narrowed down.

Despite those setbacks, Directive 2006/123/EC of the European Parliament and of the Council of 12 December 2006 on services in the internal market ([2006] OJ L376/36) constitutes an important step towards further liberalisation of services.

15.3.4.1 Scope of application of the Directive

Directive 2006/123/EC ('the Services Directive') is a horizontal framework directive, the purpose of which is to establish 'general provisions facilitating the exercise of the freedom of establishment for service providers and the free movement of services, while maintaining a high quality of services' (Article 1(1)).

However, Article 2(2) excludes a number of services from its scope of application by reason of their nature, such as:

- non-economic services of general interest
- services of temporary work agencies

- healthcare services
- social services relating to social housing, childcare, and support of families and persons in need
- gambling activities
- activities connected with the exercise of official authority as set out in Article 51 TFEU (see **15.6.2**).

Other services already covered by other directives are also excluded. This is the case as regards:

- financial services (eg, banking, credit, insurance, etc) listed in Annex I to Directive 2006/48/EC on the taking up and pursuit of the business of credit institutions ([2008] OJ L177/1)
- electronic communications services and networks covered by four 2002 Directives
- services in the field of transport, including port services
- audiovisual services.

Further '[a]dditional derogations from the freedom to provide services' are also provided for under Article 17 of the Services Directive. This provision excludes the application of the Directive to services of general economic interest, and to sectors and activities already covered by EU legislation, such as services in the postal, electricity and gas sectors, water distribution and supply services, and waste water services and treatment of waste. Amongst others, matters covered by Directive 96/71/EC on the Posting of Workers ([1997] OJ L18/1), Directive 95/46/EC on the protection of personal data and on the free movement of such data ([1995] OJ L281/314), and Council Directive 77/249/EEC on lawyers' freedom to provide services ([1977] OJ L78/17), as well as a variety of disparate areas (eg, judicial recovery of debts, acts requiring by law the involvement of a notary, registration of vehicles leased in another Member State, etc) are also excluded.

Within its scope of application, the Services Directive reinforces the principles of freedom of establishment (Chapter III) and of free provision of services (Chapter IV).

15.3.4.2 Freedom of establishment for providers

The Services Directive simply consolidates the case law of the Court on the conditions for the lawfulness of national schemes of authorisation and of national requirements for access to, and exercise of, a service activity.

Under Article 9, access to a service activity and its exercise cannot be subject to an authorisation scheme unless:

(a) it does not discriminate against the service provider;
(b) it is justified by an overriding reason relating to the public interest; and
(c) the objective pursued cannot be attained by means of a less restrictive measure (see **15.4.4**).

Furthermore, an authorisation scheme must fulfil clear criteria listed under Article 10 and be:

(a) non-discriminatory;
(b) justified by an overriding reason relating to the public interest;
(c) proportionate to that public interest objective;
(d) clear and unambiguous;
(e) objective;
(f) made public in advance; and

(g) transparent and accessible.

With regard to national requirements imposed on service activities, the Services Directive distinguishes between 'prohibited requirements' and those 'subject to evaluation'. Article 14 prohibits notably all discriminatory requirements based directly or indirectly on nationality or the location of the registered office of companies, residence requirements or conditions of reciprocity with the Member State in which the service provider is already established, etc. Furthermore, Article 15 provides that Member States must assess whether, under their legal systems, certain requirements (such as, amongst others, quantitative or territorial restrictions, requirements relating to the shareholding of a company, the obligation to have one establishment only in the territory of the same State or to have a minimum number of employees, etc) comply with the principles of non-discrimination, necessity and proportionality (see **15.4.4**).

As recital 43 of the Directive states:

> One of the fundamental difficulties faced, in particular by [small and medium-sized enterprises], in accessing service activities and exercising them is the complexity, length and legal uncertainty of administrative procedures.

In order to remove such obstacles, the Services Directive lays down the principle of administrative simplification (Article 5), and requires Member States to set up points of single contact (one-stop shops), where service providers can obtain all relevant information (Article 7) and complete, at the contact point itself or 'at a distance or by electronic means' (Article 8), all necessary procedures and formalities relating to their activities (Article 6).

15.3.4.3 Free provision of services

Subject to the derogations of Article 17 (see above **15.3.4.1**), Article 16 of the Services Directive lays down the 'freedom to provide services' clause, which guarantees 'the right of providers to provide services in a Member State other than that in which they are established' and under which the host Member State 'shall ensure free access to and free exercise of a service activity within its territory'. However, Article 16(1), third paragraph allows Member State to restrict the activities of service providers by imposing proportionate, non-discriminatory national requirements, 'justified for reasons of public policy, public security, public health or the protection of the environment'. It is to be noted, though, that, in contrast with restrictions on the freedom of establishment, restrictions on the freedom to provide services cannot be justified by 'overriding reasons relating to the public interest', as recognised and developed in the settled case law of the Court of Justice (see **15.4.4**) and defined in point 8 of Article 4 of the Directive.

Furthermore, Article 18 allows Member States to take, in exceptional circumstances, measures relating to the safety of services against a provider established in another Member State.

The Services Directive also enhances the rights of consumers and businesses that are service recipients. Beside requiring the removal of all restrictions on the use of services supplied by providers from another Member State, and prohibiting all discrimination based on nationality or place of residence (Article 20), the Directive aims to guarantee full protection of service recipients through detailed information on providers and services (Article 22), and by the requirement for professional liability insurance or equivalent guarantees imposed on service providers presenting a direct risk to the health and safety of recipients (Article 23). The Services Directive also requires

Member States to ensure that recipients can obtain, in their country of residence, information relating to consumer protection, on means of redress in the case of any dispute between a service provider and the recipient, and contact details of consumer organisations and centres of the European Consumer Centres Network in order to get practical assistance (Article 21).

15.3.4.4 Cooperation between Member States

Article 28 of the Services Directive requires Member States to cooperate with each other and provide mutual assistance, with a view to ensuring effective supervision of service providers and of the services provided. Under that provision, the competent authorities of different Member States may exchange information or carry out checks, inspections and investigations upon duly motivated requests. Furthermore, under Article 34, Member States have an obligation to alert other Member States and the Commission to 'acts or circumstances relating to a service activity that could cause serious damage to the health or safety of persons or to the environment', either in their own territory or that of other Member States. To facilitate this exchange of information, the Commission, in cooperation with Member States, set up an electronic system for the exchange of information between Member States (Article 34(1)).

15.4 The principle of non-discrimination

A cardinal rule of EU law, the principle of non-discrimination is naturally enshrined in the three Treaty provisions that guarantee the free movement of economically active migrants. Article 45(2) TFEU unambiguously provides that

> freedom of movement shall entail the abolition of any discrimination based on nationality between workers of the Member States ...

Under Article 49, second paragraph TFEU, a self-employed person has a right of establishment 'under the conditions laid down for its own nationals by the law of the country where such establishment is effected'. Similarly, a person providing a service in another Member State must be able to do so 'under the same conditions as are imposed by that State on its own nationals' (Article 57, third paragraph TFEU).

Therefore, the principle of non-discrimination implies that EU migrants are treated in the same way as the nationals of the host country. Equal treatment with nationals is not only further confirmed in secondary legislation applicable to workers and the self-employed, but also firmly established as a fundamental legal provision of the EU by the Court of Justice (see Case 2/74 *Reyners v Belgium* [1974] ECR 631, para 24).

15.4.1 Prohibition of direct and indirect discrimination

In order to give full effect to the principle of non-discrimination, the Court held that what are now Article 45 TFEU (Case 36/74 *Walrave and Koch v Association Union Cycliste Internationale and others* [1974] ECR 1405, para 17; Case C-415/93 *Union royale belge des sociétés de football association ASBL v Bosman, Royal club liégeois SA v Bosman and others and Union des associations européennes de football (UEFA) v Bosman* [1995] ECR I-4921, para 93), Article 49 TFEU (Case 2/74 *Reyners v Belgium* [1974] ECR 631, para 32) and Article 56 TFEU (Case 33/74 *Van Binsbergen v Bestuur van den Bedrijfsvereniging voor de Metaalnijverheid* [1974] ECR 1299, para 27) are capable of direct effect (see 6.3), and may therefore be relied upon in national courts. The direct effect of these provisions reinforces the obligation imposed on Member States to abolish any discrimination based on nationality and any other restrictions on the free movement of workers or self-employed persons.

As the Court unequivocally put it in Case 152/73 *Sotgiu v Deutsche Bundespost* [1974] ECR 153, the principle of non-discrimination 'forbid[s] not only overt discrimination by reason of nationality but also all covert forms of discrimination which, by the application of other criteria of differentiation, lead in fact to the same result' (para 11). For instance, restricting appointment and establishment in permanent employment to a State's own nationals would constitute such overt discrimination, as in Case 307/84 *Commission of the European Communities v French Republic* [1986] ECR 1725, regarding a nationality requirement for the appointment of nurses in permanent employment in public hospitals. So also would a nationality requirement for access to social housing and reduced-rate mortgage loans (Case 63/86 *Commission v Italy* [1988] ECR 29).

Although more difficult to identify, since they are based on factors other than nationality (such as place of residence, language requirements, etc) and are indistinctly applicable, indirectly discriminatory national measures are also prohibited. In Case C-237/94 *O'Flynn v Adjudication Officer* [1996] ECR I-2617, the Court embraced a broad interpretation of indirect discrimination and ruled that

> ... conditions imposed by national law must be regarded as indirectly discriminatory where, although applicable irrespective of nationality, they affect essentially migrant workers ... or the great majority of those affected are migrant workers ... where they are indistinctly applicable but can more easily be satisfied by national workers than by migrant workers ... or where there is a risk that they may operate to the particular detriment of migrant workers ... (para 18)
>
> ...
>
> ... [U]nless objectively justified and proportionate to its aim, a provision of national law must be regarded as indirectly discriminatory if it is intrinsically able to affect migrant workers more than national workers and if there is a consequent risk that it will place the former at a particular disadvantage.
>
> It is not necessary in this respect to find that the provision in question does in practice affect a substantially higher proportion of migrant workers. It is sufficient that it is liable to have such an effect ... (paras 20–21)

As a result, the following national measures are regarded as indirectly discriminatory:

- a residence requirement (*Sotgiu*, above: separation allowance for a worker employed away from home being lower on the ground that his residence was in another Member State; and Case C-111/91 *Commission v Luxembourg* [1993] ECR I-817: childbirth and maternity allowances made conditional on residence requirements)
- a territorial restriction (Case 305/87 *Commission v Greece* [1989] ECR 1461: prohibition on foreign, natural or legal persons acquiring ownership of immovable property situated in the border regions of the country)
- the refusal by a public body in a university open competition to take account of a candidate's previous employment in the public service in another Member State, when the competition rules did not specify that such experience had to be connected with the duties of the post (Case C-419/92 *Scholz v Opera Universitaria di Cagliari and Cinzia Porcedda* [1994] ECR I-505)

- the requirement for authorisation of the use of academic titles awarded in another Member State (Case C-19/92 *Kraus v Land Baden-Württemberg* [1993] ECR I-1663).

15.4.2 Non-discrimination and access to an economic activity

Although the Treaties draw a distinction between employment and self-employment, access to both faces similar restrictions as shown in the case law of the Court.

The principle of equal treatment with nationals is a key rule with regard to access to employment. Provided for in Article 45(2) TFEU, it is further enshrined in Regulation 492/2011/EU on freedom of movement for workers within the Union ([2011] OJ L141/1), which replaced Regulation 1612/68/EEC ([1968] OJ L257/2). Under Article 1(2) of the Regulation, any EU national has 'the right to take up available employment in the territory of another Member State with the same priority as nationals of that State'. Member States must also abolish all discrimination relating to recruitment procedures (Article 3(2)), to quotas on foreign nationals (Article 4), assistance afforded by employment offices (Article 5), or to medical, vocational or other criteria for recruitment (Article 6). The only exception to this principle is that 'relating to linguistic knowledge required by reason of the nature of the post to be filled' (Article 3(1), second subparagraph). However, the Court has interpreted it restrictively, as it does not accept this linguistic requirement where it is not necessary and proportionate to the objective pursued (see Case C-379/87 *Groener v Minister for Education and the City of Dublin Vocational Educational Committee* [1989] ECR 3967: justified requirement for permanent full-time post of lecturer in public vocational educational institution of linguistic knowledge, imposed as part of a policy for the promotion of the national language).

Article 49, second paragraph TFEU also guarantees the right to equal treatment with nationals to anyone wishing to take up an activity as a self-employed person (eg, tradesperson, craftsperson, farmer, regulated profession, etc), or to set up and manage a civil or commercial profit-making company. Thus prohibited are all forms of discrimination such as a single practice requirement, prohibiting migrant doctors, dentists and veterinary surgeons from maintaining a separate practice in another Member State (Case C-351/90 *Commission v Luxembourg* [1992] ECR I-3945), not granting the same benefits of corporation tax and shareholders' tax credits to branches in a Member State of companies registered in another State (Case 270/83 *Commission v France* [1986] ECR 273) or making reciprocity from the State of origin of the EU migrant a condition of access to certain professions (Case 168/85 *Commission v Italy* [1986] ECR 2945).

Furthermore, Article 23 of Directive 2004/38/EC grants the same rights – to take up employment or self-employment and to equal treatment – to the spouse, partner, children under the age of 21 or dependent children and dependent direct relatives of a migrant worker or self-employed person.

15.4.3 Non-discrimination and pursuit of an economic activity

Equal treatment with nationals naturally extends to the pursuit of the activity in employment or self-employment.

Article 45(2) TFEU prohibits any discrimination 'with regard to employment, remuneration and other conditions of work and employment', and Articles 7 to 9 of Regulation 492/2011 further specify those rights. Equal treatment covers:

- all conditions of employment and work, notably remuneration, dismissal, and reinstatement or re-employment (Article 7(1))
- tax advantages (Article 7(2))
- social advantages (Article 7(2)) (see below **20.2**)
- access to training in vocational schools and retraining centres (Article 7(3))
- trade-union rights (Article 8)
- rights and benefits accorded to national workers in matters of housing, including ownership of housing (Article 9).

With regard to the pursuit of an activity in self-employment, the principle of non-discrimination under Articles 49 and 56 TFEU implies that, in the absence of EU legislation, Member States have discretion to regulate, 'without discriminating between [their] own nationals and those of the other Member States', the exercise of such activity (see Case C-61/89 *Criminal proceedings against Bouchoucha* [1990] ECR I-3551, para 12: restriction of the professional practice of osteopathy exclusively to persons holding the qualification of doctor of medicine), and notably to subject it to professional rules of conduct (see Case 107/83 *Ordre des avocats au Barreau de Paris v Klopp* [1984] ECR 2971, para 19: access to and exercise of the legal profession; and Case C-106/91 *Ramrath v Ministre de la Justice and l'Institut des réviseurs d'entreprises* [1992] ECR I-3351, para 37: requirement of a permanent infrastructure for carrying out the work as an auditor within a Member State by a person who was already authorised to practise as an auditor in another Member State, in order to ensure compliance with the rules of professional practice).

15.4.4 Prohibition of non-discriminatory restrictions

Certain non-discriminatory national measures may still restrict access to, and the pursuit of, an economic activity. In *Kraus*, the Court stressed that

> Articles [45] and [49] preclude any national measure governing the conditions under which an academic title obtained in another Member State may be used, where that measure, even though it is applicable without discrimination on grounds of nationality, is liable to hamper or to render less attractive the exercise by [EU] nationals, including those of the Member State which enacted the measure, of fundamental freedoms guaranteed by the Treaty. (para 32)

Rules laid down by sporting associations, and preventing a professional footballer, on the expiry of his contract with a club, from being employed by a club of another Member State unless the latter club has paid to the former club a transfer, training or development fee, fall into this category of national rules (*Bosman*). The same is true, in principle, of legislation of a Member State that reserves the provision of services relating to the monitoring of patents for economic agents possessing certain professional qualifications, thus preventing a company established abroad from providing services to holders of patents in that Member State and preventing the latter from freely choosing how their patents should be monitored (Case C-76/90 *Säger v Dennemeyer & Co Ltd* [1991] ECR I-4221); or of a national measure liable to restrict the right of lawyers to set up chambers on a permanent basis in another Member State (*Gebhard*); or even a national measure that may prevent or deter a national from one State taking up employment in another Member State, such as the imposition of greater social security contributions than those that would have been paid had he not moved (Case C-18/95 *FC Terhoeve v Inspecteur van de Belastingdienst Particulieren/ Ondernemingen buitenland* [1999] ECR I-345).

However, in an approach similar to that regarding free movement of goods (see **Chapter 13**), the Court accepts that measures restricting the free exercise of economic activities may be justified on the ground of 'imperative requirements in the general interest'. This approach has been applied extensively to measures restricting freedom of establishment and freedom to provide services. The Court requires that 'national measures liable to hinder or make less attractive the exercise of fundamental freedoms guaranteed by the Treaty ... fulfil four conditions' (*Säger*, para 15; *Gebhard*, para 38), namely, the measures:

(a) must be applied in a non-discriminatory manner;

(b) must be justified by imperative requirements in the general interest;

(c) must be suitable for securing the attainment of the objective which they pursue; and

(d) must not go beyond what is necessary in order to attain it.

Naturally, the Court is very cautious not to give any specific definition of those 'imperative requirements', and it will simply provide national authorities with some indication of how to assess their national measures against those requirements.

As in the case of *Cassis de Dijon* 'mandatory requirements', which may justify trade restrictions (see **14.3.1**), 'imperative requirements' cannot be relied upon to protect economic interests such as, for instance, 'maintaining industrial peace in [a] sensitive area of the supply of tourist services' (see Case C-398/95 *Syndesmos ton en Elladi Touristikon kai Taxidiotikon Grafeion v Ypourgos Ergasias* [1997] ECR I-3091, para 23: national requirement for a licence constituting a barrier to the freedom of tourist guides from other Member States to provide services in Greece as self-employed guides). Nevertheless, national authorities have some discretion in determining whether a restriction on the exercise of fundamental freedoms may be justified by, amongst other things:

- professional rules 'justified by the general good, such as rules relating to organization, qualifications, professional ethics, supervision and liability' (see Case C-71/76 *Thieffry v Conseil de l'Ordre des Avocats à la Cour de Paris* [1977] ECR 765, para 12; and *Gebhard,* para 35)
- the effectiveness of fiscal supervision (see Case C-250/95 *Futura Participations SA and Singer v Administration des contributions* [1997] ECR I-2471, para 31: measures enabling authorities to ascertain clearly and precisely the amount of income taxable in a State and losses which can be carried forward there)
- social protection for victims of road traffic accidents (see Case C-518/06 *Commission v Italy* [2009] ECR I-3491, paras 81–82: Italian legal obligation to provide coverage for third-party motor vehicle liability insurance, imposed on insurance undertakings, including those based in another Member State and pursuing their business in Italy)
- the protection of public health (see Case C-531/06 *Commission v Italy* [2009] ECR I-4103, paras 51–52: Italian law restricting the right to operate a pharmacy to pharmacists alone)
- the protection of the consumers (see Case C-390/99 *Canal Satélite Digital SL v Adminstración General del Estado and Distribuidora de Televisión Digital SA (DTS)* [2002] ECR I-607, para 34: Spanish legislation requiring operators of conditional-access television services to register in a national register)
- consumer protection, the prevention of both fraud and incitement to squander on gaming, and the general need to preserve public order (see Joined Cases C-338/04,

C-359/04 and C-360/04 *Criminal proceedings against Placanica, Palazzese and Sorricchio* [2007] ECR I-1891, para 46: Italian law imposing certain conditions on operators of activities in the betting and gaming sector, such as, notably, the obligation to obtain a licence and police authorisation), or

- the protection of patients or clients (see Case C-351/90 *Commission v Luxembourg* [1992] ECR I-3945, para 13: Luxembourg law prohibiting migrant doctors, dentists and veterinary surgeons from maintaining a separate practice in another Member State).

However, even if a non-discriminatory restrictive measure appears to be justified by an imperative requirement in the general interest, it will ultimately be fully justified only if the Court is absolutely satisfied that it meets the last two conditions of suitability and proportionality (see *Säger* and *Gebhard*).

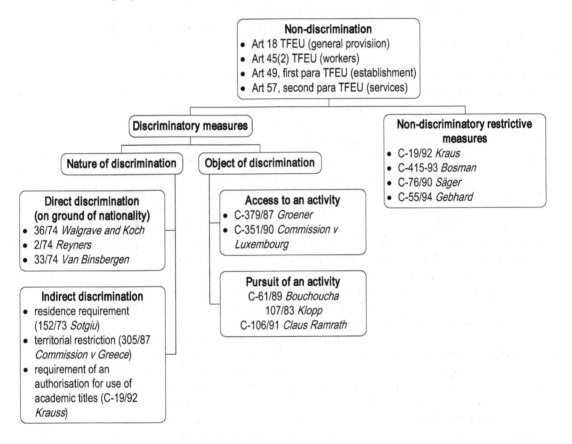

Figure 15.3   The principle of non-discrimination

15.5   Mutual recognition of professional qualifications

If the Court recognises that Member States may restrict access to, and the exercise of, certain economic activities to 'holders of a diploma, certificate or other evidence of formal qualifications' (*Gebhard*, para 35), EU migrants may face an 'invisible barrier', preventing them from taking up such activity. For that reason, Article 53(1) TFEU (and, by reference, Article 62 TFEU) provides:

> In order to make it easier for persons to take up and pursue activities as self-employed persons, the Council shall, acting in accordance with the ordinary legislative procedure, issue directives for the mutual recognition of diplomas, certificates and other evidence of formal qualifications ...

Directives on the mutual recognition of diplomas and professional qualifications adopted under these provisions apply naturally to professional activities pursued by employed and self-employed persons, since the same qualifications are required for their practise as is the case, for instance, of the professional activities of employed and self-employed medical doctors, pharmacists or lawyers.

15.5.1 The original legislative movement

The original approach to mutual recognition of diplomas and professional qualifications consisted of the harmonisation of rules in respect of specific professions or economic sectors. Following this approach, 'sectorial' directives were adopted in three specific sectors: professions in the health sector, the profession of architect, and the legal profession.

15.5.1.1 The health professions

Professional qualifications in the health sector were the first to be covered by mutual recognition directives. Each profession was covered by two directives: one on the actual recognition of qualifications, and the other on the minimum harmonisation of training leading to the qualifications. The directives applicable to medical doctors (Directives 75/362/EEC and 75/363/EEC) were the first to be adopted, and served as a template for other professional qualifications and training, such as:

- Directives 77/452/EEC and 77/453/EEC on qualifications and the training of nurses responsible for general care
- Directives 78/686/EEC and 78/687/EEC on qualifications and the activities of dental practitioners
- Directives 78/1026/EEC and 78/1027/EEC on qualifications and the training of veterinary surgeons
- Directives 80/154/EEC and 80/155/EEC on qualifications and the activities of midwives
- Directives 85/432/EEC and 85/433/EEC on activities and the qualifications of pharmacists.

15.5.1.2 Architects

Mutual recognition of qualifications in architecture was originally covered by Directive 85/384/EEC ([1985] OJ L223/15). Unlike the directives listed in 15.5.1.1 above, it did not harmonise the minimum training requirements, but rather established mutual recognition of diplomas and qualifications acquired at the end of a period of education or training of four to six years (Article 4) and ensuring the acquisition of specific skills (Article 3).

15.5.1.3 The legal profession

For obvious reasons, the free movement of lawyers proved to be the most complex area to legislate upon. It is therefore not too surprising that the two directives that apply to the legal profession were adopted 21 years apart.

Directive 77/249/EEC to facilitate the effective exercise by lawyers of freedom to provide services ([1977] OJ L78/17) applies only to the provision of services by lawyers. It does not deal with the mutual recognition of diplomas, but rather with the professional title used by lawyers in the Member State in which they are established.

Under this Directive, a lawyer may represent a client in legal proceedings or before public authorities in another Member State, 'under the conditions laid down for lawyers established in that State, with the exception of any conditions requiring residence, or registration with a professional organisation, in that State' (Article 4(1)). However, the lawyer may be required to be introduced to the presiding judge and to the President of the relevant Bar in the host Member State, or to work in conjunction with a lawyer who practises before the judicial authority in that State (Article 5). In any case, the lawyer must observe the rules of professional conduct of the host Member State (Article 4(2)).

Long-awaited Directive 98/5/EC to facilitate practice of the profession of lawyer on a permanent basis in a Member State other than that in which the qualification was obtained ([1998] OJ L77/36) enables a lawyer who has registered with the competent authority (Article 3), to practise in any other Member State, on a permanent basis and under his home-country professional title (Article 2), activities in the field of the law of his home Member State, on EU law, on international law and on the law of the host Member State (Article 5). However, the host Member State may exclude certain activities relating to the preparation of 'deeds for obtaining title to administer estates of deceased persons and for creating or transferring interests in land' and which are reserved for other professions (such as notaries); it may also require a lawyer representing or defending a client to work in conjunction with a national lawyer. Under Article 6, the migrant lawyer will be subject to the rules of professional conduct in both his home and host Member States.

Migrant lawyers wishing to gain admission to the profession of lawyer in the host Member State and to practise under its title, may either take an aptitude test demonstrating their knowledge of the host State law, or simply 'effectively and regularly [pursue] for a period of at least three years an activity in the host Member State in the law of that State including [EU] law' (Article 10).

15.5.2 The new approach to harmonisation

Progress under the original approach proved to be too slow, and sectorial directives, seen as inadequate to meet the new challenges of the completion of the internal market in the 1990s, gave way to a new general system for the mutual recognition of diplomas.

15.5.2.1 The first wave of legislation

This new approach was first introduced by Directive 89/48/EEC on a general system for the recognition of higher-education diplomas awarded on completion of professional education and training of at least three years' duration ([1989] OJ L19/16). The Directive covered 'regulated professions' other than those already covered by a sectorial directive, that is professions whose exercise in a Member State is subject by law to the possession of a diploma, certificate or other evidence of formal qualifications awarded on completion of a course lasting at least three years (eg, chartered accountants, engineers, lawyers, etc).

The system of mutual recognition introduced by the 1989 Directive was later extended, by Directive 92/51/EEC on a second general system for the recognition of professional education and training to supplement Directive 89/48/EEC ([1992] OJ L209/25), to those professions for which a lower post-secondary education level of training was required.

This new system no longer relies on an automatic mutual recognition of diplomas, as is the case under sectorial directives, but on the presumption that the professional education and professional training obtained in different Member States are comparable. Nationals of the EU cannot be denied, in the host Member State, access to, and the exercise of, a regulated profession subject to the possession of a diploma, on the grounds of inadequate qualifications, if they possess an equivalent diploma required for that profession in another Member State (Article 3). However, they could be required to provide evidence of professional experience should their education or training period be shorter than that required in the host State (Article 4(1)(a)). They could also be required to complete an adaptation period not exceeding three years, or take an aptitude test where, notably, the matters covered by their education and training differ substantially from those covered by the diploma required in the host Member State. In such circumstances, an EU national then has the right to choose between an adaptation period and an aptitude test, except 'for professions whose practice requires precise knowledge of national law and in respect of which the provision of advice and/or assistance concerning national law is an essential and constant aspect of the professional activity' (Article 4(1)(b)), in which case the host Member State may stipulate either an adaptation period or an aptitude test. For instance, an English solicitor wishing to practise law in France would have to take the French aptitude test.

Directive 1999/42/EC ([1999] OJ L201/77) established a third general system for the recognition of qualifications in respect of the professional activities covered by the directives on liberalisation, notably in regard to commerce, industry and craft trades.

Although this new approach represented clear progress in the mutual recognition of qualifications, the Commission observed in its 2001 Communication *New European Labour Markets, Open to All, with Access for All* (COM(2001) 116 Final) that '[t]he gaps in the recognition of professional, academic and vocational qualifications from another Member State [still form] a particular obstacle to people working in Europe' (at 9). Notably, it recognised that

> [m]eans need to be found to extend the scope for more automatic recognition within the existing systems. At the same time, the rules of the General System and directives on individual professions can be consolidated and a more flexible overall framework provided for EU enlargement. (at 9–10)
>
> General rules guaranteeing professional recognition based on a minimum coordination of education and training are also no longer sustainable in their present form. (at 10)

Further to these findings, the European Council of Stockholm, on 23 and 24 March 2001, requested the Commission to draft proposals 'for a uniform, transparent and flexible regime of recognition of qualifications' (recital 2 of Directive 2005/36/EC). This led to the adoption of Directive 2005/36/EC.

15.5.2.2   Consolidation under Directive 2005/36

The stated objective of Directive 2005/36 on the recognition of professional qualifications ([2005] OJ L255/22) is 'the rationalisation, simplification and improvement of the rules for the recognition of professional qualifications' (recital 40). Indeed, it repealed and replaced the sectorial directives and the three directives that set up the general system for recognition. Applying to

> ... all nationals of a Member State wishing to pursue a regulated profession in a Member State, including those belonging to the liberal professions, other than that in which they obtained their professional qualifications, on either a self-employed or employed basis ... (Article 2(1))

the Directive revamps and consolidates the three pre-existing models of mutual recognition. It provides for the following:

(a) A general system for the recognition of evidence of training (Articles 10–15), which applies to all professions not covered by the other two systems of recognition under (b) and (c) below. Under this system, professional qualifications are grouped in five levels (Article 11, first paragraph (a)–(e)):

(i) an attestation of competence based on a general training course, or based on general primary or secondary education;

(ii) a certificate attesting to a successful completion of a secondary course, either general or technical or professional in character;

(iii) a diploma certifying successful completion of training at post-secondary level of a duration of at least one year and not exceeding three years;

(iv) a diploma certifying successful completion of training at post-secondary level of at least three and not more than four years' duration, or the equivalent on a part-time basis, at a university or higher education establishment, or at another establishment providing the same level of training;

(v) a diploma certifying the completion of a post-secondary course of at least four years' duration, or the equivalent on a part-time basis, at a university or higher education establishment, or at any other establishment of equivalent level.

The principle of mutual recognition applies if the level of qualification of the EU migrant is 'at least equivalent to the level immediately prior to that which is required in the host Member State'. Mutual recognition operates whether the profession is regulated in the host State and the EU migrant's home State (Article 13(1)), or in the host State alone. In the latter case, access to the profession will be given to an EU migrant who has pursued that profession 'on a full-time basis for two years during the previous 10 years in another Member State which does not regulate that profession', and who possesses attestations of competence or has evidence of formal qualifications (Article 13(2)). However, Article 14 provides for 'compensatory measures', in the form of an aptitude test or an adaptation period of up to three years, from which EU migrants may be required to choose, should the training they have received be shorter or substantially different from that required in the host State, or should the regulated profession in the host State comprise regulated professional activities that are not part of the equivalent profession in the EU migrants' home State (para (1)(a)–(c)).

(b) Recognition of professional experience (Articles 16–20), which applies in the same way as it did under Directive 1999/42 (see above **15.5.2.1**).

(c) Automatic recognition on the basis of coordination of minimum training conditions (Articles 21–52), which applies to all the health professions and the profession of architect previously covered by the sectorial directives (see 15.5.1.1 and 15.5.1.2). The legal profession remains regulated by the 1977 and 1998 Directives, and the 2005 Directive covers the recognition of qualifications for lawyers only for the purpose of immediate practice under the professional title of the host Member State (recital 42).

The 2005 Directive gives professionals moving on a temporary and occasional basis more flexibility to practise in any EU Member State. Under its Article 5, they may work or provide services in another Member State on that basis without any prior check of their qualifications – unless their professional activities have public health or safety implications – and without applying for recognition in the host State. However, on their first move from one State to another, they could be required to provide information on their establishment, insurance and professional competence in other Member States.

15.5.2.3 Modernisation of Directive 2005/36

Recognition of professional qualifications has become an essential instrument for a more effective exercise of the fundamental freedoms within the internal market. Yet, despite the consolidation of 15 directives into a single instrument by the 2005 Directive, mobility of qualified professionals has remained low in the EU. Furthermore, Member States are facing shortages of skilled workers, which, as the Commission pointed out, 'are projected to increase in particular in the health sector, in the education sector, and also in growth sectors, such as construction or business services' (Proposal of 19 December 2011 (COM(2011) 883 final, at 2).

Complex recognition procedures, the lack of readily available information on ways of seeking and obtaining recognition of qualifications, and outdated minimum training requirements for the health professions, all contribute to preventing EU migrant professionals from responding rapidly to job opportunities in other Member States. In order to adapt the 2005 Directive to the needs of an evolving EU labour market, the Commission submitted a proposal for its modernisation, rather than its replacement by a completely new directive, which resulted in the adoption of Directive 2013/55/EU amending Directive 2005/36/EC on the recognition of professional qualifications and Regulation (EU) No 1024/2012 on administrative cooperation through the Internal Market Information System ([2013] OJ L354/132).

The amending Directive does not radically change the system of recognition of professional qualifications and, whilst confirming the philosophy of mutual recognition based on trust between the Member States, it intends to turn it into a more effective tool through, notably, a greater use of the Internal Market Information System (an electronic tool for improved communication and cooperation between national authorities) and Points of Single Contact (e-government portals, allowing individuals and businesses to obtain online relevant information relating to their activities and to complete electronically all relevant administrative procedures).

The key elements of this modernisation process are as follows:

- The creation of a European professional card as an option for interested professions, in the form of an electronic certificate exchangeable between Member States' authorities via the Internal Market Information System, designed to streamline recognition of qualifications and to make it easier for professionals to exercise their activity in another Member State on a permanent or temporary basis.

- Improved access to information about recognition of qualifications and completion of recognition procedures through the Points of Single Contact created under the Services Directive (see **15.3.4**).
- The modernisation of harmonised minimum training requirements for the professions benefiting from automatic recognition (doctors, nurses, midwives, dentists, pharmacists, veterinary surgeons and architects); and the possibility for those professions of continuous professional development to be ensured by Member States.
- An alert mechanism, whereby national competent authorities must inform those in other Member States about professionals who have been barred from exercising professional activities that have implications for patient safety or which concern the education of minors, childcare and early childhood education.
- The introduction of 'common training frameworks' and 'common training tests', based on a common set of knowledge, skills and competences necessary to access and practise a profession, in order to facilitate automatic recognition.
- Greater transparency through the provision of national lists of regulated professions and activities reserved for them, and justification for their regulation.
- New rules on access to part of the activities reserved to a particular profession.
- An extension of the scope of the 2005 Directive to professionals who hold a diploma but have not yet completed the required professional training to achieve full access to the profession.
- The non-application of the Directive to notaries appointed by an official act of government.
- The reduction from two years to one year of the professional experience requirement, under Article 13(2) of the 2005 Directive, for professionals coming from Member States where the profession is not regulated.
- The removal of the former requirement, under Article 13(1)(b) and (2)(b), that the level of qualification of the EU migrant be at least equivalent to the level immediately prior to that which is required in the host Member State.
- The introduction of new rules on the checking of language knowledge necessary for the practice of a profession.

Legislation modernising and simplifying the system of recognition of professional qualifications is one of the 12 levers to boost growth in the single market and the key action for improving mobility of EU citizens in the single market, as identified by the Commission in the 2011 Single Market Act (see **11.2.3**). To have their professional qualifications and experience recognised throughout the EU would enable and should encourage European citizens to seek and take up work in other Member States more quickly, thus helping employers recruit staff with appropriate skills more easily in a labour market affected by slow growth and an ageing population. The creation of a European professional card particularly is seen as a major tool to enhance mobility for highly qualified workers and professionals, and to boost the competitiveness of the European economy.

15.6 Activities falling outside the scope of those freedoms

Traditionally, public international law recognises the right of States to reserve certain activities connected to the exercise of State authority or sovereign rights for their nationals only, thus emphasising the special relationship between a State and its own citizens. In this respect, the EC and the EU Treaties have always embraced this approach, in so far as they exclude from the scope of application of the provisions on the free movement of workers and of self-employed persons specific activities in the public service or involving the exercise of official authority under Articles 45(4) and 51 and 62 TFEU respectively. However, the Court of Justice has always interpreted those public service and official authority exceptions restrictively, thus promoting the idea that the EU national has a special status compared to that of non-EU nationals.

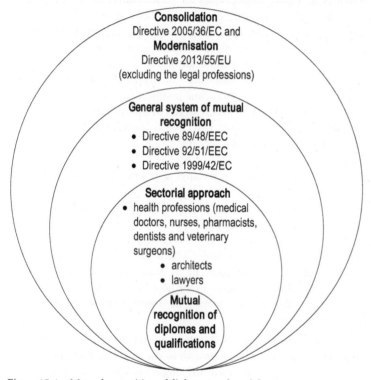

Figure 15.4   Mutual recognition of diplomas and qualifications

15.6.1 Public service

Article 45(4) TFEU unambiguously provides that

> The provisions of [Article 45] shall not apply to employment in the public service.

However, it cannot be interpreted as giving Member States full discretion as to how to interpret the term 'employment in the public service', and therefore as giving them the right to exclude from the application of Article 45 TFEU all activities in services performed by public authorities or entities. Like the concept of 'worker' (see 15.2.1.1), that of 'employment in the public service' was given an autonomous European meaning. In *Lawrie-Blum* (see 15.2.1.1), the Court ruled that 'employment in the public service' did not cover the period of preparatory service for the teaching profession, the reason being that the activities of a teacher or a trainee teacher do not involve the exercise of powers conferred by public law.

In Case 149/79 *Commission v Belgium* [1980] ECR 3881, the Commission brought an enforcement action against Belgium for making the possession of Belgian nationality – or allowing it to be made – a condition of recruitment to posts not covered by the public service exception. The posts in question were advertised by the Belgian national and local railways, the City of Brussels and the Commune of Auderghem, and covered a wide range of jobs, from head technical office supervisor, principal supervisor, works supervisor, stock controller and night watchman to electricians, garden hands, joiners, children's nurses, signalmen, drivers, office cleaners, etc. Adopting a functional rather than an institutional or organisational interpretation of the notion of 'public service', the Court held that

> [s]uch a classification depends on whether or not the posts in question are typical of the specific activities of the public service *in so far as the exercise of powers conferred by public law and responsibility for safeguarding the general interests of the State are vested in it.* (para 12, emphasis added)

The two criteria (the exercise of powers conferred by public law and safeguarding general interests) are not to be regarded as alternative but cumulative, and must be assessed on a case-by-case basis in light of the nature of the tasks and responsibilities involved.

Only those activities fitting this functional definition can be covered by the public service exception, on the ground that they 'require a special relationship of allegiance to the State on the part of persons occupying them and reciprocity of rights and duties which form the foundation of the bond of nationality' (*Lawrie-Blum*, para 27).

The direct result of this restrictive interpretation of the public service exception was to make accessible to all EU nationals jobs in the public service traditionally reserved by a Member State for its own nationals. These include notably posts in the education sector (*Lawrie-Blum*: trainee teachers; Case 33/88 *Allué and Coonan v Università degli studi di Venezia* [1989] ECR 1591: university foreign-language assistants); posts in the railways and employment for municipal authorities (Case 149/79 *Commission v Belgium* [1982] ECR 1845: drivers, loaders, electricians, gardeners); posts in the health service (Case 307/84 *Commission v France* [1986] ECR 1725: nurses); posts in the utility sector (Case C-173/94 *Commission v Belgium* [1996] ECR I-3265: officials or public employees of the public bodies responsible for the distribution of water, gas and electricity); and posts in non-military research (Case 225/85 *Commission v Italy* [1987] ECR 2625: researchers employed by a national research council), etc.

In 1988 the Commission addressed to the Member States a Communication on *Freedom of workers and access to employment in the public service of member states – Commission action in respect of the application of Article 48(4) of the EEC Treaty* ([1988] OJ C72/2), to monitor the application of the Court's case law regarding access to employment in four sectors: commercial services administered by public bodies; public healthcare services; the teaching sector; and non-military research. In this Communication, the Commission considered that the public service exception covers 'specific functions of the State and similar bodies such as the armed forces, the police and other forces of the maintenance of order, the judiciary, the tax authorities and the diplomatic corps', but not those functions in these fields that do not involve the exercise of public authority, such as administrative, technical or maintenance tasks. The latter functions or posts may not be restricted by a Member State to its own nationals (Commission Communication on *Free movement of workers – Achieving the full benefits and potential* (COM(2002) 694 Final) at 19).

Combined with some enforcement procedures (see Cases C-473/93 *Commission v Luxembourg* [1996] ECR I-3207; C-173/94 *Commission v Belgium* [1996] ECR I-3265; and C-290/94 *Commission v Greece* [1996] ECR I-3285), the 1988 Commission action encouraged Member States to adopt reforms to open up their public sectors to EU nationals (eg, The Netherlands in 1988, and France in 1991 and 2005). However, in its Staff Working Document, *Free movement of workers in the public sector* (SEC(2010) 1609 final), the Commission deplored that,

> [i]n many Member States, the functional criteria established by the case law have been transformed into organisational criteria: what is contained in the national provisions or application rules are lists of posts according to sectors, departments, categories, etc, and no further distinction is made in relation to the different posts. (at 15)

As a result, many Member States are still reserving for their own nationals all posts in specific government departments, posts at a high and middle management level in administrative authorities, or all posts in the civil service.

15.6.2 Exercise of official authority

The freedom of establishment and the freedom to provide services are also subject to a similar exception. With regard to services, Article 62 TFEU simply refers to Article 51, first paragraph TFEU, which, limiting the right to establishment, provides:

> The provisions [on the right of establishment] shall not apply, so far as any given Member State is concerned, to activities which in that State are connected, even occasionally, with the exercise of official authority.

Like the public service exception, the official authority exception has been interpreted narrowly by the Court. However, unlike the former, the latter does not concern so much access to a profession as the right to exercise certain activities within that profession.

case example

In Case 2/74 *Reyners v Belgium* [1974] ECR 631, a Dutch national, who held a Belgian legal diploma giving him the right to take up the profession of '*avocat*' in Belgium, was excluded from that profession by reason of his nationality as a result of a 1972 Royal Decree on the title and exercise of this profession.

The Belgian lawyers' professional body and the Luxembourg Government argued that the Treaty provisions on the right of establishment could not apply to the whole profession of '*avocat*', because it was 'connected organically with the functioning of the public service of the administration of justice' (para 35) and, notably, because the activities of '*avocats*' made them 'indispensable [auxiliaries] of the administration of justice, [and] form a coherent whole, the parts of which [could not] be separated' (para 37).

The Court ruled that

> [the] exception to freedom of establishment provided for by the first paragraph of Article [51] must be restricted to those of the activities referred to in Article [49] *which in themselves involve a direct and specific connexion with the exercise of official authority*. (para 55, emphasis added)

A lawyer's activities of consultation, legal assistance, or representation and defence of parties in court do not fit this description and cannot therefore be covered by this exception.

Equally, the activities of Court experts who are professional translators (Joined Cases C-372/09 and C-373/09 *Peñarroja Fa* [2011] ECR I-1785), or even those of civil law notaries (Cases C-47/08 *Commission v Belgium* [2011] ECR I-4105; Case C-50/08 *Commission v France* [2011] ECR I-4195; and C-53/08 *Commission v Austria* [2011] ECR I-4309) do not constitute activities connected with the exercise of official authority.

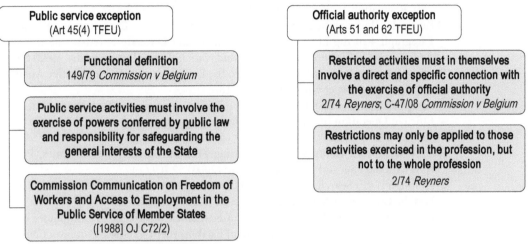

Figure 15.5   Public service and official authority exceptions

15.7   Further reading

Barnard C, 'Unravelling the Services Directive' (2008) 45 *CML Rev* 323.

Castro Olivera A, 'Workers and other Persons: Step-by-Step from Movement to Citizenship' (2002) 39 *CML Rev* 77.

Daniele L, 'Non-Discriminatory Restrictions to the Free Movement of Persons', (1997) 22 *EL Rev* 191.

De La Rosa S, 'The Directive on Cross-Border Healthcare or the Art of Codifying Complex Case Law' (2012) 49 *CML Rev* 15.

Demmke C and Linke U, 'Who's a National and Who's a European? Exercising Public Power and the Legitimacy of Art 39.4 EC in the 21st Century' (2003) 2 *Eipascope* 1.

Ellis E, 'Social Advantages: a New Lease of Life?' (2003) 40 *CML Rev* 639.

Golynker O, 'Jobseekers' Rights in the European Union' (2005) 30 *EL Rev* 111.

Handoll J, 'Article 48(4) EEC and Non-National Access to Public Employment' (1988) 13 *EL Rev* 223.

Lombay J, 'Assessing the European Market for Legal Services: Developments in the Free Movement of Lawyers in the European Union' (2010) 33 *Fordham International Law Journal* 1629.

Mancini GF, 'The Free Movement of Workers in the Case-Law of the European Court of Justice' in Curtin D and O'Keeffe D (eds), *Constitutional Adjudication in European Community and National Law* (Butterworths, 1992) 67.

Martín Fernández J-M, 'Re-defining Obstacles to the Free Movement of Workers' (1996) 21 *EL Rev* 313.

Mörsdorf O, 'The Legal Mobility of Companies within the European Union through Cross-Border Conversion' 49 (2012) *CML Rev* 629.

O'Brien C, 'Real Link, Abstract Rights and False Alarms: The Relationship between the ECJ's "Real Link" Case Law and National Solidarity' (2008) 33 *EL Rev* 643.

O'Brien C, 'Social Blind Spot and Monocular Policy Making: The ECJ's Migrant Worker Model' (2009) 46 *CML Rev* 1107.

O'Keeffe D, 'Practical Difficulties in the Application of Article 48 of the EEC Treaty' (1982) 19 *CML Rev* 35.

O'Keeffe D, 'Equal Rights for Migrants: the Concept of Social Advantages in Article 7(2), Regulation 1612/68' (1985) 5 *Yearbook of European Law* 92.

O'Keeffe D, 'Judicial Interpretation of the Public Service Exception in Article 48, Paragraph 4 of the EEC Treaty' in Curtin D and O'Keeffe D (eds), *Constitutional Adjudication in European Community and National Law* (Butterworths, 1992) 89.

Pravita M-I, 'The Access of EU Citizens to the Public Service: A Comparative Analysis' (2010) 2(2) *Review of European Studies* 18.

Rentrop T, 'The Mutual Recognition of Diplomas. A Quest for a more Effective/ Efficient Operation of the System While "Living in the Shadows"' (2002) 1 *Eipascope* 18.

Roth W-H, 'From Centros to Überseering: Free Movement of Companies, Private International Law and Community Law' (2003) 52 *ICLQ* 177.

Tryfonidou A, 'In Search of the Aims of the EC Free Movement of Persons Provisions: Has the Court of Justice Missed the Point?' (2009) 46 *CML Rev* 1591.

Vossenstein G, 'Cross-Border Transfer of Seat and Conversion of Companies under the EC Treaty Provisions on Freedom of Establishment' (2009) 6 *European Company Law* 115.

White C, 'Revisiting Free Movement of Workers' (2010) 33 *Fordham International Law Journal* 1564.

Since the original Treaty of Rome, EU migrants have had the right to move to, and reside in, another Member State with the view to taking up and pursuing an economic activity. They may enjoy this freedom to exercise an economic activity either as workers under Article 45 TFEU, or as self-employed persons, by setting up a business under Article 49 TFEU or otherwise providing services under Article 56 TFEU. The last two rights also benefit companies incorporated in a Member State of the EU.

This freedom would not be fully effective, however, were it not supported by the principle of non-discrimination on the ground of nationality, as enshrined in the above provisions. Firmly established as a cardinal rule of the EU by the Court of Justice, it guarantees that EU migrants are given the same treatment as the nationals of the host Member States with regard to access to and pursuit of an economic activity. Access to, and exercise of, certain economic activities may nevertheless be legitimately restricted by Member States to holders of a diploma or formal qualifications. For that reason, and in order to facilitate the exercise of those activities, the EU legislature undertook an ambitious and complex programme of mutual recognition of professional qualifications, which culminated in the adoption of Directive 2005/36 as amended by Directive 2013/55.

Equally, Member States are permitted to restrict to their own nationals access to, and pursuit of, certain activities that involve either the exercise of powers conferred by public law (Article 45(4) TFEU), or the exercise of official authority (Article 51, first paragraph TFEU). However, those exceptions are consistently interpreted narrowly by the Court of Justice, so as to limit their restrictive effects on this fundamental freedom.

1 Christian, a Danish national, entered France at the beginning of the year, having accepted the position in Paris of assistant editor of *La Taupe*, a radical political journal. The association that publishes *La Taupe* is a non profit-making organisation, which finances the journal through donations and subscriptions. Christian was told when he arrived in France that he would receive remuneration below the minimum wage, but that the organisation would provide him with accommodation. He was joined one month later by Minh, his Vietnamese wife, with whom he had lived in Copenhagen for six years. A former lecturer in employment law from Hanoi Law University, Minh obtained her PhD in Comparative Employment Law at Copenhagen University and hopes to find work in Paris in her field of expertise. She has applied for a post as lecturer in Asian Legal Studies at Paris-Pantheon-Sorbonne University.

Can Christian be regarded as a worker and, if so, what are his rights under EU law and those of his wife?

2 Elisa lives in Paris. She is a former horse-riding champion who wants to set up 'Equus', an Internet business specialising in selling horse-riding equipment. On the advice of a chartered accountant, she decides to set up this business in London and its subsidiary in Paris, as UK company law does not require the payment of a minimum share capital.

What are Elisa's rights to set up her Internet business in the UK, and could the French authorities object to the creation of its subsidiary in Paris?

3 Christopher is a UK citizen. He has successfully completed his LLB and the Bar Professional Training Course (BPTC) at a London university. Wanting to take advantage of the opportunities in Eastern Europe, he decides to migrate to Lithuania and join Inga, his new partner, who runs her own family law firm in Vilnius. Christopher wants to join Inga's law firm and practise law in the Lithuanian courts.

What are Christopher's rights and obligations to establish himself as a practising lawyer in Lithuania?

part

V

COMPETITION LAW

Core Concepts of Competition Law

After reading this chapter, you will be able to understand:

- the objectives of EU competition law
- the concept of 'undertaking'
- the concept of relevant market
- the concept of 'effect on trade between Member States'.

16.1 Introduction

European competition law has played an essential role in economic integration and the completion of the internal market. The original structure of the Treaty of Rome was evocative in this respect. Prior to the Maastricht Treaty, the competition rules were laid down in the first chapter of Part Three of the EEC Treaty on 'Community policies'. This was no coincidence but a clear indication that the foundations of the European Community, notably the free movement of goods, services and establishment, could not be effective without rules ensuring fair competition. In essence, the internal market was completed in order to allow firms to compete on a level playing field in all Member States.

The essential mission of competition law was clearly enshrined in former Article 3(1)(g) TEC (formerly 3(f) TEEC), namely to ensure that 'competition in the internal market is not distorted'. The important place originally given to competition law was confirmed in the policy followed by the European institutions. The priority of competition law in the 1960s and 1970s was first to support the dismantling of all State-imposed barriers and restrictions to trade and, subsequently, to prevent companies from endorsing practices, such as market sharing and partitioning, price discrimination or restrictions of parallel trade, which would result in artificially dividing the internal market. Merger control was also introduced in the late 1980s to take account of the growing opportunities for European companies to merge and acquire assets across borders in the newly created internal market. The 1989 Merger Regulation, which aimed at eliminating risks of consumer harm as a result of the creation and strengthening of dominant positions through mergers, gradually led the way to a competition policy with an increased focus on consumer welfare based on a more rigorous economic analysis and on an effects-based approach. In the late 1990s and early 2000s, a new generation of competition regulations on vertical and horizontal agreements enabled the Commission to focus on agreements concluded by companies enjoying market power and more likely to cause consumer harm and damage the internal market, notably hardcore cartels. A more sophisticated economic approach and analysis further led to the adoption in the 2004 Merger Regulation of the 'substantive test' which is used to assess whether an economic operation may lead or not to a significant impediment to effective competition (SIEC). It is clear from the horizontal merger guidelines and the guidance on the Commission's enforcement priorities regarding exclusionary abuses of dominant undertakings, that the economic approach with a focus on the maximisation of consumer welfare is now solidly anchored in competition enforcement policy. Competition rules now ensure that consumers benefit from the best prices, quality and diversity of products and services markets can deliver. Yet, they are also crucial in preserving the integrity of the internal market as a level playing field.

As a result, European competition rules and policies have a direct impact on the daily lives of consumers and businesses of the European Union. Wider access to air transport at lower prices, the possibility of buying a car in another EU country at a cheaper price, and the reduction in telecommunication costs and roaming charges are among the many benefits directly enjoyed by European consumers. Any business which plans, for example, to set up a distribution network, enter into a cooperation agreement with another business, conclude an agreement on patent licensing, or set up a joint subsidiary with another business can no longer afford to ignore European competition rules without taking the risk of breaching them and dividing the internal market.

16.2   The concept of 'undertaking'

As the majority of competition rules apply to the behaviour of 'undertakings', this term is one of the key concepts in EU competition law. It has the same meaning for the purpose of Articles 101 and 102 TFEU, the Merger Regulation and State aids rules. The lack of definition in the Treaty has allowed the ECJ to construe this term widely and adopt a pragmatic approach which distances itself from its legal and formal meaning.

16.2.1   Irrelevance of the form or legal status

Very early on, the Court made it quite clear that, for the purpose of competition rules, an undertaking could not be defined solely in accordance with its legal form or status. In Case 155/73 *Sacchi* [1974] ECR 409, the Court ruled that an undertaking has to be capable of having an effect on competition whether it was set up for an economic purpose or not. In this case, the undertaking was a limited company on which a Member State had conferred by law the exclusive right to carry out television broadcasts of all kinds including those transmitted by cable. The fact that an undertaking, public or not, may be granted special or exclusive rights by a Member State under Article 106(1) TFEU or is entrusted with the operation of services of general economic interest under Article 106(2) TFEU does not exempt it from the application of the rules contained in Articles 101 and 102 TFEU (paras 14 and 15).

It is also irrelevant that the undertaking is a legal or natural person. According to Commission Decision 76/29/EEC ([1976] OJ L6/8) in *AOIP/Beyrard*, an individual trader (here an inventor who commercialises his invention) can be regarded as an undertaking.

The concept can also embrace a trust company set up to police a cartel, as in the *Italian flat glass* case (Commission Decision 81/881/EEC ([1981] OJ L326/32)) which concerned a company established by four other firms for the sole purpose of supervising a quota-fixing agreement; or a partnership as in *GVL* (Commission Decision 81/1030/EEC ([1981] OJ L370/49)), a case in which artists were deemed to be 'commercial partners' as their works were recorded, broadcast on radio and television or performed publicly for the consideration of payment of fees and royalties. Even associations may be regarded as undertakings provided they act as economic operators.

Whether the undertaking is private or State-owned is equally irrelevant. Competition rules apply not only to private entities but also to public bodies or corporations, which are directly or indirectly controlled by public central or local authorities. As a result, a German public employment agency operating under statutory powers (see Case C-41/90 *Höfner and Elser v Macrotron GmbH* [1991] ECR I-1979) and an Italian public placement office with an exclusive right to procure employment (Case C-55/96 *Job Centre coop arl* [1997] ECR I-7119) were deemed to be undertakings. So was ADP, the Paris Airport Authority, a public undertaking in charge of the management and operation of the Paris airports even though it operated under official powers and occupied government land (Case T-128/98 *Aéroports de Paris v Commission* [2000] ECR II-3929, para 109 and Case C-82/01 P *Aéroports de Paris v Commission* [2002] ECR I-9297, paras 68–83).

The concept of undertaking is not so much a concept that is determined by the legal status or personality of the entity concerned but rather by the economic nature of its activity.

16.2.2 The economic nature of the activity

In its *Polypropylene Cartel* decision (Commission Decision 86/398/EEC ([1986] OJ L230/1)), the Commission stated that

> [t]he subjects of [EU] competition rules are undertakings, a concept which is not identical with the question of legal personality for the purposes of company law or fiscal law ... It may, however, refer to any entity engaged in commercial activities and in the case of corporate bodies may refer to a parent or to a subsidiary or to the unit formed by the parent and subsidiaries together.

This broader interpretation of the term 'undertaking' was embraced in *Höfner and Elser v Macrotron*, in which the Court of Justice stated:

> It must be observed, in the context of competition law, first that the concept of an undertaking encompasses every entity engaged in an economic activity, regardless of the legal status of the entity and the way in which it is financed and, secondly, that employment procurement is an economic activity.
>
> The fact that employment procurement activities are normally entrusted to public agencies cannot affect the economic nature of such activities ...
>
> It follows that an entity such as a public employment agency engaged in the business of employment procurement may be classified as an undertaking for the purpose of applying the [Union] competition rules. (paras 21–23)

As such, an economic activity must involve the offering of goods or services on the market.

In Case C-475/99 *Ambulanz Glöckner v Landkreis Südwestpfalz* [2001] ECR 8089, a German medical organisation providing emergency and routine ambulance services for which it received payment from the Land of Rhineland-Palatinate and from insurers was regarded as an undertaking on the ground that

... [t]he concept of an undertaking, in the context of competition law, covers any entity engaged in an economic activity, regardless of the legal status of the entity or the way in which it is financed ... Any activity consisting in offering goods and services on a given market is an economic activity ... (para 19)

The fact that an entity is a cooperative set up in accordance with the law of a Member State (Case T-61/89 *Dansk Pelsdyravlerforening v Commission* [1992] ECR II-1931) or that it is a non-profit organisation (see Commission Decision 82/371/EEC ([1982] OJ L167/39) in *NAVEWA-ANSAEU* regarding an association of water supply companies and Case C-244/94 *Fédération Française des Sociétés d'Assurances and others v Ministère de l'Agriculture et de la Pêche* [1995] ECR I-4013, paras 14–22 in the case of an organisation managing an optional supplementary social security scheme) does not affect the economic nature of its activity and does not shield it from the application of competition rules.

However, where a body's activities are by 'their nature, their aim, and the rules to which they are subject, connected with the exercise of powers which are typically those of a public authority', they cannot be of an economic nature justifying the application of the EU competition rules. Thus, the body concerned cannot be treated as an undertaking within the meaning of those rules. This is the case of Eurocontrol which exercises, on behalf of contracting States, powers of control and supervision of air space and carries out tasks in the public interest in relation to air navigation safety (Case C-364/92 *SAT Fluggesellschaft mbH v Eurocontrol* [1994] ECR I-43, para 30), including its other activities of assisting national administrations in connection with tendering procedures carried out for the acquisition of equipment and systems in the field of air traffic management, and of technical standardisation (Case C-113/07P *SELEX Sistemi Integrati SpA v Commission* [2009] ECR I-2207, paras 82, 92–93). The same principle applied to SEPG, a private limited company, which was entrusted by the port authority of Genoa with anti-pollution surveillance and intervention in the oil port, which are tasks in the public interest and forming part of the essential functions of the State (Case C-343/95 *Cali & Figli Srl v Servizi ecologici porto di Genova SpA (SEPG)* [1997] ECR I-1547, para 23).

Naturally, when an entity performs in parallel activities falling within the exercise of public powers and economic activities, an assessment must be carried out separately for each activity. This assessment might then justify the application of competition rules to some but not all of its activities (Case C-49/07 *Motosykletistiki Omospondia Ellados NPID (MOTOE) v Elliniko Dimosio* [2008] ECR I-4863 concerning a non-profit-making association representing in Greece the International Motorcycling Federation in charge of authorising the organisation of motorcycling events and of entering into sponsorship, advertising and insurance contracts when organising such events itself).

16.2.3 Specific sectors of activities

The Court was also called upon to examine the application of competition rules to liberal professions and to insurance and social security funds.

16.2.3.1 The liberal professions

For many years, the liberal professions were regarded as operating outside commerce, and therefore law firms or offices were not treated as undertakings. This view is no longer true since the ECJ ruling in Case C-309/99 *JCJ Wouters, JW Savelbergh and Price Waterhouse Belastingadviseurs BV v Algemene Raad van de Nederlandse Orde van Advocaten* [2002] ECR I-1577.

In *Wouters, Savelbergh and Price Waterhouse* the Court ruled that members of the Amsterdam bar were undertakings as they

> ... offer, for a fee, services in the form of legal assistance consisting in the drafting of opinions, contracts and other documents and representation of clients in legal proceedings. In addition, they bear the financial risks attaching to the performance of those activities since, if there should be an imbalance between expenditure and receipts, they must bear the deficit themselves. (para 48)

As such activities clearly consist of offering services on a given market making them economic activities, Members of the Bar are therefore undertakings despite the complexity and technical nature of their services and the fact that the practice of their profession is regulated. This then justifies the application of competition rules to the legal professions.

The same principle applies to members of the medical profession, as ruled in Joined Cases C-180/98 to C-184/98 *Pavlov and Others v Stichting Pensioenfonds Medische Specialisten* [2000] ECR I-6451. In this case, the Court regarded medical specialists who were members of the National Association of Specialists of the Royal Netherlands Society for the Promotion of Medicine as self-employed economic operators providing services on the market in specialist medical services for which they were paid by their patients and for which they assumed the financial risks attached to this activity (para 76). As with lawyers, the complexity and technical nature of the services they provide and the fact that the exercise of their profession is regulated cannot shield them from the application of competition rules (para 77).

Likewise, Italian independent customs agents are regarded as 'undertakings' by the Commission (see Commission Decision 93/438/EEC ([1993] OJ L203/27) *Consiglio Nazionale degli Spedizionieri Doganali (CNSD)*, recitals 40–41) and the Courts (Case C-35/96 *Commission v Italy* [1998] ECR I-3851, para 37 and Case T-513/93 *Consiglio Nazionale degli Spedizionieri Doganali v Commission* [2000] ECR II-1807, para 37) as

> [t]hey offer, for payment, services consisting in the carrying out of customs formalities, relating in particular to the importation, exportation and transit of goods, as well as other complementary services such as services in monetary, commercial and fiscal areas.

In addition, they must assume the financial risks involved in the exercise of those activities and, notably, bear the deficit themselves, should there be an imbalance between expenditure and receipts.

16.2.3.2 Insurance, pension and social security funds

A great number of cases also involved insurance, pension and social security funds.

In Case C-244/94 *Fédération Française des Sociétés d'Assurances and others v Ministère de l'Agriculture et de la Pêche* [1995] ECR I-4013, the French federation of insurance companies challenged in the Conseil d'Etat, the highest administrative court, the legality of a decree laying down the organisation and rules for the operation of a supplementary old-age insurance scheme for self-employed farmers, financed by voluntary contributions deductible from taxable earnings. The decree also provided that the scheme was to be managed by the Caisse Centrale de la Mutualité Sociale Agricole (CCMSA), a non-profit-making organisation. Following a preliminary ruling by the Conseil d'Etat, the French government argued before the ECJ that, owing to its nature, CCMSA could not be treated as an undertaking and that the scheme it managed was not competitive in essence since it pursued a social purpose, it was based on the principle of social solidarity, and the legal relations between CCMSA and the persons insured were governed by public law and not by a contract under private law.

The Court first noted that membership of the scheme was optional as farmers wishing to supplement their basic pension could opt for better investment between the CCMSA and an insurance company. Secondly, it found that the scheme operated according to the capitalisation method rather than on a redistributive basis, and thirdly that the benefits to which farmers were entitled depended exclusively on the amount of contributions they paid and the financial return on the investments made by CCMSA. Fourthly, the Court considered that, although the scheme had elements of solidarity reflected in the fact that contributions were not linked to the risks incurred, these were limited in scope as a result of the optional nature of the scheme.

For those reasons, the Court concluded that CCMSA carried on an economic activity in competition with life assurance companies and, on that basis, that

> a non-profit-making organization which manages an old-age insurance scheme intended to supplement a basic compulsory scheme, established by law as an optional scheme and operating according to the principle of capitalization in keeping with the rules laid down by the authorities in particular with regard to conditions for membership, contributions and benefits, is an undertaking within the meaning of Article [101] et seq of the Treaty. (para 22)

Following this judgment, in Case C-97/96 *Albany International BV v Stichting Bedrijfspensieonfonds Textielindutrie* [1999] ECR I-5751, the Court held that

> … a pension fund charged with the management of a supplementary pension scheme set up by a collective agreement concluded between organisations representing employers and workers in a given sector, of which membership had been made compulsory by the public authorities for all workers in that sector, [was] an undertaking within the meaning of Article [101] et seq of the Treaty. (para 87)

The Court applied the same reasoning to a sectoral pension fund responsible for managing a supplementary medical specialists' pension scheme set up by the medical specialists' representative body. Although membership was made compulsory by law for all members of that profession, medical specialists could opt to purchase their basic pension either from the fund or from an authorised insurance company, and some of them could be granted exemption from membership with regard to the other components of the pension scheme. Together with the fact that this fund operated on the basis of the principle of capitalisation and that the level of its benefits depended on the performance of its investments and was subject to control by the Insurance Board, this was a clear indication that its activity was carried out in competition with insurance companies.

Carrying on an economic activity in competition with insurance companies is therefore the key criterion justifying the application of competition rules to such a body managing a pension fund. This in turn can be implied by the '[o]ptional affiliation, application of the principle of capitalisation and the fact that benefits depended solely on the amount of the contributions paid by the beneficiaries and on the financial results of the investments made by the managing organisation' (*Albany International BV*, para 79).

The economic nature of the activity of the organisation managing the fund cannot be altered by the fact that the organisation is non-profit-making, pursues a social objective, partially applies the principle of solidarity, or is subject to restrictions in making investments.

By contrast, this is not the case of a body managing a compulsory social security scheme based solely on the principle of national solidarity (Joined Cases C-159 and 160/91 *Poucet v Assurances Générales de France (AGP) and Pistre v Caisse Autonome Nationale de Compensation de l'Assurance Vieillesse des Artisans* [1993] ECR I-637). In this case, compulsory social protection applied to self-employed persons in non-agricultural and craft occupations against the risks of sickness, old age, death and invalidity. The Court found that all the schemes embraced the principle of solidarity in the fact that:

- contributions to the sickness and maternity scheme were proportional to income but benefits were identical for all beneficiaries;
- pensions under the old-age pension scheme were funded by those in employment but statutory pension entitlements were not proportional to the contributions paid into the scheme; and
- the financial equilibrium of those schemes was guaranteed by a financial contribution from the schemes with a surplus to those with structural financial difficulties.

The element of solidarity was even stronger in Case T-319/99 *Federación Nacional de Empresas de Instrumentación Científica, Médica, Técnica y Dental (FENIM) v Commission* [2003] ECR II-360, para 37, which involved an association of undertakings marketing medical goods to Spanish hospitals. The Court of First Instance ruled that SNS, the Spanish Health Service, purchased medical goods and equipment to provide free health services, an activity of a purely social nature, and not for the purpose of offering goods or services. SNS could not be seen as pursuing an economic activity in this respect and therefore could not be regarded as being an undertaking.

Likewise, the Italian National Institute for Insurance against Accidents at Work, a body entrusted by law with a scheme providing insurance against accidents at work and occupational diseases, was not deemed an undertaking because the amount of benefits and of contributions was fixed by the State (Case C-218/00 *Cisal di Battistello Venanzio & C Sas v Istituto nazionale per l'assicurazione contro gli infortuni sul lavoro (INAIL)* [2002] ECR I-691, paras 43–46).

This line of cases shows that the distinction between bodies running social security schemes which are regarded as undertakings and those which are not is a fine one. What the European authorities focus on to make such distinction are the actual functions of the entity.

16.2.4 Single economic entity

Whatever its form or legal status, whether it has a separate legal personality or not, an entity will be treated as an undertaking for the purpose of EU competition rules if it constitutes a single economic entity under the control of the same person enjoying sufficient autonomy in determining its conduct on the market.

As the Court put it in Case 170/83 *Hydrotherm v Compact* [1984] ECR 2999:

> In competition law, the term 'undertaking' must be understood as designating an economic unit for the purpose of the subject-matter of the [competition rule] in question even if in law that economic unit consists of several persons, natural or legal. (para 11)

This will be the case of 'undertakings belonging to the same concern and having the status of parent company and subsidiary, if the undertakings form an economic unit within which the subsidiary has no real freedom to determine its course of action on the market' (Case 15/74 *Centrafarm BV and de Peijper v Sterling Drug Inc* [1974] ECR 1147, para 41 and Case 66/86 *Ahmed Saeed Flugreisen and others v Zentrale zur Bekämpfung unlauteren Wettbewerbs* [1989] ECR 803, para 35).

In Case C-73/95P *Viho Europe BV v Commission of the European Communities* [1996] ECR I-5457, a group of subsidiaries which operated under the tight control of their parent company was treated as a single entity and any 'agreement' between them amounted in effect to a 'distribution of tasks within a single economic entity'.

Viho Europe BV, a company which marketed office equipment on a wholesale basis and which imported and exported that equipment, attempted without success to enter into business relations with Parker Pen Ltd – a producer of a wide range of writing utensils, which it sold throughout Europe through subsidiary companies or independent distributors – and to obtain Parker products on conditions equivalent to those granted to Parker's subsidiaries and independent distributors. Viho lodged a complaint with the Commission in which it claimed that Parker was prohibiting the export of its products by its distributors, dividing the common market into national markets and maintaining artificially high prices for Parker products on those national markets. In a second complaint, it claimed that the distribution policy pursued by Parker, whereby it required its subsidiaries to restrict the distribution of Parker products to their allocated territories, was in breach of Article 101 TFEU on prohibited anti-competitive agreements.

Having analysed the nature of the relationship between Parker Ltd and its subsidiaries, and having notably noted that Parker owned 100% of the capital of its subsidiaries and that the operation, the sales and marketing activities of its subsidiary companies were directed and controlled by an area team which was appointed by Parker (para 48), the Court concurred with the Commission that the Parker group could be classified as 'one economic unit within which the subsidiaries do not enjoy real autonomy in determining their course of action in the market' (para 49).

This sort of situation arises not only in the case of relationships between parent and subsidiary companies but also in relationships between a company and its commercial representative or between a principal and its agent. In Joined Cases 40–48, 50, 54–56, 111, 113 and 114/73 *Coöperatieve Vereniging 'Suiker Unie' UA and others v Commission (Re Sugar Cartel)* [1975] ECR 1663, the Court stated that

> ... if such an agent works for his principal he can in principle be regarded as an auxiliary organ forming an integral part of the latter's undertaking bound to carry out the principal's instructions and thus, like a commercial employee, forms an economic unit with this undertaking. (para 480)

In that regard, unlike dealers acting as agents under exclusive agency agreements for a manufacturer's subsidiary primarily engaged in leasing (Case C-266/93 *Bundeskartellamt v Volkswagen AG and VAG Leasing GmbH* [1995] ECR I-3477, para 19), genuine commercial agents whose commercial freedom is limited and who bear no commercial risks (see Case T-325/01 *DaimlerChrysler AG v Commission* [2005] ECR II-3319, paras 100–101) cannot be deemed to be independent undertakings. Nor can company employees, taken individually or collectively, '[s]ince they are, for the duration of [the employment] relationship, incorporated into the [undertaking] and thus form an economic unit with [it]' (see Case C-22/98 *Criminal proceedings against Becu, Verweire, Smeg NV and Adia Interim NV* [1999] ECR I-5665, paras 26–27).

From this it follows that, where an entity within a group of companies does not enjoy real autonomy to determine its own course of action, 'relations within an economic unit cannot amount to an agreement or concerted practice between undertakings which restricts competition within the meaning of Article [101(1)] of the Treaty' (*Viho Europe BV*, para 51) (see **17.1**). However, the conduct of such a unit on the market is liable to come under Article 102 TFEU on abuse of a dominant position (*Ahmed Saeed Flugreisen*, para 35) (see **17.2**).

This also means that companies deemed to be an economic unit are jointly and severally responsible for their united action or conduct (Joined Cases 6 and 7/73 *Istituto Chemioterapico Italiano Spa and Commercial Solvents Corporation v Commission* [1974] ECR 223, para 41). Thus, the conduct of a subsidiary may be attributed to a parent company 'where the subsidiary does not decide independently upon its own conduct in the market but carries out, in all material respects, the instructions given to it by the parent company' (Case T-65/89 *BPB Industries Plc and British Gypsum Ltd v Commission* [1993] ECR II-389 para 149).

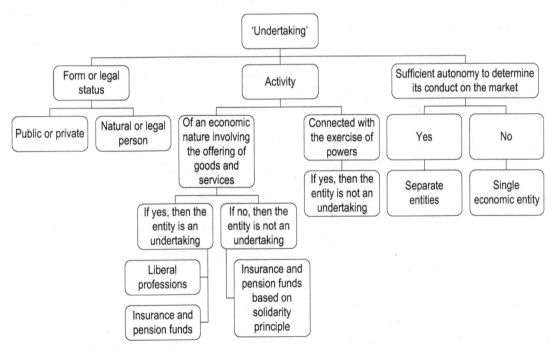

Figure 16.1   Undertakings

16.3 Market definition

When considering suspected infringements of competition rules, the relevant market is the first element that competition authorities, whether European or national, must analyse and assess, as the definition of the relevant market will help determine the scope of application of competition rules in respect of restrictive agreements, abuses of dominant positions and mergers.

16.3.1 The importance of the concept of relevant market

The importance of defining the relevant market was recognised in the early case law of the Court of Justice.

Case 6/72 *Europemballage Corporation and Continental Can Company Inc v Commission* [1973] ECR 215. On 9 December 1971, the Commission adopted a decision accusing Continental Can, an American company manufacturing metal packages, paper and plastic packaging and machines for the production and use of these packages, of abusing its dominant position allegedly held through SLW AG, its German subsidiary, in the market for light metal containers for meat, meat products, fish and crustaceans and in the market for metal closures for glass jars. According to Article 1 of the decision, the abuse consisted in Continental Can having acquired in April 1970, through its subsidiary Europemballage, about 80% of the shares and debentures of the company Thomassen and Drijver-Verbliva NV (TDV). By this acquisition, the Commission alleged, competition in the above-mentioned packaging product markets was practically eliminated in a substantial part of the then Common Market.

After stressing that

... the definition of the relevant market is of essential significance, for the possibilities of competition can only be judged in relation to those characteristics of the products in question by virtue of which those products are particularly apt to satisfy an inelastic need and are only to a limited extent interchangeable with other products[,] (para 32)

the Court quashed the Commission's decision on the ground that it did not

... give any details of how these three markets [differed] from each other, and must therefore be considered separately. Similarly, nothing [was] said about how these three markets [differed] from the general market for light metal containers, namely the market for metal containers for fruit and vegetables, condensed milk, olive oil, fruit juices and chemico-technical products. In order to be regarded as constituting a distinct market, the products in question must be individualized, not only by the mere fact that they are used for packing certain products, but by particular characteristics of production which make them specifically suitable for this purpose. Consequently, a dominant position on the market for light metal containers for meat and fish cannot be decisive, as long as it has not been proved that competitors from other sectors of the market for light metal containers are not in a position to enter this market, by a simple adaptation, with sufficient strength to create a serious counterweight. (para 33)

Generally, however, the ECJ would uphold the Commission's definition of the relevant market. The Commission will of course tend to define the market narrowly where the effect of doing so will be to enlarge a given firm's market share.

Illustration of this trend can be found in cases such as Case 226/84 *British Leyland plc v Commission* [1986] ECR 3263, where the ECJ upheld the Commission's finding that British Leyland held a form of administrative monopoly under British rules whereby someone seeking to register commercially imported vehicles for use on UK roads had to produce a certificate of conformity certifying that the vehicle conformed to a previously approved type vehicle to be issued by the manufacturer of the vehicle on the basis of the national type approval certificate. The relevant market was not cars, nor even left-hand drive cars but national type approval certificates for left-hand drive cars. In Case T-30/89 *Hilti AG v Commission* [1991] ECR II-1439, Hilti, the then largest European producer of powder-actuated fastening (PAF) nail guns, nails and cartridge strips, which carried on its main manufacturing operations in Liechtenstein where it was incorporated but also in the United Kingdom and other European countries, was found to be in a dominant position in not one (construction fastening systems as argued by Hilti) but three relevant product markets.

The Court of First Instance (now General Court) agreed that

> [i]n order to determine, therefore, whether Hilti, as a supplier of nail guns and of consumables designed for them, enjoys such power over the relevant product market as to give it a dominant position within the meaning of Article [102], the first question to be answered is whether the relevant market is the market for all construction fastening systems or whether the relevant markets are those for PAF tools and the consumables designed for them, namely cartridge strips and nails.

> The Court takes the view that nail guns, cartridge strips and nails constitute three specific markets. Since cartridge strips and nails are specifically manufactured, and purchased by users, for a single brand of gun, it must be concluded that there are separate markets for Hilti-compatible cartridge strips and nails, as the Commission found in its decision (paragraph 55). (paras 65 and 66)

16.3.2 Purpose of market definition

In 1997 the Commission introduced a Notice on the definition of relevant market for the purposes of Community competition law ([1997] OJ C372/5) ('the Notice') which offers valuable guidance on the method used by the Commission to define the relevant market.

Market definition is viewed as

> ... a tool to identify and define the boundaries of competition between firms. It serves to establish the framework within which competition policy is applied by the Commission[,]

and its main purpose

> ... is to identify in a systematic way the competitive constraints that the undertakings involved face. The objective of defining a market in both its product and geographic dimension is to identify those actual competitors of the undertakings involved that are capable of constraining those undertakings' behaviour and of preventing them from behaving independently of effective competitive pressure. It is from this perspective that the market definition makes it possible inter alia to calculate market shares that would convey meaningful information regarding market power for the purposes of assessing dominance or for the purposes of applying Article [101].

This objective of defining the relevant market is further confirmed in the DG Competition discussion paper on the application of Article 82 of the Treaty to exclusionary abuses of December 2005 (para 12).

In this respect, 'relevant market' cannot be equated to the usual understanding of markets, such as the area within which a company sells its products or the industry or sector where it operates.

Rather, the concept of relevant market 'is closely related to the objectives pursued under [Union] competition policy' and will be regarded in light of the nature of the competition inquiry, ie prospective as in the case of merger control or analytical in the case of other types of inquiries, notably abuse of a dominant position by a company or group of companies or in the application of Article 101 TFEU 'in particular, in determining whether an appreciable restriction of competition exists or in establishing if the condition pursuant to Article [101(3)(b)] for an exemption from the application of Article [101(1)] is met'.

16.3.3 Definition of relevant market

The concept of relevant market can be broken down into three separate issues: the relevant product market, the relevant geographic market, and (very rarely) the relevant temporal market.

16.3.3.1 The relevant product market

The Notice defines the relevant product market as a market that

> comprises all those products and/or services which are regarded as interchangeable or substitutable by the consumer, by reason of the products' characteristics, their prices and their intended use. (para 7)

The key issue for the Commission and the Court is interchangeability: if the consumer regards two different products as being interchangeable, then they are within the same product market. But how is interchangeability to be measured? The Court has suggested two ways: either by checking the cross-elasticity of demand between the products alleged to be within the relevant product market; or to look at the special features of the goods in question, such as their physical characteristics or the use to which the purchaser will put them.

case example

In Case 27/76 *United Brands v Commission* [1978] ECR 207, United Brands, an American company which was at the time the largest group on the world banana market and accounting for 35% of world exports in 1974, was alleged to have abused its dominant position in the banana market. The Court dismissed United Brands' argument that bananas were in the same market as other fruit because of their limited interchangeability.

The physical characteristics approach can be seen in the *United Brands* case where the Court looked at the special features of bananas. The Court notably observed that

> [f]or the banana to be regarded as forming a market which is sufficiently differentiated from other fruit markets it must be possible for it to be singled out by such special features distinguishing it from other fruits that it is only to a limited extent interchangeable with them and is only exposed to their competition in a way that is hardly perceptible. (para 22)

> The studies of the banana market on the Court's file show that on the latter market there is no significant long term cross-elasticity anymore than – as has been mentioned – there is any seasonal substitutability in general between the banana and all the seasonal fruits, as this only exists between the banana and two fruits (peaches and table grapes) in one of the countries (West Germany) of the relevant geographic market. (para 28)

As far as concerns the two fruits available throughout the year (oranges and apples) the first are not interchangeable and in the case of the second there is only a relative degree of substitutability. (para 29)

This small degree of substitutability is accounted for by the specific features of the banana and all the factors which influence consumer choice. (para 30)

The banana has certain characteristics, appearance, taste, softness, seedlessness, easy handling, a constant level of production which enable it to satisfy the constant needs of an important section of the population consisting of the very young, the old and the sick. (para 31)

The particular use approach can also be seen in *Istituto Chemioterapico Italiano* (ICI) *and Commercial Solvents Corporation* (CSC). Zoja, a customer of CSC and ICI, had been refused a supply of aminobutanol as a raw material for the manufacture of ethambutol and ethambutol-based specialities used as an anti-tuberculosis drug. Without it, Zoja was unable to produce its own goods based on other raw materials without making expensive and difficult changes to its installations and manufacturing processes. CSC and ICI disputed the Commission's findings that CSC held a dominant position in the world market of the raw materials for the production of ethambutol, namely nitropropane and aminobutanol, on the ground that ethambutol could be produced from other raw materials than those produced by CSC.

On the other hand, CSC asserted the relevant market to be that of anti-tuberculosis drugs in which ethambutol was 'in competition with other drugs that were to a large extent interchangeable'. Furthermore according to CSC, 'since a market in ethambutol [did] not exist, it [was] impossible to establish a separate market in the raw material for the manufacture of this product' (para 19). Focusing on the inability of Zoja's to use other raw materials to manufacture derivatives such as ethambutol, the Court ruled that

> [c]ontrary to the arguments of the applicants it is in fact possible to distinguish the market in raw material necessary for the manufacture of a product from the market on which the product is sold. An abuse of a dominant position on the market in raw materials may thus have effects restricting competition in the market on which the derivatives of the raw material are sold and these effects must be taken into account in considering the effects of an infringement, even if the market for the derivative does not constitute a self-contained market ... (para 22)

Likewise in Case 22/78 *Hugin Kassaregister AB and Hugin Cash Registers Ltd v Commission* [1979] ECR 1869, the Commission had found that Hugin was dominant in the market for spare parts for its own cash registers because Liptons, an independent company which serviced the machines outside the Hugin distribution system, could not get spares from anywhere else without committing a breach of copyright. Hugin challenged the Commission's definition of the relevant market, notably on the ground that 'the supply of spare parts and of maintenance services is certainly not a separate market but is an essential parameter of competition in the market for cash registers as a whole' (para 4).

The Court firstly observed that

> [w]hile there certainly exists amongst users a market for maintenance and repairs which is distinct from the market in new cash registers, it is essentially a market for the provision of services and not for the sale of a product such as spare parts ... (para 6)

It further stated at paragraph 7 that

> there exists a separate market for Hugin spare parts at another level, namely that of independent undertakings which specialize in the maintenance and repair of cash registers, in the reconditioning of used machines and in the sale of used machines and the renting out of machines ...

and finally, that

> [i]t is, moreover, established that there is a specific demand for Hugin spare parts, since those parts are not interchangeable with spare parts for cash registers of other makes. (para 7)

This led the Court to find that there was a narrow market for Hugin spare parts.

A difficult case was that of Case 85/76 *Hoffmann-La Roche & Co AG v Commission* [1979] ECR 461 because here two groups of vitamins, C and E, could be used for two different purposes. They could be used for bio-nutritive purposes (ie in health products) in which case they could not be interchanged; but they could also be used as anti-oxidants (preservatives in foodstuffs) where they could be interchanged with other products. Nevertheless, the Commission, upheld by the ECJ, persisted in defining the product market as narrowly as possible, though it overlooked the fact that had the applicants abused their power in one market, eg by raising the price of the product unilaterally, they would have left themselves open to competitive attack in the other.

Regarding the way the market definition will be conducted, the Commission will inquire into demand substitutability (as in the *United Brands* case; paras 15–19 of the Notice), supply substitutability (as in the *Continental Can* case; paras 20–23 of the Notice) and potential competition (para 24 of the Notice). In applying these principles, the Commission has adopted the SSNIP test, which stands for 'Small but Significant and Non-transitory Increase in Prices'. Indeed in para 17 of the Notice, the Commission indicates that

> [t]he question to be answered is whether the parties' customers would switch to readily available substitutes or to suppliers located elsewhere in response to a hypothetical small (in the range 5% to 10%) but permanent relative price increase in the products and areas being considered. If [demand] substitution were enough to make the price increase unprofitable because of the resulting loss of sales, additional substitutes [products] and areas are included in the relevant market.

The Commission considers that the similarity of products' characteristics and intended use are no longer sufficient to demonstrate that two products are demand substitutes. This is equally the case for functional interchangeability (as used by the ECJ in the *Continental Can* case) as the responsiveness of customers to price changes may be determined by other factors. The Commission will consider evidence of substitution in the recent past, quantitative econometric tests, the views of consumers and competitors, consumer preferences, barriers and costs associated with switching demand to potential substitutes and different categories of customers and price discrimination (see paras 38–43).

The SSNIP test was mentioned for the first time by the General Court in Case T-340/03 *France Télécom SA v Commission* [2007] ECR II-107, in which France Télécom challenged the Commission's findings in its 2005 Wanadoo decision (Case COMP/38.233 *Wanadoo Interactive*) that the French market for high-speed internet access for residential customers was the relevant market. Besides referring to the ECJ case law regarding characteristics and use of products for the identification of their substitutability (paras 78–80), the General Court indeed stated that

> ... the assessment of demand substitution entails a determination of the range of products which are viewed as substitutes by the consumer. One way of making this determination can be viewed as a speculative experiment, postulating a hypothetical small but lasting change in relative prices and evaluating the likely reactions of customers to that increase. In paragraph 17 of the notice, the Commission states '[t]he question to be answered is whether the parties' customers would switch to readily available substitutes ... in response to a hypothetical small (in the range 5 to 10%) but permanent relative price increase in the products and areas being considered'. (para 87)

The Court then concluded that

> ... the Commission was right to find that a sufficient degree of substitutability between high-speed and low-speed access did not exist and to define the market in question as that of high-speed internet access for residential customers. (para 91)

16.3.3.2 The relevant geographic market

According to the 1997 Notice:

> The relevant geographic market comprises the area in which the undertakings concerned are involved in the supply and demand of products or services, in which the conditions of competition are sufficiently homogeneous and which can be distinguished from neighbouring areas because the conditions of competition are appreciably different in those area. (para 8)

In the *United Brands* case, the ECJ stressed the need to consider a

> clearly defined geographic area in which the product is marketed and where the conditions are sufficiently homogenous for the effect of the economic power of the undertaking concerned to be able to be evaluated. (para 11)

However, the Court did not identify which issues are relevant in defining the geographic market, other than saying that

> [t]he conditions for the application of article [102] to an undertaking in a dominant position presuppose the clear delimitation of the substantial part of the [internal] market in which it may be able to engage in abuses which hinder effective competition and this is an area where the objective conditions of competition applying to the product in question must be the same for all traders. (para 44)

In many cases the Commission and Court both seem to assume that the geographical market cannot extend beyond the EU. Two cases where there was a conveniently defined geographical market involving two Member States are, first, Decision 89/205/EEC in Case *Magill TV Guide/ITP, BBC and RTE* ([1989] OJ L78/43) where Magill challenged the refusal of the three broadcasting companies to license the copyright in their programme listings for Northern Ireland and Eire, all three stations being receivable either side of the Irish border. The Commission Decision was confirmed by the General Court in Case T-69/89 *Radio Telefis Eireann v Commission* [1991] ECR II-489 (para 64).

Secondly, in the *BPB Industries plc* case (Decision 89/22/EEC [1989] OJ L10/50), the Commission treated the whole of the Irish island as the relevant geographical market in holding that the two companies, BPB Industries and British Gypsum Ltd, were in breach of former Article 86 TEEC (now Article 102 TFEU) by operating a system of fidelity rebates and more favourable delivery dates to those builders' merchants who stocked their products only, the market share being 90% of the market for plasterboard.

However, not all cases are as simple. In *Virgin/British Airways* (Decision 2000/74/EC [2000] OJ L30/1), taking into account that the 'distribution of airlines tickets takes place at national level' and that 'airlines normally purchase the services for distributing those tickets on a national basis', the Commission defined the geographic market for air travel agency services as the UK only since

> [t]ravel agents tend to operate within national boundaries, since customers normally book tickets in their country of residence. In the present case, customers residing in the United Kingdom purchase their tickets from travel agents in the United Kingdom; transactions are generally made in pounds sterling; and travel agents operate on the basis that the markets they are serving are delineated on national boundaries. The carriers therefore market their services and purchase air travel agency services within the same boundaries. (para 78)

The Commission's view was subsequently upheld by the General Court in Case T-219/99 *British Airways Plc v Commission* [2004] 4 CMLR 1008. After reiterating that

> [a]s for the geographic market to be taken into consideration, consistent case-law shows that it may be defined as the territory in which all traders operate in the same or sufficiently homogeneous conditions of competition in so far as concerns specifically the relevant products or services, without it being necessary for those conditions to be perfectly homogeneous (Case T-83/91 *Tetra Pak v Commission* [1994] ECR II-755, paragraph 91, confirmed on appeal by judgment in Case C-333/94 P *Tetra Pak v Commission (Tetra Pak II)* [1996] ECR I-5951) [...] (para 108)

and after observing that

> [i]t can hardly be denied that, in the overwhelming majority of cases, travellers reserve airline tickets in their country of residence. Although BA has argued that not all tickets sold by travel agents in the United Kingdom are necessarily sold to residents of that country, it has acknowledged that transactions taking place outside the United Kingdom could not be quantified [...] (para 109)

the Court concluded that

> [i]t does not therefore appear that the Commission erred in defining the relevant geographic market as the United Kingdom market, for the purposes of demonstrating that BA held a dominant position on that market in its capacity as the purchaser of air travel agency services provided by agents established in the United Kingdom. (para 116)

This case reflects the Commission's approach to the geographic market definition as explained at length in its Notice on market definition. As the Commission explains,

> ... it will take a preliminary view of the scope of the geographic market on the basis of broad indications as to the distribution of market shares between the parties and their competitors, as well as a preliminary analysis of pricing and price differences at national and [EU] or EEA level. This initial view is used basically as

a working hypothesis to focus the Commission's enquiries for the purposes of arriving at a precise geographic market definition. (para 28)

On that basis, the Commission will notably take into consideration the following types of evidence to define the relevant geographic market, ranging from a local to a global dimension (paras 44–50):

- past evidence of orders to other areas;
- basic demand characteristics;
- views of customers and competitors;
- geographic patterns of demand;
- trade flows;
- barriers and switching costs; and
- the continuing process of integration.

16.3.3.3   The relevant temporal market

Although this dimension is generally ignored and is not mentioned in the Commission Notice, the relevant market can also be defined by reference to time. Though perhaps it should have done so, the Commission did not consider the relevant temporal market in the *United Brands* case where there was evidence of seasonal fluctuations in the demand for bananas. Equally the Court's view was that there was no seasonable substitutability between the banana and other fruits 'since the banana is a fruit which is always available in sufficient quantities' (paras 26 and 27).

However, the Commission did so in *Ardolie Belanger Gemeenschap (ABG) BV/Oil Companies Operating in the Netherlands* (Decision 77/327/EEC [1977] OJ L117/1), where it took into account a short-term crisis in the oil industry in the early 1970s. In this Decision, the Commission accused Benzine Petroleum Maatschapij BV of having abused its dominant position on the market in question by reducing its supplies to ABG substantially and proportionately to a much greater extent than in relation to all its other customers and of having been unable to provide any objective reasons for its behaviour.

RELEVANT MARKET

Importance of the concept

The possibilities of competition can only be judged in relation to the relevant market

(Case 6/72 *Europemballage and Continental Can v Commission*)

▶

RELEVANT MARKET

Purpose of market definition

(1997 Commission Notice on the definition of relevant market)

- a tool to identify and define boundaries of competition between firms
- to identify competitive constraints faced by those firms

▶

RELEVANT MARKET

Definition

- Relevant product market (demand and supply substitutability of products) (Case 27/76 *United Brands v Commission*)
- Relevant geographic market (Case T-219/99 *British Airways Plc v Commission*)
- Relevant temporal market (Case 27/76 *United Brands v Commission*)

Figure 16.2   Relevant market

16.4 The concept of 'effect on trade between the Member States'

Articles 101 and 102 TFEU require there to be a conduct or an abuse of a dominant position affecting trade between Member States.

Originally developed and clarified by the EU courts, the concept was 'codified' by the Commission in its 2004 Notice on Guidelines on the effect on trade concept contained in Articles 81 and 82 of the Treaty ([2004] OJ C101/81) ('the 2004 Notice'), setting out a methodology for, and guidance on, its application, and spelling out 'a rule indicating when agreements are in general unlikely to be capable of appreciably affecting trade between Member States (the non-appreciable affectation of trade rule or NAAT-rule)' (para 3).

As specified very clearly in para 4 of the 2004 Notice, a clear distinction is made between this concept which deals with 'the ability of agreements to appreciably affect trade between Member States' and the concept of appreciable restriction of competition under Article 101(1) TFEU, which is covered under the de minimis rule in the 2014 Commission Notice on agreements of minor importance which do not appreciably restrict competition under Article 101(1) of the Treaty on the Functioning of the European Union (De Minimis Notice) (see below 17.2.2.2).

16.4.1 The purpose of the concept

This is an important requirement as it helps to define the boundary between Union and national competition law (where the Member States have retained some autonomy) (see Case 56 and 58/64 *Consten and Grundig v Commission* [1966] ECR 299, 341). As clearly stated in paragraph 12 of the 2004 Notice:

> The effect on trade criterion is an autonomous [EU] law criterion, which must be assessed separately in each case. It is a jurisdictional criterion, which defines the scope of application of [EU] competition law. [EU] competition law is not applicable to agreements and practices that are not capable of appreciably affecting trade between Member States.

Therefore, the scope of application of Articles 101 and 102 TFEU is confined to agreements and practices that are capable of (see below 16.4.2) having a minimum level effect or, in other words, an 'appreciable' effect (see below 16.4.3) on cross-border trade within the EU.

While alleged restrictions of competition may provide a clear indication that an agreement or a practice may affect trade between Member States, it cannot be assumed that non-restrictive agreements may not have cross-border effects within the EU. As a result, according to the 2004 Notice,

> [i]t is not necessary, for the purposes of establishing [EU] law jurisdiction, to establish a link between the alleged restriction of competition and the capacity of the agreement to affect trade between Member States. (para 16)

The notion of 'trade between the Member States' implies an impact on cross-border economic activities involving at least two Member States, either whole or part thereof, or where the relevant market is national or regional. In this respect, it has to be clearly differentiated from the notion of relevant geographic market (see above 16.3.3.2). The former is to be understood in its wider understanding consistent with the fundamental freedoms of movement of goods, services, persons and capital, and the competitive structure of the internal market.

16.4.2 Definition and interpretation of the concept

Articles 101(1) and 102 TFEU refer to agreements or practices that 'may affect trade between the Member States'. As mentioned in paragraph 23 of the 2004 Notice, '[t]he function of the notion "may affect" is to define the nature of the required impact on trade between Member States'.

The ECJ gave a wide interpretation to the phrase, thus extending the scope of application of EU competition law. The test was that laid down in Case 56/65 *Société Technique Minière v Maschinenbau Ulm* [1966] ECR 235 which concerned an agreement containing a clause 'granting an exclusive right of sale'. In this case, the ECJ stated that

> ... it must be possible to foresee with a sufficient degree of probability on the basis of a set of objective factors of law or of fact that the agreement in question may have an influence, direct or indirect, actual or potential, on the pattern of trade between Member States. Therefore, in order to determine whether an agreement ... comes within the field of application of article [101], it is necessary to consider in particular *whether it is capable of bringing about a partitioning of the market in certain products between member states and thus rendering more difficult the interpenetration of trade which the treaty is intended to create.* (at 249) (emphasis added)

This ruling was later confirmed in the Case 5/69 *Völk v SPRL Ets J Vervaecke* [1969] ECR 295 (para 5).

The test for assessing effect on trade, the so-called *STM (Société Technique Minière)* test, is therefore threefold and is codified in the 2004 Notice:

- a sufficient degree of probability on the basis of a set of objective factors of law or facts which means that, although subjective intent on the part of undertakings to affect trade between the Member States is relevant evidence to be considered, it is not required (para 25);
- an influence on the pattern of trade between the Member States; without being regarded as a 'condition that trade be restricted or reduced', the term 'pattern of trade' is used rather as a basis for an examination under EU competition law of agreement and practices that have cross-border effects (paras 33–35); and
- a direct or indirect, actual or potential influence on the pattern of trade. While direct effects 'normally occur in relation to the products covered by an agreement or practice', indirect ones 'often occur' in relation to those products (paras 37 and 38 of the Notice and in the *Zanussi SpA* case (Commission Decision 78/922/EEC [1978] OJ L322/36, para 11)); equally, while actual effects on trade are produced by the implementation of an agreement or practice, potential effects 'may occur in the future with a sufficient degree of probability' (paras 40 and 41 of the Notice and Case 107/82 *AEG-Telefunken v Commission* [1983] ECR 3151, para 60 and Case T-77/92 *Parker Pen Ltd v Commission* [1994] ECR II-549, paras 39–46). Indirect and potential effects do not imply speculative or hypothetical effects however (para 43 of the Notice and Case T-374/94 *European Night Services Ltd (ENS) and others v Commission* [1998] ECR II-3141, paras 102–103).

Furthermore, the Court of Justice has developed a test based on whether or not the agreement or practice affects the competitive structure (Joined Cases T-24/93 and others, *Compagnie maritime belge* [1996] ECR II-1201, para 203). As noted in para 20 of the 2004 Notice:

Agreements and practices that affect the competitive structure inside the [EU] by eliminating or threatening to eliminate a competitor operating within the [EU] may be subject to the [EU] competition rules.

This is notably the case in the context of an undertaking in a dominant position as, for instance, in *Istituto Chemioterapico Italiano SpA*, in which the Court observed that

… [w]hen an undertaking in a dominant position with the [single] market abuses its position in such a way that a competitor in the [single] market is likely to be eliminated, it does not matter whether the conduct relates to the latter's exports or its trade within the [single] market, once it has been established that this elimination will have repercussions on the competitive structure within the [single] market. (para 33)

16.4.3 Appreciability

For Articles 101 and 102 TFEU to apply, trade within the EU must be affected in a significant or appreciable way. This was clearly established by the ECJ in Case 22/71 *Béguelin Import Co v SAGL Import Export* [1971] ECR 949 which stated that

… in order to come within the prohibition imposed by article [101], the agreement must affect trade between member states and the free play of competition to an appreciable extent. (para 16)

To measure appreciability, EU authorities can take into account the turnover of the undertakings concerned (absolute terms) and their respective position on the relevant market in light of their market shares (relative terms). Appreciability must therefore be assessed on the basis of 'the circumstances of each individual case, in particular the nature of the agreement and practice, the nature of the products covered and the market position of the undertakings concerned' (para 45 of the 2004 Notice).

However, such measurements might not be necessary if it is possible to infer from the very nature of an agreement or concerted practice that it is liable to affect trade within the EU, 'for example because they concern imports or exports or because they cover several Member States' (para 48).

In principle, some agreements will not appreciably affect trade between Member States when cumulative conditions are met. These are spelled out in para 52 of the 2004 Notice:

- the aggregate market share of the parties on any relevant market within the EU does not exceed 5%;
- the aggregate annual EU turnover of the undertakings party to horizontal agreements does not exceed €40 million; and
- the aggregate annual EU turnover of the supplier in the products covered by vertical agreements does not exceed €40 million.

The presumption that agreements and practices do not appreciably affect trade within the EU still applies 'where during two successive calendar years the above turnover threshold is not exceeded by more than 10% and the above market threshold is not exceeded by more than 2 percentage points' (para 52).

16.4.4 The applicability of the concept to agreements or abuses covering one, or part of a, single Member State

Although, as mentioned above, the impact on cross-border economic activities must involve at least two Member States, it is irrelevant that the parties to the agreement or practice are from the same Member State, or an undertaking holds a dominant position in a part or the whole of a single Member State.

In Case 8/72 *Vereeniging van Cementhandelaren v Commission (Re Cement Cartel)* [1972] ECR 977, the ECJ upheld the Commission's finding that a price-fixing scheme limited to the Dutch cement market was capable of affecting trade between Member States and infringed former Article 85 TEEC (now Article 101 TFEU) on the ground that

> [a]n agreement extending over the whole of the territory of a member state by its very nature has the effect of reinforcing the compartmentalization of markets on a national basis, thereby holding up the economic interpenetration which the treaty is designed to bring about and protecting domestic production. (para 29)

This view was reiterated by the General Court in Joined Cases T-259/02 to T-264/02 and T-271/02 *Raiffeisen Zentralbank Österreich AG and Others v Commission (Re The Lombard Club)* [2006] ECR II-5169, para 180.

However, such presumption can be rebutted by an analysis of the characteristics of the agreement and its economic context demonstrating the contrary (see Joined Cases C-215/96 and C-216/96 *Bagnasco and Others* [1999] ECR I-135, paras 51–53).

In Joined Cases 43/82 and 63/82 *VBVB & VBBB v Commission (Re Dutch Books)* [1984] ECR 19, the Court held that there was no justification for the view that there could be no inter-State trade between the Flemish-speaking part of Belgium and Holland and that the geographical region to be taken into account was not the political territory of the two States but the Dutch-language territory thus forming a single entity. It therefore ruled that

> [t]hat line of argument on the part of the applicants [disregarded] the express wording of article [101], which refers to 'trade between member states'. In this case the agreement indisputably [affected] trade between two member states, notwithstanding the linguistic links between them.

This issue is also extensively covered in paras 77–99 of the 2004 Notice.

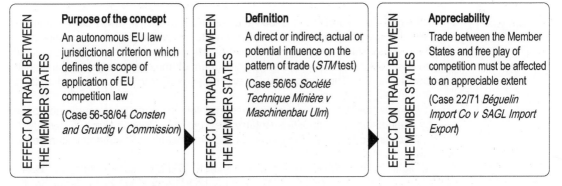

Figure 16.3   *'Effect on trade between the Member States'*

16.5   Further reading

Baker JB, 'Market Definition: An Analytical Overview' (2007) 74 *Antitrust Law Journal* 129.

Coate MB and Fischer JH, 'Is Market Definition Still Needed After All These Years' (2014) 2(2) *Journal of Antitrust Enforcement* 422–450.

Coscelli A and Overd A, 'Market Definition in the Pharmaceutical Sector' (2007) 28(5) *ECLR* 294.

Dunne N, 'Knowing When to See it: State Activities, Economic Activities, and the Concept of Undertaking' (2009–2010) 16 *Columbia Journal of European Law* 427.

Nowag J, 'SELEX Sistemi Integrati SpA v Commission of the European Communities (C-113/07 P) [2009] E.C.R. I-2207: Redefining the Boundaries between Undertaking and the Exercise of Public Authority' (2010) 31(12) *ECLR* 483.

Lasok KPE, 'When is an Undertaking not an Undertaking' (2004) 25(7) *ECLR* 383.

Šilhán J, 'The Concept of Relevant Market: Some Critical Remarks' (2012) 33(12) *ECLR* 589.

Sinclair D, '"Undertakings" in Competition Law at the Public-Private Interface – an Unhealthy Situation' (2014) 34(4) *ECLR* 167.

Wils WPJ, 'The Undertaking as Subject of E.C. Competition Law and the Imputation of Infringements to Natural or Legal Persons' (2000) 25 *EL Rev* 99.

summary

From the very inception of the European economic integration process, competition rules have played a pivotal role which has evolved from an originally formalistic and legalistic approach to a more economic and consumer welfare-oriented one. Competition rules are also crucial to preserve the integrity of the internal market as a level playing field against interference with competition by undertakings' behaviour that might affect trade between the Member States within a defined market. The key concepts that apply across competition rules on concerted behaviour, abuse of dominant position and mergers are those of: 'undertakings', 'relevant market' and 'effect on trade between the Member States'. These concepts have been defined by the Commission and the Court in a rather broad manner for the benefit of ensuring a fair, competitive market within the EU.

test your knowledge

1   'One of the most important issues in competition (antitrust) law is determination of relevant market boundaries. Be it prohibited cartel agreements, regulation of dominant position, or merger control, the definition of relevant market is regularly an essential and usually also initial component of any case analysis in competition law.' (Šilhán J, 'The Concept of Relevant Market: Some Critical Remarks' (2012) 33(12) ECLR 589)

   Discuss how this concept of 'relevant market' has been interpreted and applied by competition law authorities, notably the European Commission and the CJEU.

   Discuss the benefits of this concept and whether it is still needed in competition law.

2   In light of the ruling in Case C-113/07P *SELEX Sistemi Integrati SpA v Commission* [2009] ECR I-2207, discuss how the concept of 'undertaking' has been defined in the case law of the CJEU.

3   Analyse the application of the SNIPP test in Case T-340/03 *France Télécom Sa v Commission* [2007] ECR II-107.

chapter 17

Substantive Competition Rules Applicable to Undertakings

study
points

After reading this chapter, you will be able to understand:

- the control of horizontal and vertical restraints
- the individual and block exemptions from such control
- the concept of dominance
- the concept of abuse of dominance
- control of concentrations.

17.1 Introduction

The Treaty provisions applicable to undertakings relate to two familiar types of anti-competitive behaviour on the market: anti-competitive agreements covered by Article 101 TFEU and abuse of dominant position prohibited under Article 102 TFEU. These two breaches of competition rules are fundamentally distinct and different. The former is the result of bilateral or collective collusion, whilst the latter is the expression of unilateral action by one or more undertakings taking advantage of their power on the market. While Article 101 prohibits the anti-competitive effects of collusion between several economic operators, Article 102 prohibits the restrictive effects of dominance on competition in the market within which an undertaking operates. Furthermore, while the prohibition of anti-competitive agreements laid down in Article 101(1) TFEU can be mitigated by the exemptions provided for under Article 101(3), the prohibition of abuse of dominance under Article 102 is absolute.

Yet both provisions 'seek to achieve the same aim on different levels, viz. the maintenance of effective competition within the [internal] market' (Case 6/72 *Europemballage Corporation and Continental Can Company Inc v Commission* [1973] ECR 215). In this respect, even though this is not explicitly suggested in the Treaty, they can be seen as complementary. The application of one of the provisions is not necessarily exclusive of the other. Rather, as suggested in Case 66/86 *Ahmed Saeed Flugreisen and others v Zentrale zur Bekämpfung unlauteren Wettbewerbs eV* [1989] ECR 803, 'the possibility that Articles [101] and [102] may both be applicable cannot be ruled out' (para 37). In this case, the Court examined whether an undertaking in a dominant position could also be in breach of former Article 85 TEEC (now Article 101 TFEU). It is then possible to apply Articles 101 and 102 to situations where an undertaking in a dominant position is also party to an agreement as in Case 85/76 *Hoffmann-La Roche & Co AG v Commission* [1979] ECR 461 or where a collective dominance originates from an agreement (see Joined Cases T-68/89, T-77/89 and T-78/89 *Società Italiana Vetro SpA, Fabbrica Pisana SpA and PPG Vernante Pennitalia SpA v Commission (Re Italian Flat Glass)* [1992] ECR II-1403).

Depending on the particulars of the case, Articles 101 and 102 TFEU can also apply to concentrations (mergers of companies or acquisition of a company by another).

However, even if concentrations are not seen as anti-competitive per se and are not prohibited as such under the Treaty provisions on competition, a special and complex ex ante or preventive regime of control of concentrations was deemed necessary and set up by way of secondary legislation.

17.2 Control of horizontal and vertical restraints under Article 101 TFEU

Article 101 TFEU is the first fundamental provision of EU competition law. It is designed to protect a competitive economic environment within the European internal market from all forms of anti-competitive agreements or behaviour, whether horizontal or vertical, between businesses operating within that market.

While its first and second paragraph lay down a strict prohibition leading to the voidance of any anti-competitive agreement or behaviour, its third paragraph recognises that, in certain limited circumstances, such anti-competitive behaviour may be exempted from the application of paragraph 1.

Article 101(1) TFEU provides:

> The following shall be prohibited as incompatible with the internal market: all agreements between undertakings, decision by associations of undertakings and concerted practices which may affect trade between Member States and which have as their object or effect the prevention, restriction or distortion of competition within the internal market ...

17.2.1 The general economy of Article 101(1) TFEU

The Commission Notice 'Guidelines on the application of Article 81(3) of the Treaty' ([2004] OJ C101/97) clearly explains the general economy and objective of the prohibition rule under Article 101(1). It notably states that

> [t]he objective of Article [101] is to protect competition on the market as a means of enhancing consumer welfare and of ensuring an efficient allocation of resources. Competition and market integration serve these ends since the creation and preservation of an open single market promotes an efficient allocation of resources throughout the [Union] for the benefit of consumers. (para 13)

Prohibiting restrictive agreements and concerted practices between undertakings which affect trade between Member States, Article 101(1) is based on the general principle 'that each economic operator must determine independently the policy, which he intends to adopt on the market' (Joined Cases 40/73 to 48/73 and others, *Suiker Unie v Commission (Re Sugar Cartel)* [1975] ECR 1663, para 173; Case C-49/92 P *Commission v Anic Partecipazioni SpA* [1999] ECR I-4125, para 116; Joined Cases C-89/85, C-104/85, C-114/85, C-116/85, C-117/85 and C-125/85 to C-129/85 *A Ahlström Osakeyhtiö and others v Commission* [1993] ECR I-1307, para 63).

17.2.2 The constituent elements of Article 101(1) TFEU

The prohibition rule of Article 101(1) TFEU applies to:

- agreements, concerted practices between undertakings and decisions by associations of undertakings;
- whose object or effect is to prevent, restrict or distort competition within the internal market;

- in so far as they are capable of affecting trade between Member States (see **16.4**).

17.2.2.1 The different forms of collusion

Agreements, decisions and concerted practices have been defined by the EU Courts as autonomous EU law concepts whereby they clearly distinguished between coordination of behaviour or collusion between undertakings and unilateral conduct of an undertaking, the latter being subject only to Article 102 TFEU.

In many ways it is not necessary to know the precise meaning of these concepts because of the wide meaning given to 'concerted practice' (see **Concerted practice** below). The term embraces both legally enforceable contracts and the constitution of trade associations.

Joint intention

The parties' joint intention or concurrence of wills to act in a specific way on the market is the minimum requirement for such conduct to be caught by Article 101(1) TFEU (see Case T-6/89 *Enichem Anic SpA v Commission* [1991] ECR II-1623, para 198; Case 41/69 *ACF Chemiefarma NV v Commission (Re Quinine Cartel)* [1970] ECR 661, para 112 and Joined Cases 209 to 215 and 218/78 *van Landewyck Sàrl v Commission (FEDETAB)* [1980] ECR 3125, para 86). In *Enichem Anic SpA*, the Court held that the Commission was entitled to treat as agreements the common intentions existing between the applicant and other polypropylene producers which related to price initiatives, sales volume targets for 1979 and 1980 and measures for restricting monthly sales for 1981 and 1982.

Such intention of the parties need not be expressed in a valid and binding contract in national law (Case C-277/87 *Sandoz prodotti farmaceutici SpA v Commission* [1990] ECR I-45, para 13). Nor does it need to be explicit. For example, in Case T-35/92 P *John Deere Ltd v Commission* [1994] ECR II-957, para 66, the Court found that the provision of information collected upon registration of every vehicle presupposed a tacit agreement between traders in order to define the boundaries of the distributors' sales territories, without which the information disseminated could not have been exploited in the same way. Similarly, the Court found joint intention in Case T-43/92 *Dunlop Slazenger International Ltd v Commission* [1994] ECR II-441, para 61, in which Dunlop provided, in unwritten terms, its exclusive distributors with absolute territorial protection and imposed on them an unwritten condition of sale prohibiting them from exporting its products to the territories of each of its distributors within the European market.

By contrast, a gentleman's agreement may be regarded as an agreement under Article 101 TFEU if its clauses amount to a 'faithful expression of the joint intention of the parties to the agreement and restrict competition' (see *Quinine Cartel*, paras 110–113; Case 44/69 *Buchler & Co v Commission* [1970] ECR 733, paras 25–26 and Case T-141/89 *Tréfileurope Sales SARL v Commission (Re Welded Steel Mesh Sector)* [1995] ECR II-791, para 96).

The mere participation of an undertaking, even not actively, in meetings between undertakings with an anti-competitive intention, will make it a party to an agreement or practice. This will notably be the case if the undertaking does not publicly distance itself from what is discussed at those meetings and gives the 'impression to the other participants that it subscribes to the outcome of the meetings and will act in conformity with it' (see Case T-9/99 *HFB Holding für Fernwärmetechnik Beteiligungsgesellschaft mbH & Co KG and Others v Commission* [2002] ECR II-1487, para 223; Case T-61/99 *Adriatica di Navigazione SpA v Commission* [2003] ECR II-5349, paras 91, 112, 118, 135–136; Case T-48/00 *Corus UK Ltd (Re Seamless Steel) v Commission* [2004] ECR II-2325, para 116 and Joined Cases T-67/00, T-68/00, T-71/00 and T-78/00 *JFE Engineering v Commission (Re Seamless Steel Tubes and Pipes)* [2004] ECR II-2501, para 327).

Even participation in meetings with an anti-competitive object against its will or under alleged constraint from other undertakings with greater economic power is no defence as the undertaking 'can always report the anti-competitive activities in question to the Commission rather than continue to participate in the meetings' (see *HFB Holding*, para 226; *Welded Steel Mesh Sector*, para 58; Case T-308/94 *Cascades SA v Commission* [1998] ECR II-925, para 122 and Case T-17/99 *KE KELIT v Commission (Re District Heating Pipes)* [2002] ECR II-1647, para 50).

As the Court put it in Case T-41/96 *Bayer AG v Commission* [2000] ECR II-3383, proof of an agreement between undertakings must be based on

> ... the direct or indirect finding of the existence of the subjective element that characterises the very concept of an agreement, that is to say a concurrence of wills between economic operators on the implementation of a policy, the pursuit of an objective, or the adoption of a given line of conduct on the market, irrespective of the manner in which the parties' intention to behave on the market in accordance with the terms of that agreement is expressed. (para 173)

In this case, the Court found that the mere continuation of commercial relations with a manufacturer who adopted a new policy which it implemented unilaterally did not amount to concurrence of wills with its wholesalers whose de facto conduct was clearly contrary to that policy.

It is also very clear from this case that, by definition, unilateral conducts escape the prohibition of Article 101(1) (see Case 107/82 *AEG-Telefunken v Commission* [1983] ECR 3151, para 38; Joined Cases 25/84 and 26/84 *Ford - Werke AG and Ford of Europe Inc v Commission* [1985] ECR 2725, para 21; Case T-43/92 *Dunlop Slazenger International Ltd v Commission* [1994] ECR II-441, para 56) and that this provision is concerned only with

> ... conduct that is coordinated bilaterally or multilaterally, in the form of agreements between undertakings, decisions by associations of undertakings and concerted practices. (para 64)

A clear distinction must therefore be drawn between an undertaking's genuine unilateral measure without the express or implied participation of another undertaking and a measure whose unilateral character is merely apparent. As a result, as the Court put it,

> ... the Commission cannot hold that apparently unilateral conduct on the part of a manufacturer, adopted in the context of the contractual relations which he maintains with his dealers, in reality forms the basis of an agreement ... if it does not establish the existence of an acquiescence by the other partners, express or implied, in the attitude adopted by the manufacturer. (para 72)

Article 101 TFEU may, however, be applicable to unilateral conducts in the context of long-term contracts with selected dealers such as in *AEG-Telefunken v Commission*, in which the Court found that the operation of a selective distribution system, where AEG, the manufacturer, refused to approve distributors who satisfied the qualitative criteria of the system in order to maintain a high level of prices or to exclude certain modern channels of distribution, was unlawful. The attitude of the manufacturer could not constitute unilateral conduct as, 'in the case of the admission of a distributor, approval [was] based on the acceptance, tacit or express, by the contracting parties of the policy pursued by AEG' (para 38).

Equally, in Joined Cases 25 and 26/84 *Ford - Werke AG and Ford of Europe Inc v Commission* [1985] ECR 2725, para 21, a decision of the motor manufacturer not to supply right-hand drive cars to German dealers so as to prevent them from exporting those cars to the UK market was assimilated to an agreement (see also Case T-62/98 *Volkswagen AG v Commission* [2000] ECR II-2707, para 236, as confirmed on appeal in Case C-338/00 *Volkswagen AG v Commission* [2003] ECR I-9189, para 60).

Article 101 is also applicable to agreements which produce their effects even after they have formally ceased to be in force (Case 51/75 *EMI Records Ltd v CBS United Kingdom Ltd* [1976] ECR 811, para 30). In this case, in which the proprietor of a trade mark in a Member State of the EU exercised his exclusive right to prevent the importation or marketing in that Member State of products bearing the same mark coming from a third country or manufactured in the EU by a subsidiary of the proprietor of the mark in that country, the ECJ ruled that

> [a]n agreement is only regarded as continuing to produce its effects if from the behaviour of the persons concerned there may be inferred the existence of elements of concerted practice and of coordination peculiar to the agreement and producing the same result as that envisaged by the agreement. (para 31)

This principle was confirmed in later cases such as Case 243/83 *SA Binon & Cie v Agence et Messagerie de la Presse SA* [1985] ECR 2015, para 17 and Case T-10/89 *Hoechst AG v Commission* [1992] ECR II-629, para 288, the latter concerning the participation of polypropylene producers in agreements and concerted practices for the determination of their commercial and pricing policies.

Decision by associations of undertakings

Article 101(1) TFEU does not prohibit the creation of associations of undertakings but rather the common intention to make decisions having an anti-competitive object (Case C-235/92 P *Montecatini SpA v Commission* [1999] ECR I-4539). This phrase is therefore particularly relevant to the conduct of trade associations.

In Case T-25/95 *Cimenteries CBR and Others v Commission* [2000] ECR II-491, the Court confirmed that it is not necessary for trade associations to have a commercial or economic activity of their own and Article 101(1) TFEU

> ... applies to associations in so far as their activities or those of the undertakings belonging to them are calculated to produce the results which it aims to suppress. (para 1320)

The concept of association of undertakings is broadly interpreted so as to include all forms of groupings of undertakings: commercial companies, non-profit associations, professional associations (Case C-309/99 *JCJ Wouters, JW Savelbergh, Price Waterhouse Belastingadviseurs BV v Algemene Raad van de Nederlandse Orde van Advocaten* [2002] ECR I-1577), economic interest groups, cooperative societies (Case T-61/89 *Dansk Pelsdyravlerforening v Commission* [1992] ECR II-1931), groupings without legal personality (*Cement* Commission Decision 94/815/EC ([1994] OJ L343/1)) or even a public law body (*AROW/BNIC* Commission Decision 82/896/EEC ([1982] OJ L379/1)).

'Decision' has to be understood as 'faithful expression of the applicants' intention to conduct themselves' in the internal market (see *van Landewyck Sàrl v Commission*

FEDETAB, para 86). The decision can take the form of a recommendation. According to Joined Cases 96-102, 104, 105, 108 and 110/82 *NV IAZ International Belgium v Commission (IAZ)* [1983] ECR 3369, it does not matter that the decision is not legally binding on the members of the association, as long as there is evidence that members complied with it so producing significant effects (*IAZ*, para 20 and *FEDETAB*, para 88). Here, an association of water supply undertakings recommended to its members not to connect certain dishwashers to the mains supply if they did not bear a conformity label issued by a Belgian manufacturers' association; this was held contrary to former Article 85 TEEC (now Article 101 TFEU) because it discriminated against non-Belgian machines.

Although a recommendation to members of an association, for instance to raise prices or boycott certain customers, could be challenged as a 'concerted practice' of its members, the word decision means that the trade association itself could be fined, and the making of the decision would be easier to prove than a concerted practice.

Concerted practice

The insertion of this phrase was intended to be an anti-avoidance device. However, its interpretation by the ECJ goes beyond the concept of a 'gentleman's agreement' to encompass the intentional coordination of market behaviour.

Two questions are raised here: what degree of coordination suffices and what sort of evidence is required?

The notion of concerted practice

The first question is answered in Case 48/69 *Imperial Chemical Industries Ltd v Commission (Re Dyestuffs)* [1972] ECR 619.

In the *Dyestuffs* case, the ECJ upheld the Commission's decision that there had been a concerted practice, as evidenced by the similarity of amount and timing of price increases, instructions issued by parents to subsidiaries and the fact that the various companies maintained informal contacts.

The Court describes a concerted practice as

> ... a form of coordination between undertakings which, without having reached the stage where an agreement properly so-called has been concluded, knowingly substitutes practical cooperation between them for the risks of competition. (para 64)

The Court carries on, stating that

> [b]y its very nature, then, a concerted practice does not have all the elements of a contract but may inter alia arise out of coordination which becomes apparent from the behaviour of the participants. (para 65)

In the following Case 40/73 *Suiker Unie v Commission (Re Sugar Cartel)* [1975] ECR 1663, the Court dismissed the argument put forward by sugar producers accused of acting to protect the position of two Dutch producers that there had been no plan worked out beforehand. Such a plan was not necessary. What mattered was direct or indirect contact between operators, the object or effect of which was to influence the conduct of the market or to disclose to a competitor a course of conduct proposed to be adopted.

From these two cases it can be seen that there must be

practical cooperation between [undertakings] which leads to conditions of competition which do not correspond to the normal conditions of the market, having regard to the nature of the products, the importance and number of the undertakings as well as the size and nature of [their] market. (*Suiker Unie*, para 26)

In other words, there must be a mental consensus to substitute cooperation for competition without it being achieved verbally as long as there is direct or indirect contact.

Evidence of a concerted practice

Proof of a concerted practice depends on circumstantial evidence. Much depends on the nature of the product, the size and nature of the undertakings and the volume of the market.

In the *Dyestuffs* case, the correspondence of behaviour showed a high degree of coordination between the various producers:

- price rises by similar amounts on three separate occasions;
- identical rates of individual increases;
- price rises applied to same dyestuffs;
- price rises effected on almost the same day;
- orders sent out on same day by producers had very similar wording; and
- attendance by producers at meetings.

However, although the ECJ stated in the *Sugar Cartel* case that the inference that there was a market sharing arrangement should not be too readily drawn as there might be other valid explanations as to why the market has been partitioned, in Case 107/82 *AEG-Telefunken v Commission* [1983] ECR 3151 the Court seemed prepared to accept the Commission's inference that supplier and distributors had reached a mutual understanding in addition to their existing contractual relationship.

A key issue here is whether coordinated behaviour enables the companies involved to foresee clearly and unequivocally the future conduct of their competitors.

In the *Wood Pulp Cartel case* (Commission Decision 85/202/EEC ([1985] OJ L85/1)), the Commission decided that 41 firms and two trade associations were parties to a concerted practice to fix the price of wood pulp although there was virtually no evidence of contact between the firms in question. As explained by the Court in Joined Cases C-89/85, C-104/85, C-114/85, C-116/85, C-117/85 and C-125/85 to C-129/85 *A Ahlström Osakeyhtiö and others v Commission* [1993] ECR I-1307, according to the Commission this was done through a system of quarterly price announcements

> ... which was deliberately introduced by the pulp producers in order to enable them to ascertain the prices that would be charged by their competitors in the following quarters. The disclosure of prices to third parties, especially to the press and agents working for several producers, well before their application at the beginning of a new quarter gave the other producers sufficient time to announce their own, corresponding, new prices before that quarter and to apply them from the commencement of that quarter. (para 60)

For the Commission,

> ... the implementation of that mechanism had the effect of making the market artificially transparent by enabling producers to obtain a rapid and accurate picture of the prices quoted by their competitors. (para 61)

Thus, in the Commission's view, the charging of parallel prices in a competitive market for heterogeneous goods where the producers were established in different countries facing different cost structures must have meant that there was a concerted practice. On appeal, the Court appeared to be more cautious and, after reiterating its definition of a concerted practice from the *Suiker Unie* case (para 63), came to the conclusion that

> [i]n this case, the communications arise from the price announcements made to users. *They constitute in themselves market behaviour which does not lessen each undertaking's uncertainty as to the future attitude of its competitors. At the time when each undertaking engages in such behaviour, it cannot be sure of the future conduct of the others.*
>
> Accordingly, the system of quarterly price announcements on the pulp market is not to be regarded as constituting in itself an infringement of Article [101(1)] of the Treaty. (paras 64–65, emphasis added)

Concerted practice and parallel behaviour

It is necessary to distinguish a firm's response to a competitor's conduct from consensual coordination. Parallel behaviour may be unobjectionable if products are interchangeable and there is an open price structure even if there are few competitors (*Dyestuffs* case).

The dividing line between mere parallel behaviour and a concerted practice is a hard one to spot especially in an oligopolistic market or industry. In such a market, the competition authorities are forced to rely on parallel conduct which, in the absence of evidence of contact, may simply be the natural result of having so few players on the market. In such case, economic theory suggests that similar behaviour (eg, price rises at the same time) by companies may just be the way an oligopolistic market operates.

As the Court observes in *A Ahlström Osakeyhtiö*, as confirmed in Case T-30/91 *Solvay SA v Commission* [1995] ECR II-1775, para 75:

> In determining the probative value of those different factors, it must be noted that parallel conduct cannot be regarded as furnishing proof of concertation unless concertation constitutes the only plausible explanation for such conduct. It is necessary to bear in mind that, although Article [101] of the Treaty prohibits any form of collusion which distorts competition, *it does not deprive economic operators of the right to adapt themselves intelligently to the existing and anticipated conduct of their competitors ...* (emphasis added)
>
> Accordingly, it is necessary in this case to ascertain whether the parallel conduct alleged by the Commission cannot, taking account of the nature of the products, the size and the number of the undertakings and the volume of the market in question, be explained otherwise than by concertation. (paras 71–72)

What should companies do to avert suspicion?

Although it might not always be easy for competition authorities to differentiate a concerted practice from parallel behaviour, undertakings should not feel overconfident and always seek to avert suspicion, as advised by the General Court.

in practice

In Case T-1/89 *Rhône-Poulenc SA v Commission (Re Polypropylene cartel)* [1991] ECR II-867, para 103, the Court set out the following guidance to undertakings:

- to have no contact, whether direct or indirect, with competitors;
- if such contact is intended, not to influence the conduct of a competitor or disclose to such competitors one's intended or possible conduct;
- undertakings must work out their policies for themselves;
- yet, they can adapt their policies intelligently to respond to the existing and anticipated conduct of their rivals.

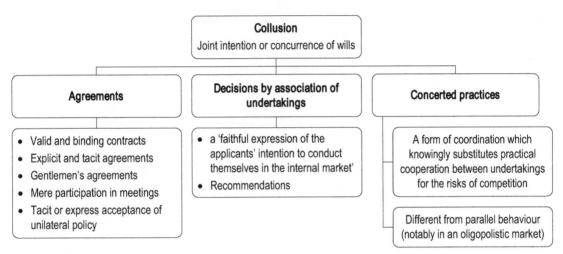

Figure 17.1   Collusion

17.2.2.2   Interference with competition

Article 101(1) TFEU will apply only where the agreement, decision or practice has 'as their object or effect to prevent, restrict or distort competition'. As the Court made it clear in Case 56/65 *Société Technique Minière v Maschinenbau Ulm* [1966] ECR 235:

> This interference with competition referred to in Article [101(1)] must result from all or some of the clauses of the agreement itself. Where, however, an analysis of the said clauses does not reveal the effect on competition to be sufficiently deleterious, the consequences of the agreement should then be considered and for it to be caught by the prohibition it is then necessary to find that those factors are present which show that competition has in fact been prevented or restricted or distorted to an appreciable extent. (at 249)

The determination and assessment of any interference with competition (inter-brand, namely between suppliers of competing brands, and/or intra-brand, that is between distributors of the same brand) is necessarily the result of a complex analysis of several elements of the agreement or practice.

The object or effect of the agreement or practice

The *STM* case made it clear that the words 'object or effect' are not 'cumulative but alternative requirements, indicated by the conjunction "or"' (at 249) and have to be read disjunctively. Therefore, it is first necessary to consider the purpose of the agreement; if that is unclear, then it must be decided whether the agreement might have harmful effects on competition.

As expressed in the Commission Guidelines on the application of Article 81(3) of the Treaty:

> The distinction between restrictions by object and restrictions by effect is important. Once it has been established that an agreement has as its object the restriction of competition, there is no need to take account of its concrete effects. In other words, for the purpose of applying Article [101(1)] no actual anti-competitive effects need to be demonstrated where the agreement has a restriction of competition as its object. (para 20)

There are therefore two categories of agreements: those whose anti-competitive effect can be assumed and those whose anti-competitive effect has to be demonstrated by analysing their economic context. According to the Court in Case C-8/08 *T-Mobile Netherlands BV, KPN Mobile NV, Orange Nederland NV and Vodafone Libertel NV v Raad van bestuur van de Nederlandse Mededingingsautoriteit* [2009] ECR I-4529:

> The distinction between 'infringements by object' and 'infringements by effect' arises from the fact that certain forms of collusion between undertakings can be regarded, *by their very nature*, as being injurious to the proper functioning of normal competition. (para 29, emphasis added)

More specifically, according to the Commission Guidelines on the application of Article 81(3) of the Treaty:

> Restrictions of competition by object are those that by their very nature have the potential of restricting competition. These are restrictions which in light of the objectives pursued by the [EU] competition rules have such a high potential of negative effects on competition that it is unnecessary for the purposes of applying Article [101(1)] to demonstrate any actual effects on the market. This presumption is based on the serious nature of the restriction and on experience showing that restrictions of competition by object are likely to produce negative effects on the market and to jeopardise the objectives pursued by the [EU] competition rules. Restrictions by object such as price fixing and market sharing reduce output and raise prices, leading to a misallocation of resources, because goods and services demanded by customers are not produced. They also lead to a reduction in consumer welfare, because consumers have to pay higher prices for the goods and services in question. (para 21)

Guidance on restrictions of competition by object can also be found in the Commission block exemption regulations and guidelines (see 17.2.4.2). Restrictions that are black-listed and/or identified as hardcore restrictions are regarded as restrictions by object. These usually include price-fixing, export bans, output limitation, sharing of markets and customers, fixed and minimum resale price maintenance; restrictions providing absolute territorial protection, and restrictions on passive sales.

In order to assess whether an agreement or practice contains restrictions by object, the facts surrounding it and the circumstances in which it operates will be examined:

content of the agreement, aims, context of its application, conduct and behaviour of the parties on the market, actual implementation (see *T-Mobile*, paras 27–28).

If the restriction by object is unclear, attention is then turned to the actual and potential restrictive effects of the agreement or practice. As explained in Case 23/67 *SA Brasserie de Haecht v Wilkin* [1967] ECR 525, it will be necessary to examine the particular product, measure competition in the rest of the relevant market (see **16.3**) and analyse how other competitors behave.

Article 101(1) TFEU provides a non-exhaustive list of agreements which have as their object the restriction of competition. These are agreements which:

(a) directly or indirectly fix purchase or selling prices or any other trading conditions (eg *Dyestuffs*: a concerted practice leading to parallel pricing over a number of years; Case 8/72 *Vereeniging van Cementhandelaren v Commission (Re Cement Cartel)* [1972] ECR 977: recommended prices issued by a trade association to its members; Joined Cases 43/82 and 63/82 *VBVB & VBBB v Commission (Re Dutch Books)* [1984] ECR 19: agreement relating to resale price maintenance; *Vitamins Cartel* Commission Decision 2003/2/EC ([2003] OJ L6/1) and Joined Cases T-22/02 and T-23/02 *Sumitomo Chemical Co Ltd and Sumika Fine Chemicals Co Ltd v Commission* [2005] ECR II-4065: price-fixing on the market of vitamin products; Case T-588/08 *Dole Food Company, Inc and Dole Germany OHG v Commission*, 14 March 2013, ECLI:EU:T:2013:130: coordination of quotation prices for bananas marketed in Northern Europe);

(b) limit or control production, markets, technical development, or investment (eg *Quinine Cartel*; *Zinc Producer Group* Commission Decision 84/405/EEC ([1984] OJ L220/27): quotas and restrictions on production);

(c) share markets or sources of supply (eg Joined Cases 56 and 58/64 *Établissements Consten SàRL and Grundig-Verkaufs-GmbH v Commission* [1966] ECR 429; *Quinine Cartel*; *Peroxygen products* Commission Decision 85/74/EEC ([1985] OJ L35/1); *Methylglucamine* Commission Decision 2004/104/EC ([2004] OJ L38/18): market sharing);

(d) apply dissimilar conditions to equivalent transactions with other trading parties, thereby placing them at a competitive disadvantage (eg *IAZ*: recommendation by an association of water supply undertakings not to connect certain dishwashers to the mains supply if they did not bear a conformity label; Case 26/76 *Metro SB-Grossmärkte GmbH & Co KG v Commission (Metro I)* [1977] ECR 1875: appointment of several distributors selected on the basis of other criteria);

(e) make the conclusion of contracts subject to acceptance by the other parties of supplementary obligations which, by their nature or according to commercial usage, have no connection with the subject of such contracts.

The prevention, restriction or distortion of competition

In *Consten and Grundig* the Court ruled that

> ... what is particularly important is whether the agreement is capable of constituting a threat, either direct or indirect, actual or potential, to freedom of trade between Member States in a manner which might harm the attainment of the objectives of a single market between States. Thus the fact that an agreement encourages an increase, even a large one, in the volume of trade between States is not sufficient to exclude the possibility that the agreement may 'affect' such trade ... (at 341)

What matters is therefore that the pattern of trade has changed. The key word is therefore 'distortion', namely an unlawful manipulation of the market.

Actual or potential competition must be restricted 'to such an extent that on the relevant market negative effects on prices, output, innovation or the variety or quality of goods and services can be expected with a reasonable degree of probability' (Guidelines, para 24). However, those negative effects must be appreciable. Should they be insignificant, the prohibition rule of Article 101(1) does not apply. In line with the economic approach of the Commission, the appreciability of those anti-competitive effects has to be based on a proper analysis of the relevant market.

The 'appreciable effect' concept, which appears to be a gloss added by the Court to Article 101(1), was first formulated in Case 5/69 *Franz Völk v SPRL Ets J Vervaecke* [1969] ECR 295 and confirmed in further cases such as Case C-238/05 *Asnef-Equifax, Servicios de Información sobre Solvencia y Crédito, SL v Asociación de Usuarios de Servicios Bancarios (Ausbanc)* [2006] ECR I-11125, para 50.

In the latter case, the Court stated that

> ... it should be emphasised that the appraisal of the effects of agreements or practices in the light of Article [101 TFEU] entails the need to take into consideration the actual context to which they belong, in particular the economic and legal context in which the undertakings concerned operate, the nature of the goods or services affected, as well as the real conditions of the functioning and the structure of the market or markets in question ...
>
> ... while Article [101(1) TFEU] does not restrict such an assessment to actual effects alone, as that assessment must also take account of the potential effects of the agreement or practice in question on competition within the [internal] market, an agreement will, however, fall outside the prohibition in Article [101] if it has only an insignificant effect on the market ... (paras 49–50)

If the aggregate market share involved is minute (eg 0.5% as in the *Völk* case) then the restrictive effect of the agreement will be deemed insignificant and the infringement of Article 101 will be ignored.

This gave rise to the de minimis doctrine, which was codified for the first time in the 1970 Commission Notice on agreements of minor importance which do not appreciably restrict competition under Article 85(1) of the Treaty Establishing the European Economic Community (De Minimis Notice).

The third version of 1986 laid down two criteria:

- the relevant products could not represent more than 5% of the total market for such products; and
- the participating undertakings could not have an aggregate turnover in excess of 300 million Ecus.

This threshold approach based on market share and aggregate turnover was abandoned in the 1997 version of the Notice. The Commission focused then on market shares alone. Paragraph 9 provided that agreements concerning goods and services would not fall within former Article 85 (now Article 101 TFEU) if the market share of the participating undertakings on the relevant markets did not exceed 5% in the case of horizontal or mixed horizontal/vertical agreements and 10% in the case of vertical agreements.

Those criteria were again modified under the 2001 De Minimis Notice and in its latest version of 2014 (Notice on agreements of minor importance which do not appreciably restrict competition under Article 101(1) of the Treaty on the Functioning of the European Union (De Minimis Notice) ([2014] OJ C291/1)).

Under paragraphs 8, 9 and 11 of the 2014 Notice, the focus is no longer on the horizontal/vertical agreement divide but on that between agreements involving competitors and those between non-competitors:

> The Commission holds the view that agreements between undertakings which may affect trade between Member States and which may have as their effect the prevention, restriction or distortion of competition within the internal market, do not appreciably restrict competition within the meaning of Article 101(1) of the Treaty:
>
> (a) if the aggregate market share held by the parties to the agreement does not exceed 10 % on any of the relevant markets affected by the agreement, where the agreement is made between undertakings which are actual or potential competitors on any of those markets (agreements between competitors); or
>
> (b) if the market share held by each of the parties to the agreement does not exceed 15 % on any of the relevant markets affected by the agreement, where the agreement is made between undertakings which are not actual or potential competitors on any of those markets (agreements between non-competitors). (para 8)
>
> In cases where it is difficult to classify the agreement as either an agreement between competitors or an agreement between non-competitors the 10 % threshold is applicable. (para 9)
>
> ...
>
> The Commission also holds the view that agreements do not appreciably restrict competition if the market shares of the parties to the agreement do not exceed the thresholds of respectively 10 %, 15 % and 5 % set out in points 8, 9 and 10 during two successive calendar years by more than 2 percentage points. (para 11)

Having said that, it should be noted that the economic impact of an agreement should be assessed in a wider context as an apparently minor agreement may fall foul of Article 101 if it is part of a network of similar agreements (see *Brasserie de Haecht,* at 415 and Case C-234/89 *Delimitis v Henninger Bräu* [1991] ECR I-935, para 14), as clearly expressed in paragraph 10 of the De Minimis Notice:

> Where, in a relevant market, competition is restricted by the cumulative effect of agreements for the sale of goods or services entered into by different suppliers or distributors (cumulative foreclosure effect of parallel networks of agreements having similar effects on the market), the market share thresholds set out in point 8 and 9 are reduced to 5 %, both for agreements between competitors and for agreements between non-competitors. Individual suppliers or distributors with a market share not exceeding 5 %, are in general not considered to contribute significantly to a cumulative foreclosure effect. A cumulative foreclosure effect is unlikely to exist if less than 30 % of the relevant market is covered by parallel (networks of) agreements having similar effects.

The market shares are calculated 'on the basis of sales value data or, where appropriate, purchase value data' (para 12) within the relevant product and geographic market as defined by reference to the Notice on the definition of relevant market (see **16.3**).

The De Minimis Notice therefore creates a 'safe harbour' for:

(a) categories of agreements not covered by a Commission block exemption regulation (see below **17.2.4.2**), such as, for instance, trade mark licence agreements and most categories of agreements between competitors; and

(b) agreements covered by a block exemption regulation containing an excluded restriction which, although not a hardcore restriction, does not benefit from the exemption of the application of Article 101(1) under the regulation (such as those in Article 5 of Commission Regulation 330/2010 on the application of Article 101(3) TFEU to categories of vertical agreements and concerted practices; Article 6 of Commission Regulation 1217/2010 on the application of Article 101(3) TFEU to certain categories of research and development agreements; and Article 5 of Commission Regulation 316/2014 on the application of Article 101(3) TFEU to categories of technology transfer agreements).

This Notice does not apply, however, to agreements which have as their object the prevention, restriction or distortion of competition within the internal market, such as:

- the fixing of prices when selling products to third parties;
- the limitation of output or sales; or
- the allocation of markets or customers.

Nor will the Notice cover agreements containing any of the restrictions that are listed as hardcore restrictions in one of the block exemption regulations.

According to paragraph 7, the De Minimis Notice is without prejudice to the interpretation of Article 101 TFEU by the Courts. For instance, in Case 30/78 *Distillers Company Limited v Commission* [1980] ECR 2229, the ECJ seemed to have felt that the quantitative approach in the 1977 Notice was inappropriate, holding that an agreement relating to the terms of supply for 'Pimms' was caught by former Article 85 TEEC (now Article 101 TFEU); sales of the drink outside the UK were minimal compared with other spirits but this was outweighed by the size of the applicants in relation to the drinks market as a whole.

The non-binding nature of the De Minimis Notice was confirmed by the Court in Case C-226/11 *Expedia Inc v Autorité de la concurrence and others*, 25 January 2013, ECLI:EU:C:2012:795, in which it stated that

> … in order to determine whether or not a restriction of competition is appreciable, the competition authority of a Member State may take into account the thresholds established in paragraph 7 of the *de minimis* notice but is not required to do so. Such thresholds are no more than factors among others that may enable that authority to determine whether or not a restriction is appreciable by reference to the actual circumstances of the agreement. (para 31)

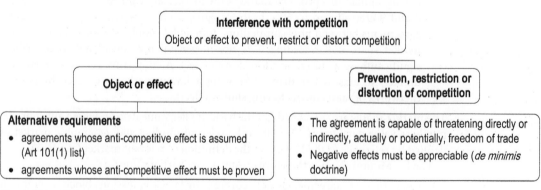

Figure 17.2   Object or effect on competition

17.2.3 Article 101(1) TFEU applies to horizontal and vertical agreements alike

At one time it was thought that former Article 85 TEEC (now Article 101 TFEU) only applied to horizontal agreements between competitors operating at the same level of the market (eg between manufacturers or between distributors) rather than vertical constraints between parties operating at a different level of the market (eg between manufacturers and distributors).

The ECJ dismissed this assumption in *Consten and Grundig*. Here there had been the appointment of an exclusive distributor in France which precluded other distributors competing with it for the sale of Grundig's products. This was caught by former Article 85 TEEC, it being irrelevant that the parties concerned operated at different levels in the market and that the agreement restricted intra-brand competition (the way Grundig's goods were dealt with) rather than inter-brand competition (preventing retailers selling rivals' products).

In this case, the Court ruled that

> Article [101] refers in a general way to all agreements which distort competition within the [internal] market and does not lay down any distinction between those agreements based on whether they are made between competitors operating at the same level in the economic process or between non-competing persons operating at different levels. In principle, no distinction can be made where the treaty does not make any distinction. (at 339)

17.2.3.1 Horizontal agreements

Apart from the obvious horizontal anti-competitive agreements in the form of cartels which are entered into to limit competition, there exist a number of horizontal 'cooperation agreements' which are entered into for pro-competitive reasons which may outweigh their anti-competitive effects.

The Commission in its Guidelines on the applicability of Article 101 of the Treaty on the Functioning of the European Union to horizontal co-operation agreements ([2011] OJ C11/01) recognises fully the dual nature of horizontal cooperation agreements which on the one hand

> ... can lead to substantial economic benefits, in particular if they combine complementary activities, skills or assets [and] can be a means to share risk, save costs, increase investments, pool know-how, enhance product quality and variety, and launch innovation faster,

while

> on the other hand ... may lead to competition problems ... for example ... if the parties agree to fix prices or output or to share markets, or if the co-operation enables the parties to maintain, gain or increase market power and thereby is likely to give rise to negative market effects with respect to prices, output, product quality, product variety or innovation. (paras 2–3)

These Guidelines provide an analytical framework based on legal and economic criteria for most categories of horizontal cooperation agreements, namely:

- research and development agreements which may concern the acquisition of know-how, theoretical analyses, studies and experiments relating to products or process, and may be structured in various ways including a joint venture;
- production agreements including subcontracting (whereby a contractor entrusts production of a product to a subcontractor), unilateral specialisation (whereby one

firm gives up the manufacture of certain products or provision of services in favour of another party), reciprocal specialisation (whereby each participant gives up the manufacture of certain products or provision of certain services in favour of another party) and joint production (the participants jointly manufacture certain products or provide services);

- purchasing agreements, often concluded by small and medium-sized companies, concerning the joint buying of products;
- commercialisation agreements which involve cooperation between competitors in the selling, distribution or promotion of their products;
- standardisation agreements, including standard contracts and information exchange, aiming at defining technical or quality requirements with which current or future products, processes or methods may comply; and
- environmental agreements whereby the parties undertake to achieve pollution abatement or environmental objectives.

17.2.3.2 Vertical agreements

The Commission Guidelines on Vertical Restraints ([2010] OJ C130/01) define a vertical agreement as an

> ... agreement or concerted practice entered into between two or more undertakings each of which operates, for the purposes of the agreement or the concerted practice, at a different level of the production or distribution chain, and relating to the conditions under which the parties may purchase, sell or resell certain goods or services. (para 24)

A producer of goods or services faces the choice of vertical integration (by arranging its own distribution through its own organisation or via a subsidiary company) or by appointing an agent. The Commission has tended to adopt a benevolent attitude here because there may be beneficial effects on both sides. As stated in paragraph 6:

> For most vertical restraints, competition concerns can only arise if there is insufficient competition at one or more levels of trade, that is, if there is some degree of market power at the level of the supplier or the buyer or at both levels. Vertical restraints are generally less harmful than horizontal restraints and may provide substantial scope for efficiencies.

Examples of vertical agreements include:

- exclusive distribution whereby a supplier agrees to sell its products to only one distributor for resale in particular territory;
- exclusive customer allocation whereby a supplier agrees to sell its products to only one distributor for resale to particular class of customer;
- selective distribution whereby a supplier agrees to sell its products to selected (or authorised) distributors;
- franchising, under which a franchiser licenses the franchisee to use intellectual property rights (trade marks, signs, know-how) for the use and distribution of goods and services and also provides the franchisee with commercial and technical assistance;
- exclusive supply: for a particular final product, only one buyer inside the EU to which the supplier may sell it; and for intermediate goods or services, only one buyer in the EU or only one buyer in the EU for the purpose of a specific use (also known as industrial supply);

- single branding whereby the buyer has an obligation or incentive to purchase practically all its requirements on a particular market from one supplier only;
- tying whereby the supplier makes the sale of one product (tying product) conditional upon the purchase of another distinct product (tied product) from the supplier or someone designated by the supplier;
- recommended and maximum resale prices whereby the supplier recommends a resale price to the reseller or requires the reseller to respect a maximum resale price.

Some agreements, such as technology transfer agreements (TTAs), are regarded as mixed agreements as they combine horizontal and vertical aspects.

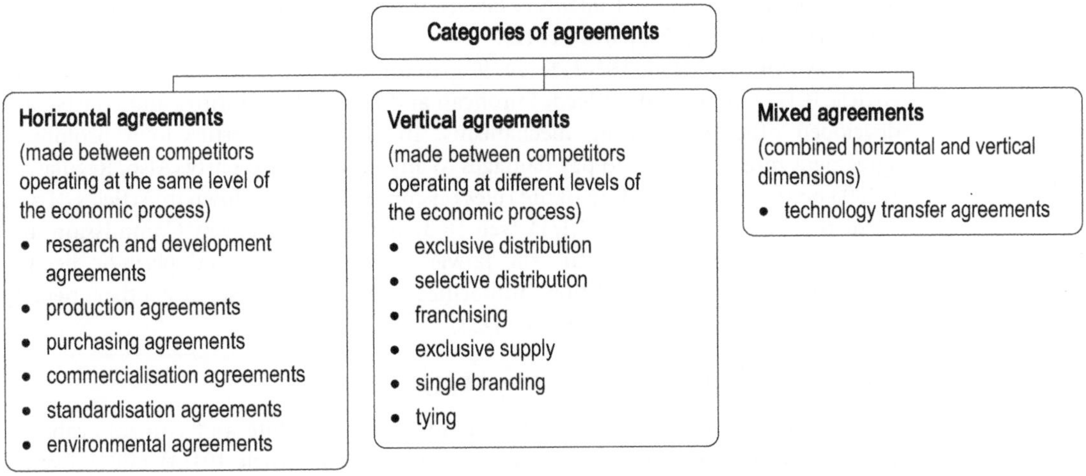

Categories of agreements

Horizontal agreements
(made between competitors operating at the same level of the economic process)
- research and development agreements
- production agreements
- purchasing agreements
- commercialisation agreements
- standardisation agreements
- environmental agreements

Vertical agreements
(made between competitors operating at different levels of the economic process)
- exclusive distribution
- selective distribution
- franchising
- exclusive supply
- single branding
- tying

Mixed agreements
(combined horizontal and vertical dimensions)
- technology transfer agreements

Figure 17.3   Categories of agreements

17.2.4   The nullity of a restrictive agreement under Article 101(2) TFEU

Article 101(2) TFEU provides that:

> All agreements or decisions prohibited pursuant to this Article shall be automatically void.

The effect of this paragraph was stressed by the ECJ notably in Case C-453/99 *Courage Ltd v Crehan and Crehan v Courage Ltd and Others* [2001] ECR I-6297:

> … according to Article 3(g) of the EC Treaty … Article [101] of the Treaty constitutes a fundamental provision which is essential for the accomplishment of the tasks entrusted to the [EU] and, in particular, for the functioning of the internal market …
>
> Indeed, the importance of such a provision led the framers of the Treaty to provide expressly, in Article [101(2)] of the Treaty, that any agreements or decisions prohibited pursuant to that article are to be automatically void …
>
> That principle of automatic nullity can be relied on by anyone, and the courts are bound by it once the conditions for the application of Article [101(1)] are met and so long as the agreement concerned does not justify the grant of an exemption under Article [101(3)] of the Treaty … Since the nullity referred to in Article [101(2)] is absolute, an agreement which is null and void by virtue of this

provision has no effect as between the contracting parties and cannot be set up against third parties .... Moreover, it is capable of having a bearing on all the effects, either past or future, of the agreement or decision concerned ... (paras 20–22)

However, as the Court stated in the *STM* case:

... automatic nullity in question only applies to those parts of the agreement affected by the prohibition, or to the agreement as a whole if it appears that those parts are not severable from the agreement itself. (at 250)

The consequences of such nullity for the remaining part of the agreement are not to be determined under EU law but by national courts according to their own law (Case 319/82 *Société de Vente de Ciments et Bétons de l'Est SA v Kerpen & Kerpen GmbH und Co KG* [1983] ECR 4173, paras 11–12).

The wording of Article 101(2) leaves it open for other sanctions for infringements of Article 101(1) to be used. Indeed, European and national authorities and courts have developed other sanctioning mechanisms. In effect, the parties to a prohibited agreement might be liable to pay damages to any injured third party. Also, Regulation 1/2003 on the implementation of the rules on competition laid down in Articles 81 and 82 of the Treaty ([2003] OJ L1/1) (see 18.3) gives the European Commission and national competition authorities the power to impose fines and periodic penalty payments. National competition authorities can also impose any other penalty provided for in their national law (see 18.3).

17.2.5 Exemptions under Article 101(3) TFEU

The prohibition rule of Article 101(1) TFEU is not absolute and is inapplicable to agreements which satisfy the conditions provided for in Article 101(3) TFEU. Even if they affect competition, agreements are a constituent part of the market and may have beneficial effects. For instance, agreements whose purpose is to promote technical and technological progress might contribute to economic and social progress. Far from prohibiting such agreements – which could prove counter-productive – EU competition law endeavours rather to promote them. As the Commission Guidelines on the application of Article 81(3) of the Treaty state:

The assessment of restrictions by object and effect under Article [101(1)] is only one side of the analysis. The other side, which is reflected in Article [101(3)], is the assessment of the positive economic effects of restrictive agreements. (para 32)

While competition rules aim to protect competition on the market as a way of 'enhancing consumer welfare and of ensuring an efficient allocation of resources', agreements which restrict competition may equally have pro-competitive effects by way of efficiency gains. Agreements whose pro-competitive effects outweigh its anti-competitive effects will then be deemed to be 'on balance pro-competitive and compatible with the objectives of the [EU] competition rules' (Guidelines, para 33).

For this reason, Article 101(3) TFEU 'sets out an exception rule, which provides a defence to undertakings against a finding of an infringement of Article [101(1)] of the Treaty' (Guidelines, para 1) in the form of individual and collective exemptions.

Article 101(3) TFEU provides that:

The provisions of paragraph 1 may, however, be declared inapplicable in the case of:

- any agreement or category of agreements between undertakings,
- any decision or category of decisions by associations of undertakings,
- any concerted practice or category of concerted practices,

which contributes to improving the production or distribution of goods or to promoting technical or economic progress, while allowing consumers a fair share of the resulting benefit, and which does not:

(a) impose on the undertakings concerned restrictions which are not indispensable to the attainment of these objectives;

(b) afford such undertakings the possibility of eliminating competition in respect of a substantial part of the products in question.

Until the coming into force on 1 May 2004 of Regulation 1/2003, Regulation 17/62 granted exclusive powers to the Commission to grant exemptions under former Articles 85(3) TEEC and 81(3) TEC (now Article 101(3) TFEU). While this centralised enforcement of European competition law made sense and was necessary in the early stages of the European integration when economic markets were still defined along national borders, it became increasingly cumbersome. In the wake of the 2004 enlargement to Eastern and Central European countries, Regulation 1/2003 decentralised the exemption procedure and transferred those powers to national competition authorities and courts (see **18.2**).

17.2.5.1 The general economy of Article 101(3) TFEU

By definition, Article 101(3) TFEU applies only to an agreement between undertakings that distorts competition and is caught under Article 101(1). There is therefore no need to examine any benefits generated by non-restrictive agreements.

Article 101(3) can be invoked as a defence where the restrictive agreement satisfies four cumulative requirements (see Case T-185/00 *Métropole télévision SA (M6) v Commission* [2002] ECR II-3805, para 86 and Case T-17/93 *Matra Hachette SA v Commission* [1994] ECR II-595, para 104). This means that all conditions must be fulfilled for the exemption to be granted. Failing that, the application of the exception rule is refused and the agreement will be deemed to be null and void under Article 101(2) TFEU (see Case T-213/00 *CMA CGM and others v Commission* [2003] ECR II-913, para 226; see also above at **17.2.3**). Furthermore, those requirements are exhaustive (see Case 26/76 *Metro I* [1977] ECR 1875, para 43 and *Matra*, para 139).

While, in principle, all anti-competitive agreements and practices fulfilling Article 101(3) conditions are covered by the exception rule (see *Matra*, para 85), agreements containing hardcore or black-listed restrictions are very unlikely to be as they would generally fail to satisfy the first two conditions (objective benefits and a fair share for consumers) (Case T-29/92 *Vereniging van Samenwerkende Prijsregelende Organisaties in de Bouwnijverheid and others v Commission* [1995] ECR II-289, para 256) and the third one (no indispensable restrictions, known as the indispensability test) (Case 258/78 *LC Nungesser KG and Eisele v Commission* [1982] ECR 2015, para 77).

The first two requirements are positive conditions (objective benefits and a fair share for consumers) and the last two negative ones (no indispensable restrictions and no substantial elimination of competition).

Objective benefits

In the words of the Article, the restrictive agreement must 'contribute to improving the production or distribution of goods' or it must 'promote technical or economic progress'. Although express reference is made to goods only, services are also covered by Article 101(3).

According to the settled case law, only objective benefits or efficiency gains can be taken in consideration. As the Court stated in *Consten and Grundig*,

> … improvement must in particular show *appreciable objective advantages of such a character as to compensate for the disadvantages* which they cause in the field of competition. (at 348, emphasis added)

As Article 101(3) applies only where the pro-competitive effects of an agreement outweigh its anti-competitive ones, an analysis has to be made to determine what the objective benefits of the agreements are and the economic value of those claimed efficiencies. A direct causal link between the agreement and the claimed benefits must therefore be established. As explained in the Commission Guidelines on the application of Article 81(3):

> All efficiency claims must therefore be substantiated so that the following can be verified:
>
> (a) The nature of the claimed efficiencies;
> (b) The link between the agreement and the efficiencies;
> (c) The likelihood and magnitude of each claimed efficiency; and
> (d) How and when each claimed efficiency would be achieved. (para 51)

The case law also shows that there can be a considerable overlap between these benefits as the categories of efficiencies covered in Article 101(3) are very broadly defined. Objective benefits, such as cost and quality efficiencies, usually result from an integration of economic activities and assets, enabling parties to an agreement to achieve certain objectives more efficiently together that they would separately. Examples include specialisation agreements, research and development agreements, and exclusive or selective dealership agreements.

Fair share for consumers

The second condition of Article 101(3) provides that consumers must receive 'a fair share of the resulting benefit' generated by the agreement. The 'consumers' to be benefited need not be members of the public, but can be direct or indirect customers of one of the parties, namely manufacturers of other products, wholesalers, retailers and final consumers.

'Fair share' must be understood as the pass-on of benefits to consumers, compensating the latter for the negative effects of the restriction of competition they would suffer.

Either the negative effects on the consumers are outweighed or at least neutralised by the positive effects of the agreement and the agreement then fulfils the second condition, or they are not and the agreement does not satisfy the condition. It is not expected that consumers receive a share of every single claimed improvement but sufficient benefits outweighing and compensating the negative impact of the agreement, as demonstrated in the *Metro I* case.

In *Metro I*, Metro challenged the Commission's decision to grant negative clearance to SABA's selective distribution system for its TVs, SABA having refused to supply Metro because it did not meet the stipulated conditions. The ECJ upheld the idea of selective distribution agreements, but stated that:

- the goods must be of a type where it is legitimate to restrict the number and type of retail outlets. Hence watches, jewellery, perfume, cars, consumer durables and personal computers are all suitable goods for selective distribution, but plumbing fittings are not;
- the outlets must be chosen on the basis of objective, qualitative criteria, eg that the distributor has a specialised department dealing in the goods; employs trained staff; offers after-sales service; displays the goods in an attractive manner; deals in a wide and varied range of the contract goods; has a favourable credit rating. However, dealers must not be selected on the basis of quantitative criteria;
- the restrictions must be no more than is necessary to protect the quality of the goods (proportionality);
- there must be no refusal to supply a qualified retailer because this may be a disguised attempt to maintain prices or divide the market.

With regard to the fair share of benefits for consumers, the Court pointed out that

> ... regular supplies represent a sufficient advantage to consumers for them to be considered to constitute a fair share of the benefit resulting from the improvement brought about by the restriction on competition permitted by the Commission. (para 48)

A claim of general consumer welfare is often dismissed, however, as in *VBBB and VBVB Agreement* (Commission Decision 82/123/EEC ([1982] OJ L54/36)). In this case, the rejoinder was that the resale price maintenance scheme for books in the Flemish language in fact deprived consumers of choice and prevented them from getting discounts.

No indispensable restrictions

The third condition of Article 101(3) is that the agreement must not 'impose on the undertaking concerned restrictions which are not indispensable to the attainment' of the benefits above.

The concept of proportionality is relevant here. The agreement itself and the restrictions of competition it contains must be necessary to achieve those benefits. The issue is whether or not more benefits are produced as the result of a more efficient activity under the restrictive agreement than there would be without such an agreement. The parties to the agreement must demonstrate that the efficiencies produced by the agreement are specific to it and that there are no other realistic and less restrictive alternatives to achieve those efficiencies, and that they could not have achieved them on their own.

If the agreement is found to be necessary to achieve those benefits, it must then be assessed if the restrictions of competition it contains are reasonably necessary. The more serious the restriction, the stricter the test, as demonstrated in Case T-86/95 *Compagnie générale maritime and others v Commission* [2002] ECR II-1011, concerning an agreement between ship owners which fixed the price of transport services and the transport capacity management programme for containers to the Far East. In this case, the Court stated that

... the contested agreement entails restrictions of competition that are not only extremely serious, but are, above all, not indispensable for attaining the objective of stability alleged by the applicants. (para 396)

By definition, as the Guidelines state:

Restrictions that are black listed in block exemption regulations or identified as hardcore restrictions in Commission guidelines and notices are unlikely to be considered indispensable. (para 79)

Should a restriction of competition be indispensable for a certain period of time only, exemption from Article 101(1) TFEU will apply only for that time, in which case a detailed assessment of the length of time required to achieve the benefits has to be made, notably of the period of time required to ensure a proper return on the investments needed to achieve those benefits (see Case T-374/94 *European Night Services Ltd (ENS) and others v Commission* [1998] ECR II-3141, para 230).

No substantial elimination of competition

Finally, Article 101(3) provides that the agreement must not 'afford [the] undertakings the possibility of eliminating competition in respect of a substantial part of the products in question'. As the aim of Article 101 TFEU is to maintain and protect competition between undertakings as a driver for economic efficiency, no elimination of competition can ever be justified by short-term benefits.

It is necessary here to define the relevant product and geographical markets (see **16.3**) before deciding whether the agreement has no eliminating effect. The Commission tends to be sceptical of this claim in the case where an undertaking controls a large market share. The Commission examines not only the terms of the agreement but also how they are implemented and what their practical effects are. For instance, in *Ford - Werke AG*, the Commission refused to approve a standard distribution agreement entered into by Ford Germany with all its main dealers because, as implemented, it did affect competition in that Ford ceased to supply right-hand drive models to its German distributors so as to protect Ford of UK. This deprived consumers of the possibility of making personal imports. The ECJ agreed with the Commission's conclusion that the refusal to supply compartmentalised markets.

An agreement eliminating any important expression of competition such as, for instance, price competition (see *Metro I*, para 21; Case 161/84 *Pronuptia de Paris GmbH v Pronuptia de Paris Irmgard Schillgallis* [1986] ECR 353: clauses limiting the franchisee's activities, such as price determination clauses, are not considered acceptable) will never satisfy this fourth condition.

Finally, elimination of competition must occur 'in respect of a substantial part of the products in question', an autonomous EU law concept specific to Article 101(3) (see Case T-395/94 *Atlantic Container Line AB and Others v Commission* [2002] ECR II-875, para 330).

Once those four conditions are met, the agreement is regarded as improving competition by providing consumers cheaper or better products, thus outweighing its adverse effects on competition. It is to be noted, however, that the compatibility of an agreement with Article 101 TFEU does not prejudice the application of, and its compatibility with, Article 102 TFEU on abuse of dominant position (see below **17.3**) (see Case T-51/89 *Tetra Pak Rausing SA v Commission* [1990] ECR II-309, para 29 and

Joined Cases T-191/98, T-212/98 to T-214/98 *Atlantic Container Line AB and Others v Commission* [2003] ECR II-3275, para 1456).

Individual exemptions	**Article 101(3) TFEU**	**Block exemptions**
• applied by the European Commission and national competition authorities and courts • under Articles 5, 6 and 10 of Regulation 1/2003	• Economic benefits: improving production or distribution of goods, or promoting technical or economic progress • fair share for consumers • no indispensable restriction of competition • no elimination of competition	• apply to categories of horizontal, vertical or mixed agreements • adopted by the Council under Article 103(2)(b) TFEU and the Commission under delegated powers under Article 105(3) TFEU

Figure 17.4   Article 101(3)

Article 101(3) applies to individual agreements as well as to categories of agreements by way of block exemption regulations.

17.2.5.2 Block exemptions

In order to alleviate its own pressure of work and to enable undertakings to be able to implement agreements without having to wait for clearance (see **18.3.2**), the Commission drafted a series of regulations dealing with certain types of standard agreements on the basis of Article 105(3) TFEU. Used since the late 1960s (Regulation 67/67 on exclusive dealing agreements ([1967] OJ L57/849) was the first one), block exemption regulations (BERs) have become a well-established means of application of EU competition rules. Since then, many generations of regulations have reflected the economic development and evolution of European competition law.

Taking more account of market power usually assessed on the market shares of the parties to an agreement, the European Commission has gradually abandoned a formalistic and legalistic approach to espouse a more sophisticated economic analysis. This new approach materialised in the adoption of the second generation of regulations at the turn of this century.

The first regulation of this new generation was Regulation 2790/99 ([1999] OJ L336/21), a single exemption regulation on vertical agreements and concerted practices which replaced a series of three individual ones on distribution agreements.

It was soon followed by the adoption of two regulations on horizontal agreements: Regulation 2658/2000 on specialisation ([2000] OJ L304/3) and Regulation 2659/2000 on research and development (R&D) ([2000] OJ L304/7), which replaced their respective predecessors of 1985.

On the expiry of those BERs, a third generation of regulations and new guidelines were adopted in 2010 (Regulation 330/2010 on vertical agreements ([2010] OJ L102/1)) and 2011 (Regulations 1218/2010 on specialisation ([2010] OJ L335/43) and 1217/2010 on R&D ([2010] OJ L335/36)) with the view to modernising the previous regulations.

While agreements are generally classified as vertical and horizontal agreements, some, such as technology transfer agreements (TTAs) covered by Regulation 316/2014 ([2014] OJ L93/17), are regarded as mixed ones since they may contain horizontal and vertical restraints.

First generation	Second generation	Third generation
• Regulation 67/67 on exclusive dealings	• Regulation 2790/1999 on vertical agreements and concerted practices	• Regulation 330/2010 on vertical agreements and concerted practices
• Regulation 1983/83 on exclusive distribution agreements	• Regulation 2658/2000 on specialisation agreements	• Regulations 1218/2010 on specialisation agreements
• Regulation 1984/83 on exclusive purchasing agreements	• Regulation 2659/2000 on research and development agreements	• Regulation 1217/2010 on research and development agreements
• Regulation 4087/88 on franchise agreements	• Regulation 1400/2002 on vehicle distribution agreements	• Regulation 461/2010 on vehicle distribution agreements
• Regulation 417/85 on specialisation agreements	• Regulation 823/2000 on agreements between liner shipping companies (consortia)	• Regulation 316/2014 on technology transfer agreements
• Regulation 418/85 on research and development agreements	• Regulation 258/2003 on agreements in the insurance sector	• Regulation 487/2009 on air transport sector
	• Regulation 772/2004 on technology transfer agreements	• Regulation 267/2010 on agreements in the insurance sector
	• Regulation 1459/2006 on passenger tariffs on scheduled air services and slot allocations at airports	• Regulation 906/2009 as amended by Regulation 697/2014 on agreements between liner shipping companies (consortia)
	• Regulation 169/2009 applying rules of competition to transport by rail, road and inland waterway	

Figure 17.5   Block exemption regulations

Compared to individual exemptions, BERs have two main benefits:

• they simplify the exemption procedure for economic agents and operators; and
• they offer greater legal certainty to undertakings which no longer have to seek individual negative clearance from the Commission.

They also provide undertakings with valuable information on standard agreements and their compatibility with competition rules. Provided an agreement complies with the model prescribed by the relevant regulation, it will be deemed compatible with Article 101(1) TFEU. This presumption is not without limits, however, as the European Commission and national competition authorities have, within their respective jurisdiction, the power to withdraw such exemption provided they can demonstrate that the agreement concerned does not satisfy the conditions of Article 101(3) TFEU.

All BERs follow a set pattern:

• they commence with a preamble (which is an important guide to subsequent interpretation);
• they define the agreements they apply to and grant exemption from Article 101(1) to those which comply with the regulation terms;
• they set aggregate market share thresholds beyond which exemption is not applicable (eg, 20% for specialisation and technology transfer agreements; 25% for

research and development agreements; and 30% for vertical agreements). This is an indication that the higher the threshold, the less harmful to competition an agreement is viewed; and

- they list prohibited hardcore restrictions (which prevent exemption) and the severable non-exempted restrictions (although prohibited, they do not prevent the remainder of the agreement from the benefit of the block exemption, so long as they can be severed from the agreement).

Those regulations need to be read in light of their respective guidelines, the purpose of which is to provide guidance on the application of the BERs. They are without prejudice to the interpretation of Article 101 TFEU and those rulings that the Courts may give. These are:

- Guidelines on vertical restraints ([2010] OJ C130/01);
- Supplementary guidelines on vertical restraints in agreements for the sale and repair of motor vehicles and for the distribution of spare parts for motor vehicles ([2010] OJ C138/05);
- Guidelines on the application of Article 101 TFEU to horizontal co-operation agreements ([2011] OJ C11/01); and
- Guidelines on the application of Article 101 TFEU to technology transfer agreements ([2014] OJ C89/03).

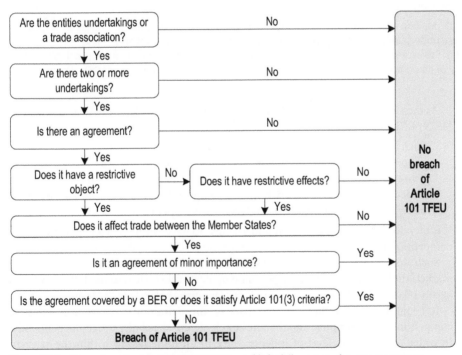

Figure 17.6 How a breach of Article 101 TFEU is established ('agreement' covers agreements, decisions of associations of undertakings and concerted practices)

17.3 Abuse of dominant position

There are various economic objections to a monopoly. However, a pure monopoly, just like pure competition, is extremely rare, and competition law has to concern itself with firms with a sufficiently large market share to be able to derive benefits analogous to those of a monopolist. Article 102 TFEU places great emphasis on the idea of market power, a concept which has to be broken down into three separate issues:

- the relevant product and geographical market (see **16.3**);
- the market power within that relevant market; and
- within a substantial part of the internal market

Under Article 102 TFEU:

> Any abuse by one or more undertakings of a dominant position within the internal market or a substantial part of it shall be prohibited as incompatible with the internal market in so far as it may affect trade between Member States.

17.3.1 Market power

Unlike Article 66(7) of the now expired ECSC Treaty (see **1.5**), which defined dominant position as protecting undertakings from effective competition in a substantial part of the (common) market, Article 102 TFEU offers no such definition. The relevant test is that laid down in Case 27/76 *United Brands v Commission* [1978] ECR 207 (see **16.3**).

In *United Brands*, the Court ruled that

[t]he dominant position thus referred to relates to a position of economic strength enjoyed by an undertaking which enables it to prevent effective competition being maintained on the relevant market by affording it the power to behave to an appreciable extent independently of its competitors, customers and ultimately of its consumers. (para 65)

case example

As the Court further put it in Case 85/76 *Hoffmann-La Roche & Co AG v Commission* [1979] ECR 461:

> Such a position does not preclude some competition, which it does where there is a monopoly or a quasi-monopoly, but enables the undertakings which profit by it, if not to determine, at least to have an appreciable influence on the conditions under which that competition will develop and in any case to act largely in disregard of it so long as such conduct does not operate to its detriment. (para 39)

It is therefore not necessary for an undertaking 'to have eliminated all opportunity for competition in order to be in a dominant position' (*United Brands*, para 113).

Such dominance can exist not only in the supplier market but also in the buyer market, such as, for instance, the purchase of air travel services in the UK from travel agents (Case T-219/99 *British Airways Plc v Commission* [2003] ECR II-5917).

It could be argued that the first part of the definition – preventing effective competition – is descriptive and that the key element is the ability to act independently. In order to assess the level of independence of an undertaking within the relevant market, the size of the firm's market share is obviously a key question, though by no means conclusive. Save in exceptional circumstances, very large shares are in themselves evidence of the existence of a dominant position (see *Hoffmann-La Roche*, para 41). The case law shows that a market share of over 50% in itself constitutes a rebuttable presumption of the existence of a dominant position on the market in question (Case C-62/86 *AKZO Chemie BV v Commission* [1991] ECR I-3359, para 60). This view is corroborated in the Guidance on the Commission's enforcement priorities in applying Article 82 of the EC Treaty to abusive exclusionary conduct by dominant undertakings ([2009] OJ C45/2), in which the Commission indicates that

> [e]xperience suggests that the higher the market share and the longer the period of time over which it is held, the more likely it is that it constitutes an important preliminary indication of the existence of a dominant position and, in certain circumstances, of possible serious effects of abusive conduct … (para 15)

Typical examples of such large market shares can be found in Case T-201/04 *Microsoft Corp v Commission* [2007] ECR II-3601 (over 90% of client PC operating systems and at least 60% of work group server operating systems market shares), Joined Cases T-24/93, T-25/93, T-26/93 and T-28/93 *Compagnie maritime belge transports SA and Compagnie maritime belge SA, Dafra-Lines A/S, Deutsche Afrika-Linien GmbH & Co and Nedlloyd Lijnen BV v Commission* [1996] ECR II-1201 (90% of maritime transport between Zaire and ports in northern Europe market share), *Hoffmann-La Roche* (85% of the vitamins A, B2, B3, B6, C and E markets), Case T-83/91 *Tetra Pak International SA v Commission* [1994] ECR II-755 (90% of the markets in aseptic machines and cartons intended for the packaging of liquid foods), Case T-228/97 *Irish Sugar plc v Commission* [1999] ECR II-2969 (market share of industrial sugar market and retail sugar market over 90%) and Case T-30/89 *Hilti AG v Commission* [1991] ECR II-1439 (70 to 80% of the market of powder-actuated fastening nails and cartridge strips and 55% of the nail guns market).

But how small a share can a firm hold and yet still have a dominant position? While it is clear that a 10% market share is too small to constitute dominant position if there are no exceptional circumstances (see Case 75/84 *Metro SB-Großmärkte v Commission (Metro II)* [1986] ECR 3021), the case law shows that even firms with less than 50% of the market can be caught by Article 102. In some of the decisions such as *United Brands*, it can be queried whether by drawing the relevant product and geographical market too narrowly, the Commission then has the chance to overstate the market share, particularly as it tends to ignore pressures placed on the relevant undertaking from outside the relevant market. It would seem, however, that a market share of between 40 and 45% is generally enough to give rise to a dominant position, especially if all the rival firms have very small shares. In *Virgin/British Airways* Commission Decision 2000/74/EC ([2000] OJ L30/1), the Commission held British Airways to be in a dominant position in the market for air travel agency services, its share being 39.7% while that of Virgin, its nearest rival, was only 5.5%. The relationship between the market shares of the leading undertaking and of its next largest competitors therefore enables the competitive strength of the undertaking to be accurately assessed.

The way the market share is calculated is clearly explained in the Commission Notice on the definition of relevant market for the purposes of Community competition law ([1997] OJ C372/5). Paragraph 53 states that

> [t]he definition of the relevant market in both its product and geographic dimensions allows the identification the suppliers and the customers/consumers active on that market. On that basis, a total market size and market shares for each supplier can be calculated on the basis of their sales of the relevant products in the relevant area.

These are usually available from 'companies' estimates, studies commissioned from industry consultants and/or trade associations'.

While a substantial market share as evidence of the existence of a dominant position is a highly important factor, it is not a constant one and its importance may vary from market to market in accordance with their structure. In *Hoffmann-La Roche*, the Court also recognised that 'the existence of a dominant position may derive from several factors' (para 39). Such relevant factors in assessing market power include, among others:

- technical and commercial advantages such as the technological lead of an undertaking over its competitors (*Hoffmann-La Roche*) and the existence of a highly developed sales network (Case 322/81 *NV Nederlandsche Banden Industrie Michelin v Commission (Michelin I)* [1983] ECR 3461);
- the absence of potential competition as the consequence of the existence of barriers preventing new competitors from having access to the market (Case 22/78 *Hugin Kassaregister AB and Hugin Cash Registers Ltd v Commission* [1979] ECR 1869; *Tetra Pak II*; *United Brands*);
- access to capital and vertical integration (*United Brands*; Case T-340/03 *France Télécom SA v Commission* [2007] ECR II-107); and
- advertising campaigns and brand image (*United Brands*).

The criticism can be made, however, that many of these factors are not considered true barriers to entry in orthodox economic theory because there is no reason why other firms cannot do the same. In particular, with regard to superior technology, it might seem difficult to see why the fact a defendant undertaking has invested in technology should prevent other firms starting up, since presumably the technology is open to all at no greater cost than it was to the defendant.

Although Article 102 TFEU refers to 'one or more undertakings', the ECJ rejected in *Hoffmann-La Roche* the view that Article 102 could be used to control oligopolies (para 39). This view was reiterated in Joined Cases C-395/96 P and C-396/96 P *Compagnie maritime belge transports SA, Compagnie maritime belge SA and Dafra-Lines A/S v Commission* [2000] ECR I-1365, paras 20–22. Article 102 can apply only exceptionally to an agreement between two undertakings (Case 66/86 *Ahmed Saeed Flugreisen and others v Zentrale zur Bekämpfung unlauteren Wettbewerbs* [1989] ECR 803, para 36 et seq). Rather, what the phrase implies is that the market power and behaviour of organically related undertakings can be aggregated. The issue then becomes whether the companies are so closely related to each other that they can be regarded as one economic unit, in other words, whether there is collective or joint dominance. As the Court stated in *Compagnie maritime belge* (2000):

> It follows that the expression 'one or more undertakings' in Article [102] of the Treaty implies that a dominant position may be held by two or more economic entities legally independent of each other, provided that from an economic point of view they present themselves or act together on a particular market as a collective entity. That is how the expression 'collective dominant position' … should be understood. (para 36)

In an appeal heard from Commission Decision 89/93/EEC in *Flat glass* ([1989] OJ L33/44), where it ruled that a three-company oligopoly could be liable under both former Articles 85 and 86 TEEC (now Articles 101 and 102 TFEU) for collective abuse of its dominant position in the Italian flat glass industry, the Court agreed that collective dominance might exist when two or more undertakings sharing a technological lead through a technological agreement or licence could, being 'united by such economic links', be able to behave to an appreciable extent independently from their competitors on the same market (Joined Cases T-68/89, T-77/89 and T-78/89 *Società Italiana Vetro SpA, Fabbrica Pisana SpA and PPG Vernante Pennitalia SpA v*

Commission (Re Italian Flat Glass) [1992] ECR II-1403, para 358 and *Compagnie maritime belge* (1996), para 60).

Undertakings may be linked as to their conduct on a particular market by an agreement, decision or concerted practice covered by Article 101 TFEU to such an extent that they will appear on that market to their competitors, trading partners and consumers as a collective entity. As the Court stated in *Compagnie maritime belge* (2000), although the existence of an agreement or other links in law is not indispensable to establish a collective dominant position, such dominance may

> ... flow from the nature and terms of an agreement, from the way in which it is implemented and, consequently, from the links or factors which give rise to a connection between undertakings which result from it. (para 45)

Also, quite logically, as the Court put it in Case C-413/06 P *Bertelsmann AG and Sony Corporation of America v Independent Music Publishers and Labels Association (Impala)* [2008] ECR I-4951, in the case of an alleged creation or strengthening of a collective dominant position, it must be assessed whether a concentration (see **17.4**) may lead to effective competition being significantly impeded by undertakings which are parties to it and

> ... which together, in particular because of correlative factors which exist between them, are able to adopt a common policy on the market ... in order to profit from a situation of collective economic strength, without actual or potential competitors, let alone customers or consumers, being able to react effectively. (para 120)

17.3.2 Dominance in a substantial part of the internal market

Article 102 requires that the abuse of dominant position takes part 'within the internal market or in a substantial part of it'. Read in conjunction with the condition that the abuse of dominance has an effect on trade between the Member States (see **16.4**), this requirement is designed to delineate the jurisdiction of the EU. It is this element which has received the least attention in the case law, and there is no precise test.

The issue is not simply one of geography because, as the Court ruled in *Suiker Unie*,

> [f]or the purpose of determining whether a specific territory is large enough to amount to 'a substantial part of the [internal] market' within the meaning of Article [102] of the Treaty *the pattern and volume of the production and consumption of the said product as well as the habits and economic opportunities of vendors and purchasers must be considered.* (para 371, emphasis added)

Equally, no particular percentage is critical in deciding what is substantial, nor has the Court ever specified one. However, in Case *77/77 Benzine en Petroleum Handelsmaatschappij BV and others v Commission* [1978] ECR 1513, Advocate-General Warner considered the Dutch market for petrol amounting to some 4.6% of the then European Community market as a whole to be substantial (at 1537). To a certain extent this could be seen as a parallel with the de minimis doctrine under Article 101 (see **The prevention, restriction or distortion of competition** above).

Not only individual Member States are likely to constitute a substantial part of the internal market (eg, the UK in Case 226/84 *British Leyland plc v Commission* [1986] ECR 3263 or Belgium in Case 127/73 *Belgische Radio en Televisie and société belge des auteurs, compositeurs et éditeurs v SV SABAM and NV Fonior* [1974] ECR 51), but also parts of them, such as South Germany (*Suiker Unie*) or even a small area of the French territory for which insemination centres were each granted an exclusive licence by the French government (Case C-323/93 *Société Civile Agricole du Centre d'Insémination de la Crespelle v Coopérative d'Elevage et d'Insémination Artificielle du Département de la Mayenne* [1994] ECR I-5077). Even a port can be regarded as such, as in Case C-179/90 *Merci convenzionali porto di Genova SpA v Siderurgica Gabrielli SpA* [1991] ECR I-5889 in which the Italian port of Genova was deemed to play an important part in the trade between Italy and the rest of the European Union (see also *B&I/Sealink, Holyhead* Commission Decision [1992] 5 CMLR 255 and *Sea Containers v Stena Sealink* Commission Decision 94/19/EC ([1994] OJ L15/8).

This concept means that Article 102 is not reserved just for the industrial giants of this world and that even a comparatively small firm could find itself caught.

17.3.3 Abuse

Article 102 TFEU does not prohibit an undertaking from acquiring, on its own merits, a dominant position in a market. As such, the finding that an undertaking has a dominant position is not in itself a ground of criticism or a recrimination (see Case 322/81 *NV Nederlandsche Banden-Industrie-Michelin v Commission* [1983] ECR 3461, para 57 and *Compagnie maritime belge* (2000), para 37).

Nonetheless, according to settled case law (see, in particular, *Tetra Pak II*, para 114 and Case C-202/07 P *France Télécom SA v Commission* [2009] ECR I-2369, para 105), an undertaking in a dominant position

> … has a special responsibility not to allow its conduct to impair genuine undistorted competition in the internal market.

Article 102 refers to the abuse of dominant position and, while it provides no definition of this concept, it offers a non-exhaustive enumeration of certain types of monopoly behaviour (see Case T-321/05 *AstraZeneca AB and AstraZeneca plc v Commission* [2010] ECR II-2805, adding to this list misleading representations and deregistration of marketing authorisations).

As Article 102 TFEU states:

> Such abuse may, in particular, consist in:
>
> (a) directly or indirectly imposing unfair purchase or selling prices or other unfair trading conditions;
> (b) limiting production, markets or technical development to the prejudice of consumers;
> (c) applying dissimilar conditions to equivalent transactions with other trading parties, thereby placing them at a competitive disadvantage;
> (d) making the conclusion of contracts subject to acceptance by the other parties of supplementary obligations which, by their nature or according to commercial usage, have no connection with the subject of such contracts.

17.3.3.1 Concept of abuse

Save in some cases (eg predatory pricing, selective discount or refusal to supply), there is no need for intention or fault since the concept of abuse is

> … an objective concept relating to the behaviour of an undertaking in a dominant position which is such as to influence the structure of a market where, as a result of the very presence of the undertaking in question, the degree of competition is weakened and which, through recourse to methods different from those which

condition normal competition in products or services on the basis of the transactions of commercial operators, has the effect of hindering the maintenance of the degree of competition still existing in the market or the growth of that competition. (*Hoffmann-La Roche*, para 91)

As explained in Case C-333/94 P *Tetra Pak International SA v Commission* [1996] ECR I-5951, the application of Article 102 presupposes

> ... a link between the dominant position and the alleged abusive conduct (para 27)

Consequently, conduct must produce effects on the dominated market. However, in *Tetra Pak*, the Court accepted that if conduct has effects on a distinct, but associated, non-dominated market, the application of Article 102 to that conduct can only be justified by special circumstances (see para 27).

17.3.3.2 Types of abuse

Exploitative and exclusionary (or anti-competitive) abuses are the two main categories of abuse, but many kinds of abusive behaviour can be both exploitative and exclusionary at the same time. This distinction originates from the *Continental Can* case in which the Court stated that

> ... the provision is not only aimed at practices which may cause damage to consumers directly, but also at those which are detrimental to them through their impact on an effective competition structure .... Abuse may therefore occur if an undertaking in a dominant position strengthens such position in such a way that the degree of dominance reached substantially fetters competition ... (para 26)

According to the Guidance on the Commission's enforcement priorities in applying Article 82 of the EC Treaty to abusive exclusionary conduct by dominant undertakings, exclusionary abuses (anti-competitive foreclosure) cover situations

> ... where effective access of actual or potential competitors to supplies or markets is hampered or eliminated as a result of the conduct of the dominant undertaking whereby the dominant undertaking is likely to be in a position to profitably increase prices to the detriment of consumers. (para 19)

It appears from this definition that exclusionary abuse includes:

- foreclosure ('access of actual or potential competitors to supplies or markets is hampered or eliminated'), thus preventing or weakening competition from other competitors in the same market; and
- harm to consumers ('the dominant undertaking is likely to be in a position to profitably increase prices to the detriment of consumers'), the exploitation of consumers being the logical consequence of the elimination of competitors.

For the Court, the latter element is the defining one, as is clear from Case C-52/09 *Konkurrensverket v TeliaSonera Sverige AB* [2011] ECR I-527, para 24 and Case C-209/10 *Post Danmark A/S v Konkurrencerådet*, 27 March 2012, ECLI:EU:C:2012:172:

> It is apparent from case-law that Article [102 TFEU] covers not only those practices that directly cause harm to consumers but also practices that cause consumers harm through their impact on competition .... It is in the latter sense that the expression 'exclusionary abuse' ... is to be understood. (para 20)

Examples of such abuse are:

- exclusive dealing: obligation or incentive for the buyer to make all its purchases from one dealer only (*Hoffmann-La Roche*);
- tying and bundling: the purchase of the main product or service is made conditional on the purchase of other products or services (tie-in); when the latter product (tied product) is already incorporated into the former (tying product), this is bundling (*Hilti AG*; *Tetra Pak II*; *Microsoft* Commission Decision COMP/C-3/37.792 (C(2004)900 final) and *Microsoft Corp*);
- import and export bans (*Suiker Unie*);
- refusing to supply an existing customer (*ICI & CSC*; *Hugin* and *Microsoft Corp*). However, non-discriminatory and objectively justified refusals are permissible;
- refusing to licence intellectual property rights: this is a more difficult area as mere ownership of intellectual property rights does not establish dominance, and the outcome of the case would seem to depend on the nature of the product and whether the licence relates to initial marketing or the sale of replacement parts (Joined Cases C-241 and 242/91 P *Radio Telefis Eireann (RTE) and Independent Television Publications Ltd (ITP) v Commission (Magill)* [1995] ECR I-743: the refusal to licence the copyright in TV programme listings was held to be an abuse; by contrast, Case 238/87 *AB Volvo v Erik Veng (UK) Ltd* [1988] ECR 6211 and Case 53/87 *CICRA v Régie nationale des usines Renault* [1988] ECR 6039: the refusal to licence the copyright in the design for replacement car body panels was held not to be abusive);
- denying access to essential facilities, such as intellectual property rights, bus stations, ports, etc. A facility is said to be essential if access to it is indispensable to compete in a related market and whose duplication is impossible or very difficult for physical geographic or legal constraints, or is not desirable for reasons of public policy (see *Magill* and Case C-7/97 *Oscar Bronner GmbH & Co KG v Mediaprint Zeitungs* [1998] ECR I-7791: refusal of a media undertaking holding a dominant position in the territory of a Member State to include a rival daily newspaper of another undertaking in the same Member State in its newspaper home-delivery scheme). The refusal of access to an essential facility is abuse if:
  - it is likely to eliminate competition in the downstream market from the person requiring access to the essential facility;
  - it is not objectively justified;
  - access to the facility is indispensable for carrying on business; and
  - there is no actual or potential substitute for the essential facility.
  However, in Case C-418/01 *IMS Health GmbH v NDC Health GmbH* [2004] ECR I-5039, concerning a brick structure used to supply regional sales data for pharmaceutical products in a Member State, the ECJ attempted to readjust balance between protection of intellectual property rights and innovation;
- loyalty bonuses or rebates: though in themselves they are not abuses, they may breach Article 102 if they are not based on economic considerations and restrict the purchaser's freedom to choose other sources of supply or restrict market access to competitors, etc (*Hoffmann-La Roche*; *Hilti AG*; *Compagnie maritime belge* (1996); *Michelin I*; Case T-203/01 *Manufacture française des pneumatiques Michelin v Commission (Michelin II)* [2003] ECR II-4071; *British Airways plc*; Case T-286/09 *Intel Corp v Commission*, 12 June 2014, ECLI:EU:T:2014:547);
- predatory pricing: the dominant undertaking drops its prices below costs over a certain period of time with the view to driving competitors out of the market or stopping potential competitors from accessing it, thus gaining long-term profit in a

more solidified market position (*AKZO Chemie BV*; *Wanadoo Interactive* Commission Decision COMP/38.223 and *France Télécom SA*).

Exploitation, on the other hand, imposes unfair conditions on consumers. It notably includes:

- unfairly high (excessive) pricing: prices are deemed excessive if there is 'no reasonable relation to the economic value of the product supplied' (*United Brands*; Case 26/75 *General Motors Continental NV v Commission* [1975] ECR 1367; Case 226/84 *British Leyland plc v Commission* [1986] ECR 3263);
- unfair trading conditions (*United Brands*; *1998 Football World Cup* Commission Decision 2000/12/EC ([2000] OJ L5/55)).

Discrimination and reprisals are two other forms of abuse:

- discriminatory pricing of a uniform product (*United Brands*); discriminatory discounts (*Michelin* and *Hilti*);
- discriminatory treatment (*British Airways plc*; *Hilti*);
- discriminatory prices (*United Brands*; Case C-497/99 P *Irish Sugar plc v Commission* [2001] ECR I-5333);
- retaliatory refusal to supply an existing customer (*ICI & CSC*; *United Brands*).

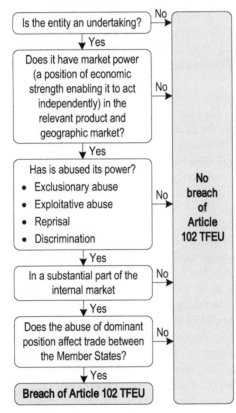

Figure 17.7   How a breach of Article 102 TFEU is established

One particularly important area of anti-competitive abuse is concentrations. In *Continental Can*, the Court ruled that it would be an abuse for a dominant undertaking to increase that dominance through the acquisition of a competitor although, in this case, it held that the Commission had failed to establish on the facts that competition would be eliminated.

The use of Article 102 for control of concentrations laid dormant until Commission Decision 88/501/EEC in *Tetra Pak I* ([1988] OJ L272/27). Here, Tetra Pak took over a competitor (Liquipak) with the result that it also acquired an exclusive patent licence granted to Liquipak concerned with the packaging of long-life milk. This excluded Elopak, which had been cooperating in the new technology, from access to the information. The Commission upheld Elopak's complaint that Tetra Pak had strengthened its own dominant position and withdrew from Tetra Pak the benefit of the Patent Licensing Block Exemption. Tetra Pak's appeal against the Commission Decision was rejected by the Court in Case T-51/89 *Tetra Pak Rausing SA v Commission* [1990] ECR II-309.

17.4 Concentrations

Concentration is a generic term to designate the process whereby companies either merge into one or whereby one company takes control of another by acquisition. On the one hand, concentrations can have a significant market impact on competition, can be used to strip the assets of the acquired firm and, through rationalisation of existing plants, may have an adverse impact on employment and regional vitality. On the other, concentrations contribute to improving economic and managerial efficiency. They render possible economies of scale and increase distributional efficiency. They also increase management efficiency through fear or threat of takeover, and improve dissemination of technology. Furthermore, within the context of the European single market, concentrations can lead to integration and greater rationalised market interpenetration.

Yet, as with oligopolies, there is no specific provision in the EU Treaties which addresses the issue of concentrations. The reason for this is that, in the 1950s, the main post-war concern was reconstruction and the fragmentation of the European industry. Concentrations were thus seen as a good thing that needed to be encouraged rather than prevented. Member State governments, which controlled the major industrial companies or groups, were also keen to operate concentrations to their own benefit and were not ready at the time to relinquish control of those to the European Community institutions. This explains why the framers of the original Treaties treaded carefully in this domain and why only the 1951 ECSC Treaty (see **1.5**) provided, under Article 66, comprehensive rules on concentrations of companies in the steel and coal industry.

In a Memorandum on mergers within the common market of 1965, the European Commission, concerned by the increasing number of concentrations in the 1960s and 1970s, advocated, however, the need for control of concentrations, albeit limited to those potentially leading to monopolies. Nonetheless, with the exception of a few countries (the German 1957 Gesetz gegen Wettbewerbsbeschränkungen (GWB) and the UK 1965 Monopolies and Mergers Act, replaced by the 1973 Fair Trading Act), national legislation on mergers and takeovers was slow to come and the pace only started to quicken in the late 1980s. By 1989 Germany, France, the UK and Ireland had full concentration legislation. They were joined by the Netherlands (Medelinngingswet) and Finland (Laki Kilpailunrajoituksista) in 1998, and Denmark (Lov om ændring af Konkurrenceloven) in 2000. Luxembourg remains the only Member State with no specific law on concentration.

At EU level, it was not until 1989 that Regulation 4064/1989 on the control of concentrations between undertakings (the EC Merger Regulation) ([1989] OJ L395/1) was adopted and later amended in 1998 by Regulation 1310/1997 ([1997] OJ L180/1). It was the first serious attempt at consolidating EC rules on mergers.

Following the Green Paper of 11 December 2001 on the review of the 1989 Regulation (COM(2001) 745 final), a wide reform dealing with substantive, jurisdictional and procedural issues was launched. This overall review of merger legislation led to the adoption in January 2004 of Regulation 139/2004 ([2004] OJ L24/1) which came into force on 1 May 2004, the day of the enlargement to include 10 Mediterranean, Central and Eastern European countries (see **1.4**).

Compared to the reform of procedure under Regulation 1/2003 on the implementation of the rules on competition laid down in Articles 81 and 82 of the Treaty ([2003] OJ L1/1) (see **18.2**), the reform of merger legislation was of limited amplitude. This can be explained by the fact that the former system had produced satisfactory results on the whole over its 14 years of existence.

The basic principles of control of concentrations remained unchanged:

- EU control is ex ante and based on the obligation to notify to the Commission the proposed merger;
- the definition of a concentration remains unchanged – most of the proposed suggestions having then been rejected; and
- the emphasis on the change of control which must be on a lasting basis remains.

Essentially, however, the 2004 EC Merger Regulation re-delineated the powers and competence between the Commission and the national authorities (jurisdictional thresholds), improved the control procedure and modified the concentration assessment criteria.

It is widely recognised that the 2004 Regulation has certainly rendered the control of concentrations within the EU more efficient and contributed to preserving effective competition in the European internal market. Yet 10 years of experience have also highlighted that some aspects of this control regime still needs improvement. For this reason, in July 2014, the European Commission launched a public consultation on proposals to improve control of concentrations. These are outlined in a White Paper, 'Towards more effective EU merger control' (COM(2014) 449 final). Their primary aim is to:

- allow the Commission to deal more efficiently with non-controlling minority shareholdings which may have harmful effects on competition;
- make referral procedures between Member States and the Commission simpler and faster;
- make procedures simpler; and
- foster coherence and convergence between Member States.

The 2004 Regulation must be read in conjunction with:

- the Guidelines on the assessment of horizontal mergers under the Council Regulation on the control of concentrations between undertakings ([2004] OJ C31/5); and
- the Guidelines on the assessment of non-horizontal mergers under the Council Regulation on the control of concentrations between undertakings ([2008] OJ C265/7).

According to its first Article,

> … this Regulation shall apply to all concentrations with a [Union] dimension as defined in this Article.

In other words, to be appraised under the EU merger control regime, a concentration operation must satisfy two conditions:

- it must fall within the definition of concentration provided for under Article 3 of the Regulation; and
- it must have a Union dimension.

17.4.1 Definition of a concentration

Under Article 3(1) of the 2004 Merger Regulation:

> A concentration shall be deemed to arise where a change of control on a lasting basis results from:

(a) the merger of two or more previously independent undertakings or parts of undertakings, or

(b) the acquisition, by one or more persons already controlling at least one undertaking, or by one or more undertakings, whether by purchase of securities or assets, by contract or by any other means, of direct or indirect control of the whole or parts of one or more other undertakings.

Two elements are to be considered here:

- first, as recital 20 in the preamble to the 2004 Merger Regulation explains, the concept of concentration is intended to relate to operations which bring about a lasting change in the structure of the market;
- secondly, as the Commission makes it clear in its Consolidated Jurisdictional Notice under Council Regulation (EC) No 139/2004 on the control of concentrations between undertakings ([2008] OJ C95/01), 'the test in Article 3 is centred on the concept of control [and] the existence of a concentration is to a great extent determined by qualitative rather than quantitative criteria' (para 7).

A distinction is made between concentrations resulting from a merger and those from acquisition of control.

The former occurs when a new undertaking is created from the amalgamation of two or more undertakings that cease to exist as separate legal entities, or from the absorption of one undertaking by another that will retain its legal identity. Examples of such concentrations can be found in cases COMP/M.1673 *VEBA/VIAG* ([2001] OJ L188/1), COMP/M.1806 *AstraZeneca/Novartis* ([2004] OJ L110/1), COMP/M.2208 *Chevron/ Texaco* ([2001] OJ C128/2) and COMP/M.3294 *ExxonMobil/BEB* ([2004] OJ C8/7).

In the case of the latter, control is acquired by one undertaking acting alone or by several undertakings acting jointly. Under Article 3(1)(b) of the 2004 Merger Regulation, a concentration may be a legal or a de facto operation in the form of sole or joint control, and extend to the whole or parts of one or more undertakings. Control is defined in Article 3(2) of the 2004 Merger Regulation as the 'possibility of exercising decisive influence on an undertaking' on the basis of 'rights, contracts or any other means ..., either separately or in combination ...'. Such influence need not be actually exercised but the possibility of such influence must be effective (Case T-282/02 *Cementbouw Handel & Industrie BV v Commission* [2006] ECR II-319, para 58).

A third category of concentration is covered by Article 3(4) of the 2004 Merger Regulation, namely 'the creation of a joint venture performing on a lasting basis all the functions of an autonomous economic entity', known as a full-function joint venture. Full functionality means that the entity enjoys operational autonomy. This does not require, however, that the entity has autonomy with regard to the adoption of strategic decisions (see *Cementbouw*, para 62).

In order for it to have full functionality, a joint venture must 'operate on a market, performing the functions normally carried out by undertakings operating on the same market' (Commission Notice, para 94). This implies the management of its day-to-day operations and access to sufficient resources to be able to conduct long-term activities assigned to it in the joint-venture agreement. Thus, taking over one specific function within the parent companies' activities without having access to, or a presence of its own on, the market will not be sufficient to make it a full-function joint venture.

Furthermore, the joint venture must be able to operate on a lasting basis. This will usually be demonstrated by the resources committed by the parent companies to the joint venture. By contrast, a joint venture established for a short period of time will not satisfy this criterion and will not be covered by Article 3(4) of the Merger Regulation. This will be the case where the joint venture is created for the sole purpose of dealing with a specific project without involving it in the management and operation of the object of that project once completed.

However, where a joint venture covered by Article 3(4) of the Regulation 'has as its object or effect the coordination of the competitive behaviour of undertakings that remain independent', Article 2(4) provides that the compatibility with the internal market of such coordination is to be assessed under Article 101(1) and (3) TFEU.

17.4.2 The Union dimension of concentrations

Not all concentrations fall within the scope of application of the 2004 EC Merger Regulation. Only those that satisfy a very specific criterion, namely those with a Union dimension, will. This is an important criterion as it delineates the jurisdiction between the European Commission and national competition authorities.

According to its Article 1(1), the 2004 Merger Regulation

> shall apply to all concentrations with a [Union] dimension as defined in this Article.

This is the second limb of a twofold test to determine whether the Merger Regulation applies to an operation or not. Once the operation is identified as a concentration in accordance with Article 3 of the 2004 Merger Regulation, it will be necessary to assess whether it has an impact upon the Union and then be deemed to be with a 'Union dimension'.

Article 1 provides two sets of turnover thresholds to establish whether a concentration has a Union dimension or not.

Under Article 1(2), a concentration will have such dimension if:

- the combined aggregate worldwide turnover of all undertakings exceeds EUR 5,000 million; and
- the aggregate Union-wide turnover of at least two of the undertakings exceeds EUR 250 million,

unless each of the companies achieves more than two-thirds of its aggregate Union-wide turnover in one and the same Member State.

The first criterion aims to measure the overall dimension of the companies involved in the concentration; the second one is intended to determine whether the concentration involves a minimum level of activities within the Union; and the purpose of the third one is to distinguish purely domestic operations from Union ones.

Should a concentration fall short of meeting those criteria to achieve Union dimension under Article 1(2) and yet, should it still have a substantial impact in at least three Member States, Article 1(3) provides for another set of lower world- and Union-wide turnover thresholds. Those are:

- the combined aggregate worldwide turnover of all undertakings exceeds EUR 2,500 million;
- in each of at least three Member States, the combined aggregate turnover exceeds EUR 100 million;
- in each of at least three Member States, the turnover of at least two undertakings exceeds EUR 25 million; and
- the aggregate Union-wide turnover of each of at least two of the undertakings exceeds EUR 100 million,

unless each of them achieves more than two-thirds of its aggregate Union-wide turnover in one and the same Member State.

As the Commission Notice explains, those thresholds, based on turnover calculation rather than market shares, are 'purely quantitative' and are only designed to provide a simple mechanism to enable companies involved in a concentration operation to determine whether it has a Union dimension and, consequently, whether it is notifiable to the European Commission or not.

The sole purpose of Article 1 is to determine jurisdiction, not to explain how aggregate turnovers should be calculated in a way that they accurately reflect economic reality. This point is explained in great detail in Article 5 of the 2004 Merger Regulation.

17.4.3 Appraisal of concentrations

The appraisal of concentrations is designed to establish whether or not they are compatible with the internal market.

Such appraisal will be done on the basis of the necessity of ensuring effective competition within the internal market and the market position of the undertakings involved in the concentration operation, notably taking account of their economic and financial power, legal or other barriers to entry, the supply and demand trends for the relevant goods or services, the interests of intermediate and final consumers, and the development of technical and economic progress.

Article 2(2) of the 2004 Merger Regulation describes in general terms the conditions under which a concentration is compatible with EU law, namely:

A concentration which would not *significantly impede effective competition* in the [internal] market or in a substantial part of it, in particular as a result of the creation or strengthening of a dominant position, shall be declared compatible with the [internal] market. (emphasis added)

This should be contrasted with Article 2(2) of the 1989 Merger Regulation which provided that

[a] concentration which does not create or strengthen a dominant position as a result of which effective competition would be significantly impeded in the common market or in a substantial part of it shall be declared compatible with the common market.

The 1989 provision put the emphasis on the existence or the strengthening of a dominant position. By contrast, the 2004 version gives preference to the effect on competition and applies the *significant impediment of effective competition* (SIEC) economic criterion, which is close to the American *substantial lessening of competition* criterion.

This wide-meaning phrase gives the European Commission wide discretion when taking into consideration the 'need to maintain and develop effective competition' and the 'market position of the undertakings concerned' (Article 2(1)(a) and (b) of the 2004 Merger Regulation).

It is clear from the Guidelines on the assessment of horizontal mergers under the Council Regulation on the control of concentrations between undertakings that, for the Commission, the need to maintain effective competition is paramount. As stated in paragraph 8 of the Guidelines:

Effective competition brings benefits to consumers, such as low prices, high quality products, a wide selection of goods and services, and innovation. Through its control of mergers, the Commission prevents mergers that would be likely to deprive customers of these benefits by significantly increasing the market power of firms.

As explained in paragraph 10 of the Guidelines, the Commission's assessment of mergers will normally entail a definition of the relevant product and geographic markets and a competitive assessment of the merger.

The Commission will notably base this assessment on:

- an analysis of market shares held by the undertakings involved in the concentration and the concentration thresholds;
- the potential anti-competitive effects in the relevant markets of the merger in the absence of countervailing factors;
- the existence of countervailing factors such as buyer power, efficiencies brought about by a merger and likelihood of market entry; and
- whether one of the merging parties is a failing firm, thus rendering a problematic merger compatible with the internal market. (Guidelines, para 11)

Nonetheless, if the Commission is given wide discretion by the 2004 Merger Regulation in its assessment of compatibility of mergers with the internal market, the Court became increasingly critical of the Commission's economic analysis of the effects of concentration within the internal market, and has required the Commission to provide more accurate, reliable and coherent supporting evidence. Cases such as Case T-342/299 *Airtours plc v Commission* [2002] ECR II-2585, Case T-310/01 *Schneider Electric SA v Commission* [2002] ECR II-4071, Case T-80/02 *Tetra Laval BV v Commission* [2002] ECR II-4519 and Case C-12/03 P *Commission v Tetra Laval BV* [2005] ECR I-987 provide a clear illustration of the more stringent review exercised by the Court over Commission decisions declaring a concentration to be incompatible with the internal market, thus forcing the Commission to improve dramatically its decision-making process. In the absence of a sufficiently and accurately substantiated analysis, the Court will not hesitate to annul the Commission's decisions.

With the exception of certain controversial decisions declaring a concentration incompatible with EU competition rules, such as in Case IV/M53 *Aerospatiale-Alenia/ de Havilland* ([1991] OJ L334/42), the majority of the Commission decisions have been decisions declaring a concentration compatible. This is notably the result of a direct dialogue and negotiation process between the Commission Merger task force and companies regarding commitments (usually in the form of relinquishment of business activities to third companies) and corrective measures that the latter must make in order to secure a Commission decision of compatibility (see Commission notice on remedies acceptable under Council Regulation (EC) No 139/2004 and under Commission Regulation (EC) No 802/2004 ([2008] OJ C267/01)).

Examples of such decisions can be found in the following cases:

- IV/M.877 *Boeing/McDonnell Douglas* ([1997] OJ L336/16): Boeing had to renounce exclusive supply agreements;
- COMP/M.1628 *TotalFina/Elf* ([2001] OJ L143/1): as a condition for acquiring Elf Aquitaine, TotalFina had to sell 70 service stations on the French motorway network;
- COMP/M.2016 *France Télécom/Orange* ([2000] OJ C261/07): the acquisition by France Télécom of Orange was conditional on the obligation to sell its shares in a Belgian mobile phone company;

- COMP/M.3225 *Alcan/Pechiney (II)* ([2003] OJ C299/19): acquisition of French aluminium producer Pechiney by Alcan of Canada after Alcan offered to divest a number of businesses; and
- COMP/M.5440 *Lufthansa/Austrian Airlines* ([2010] OJ C16/10): acquisition of Austrian Airlines by Deutsche Lufthansa AG of Germany conditional upon the implementation of a set of remedies offered by Lufthansa addressing competition concerns on routes Vienna–Frankfurt, Vienna–Munich, Vienna–Stuttgart, Vienna–Cologne and Vienna–Brussels.

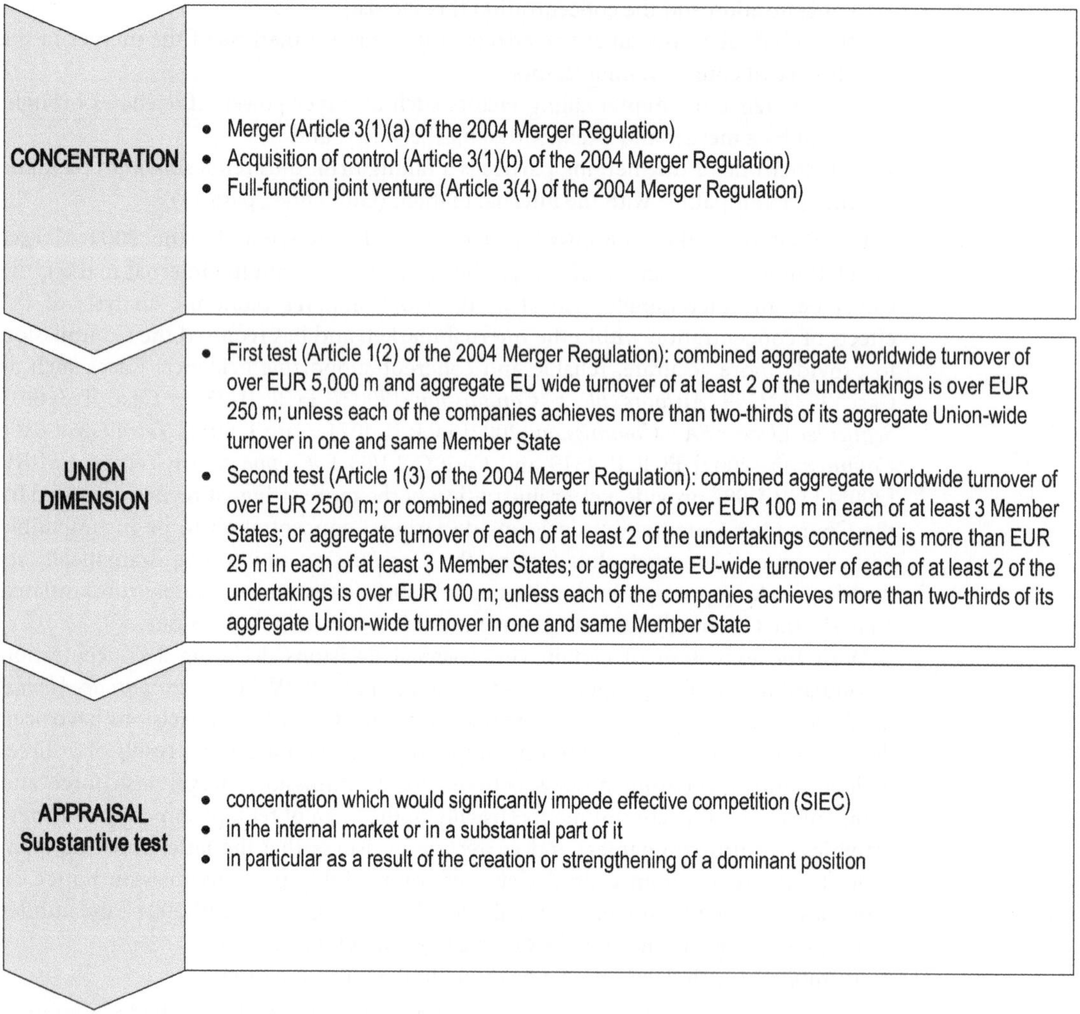

CONCENTRATION

- Merger (Article 3(1)(a) of the 2004 Merger Regulation)
- Acquisition of control (Article 3(1)(b) of the 2004 Merger Regulation)
- Full-function joint venture (Article 3(4) of the 2004 Merger Regulation)

UNION DIMENSION

- First test (Article 1(2) of the 2004 Merger Regulation): combined aggregate worldwide turnover of over EUR 5,000 m and aggregate EU wide turnover of at least 2 of the undertakings is over EUR 250 m; unless each of the companies achieves more than two-thirds of its aggregate Union-wide turnover in one and same Member State
- Second test (Article 1(3) of the 2004 Merger Regulation): combined aggregate worldwide turnover of over EUR 2500 m; or combined aggregate turnover of over EUR 100 m in each of at least 3 Member States; or aggregate turnover of each of at least 2 of the undertakings concerned is more than EUR 25 m in each of at least 3 Member States; or aggregate EU-wide turnover of each of at least 2 of the undertakings is over EUR 100 m; unless each of the companies achieves more than two-thirds of its aggregate Union-wide turnover in one and same Member State

APPRAISAL Substantive test

- concentration which would significantly impede effective competition (SIEC)
- in the internal market or in a substantial part of it
- in particular as a result of the creation or strengthening of a dominant position

Figure 17.8   Control of concentrations

17.5 Further Reading

Article 101 TFEU

Bailey D, 'Overall, Single Agreement in EU Competition Law' (2010) 47 *CML Rev* 473.

Bailey D, 'Restriction of Competition by Object' (2012) 49 *CML Rev* 559.

Coumes J-M and Wilson K, 'New Rules on Supply and Distribution Agreements: Main Changes of the New System' (2010) 31(11) *ECLR* 439.

De Stefano G, 'The New EU "Vertical Restraints Regulation": Navigating the Vast Sea Beyond' (2010) 31(12) *ECLR* 487.

Ibanez Colomo P, 'Intel and Article 102 TFEU Case Law: Making Sense of a Perpetual Controversy', *LSE Working Paper Series* 29-2014, December 2014.

Joshua J, 'Single Continuous Infringement of Article 81 EC: Has the Commission Stretched the Concept beyond the Limit of its Logic?' (2009) 5(2) *European Competition Journal* 451.

Loozen E, 'Case Comment. The Workings of Article 101 TFEU in Case of an Agreement that Aims to Limit Parallel Trade (GlaxoSmithKline Services (C-501/06 P, C-513/06 P, C-515/06 P and C-519/06 P))' (2010) 31(9) *ECLR* 349.

Monti G, 'The New Substantive Test in the EC Merger Regulation – Bridging the Gap Between Economics and Law?', *LSE Working Paper Series* 10-2008, August 2008.

Nagy CI, 'The New concept of Anti-competitive Object: a Loose Cannon in EU Competition Law' (2015) 36(4) *ECLR* 154.

Ortega González A, 'Case Comment. Restrictions by Object and the Appreciability Test: the Expedia Case, a Surprising Judgment or a Simple Clarification?' (2013) 34(9) *ECLR* 457.

Whish R and Bailey D, 'Regulation 330/2010: The Commission's New Bock Exemption for Vertical Agreements' (2010) 47 *CML Rev* 1747.

Article 102 TFEU

Akman P, 'Searching for the Long-Lost Soul of Article 82EC' (2009) 29(2) *Oxford Journal of Legal Studies* 267.

Albors-Llorens A, 'The Role of Objective Justification and Efficiencies in the Application of article 82 EC' (2007) 44 *CML Rev* 1727.

Borlini L, 'Methodological Issues of the "More Economic Approach" to Unilateral Exclusionary Conduct. Proposal of Analysis Starting from the Treatment of Retroactive Rebates' (2009) 5(2) *Competition Law Review* 409.

Gormsen L, 'Article 82 EC: Where Are we Coming from and Where Are we Going to?' (2005) 2(2) *Competition Law Review* 5.

Gormsen L, 'The Conflict between Economic Freedom and Consumer Welfare in the Modernisation of Article 82 EC' (2007) 3(2) *Competition Law Review* 329.

Gravengaard MA and Kjaersgaard N, 'The EU Commission Guidance on Exclusionary Abuse of Dominance - and its Consequences in Practice' (2010) 31(7) *ECLR* 285.

Szyszczak E, 'Controlling Dominance in European Markets' (2010) 33 *Fordham International Law Journal* 1738.

Verhaert J, 'The Challenges Involved with the Application of Article 102 TFEU to the New Economy: A Case Study of Google' (2014) 35(6) *ECLR* 265.

Wills W, 'The Judgment of the EU General Court in Intel and the So-Called More Economic Approach to Abuse of Dominance' (2014) 37(4) *World Competition* 405

Witt A, 'The Commission's Guidance Paper on Abusive Exclusionary Conduct – More Radical than it Appears?' (2010) 35(2) *EL Rev* 214.

Control of concentrations

Doleys T, 'Incomplete Contracting, Commission Discretion and the Origins of EU Merger Control' (2009) 47(3) *Journal of Common Market Studies* 483.

Kratsas G, 'Structural or not? A Critical Analysis of the Commission's New Notice on Remedies' (2008–2009) 15 *Columbia Journal of European Law* 549.

Moeschel W, 'European Merger Control' (2013) 34(6) *ECLR* 283.

Weitbrecht A, 'Mergers in an Economic Crisis - EU Merger Control 2008/2009' (2010) 31(7) *ECLR* 276.

Witt A, 'From *Airtours* to *Ryanair*: Is the More Economic Approach to EU Merger Law Really About More Economics?' (2012) 49 *CML Rev* 217.

summary

The framers of the original Treaty of Rome understood very well that an internal market without competition rules would never be an effective market. For this reason, companies may not engage into behaviour that may distort or restrict competition. The Treaty rules on competition prohibit two specific anti-competitive behaviours: collusion between undertakings in the form of restrictive agreements or concerted practices (Article 101 TFEU) and unilateral conduct in the form of abuse of a dominant position (Article 102 TFEU). While the latter is strictly prohibited, the former may be exempted from prohibition if it satisfies specific conditions set out in the third paragraph of Article 101 TFEU.

Both provisions seek to achieve, in different ways, the same aim of maintaining effective competition within the internal market and operate only in so far as the behaviour concerned affects trade between the Member States.

It is to be noted also that the wording of Articles 101 and 102 have remained untouched since the adoption of the Treaty of Rome in 1957.

Concentration, in the form of merger or acquisition of companies, is another type of behaviour which, per se, is not necessarily viewed as anti-competitive, yet may have a significant impact on competition and the internal market. As they are not covered by Treaty provisions, concentrations were originally dealt with primarily under the concept of collective dominant position. It was not until 1989 that an effective regime of control of concentrations was set up under Regulation 4064/1989, later amended by Regulation 139/2004 (Merger Regulations). Unlike Articles 101 and 102 which establish a system of a posteriori enforcement of competition rules, the Merger Regulations set up a preventive control.

test your knowledge

1   Robotica SpA, an Italian company, has developed a voice-activated word processor which was patented under the name 'VOX'. Owing to its lack of marketing experience, Robotica enters into an agreement with Omega SA, a French company, whereby Omega must use its best efforts to market the processor in France.

The agreement notably provides that Omega will be the only distributor of VOX in France, will not sell VOX to distributors in other Member States and will register the 'VOX' trade mark in France.

Alpha SaRL has complained that it is unable to stock the VOX processors and that the agreement between Robotica and Omega is unlawful under Article 101 TFEU.

Discuss.

2 '[B]ecause both the agreement and the concerted practice fall within Article 101, there may be little point distinguishing between them. However, it remains crucial to differentiate collusion, whether agreement or concerted practice, from mere parallel behaviour, for the latter remains perfectly lawful.'
(per S Weatherill, *Cases & Materials on EU Law* (10th edn, Oxford University Press) at 457)

Discuss how the distinction between collusion and parallel behaviour has been drawn by the EU authorities.

3 Pfuezer SA, a French firm, Pharmacom Plc, a UK-based firm, Pharmatica SpA, an Italian firm, and Advent Inc, an American firm, are the four major producers of anti-tuberculosis drugs in the world.

Their respective shares of the world market are 39%, 23%, 18% and 12%. Three other firms produce the remaining 8%.

Since 2009, the prices of the four companies have never diverged by more than 5% and their respective market shares have been constant throughout this period.

In 2011 and 2013, the price of aminobutanol, the raw material necessary to make those drugs, increased considerably, and all four firms' prices went up simultaneously by an equal amount.

Pfuezer put its prices up before the other three major firms. However, those followed the lead of Pfuezer within a matter of days.

All four firms belong to the International Association of Pharmaceutical Producers (IAPP), to which they send details of their prices, production and sales on a quarterly basis. The Association collates this information and sends it to its members at regular intervals.

Discuss the liability of the parties under Article 101 TFEU.

4 Explain the de minimis doctrine and how it has developed in its application since its original formulation.

5 TG Ltd has developed a fruit called peap, a cross between a peach and an apricot. It is extremely popular in shops and supermarkets. Other rivals also produce peap, but TG still retains 48% share of the total peap market in the EU, although only 5% of the total market of fresh fruit.

TG supplies peap to shops which agree to sell only peap and no other soft fruit. It also insists on charging retailers 75 cents per peap (production and cultivation costs amount to only 5 cents per fruit). Gerhard Merkel, a small grocer, wishes to stock peap. However, TG refuses to supply him because he would not agree to comply with TG's conditions.

Advise Gerhard Merkel on his position and TG Ltd on its practices.

6 Billard SA is a French company which manufactures billiard tables and cues, primarily for export to the UK where it has 40% of the market for billiard tables and 65% of the market for cues.

In January 2015, three of its former employees moved to the UK and set up a small company, Q Ltd, to manufacture and sell top quality cues. By March 2015, Q had captured a 15% share of the UK market and its customers include top professional players.

Concerned about the erosion of its market share, Billard SA cuts the price of its cues in the UK by 20%. This results in Q seeing its own share of the market falling to 8% within just five weeks. At this level, it will be difficult for Q to survive for long. Q decides to take urgent action.

Q complains to the UK Competition and Markets Authority about the behaviour of Billard, alleging that Billard is guilty of breaching Article 102 TFEU. The complaint specifically states that Billard is selling its cues in the UK below the prices at which it could make a profit.

Advise Q Ltd whether or not there is a prima facie breach of Article 102 TFEU considering all the elements of this Article.

18 Enforcement of Competition Rules

study points

After reading this chapter, you will be able to understand:

- the territoriality principle
- the public enforcement mechanism
- the private enforcement of competition rules and damages action.

18.1 Introduction

There are multiple enforcers of EU competition rules: the European Commission, under the supervision of the Court of Justice, and national competition authorities and courts.

Regulation 17/62 (OJ English special edition: Series I Chapter 1959-1962 at 87), the first Regulation implementing former Articles 85 and 86 TEEC (Regulation 17), set up the original highly centralised system of supervision and enforcement of competition rules. In this system, the European Commission, national courts and national competition authorities (NCAs) could all apply former Articles 85(1) and 86 TEEC (now Articles 101(1) and 102 TFEU), but the Commission alone was vested with the exclusive power to grant exemptions under former Article 85(3) TEEC (now Article 101(3) TFEU).

Regulation 1/2003/EC on the implementation of the rules laid down under Articles 81 and 82 EC ([2003] OJ L1/1) brought about the first landmark reform in the development of European competition law to enable the enforcement system to cope with the challenges of further enlargement and the creation of an economic and monetary union. It not only extended the powers of national competition authorities and national courts to apply all EU competition rules, but also established new forms of cooperation between the Commission and NCAs within the framework of a European Competition Network (ECN).

If public enforcement of competition law is a major tool to deter anti-competitive practices and to protect businesses and consumers from such practices, private enforcement is also regarded as an important part of a common enforcement system serving the same aims of maintaining a competitive economy. Compared to public enforcement, private enforcement was, however, in a state of complete underdevelopment. This imbalance was corrected by the second landmark reform in the history of EU competition law with the adoption of Directive 2014/104/EU on certain rules governing actions for damages under national law for infringements of the competition law provisions of the Member States and of the European Union ([2014] OJ L349/1).

Another important aspect of the EU's jurisdiction is the extent to which Articles 101 and 102 TFEU apply to firms that are incorporated outside the European Union. This controversial issue in turn raises questions of enforcement.

18.2 The territoriality principle in EU competition law

According to the **principle of territoriality**, wrongly referred to as the extraterritoriality principle, EU competition rules apply to agreements, abuse of dominant position and concentrations which may distort competition within the internal market even if they involve, partially or fully, undertakings which are registered outside the European Union.

It is clear that an agreement between an EU firm and a non-EU firm to limit imports into the internal market is caught by Article 101 TFEU, as is an agreement between two EU firms to restrict exports from the internal market, at least if the effect is to change trade patterns (as in Joined Cases 40 to 48, 50, 54 to 56, 111, 113 and 114/73 *Coöperatieve Vereniging 'Suiker Unie' UA and others v Commission* [1975] ECR 1663). This was the case, for instance, in *Franco-Japanese ball-bearings agreement* (Commission Decision 74/634/EEC ([1974] OJ L343/19)), in which major French and Japanese ballbearing manufacturers entered into a written agreement to increase the prices of Japanese ballbearings imported into France so as to make them level with the prices of bearings manufactured in France.

Generally, the EU authorities have not been diffident about applying Article 101 to non-EU firms. They are treated as being subject to the law either because their behaviour is within the European Union's territory or because they have a subsidiary company within the Union's territory. In Case 48/69 *Imperial Chemical Industries Ltd v Commission (Re Dyestuffs)* [1972] ECR 619, the ECJ decided that three non-EU undertakings had participated in an illegal price-fixing scheme within the internal market through subsidiary companies located there and under their control. In reality, each parent and subsidiary formed one economic entity and, therefore, Imperial Chemical Industries Ltd

> ... was able to exercise decisive influence over the policy of the subsidiaries as regards selling prices in the Common Market and in fact used this power upon the occasion of the three price increases in question. (para 137)

Further, the Commission and the Court espoused the so-called 'effects doctrine' from US antitrust law.

case example

In *Wood Pulp Cartel* (Commission Decision 85/202/EEC ([1985] OJ L85/1)), the Commission found that 43 non-EU wood pulp manufacturers had through a concerted practice imposed resale and export bans. They were found liable on the basis of the effect of the conduct on the then EC market (see **17.2.2.1**). On appeal to the Court (Joined Cases 89, 104, 114, 116, 117 and 125 to 129/85 *A Ahlström Osakeyhtiö and others v Commission (Re Wood Pulp Cartel)* [1988] ECR 5193, decided initially only on the question of jurisdiction, it was held that

> ... [i]f the applicability of prohibitions laid down under competition law were made to depend on the place where the agreement, decision or concerted practice was formed, the result would obviously be to give undertakings an easy means of evading those prohibitions. The decisive factor is therefore the place where it is implemented.
>
> The producers in this case implemented their pricing agreement within the [internal] market. It is immaterial in that respect whether or not they had recourse to subsidiaries, agents, sub-agents, or branches within the [Union] in order to make their contacts with purchasers within the [Union]. (paras 16–17)

As the Court put it, the decisive factor in applying competition rules is therefore the *place of implementation of the restrictive agreement, not its place of formation.*

By contrast, in *Zinc Producer Group* (Commission Decision 84/405/EEC ([1984] OJ L220/27)) – which was not referred to by the Court in the *Wood Pulp Cartel* case – liability was founded on the presence of a subsidiary in the then Community's territory.

The *Vitamins Cartel* case (Commission Decision 2003/2/EC ([2003] OJ L6/1) and Cases T-22/02 and T-23/02 *Sumitomo Chemical Co Ltd and Sumika Fine Chemicals Co Ltd v Commission* [2005] ECR II-4065), which involved price-fixing on the market of vitamin products by 15 European and non-European pharmaceutical companies, is another good example of the application of the territoriality principle in EU competition law.

The Commission also found the American company Continental Can guilty of abuse of a dominant position (see Case 6/72 *Europemballage Corporation and Continental Can Company Inc v Commission* [1973] ECR 215). In this case, the Court stated that

> [t]he circumstance that Continental does not have its registered office within the territory of one of the Member States is not sufficient to exclude it from the application of [Union] law. (para 16)

Article 102 also applied to the US-based company Microsoft, which was found to be guilty of abuse of its dominant position on the markets of client PC operating systems and of work group server operating systems (see *Microsoft* COMP/C-3/37.792 (C(2004)900 final) and Case T-201/04 *Microsoft Corp v Commission* [2007] ECR II-3601).

With regard to concentrations (mergers and acquisitions), cases such as Case COMP/M.2220 *General Electric/Honeywell* ([2004] OJ L48/1) prohibiting the acquisition of Honeywell by General Electric and Case IV/M.877 *Boeing/McDonnell Douglas* ([1997] OJ 1997 L336/16) demonstrate that EU rules on concentrations can apply to mergers involving American companies. In the latter case, Boeing even accepted the negotiation with the European Commission of corrective measures necessary to secure a decision of compatibility of the merger with EU rules.

As the Court put it in the *Wood Pulp Cartel* case, the EU's jurisdiction to apply its competition rules to such anti-competitive conduct on the part of non-EU based companies

> ... is covered by the territoriality principle as universally recognized in public international law. (para 18)

This principle suffers serious limits however. If the Commission has the power to notify non-EU companies of its intention to start infringement proceedings against them, request information from them or even impose penalties on them, it has no powers of enforcement.

This is the reason why it has been necessary for the European Commission to engage in cooperation with competition authorities of third countries, either by way of:

- bilateral international cooperation agreements on competition, known as 'dedicated agreements': United States of America (1995 and 1998), Canada (1999), Japan (2003), Korea (2009) and Switzerland (2014);
- memoranda of Understanding on Cooperation, such as those with Brazil (2009), China (2012), India (2013) and Russia (2011); or
- specific competition provisions as part of:
  - the EEA Agreement: Iceland and Norway (1994);

- Stabilisation and Association Agreements: FYROM (2004), Albania (2006), Montenegro (2007) and Bosnia and Herzegovina (2008);
- Free Trade Agreements: South Korea (2010), Columbia and Peru (2011), Singapore (1914) and Vietnam (2015);
- Agreements on Trade, Development and Cooperation: South Africa (1999);
- Partnership and Cooperation Agreements: Russia (1997), Mexico (1997), Moldova and Ukraine (1998), Armenia, Azerbaijan and Georgia (1999), ACP countries (2000 Cotonou agreement), and Caribbean Community (CARIFORUM) (2008); and
- Association Agreements: Turkey (1995), West Bank and the Gaza Strip (1997), Tunisia (1998), Morocco (2000), Chile (2002), Egypt (2004), Algeria and Israel (2005) and Lebanon (2006).

The need for further international cooperation has also driven the EU and third countries to set up in 2001 an International Competition Network which brings together more than 132 national competition authorities. Its purpose is to facilitate substantial and procedural convergence of national competition rules.

18.3 Public enforcement of competition rules

18.3.1 The modernisation of European competition law

Though it was necessary in the 1960s, 1970s and 1980s, the centralised system of competition regulation and enforcement designed for an original European Community of six Member States, 170 million inhabitants, working in four different languages, was no longer appropriate at the turn of this century for a Community of 15 Member States, 11 languages and over 380 million inhabitants, heading for its ever biggest enlargement in 2004.

At that time, the European competition policy was facing three major challenges:

- the enlargement of the then European Community to the countries of Central and Eastern Europe, Malta and Cyprus;
- the creation of an economic and monetary union entailing further economic integration; and
- the increasing internationalisation of the European economy.

'In a European Union with more than 20 Member States, the rules for implementing Articles [101] and [102] [had to] be modernised if competition policy [was] to continue to operate efficiently.' This was the diagnosis made by the Commission in its White Paper on the modernisation of the rules implementing Articles 85 and 86 of the EC Treaty ([1999] OJ C132/1) (para 7). The need for reform of the EC competition legal framework was inevitable indeed.

To carry out this reform most effectively, the Commission focused its efforts on two main objectives:

- the decentralisation of the enforcement of competition rules, thus empowering NCAs and national courts to apply the then EC antitrust rules in their entirety, with the effect of creating multiple enforcers and ensuring their wider application; and
- the abolition of the Commission's monopoly in the notification and exemption systems for business agreements by making the criteria of former Article 85(3) TEEC (now Article 101(3) TFEU) on individual exemptions (see **17.2.4**) directly

applicable by national courts and NCAs without prior decision of the Commission. This would enable the Commission to focus its resources on the fight against major cartels and other serious violations of antitrust rules.

18.3.2 The enforcement of Articles 101 and 102 TFEU

The modernisation and decentralisation of the enforcement of European competition rules was achieved with the adoption of Regulation 1/2003/EC. By replacing Regulation 17, it laid down a new system of supervision and enforcement procedures.

It is supplemented by Regulation 773/2004 relating to the conduct of proceedings by the Commission pursuant to Articles 81 and 82 of the EC Treaty ([2004] OJ L123/18) as amended by Regulation 622/2008 on the conduct of settlement procedures in cartel cases ([2008] OJ L171/3).

The abolition of the prior notification procedure under Regulation 1/2003 means that an agreement is presumed compatible with competition rules unless the Commission or NCAs prove otherwise. However, it falls on the undertakings claiming the benefit of Article 101(3) TFEU to prove that their agreement fulfils the conditions of that provision (Article 2 of Regulation 1/2003). Under this new regime, it is for the undertakings to assess the compatibility of their behaviour with competition rules. Such self-assessment can be quite complex and can only be based on Commission decisions, notices and guidelines as well as the case law of the Court.

However, the possibility of requesting negative clearance from the Commission available under Regulation 17 in order to guarantee the non-application of Articles 101 and 102 TFEU has not been abolished but made optional for companies seeking greater legal certainty. Furthermore, as a preventive measure, individual undertakings may request guidance letters from the Commission in the case of 'novel or unresolved questions' for the application of competition rules giving rise to genuine legal uncertainty (recital 38 of the preamble to Regulation 1/2003). The conditions under which informal guidance might be provided by the Commission are explained in the Notice on informal guidance relating to novel questions concerning Articles 81 and 82 of the EC Treaty that arise in individual cases (guidance letters) ([2004] OJ C101/78).

18.3.2.1 The role of the Commission

While abolishing the centralised notification system and putting an end to the Commission's monopoly in the exemption procedure, Regulation 1/2003 also had the effect of strengthening the Commission's powers, which is visible at both stages of investigation and in the final decision.

Investigation by the Commission

The entire supervision and enforcement procedure takes place in three stages: initiation of the investigation, the investigation process and the decision-making process.

Initiation of the investigation

According to Article 7(1) of Regulation 1/2003, the Commission can act on the basis of a complaint or on its own initiative. In the former case, the complaint may originate from natural or legal persons who 'can show a legitimate interest' (Article 7(2)). These can be the parties to an agreement itself (eg, distributors), the rivals of the parties to an agreement or third persons such as suppliers, customers or consumers' associations (see Case T-37/92 *Bureau Européen des Unions des Consommateurs and National*

Consumer Council v Commission [1994] ECR II-285). Member States may also lodge complaints with the Commission. In the latter case, the Commission will act on the basis of information collected by its services following informal complaints or given by national authorities.

The Commission has full discretion to decide to take action if there is a legitimate Union interest (see Case T-77/95 *Union française de l'express (Ufex), DHL International, Service CRIE and May Courier v Commission* [2000] ECR II-2167, para 40 and Commission Notice on the handling of complaints by the Commission under Articles 81 and 82 of the EC Treaty ([2004] OJ C101/65), para 28).

The Commission is expected, however, to

> ... consider attentively all the matters of fact and law brought to its attention by complainants in order to decide whether they disclose conduct of such a kind as to distort competition in the [internal] market and affect trade between Member States ... (*Ufex*, para 37)

Furthermore, according to the settled case law of the Court (see Case T-24/90 *Automec Srl v Commission* [1992] ECR II-2223, para 86; Joined Cases T-189/95, T-39/96 and T-123/96 *Service pour le groupement d'acquisitions (SGA) v Commission* [1999] ECR II-3587, para 52; Joined Cases T-185/96, T-189/96 and T-190/96 *Riviera Auto Service Etablissements Dalmasso SA, Garage des quatre vallées SA, Tosi, Palma SA (CIA - Groupe Palma) and Palma v Commission* [1999] ECR II-93, para 46; and Case T-201/11 *Si.mobil telekomunikacijske storitve d.d. v Commission*, 17 December 2014, ECLI:EU:T:2014:1096, para 83), in its assessment of the Union interest, the Commission must

> ... take account of the circumstances of the case, and must in particular balance the significance of the damage which the alleged infringement may cause to the functioning of the [internal] market against the probability of its being able to establish the existence of the infringement and the extent of the investigative measures required for it to perform, under the best possible conditions, its task of ensuring that Articles [101 and 102] of the Treaty are complied with ... (*Automec*, para 86)

The Commission's discretion in defining priorities is therefore not unlimited and is reviewable by the Court. Not only are complainants 'entitled to have the fate of their complaint settled by a decision of the Commission against which an action may be brought' (Case C-282/95 P *Guérin automobiles v Commission* [1997] ECR I-1503, para 36 and *Ufex*, para 37), but also the Commission is notably obliged to give sufficiently precise and detailed reasons for its decision to decline to continue with the examination of a complaint (see *Automec*, para 80 and *Ufex*, para 42).

This obligation is now formally incorporated in Article 7(1) of Regulation 773/2004:

> Where the Commission considers that on the basis of the information in its possession there are insufficient grounds for acting on a complaint, it shall inform the complainant of its reasons and set a time-limit within which the complainant may make known its views in writing.

Powers of investigation

Under Regulation 17, the Commission had three types of powers, namely:

- to conduct inquiries into sectors of the economy (Article 12);
- to request information (Article 11); and

- to undertake all necessary investigations into undertakings and associations of undertakings (Article 14).

Under Regulation 1/2003, the Commission keeps those powers and gain a new one, that of taking statements.

Conduct of inquiries   Under Article 17(1) of the Regulation, the Commission may conduct general inquiries into a particular sector of the economy if it has reasons to believe that competition may be restricted or distorted in that sector. For that purpose, it may request undertakings concerned to supply information, notably on all agreements, decisions and concerted practices in which they may be involved, and carry out all necessary inspections.

The results of its inquiry may be published in a report and interested parties may be invited to comment upon them.

Request for information   Article 18(1) of the Regulation provides that

> … the Commission may, by simple request or by decision, require undertakings and associations of undertakings to provide all necessary information.

In this case, the legal basis and the purpose of the request, the information required, the time limit within which the information is to be provided, and the penalties provided for in Articles 23 and 24 of the Regulation for supplying incorrect or misleading information, or for failing to supply information within the required time limit, must be specified.

Power to take statements   Article 19(1) of the Regulation gives the Commission the power to interview any natural or legal person with the view to collecting any information relating to the investigation provided they consent to be interviewed (on the conduct of proceedings, see Regulation 773/2004, Article 3).

The competition authority of the Member State in whose territory the interview takes place must be informed by the Commission and, if it requests it, its officials may assist the Commission's officials in conducting the interview (Regulation 1/2003, Article 19(2)).

Powers of inspection   Under Article 20(1) of the 2003 Regulation, the Commission has wide powers to conduct all necessary inspections of undertakings and associations of undertakings. Upon production of a written authorisation specifying the subject matter and purpose of the inspection and after giving notice of the inspection to the competition authority of the country where it is to be conducted (Article 20(3)), its officials may:

- enter any premises, land and means of transport of the companies under investigation; and
- examine their books and other records, take copies of those books or records and seal any business premises, books or records for the period necessary for the inspection.

In the exercise of those powers, at their request, the Commission officials must be actively assisted by officials of the relevant national competition authority who will then enjoy the same powers (Article 20(5)).

Undertakings must submit to inspections ordered by the decision of the Commission taken after consulting the relevant national competition authority. Such decision is challengeable in the Court of Justice however (see Case T-23/09 *Conseil national de l'Ordre des pharmaciens (CNOP) and Conseil central de la section G de l'Ordre national des pharmaciens (CCG) v Commission* [2010] ECR II-5291).

In the case where the undertaking under inspection opposes it, the Member State concerned must provide the Commission officials with the necessary assistance, including the assistance of the police or of any other enforcement authority (Article 20(6)), in which case authorisation from a national judicial authority is required (Article 20(7)). In such case, the jurisdiction of the national judicial authority is limited under Article 20(8) to 'control that the Commission decision is authentic and that the coercive measures envisaged are neither arbitrary nor excessive' (see Case C-94/00 *Roquette Frères SA v Directeur général de la concurrence, de la consommation et de la répression des fraudes, and Commission* [2002] ECR I-9011, para 40). To assess the proportionality of the coercive measures, the national judicial authority may ask the Commission 'for detailed explanations' but cannot 'question the necessity for the inspection' as the lawfulness of the Commission decision can only be challenged in the Court of Justice.

Article 21(1) of the Regulation also authorises the Commission to conduct an inspection in other premises, land and means of transport, including the homes of directors, managers and other members of staff of the undertakings, if there is a reasonable suspicion that books or other records related to the business are kept in those premises. However, the Commission cannot proceed with such inspection 'without prior authorisation from the national judicial authority of the Member State concerned' (Article 21(3)).

Hearings and professional secrecy

The inquisitorial investigation is followed by the adversarial hearings stage of the procedure, which gives the undertakings under investigation the opportunity of being heard and during which their rights of defence are fully respected.

This stage starts with the notification by the Commission to the parties concerned of a written statement of objections raised against them, to which the parties are invited to submit their written submission within a set time limit (Article 10 of Regulation 773/2004). After the notification of the statement of objections, those parties have a right of access to the files except to 'business secrets, other confidential information and internal documents of the Commission or of the competition authorities of the Member States' or any correspondence between the Commission and national competition authorities (Article 28 of Regulation 1/2003 and Article 15 of Regulation 773/2004).

Under Article 14 of Regulation 773/2004, oral hearings of the parties concerned and third parties showing sufficient interest are then conducted by a Hearing Officer acting in full independence from the head of the Competition Directorate-General. The hearings are not public. Statements made by the parties during the hearings are recorded and must be made available to the parties who attended the hearings.

Commission decisions

Decision-making is the last stage of the investigation process. This takes place after the Commission has consulted an Advisory Committee on Restrictive Practices and Dominant Positions as required under Article 14 of the 2003 Regulation. The Commission may take two types of decisions: interim measures and final decisions.

Interim measures

Originally, Regulation 17 being silent on the matter, the power of the Commission to take interim measures was recognised in the case law of the Court (see Case 792/79 R *Camera Care Ltd v Commission* [1980] ECR 119, para 14; Joined Cases 228/82 and 229/

82 R *Ford Werke AG and Ford of Europe Incorporated v Commission* [1982] ECR 3091, para 13 and Case T-44/90 *La Cinq SA v Commission* [1992] ECR II-1). In *La Cinq*, the Court ruled that interim measures were justified under two conditions:

- practices of certain undertakings are prima facie such as to constitute a breach of EU rules on competition; and
- there is 'proven urgency, in order to prevent the occurrence of a situation likely to cause serious and irreparable damage to the party applying for their adoption or intolerable damage to the public interest' (para 28).

The Commission may take such measures in order to end an infringement of competition rules before adopting a final decision (see Joined Cases 228 and 229/82 *Ford of Europe Incorporated and Ford-Werke Aktiengesellschaft v Commission* [1984] ECR 1129).

This power is now enshrined in Article 8(1) of Regulation 1/2003:

> In cases of urgency due to the risk of serious and irreparable damage to competition, the Commission, acting on its own initiative may by decision, on the basis of a prima facie finding of infringement, order interim measures.

Final decisions

The Commission may take a variety of decisions based on the nature and the extent of the infringement and EU law requirements.

Finding and termination of infringement   If the Commission finds that there is a breach of Articles 101 or 102 TFEU, Article 7(1) of Regulation 1/2003 empowers it to adopt a decision requiring the guilty undertakings to bring such infringement to an end, and imposing on them any behavioural or structural remedies in proportion to the infringement committed.

Under Article 9(1), the Commission may also by decision make binding on the undertakings concerned their commitments to meet the concerns of the Commission.

Finding of inapplicability   At the end of its investigation, the Commission may also come to the conclusion that no infringement was committed and will then issue, under Article 10 of Regulation 1/2003, a decision finding that Article 101 or 102 TFEU is not applicable.

Penalties

Following the finding of an infringement, the Commission may impose two types of penalties on the undertakings concerned: fines and periodic penalty payments.

Fines

Based on the seriousness and the duration of the infringement (Article 23(3) of Regulation 1/2003), the Commission may impose two kinds of fines.

Under Article 23(2), the Commission may impose a fine not exceeding 10% of its total turnover in the preceding business year on each undertaking which, either intentionally or negligently:

- infringed Articles 101 or 102 TFEU; or
- contravened a decision ordering interim measures; or
- failed to comply with a commitment made binding by a decision under Article 9.

Article 23(1) also empowers the Commission to impose fines of up to 1% of total turnover in the preceding business year on each undertaking for having, intentionally or negligently:

- supplied incorrect, incomplete or misleading information following an Article 17 or 18 request for information (see above); or failed to supply information within the required time limit;
- produced the required books or other records related to the business in incomplete form or refused to submit to inspections;
- given, or failed to correct, an incorrect or misleading answer, failed or refused to provide a complete answer; or
- broken seals affixed by the Commission.

Periodic penalty payments

Periodic penalty payments are designed to compel undertakings to:

- put an end to an infringement of Articles 101 or 102 TFEU;
- comply with interim measures;
- comply with a commitment made binding by a decision under Article 9;
- supply complete and correct information as requested; or
- submit to an inspection.

These payments cannot exceed 5% of the average daily turnover of the undertakings in the preceding business year per day.

However, considering that the penalties imposed on undertakings may reach extremely high levels, the Commission developed since 1996 a general leniency programme. The latest one can be found in the Commission Notice on Immunity from fines and reduction of fines in cartel cases ([2006] OJ C298/17). Such programme is designed to '[reward] cooperation in the Commission investigation by undertakings which are or have been party to secret cartels affecting the [Union]' (first recital). The reward might consist either in:

- an immunity of fines for undertakings who are the first to provide information and evidence which will enable the Commission to carry out targeted inspections or find an infringement of Article 101 TFEU in connection with the alleged cartel; or
- a reduction of the fine for undertakings which provide the Commission with evidence of the alleged infringement representing significant added value with respect to the evidence already in the Commission's possession.

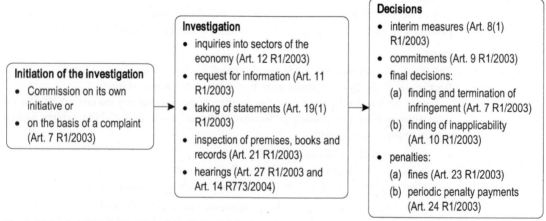

Figure 18.1   Investigating powers of the Commission

18.3.2.2 Cooperation between the Commission and national competition authorities and courts

The distribution of powers between the European and national authorities with regard to Articles 101 and 102 TFEU has been fundamentally overhauled as a result of the modernisation and decentralisation of the enforcement system of EU competition rules. By introducing a system based on the direct effect of EU competition rules, Regulation 1/2003/EC empowered NCAs and national courts to apply all aspects of EU competition law.

Thus, the Regulation offered two evolutions: a decentralised enforcement of EU competition rules in favour of NCAs (see the Commission Notice on cooperation within the Network of Competition Authorities ([2004] OJ C101/43)) and greater cooperation between the European Commission and national courts (see the Commission Notice on the co-operation between the Commission and the courts of the EU Member States in the application of Articles 81 and 82 EC ([2004] OJ C101/54)).

Cooperation between the Commission and national competition authorities

Under Article 11(1) of Regulation 1/2003, the Commission and NCAs must apply EU competition rules in close cooperation. Together, they form a European Competition Network (ECN). In this respect, Member States have an obligation to set up authorities responsible for the enforcement of competition rules. This obligation applied to all new Member States which joined the EU in 2004 and later (hence the coming into force of Regulation 1/2003 on 1 May 2004, the official day of that enlargement). In the United Kingdom, the relevant competition authority is the Competition and Markets Authority, which, from 1 April 2014, took over many of the functions of the Competition Commission (CC) and the Office of Fair Trading (OFT).

Clearly specified under Article 5, first paragraph of the Regulation, the powers of NCAs are to 'apply Articles [101] and [102] of the Treaty in individual cases'. For this purpose, acting on their own initiative or on a complaint, they are competent to:

- require that an infringement be brought to an end;
- order interim measures;
- accept commitments made by undertakings;
- impose fines, periodic penalty payments or any other penalty provided for in their national law; or
- decide that there are no grounds for action.

Cooperation between the Commission and NCAs has been solidly established and takes many forms:

- first, they have the power to exchange information, including any evidence used in any matter of fact or of law and confidential information (Article 12(1));
- secondly, when acting under EU competition rules, NCAs must inform the Commission in writing before or without delay after commencing the first formal investigative measure, as well as the NCAs of other Member States (Article 11(3)). Conversely, the Commission also has an obligation, under Article 11(2), to transmit to NCAs copies of the most important documents it has collected in the course of an investigation and, at the request of a NCA, to provide it with a copy of other existing documents necessary for the assessment of the case;

- more generally, NCAs may consult the Commission on any case involving the application of EU competition law (Article 11(5)), and have an obligation to assist Commission officials in the conduct of investigations (Article 22(2)); and
- finally, under Article 13(1), the Commission may reject a complaint if a competition authority of a Member State is already dealing with the case (for a first interpretation of the conditions of application of this provision, see *Si.mobil*, paras 30–77).

Nonetheless, the Commission retains an important regulatory role within the ECN. Under Article 11(6) of the Regulation, subject only to consultation of the national authority concerned, the Commission retains the option of initiating proceedings for the adoption of a decision, even where a national authority is already acting in the matter (see also Case T-339/04 *France Télécom SA v Commission* [2007] II-521, para 80). Furthermore, a NCA can never make a decision running counter to a Commission decision (Article 16(2)). Nor can it take a decision stating that there is no breach of Article 101 or 102 TFEU (negative decision) since the power of NCAs is limited to the adoption of a decision stating that there are no grounds for action (Article 5, second paragraph). Indeed, as the Court put it in Case C-375/09 *Prezes Urzedu Ochrony Konkurencji i Konsumentów v Tele2 Polska sp z oo, devenue Netia SA* [2011] ECR I-3055:

> Empowerment of national competition authorities to take decisions stating that there has been no breach of Article 102 TFEU would call into question the system of cooperation established by the Regulation and would undermine the power of the Commission.
>
> Such a 'negative' decision on the merits would risk undermining the uniform application of Articles 101 TFEU and 102 TFEU, which is one of the objectives of the Regulation highlighted by recital 1 in its preamble, since such a decision might prevent the Commission from finding subsequently that the practice in question amounts to a breach of those provisions of European Union law. (paras 27–28)

Cooperation between the Commission and national courts

Regulation 1/2003/EC has formalised the relations between the Commission and national courts and has extended their powers to the application of Article 101(3) TFEU.

The importance of the role of national courts in the application of EU competition rules is particularly stressed in the Notice on the handling of complaints by the Commission under Articles 81 and 82 of the EC Treaty, in which the Commission analyses the advantages for complainants to take action before a national court which may notably:

- award damages for loss suffered as a result of a breach of Article 101 or 102 (see 18.4.1);
- deal with claims for payment or contractual obligations based on an agreement covered by Article 101 TFEU;
- apply the civil sanction of nullity of Article 101(2) TFEU in contractual relationships between individuals;
- adopt interim measures;
- hear combined claims under EU competition law with other claims under national law; and
- award legal costs to the successful applicant.

The basic principles governing the relations between the Commission and national courts are untouched. First, the **principle of institutional and procedural autonomy** continues to apply (see Case C-234/89 *Delimitis v Henninger Bräu AG* [1991] ECR I-935: a national court may not declare Article 101(1) TFEU inapplicable to an agreement under Article 101(3) but may declare the agreement void under Article 101(2) if it is certain that the agreement cannot be exempted under Article 101(3) (para 55)).

Secondly, Commission decisions always take precedence (see Case C-344/98 *Masterfoods Ltd v HB Ice Cream Ltd* [2000] ECR I-11369: a national court ruling on the compatibility of an agreement or practice with Articles 101(1) and 102 TFEU which is already the subject of a Commission decision, cannot take a decision running counter to that of the Commission even if the latter's decision conflicts with a decision given by a national court of first instance (para 60)). This principle is now enshrined in Article 16(1) of Regulation 1/2003. Article 15 of the Regulation, which defines the different modes of cooperation between the Commission and national courts, is more innovative however. First, national courts 'may ask the Commission to transmit to them information in its possession or its opinion on questions concerning the application of the [Union] competition rules' (Article 15(1)). Secondly, copies of written judgments of national courts on the application of Article 101 or Article 102 TFEU must be forwarded to the Commission 'without delay after the full written judgment is notified to the parties' (Article 15(2)). Thirdly, in order to ensure a coherent application of Articles 101 and 102, the Commission, acting on its own initiative, may submit written and, with their permission, oral observations to national courts (Article 15(3)).

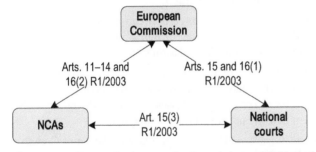

Figure 18.2   Cooperation between the Commission and NCAs and national courts

18.3.2.3   Review of public enforcement under Regulation 1/2003

The Commission reviewed the working of the new enforcement system in its Communication, 'Ten Years of Antitrust Enforcement under Regulation 1/2003: Achievements and Future Perspectives' (COM(2014) 453).

Following a detailed analysis of public enforcement of competition rules under the 2003 Regulation, the Commission concludes that 'Regulation 1/2003 has transformed the competition enforcement landscape', notably by increasing the achievements of the Commission, the ECN and NCAs. Not only has the Regulation enabled the Commission to strengthen its enforcement record by devoting greater resources to investigating cases and conducting inquiries in key sectors of the economy suffering from market distortions, it has also fostered 'a dynamic development of close cooperation within the ECN, which has underpinned the coherent application of the

EU competition rules throughout the EU' (para 43) by turning NCAs into key pillars of the enforcement of EU competition rules.

The Commission believes that a 'truly common competition enforcement area in the EU' can be created on the basis of those achievements. For that purpose it has identified a few key areas for further improvement, namely (para 46):

- the strengthening of NCAs' independence by providing them with sufficient resources;
- NCAs with full effective investigative and decision-making powers at their disposal;
- the existence of powers to impose effective and proportionate fines and of well-designed national leniency programmes; and
- the existence of measures to remove disincentives for corporate leniency applicants.

18.4 Private enforcement of competition rules

Competition rules are enforced both by public and private enforcement systems which serve the same aims of deterring anti-competitive practices, protecting companies and consumers from these practices and making available damages caused by them.

However, compared to US antitrust law, private enforcement under EU law had been lagging behind public enforcement. In the Green Paper on Damages actions for breach of the EC antitrust rules (COM(2005) 672 final), the Commission observed that

[w]hile [Union] law ... demands an effective system for damages claims for infringements of antitrust rules, this area of the law in the 25 Member States presents a picture of 'total underdevelopment'. (at 3)

There was therefore a need to address the imbalance between a modernised public enforcement system and a deficient system for bringing damages claims for infringements of EU competition rules. In the Commission's view:

Facilitating damages claims for breach of antitrust law will not only make it easier for consumers and firms who have suffered damages arising from an infringement of antitrust rules to recover their losses from the infringer but also strengthen the enforcement of antitrust law. (Green Paper at 1)

As the Court rightly stated in Case C-453/99 *Courage Ltd v Crehan and Crehan v Courage Ltd and Others* [2001] ECR I-6297:

The full effectiveness of Article [101] of the Treaty and, in particular, the practical effect of the prohibition laid down in Article [101(1)] would be put at risk if it were not open to any individual to claim damages for loss caused to him by a contract or by conduct liable to restrict or distort competition.

Indeed, the existence of such a right strengthens the working of the [Union] competition rules and discourages agreements or practices, which are frequently covert, which are liable to restrict or distort competition. From that point of view, actions for damages before the national courts *can make a significant contribution to the maintenance of effective competition in the [Union]*. (paras 26–27, emphasis added)

Actions for damages for breaches of EU competition rules have therefore a dual purpose:

- to compensate those who have suffered a loss as a consequence of anti-competitive behaviour, thus involving companies and consumers more closely in competition law; and
- to ensure the full effectiveness of competition rules by deterring anti-competitive behaviour.

18.4.1 Private enforcement in the national courts

As there was no effective system of damages claims under EU law and the EU Courts had no jurisdiction for such claims, this area of law enforcement was left to the national courts (subject to the preliminary rulings procedure, see **Chapter 9**).

On the basis of the settled case law of the Court relating to the effective protection of EU rights by national courts, and following the same principles as those applied in State liability actions (see 7.3), the Court ruled in *Courage v Crehan*:

> ... in the absence of [Union] rules governing the matter, it is for the domestic legal system of each Member State to designate the courts and tribunals having jurisdiction and to lay down the detailed procedural rules governing actions for safeguarding rights which individuals derive directly from [Union] law, provided that such rules are not less favourable than those governing similar domestic actions (principle of equivalence) and that they do not render practically impossible or excessively difficult the exercise of rights conferred by [Union] law (principle of effectiveness) ... (para 29)

However, the effectiveness of the system of damages actions for infringement of EU competition rules was significantly impeded by the diversity and sometimes underdevelopment of national rules. This can result in great legal uncertainty and, in practice, in victims of EU competition breaches rarely obtaining adequate reparation for the harm suffered. These obstacles are analysed in great detail in the Commission Staff Working Paper annexed to the Green Paper (SEC(2005) 1732) in paragraphs 28 to 44.

The Commission consequently concluded in the White Paper on Damages actions for breach of the EC antitrust rules (COM(2008) 165 final) that, in order to create a better level playing field and legal certainty within the internal market, the 'ineffectiveness of antitrust damages actions [was] best addressed by a combination of measures at both [Union] and national levels' (at 2).

18.4.2 The new EU regime governing actions for damages under national law for breaches of competition law

On the basis of the White Paper, in 2009, the Commission made an initial proposal for a Directive on the rules governing damages actions for infringements of Articles 81 and 82 of the Treaty, which was soon abandoned as a result of the many divergent views from the Member States.

Following years of further and hard negotiations, Directive 2014/104/EU on certain rules governing actions for damages under national law for infringements of the competition law provisions of the Member States and of the European Union was finally adopted on 26 November 2014. Member States have until 27 December 2016 to transpose the Directive into national law.

In the UK, reforms of the private enforcement of competition law were also adopted in March 2015 under s 81 and Sch 8 of the Consumer Rights Act 2015, which focus mainly on increasing the use of collective actions for breaches of competition rules and the powers of the Competition Appeal Tribunal.

18.4.2.1 Aims and objectives of the Directive

The 2014 Directive first aims to harmonise certain procedures across the European Union for claimants seeking to bring damages actions for harm caused by breaches of competition law.

The Directive is designed to smooth out the discrepancies between the national rules on actions for damages leading to an uneven playing field with regard to such actions and potentially affecting competition on the markets. Uneven enforcement of the right to compensation in EU law affects not only competition within the internal market by providing a competitive advantage for some undertakings breaching EU rules, but also the proper functioning of the internal market by potentially deterring companies from exercising their rights of establishment or from providing goods or services in Member States where the right to reparation is more effectively enforced.

It also seeks to correct the imbalance between an effective public enforcement at EU and national levels and an ineffective access to private enforcement of competition law in national courts, and to create better interaction between both forms of enforcement to ensure maximum effectiveness of competition rules by '[regulating] the coordination of those two forms of enforcement in a coherent manner' (recital 6 of the preamble to the Directive).

Finally, regarding actions for damages as 'only one element of an effective system of private enforcement of infringements of competition law', it seeks to provide alternative measures of redress, such as consensual dispute resolution and public enforcement decisions giving parties an incentive to provide compensation as a complement (see recital 5 of the preamble to the Directive).

This is summed up in Article 1 of the Directive, which states:

> 1. This Directive sets out certain rules necessary to ensure that anyone who has suffered harm caused by an infringement of competition law by an undertaking or by an association of undertakings can effectively exercise the right to claim full compensation for that harm from that undertaking or association. It sets out rules fostering undistorted competition in the internal market and removing obstacles to its proper functioning, by ensuring equivalent protection throughout the Union for anyone who has suffered such harm.
>
> 2. This Directive sets out rules coordinating the enforcement of the competition rules by competition authorities and the enforcement of those rules in damages actions before national courts.

18.4.2.2 Key provisions of the Directive

Right to full compensation

The whole Directive lies on the fundamental principle of the right to full compensation. This is expressed in Article 3(2), which states:

> Full compensation shall place a person who has suffered harm in the position in which that person would have been had the infringement of competition law not been committed. It shall therefore cover the right to compensation for actual loss and for loss of profit, plus the payment of interest.

The right must be guaranteed in all Member States (Article 3(1)) so as to avoid 'forum shopping', that is seeking the most favourable jurisdiction in which to bring a claim.

As stated in Joined Cases C-295/04 to C-298/04 *Manfredi v Lloyd Adriatico Assicurazioni SpA, Cannito v Fondiaria Sai SpA and Tricarico and Murgolo v Assitalia SpA* [2006] ECR I-6619, para 95

> … compensation includes reparation not only for actual loss suffered (*damnum emergens*), but also for loss of profit (*lucrum cessans*) and the payment of interest. (para 95)

This definition of compensation is now provided in Article 3(2) and can in no way include 'overcompensation, whether by means of punitive, multiple or other types of damages' (Article 3(3)).

Under the Directive, both direct purchasers (anyone who bought directly from an infringer, products or services that were the object of the breach of competition rules) and indirect purchasers (anyone who bought products or services that were the object of a breach of competition rules from a direct purchaser or a subsequent purchaser rather than directly from the infringer) of the goods or services sold by an infringer can claim compensation of harm (Article 12(1)).

Under Article 14(2), indirect purchasers may rely on a rebuttable presumption (as recommended by the Commission in the White Paper, para 2.6) that they have suffered a loss as a result of a passing-on of an illegal overcharge when it can be shown that:

- the defendant has committed an infringement of competition law;
- the latter has resulted in overcharge for a direct purchaser of the defendant; and
- the indirect purchaser purchased from the direct purchaser the goods or services that were the object of the infringement.

This is an important development for indirect purchasers as it is more difficult for them to prove the existence and extent of a passing-on of an illegal overcharge since, by definition, they are at or close to the end of the distribution chain and therefore farther from the infringement of a competition rule.

Proof of a breach of competition rules

As explained above (see **18.3.2.2**), it is a settled principle of EU law that national courts cannot take decisions running counter to decisions of the European Commission. Infringement decisions of the Commission are binding on national courts.

Article 9 extends the binding effect on national courts to infringement decisions of NCAs. This is designed to facilitate the bringing of actions for antitrust damages, increase their effectiveness and procedural efficiency, and increase legal certainty by ensuring a consistent application of Articles 101 and 102 by national bodies.

It would make little sense indeed if defendants could challenge in an action for damages their own breach of Article 101 or 102 already established in a final decision by an NCA, confirmed by a review court. This would oblige the national court to re-examine the facts and legal issues already investigated and assessed by those bodies, thus potentially increasing the duration of the damages action and therefore making it considerably more costly and imponderable.

For that reason, a national court ruling in a follow-on action for antitrust damages cannot take decisions running counter to a final decision of a NCA or of a review court of the same State. The infringement found in those decisions is thus deemed to be irrefutably established (Article 9(1)).

Equally, a national court must treat the finding of an infringement in a final decision of a NCA or of a review court in a different Member State as at least prima facie evidence, and may assess that decision along with any other evidence provided in court (Article 9(2)).

These obligations do not prevent, however, national courts from seeking clarification on the interpretation of Articles 101 or 102 TFEU under Article 267 TFEU (see **Chapter 9**).

Limitation periods

Limitation periods or prescriptions play an important role in providing legal certainty, but they can also be a major obstacle to recovering damages, either in stand-alone or follow-on cases (on the diversity of the rules on limitation periods in national and EU laws, see the Staff Working Document annexed to the Green Paper, paras 261–272).

The commencement of limitation periods presents many difficulties, in particular in the case of continuous or repeated infringements or when the victim cannot reasonably be aware of them. This is frequently the case for cartels, which by definition are covert during their whole existence.

Consequently, the Directive gives claimants a period of at least five years to bring actions for damages (Article 10(3)), which cannot start before the infringement of competition law has ceased and before the claimants know, or can reasonably be expected to know of its existence, the harm caused to them by the infringement and the identity of the infringer (Article 10(2)).

Contrary to the Commission's recommendation in the White Paper (para 2.7), Article 10(4) provides for the limitation period to be suspended or interrupted where a NCA decides to initiate an investigation or proceedings with respect to an infringement relating to the damages claim. The suspension should then continue for at least a year following the final NCA decision or the termination of the proceedings.

These new rules should potentially give rise to actions for competition law breaches running over decades.

Joint and several liability

With a limited exception for small or medium-sized enterprises (SMEs) as defined in Commission Recommendation 2003/361/EC, undertakings which have infringed competition law through joint behaviour, such as in cartels, are to be held jointly and severally liable for the harm caused as a result of this infringement (Article 11(1) and (2) of the Directive). The victim of an infringement can therefore choose to sue one or more infringers until fully compensated. Should one of the infringers not be sued, another co-infringer might still try to recover a contribution for its share in the infringement.

Nonetheless, in order to preserve the efficiency of the Commission and national leniency programmes (see **18.3.2.1**), the civil liability of successful immunity applicants could be limited. As suggested by the Commission in the White Paper (para 2.9), Article 11(4) of the Directive provides that the liability of immunity recipients (an undertaking or natural person who was granted immunity from fines by the Commission or a NCA under a leniency programme) is limited to the harm they caused to their own direct and indirect purchasers or providers, and to other victims unless full compensation cannot be obtained from the other co-infringers. In the latter case, the right to full compensation is thus protected by maintaining the full liability of the immunity recipients.

Disclosure of evidence

Article 5(1) and (2) stipulates that, when claimants have presented a reasoned justification demonstrating the plausibility of their claim for damages, national courts must have the power to order the defendant or a third party to disclose relevant evidence in their control, and notably to order the disclosure of specified items of evidence or relevant categories of evidence defined as precisely and as narrowly as possible. Equally, national courts must be able, upon request of the defendant, to order the claimant or a third party to disclose relevant evidence. Disclosure must be proportionate, taking account of the legitimate interests of all parties and third parties (Articles 5(3) and 6(4)).

Where confidential documents must be disclosed, national courts must 'have at their disposal effective measures to protect such information' (Article 5(4)).

This power of disclosure is, however, subject to two limitations:

- under Article 6(5), information prepared specifically for the proceedings of a NCA, or information prepared by the NCA and sent to the parties during its proceedings, and withdrawn settlement submissions are temporarily protected against disclosure until the closure of the NCA's proceedings; and
- under Article 6(6), leniency statements and settlement submissions are fully protected from disclosure.

Passing-on defence

Passing-on defence means that the defendant argues that the direct purchaser, as claimant in the damages action, should either be entitled to no or limited reparation on the ground that the whole or part of the overcharge resulting from the infringement was passed on to the claimant's customers.

The right to invoke such defence is now enshrined in Article 13 of the Directive. In support of this defence, the defendant may require disclosure from the claimant or from third parties in order to prove that the overcharge was passed on.

Quantification of harm

As compensation for harm caused is designed to place the victims of the antitrust infringement in the position in which they would have been before it occurred, their post-infringement position has to be compared with their pre-infringement one (the 'non-infringement or counterfactual scenario') in an assessment which is usually referred to as the 'but-for analysis'.

Once a national court has determined whether the claimant has suffered harm because of an antitrust breach – namely that it has made a finding of an infringement and the causal link between this infringement and the harm suffered – it has then to award an amount to the claimant as compensation for that harm.

Assessing and proving the quantum of damages or quantification is often difficult, however, as this is based on a hypothetical situation and on a form of estimation necessary to build up a counterfactual scenario with which to compare the post-infringement position of the claimant. Nevertheless, this is the central question in all antitrust damages actions.

Under Article 17(1) of the Directive, national courts are

> … empowered, in accordance with national procedures, to estimate the amount of harm if it is established that a claimant suffered harm but it is practically impossible or excessively difficult precisely to quantify the harm suffered on the basis of the evidence available.

In this respect, a NCA may, at their request, assist national courts if it considers such assistance to be appropriate (Article 17(3)).

Article 17(2) also provides a rebuttable presumption that a cartel causes harm. This should help lower claimants' costs since it will no longer be required to prove that a cartel caused higher prices.

Consensual dispute resolution

As clearly stated in recital 5 of the preamble to the Directive:

> Actions for damages are only one element of an effective system of private enforcement of infringements of competition law and are complemented by alternative avenues of redress, such as consensual dispute resolution and public enforcement decisions that give parties an incentive to provide compensation.

The promotion of consensual dispute resolution (CDR) is in line with the overall objective of the Directive to ensure that all victims of breaches of competition rules can enforce their right to claim full compensation from the infringer(s), since it is deemed to be a cheaper and faster way of resolving disputes by involving out-of-court settlements, arbitration, mediation or conciliation.

Under Article 18(1) of the Directive, the limitation period for bringing an action for damages must be suspended for the duration of any consensual dispute resolution process 'with regard to those parties that are or that were involved or represented in the consensual dispute resolution'.

Where the parties are involved in CDR, courts' proceedings can be suspended for up to two years (Article 18(2)).

In order to protect settling co-infringers, Article 19(2) provides that non-settling co-infringers cannot be permitted to recover contribution for the remaining claim from the former. Settling co-infringers will, however, be held jointly and severally liable for the award of damages made against non-settling co-infringers only if the latter are unable to pay the compensation owed (Article 19(3)).

In order to avoid overcompensation of claimants, when awarding damages, national courts must take account of any damages paid in accordance with a prior consensual settlement relating to a particular breach of competition (Article 19(4)).

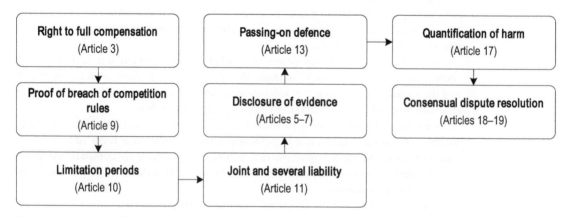

Figure 18.3   Damages for breaches of competition rules under the 2014 Directive

18.5 Further reading

Breathnach S, 'Sweetening the Carrot: the Role of Leniency Programmes in the Fight against Cartels' (2013) 34(1) *ECLR* 12.

Camilleri E, 'A Decade of EU Antitrust Private Enforcement: Chronicle of a Failure Foretold?' (2013) 34(10) *ECLR* 531.

Cengiz F, 'Multi-Level Governance in Competition Policy: the European Competition Network' (2010) 35(5) *EL Rev* 660.

Ehlermann C, 'The Modernisation of EC Anti-trust Policy: A Legal and Cultural Revolution' (2000) 37 *CMLRev* 537.

Ford S, 'Claims for Contribution in Competition Damages Actions: the Impact of the EU Damages Directive' (2015) 36(8) *ECLR* 327.

Gamble R, 'The European Embrace of Private Enforcement: this Time with Feeling' (2014) 35(10) *ECLR* 469.

Killeen D, 'Following in "Uncle Sam's" Footsteps? The Evolution of Private Antitrust Enforcement in the European Union' (2013) 34(9) *ECLR* 480.

Komninos A, 'Public and Private Antitrust Enforcement in Europe: Complement? Overlap?' (2006) 3(1) *Competition Law Review* 5.

Lianos I, 'Causal Uncertainty and Damages Claims for Infringement of Competition Law in Europe' (2015) *CLES Research Paper Series* 2/2015.

Mateus A, 'Ensuring a More Level Playing Field in Competition Enforcement Throughout the European Union' (2010) 31(12) *ECLR* 514.

Nazzini R, 'Fundamental Rights beyond Legal Positivism: Rethinking the *ne bis in idem* Principle in EU Competition Law' (2014) 2(2) *Journal of Antitrust Enforcement* 270.

Segal I and Whinston M, 'Public vs Private Enforcement of Antitrust Law: A Survey' (2007) 28(5) *ECLR* 306.

de Sousa e Alvim M, 'The New EU Directive on Antitrust Damages – a Giant Step Forward?' (2015) 36(6) *ECLR* 245.

Slot P, 'A View from the Mountain: 40 Years of Developments in EC Competition Law' (2004) 41 *CML Rev* 443.

Wils W, 'The Relationship Between Public Antitrust Enforcement and Private Actions for Damages' (2009) 32(1) *World Competition* 3.

summary

The enforcement system of competition rules serves the aims of deterring anti-competitive practices and protecting companies and consumers from these practices. It must also offer damages to parties injured by such practices.

Both public and private enforcement are therefore an important part of a common enforcement system aimed at guaranteeing a competitive economy.

Compared to the American antitrust enforcement system where private enforcement is predominant, public enforcement has prevailed in the European Community and Union. This was a natural development in the initial creation of a European common market. Furthermore, as part of the integration process, the original system of supervision and enforcement of competition rules could only be highly centralised. However, in order to face successfully the challenges of further enlargement to Eastern and Central Europe and further economic and monetary integration, public enforcement undertook a complete overhaul under Regulation 1/2003, leading to the modernisation and decentralisation of the enforcement of competition rules, thus involving fully national competition authorities and national courts in the application of EU competition rules. This, in turn, revolutionised the relationship between the European Commission and national competition authorities on the one hand, and between national competition authorities themselves on the other. It also changed the nature of the cooperation between the Commission and national courts.

In parallel, while private enforcement under EU law was lagging behind public enforcement and while, in the absence of an effective system of damages claims under EU law, this area of law enforcement was left to the national courts, it was soon recognised by the Commission that facilitating damages claims for breach of competition law would strengthen the enforcement of European antitrust law and that the ineffectiveness of damages actions would be best addressed by a combination of measures at both Union and national levels. After more than 10 years of negotiations, this imbalance between the two legs of the EU enforcement system of competition rules was corrected by the adoption of the 2014 Directive on damages actions for breaches of competition law.

Naturally, private and public enforcement of competition rules would be seriously limited, should EU competition rules not apply to undertakings located outside the European Union. The principle of territoriality enables the European authorities to reach out to such entities. Furthermore, the European Union has also engaged in international cooperation with competition authorities of third countries by way of bilateral competition agreements or a variety of association, partnership and free trade agreements.

test your knowledge

1   Critically analyse the ruling of the CJEU in Case C-17/10 *Toshiba Corporation and Others v Úřad pro ochranu hospodářské soutěže*, 14 February 2012, ECLI:EU:C:2012:72 on the parallel application of national and Union competition law.

2   It could be stated that the public enforcement of Articles 101 and 102 TFEU does not suffer from the deficiencies of US public enforcement and that there is no reason therefore to import into the European Union the American conception of actions for damages as an instrument of deterrence and punishment.
    Discuss.

3   Critically analyse Case C-557/12 *Kone AG v OBB-Infrastruktur AG*, 24 October 2013, ECLI:EU:C:2014:1317 on damages for losses caused by a cartel.

4   In your opinion, is Directive 2014/104/EU on certain rules governing actions for damages under national law for infringements of the competition law provisions of the Member States and of the European Union ([2014] OJ L349/1) likely to endanger the effectiveness of the EU public enforcement of competition law whilst failing to achieve the objectives underpinning private enforcement?

EUROPEAN CITIZENSHIP AND THE FREE MOVEMENT OF EUROPEAN CITIZENS

19 European Citizenship

study points

After reading this chapter, you will be able to understand:
- the concept of European citizenship
- the status of European citizens
- the political and legal rights of European citizens.

19.1 Introduction

The concept of European citizenship, additional to national citizenship, is the necessary corollary of the European integration process. The Maastricht Treaty of 1992 was the first stone laid down for the establishment of 'a citizenship common to nationals of their countries' (recital 8 of the preamble to the Maastricht Treaty on European Union). The clear intention of the Member States materialised in Article 8 of the Maastricht Treaty establishing the European Community, which simply states that 'Citizenship of the Union is hereby established'.

The concept of European citizenship is now firmly enshrined in Articles 9 TEU and 20(1) TFEU, and in Chapter V (Articles 39–46) of the Charter of Fundamental Rights of the European Union (ECFR).

Uneasy to define, the Court of Justice elevated this concept to one that is 'destined to be the fundamental status of nationals of the Member States' (Case C-184/99 *Grzelczyk v Centre public d'aide sociale d'Ottignies-Louvain-la-Neuve* [2001] ECR I-6193, para 31) which confers a number of political and legal rights to citizens of the Union. However, as the Court's case law shows, the concept of European citizenship is still affected by its ambiguous nature and its own limits, and has been developed through a pragmatic approach.

19.2 From a People's Europe to European citizenship

19.2.1 People's Europe and citizens' Europe

The concept of a People's Europe was first coined at the European Council meeting at Fontainebleau of 25–26 June 1984 (Conclusions of the presidency are available at <http://www.consilium.europa.eu> – search 'Fontainebleau 1984') in order for the former European Community to 'respond to the expectations of the people of Europe by adopting measures to strengthen and promote its identity and its image both for its citizens and for the rest of the world' (at 8).

The European Council decided to set up an ad hoc Committee (the Adonnino Committee), composed of representatives of the Heads of State or of Government of the Member States, to prepare and coordinate this action.

The Committee made a number of proposals in its report, 'A People's Europe' (Bulletin of the European Communities, Supplement 7/85). The first report of March 1985 focused on:

- easing the rules and practices causing irritation to Community citizens and undermining the credibility of the Community, notably 'the abolition of all police and customs formalities for people crossing intra-Community frontiers' (at 8);
- extending Community citizens' rights with regard to the right of establishment, mutual recognition of professional qualifications and the right of residence.

The second report of June 1985 extended the issue to special rights of citizens, such as:

- greater participation in the political process in the Community (voting rights and eligibility in local elections);
- same rights as nationals to freedom of speech and of assembly; consultation of citizens on transfrontier issues (eg, major public works, environmental issues, transport, and health and safety matters) within the Community; and
- codification and simplification of Community law.

A number of those rights recognised in A People's Europe are certainly rights that are inherent to the concept of European citizenship and in particular its political aspect. But most of those rights are also attached to the economic integration process and are part of a wider, modern conception of citizenship.

Although the division between the two concepts of a People's Europe and European citizenship might be blurred, the former ignores the human rights dimension of European citizenship. For that reason, in its 'Resolution on the functioning of the Treaty on European Union with a view to the 1996 Intergovernmental Conference – Implementation and development of the Union', 17 May 1995 ([1995] OJ C151/56), the European Parliament called for the concept of EU citizenship to be given greater substance through the development of the special rights linked to EU citizenship, notably by means of:

- accession of the European Union to the European Convention on Human Rights and Fundamental Freedoms (ECHR);
- a new right of all EU citizens to information on EU matters;
- the inclusion of an explicit reference in the Treaty to the principle of equal treatment irrespective of race, sex, age, handicap or religion and the incorporation of a specific reference to a ban on capital punishment;
- the development of political citizenship through measures facilitating participation in political life in a Member State of Union citizens residing in that State;
- the strengthening of the provisions on the free movement of persons;
- the preservation of Europe's diversity through special safeguards for traditional national minorities, democracy and the rule of law;
- the application of the Treaty provisions on equal rights not only to economic rights but to all aspects of equality for women; and
- the adoption of Treaty provisions rejecting racism, xenophobia, sexism, discrimination on grounds of a person's sexual orientation, antisemitism, revisionism and all forms of discrimination, and guaranteeing adequate legal protection against discrimination for all individuals resident within the EU.

It is this concept of European citizenship that has been enshrined in the Treaty on European Union.

19.2.2 European citizenship under the EU treaties

European citizenship was first created in the Maastricht Treaty of 1992 (see 1.5) with the view to bringing European citizens closer to the European Union integration process.

The new Article 8 TEC (as inserted by the Maastricht Treaty) simply provided that:

1. Citizenship of the Union is hereby established.

Every person holding the nationality of a Member State shall be a citizen of the Union.

2. Citizens of the Union shall enjoy the rights conferred by this Treaty and shall be subject to the duties imposed thereby.

Articles 8a–8e described a range of rights linked to European citizenship but no definition of the concept is to be found.

Those original provisions on European citizenship have hardly been amended by successive Treaties and can now be found in Article 9 TEU and Articles 20 to 25 TFEU.

19.2.3 European citizenship and national citizenship

If European citizenship is naturally linked to national citizenship, it is essentially different from it.

European citizenship is conditional on having the nationality of one of the Member States. Under Article 9, third sentence TEU and Article 20(1), second sentence TFEU, '[e]very national of a Member State shall be a citizen of the Union'. It is therefore for each Member State's laws to determine the conditions for the granting, refusal or loss of nationality.

This has been reiterated on many occasions by the Court of Justice in settled case law since Case C-369/90 *Micheletti and others v Delegación del Gobierno en Cantabria* [1992] ECR I-4239:

Under international law, it is for each Member State, having due regard to [Union] law, to lay down the conditions for the acquisition and loss of nationality. However, it is not permissible for the legislation of a Member State to restrict the effects of the grant of the nationality of another Member State by imposing an additional condition for recognition of that nationality with a view to the exercise of the fundamental freedoms provided for in the Treaty. (para 10)

(See also Case C-200/02 *Zhu and Chen v Secretary of State for the Home Department* [2004] ECR I-9925, para 37.)

However, the limits of this approach can be found in Case C-135/08 *Rottman v Freistaat Bayern* [2010] ECR I-1449.

case example

The case of *Rottman* concerned the loss with retroactive effect of Mr Rottman's German nationality. An Austrian national, he had acquired German nationality by naturalisation on account of deception practised in that acquisition. As the acquisition of his German nationality automatically led to the loss of his Austrian nationality, Mr Rottman found himself stateless, leading to the loss of the status of citizen of the European Union. The Court accepted that

... it is not contrary to European Union law, in particular to Article [20(1) TFEU], for a Member State to withdraw from a citizen of the Union the nationality of that State acquired by naturalisation when that nationality has been obtained by deception, on condition that the decision to withdraw observes the principle of proportionality. (para 59)

The Court noted, however, that, at the time of its judgment, the withdrawal of the German nationality by naturalisation had not become definitive and that no decision concerning Rottman's status has been taken by Austria. As a result, the Court could not draw any conclusion as to the compatibility of a national decision that had not yet been taken with EU law. However, as the Court put it,

> ... the fact that a matter falls within the competence of the Member States does not alter the fact that, in situations covered by European Union law, the national rules concerned must have due regard to the latter ... (para 39)

Mr Rottman, faced with a decision withdrawing his German naturalisation, and after losing his Austrian nationality, would be placed in a position of losing his status of European citizen and the rights attached to it. Such a situation would therefore be covered by European Union law (para 40). It is therefore clear that the Member States would have to take a decision, such as reinstating the original nationality, so as not to deprive an EU national, such as Mr Rottman, of his EU citizen status.

Conditional on national citizenship, as Article 9, third sentence TEU and Article 20(1), third sentence TFEU provide, European citizenship is 'additional to national citizenship and shall not replace it'.

Initially, following the amendment under the 1997 Treaty of Amsterdam (see 1.5), former Article 8(1) TEC stated that '[c]itizenship of the Union shall complement and not replace national citizenship'. The word 'complement' was unfortunate as it suggested that European citizenship was a subsidiary element of national citizenship. By contrast, the word 'additional' rather suggests that EU nationals have the benefit of a dual citizenship. Every British national, like every national of other Member States, is therefore also a European citizen.

Yet the two citizenships are fundamentally different. First, European citizenship is governed by Union law, and national citizenship by the national laws of the Member States. Secondly, European citizenship does not overrule the rights conferred upon EU nationals by their respective national citizenship but grants additional rights to be exercised under EU law, such as the right of free movement and residence in another Member State, and the right to vote, or to stand, at European or local elections.

19.3 The status of European citizens

Under Article 20(2) TFEU:

> Citizens of the Union shall enjoy the rights and be subject to the duties provided for in the Treaties.

The wording of this provision gives the impression that rights and duties are on the same footing. The prohibition of discrimination on the ground of nationality (Article 18 TFEU) or the respect of the principle of equal pay for male and female workers for equal work or work of equal value (Article 157(1) TFEU) might be regarded as such duties, yet the Treaty on European Union and the Treaty on the Functioning of the European Union are not specific in this regard. Duties are nowhere to be found. By contrast, the legal and political rights deriving from EU citizenship are clearly and specifically listed in Articles 20(2), 21(1) and 22–24 TFEU.

European citizenship has become a status that not only confers on EU nationals rights and duties which are additional to those deriving from national citizenship, but also draws a distinction between EU nationals and third country nationals.

19.3.1 Citizenship as the fundamental status of EU nationals

In the past 15 years, the Court has developed a remarkable case law on the concept of European citizenship and its effects, giving it a strong symbolic and practical value.

In Case C-184/99 *Grzelczyk v Centre public d'aide sociale d'Ottignies-Louvain-la-Neuve* [2001] ECR I-6193, which concerned the right of residence for students and to national minimum subsistence allowance, the Court ruled that

Union citizenship is destined to be the *fundamental status of nationals of the Member States*, enabling those who find themselves in the same situation to enjoy the same treatment in law irrespective of their nationality, subject to such exceptions as are expressly provided for. (emphasis added)

... a citizen of the European Union, lawfully resident in the territory of a host Member State, can rely on Article [18 TFEU] in all situations which fall within the scope *ratione materiae* of [Union] law. (paras 31–32)

Case C-413/99 *Baumbast and R v Secretary of State for the Home Department* [2002] ECR I-7091 is a good illustration of what European citizenship as a fundamental status actually means. Mr Baumbast was a German migrant worker in the UK where he met and married his Colombian wife in 1990. They had two daughters: the elder one was Mrs Baumbast's daughter from an earlier relationship and had Colombian nationality; the second daughter had dual German and Colombian nationality. The family was granted a residence permit valid for five years until 1995. While initially Mr Baumbast was a worker and then a self-employed person, he was later on engaged on temporary contracts by German companies in China and Lesotho following his own company's failure. At different times, he had sought work in the United Kingdom but without success. During that time, the couple owned a house on a mortgage and the children attended school in the United Kingdom. The family never had recourse to public funds and had comprehensive medical insurance in Germany. In 1995, the Baumbasts applied for indefinite leave to remain in the UK, but their application was turned down by the Secretary of State. While the British authorities recognised that the children had a right of residence under Article 12 of Regulation No 1612/68 (now Article 10 of Regulation 492/2011, see **15.4.2** and **15.4.3**) and that Mrs Baumbast had a right to stay in connection with the right of residence of her children, Mr Baumbast was refused leave to stay as he was no longer a worker and was not insured in the UK.

Before the Court of Justice, in the preliminary procedure (see **Chapter 9**), the British Government notably argued that, where a host Member State has a duty to allow children to reside on its territory in order to attend general educational courses under Article 12 of Regulation 1612/68, such duty may not be interpreted as requiring that State to allow the person who is their carer to reside with them. Should refusal of the right of residence to the carer interfere with family life as protected by Article 8 ECHR, the Home Office might grant that parent exceptional leave to remain in derogation from the British Immigration Rules.

The Court responded that to refuse to grant permission to remain to a parent as primary carer of the child exercising his right to pursue his studies in the host Member State would infringe that right. Article 12 of Regulation 1612/68 must therefore be interpreted as

... entitling the parent who is the primary carer of those children, irrespective of his nationality, to reside with them in order to facilitate the exercise of that right notwithstanding the fact ... that the parent who has the status of citizen of the European Union has ceased to be a migrant worker in the host Member State. (para 75)

Furthermore, the British Government argued that a right of residence could not be derived directly from former Article 18(1) TEC (now Article 21(1) TFEU) and that the limitations and conditions referred to in that paragraph showed that it was not intended to be a free-standing provision (para 78). Again, the Court did not embrace this narrow interpretation of that provision, pointing out that

[a]lthough, before the Treaty on European Union entered into force, the Court had held that that right of residence, conferred directly by the [former] EC Treaty, was subject to the condition that the person concerned was carrying on an economic activity ... it is none the less the case that, since then, Union citizenship has been introduced into the [then] EC Treaty and Article 18(1) EC [now Article 21(1) TFEU] has conferred a right, for every citizen, to move and reside freely within the territory of the Member States. (para 81)

Reaffirming that 'Union citizenship is destined to be the fundamental status of nationals of the Member States' (para 82), the Court stated that the Treaty on European Union does not require that EU citizens pursue a professional or trade activity in order to enjoy the rights deriving from European citizenship. Nor does it provide that EU nationals should be deprived of their rights as EU citizens after their professional activity has come to an end (para 83).

Most importantly, the Court came to the conclusion that

... a citizen of the European Union *who no longer enjoys a right of residence as a migrant worker in the host Member State can, as a citizen of the Union, enjoy there a right of residence by direct application of Article [21(1) TFEU]*. The exercise of that right is subject to the limitations and conditions referred to in that provision, but the competent authorities and, where necessary, the national courts must ensure that those limitations and conditions are applied in compliance with the general principles of [Union] law and, in particular, the principle of proportionality. (para 94, emphasis added)

Not only did Mr Baumbast have a right of residence derived from his children's right to a general education in the host Member State (see also in this respect Case C-480/08 *Teixeira v London Borough of Lambeth and Secretary of State for the Home Department* [2010] ECR I-1107 and Case C-310/08 *London Borough of Harrow v Nimco Hassan Ibrahim and Secretary of State for the Home Department* [2010] ECR I-1065, see **20.3**), but he also had a general right of residence as an EU citizen, irrespective of pursuing an economic activity or not, 'conferred directly on every citizen of the Union by [the] clear and precise provision of [Article 21(1) TFEU]' (para 84).

The fundamental status as European citizen can also protect EU nationals against discrimination in areas of law that are normally regarded as the exclusive domain of national law, such as rules on patronymic surnames, insofar as such discrimination does not occur in purely internal situations with no link with EU law (Joined Cases C-64/96 and C-65/96 *Land Nordrhein-Westfalen v Uecker and Jacquet v Land Nordrhein-Westfalen* [1997] ECR I-3171, para 23). Such a link existed in Case C-148/02 *Carlos Garcia Avello v Belgium* [2003] ECR I-11613. In this case, children who had dual

Spanish and Belgian nationality were prevented under Belgian law from changing their patronymic surnames from Garcia Avello to Garcia Weber, in accordance with the well-established usage in Spanish law whereby the surname of children of a married couple consists of the first surname of the father followed by that of the mother, on the ground that in Belgium children take the name of their father. The Court of Justice found that the Belgian law and administrative practice on the change of patronymic surnames constituted discrimination on ground of nationality contrary to former Article 12 TEC (now Article 18 TFEU) (para 45).

Citizenship of the Union has not been used, however, to extend the scope of Article 21 TFEU to prevent a Member State from refusing to recognise the patronymic surname of one of its citizens which included a title of nobility acquired by means of adoption by a citizen from another EU Member State who was permitted to bear that title as a constituent element of his name (see Case C-208/09 *Sayn-Wittgenstein v Landeshauptmann von Wien* [2010] ECR I-13693, para 95).

The concept of European citizenship took a new turn in the recent case law of the Court with a new emphasis on national measures depriving EU citizens of the genuine enjoyment of the substance of their rights attaching to their status of European citizens.

case example

This approach was first developed in Case C-34/09 *Ruiz Zambrano v Office national de l'emploi (ONEm)* [2011] ECR I-1177. Mr Zambrano and his wife, both of Columbian nationality, fled the civil war in Columbia to Belgium where they applied for asylum. Their application was rejected and they were ordered to leave Belgium. While residing in Belgium during the processing of their application, their first two children were born in Belgium and acquired Belgian nationality. Despite having no work permit, Mr Zambrano was employed full time by a Belgium company and had sufficient resources to provide for his family.

Following periods of unemployment, Mr Zambrano applied for unemployment benefit. Although he had contributed to social security, his claim was rejected on the ground that he did not meet the Belgian foreigners' residence requirements and was not entitled to work in Belgium.

The Zambranos also applied for residence in Belgium as parents of Belgian nationals, but their application was rejected on the ground that they deliberately failed to have their children recognised as Columbian citizens, a necessary step prior to regularising their own residence in Belgium.

Mr Zambrano challenged the refusal of his applications for residence and unemployment benefit before a Belgian labour court on the ground that he was entitled to reside and work in Belgium as a parent and carer of minor children holding Belgian nationality.

The Court of Justice observed first that, since Mr Zambrano's children possessed Belgian nationality, Article 20 TFEU confered upon them the status of citizen of the Union, and secondly that

> ... Article 20 TFEU precludes national measures which have the effect of depriving citizens of the Union of the *genuine enjoyment of the substance of the rights* conferred by virtue of their status as citizens of the Union ... (para 42, emphasis added)

Considering that the refusal to grant a right of residence to Mr Zambrano upon whom his minor children were dependent would result in the children having to leave the EU in order to accompany their parents, and, equally, that the refusal to grant Mr Zambrano a work permit would mean running the risk of him not having sufficient resources to support his family and forcing them to leave the EU, the Court concluded that

> Article 20 TFEU is to be interpreted as meaning that it precludes a Member State from refusing a third country national upon whom his minor children, who are European Union citizens, are dependent, a right of residence in the Member State of residence and nationality of those children, and from refusing to grant a work permit to that third country national, in so far as such decisions deprive those children of the genuine enjoyment of the substance of the rights attaching to the status of European Union citizen. (para 45)

It was argued by other Governments and by the European Commission which submitted observations to the Court in this case that the situation of Mr Zambrano's children who resided in Belgium and had never left its territory was not covered by the provisions on freedoms of movement and residence guaranteed under EU law. In other words, such a situation was a purely internal one. However, while Directive 2004/38/EC on the right of citizens of the Union and their family members to move and reside freely within the territory of the Member States ([2004] OJ L158/77) (see **20.1**) did not apply to such a situation (para 39), Article 20 TFEU did, despite the lack of cross-border movement.

This new concept of 'genuine enjoyment of the substance of rights' was seized upon by Mrs McCarthy in Case C-434/09 *McCarthy v Secretary of State for the Home Department* [2011] ECR I-3375. Mrs McCarthy was a UK national who was born and has always resided in the UK. She never exercised her rights of free movement and residence in other EU Member States. After marrying a Jamaican national, she applied for and obtained an Irish passport. She then applied for a residence permit in the UK as an Irish national. Her husband also applied for a residence permit as the spouse of an EU citizen. Both applications were refused on the ground that Mrs McCarthy had never exercised her right to move and reside in Member States other than the UK.

First, the Court ruled that Directive 2004/38/EC could not apply to EU citizens in the situation of Mrs McCarthy who reside in the Member State of which they are a national since they enjoy an unconditional right of residence in that State. The Court also noted that being the national of more than one Member State does not entail that the EU national has made use of the right of free movement. Therefore, the Court found that someone in Mrs McCarthy's situation could not rely on the Directive.

Furthermore, the Court observed that, although a person such as Mrs McCarthy enjoys the status of a Union citizen under Article 20(1) TFEU, the refusal by the British authorities to grant her a residence permit in the UK on the basis of her Irish nationality did not have

> the effect of depriving her of the genuine enjoyment of the substance of the rights associated with her status as a Union citizen, or of impeding the exercise of her right to move and reside freely within the territory of the Member States, in accordance with Article 21 TFEU ... (para 49)

According to the Court, Mrs McCarthy was not put in the same situation as the Zambrano children who would have been obliged to leave the EU (para 50). Rather, her situation had no factor linking it with EU law and was covered exclusively by national law.

Case C-256/11 *Dereci and Others v Bundesministerium für Inneres* [2011] ECR I-11315 gave the Court another opportunity to clarify the conditions of application of Article 20 TFEU and the concept of 'substance of rights'. In this case, the applicants were all third country nationals who wished to live with their family members, who were Austrian nationals, and therefore EU citizens, resident in Austria. The latter had, however, never exercised their right to free movement and were not maintained by the applicants. All applicants had their applications for residence permits in Austria rejected and some of them were subject to expulsion orders. Confirming its rulings in *Zambrano* and *McCarthy*, the Court specified that

> ... the criterion relating to the denial of the genuine enjoyment of the substance of the rights conferred by virtue of European Union citizen status refers to situations in which *the Union citizen has, in fact, to leave not only the territory of the Member*

State of which he is a national but also the territory of the Union as a whole. (para 66, emphasis added)

The fact that it might be desirable to EU nationals that their family members who are third country nationals reside with them within an EU Member State 'is not sufficient in itself to support the view that the Union citizen will be forced to leave Union territory if such a right [of residence] is not granted' to those family members (para 68). In other words, as long as EU citizens are not deprived of the option of living with their non-EU family members in another Member State, Article 20 TFEU is not breached. This criterion clearly draws the line between the *McCarthy* and the *Dereci* cases on the one hand and *Zambrano* on the other.

The clarification made by the Court in *Dereci* was confirmed in subsequent cases such as Case C-40/11 *Iida v Stadt Ulm*, 8 November 2012, ECLI:EU:C:2012:691 (a Japanese national who could not claim a right of residence in Germany derived from the right of his two children as Union citizens who had moved with their mother to Austria); Joined Cases C-356/11 and C-357/11 *O and S v Maahanmuuttovirasto and Maahanmuuttovirasto v L*, 6 December 2012, ECLI:EU:C:2012:776 (Mr O, an Ivorian national, sought to reside in Finland with his spouse, Mrs S, a Ghanaian national and lawful resident in that State, and with their Ghanaian child. Mrs S was also the mother of a child from a previous marriage who had Finnish nationality. The Finnish authorities' refusal to grant Mr O a residence permit on the basis of family reunification was not deemed to be in breach of Article 20 TFEU); Case C-87/12 *Ymeraga and Others v Ministre du Travail, de l'Emploi et de l'Immigration*, 8 May 2013, ECLI:EU:C:2013:291 (refusal by Luxembourg to grant residence permits to Kosovan nationals who wished to reside with a family member residing in Luxembourg and holding Luxembourg nationality but who had never exercised his free movement rights as a Union citizen); and Case C-86/12 *Alokpa and Others v Ministre du Travail, de l'Emploi et de l'Immigration*, 10 October 2013, ECLI:EU:C:2013:645 (Luxembourg's refusal to grant a residence permit to a Togolese woman who had sole care for her twin minor children who were granted French nationality as a result of their father's nationality, and who had resided with her in Luxembourg since their birth, but without possessing Luxembourg nationality and making use of their free movement rights).

Figure 19.1   European citizenship

19.3.2   The political rights of European citizens

As recognised by international law, the right for citizens to participate in public affairs through the right to vote or to stand at national elections is usually reserved to the nationals of a State. The extension of this right to other EU nationals residing in a Member State other than their own constitutes an essential element of European citizenship and considerable progress towards European integration. Political citizenship has developed at European level – through the European Parliament elections and the creation of the European citizens' initiative under the Lisbon Treaty – and at national level – through the right to vote and to stand at municipal elections.

19.3.2.1 The right to vote and to stand at European and municipal elections

The right to vote and to stand at European elections is aimed at increasing European citizens' participation in European affairs and at reducing the democratic deficit within the EU. It was under the Decision of the representatives of the Member States meeting in the Council of 20 September 1976 relating to the Act concerning the election of the representatives of the Assembly by direct universal suffrage (76/787/ECSC, EEC, Euratom) ([1976] OJ L278/1) that European nationals were granted the right to directly elect their representatives in the European Parliament every five years as from 1979. Although this was a major step towards the democratisation of the then EEC, it was not until the adoption of the Maastricht Treaty on European Union that this right was extended to EU nationals residing in a Member State other than their own. Until then, with the exception of a few countries, this right to vote and stand at European elections was the exclusive right of the nationals of each Member State.

Under Article 22(2), first sentence TFEU (formerly Article 8b(2) TEC post-Maastricht):

> Without prejudice to Article 223(1) and to the provisions adopted for its implementation, every citizen of the Union residing in a Member State of which he is not a national shall have the right to vote and to stand as a candidate in elections to the European Parliament in the Member State in which he resides, under the same conditions as nationals of that State.

The detailed arrangements for the exercise of those rights were laid down in Council Directive 93/109/EC as amended ([1993] OJ L329/34).

The principle is simply that Union citizens have the right to take part in European elections as a voter and/or candidate under the same conditions as the nationals of their State of residence provided that they satisfy the conditions set out in Articles 3 (being an EU national and not being a national of the country of residence) and 6 (condition of residence) of the Directive. As such, these rights cannot be denied by a Member State to its own nationals living in that State's overseas countries and territories (see Case C-300/04 *Eman and Sevinger v College van burgemeester en wethouders van Den Haag* [2006] ECR I-8055: requirement of residence in the Netherlands for Dutch citizens of Aruba). Under Article 4 of the Directive, EU citizens can choose to exercise this right in either the country of origin or of residence but can exercise it in one of them only. A citizen who has been deprived, through an individual criminal law or civil law decision, of the right to stand at elections in either the home or the host country is precluded from exercising that right in the Member State of residence in European elections (Article 6). Any citizen who has been deprived of the right to vote in the home country may also be deprived of that right in the country of residence (Article 7).

The right to vote and to stand as a candidate in municipal elections is the second political right created under the Maastricht Treaty. This right may be regarded as a major means to foster the integration of EU nationals in their new country of residence. It is enshrined in Article 22(1) TFEU (formerly Article 8b(1) TEC post-Maastricht). The detailed arrangements for the exercise of those rights are laid down in Council Directive 94/80/EC as amended ([1994] OJ L368/38). This Directive follows the same pattern as that of the 1993 Directive on European elections and provides in its annex a list of the 'basic local government units', the bodies which are elected by direct suffrage and administer local affairs. In the UK, these would include the London boroughs, counties, districts and parishes in England; counties, county boroughs and communities in Wales; regions, districts and Islands in Scotland; and districts in Northern Ireland.

In contrast with European elections, EU nationals exercising their right to vote and to stand as a candidate in municipal elections in the Member State of residence do not lose the right to vote and to stand as a candidate in their own Member State (see recital 6 of the preamble to the Directive).

19.3.2.2 The European citizens' initiative

The European citizens' initiative (see 2.2.1) is a recent creation of the unratified Treaty establishing a constitution for Europe of 2005 and incorporated into the Lisbon Treaty. It gives European citizens the right to take part in the law-making process of the Union by taking the initiative of inviting the Commission to propose new EU legal acts within a specific legal framework. Although very similar to the popular initiative, a direct democracy instrument which enables citizens in certain countries, like Switzerland, to suggest new laws, the European citizens' initiative is much more limited.

Under Title II on Provisions on democratic principles, Article 11(4) TEU provides:

> Not less than one million citizens who are nationals of a significant number of Member States may take the initiative of inviting the European Commission, within the framework of its powers, to submit any appropriate proposal on matters where citizens consider that a legal act of the Union is required for the purpose of implementing the Treaties.
>
> The procedures and conditions required for such a citizens' initiative shall be determined in accordance with the first paragraph of Article 24 of the Treaty on the Functioning of the European Union.

And according to this provision (Part Two of the TFEU on Non-discrimination and citizenship of the Union, Article 24, first paragraph):

> The European Parliament and the Council, acting by means of regulations in accordance with the ordinary legislative procedure, shall adopt the provisions for the procedures and conditions required for a citizens' initiative within the meaning of Article 11 of the Treaty on European Union, including the minimum number of Member States from which such citizens must come.

It was on the basis of the latter provision that Regulation 211/2011/EU on the citizens' initiative ([2011] OJ L65/1) was adopted. This Regulation specifies the procedures and conditions required for a citizens' initiative.

Article 11(4) TEU sets out two series of conditions:

(a) first, the initiative must concern matters falling within the scope of application of the Treaties and within the framework of the powers of the European Commission; and

(b) secondly, the initiative must be supported by at least one million citizens who are nationals of a significant number of Member States. Article 3(4) of the 2011 Regulation specifies that the signatories of a proposed citizens' initiative must be citizens of the Union and be entitled to vote in elections to the European Parliament.

To guarantee sufficient representation of European citizens, Article 7 of the Regulation lays down a dual condition:

(a) the signatories of the initiative must come from at least one quarter of Member States (therefore 7 currently) (Article 7(1)); and

(b) the number of signatories must be equal to or more than the minimum number of citizens set out for each EU Member State in Annex 1 of the Regulation. This number is calculated on the basis of the number of Members of the European Parliament for each Member State, multiplied by 750 (Article 7(2)).

The procedure established under the Regulation is designed to be 'clear, simple, user-friendly and proportionate to the nature of the citizens' initiative so as to encourage participation by citizens' (recital 2) and to undercut frivolous, vexatious or abusive initiatives. For that reason, Article 3 requires the organisers of the initiative to set up a citizens' committee of at least seven persons who are residents of at least seven different Member States, and Article 4(1) requires that the proposed initiative be registered with the Commission prior to collecting statements of support from signatories. This enables the Commission to verify that the initiative meets the main requirements, notably, that it falls within the framework of the Commission's powers to submit a proposal for an EU act, is not manifestly abusive and is not contrary to the values of the Union (Article 4(2)). Once the proposed initiative has been registered and made public, signatures and statements of support can be collected in paper form or electronically within 12 months of the date of registration (Article 5). If the minimum number of signatures and statements of support required is reached, the proposed initiative will undergo a process of verification and certification by national authorities (Articles 7 and 8). It is only then that the proposed initiative is submitted to the Commission for examination (Articles 9 and 10), at which stage the Commission must 'receive the organisers at an appropriate level to allow them to explain in detail the matters raised by the citizens' initiative' (Article 10(1)(b)) before, within three months, stating in a communication to be notified to the organisers, the European Parliament and the Council and made public (Article 10(2)) the action it intends to take and the reasons for taking or not taking it (Article 10(1)(c)).

According to the Commission's Report on the application of Regulation (EU) No 211/2011 on the citizens' initiative (COM(2015) 145 final), since April 2012, 51 requests for registration of proposed citizens' initiatives were made, of which 31 were registered and 18 had reached the end of their collection period. Only three initiatives reached the required number of statements of support and were submitted to the Commission: 'Right2Water' (call for legislation implementing the human right to water and sanitation), 'One of us' (call to end the financing of activities which presuppose the destruction of human embryos) and 'Stop vivisection' (call for the abrogation of Directive 2010/63/EU on the protection of animals used for scientific purposes), all of which received a formal response from the Commission.

The Commission responded positively to the first initiative on 19 March 2014 (COM(2014) 177 final) but negatively to the second one on 28 May 2014 (COM(2014) 355 final) and to the third one on 3 June 2015 (C(2015) 3773 final).

19.3.3 The legal protective rights of European citizens

Besides the right of free movement and residence (see 20.2 and 20.3) and the political rights discussed above, the TEU and TFEU also include four major protective rights within the concept of European citizenship, the first three having been introduced by the 1992 Maastricht Treaty and the last one by the 1997 Amsterdam Treaty. Of a different nature, the first one (right to diplomatic and consular protection) is to be implemented by Member States, while the other three fall within the competence of the Union.

19.3.3.1 The right to diplomatic and consular protection

Article 23, first paragraph TFEU simply provides:

> Every citizen of the Union shall, in the territory of a third country in which the Member State of which he is a national is not represented, be entitled to protection by the diplomatic or consular authorities of any Member State, on the same conditions as the nationals of that State.

This is an important protection since many EU nationals travel outside the European Union (from 80 million trips in 2005 to over 90 million in 2008 according to the Commission EU Citizenship Report 2010, Dismantling the obstacles to EU citizens' rights (COM(2010) 603 final) at 9) and/or live in a third country (30 million, *ibid*), yet the totality of the EU Member States have full diplomatic representation in only five non-EU States (China, Japan, Russia, Switzerland and the United States). There is therefore an increasing need for consular assistance of unrepresented EU nationals. Reiterated in Article 46 ECFR, this right can only be guaranteed by national authorities and covers both diplomatic and consular protection in accordance with public international law, notably the Vienna Conventions of 18 April 1961 and 24 April 1963.

Since the third State in which this right is exercised is not bound by it, Article 23, first paragraph, second sentence provides that 'Member States shall adopt the necessary provisions and start the international negotiations required to secure this protection'.

Unfortunately, very little has been done in this domain, and according to the Commission in its 2010 report,

> [t]he effectiveness of EU citizens' right to consular protection remains to be proven. Even though there is a lack of systematic data, it is clear from complaints and reported cases that EU citizens and, at times, consular officials, are not yet sufficiently aware that EU citizens have the right to turn to other embassies or consulates and are not sure what kind of help can be given. (at 10)

On 14 December 2011, the Commission adopted a proposal for a Directive on consular protection for Union citizens abroad, with the view to establishing 'clear and legally binding rules on cooperation and coordination between Member States' consular authorities to ensure that unrepresented EU citizens have non-discriminatory access to protection from other Member States' diplomatic or consular representations in a third country' (Commission report, On progress towards effective EU Citizenship 2011-2013 (COM(2013) 270 final) at 7). Yet, it took until 20 April 2015 for Directive 2015/637/EU on the coordination and cooperation measures to facilitate consular protection for unrepresented citizens of the Union in third countries and repealing Decision 95/553/EC ([2015] OJ L106/1) to be adopted.

It clarifies the conditions under which EU nationals in distress in a third country can exercise their right to receive assistance from other EU countries' embassies or consulates. It is also designed to facilitate cooperation between national consular authorities and reinforce EU nationals' right to consular protection.

19.3.3.2　The right to petition the European Parliament

The right to petition is the right to make representations to a political institution in order either to prevent an unjust situation from occurring or to make it cease. Recognised in many parliamentary democracies, this right is unequally exercised and implemented.

Introduced by the Maastricht Treaty, this right is enshrined in Article 24 TFEU and Article 44 ECFR. Article 24, second paragraph TFEU states that '[e]very citizen of the Union shall have the right to petition the European Parliament in accordance with Article 227' on Union matters which affect them directly.

The procedure and the conditions for petition are very loose as a petition may be sent to the European Parliament's Committee on Petitions in writing by post or electronically in one of the official languages of the EU. The petition may be an individual or a collective one.

Of the 1,746 petitions that were received in 2010, the 2,091 in 2011 and the 1,964 in 2012, 60%, 71% and 72% respectively were declared inadmissible; those that were admissible were either referred to an institution or body or closed with a direct reply to the petitioner. (See Commission report, On progress towards effective EU Citizenship 2011-2013 at 7.)

19.3.3.3　The right to complain to the European Ombudsman

Article 24, third paragraph TFEU states that '[e]very citizen of the Union may apply to the Ombudsman ...' This provision is further confirmed by Article 43 ECFR and Article 41 ECFR (right to good administration).

Although widely known and strongly established in most European Member States, the ombudsman institution (see 2.3.3) was not established within the EC until the adoption of the 1992 Maastricht Treaty (Article 195 TEC, now Article 228 TFEU).

Elected by the European Parliament 'after each election of the European Parliament for the duration of its term of office' (Article 228(2), sub-paragraph 1 TFEU), the Ombudsman must perform her duties in total independence and may not seek or take instructions from any Government, institution, body, office or agency, and may not engage in any other occupation (Article 228(4) TFEU). The current European Ombudsman is Emily O'Reilly. Under Article 228(1), first sub-paragraph TFEU, the European Ombusdman is

> [e]mpowered to receive complaints from any citizen of the Union or any natural or legal person residing or having its registered office in a Member State concerning instances of maladministration in the activities of the Union institutions or bodies, with the exception of the Court of Justice acting in its judicial role.

Although the main role of the Ombudsman is to 'examine such complaints and report on them', Article 228(1), second sub-paragraph also gives her the power to 'conduct inquiries for which [s]he finds grounds' on her own initiative. The Ombudsman has used such power to initiate inquiries on public access to documents of EU institutions and bodies, and to assess the Commission's response to complaints relating to breaches of EU law.

Unlike petitions to the European Parliament, which apply to matters coming within the Union's fields of activity and which affect the petitioner directly, complaints to the Ombudsman concern only 'instances of maladministration in the activities of the Union institutions or bodies'. Not defined in the EU Treaties or in the Statute of the

Ombudsman, the notion of 'maladministration' covers instances where '[an EU] institution or body fails to act in accordance with the Treaties and with the [EU] acts that are binding upon it, or if it fails to observe the rules and principles of law established by the Court of Justice and Court of First Instance' (First Annual Report of The European Ombudsman 1995, 22 April 1996, at 8). Maladministration includes, amongst other things, administrative irregularities, administrative omissions, abuse of power, negligence, unlawful procedures, unfairness, malfunction or incompetence, discrimination, avoidable delay, and lack or refusal of information.

Should the Ombudsman declare a complaint admissible, EU institutions and bodies have an obligation to supply her with any information she has requested from them and give her access to the files concerned (Article 3(2) of the Ombudsman Statute). She may also request information from Member States' authorities 'that may help to clarify instances of maladministration by [EU] institutions or bodies unless such information is covered by laws or regulations on secrecy or by provisions preventing its being communicated' (Article 3(3) of the Statute).

The institution or body concerned will be informed of any maladministration established by the Ombudsman, who may make draft recommendations. The institution or body concerned will then send the Ombudsman a detailed opinion within three months (Article 3(6) of the Statute). The Ombudsman must then send a report to the European Parliament and the institution or body concerned in which she may make recommendations. She will inform the complainant of the outcome of her inquiries, of the opinion expressed by the institution or body concerned and of her recommendations (Article 3(7) of the Statute).

The increasing number of registered complaints (over 2,000 complaints a year over the period 2010–2014) is evidence of the success of the Ombudsman institution. Yet the Ombudsman was able to secure a positive outcome in only 20% of all inquiries, a great number of which focused on lack of transparency in EU administration (see Annual Report 2014 of 16 February 2015, at 7).

19.3.3.4 The right to use any EU official language in correspondence with EU institutions and bodies

A rather peculiar addition under the Amsterdam Treaty, Article 24, fourth paragraph TFEU provides:

> Every citizen of the Union may write to any of the institutions or bodies referred to in this Article or in Article 9 of the Treaty on European Union in one of the languages mentioned in Article 53(1) of the Treaty on European Union and have an answer in the same language.

This right is reiterated in Article 41(4) ECFR:

> Every person may write to the institutions of the Union in one of the languages of the Treaties and must have an answer in the same language.

This right is rather vaguely defined and cannot be regarded as benefiting only European citizens, and seems to be more about effective communication with EU institutions and bodies and transparency of EU administration. In this respect, it would have been more judicious to link it directly to the right to access to documents of the Union institutions, bodies, offices and agencies as provided for under Article 15(3) TFEU and under Article 42 ECFR.

Political rights	Legal rights
• right to vote and stand at European elections (Arts 22(2) TFEU and 39 ECFR) • right to vote and stand at municipal elections (Arts 22(1) TFEU and 40 ECFR) • European citizenship initiative (Arts 11(4) TEU and 24, first para TFEU)	• right to diplomatic and consular protection (Arts 23, first para TFEU and 46 ECFR) • right to petition the EP (Arts 24, second para TFEU and 44 ECFR) • right to apply to the European Ombudsman (Arts 24, third para TFEU and 43 ECFR) • right to use any EU official language in correspondence with EU institutions and bodies (Arts 24, fourth para TFEU and 41(4) ECFR)

Figure 19.2   Citizens' rights

19.4   Further reading

Barber N, 'Citizenship, Nationalism and the European Union' (2002) 27(3) *EL Rev* 241.

Davis R, 'Citizenship of the Union … Rights for All?' (2002) 27(2) *EL Rev* 121.

Hinarejos A, 'Citizenship of the EU: Clarifying "Genuine Enjoyment of the Substance" of Citizenship Rights' (2012) 71(2) *Cambridge Law Journal* 279.

Jacobs F, 'Citizenship of the European Union—A Legal Analysis' (2007) 13(5) *European Law Journal* 591.

Jacqueson C, 'Union Citizenship and the Court of Justice: Something New under the Sun? Towards Social Citizenship' (2002) 27(3) *EL Rev* 260.

Kochenov D, 'A Real European Citizenship: A New Jurisdiction Test: a Novel Chapter in the Development of the Union in Europe' (2011) 18 *Columbia Journal of European Law* 55.

Kochenov D, 'The Essence of EU Citizenship Emerging from the Last Ten Years of Academic Debate: Beyond the Cherry Blossoms and the Moon?' (2013) 62(1) *ICLQ* 97.

Kochenov D and Plender R, 'EU Citizenship: from an Incipient Form to an Incipient Substance? The Discovery of the Treaty Text' (2012) 37(4) *EL Rev* 369.

Konstadinides T, 'La Fraternité Européenne? The Extent of National Competence to Condition the Acquisition and Loss of Nationality from the Perspective of EU Citizenship' (2010) 35(3) *EL Rev* 401.

Reich N, 'Citizenship and Family on Trial: A Fairly Optimistic Overview of Recent Court Practice with regard to Free Movement of Persons' (2003) 40 *CML Rev* 615.

Shuibhne N, 'The Resilience of the EU Market Citizenship' (2010) 47 *CML Rev* 1597.

Van Der Mei A, 'Union Citizenship and the Legality of Durational Residence Requirements for Entitlement to Student Financial Aid' (2009) 16 *Maastricht J Eur & Comp L* 477.

White R, 'Free Movement, Equal Treatment, and Citizenship of the Union' (2005) 54(4) *ICLQ* 885.

As an 'experimental form of non-state membership' (Editorial, 'Three Paradoxes of EU Citizenship' (2010) 35(2) *EL Rev* 129 at 130), European citizenship has certainly become a core concept of EU law which has added a political dimension to the original economic nature of the European integration process. Additional to national citizenship, European citizenship has been elevated to the fundamental status of EU nationals upon whom it confers a set of specific legal and political rights.

In particular, with European citizenship being recognised by the Court as a source of free movement rights, European citizens are entitled to enter and reside in another Member State purely as citizens of the Union but also to enjoy the same treatment in law as the nationals of the host States irrespective of their nationality.

Attached to this status are a number of political rights (right to vote and stand at local and European elections and the European citizens' initiative) and legal rights (right to diplomatic and consular protection, right to petition the European Parliament and right to complain to the European Ombudsman).

test your knowledge

1 'The legal, political and social threads of citizenship are not sufficiently joined up but we may need to reflect on this more creatively than we might like. EU citizenship is an experimental form of non-state membership. The same rules do not necessarily apply.' (Editorial, 'Three Paradoxes of EU Citizenship' (2010) 35(2) *EL Rev* 129 at 130)

    Discuss.

2 The Court's case law on European citizenship has often been criticised for promoting a legal concept which is not supported by clear and adequate political and social foundations.

    Critically analyse the contribution of the Court to the development of this concept.

chapter 20

The Free Movement of European Citizens

After reading this chapter, you will be able to understand:

- the right of EU citizens to enter and reside in another Member State
- the concept of EU citizens' family members and their right of free movement and residence
- the right to equal treatment
- the limits to the right of free movement.

20.1 Introduction

The freedom of movement and residence has profoundly changed since the origins of the European Union. As a result of the predominantly economic dimension of the Treaty of Rome, free movement rights were enjoyed exclusively by nationals of Member States who were economically active, namely workers and self-employed persons.

The freedom of movement developed in different ways. First, beyond the economic dimension and as a result of the creation of European citizenship (see 19.2), the free movement of economically active migrants developed into the freedom of movement of European citizens, thus offering more rights to a greater number of beneficiaries. Secondly, the Schengen agreements of 1985 and 1990, acting as instruments of generalisation and intensification of the free movement of persons, including that of third country nationals, have contributed to the creation of an area of freedom, security and justice beyond a purely economic area, later set up in the 1997 Amsterdam Treaty and elevated to a Union objective by the 2007 Lisbon Treaty.

Closely linked to the principle of equal treatment, the freedom of movement is, however, subject to certain limitations which are clearly defined in the Treaties and secondary legislation, and strictly interpreted by the Court of Justice.

20.2 Free movement within the area of freedom, security and justice

Under Article 3(2) TEU, one of the Union's major objectives is to

> ... offer its citizens an area of freedom, security and justice without internal frontiers, in which the free movement of persons is ensured in conjunction with appropriate measures with respect to external border controls, asylum, immigration and the prevention and combating of crime.

Originally limited to economically active persons, namely workers, self-employed persons and their families (see 15.2 and 15.3), the right of free movement is now enjoyed not only by all EU nationals but also, in 'the absence of internal border controls for persons', by third country nationals (Article 67(2) TFEU).

Further integration, together with growing immigration, has gradually led to the creation of an area without frontiers for persons. Originally created step by step through intergovernmental cooperation, this area of freedom, security and justice was formally established under the 1997 Amsterdam Treaty and completed by the 2007 Lisbon Treaty.

20.2.1 Genesis of the area of freedom, security and justice

Amongst all measures adopted by way of intergovernmental cooperation, the Schengen agreements constitute the foundation of this area of freedom, security and justice. Disagreements between the then nine EEC Member States on the abolition of border controls led five of its original Member States (Belgium, the Federal Republic of Germany, France, Luxembourg and the Netherlands) to go ahead with the project of abolishing border controls between them, adopting common rules on visas and establishing police and judicial cooperation. These objectives were achieved through the adoption of the Schengen Agreement of 14 June 1985 and the Schengen Convention of 19 June 1990, thus creating what is now known as the Schengen area. Independent of EEC law and governed by public international law, the Schengen agreements were a form of experimental project in anticipation of the creation of a borderless area within the then European Community.

The Schengen area gradually enlarged to include currently 22 out of 28 EU Member States (Ireland and the UK are maintaining their opt-outs – see current Protocol on the Schengen acquis integrated into the framework of the European Union; Bulgaria, Croatia, Cyprus and Romania have a legal obligation to join once ready to do so) and four non-EU States (Iceland, Norway, Switzerland and Liechtenstein). It also includes de facto the three micro-States of Monaco, San Marino and the Vatican City.

The Schengen area is first an area of freedom within which EU nationals and third country nationals (the latter are entitled to move within Schengen for three months or for a longer period depending on their visa) may move freely and without being subject to individual border controls. It is also an area of security where individual border controls are transferred from the Member States' borders to the external borders of the Union, and within which national judicial, police and border control authorities have developed closer cooperation based notably on the Schengen Information System (SIS), a database permanently available to them. The abolition of internal border controls was therefore accompanied by the necessary harmonisation of national rules applicable to non-EU nationals and closer police cooperation based on the principle of mutual trust between Member States.

Originally based on some form of coordination between police authorities and government home affairs departments, or bilateral conventions between certain Member States, police cooperation was formalised under the third pillar established under the Maastricht Treaty on cooperation in the fields of justice and home affairs, covering notably asylum policy, rules governing the crossing by persons of the external borders of the Member States, immigration policy and policy regarding nationals of third countries, judicial cooperation in civil and criminal matters, and customs and police cooperation (for pillar structure, see 1.5).

The 1997 Amsterdam Treaty incorporated into the EC Treaty those matters covered in the third pillar with the exception of judicial and police cooperation in criminal matters (Title IV on Visas, asylum, immigration and other policies related to free movement of persons, Articles 61 to 69 TEC) 'in order to establish progressively an area of freedom, security and justice' (Article 61 TEC). Its second Protocol also integrated the Schengen agreements or *acquis* into the framework of the EU.

Under the Amsterdam Treaty, a new impetus was given to the creation of an area of freedom, security and justice with the adoption of the programmes of Tampere (1999–2004) and The Hague (2004–09).

20.2.2 The area of freedom, security and justice under the Lisbon Treaty

Following the abolition of the pillar structure under the Lisbon Treaty, all the provisions on the area of freedom, security and justice (AFSJ) were incorporated into Title V of the Treaty on the Functioning of the European Union (TFEU) (Articles 67 to 89 TFEU). Title V covers policies on border checks, asylum and immigration (Articles 77 to 80), judicial cooperation in civil matters (Article 81), judicial cooperation in criminal matters (Articles 82 to 86) and police cooperation (Articles 87 to 89).

The Lisbon Treaty has reinforced some of the previous provisions, notably those relating to Europol (Article 88), Eurojust (Article 85) from which a European Public Prosecutor's Office can be established (Article 86), the common asylum policy (Article 78) and the common immigration policy (Article 79). It also establishes the power of the European Council to 'define the strategic guidelines for legislative and operational planning within the area of freedom, security and justice' (Article 68), a role it fulfilled when it adopted in December 2009 the Stockholm programme ([2010] OJ C115/1).

The incorporation of the third pillar provisions into the TFEU also means that qualified majority voting (see 2.3.2.3) applies in principle in the adoption of AFSJ measures. Exceptions remain, however, where unanimity in the Council is required, notably for measures concerning:

- national identity cards and passports, residence permits or any similar documents (Article 77(3));
- family law with cross-border implications (Article 81(3));
- the establishment of a European Public Prosecutor's Office (Article 86(1));
- the conditions under which national criminal courts and law enforcement authorities can operate in the territory of another Member State (Article 89); and
- operational cooperation between national police, customs and specialised law enforcement services (Article 87(3)).

In the absence of unanimity in the Council, the procedure may be suspended (emergency brake) and a minimum of nine Member States may request that the draft measures be referred to the European Council. Should disagreement persist, those nine Member States may establish enhanced cooperation (see 3.3.4) on the basis of those draft measures in accordance with Article 20(2) TEU and Article 329(1) TFEU (Article 87(3), sub-paragraphs 2 and 3).

It is to be noted also that the UK, Ireland and Denmark benefit from 'opt-outs' and 'opt-ins' in the areas of judicial and police cooperation (see Protocol 21 on the position of the United Kingdom and Ireland in respect of the area of freedom, security and justice, and Protocol 22 on the position of Denmark [2012] OJ C326/1).

20.3 European Union migrants and family members' right to free movement and residence

Article 21(1) TFEU provides the right for every citizen of the Union

... to move and reside freely within the territory of the Member States ...

Such freedom is not absolute, however, and is 'subject to the limitations and conditions laid down in the Treaties and by the measures adopted to give them effect' (see **20.5**).

The scope of application and conditions for the exercise of the right of free movement and residence are further specified in Directive 2004/38/EC on the right of citizens of the Union and their family members to move and reside freely within the territory of the Member States amending Regulation (EEC) No 1612/68 and repealing Directives 64/221/EEC, 68/360/EEC, 72/194/EEC, 73/148/EEC, 75/34/EEC, 75/35/EEC, 90/364/EEC, 90/365/EEC and 93/96/EEC ([2004] OJ L158/77). As the full title of the Directive shows, the 2004 Directive (the Citizenship Directive) consolidated nine former directives. Incorporating also the case law of the Court of Justice interpreting this former body of law, it not only constitutes a full codification of the right of free movement and residence but also extends the scope of this right.

20.3.1 Economically active and inactive EU migrants

The regulation of the right to the freedom of movement and residence in other EU Member States has fundamentally evolved. Originally conceived as a corollary of the freedom to exercise an economic activity (see **Chapter 15**), this right is now regarded as a fundamental right of all European citizens (see **Chapter 19**). As a result, the beneficiaries of this right include not only economically active but also economically inactive EU migrants, such as persons with sufficient resources, persons who have reached retirement age, and students. This extension of the right of free movement and residence to economically inactive persons was initiated in 1990 with the adoption of three directives: Directive 90/364/EEC on the right of residence ([1990] OJ L180/26), Directive 90/365/EEC on the right of residence for employees and self-employed persons who have ceased their occupational activity ([1990] OJ L180/28) and Directive 90/366/EEC replaced by Directive 93/96/EEC on the right of residence for students ([1993] OJ L317/59).

Economically active EU migrants (Article 7(1)(a) of the Citizenship Directive):
- workers
- self-employed persons

Economically inactive EU migrants (Article 7(1)(b) of the Citizenship Directive):
- self-sufficient or retired persons with sufficient financial resources and with comprehensive sickness insurance cover

---

Economically inactive EU migrants (Article 7(1)(c) of the Citizenship Directive):
- persons who are enrolled at a private or public establishment, accredited or financed by the host Member State for the purpose of studying, who have sufficient financial resources and comprehensive sickness insurance cover

---

Figure 20.1   The direct beneficiaries of the freedom of movement and residence

Those provisions are now incorporated into Article 7(1)(b) of the Citizenship Directive with regard to economically inactive (self-sufficient and retired) persons and Article 7(1)(c) for students enrolled on a course of study or vocational training 'in a private or public establishment, accredited or financed by the host Member State'.

However, their right of residence (and that of their family members) is subject to the dual condition that they do not 'become a burden on the social assistance system of the host Member State during their period of residence and have comprehensive sickness insurance cover in the host Member State'.

20.3.2 Migrants' family members

The right of economically active migrants to be joined by their families was recognised very early on in Community legislation. Recital 5 of the preamble to Regulation 1612/68/EEC on freedom of movement for workers within the Community ([1968] OJ L257/2) (now recital 6 of the preamble to Regulation 492/2011/EU on freedom of movement for workers within the Union ([2011] OJ L141/1)) provided that

> ... the right of freedom of movement, in order that it may be exercised, by objective standards, in freedom and dignity, requires that ... obstacles to the mobility of workers shall be eliminated, in particular as regards the worker's right to be joined by his family and the conditions for the integration of that family into the host country.

This right was clearly established in Article 10 of Regulation 1612/68 and in Article 1 of Directive 73/148/EEC on the abolition of restrictions on movement and residence within the Community for nationals of Member States with regard to establishment and the provision of services ([1973] OJ L172/14). The purpose of those provisions was not only to facilitate mobility of workers and self-employed persons but also to ensure that their right to family life, as protected under Article 8 ECHR, was respected.

This right to be joined by their family, irrespective of their nationality (see Case C-370/90 *R v Immigration Appeal Tribunal and Singh, ex parte Secretary of State for Home Department* [1992] ECR I-4265; Case C-291/05 *Minister voor Vreemdelingenzaken en Integratie v Eind* [2007] ECR I-10719; Case C-127/08 *Metock and Others v Minister for Justice, Equality and Law Reform* [2008] ECR I-6241 and Case C-456/12 *O v Minister voor Immigratie, Integratie en Asiel and Minister voor Immigratie, Integratie en Asiel v B,* 12 March 2014, ECLI:EU:C:2014:135), has been extended to all EU migrants under the Citizenship Directive (see recital 5).

For the purposes of the Directive, the definition of 'family member' was enlarged under Article 2(2) so as to include:

(a) the spouse. This term refers exclusively to a marital relationship (see Case 59/85 *Netherlands v Reed* [1986] ECR 1283, para 15) and does not include unmarried partners unless, as in *Reed,* an EU migrant has the right to live with their unmarried partner if that right is granted to the nationals of the host State. Such marital relationship must of course be a genuine one and not one of convenience (see Case C-109/01 *Secretary of State for the Home Department v Akrich* [2003] ECR I-9607). Partners may live separately and will be regarded as married until their marital relationship is officially dissolved (see Case 267/83 *Diatta v Land Berlin* [1985] ECR 567, para 20);

(b) the partner – of the same or different gender – with whom the EU migrant has entered into a registered partnership, under the law of a Member State, 'if the legislation of the host Member State treats registered partnerships as equivalent to marriage and in accordance with the relevant legislation of the host Member State'. Where the registered partnership is not treated in the host Member State as equivalent to marriage, the registered partner would enjoy the same right as other family members under Article 3(2) (see below);

(c) the direct descendants who are under the age of 21 or are dependants and those of the spouse or registered partner (ie children and grandchildren, etc); and

(d) the direct dependent ascendants and those of the spouse or registered partner (ie parents and grandparents, etc).

With regard to those family members joining or accompanying an EU migrant, the Member States have little scope for discretion in recognition of their rights of free movement and residence under the Citizenship Directive.

Furthermore, as recital 6 of the preamble to the Citizenship Directive states:

> In order to maintain the unity of the family in a broader sense and without prejudice to the prohibition of discrimination on grounds of nationality, the situation of those persons who are not included in the definition of family members under this Directive, and who therefore do not enjoy an automatic right of entry and residence in the host Member State, should be examined by the host Member State on the basis of its own national legislation, in order to decide whether entry and residence could be granted to such persons, taking into consideration their relationship with the Union citizen or any other circumstances, such as their financial or physical dependence on the Union citizen.

On this basis, Article 3(2)(a) covers any other family members, whether EU or non-EU nationals, such as siblings, cousins, aunts and uncles and other relatives if they are dependants or are members of the EU migrant's household (see Case C-1/05 *Jia v Migrationsverket* [2007] ECR I-1) or 'where serious health grounds strictly require personal care' by the EU migrant. Equally, Article 3(2)(b) confers rights of free movement and residence to the partner with whom the EU migrant has a durable, duly attested relationship, which covers same and different gender relationships and, notably, de facto ones such as cohabitation.

The close family members (Article 2(2) of the Citizenship Directive):

- the spouse
- the registered partner
- the direct descendants who are under the age of 21 or are dependants and those of the spouse or partner
- the dependent direct relatives in the ascending line and those of the spouse or partner

---

Any other family members, irrespective of nationality (Article 3(2)(a) of the Citizenship Directive):

- dependants or members of the household of the EU migrant having the primary right of residence, or
- requiring personal care from the EU migrant in case of serious health conditions

---

The partner with whom the EU migrant has a durable relationship duly attested (Article 3(2)(b) of the Citizenship Directive)

Figure 20.2   The EU migrant's family members

20.3.3   Right to move and reside in another Member State

20.3.3.1   The right to move freely

The right of free movement consists of the rights to exit and to enter any Member State.

The right of exit

Based on Article 2(1) of Protocol 4 to the ECHR ('Everyone shall be free to leave any country, including his own') and inherent in the status of European citizen, the right 'to leave the territory of a Member State to travel to another Member State' is guaranteed for all Union citizens and their family members under Article 4(1) of the Citizenship Directive and may only be restricted on the ground that 'the personal conduct of that [Union citizen] constitutes a genuine, present and sufficiently serious threat to one of the fundamental interests of society' (see Case C-33/07 *Ministerul Administraţiei şi Internelor - Direcţia Generală de Paşapoarte Bucureşti v Jipa* [2008] ECR I-5157, para 30; see below 20.5). For that purpose, Article 4(3) of the Directive requires that Member States 'issue to their own nationals, or renew, an identity card or passport stating their nationality', and Article 4(2) prohibits the requirement for exit visas or equivalent formalities.

The right of entry

The right of nationals of a Member State to enter the territory of another Member State, now established under Article 5 of the Citizenship Directive, has been regarded by the Court of Justice as '… a right conferred directly by the Treaty, or, as the case may be, by the provisions adopted for its implementation', with the effect that it 'is acquired independently of the issue of a residence permit by the competent authority of a Member State' (see Case 48/75 *Royer* [1976] ECR 497, paras 31–32). Like former Directive 68/360/EEC on the abolition of restrictions on movement and residence within the Community for workers of Member States and their families ([1968] OJ English special edition: Series I Volume 1968(II) 485) and Directive 73/148/EEC, Article 5(1) of the Citizenship Directive provides that Union citizens have the right to enter the territory of a Member State on the production of a valid identity card or passport. National authorities may require a person, under threat of criminal penalties, to hold identity papers with the view to establishing nationality upon entry into the territory of a Member State provided that those penalties are not disproportionate 'thus creating an obstacle to the free movement of workers' (Case C-378/97 *Criminal proceedings against Wijsenbeek* [1999] ECR I-6207, para 45; Case C-265/88 *Criminal proceedings against Messner* [1989] ECR 4209, para 14; Case C-24/97 *Commission v Germany* [1998] ECR I-2133, paras 13 and 14).

The Citizenship Directive also prohibits the imposition of entry visas or equivalent formalities (Article 5(1), second sentence; see also Case 157/79 *R v Pieck* [1980] ECR 2171, para 10).

Family members who are not EU nationals are required to hold a valid passport (Article 5(1)) and to have an entry visa in accordance with Regulation 539/2001/EC ([2001] OJ L81/1) listing the third countries whose nationals must be in possession of visas when crossing the external borders and those whose nationals are exempt from that requirement (Article 5(2)). However, they must be granted by national authorities every facility to obtain the necessary visas which must be 'issued free of charge as soon as possible and on the basis of an accelerated procedure'. Furthermore, the visa requirement is waived if the family member has a valid residence card of a family member of a Union citizen.

In line with the case law of the Court of Justice, Article 5(5) allows a Member State to require that migrants 'report their presence within its territory within a reasonable and non-discriminatory period of time' (see Case 118-75 *Watson and Belmann* [1976] ECR 1185, para 18; *Messner*: the requirement, subject to imprisonment or a fine, to make a declaration of residence within three days of entering a State's territory is not reasonable, para 15), failing which they could be made 'liable to proportionate and non-discriminatory sanctions'. Such sanctions cannot amount to deportation however.

Right of exit (Article 4 of the Citizenship Directive)	• right to leave a Member State to travel to another one • no exit visa
Right of entry (Article 5 of the Citizenship Directive)	• right to enter another Member State • on a valid ID card or passport • no entry visa

Figure 20.3   The right to move

20.3.3.2   The right of residence

Under Article 22 of the Citizenship Directive, Union citizens and their family have a right of residence over the whole territory of the host Member State, and territorial restrictions may be imposed only under the same conditions as those applicable to that State's own nationals (see Case 36/75 *Rutili v Ministre de l'intérieur* [1975] ECR 1219, para 53) and provided they comply with the principle of proportionality (Case C-100/01 *Ministre de l'Intérieur v Olazabal* [2002] ECR I-10981, para 45).

The Directive lays down three different regimes of residence under which administrative formalities vary.

The right of residence for up to three months

Under Article 6(1) of the Directive, Union citizens have a general right of residence in another Member State for a period of up to three months. The only requirement is to hold a valid identity card or passport. Non-EU family members in possession of a valid passport accompanying or joining an EU migrant enjoy the same right (Article 6(2)). The only restriction to this right is that the Union citizen and their family members 'do not become an unreasonable burden on the social assistance system of the host Member State' (Article 14(1)).

The right of residence for more than three months

Article 7 provides a right to mid-term residence for periods of between three months and five years but creates different conditions for different categories of EU migrants and their families. Furthermore, as a result of governments' concerns over the financing and costs of social assistance systems, and with the view to preventing the free movement of benefit seekers, this right of residence is subject to limitations.

The three categories of beneficiaries are:

(a) workers and the self-employed who have the right to reside without any conditions (see **15.2.2**);

(b) the economically inactive (self-sufficient and retired persons) who have sufficient resources for themselves and their family members and have comprehensive sickness insurance cover in the host Member State; and

(c) students who are enrolled at an establishment accredited or financed by the host Member State for the main purpose of following a course of study or vocational training and who satisfy the same conditions as the economically inactive for themselves and their family members (under Article 7(4), their spouse, registered partner and their dependent descendants having an automatic right of residence, while other members only have the right to have their entry facilitated).

For those categories of mid-term residents, administrative formalities apply under Article 8 of the Directive, such as the possible requirement to register with the relevant authorities of the host Member State to ensure that the EU migrant complies with the conditions of the right of residence. A registration certificate (replacing the residence permit) must be automatically delivered on the production of a valid identity card or passport, confirmation or certificate of employment for workers, proof of self-employment, proof of enrolment at an education establishment for students and proof of comprehensive sickness insurance cover and of sufficient resources for students and the economically inactive.

With regard to the condition of having 'sufficient resources', Article 8(4) prohibits Member States from imposing a fixed amount of resources, which in any respect may 'not be higher than the threshold below which nationals of the host Member State become eligible for social assistance, or higher than the minimum social security pension paid by the host Member State'.

The legal regime of family members of Union citizens differs on the basis of their being EU citizens themselves or not. Article 8(5) provides that the former will be issued with a registration certificate upon presentation of:

- a valid identity card or passport;
- the registration certificate or other proof of residence in the host Member State of the EU migrant;
- a document proving the existence of a family relationship, a registered partnership or a durable relationship; and
- any documentary evidence of being dependent on the EU migrant, or proof of the existence of serious health grounds requiring the personal care of the family member by the EU migrant.

Under Article 9 of the Directive, family members who are not EU citizens must apply for a 'residence card of a family member of a Union citizen' for a period of residence of more than three months. This residence card must be issued within six months of application (Article 10(1)) and be valid for five years from the date of issue or for the envisaged period of residence of the EU migrant if it is under five years (Article 11(1)).

In the event of death or departure of the EU migrant (Article 12(1)), or the termination of family ties (divorce, annulment of marriage or termination of registered partnership) (Article 13(1)), EU family members' right to reside is not affected if they are themselves workers or self-employed, students or inactive persons with comprehensive sickness insurance cover and sufficient resources, or if they are family members of a Union citizen who is dependent on them (eg, children in education).

Third country family members do not retain their right of residence in the case of the EU migrant's departure but retain it following their death provided that they have been residing in the host Member State as the migrant's family members for at least one year before their death (Article 12(2)). In any case, that right is not affected if the family members are the EU migrant's children, irrespective of their nationality, who are enrolled at an educational establishment and until the completion of their studies, or are the remaining parent who has actual custody of those children (Article 12(3)).

In case of divorce or termination of registered partnerships, a third country family member can acquire an autonomous right to reside:

- if the marriage or registered partnership has lasted at least three years, including one year in the host Member State (Article 13(2)(a)); however, this provision cannot be relied upon where the commencement of the divorce proceedings is preceded by the departure from that Member State of the spouse who is a Union citizen (see Case C-218/14 *Singh and Others v Minister for Justice and Equality*, 16 July 2015, ECLI:EU:C:2015:476, para 70); or
- if, by agreement between the spouses or the partners or by court order, the family member has custody of the EU citizen's children (Article 13(2)(b)); or
- if this family member has the right of access to the EU citizen's minor child, as long as the court ruling states that such access must be in the host Member State; the right to reside is then retained for as long as it is required (Article 13(2)(d)); or
- the marriage or the registered partnership was plagued by 'particularly difficult circumstances' and, in particular, the family member was a victim of domestic violence (Article 13(2)(c)).

The right of permanent residence

This new right is established in Article 16(1) of the Directive, which reads:

> 1. Union citizens who have resided legally for a continuous period of five years in the host Member State shall have the right of permanent residence there.

Under paragraph 2, third country family members who have legally resided with the Union citizen in the host Member State for a continuous period of five years can enjoy the same right.

The conditions applicable to the rights of residence under Articles 6 and 7 do not apply to permanent residence. Furthermore, under Article 16(3), continuity of residence will not be regarded as interrupted by temporary absences of no more than six months a year, or by longer absences for compulsory military service, or by absences for important reasons such as pregnancy and childbirth, serious illness, study or vocational training, or a posting in another Member State or a third country, and not exceeding 12 consecutive months. Periods in prison cannot be taken into account, however, for the purpose of acquiring permanent residence and, similarly, periods of imprisonment interrupt in principle the continuity of residence (see Case C-378/12 *Onuekwere v Secretary of State for the Home Department*, 16 January 2014, ECLI:EU:C:2014:13, para 32). Permanent residence will be lost, however, after an absence from the host Member State of more than two years in a row.

By derogation from Article 16, Article 17 provides that the right of permanent residence may be acquired before the completion of the five-year period by workers and self-employed persons who:

- have reached the age of entitlement to old age pension or early retirement (Article 17(1)(a)); or
- have stopped working as a result of permanent incapacity to work (Article 17(1)(b)); or
- are frontier workers (Article 17(1)(c)).

Family members, whether EU nationals or not, residing with an EU migrant are entitled to the same permanent right of residence when acquired by that migrant (Article 17(3)). Should the EU migrant die before acquiring the permanent right of residence, the family members who were residing with them are entitled to this right if, at the time of death, the EU migrant resided in the host Member State for a continuous period of two years, or the death was caused by an accident at work or an occupational disease, or even if the surviving spouse lost the nationality of that Member State following marriage to the EU migrant (Article 17(4)).

The provisions of Article 17 reflect the link that exists between free movement of persons and European citizenship and the equality of treatment between nationals of the host Member State and nationals of other Member States.

Right of short-term residence (Article 6 of the Citizenship Directive)	**Right of medium-term residence (Article 7 of the Citizenship Directive)**	**Right of permanent residence (Article 16 of the Citizenship Directive)**
• Up to three months • No conditions or formalities	• From three months to five years • Economically active migrants and economically inactive migrants with sufficient resources • Varying administrative formalities for EU citizens (Article 8 of the Directive) and for non-EU family members (Article 9 of the Directive)	• Over five continuous years of residence • All EU migrants and their EU or non-EU family members

Figure 20.4 The right of residence

20.4 Equal treatment rights

As a result of the principle of non-discrimination as laid down in Article 18 TFEU, European citizens and their family members have the right to enjoy living conditions similar to those enjoyed by the nationals of the host Member State. Originally applied only to economically active migrants (see 15.4), the principle of equal treatment was extended by the Court of Justice to all European citizens whether economically active or not. In Case C-85/96 *Martínez Sala v Freistaat Bayern* [1998] ECR I-2691, the ECJ observed that

> … a national of a Member State lawfully residing in the territory of another Member State … comes within the scope *ratione personae* of the provisions of the Treaty on European citizenship. (para 61)

As such, that national has the right

> … not to suffer discrimination on grounds of nationality within the scope of application *ratione materiae* of the Treaty. (para 62)

This line of jurisprudence was later confirmed in Case C-184/99 *Grzelczyk v Centre public d'aide sociale d'Ottignies-Louvain-la-Neuve* [2001] ECR I-6193.

case example

The *Grzelczyk* case concerned the right of residence for students and to national minimum subsistence allowance. Grzelczyk was a French national who took up residence in Belgium to study physical education at the University of Louvain-la-Neuve. During the first three years of his studies, he managed to cover his own costs of maintenance, accommodation and studies by taking on various minor jobs and by obtaining credit facilities. However, in his final year, he decided to apply for the minimex, the Belgian minimum subsistance allowance and a non-contributory social benefit. Originally granted to Grzelczyk, the minimex was withdrawn from him a few months later on the ground that Grzelczyk did not satisfy the nationality requirement and that he was an EEC national enrolled as a student.

Following the challenge of that decision by Grzelczyk before a Belgian labour court and on a preliminary reference by that court, the ECJ recalled that a social benefit providing a general guarantee of a minimum subsistence allowance, such as the Belgian minimex, constituted a social advantage granted to workers under Article 7(2) of Regulation 1612/68/EEC (now Regulation 492/2011/EU). Yet, Belgian students who found themselves in the same financial circumstances as Grzelczyk would satisfy the conditions for obtaining the minimex under Belgian law despite not being workers. It was therefore clear that Grzelczyk's nationality was the only bar to the minimex being granted to him.

In line with *Martínez Sala*, the Court held that

> [t]he fact that a Union citizen pursues university studies in a Member State other than the State of which he is a national cannot, of itself, deprive him of the possibility of relying on the prohibition of all discrimination on grounds of nationality laid down in Article [18] of the Treaty. (para 36)

After observing that, while former Directive 93/96/EC on the right of residence of students did not establish any right to payment of maintenance grants by the host Member State for students, it did not preclude those students to whom it applied from receiving social security benefits.

The Court therefore concluded that the

> entitlement to a non-contributory social benefit, such as the minimex, [could not be] made conditional, in the case of nationals of Member States other than the host State where they are legally resident, on their falling within the scope of Regulation No [492/2011/EU] when no such condition applies to nationals of the host Member State. (para 46)

The principle of equal treatment is also clearly enshrined in Article 24(1) of the Citizenship Directive:

> Subject to such specific provisions as are expressly provided for in the Treaty and secondary law, all Union citizens residing on the basis of this Directive in the territory of the host Member State shall enjoy equal treatment with the nationals of that Member State within the scope of the Treaty. The benefit of this right shall be extended to family members who are not nationals of a Member State and who have the right of residence or permanent residence.

The development of the principle of equal treatment was originally mainly driven by the recognition of social rights. These were first granted to workers under former Regulation 1612/68/EEC, now replaced by the codification Regulation 492/2011/EU ([2001] OJ L141/1), and notably its Article 7(2) which states that workers must be granted the same tax advantages (see Case C-155/09 *Commission v Greece* [2011] ECR I-65: exemption from transfer tax on the first purchase of immoveable property granted solely to persons residing in Greece and to persons of Greek origin not residing in Greece at the date of purchase) and social advantages as national workers.

The concept of 'social advantages' was first defined by the ECJ in Case 207/78 *Criminal proceedings against Even and Office national des pensions pour travailleurs salariés (ONPTS)* [1979] ECR 2019 as advantages

> ...which, *whether or not linked to a contract of employment*, are generally granted to national workers primarily because of their *objective status as workers or by virtue of the mere fact of their residence on the national territory* and the extension of which to workers who are nationals of other Member States therefore seems suitable to facilitate their mobility within the [Union]. (para 22, emphasis added)

Different from social security benefits (these are covered by Regulation 883/2004/EC on the coordination of social security systems [2004] OJ L166/1), social advantages cover a wide range of benefits, as the case law of the Court of Justice shows. These notably include fare reduction cards issued by a national railway authority to large families (Case 32/75 *Cristini v Société nationale des chemins de fer français* [1975] ECR 1085), a disability allowance for a worker's adult child (Case 63/76 *Inzirillo v Caisse d'allocations familiales de l'arrondissement de Lyon* [1976] ECR 2057), interest-free loans granted on childbirth to families with low income (Case 65/81 *Reina and Reina v Landeskreditbank Baden-Württemberg* [1982] ECR 33), a social advantage guaranteeing a minimum means of subsistence (Case 249/83 *Hoeckx v Openbaar Centrum voor Maatschappelijk Welzijn, Kalmthout* [1985] ECR 973; Case C-456/02 *Trojani v Centre public d'aide sociale de Bruxelles (CPAS)* [2004] ECR I-7573: a person in possession of a residence permit may rely on Article 18 TFEU in order to be granted a social assistance benefit such as the minimex; Case C-224/98 *D'Hoop v Office national de l'emploi* [2002] ECR I-6191: unlawful refusal by a Member State to grant a tideover allowance to one of its nationals, a student seeking her first employment, on the sole ground that that student completed her secondary education in another Member State; Case C-258/04 *Office national de l'emploi v Ioannidis* [2005] ECR I-8275; and *Grzelczyk*), the use of one's own language in proceedings before the courts of the Member State of residence (Case 137/84 *Criminal proceedings against Mutsch* [1985] ECR 2681), a special old-age allowance guaranteeing a minimum income to elderly persons (Case 157/84 *Frascogna v Caisse des dépôts et consignations* [1985] ECR 1739), the grant of a payment to cover funeral expenses incurred by a migrant worker (Case C-237/94 *O'Flynn v Adjudication Officer* [1996] ECR I-2617), and a child-raising allowance (*Martínez Sala*).

Article 12 of Regulation 1612/68/EEC (now Article 10 of Regulation 492/2011/EU) which provides that

> [t]he children of a national of a Member State who is or has been employed in the territory of another Member State shall be admitted to that State's general educational, apprenticeship and vocational training courses under the same conditions as the nationals of that State, if such children are residing in its territory[,]

has also been widely interpreted by the Court of Justice so as to include the right to financial aid to be accorded to children of EU migrant workers under the same conditions as the nationals of the host State (see Case 9/74 *Casagrande v Landeshauptstadt München* [1974] ECR 773, para 14; Case 68/74 *Alaimo v Préfet du Rhône* [1975] ECR 109, para 12).

In its interpretation of this provision, the Court of Justice went even further so as to state that the right to education of children necessarily implies that the children's parents and primary carers have a right of residence for as long as the children remain their dependants, and this despite the fact that the parents or carers do not meet the requirement of Article 7(1)(b) of the Citizenship Directive that they have sufficient resources for themselves and their family members not to become a burden on the social assistance system of the host Member State. In this situation, the Court made it clear that such requirement must be waived (see Case C-480/08 *Teixeira v London Borough of Lambeth and Secretary of State for the Home Department* [2010] ECR I-1107, para 70; Case C-310/08 *London Borough of Harrow v Ibrahim and Secretary of State for the Home Department* [2010] ECR I-1065, para 59).

Cases such as *Martínez Sala, Trojani, D'Hoop, Grzelczyk, Teixeira* and *Ibrahim* show that the principle of equal treatment has led to a recognition of social rights of economically inactive migrants exercising their right of residence in another Member State.

Nonetheless, two main derogations are provided for under Article 24(2) of the Citizenship Directive:

... the host Member State shall not be obliged to confer entitlement to social assistance during the first three months of residence or, where appropriate, the longer period provided for in Article 14(4)(b), nor shall it be obliged, prior to acquisition of the right of permanent residence, to grant maintenance aid for studies, including vocational training, consisting in student grants or student loans to persons other than workers, self-employed persons, persons who retain such status and members of their families.

First, host Member States have no obligation to provide social assistance to any migrant within the first three months of their residence. This is particularly well illustrated in Case C-138/02 *Collins v Secretary of State for Work and Pensions* [2004] ECR I-2703, para 73 (national legislation making the entitlement to a jobseeker's allowance conditional on a residence requirement which is justified on the basis of objective considerations irrespective of nationality and proportionate to the legitimate aim of the national provisions is not contrary to EU law). As the Court put it in Joined Cases C-22/08 and C-23/08 *Vatsouras and Koupatantze v Arbeitsgemeinschaft (ARGE) Nürnberg 900* [2009] ECR I-4585, although it is no longer possible to exclude from the scope of Article 48 TFEU a financial benefit intended to facilitate access to employment in the labour market of a Member State, it is nonetheless legitimate for that Member State to grant such a benefit only if a real link between the job-seeker and the labour market (or geographic employment market) of that State can be established, notably by showing that the job-seeker has, for a reasonable period of time, genuinely sought work in the host Member State (see also *D'Hoop*, para 38; *Collins*, para 70 and *Ioannidis*, para 30).

Such link to the labour market is obviously non-existent in the case of economically inactive EU citizens who move to another Member State with the sole purpose of obtaining social assistance. In Case C-333/13 *Dano and Dano v Jobcenter Leipzig*, 11 November 2014, ECLI:EU:C:2014:2358, the Court of Justice confirmed that such EU migrants may be excluded from certain social benefits.

case example

The *Dano* case concerned two Romanian nationals, a mother and her son, who had entered Germany in November 2010 to live with Ms Dano's sister who provided for them materially. They were issued by the German authorities with residence certificates in July 2011. Ms Dano received child benefit and an advance on maintenance payments for her son Florin.

Ms Dano received little education in Romania and had not been trained in a profession. Although she had some understanding of German, she had limited ability to read and write in that language. Despite her ability to work, she had never worked in Romania or Germany, and there was no indication that she was seeking work in Germany.

Nevertheless, she requested special non-contributory cash benefits by way of basic provision for job-seekers under the German Social Code, which are intended in particular to cover subsistence costs. Her request was rejected on two occasions in September 2011 and January 2012 by the Jobcentre Leipzig.

On a preliminary reference from the Leipzig social court, the Court of Justice pointed out that the Citizenship Directive distinguishes between persons who are working and those who are not. Under Article 7(1)(a) of the Directive, the first group of migrants have the right of residence without having to fulfil any other condition, while the second group of economically inactive persons are required by Article 7(1)(b) of the Directive to meet the condition that they have sufficient resources of their own. As a result, the Court added:

... Article 7(1)(b) of Directive 2004/38 seeks to prevent economically inactive Union citizens from using the host Member State's welfare system to fund their means of subsistence. (para 76)

This means therefore that Member States have the

> ... possibility of refusing to grant social benefits to economically inactive Union citizens who exercise their right to freedom of movement solely in order to obtain another Member State's social assistance although they do not have sufficient resources to claim a right of residence. (para 78)

The Court concluded that the Citizenship Directive and notably Article 24(1) did not preclude domestic law excluding nationals from other Member States, who do not have a right of residence under the Directive in the host State, from being entitled to certain non-contributory cash benefits, as those claimed by Ms Dano, even if they are granted to the nationals of the host State who are in the same situation (para 84).

As the Court observed, Ms Dano and her son did not have sufficient resources as per Article 7(1)(b) of the Directive and therefore did not have a right of residence in Germany. They could therefore not rely on the principle of equal treatment laid down in Article 24(1) of the Directive (para 81).

> Secondly, the host Member State is not obliged to grant maintenance aid for studies, including vocational training, consisting in student grants or student loans to persons who are not economically active or permanent residents. This second derogation to the principle of equal treatment must be read, however, in light of Case C-209/03 R, *on the application of Bidar v London Borough of Ealing and Secretary of State for Education and Skills* [2005] ECR I-2119.

The *Bidar* case concerned a French national who accompanied his mother who underwent medical treatment in the United Kingdom. He lived there with his grandmother as her dependant and pursued and completed his secondary education. When he started a course in economics at University College London, he received assistance with respect to tuition fees but was refused assistance to cover his maintenance costs in the form of a student loan, on the ground that he was not settled in the United Kingdom.

case example

After re-iterating that

> ... assistance, whether in the form of subsidised loans or of grants, provided to students lawfully resident in the host Member State to cover their maintenance costs falls within the scope of application of the Treaty for the purposes of the prohibition of discrimination laid down in the first paragraph of Article [18 TFEU,]

the Court observed that the condition requiring an applicant for that assistance to be settled in the United Kingdom and requiring him to have resided there prior to his studies is likely to be more easily satisfied by United Kingdom nationals. Such difference in treatment may be justified only on the basis of objective factors other than the nationality of the applicants and if it is proportionate to the legitimate aim of the national provisions. Member States certainly have the right to ensure that the assistance granted to students from other Member States to cover their maintenance costs does not become an unreasonable burden on their social assistance system and, for that purpose, may require that students have demonstrated a certain degree of integration into the society of that State (paras 56–57).

Drawing a clear distinction between this degree of integration into the host State and a link with the employment market of that State, the Court stated that the fact that a student has resided in the host Member State for a certain length of time is sufficient to establish such degree of integration (para 59).

Consequently, the Court ruled that

> [Article 18 TFEU] must be interpreted as precluding national legislation which grants students the right to assistance covering their maintenance costs only if they are settled in the host Member State, while precluding a national of another Member State from obtaining the status of settled person as a student even if that national is lawfully resident and has received a substantial part of his secondary education in the host Member State and has consequently established a genuine link with the society of that State. (para 63)

By contrast with *Bidar*, in which the grant of a student loan to a national of a Member State was made conditional on his being settled in the United Kingdom, in Case C-158/07 *Förster v Hoofddirectie van de Informatie Beheer Groep* [2008] ECR I-8507, the Dutch legislation provided that students who were nationals of another EU Member State were eligible for a maintenance grant if they had been lawfully resident in the Netherlands for an uninterrupted period of at least five years prior to their application. Such requirement of residence was not applicable to Dutch students however. The Court of Justice considered that such a requirement of five years' uninterrupted residence was appropriate, could not be held to be excessive and, being applied on the basis of clear criteria known in advance, did not go beyond what was necessary in order to guarantee that applicants for the maintenance grant were integrated into Dutch society (paras 52–59). The Court concluded that

> … a student who is a national of a Member State and travels to another Member State to study there can rely on the first paragraph of Article [18 TFEU] in order to obtain a maintenance grant where he or she has resided for a certain duration in the host Member State. The first paragraph of Article [18 TFEU] does not preclude the application to nationals of other Member States of a requirement of five years' prior residence. (para 60)

This reference to a five-year period of residence seems to reflect the wording of Article 24(2) of the Citizenship Directive – to which the Court made a specific reference in paragraph 55 of this ruling even though it was not applicable to the facts of this case – which clearly provides that there is no obligation to grant maintenance assistance to students 'prior to acquisition of the right of permanent residence' which is granted, under Article 16(1), to Union citizens who have legally resided in the host Member State for a continuous period of five years (see 20.3.3.2).

However, as the Court stresses, this does not stop Member States, that wish to do so, from awarding maintenance grants to students from other Member States who do not fulfil the five-year residence requirement (para 59).

Article 18 TFEU:
- no discrimination on the ground of nationality

Article 24(1) of the Citizenship Directive:
- equal treatment with nationals of the host Member State for all EU migrants and their family members

---

Article 24(2) of the Citizenship Directive:
- no obligation for Member State to grant social assistant during first three months of residence or during longer period of employment search;
- no obligation during the first five years of residence to grant maintenance grants for studies, student grants and loans to economically inactive persons

Figure 20.5   Equal treatment

20.5 Limits to free movement rights

As Article 21 TFEU provides, the right to move and reside freely within the territory of the Member States is 'subject to the limitations and conditions laid down in the Treaties and by the measures adopted to give them effect'.

Also provided for in Article 45(3) TFEU regarding the free movement of workers and Article 52(1) TFEU on free establishment, those limitations are further confirmed in Article 27 of the Citizenship Directive with regard to all EU citizens.

This is a reminder that, according to international law, Member States still have discretion to refuse access to, or deport from, their territory nationals of other Member States. However, regulated by EU legislation and supervised by the Court of Justice, such discretion is not unlimited, thus differentiating the status of EU citizens from that of non-EU nationals.

20.5.1 Conditions of application

Because of the contingent character and imprecise nature of the grounds on which restrictions to free movement may be relied upon by Member States, notably public policy and public security, the Court has consistently pointed out, as it recalled in *Jipa*, that

> ... while Member States essentially retain the freedom to determine the requirements of public policy and public security in accordance with their national needs, which can vary from one Member State to another and from one era to another, the fact still remains that, in the [Union] context and particularly as justification for a derogation from the fundamental principle of free movement of persons, those requirements must be interpreted strictly, so that their scope cannot be determined unilaterally by each Member State without any control by the [Union] institutions ... (para 23)

As a result, a number of conditions must be satisfied by national authorities when applying Article 27 of the Citizenship Directive.

First, as is the case with Article 36 TFEU derogations to the free movement of goods (see 14.2.1.2), those grounds for derogation cannot be 'invoked to serve economic ends'. This is now clearly enshrined in Article 27(1), second sentence.

Secondly, a measure restricting the right of freedom of movement may be justified only if it respects the principle of proportionality (see Joined Cases C-259/91, C-331/91 and C-332/91 *Allué and others v Università degli studi di Venezia and Università degli studi di Parma* [1993] ECR I-4309, para 15; Case C-413/99 *Baumbast and R v Secretary of State for the Home Department* [2002] ECR I-7091, para 91; *Olazabal*, para 43 and *Jipa*, para 29). This settled case law of the Court was formally incorporated into Article 24(2), first sub-paragraph.

Last, but not least, such a measure must be based on a fair balance between legitimate national interests 'in compliance with the general principles of EU law and, in particular, by taking proper account of respect for fundamental rights ...' (eg, the protection of family life as in Joined Cases C-482/01 and C-493/01 *Orfanopoulos and Others and Oliveri v Land Baden-Württemberg* [2004] ECR I-5257, para 100).

20.5.2 Grounds for justification

Three grounds of justification are mentioned in Article 27(1):

Subject to the provisions of this Chapter, Member States may restrict the freedom of movement and residence of Union citizens and their family members, irrespective of nationality, on grounds of public policy, public security or public health …

20.5.2.1 Public policy and public security

Public policy is, in general, interpreted as preventing the disturbance of social order, while public security covers both internal and external security with the view to preserving the integrity of the territory of a Member State and its institutions (see Cases C-423/98 *Albore* [2000] ECR I-5965, paras 18–24 and C-285/98 *Kreil v Germany* [2000] ECR I-69, paras 15–17).

Article 27(2) provides a strict frame of interpretation and states:

Measures taken on grounds of public policy or public security … shall be based exclusively on the personal conduct of the individual concerned. Previous criminal convictions shall not in themselves constitute grounds for taking such measures.

The personal conduct of the individual concerned must represent a genuine, present and sufficiently serious threat affecting one of the fundamental interests of society. Justifications that are isolated from the particulars of the case or that rely on considerations of general prevention shall not be accepted.

The Court's case law has always made it clear that the assessment of a threat to public policy, in addition to the perturbation of the social order resulting from a breach of the law, can only be based on the personal conduct of the individual whose free movement is restricted (as provided under Article 3(1) of former Directive 64/221/EEC on the co-ordination of special measures concerning the movement and residence of foreign nationals which are justified on grounds of public policy, public security or public health ([1964] OJ L56/850)). The concept of 'personal conduct' was first examined in the early Case 41/74 *Van Duyn v Home Office* [1974] ECR 1337, in which the Court considered that the fact that an individual was associated with a body or an organisation (here the Church of Scientology) whose activities were regarded as socially harmful without being unlawful in the host Member State (here the UK), amounted to personal conduct of that individual 'despite the fact that no restriction [was] placed upon [UK nationals] who [wished] to take similar employment with these same bodies or organizations' (para 24). Although this very wide interpretation of 'personal conduct' was controversial and criticised, the idea itself that measures taken on the ground of public policy or security must be based on 'personal conduct' was confirmed in Case 67/74 *Bonsignore v Oberstadtdirektor der Stadt Köln* [1975] ECR 297. In paragraph 6, the Court ruled:

As departures from the rules concerning the free movement of persons constitute exceptions which must be strictly construed, the concept of 'personal conduct' expresses the requirement that a deportation order may only be made for breaches of the peace and public security which might be committed by the individual affected.

In this respect, EU migrants may not be denied residence solely on the ground that their conduct is considered to be contrary to public policy by reason of the fact that they exercise activities which are 'suspect from the point of view of morals', notably if such activities when attributable to the State's own nationals do not give rise to repressive measures (see Joined Cases 115 and 116/81 *Adoui v Belgium and City of*

Liège; Cornuaille v Belgium [1982] ECR 1665: waitresses in a bar working as prostitutes).

Equally, as provided in Article 27(2), first sub-paragraph, previous convictions cannot automatically be regarded as personal conduct and therefore constitute ground for measures restricting free movement. This is illustrated in Case 131/79 *R v Secretary of State for Home Affairs, ex parte Santillo* [1980] ECR 1585, which concerned a deportation order made four years after the recommendation for deportation from the UK against an Italian migrant who had been sentenced to eight years' imprisonment for serious offences. Confirming its ruling in Case 30/77 *R v Bouchereau* [1977] ECR 1999 (para 27), the Court stressed that a national criminal court had to take into consideration the provisions of Article 3 of former Directive 64/221/EEC (now Article 27(2) of the Citizenship Directive) 'inasmuch as the mere existence of criminal convictions may not automatically constitute grounds for deportation measures' (para 17). However, as observed in *Bouchereau*:

> The existence of a previous criminal conviction can, therefore, only be taken into account in so far as the circumstances which gave rise to that conviction are evidence of personal conduct constituting a present threat to the requirements of public policy. (para 28)

Such threat to public policy must also be, according to Article 27(2), second sub-paragraph, 'a genuine, present and sufficiently serious threat affecting one of the fundamental interests of society'. This requirement reflects the interpretation by the Court of Justice of former Directive 64/221/EEC, notably in *Rutili* (para 28), *Bouchereau* (para 35), Case C-348/96 *Criminal proceedings against Calfa* [1999] ECR I-11 (automatic expulsion for life of an Italian national from Greece following a criminal conviction without any consideration of her personal conduct or of the danger to public policy she might represent) and *Orfanopoulos and Oliveri* (para 66).

The *Oliveri* case concerned a deportation order against an Italian national from Germany. Mr Oliveri was born in Germany and had resided in Germany since his birth. A drug addict, he became infected with HIV and chronic hepatitis C.

Following numerous offences, notably thefts and illegal sale of narcotics, he was sentenced to imprisonment in November 1999 and again in April 2000 after he interrupted his treatment in hospital during which his sentence had been suspended. Following a number of warnings, his expulsion was ordered in August 2000 on the basis of the frequency and seriousness of his offences and of the real risk of reoffending in the future because of his dependency on drugs. He was threatened with deportation to Italy without a time limit being fixed for his voluntary departure.

Mr Oliveri challenged the deportation order before the administrative court of Stuttgart. In a preliminary ruling, the Court re-iterated that measures of public policy cannot be justified by previous criminal convictions in themselves and must be based exclusively on the personal conduct of the individual concerned, representing a genuine and sufficiently serious threat to the requirements of public policy affecting one of the fundamental interests of society (para 66), before affirming that 'the *requirement of the existence of a present threat must, as a general rule, be satisfied at the time of the expulsion*' (para 79, emphasis added).

20.5.2.2 Public health

Restrictions to freedom of movement on the ground of public health may be justified under Article 29 of the Citizenship Directive in the case of

... diseases with epidemic potential as defined by the relevant instruments of the World Health Organisation and other infectious diseases or contagious parasitic diseases if they are the subject of protection provisions applying to nationals of the host Member State.

Former Directive 64/221/EEC provided a list of those diseases, which included tuberculosis, syphilis, infectious diseases or contagious parasitic diseases, diseases and disabilities which might threaten public policy or public security, drug addiction, profound mental disturbance and other mental illnesses. Member States refused to add AIDS to this list and the Citizenship Directive simply refers to diseases defined in the 'relevant instruments of the World Health Organisation'.

Under Article 29(2), this ground of derogation may not be relied upon, however, by a Member State if the disease has occurred three months after the EU migrant has entered its territory.

Nonetheless, within three months of the date of arrival, provided there are serious indications that it is necessary, EU migrants may be required to undergo, free of charge, a routine medical examination to certify that they are not suffering from any of those diseases (Article 29(3)).

20.5.3 Protection against restrictive measures

Even if the existence of a threat to public policy is established, national authorities must still take account of a number of safeguards protecting migrants.

20.5.3.1 Protection against expulsion

Normal protection

Prior to taking an expulsion decision on grounds of public policy or public security, the personal and family situation of the migrant concerned must be assessed carefully in order to ensure that the envisaged measure is appropriate and proportionate (see *Orfanopoulos*, para 100). To that effect, Article 28(1) of the Citizenship Directive provides an indicative list of factors to be taken into account, such as:

- length of residence in the host Member State;
- age and state of health of the migrant;
- family and economic situation;
- social and cultural integration into the host Member State; and
- the extent of the migrant's links with the country of origin.

Enhanced protection

Article 28(2) and (3) offers increased protection against expulsion to EU migrants and their EU or non-EU family members who are permanent residents.

Under Article 28(2), expulsion measures can only be taken 'on serious grounds of public policy or public security' against individuals who have resided in the host State between five and 10 years; and, under Article 28(3), 'on imperative grounds of public security' (but not public policy) against individuals who have resided in the host State for the previous 10 years, and children provided the expulsion is necessary for their best interests.

Therefore the expulsion decision must be taken on a clear distinction between normal, 'serious' and 'imperative' grounds. In Case C-145/09 *Land Baden-Württemberg v Tsakouridis* [2010] ECR I-11979, the Court defined the concept of 'imperative grounds of public security' as one that

… presupposes not only the existence of a threat to public security, but also that such a threat is of a particularly high degree of seriousness, as is reflected by the use of the words 'imperative reasons'. (para 41)

This concept is therefore much stricter than that of 'serious grounds' within the meaning of Article 28(2), thus reflecting the clear intention of the European Union legislature to limit measures based on Article 28(3) to 'exceptional circumstances'.

Indeed, as recital 24 of the preamble to the Citizenship Directive states:

… the greater the degree of integration of Union citizens and their family members in the host Member State, the greater the degree of protection against expulsion should be. Only in exceptional circumstances, where there are imperative grounds of public security, should an expulsion measure be taken against Union citizens who have resided for many years in the territory of the host Member State, in particular when they were born and have resided there throughout their life.

However, in Case C-348/09 *PI v Oberbürgermeisterin der Stadt Remscheid*, 22 May 2012, ECLI:EU:C:2012:300, in which it was unclear to the German referring court whether the sexual offences against a 14-year-old girl committed by Mr I, an Italian national, might be covered by the concept of 'imperative grounds of public security', the Court of Justice interpreted Article 28(3)(a) of the Directive as leaving it open to the national courts to decide whether criminal offences such as those mentioned in the second sub-paragraph of Article 83(1) TFEU (terrorism, trafficking in human beings and sexual exploitation of women and children, illicit drug trafficking, illicit arms trafficking, money laundering, corruption, counterfeiting of means of payment, computer crime and organised crime) constitute

… a particularly serious threat to one of the fundamental interests of society, which might pose a direct threat to the calm and physical security of the population and thus be covered by the concept of 'imperative grounds of public security', capable of justifying an expulsion measure under Article 28(3), as long as the manner in which such offences were committed discloses particularly serious characteristics, which is a matter for the referring court to determine on the basis of an individual examination of the specific case before it. (para 33)

Nonetheless, should an expulsion measure against Mr I be justified, the national court would still have to comply with the usual procedural requirements and safeguards imposed under EU law.

With regard to the calculation of the 10-year period of residence, the Court ruled in Case C-400/12 *Secretary of State for the Home Department v M G*, 16 January 2014, ECLI:EU:C:2014:9 that

a period of imprisonment is, in principle, capable both of interrupting the continuity of the period of residence and of affecting the decision regarding the grant of the enhanced protection provided for thereunder, even where the person concerned resided in the host Member State for the 10 years prior to imprisonment. (para 38)

20.5.3.2 Procedural requirements and safeguards

Union citizens and their family members are also protected by a number of procedural requirements and safeguards.

Notification in writing

Article 30(1) of the Citizenship Directive requires that the persons against whom a decision of refusal of entry or deportation is taken must be notified in writing 'in such a way that they are able to comprehend its content and the implications for them'.

Decisions must be fully reasoned and specify the factual and legal grounds on which they are taken to enable individuals concerned to take effective steps to prepare their defence (see *Rutili*, paras 37–39), 'unless this is contrary to the interests of State security' (Article 30(2); see Case C-300/11 *ZZ v Secretary of State for the Home Department*, 4 June 2013, ECLI:EU:C:2013:363).

The notified decision must also specify the court or administrative authority with which an appeal may be lodged and the time limit for that appeal, and the time allowed for the person concerned to leave the territory of the Member State (Article 30(3)).

Access to judicial redress

According to Article 31(1) and (2) of the Citizenship Directive, access to judicial and, where appropriate, administrative redress procedures to appeal or seek review of any decision based on the grounds of public policy, public security or public health must be made available in the host Member State to the persons concerned (see Case 48/75 *Royer* [1976] ECR 497, paras 52–62 and Joined Cases C-297/88 and C-197/89 *Dzodzi v Belgium* [1990] ECR I-3763, para 60), in such a way as to ensure an examination of the legality of the decision, together with that of the facts and circumstances on which the decision is based (Article 31(3)).

In the case where an application for an interim order to suspend enforcement of an expulsion decision is made alongside an application for appeal or judicial review against such decision, actual deportation from the territory of the host Member State cannot take place as a general rule until the decision on the interim order is taken (Article 31(2)). This rule suffers three exceptions, however, namely:

- where the expulsion decision is based on a previous judicial decision; or
- where the person concerned had previous access to judicial review; or
- where the expulsion decision is based on imperative grounds of public security under Article 28(3).

Finally, Article 31(4) grants the individuals concerned the right to present their defence in person unless their presence 'may cause serious troubles to public policy or public security or when the appeal or judicial review concerns a denial of entry to the territory'.

Exclusion ban

Under Article 32(1), expelled Union citizens and their family members who have also been excluded on grounds of public policy or public security can apply to have this ban on entry lifted after a reasonable period of time, and in any event after three years from the enforcement of the final exclusion order. For that purpose, they must demonstrate that the circumstances which justified the exclusion order have materially changed.

The national authorities of the host State must make a decision on the application within six months of its submission.

Expulsion as a legal consequence of a custodial penalty

Article 33(1) prohibits expulsion orders being issued as a penalty or legal consequence of a custodial penalty, unless they comply with the requirements of Articles 27, 28 and 29 of the Directive.

However, in the case of such an expulsion order being enforced more than two years after being issued, Article 33(2) provides that the host Member State has an obligation to check that the person concerned is currently and genuinely a threat to public policy or public security before the expulsion takes place. Also, the State must assess whether the circumstances of the person concerned have materially changed since the expulsion order was adopted.

Measures restricting free movement	**Protection against restricting measures**
taken on grounds of public policy, public security or public health (Art 27 of the Citizenship Directive)	Normal and enhanced protection against expulsion (Art 28 of the Citizenship Directive)
based on personal conduct (no previous criminal convictions alone)	Notification of decision in writing (Art 30 of the Citizenship Directive
representing a genuine, present and sufficiently serious threat affecting the fundamental interests of society	Access to judicial redress (Art 31 of the Citizenship Directive) Lifting of exclusion orders (Art 32 of the Citizenship Directive)
refusal to enter or expulsion and/or exclusion order	Prohibition of expulsion orders as penalty or legal consequence (Art 33(1) of the Citizenship Directive)

Figure 20.6   Restrictions to free movement

20.6   Further reading

Damjanovic D, 'Joined cases C-22/08 and C-23/08, *Athanasios Vatsouras (C-22/08) and Josif Koupatantze (C-23/08) v Arbeitsgemeinschaft (ARGE) Nürnberg 900*, Judgment of the Court (Third Chamber) of 4 June 2009, not yet reported' (2010) 47 *CML Rev* 847.

Ellis E, 'Social Advantages: A New Lease of Life?' (2003) 40 *CML Rev* 639.

O'Brien C, 'Social Blind Spots and Monocular Policy Making: The ECJ's Migrant Worker Model' (2009) 46 *CML Rev* 1107.

O'Brien C, 'Real Links, Abstract Rights and False Alarms: the Relationship Between the ECJ's "Real Link" Case Law and National Solidarity' (2008) 33(5) *EL Rev* 643.

Mathisen G, 'Consistency and Coherence as Conditions for Justification of Member States Measures Restricting Free Movement' (2010) 47 *CML Rev* 1021.

Peers S, 'Free Movement, Immigration Control and Constitutional Conflict' (2009) 5 *European Constitutional Law Review* 173.

Spaventa E, 'Family Rights for Circular Migrants and Frontier Workers: *O and B*, and *S and G*. Case C-456/12, *O v. Minister voor Immigratie, Integratie en Asiel and Minister voor Immigratie, Integratie en Asiel v. B*, EU:C:2014:135; and Case C-457/12, *S v. Minister voor Immigratie, Integratie en Asiel and Minister voor Immigratie, Integratie en Asiel v. G*, EU:C:2014:136, Judgments of the Court (Grand Chamber) of 12 March 2014' (2015) 52 *CML Rev* 753.

Thym D, 'Case Comment - When Union Citizens turn into Illegal Migrants: The Dano Case' (2015) 40(2) *EL Rev* 249.

Thym D, 'The Elusive Limits of Solidarity: Residence Rights of and Social Benefits for Economically Inactive Union Citizens' (2015) 52 *CML Rev* 17.

Tryfonidou A, 'In Search of the Aim of the EC Free Movement of Persons Provisions: Has the Court of Justice Missed the Point?' (2009) 46 *CML Rev* 1591.

Verschueren H, 'Preventing "Benefit Tourism" in the EU: A Narrow or Broad Interpretation of the Possibilities Offered by the ECJ in *Dano*?' (2015) 62 *CML Rev* 363.

White R, 'Revisiting Free Movement of Workers' (2010) 33 *Fordham International Law Journal* 1564.

Wiesbrock A, 'Free Movement of Third-Country Nationals in the European Union: The Illusion of Inclusion' (2010) 35(4) *EL Rev* 455.

One of the European Union's main objectives is to 'offer its citizens an area of freedom, security and justice without internal frontiers' within which all EU citizens, economically active or not, and their family members, irrespective of nationality, can enjoy the right to move and reside freely in another Member State than their own.

This right is enshrined in Article 21 TFEU and further guaranteed in Directive 2004/38/EC (the Citizenship Directive).

While the right to move can be exercised without many formalities, residence rights are variable according to the duration of residence and according to the category of beneficiaries within which the European migrant falls.

Once legally resident, European migrants are in principle entitled to enjoy the same treatment as the nationals of the host State, except in situations clearly defined in the Citizenship Directive.

Nevertheless, the right to freedom of movement may be subject to limitations and conditions under Treaty and secondary legislation provisions. Freedom of movement may be restricted on the grounds of public policy, public security and public health under certain conditions laid down by the Citizenship Directive and the case law of the Court of Justice. Furthermore, procedural requirements and safeguards are in place to protect EU migrants and their family members against disproportionate national measures restricting their right to free movement and residence.

test your knowledge

1   Cristiano is a Spanish citizen. Wanting to take advantage of the opportunities available in Germany, he decides to migrate to Berlin with Thassya, his Colombian partner, Giulietta, their child aged 15, and Joaquim, aged 19, who is Thassya's son from a previous relationship and who has dual Colombian and Spanish nationality.

   (a)   What are Cristiano's and Thassya's free movement and equality rights?
   (b)   What are the children's rights?

2   Giovanni is an Italian citizen who decided to migrate from Italy to Germany with Fernanda, his Brazilian partner, and João, aged 19, who is Fernanda's son from a previous relationship and who has dual Brazilian and Italian nationality.

   In Italy, João was arrested for dealing in Class B drugs a couple of years earlier. He was charged and convicted of the possession and use of illegal substances.

   Once in Germany, João wishes to attend university in Berlin and take advantage of both a tuition fee and maintenance fee grant available to German students studying at university.

   Although he has never worked in Italy, João also wishes to claim the German job-seeker's allowance before he starts at university.

   (a)   Can the German authorities refuse entry to João on the ground of his past criminal conviction? What would be his procedural rights against a decision of refusal of entry into Germany?
   (b)   What are João's rights to benefits and to university education, should he be allowed to enter Germany?

3   Victor, a Danish national, entered France at the beginning of the year, having accepted the position in Paris of assistant editor of *La Taupe*, a radical political journal. The association that publishes *La Taupe* is a non-profit-making organisation, which finances the journal through donations and subscriptions.

   Last month, Victor was arrested whilst lying across a road in protest against cuts in the French health service. He was charged with obstruction, found guilty and the *tribunal correctionnel* of Paris recommended deportation.

   To make things worse, Elisa, Victor's older daughter from a previous relationship, wanted to move to Paris after being offered a job as a translator of English and Danish language scientific papers into French but was refused entry by the French authorities on the ground that she had two convictions in Denmark for possession of cocaine.

   Advise Victor and Elisa as to their respective rights to stay in and enter France and their related procedural rights under EU law.

INDEX